NOTES AND QUERIES

HISTORICAL AND GENEALOGICAL

CHIEFLY RELATING TO

INTERIOR PENNSYLVANIA.

EDITED BY
WILLIAM HENRY EGLE, M. D., M. A.

FIRST AND SECOND SERIES
IN TWO VOLUMES

VOLUME I

CLEARFIELD

Originally published
Harrisburg, Pennsylvania, 1894

Reprinted with the cooperation of the
Pennsylvania State Library
Genealogical Publishing Company
Baltimore, Maryland, 1970

Library of Congress Catalog Card Number 70-114834

Reprinted for Clearfield Company by
Genealogical Publishing Company
Baltimore, Maryland, 2015

ISBN 978-0-8063-0403-8

PREFATORY TO THIS REPRINT.

Owing to the increased interest at this time taken by the descendants of the early settlers in Pennsylvania, and especially in Revolutionary ancestry, frequent demands have been made for the First and Second Series of *Notes and Queries*. Nearly one-third were never printed in pamphlet form, and except possibly in the possession of the Editor, no complete set of these are in existence.

The value and variety of these papers devoted wholly to the elucidation of the History, Biography and Genealogy of our State, has suggested their re-publication.

The papers contained in this limited edition originally appeared in the regular Saturday issue of the Harrisburg *Daily Telegraph* during the years 1878 to 1883. No contributions to any newspaper in the country have been so appreciated or more often referred to, and in a recently published Index to Local History pages of references are given to *Notes and Queries*. To the student of American history, especially of that relating to Pennsylvania, this reprint will be invaluable.

It may be here stated that all articles without signature were written by the Editor, Dr. William H. Egle.

HARRISBURG PUBLISHING COMPANY.

CONTENTS OF VOLUME ONE.

Aborigines, The,	421
Ache, or Achey,	182
Ainsworth, Samuel,	317
Alricks, James,	317
Alward, Henry,	14
Anti-Masonic Investigation,	152, 157
Atlee, William Augustus,	146
Auchmuty, Dr. Robert,	203
Audenreid, Col. Joseph C.,	354
Ayres Family,	387
Badges of the Clans of Scotland,	238
Beatty, George,	318
Beatty, Capt. James,	457
Berryhill, Alexander,	131
Bertram, Rev. William,	318
Bible, an Historic,	452
Bird, James, The Mournful Tragedy of,	260
Bizallion, Peter,	153, 251
Blasphemy, Trial for,	315
Bowman, or Bauman,	43
Bowman, John F.,	204
Boyd, Capt. Adam,	267
Boyd, Joseph,	281
Boyd, William,	81
Brady, Capt. John,	123
Brainard, Rev. David, Journal of,	274
Brisban. Capt. John.	319, 352
British Prisoners at Lancaster,	427
Brown Family,	184
Brown, John, of Upper Paxtang,	18
Brown, Dr. Mercer,	319
Brown, Capt. William, company of,	483
Bryan, John,	291
Bucher, John Jacob,	313
Buckshot War, The,	185
Buehler, George,	320
Buehler, Henry,	247
Burrs, the Two, and Gen. Hanna,	197
Calderwood, Capt. James,	447
Campbell Family,	282, 385, 419
Cathey, John,	229
Chambers Family,	52, 80, 93, 189
Chambers, Capt. Stephen,	485
"Cinquas,"	18
Clark's Valley, An Early Settler in,	410
Clocks, Old Style,	370, 377
Clokey, Joseph,	356
Clunie, James,	320
Cochran, William,	321
Conewago Church,	87
Conewago Falls Canal,	191

Contents.

Cormick's Plains, ... 119
Cowden, Capt. James, of Paxtang, ... 248
    Company of, ... 259
Covenanters, Early, in Paxtang, ... 20
    first Communion of, ... 364
Craig, Isaac, Letter of, ... 133
Culbertson, Robert, ... 465
Cumberland Valley Historical Society, ... 1, 15, 358
    Contributions to History of, ... 445, 465
    First road through, ... 447
    Scotch-Irish Settlers in, ... 448
    Early settlement of, ... 486
Darby, William, Autobiography of, ... 33
Dauphin County, history of, ... 8
    Marriages in, from 1793 to 1811, ... 182, 193, 198
    First Census of, ... 345
    Formation of, ... 412
    Bar of in 1789, ... 484
Dauphin, town of, ... 267
Debating Society, an old-time, ... 80
Denning, the blacksmith of the Revolution, ... 190
Derry, East End, Assessment lists, ... 115, 442
    West End, Assessment lists, ... 116, 401
    The Sword of, ... 356
DeWitt, Rev. William R., ... 321
Dickey, Moses, ... 250
Dixon, Richard, ... 81
Douglas, Samuel, ... 322
Downey, John, ... 219
Duncan's Island, ... 284
Duncan, Thomas, ... 485
Dundore, ... 2
"Dutchland in America," 391
Eastburn, Benjamin, Letter of, ... 9
Elder, Rev. John, Paxtang and Derry's call to, ... 16
    Family record of, ... 44
    Marriages by, ... 160
    A sermon of, ... 221
    And the Paxtang Boys, ... 484
Elder, Joshua, ... 323
Elder, Samuel, ... 14
Ellmaker, Amos, ... 328
Ettley, David, ... 144
Ewing, Rev. John, ... 397
Fahnestock, Obed, ... 324
"Fair," A, At Halifax, ... 311
Family Records, ... 273, 406
Ferries over the Susquehanna, ... 106
Fetterhoff, Philip, ... 324
Fire-proof buildings in 1810, ... 43
Fires, how formerly extinguished, ... 86
Fish, protection of, in 1792, ... 187
Fisher, George, ... 325
Fithian's Journal, ... 487
Flag, the first American, in British waters, ... 452
Fleming, Robert, ... 325
Forster, John, ... 327

Contents. vii

Forster, Thomas (1st),	326
Forster, Thomas (2d),	326
Franklin county in War of 1812-14,	448
Franklin, Walter,	327
French family,	120
"French Jacob,"	42
Fridley, Capt. Jacob, company of,	425
Fultons,	2
Garfield family,	403
Genealogies, Pennsylvania,	145
Gibbons, William, letter of,	428
Gibson, Chief Justice,	338
Gillmor, Moses,	401
Gleim, Christian,	328
Graham, Rev. William,	328
Graydon, Rachel,	329
A Matron of the Revolution,	339
William,	321
Gregg, William, of Paxtang,	250
Green, Innis,	330
Gruber, Rev. Jacob,	331
Hagerstown, Md.,	489
Haldeman, Jacob M.,	332
Hall family,	283
Hamilton, Hugh,	332
Hanna, Gen. John Andre,	484
Hanover, East, assessment lists,	83, 142, 351
West, assessment lists,	143, 404, 351
Petition against division, in 1769,	85
Spinster eighty years ago,	140, 177
Patriotism of,	149, 405
Harris, David, son of John,	388
Elizabeth, wife of John,	388
Esther,	9, 114
Family of Paxtang,	3
John,	55
Family of,	42, 59, 160
Letters from,	258, 364, 390
Robert,	90
Harrisburg in 1794,	6
In 1787,	120
In 1828,	244
In 1784,	441
Reminiscenses of,	10
Postmasters of,	46, 51, 411
Hope fire company of,	158
Manufacturing facilities of,	346
Harrison, Gen. John,	32
Hebron church, marriage record of,	461
Hendricks, Capt. William, company of,	450
Henry, John Joseph,	485
Herculaneum, MS., from,	281
Heraldic arms of Penn'a families,	53, 216
Hickok, John Hoyt,	343
Hoffman family, of Lykens Valley,	211
Hoffman's creek,	202
Hoges of Hogestown,	471

Contents.

Horter family,	347, 356
Huguenot settlement in Dauphin county,	202
Huffnagle, Peter,	485
Hummel, Frederick,	334
Hummelstown in 1771 and 1779,	396
Hutchison, Joseph,	52
Indian Town, The,	14, 162
Indian Geographical Names,	99, 109, 353
Indian Captives of Bouquet's Expedition,	182
Indian Traders, Recusant, in 1749,	403
Isenhour, Casper,	189
Jefferson, Joseph, the elder,	335
Johnson, Ovid Frazer,	335
Johnstons of Antrim,	449
"Jumping the Bullies,"	25
Juniata Island, Brainard's Visit to in 1745,	274
Jury, Abraham,	205
Keagy, Dr. John M.,	247, 335
Kean, Gen. John,	409
Kelker, Anthony,	336
Kerr, Rev. William, Call to,	58
Kingsford, Mrs., School of,	10, 105
"Kitohtening Mills," or Fort Hunter,	415
Kittera, John Wilkes,	484
Kloppen Church,	357
Kyle, James,	322
Laird, Samuel,	358
Lancaster Court Cases, Early,	446
Latin political poem of 1800,	218
Lauman, William,	359
"Laurel Hill,"	177, 198
Lee, Capt. Andrew, of Paxtang,	167, 223, 229
Legislators of 1813-14,	292, 304
Lewis, Major Eli,	359
Lewis the Robber,	446
Lind, Rev. Matthew,	19
Linn, Rev. William,	466
Local history, Scraps of,	418
Lombardy Poplar, The,	441
Londonderry in 1775,	22
Londonderry, N. H.,	250
"Long Bullets,"	5, 25
Louisburgh,	418
Ludington, James,	119
Lukens, escape of,	316
Luther, Dr. John,	269, 272
Lycans, Andrew,	264
Lytle family,	437
Lytle's ferry,	217
McCammon, James,	359
John,	94
McCosh, John,	267
Macfarlane,	353
McKinney, Mordecai,	479
Magaw, Col. Robert,	463
Maginnis, James,	360
Magnetic telegraph, first at Harrisburg,	258

Maher, Rev. Peirce, ... 360
Manning, Capt. Richard, company of, ... 425
Martinsburg, Va., ... 489
Masonic pitcher, ... 89
Masonry prior to the Revolution, ... 256
Means, Samuel, ... 224
Melish, John, ... 361
Military spirit in 1786, ... 303
   In 1821, ... 302
Miller, Col. Henry, ... 146
Millersburg, laying out of, ... 262
Minsker, Ludwig, ... 410, 436
Monteith, Capt. James, ... 1
Montgomery, Rev. Joseph, ... 152
   Rachel, ... 361
Muench, Rev. Charles Edward, ... 205
Murray, Capt. James, ... 425
   Company of, ... 7
   Col. John, ... 2, 203, 362
   Lindley, the grammarian. 27, 48, 58, 81
National capital, location of, ... 159
Newville, Dauphin county, ... 263
New York, Pennsylvania immigration into, ... 312
Oak Dale Forge, ... 378
Oath of Allegiance, in 1777-79, ... 227, 231, 286
Opickon Church, Va., ... 493
Orth Family, ... 383
Palmstown, ... 234
Partridge's Military School at Harrisburg, ... 61, 72, 84
Patterson, Mary, ... 355
   William, ... 346
Paxtang, or Paxton, ... 251
   Church, 1808, ... 82, 95
      Baptisms in, ... 430
      Deaths in, ... 422
      Marriages in, ... 380
   Volunteers in 1779, ... 349
   Assessment for 1770, ... 179
   North End, assessment of, ... 95
   Boys, ... 2, 107, 434
Peacock, James, ... 247, 362
Penn, John, visit to Harrisburg, ... 135
Perry, Oliver, Presentation of Medal to, ... 306
Peter's Mountain Road, ... 15
Peterson, Rev. John Diedrich, ... 115
Poe, Capt. James, ... 473
Politics in 1799, ... 364
Pollock, Oliver, ... 475
Potts, Stacy, ... 453
Puglia, James Philip, ... 51
Railroad Cars, first at Harrisburg, ... 460
Ramsey, Thomas, ... 363
Rankin Traitors, The, ... 235
Reily, Capt. John, ... 365
Revolution, Correspondence of, ... 145
   Officers from Lancaster co., ... 459
   Penn'a Quakers in, ... 189
   Soldiers of the, . 7, 22, 26, 141, 149, 177, 259, 349, 384, 399, 424, 450, 474, 483

Contents.

Rheumatism, Cider a cure for,	215
Ripper, John G.,	481
Roan, Rev. John, of Derry,	366
Subscription book,	458
Roddy, James,	283, 440
Rolling mill, an early,	439
Rutherford family record,	121
Capt John, company of,	399
Sallade, Simon,	206
Sawyer family,	89
Schools, early,	33
Seiler, Henry,	355
Settlers, arrival of early,	412
Sherer, Capt. Joseph, company of,	384
Shoch, John,	366
Shultze, Gov. J. Andrew,	247
Silvers of Silvers Spring,	465
Simmons, Col. Seneca G.,	337, 367
Simonton, Dr. William,	367
Simpson, John,	1, 139, 368
Smull, John Augustus,	25
Snaketown,	1, 10, 19, 41, 70
Snodgrass, Rev. James,	368, 371
Snodgrass, Rev. William Davis,	25
Spangenberg, Bishop, journey of in 1745,	117
"Soldier's Tale, The," the characters in,	54, 397
Stambaugh, Samuel C.,	247
State capital,	281
Steel, James, letter of,	8
Stevensburg, Va.,	490
Stewarts,	2, 94
Stewart, Andrew, of Paxtang,	12, 43
Stewarts of Hanover,	31
Stewart, Capt. Lazarus,	369
"Stophel" and "Christly,"	32
"Straw Jacket, a com'ab with,"	242
Susquehanna, early exploration of,	390
Swan family record,	154
Telegraph despatch, the first,	458
Templeton, Robert,	302
"Tit-for-Tat,"	32
Tobey, William Carroll,	239
"Tokens,"	5
Trenton and Princeton, officers at,	459
Trimble, James,	309
Grave of,	6
Umholtz family,	209
University of Pennsylvania, graduates of,	330
Upper Paxtang in the Revolution,	177
Assessment, 1778,	271
Walker, Capt. Thomas,	370
Wallace family,	120
Capt. Benjamin,	379, 458
William,	372
Ward the sculptor,	223
War of 1812–14, volunteers in,	280
Franklin county in,	448

Contents.

Washington's itinerary in 1794,	224
Weaver, Capt. Martin,	229
Weirick, Jacob,	373
Weise, Adam,	373
Family,	288
Whitehill, George,	375
Wiconisco in 1775,	21
Wiestling, Dr. Samuel C.,	374
Williamsburg on Swatara,	243
Williamsville,	263
Williard, John Peter,	209
Wilson family,	97
Henry,	436
Matthew,	248
Winchester, Va.,	490, 495
Winebrenner, Rev. John,	374
Wood, Nicholas Bayles,	375
Wyeth, Francis,	247
John,	376
Yeates, Jasper,	485
Yorktown, Penn'a,	488

NOTES AND QUERIES.

HISTORICAL AND GENEALOGICAL.

NOTES AND QUERIES.—I.

CAPT. JAMES MONTEITH.—Who was this individual? He appears to have been made a Mason in Perseverance Lodge, No. 21, on the 13th of February, 1781.

"SNAKETOWN."—John Burt, one of the earliest traders on the Susquehanna, resided at an Indian town on the river, forty miles above the Conestoga, called Snaketown. This would locate it at this point. An inquiry is made as to its topography.

INFORMATION WANTED concerning Wm. McCullough, ——— Darnell, James McNamara, William Wright, John McChesney, John Miller, Robert Curan, Robert Lusk, Robert Foster, Henry Laughlin, William Smith, Robert Marshall and Samuel Thompson, all of whom resided in this locality in 1779 and 1780.

CUMBERLAND VALLEY HISTORICAL SOCIETY.—A call signed by the Rev. Dr. Murray, of Carlisle, and others interested in historic research, for a meeting at Doubling Gap Springs on the 10th of July, [1879], to organize a Historical Society, has been issued. The entire Cumberland Valley is rich with incident and story, and it is to be hoped that there will be such interest manifested in the effort now making that the success of an organization may be secured. It has the good wishes of sister societies.

SIMPSON—MURRAY.—I have a commission issued in 1775 to my grandfather, John Simpson, who then lived near Fort Hunter, as a lieutenant in a battalion of associators. It is signed by John Morton, speaker of the Assembly. Were these associators called into the service? John Simpson was in the service, but in what organization I do not know. He was a son-in-law of Capt. James Murray (not of Northumberland county, but he of Paxtang), and a nephew by marriage of Col. John Murray. Capt. James, of Northumberland county, was originally from Paxtang, and according to family tradition, a nephew of the James and John above mentioned.   J. S. A.

FULTON—STEWART.—George Stewart owned a farm next to John Galbraith, but Samuel Fulton, who married Stewart's daughter Elizabeth, owned the third farm to the northwest. Stewart died in February, 1733, in Donegal. His son James got the homestead farm. His other children were, besides Mrs. Fulton, John, Frank and Mary. Samuel Fulton died in 1760, leaving his widow, sons James and Samuel. To the latter he left 139 acres of land and his " leather breeches with silver buttons." The farm was subsequently sold to his brother James. The original tract, patented in 1744, was called " Fulton's Choice." The Stewarts and Fultons were inter-married with the Allisons, Crawfords, Andersons and Clarks, of Donegal and Paxtang.
SAMUEL EVANS.

DUNDORE.—My ancestors settled in the Tulpehocken country. The first date mentioned is in the church book of the Host Church in 1749. The name of Dundore is not found in Rupp's " 30,000 Names of Immigrants," nor in any published records, save in Vol. II., p. 378 and 402, 2d series of Pennsylvania Archives, where are recorded the names of Jacob Dender and Jacob Dender, jr., which I am of opinion, if properly spelled, should be " Dundore." Can you inform me whence came Jacob Dunder or Dundore?   N. D.

[Unfortunately, the records of foreign immigration into Pennsylvania are not complete, and hence it is impossible to give the precise time of the arrival of many families. Between 1740 and 1750 there was a large emigration of French-Swiss to Pennsylvania—nearly all settling in the townships of Alsace, Oley and Tulpehocken, Berks county. With this emigration came the Dundores, father and son.]

"THE PAXTANG BOYS."—Among the number of those heroic men of 1763-4, was Capt. John Reed, who removed to the Buffalo Valley prior to the Revolution. He married in September, 1772, Margaret, daughter of William Blythe, but died in 1778, leaving three children, William, James, and a daughter, who subsequently married John Armstrong. The family left the valley with the "great runaway," and resided for several years in the Cumberland Valley. The widow subsequently married Capt. Charles Gillespie, of the army of the Revolution, and raised a second family. When a second time a widow she took refuge with her son, William Reed, where she died, and is buried in the old Kiester graveyard, on Penn's creek. William Reed, the eldest, had a son James, whose children are Robert Reed, formerly county commissioner of Union county, and subsequently a merchant at Clearfield; Dr. Uriah Reed, of Jersey Shore, and a daughter, who is the wife of ex-Governor William Bigler. Captain Reed's second son removed to the West in early life, but was never heard from.   J. B. LINN.

THE HARRIS FAMILY OF PAXTANG.

Among the early settlers of this locality was William Harris, a native of Scotland, and no doubt related to John Harris, the pioneer of Harris' ferry. He was born in 1701 and died on the 4th of April, 1754. His wife was Catharine Douglass, of the family of Sir Robert Douglass, of Scotland, born in 1709, dying August 7, 1780, aged 71 years. William Harris and his wife are buried in Old Derry graveyard, of which church he was a member. His plantation was on the Swatara, one and a half miles above Middletown. The record of the children of these pioneers, as copied from an old Bible, marked "James Harris, his Book," reads as follows:

"James Harris wass born the 16th of January, being Friday, 1739.

"Sarah Harris wass born the 20th of March, it being Saturday, 1741.

"John Harris wass born November the 20th, it being Friday, 1746.

"William Harris wass born November the 20th, it being Wednesday, 1749.

"Mary Harris was born July the 22d, it being Thursday, 1752."

There appears to have been another entry in 1753, but it is illegible. As the youngest son, Robert, was born that year it was evidently his birth record.

William Harris died the year after (1754). A distribution of his estate was not made, however, until 1763, when, on the 6th of September, the orphans' court, held at Lancaster, directed the following:

"To Catharine Harris, widow of the deceased, the interest of one-third, in lieu of her dower; James, the eldest son, one-third as the remainder, or two shares; while the other children—Sarah, John, Mary and Robert—were to receive one share; the dower to be divided among the same upon the decease of the widow. The personal property was also distributed in the same proportion.

Robert Harris, the youngest child, studied medicine and served as a surgeon of the Pennsylvania Line during the Revolution. He was a valuable officer and highly esteemed by his confreres in that glorious struggle. Dr. Harris died of quinsy at the house of John Phillips, inn-keeper, the sign of the Blue Ball, about twenty miles west of Philadelphia, in Tredyffrin township, Chester county, on the night of the 4th of March, 1785. His will was written by Andrew Gordon, at his request, and is dated March 3, 1785, "recorded May 3, 1785, and remains in the register's office in Paxtang, Dauphin county." Letters of administration with the will annexed, were granted to Mary Harris, the wife of his brother James. Dr. Harris willed the interest of a part of his personal estate to his brother John Harris during his lifetime, and then the principal to fall to Robert, son of James. His land (donation land), when surveyed, he allowed to Laird Harris, son of James. From a receipt still in existence, tombstones were purchased in Philadelphia, and as there are no records in the graveyard at Derry or Paxtang, the presumption is that he was interred at Tredyffrin. The papers of Dr. Harris, which would be of undoubted historic value, were burned by a member of the family some forty years ago, *to prevent their falling into the hands of strangers.* His medicine chest is in the possession of his grand-nephew, William L. Harris, of East Buffalo township, Union county.

Of Sarah and Mary Harris, daughters of William, we have no record.

James Harris, the eldest child, married June 2, 1768, Mary Laird, daughter of William Laird and Catharine Spencer. She was born April 28, 1750 (O. S.), and died December 13, 1842. She was interred in the cemetery at Lewisburg. James Harris died April 30, 1787, and is buried at Derry. The children of James Harris and Mary Laird were as follows:

William, born Wednesday, April 28, 1769, died February 2, 1785, and buried at Derry.

Elizabeth, born Thursday, July 18, 1770; died May 20, 1842.

Catharine, born Thursday, April 2, 1772; died December 28, 1784, and buried at Derry.

Jean, born January 6, 1774; died December 5, 1839.

Laird, born Tuesday, February 22, 1776; died June 30, 1804.

Robert, born Sunday, November 22, 1777; died at Lewisburg.

Sarah, born Saturday, September 4, 1779; died December 30, 1827.

James, born Wednesday, June 13, 1781; died July 1, 1868.

Matthew, born Friday, August 13, 1784; died February 13, 1873.

William Laird, born Thursday, May 17, 1786; died November 11, 1845.

James Harris took and subscribed the oath of allegiance and fidelity to the State and Colonies on the 14th day of July, 1777, before Joshua Elder, magistrate at Paxtang. He served in the army and was at the battles of Trenton, Princeton, Brandywine and Germantown. During the year 1778 he was in service with his wagon and team in the Jerseys. After his death his widow removed about 1792 to Buffalo Valley, then Northumberland and now Union county.

James Harris, the son of James, married October 29, 1819, Sarah Bell. Their children, William Laird, James Spencer, Samuel Bell, Mary Laird, Robert Douglass, Ann Berryhill, Sarah Clementina, Caroline Douglass and Berryhill Bell.

Of this family of Harris' none remain in this locality. Like their neighbors of a century and more agone, their descendants have sought new homes, while only the brief tombstone inscriptions in deserted graveyards, and the mere mention of a name here and there on the old records, tell of the brave and hardy ancestry.

NOTES AND QUERIES.—II.

"LONG BULLETS."—Who can explain this ancient pastime?
DAUPHIN.

"CHURCH TOKENS."—In the early days at Paxtang, Hanover and Derry, tokens were used by the officiating ministers. These were made of lead or pewter, and had raised letters on one side with date on the reverse. One in possession of the writer has the letters B. P. stamped on one side. A wag at our elbow says they stand for Bad Presbyterian, but we opine it is for Baptized Presbyterians, or the B may stand for the Pastor, Rev. Bertram. Who can give us the meaning? Recently we were shown one used by the Rev. John Cuthbertson, who missionated among Reformed Presbyterians in this section of Pennsylvania from 1751 to the close of the Revolution. On the one side were the letters R. R., which stand for Reformed Presbyterian, and L. S. (which most probably stand for Lord's Supper), and the date 1752 on the other side. The use of the token was this: The tokens were given to the intending communicants generally on the sacrament occasion, and then on the Sabbath when the communicant came forward to the table of the Lord, he presented his token to a member of session, which was the evidence that the session regarded him as entitled to participate in this ordinance.

JAMES TRIMBLE'S GRAVE.—Out in the Harrisburg cemetery is the neglected grave of James Trimble, who for fifty-six years was Deputy Secretary of the Commonwealth. From the period of his coming here until his death he took a warm interest in everything tending to the prosperity of the then borough of Harrisburg. His remains were interred in the old Presbyterian graveyard, but in the march of improvement, which does not recognize the rights of the dead—even if it chances to do that of the living, they were removed to the Harrisburg cemetery. Instead, however, of replacing the tomb in a proper manner, it was simply laid together, and at the present writing bids fair to be destroyed unless some measures are taken to have it preserved. The Presbyterian congregation, to whose interests he devoted much time and labor, cannot do a nobler act than at once see that the tombstone of the old patriot shall not be destroyed by neglect.

HARRISBURG IN 1794.—[The following interesting account of our "ancient burgh" is from the journal of Major Wm. Gould, of the New Jersey Infantry, during the so-called whisky insurrection in Western Pennsylvania, in the autumn of 1794. Brief though his record is, it contains several important items: The abounding of the Susquehanna with rock fish, salmon, shad and fowl—that previous to the founding of the town in 1785 there were quite a number of houses and people here—it again opens up the question where did Gen. Washington stop when remaining in town; and the existence of a public ferry, which was distinct from either the lower or upper ferries, taking in the island in the transit.]

Thursday, October 2d.—Marched to Hummelstown, a handsome village with kind inhabitants; we were invited into their houses and had good entertainment in taverns. Sixteen miles.

Friday, October 3d.—Marched one mile to a river called Sweet Arry; crossed on boats, and marched to Harrisburg and encamped on the banks of the Susquehanna river, a beautiful stream abounding with rock fish, salmon, and other small fish, and fowl in abundance; also shad of the best kind in the season. The founder of this town, named Harris, buried in a stockade fort by reason that the Indians prevented burying in the graveyard. Twenty-five years ago there were but three or four houses, and now it contains more than 300, beautifully situated on the banks of the river; some elegant houses, good market and full stores; a county town in Dauphin county.

At 3 o'clock p. m. paraded and marched to town from where we encamped, saluted the President of the United States, who passed by, after which returned to camp. Col. Forman, Major Kipp and myself accepted an invitation from the President to take a glass of wine with him, after which dined very agreeably, and returned to camp; the inhabitants received us with every mark of friendship; the artillery discharged fifteen guns at his entrance into town. Nine miles.

Saturday, October 4th.—Marched to the Susquehanna ferry at reveille in the morning, with the first battalion, crossed in boats to an island in the river and from thence in other boats to the other side. Suffered much with cold in crossing, it being a very cold morning. The President, General Washington, forded the river in a coach, drove it himself, &c.

CAPTAIN JAMES MURRAY'S COMPANY—1776.

In the N. and Q. (No. i) inquiry is made as to whether the battalion, or rather the company of associators of which John Simpson was lieutenant, was in actual service. We present herewith the roll of Captain James Murray's company as returned by him March 13, 1776. This company, with others, went into service in November or December, 1775, and were present at the battles of Trenton and Princeton. We give the roll as we find it, although a number of the names are evidently misspelled. The members of the company nearly all resided in what was then Upper Paxtang township, or in the section of country from the present town of Dauphin extending to Halifax. Beyond and around the latter locality was Capt. Reed's company, the roll of which is also in our possession. There is one name on the list, that of John Ayres, who was a member of Capt. Matthew Smith's company, of Paxtang, and was left with several others sick at Boston when that brave body of men marched to Quebec. The probabilities are that as they were returning home, about the time of the arrival from Philadelphia, he at least joined his friends and neighbors, and shared with them the hardships and endurance of that brief winter campaign on the Delaware.

A Return of Captain James Murray's Company of Associators of the Fourth Battalion of Lancaster County, Commanded by James Burd, Esq., March 13th, 1776.

Captain.	Brown, Peter,	Lindsey, William,
Murray, James.	Christy, John,	Linord, James,
First Lieutenant.	Cochran, George,	Lockart, Moses,
Sturgeon, Peter.	Cochran, John, sr.,	McCloskey, Henry,
Second Lieutenant.	Cochran, John, jr.,	McFadden, John,
Simpson, John.	Cochran, Samuel,	McGill, Robert,
Ensign.	Colligan, Joseph,	Mooney, Abraham,
Ryan, John.	Colligan, John,	Peacock James,
Privates.	Davis, David,	Plouge, Samuel,
Ayres, John,	Dice, John,	Richmond, John,
Bell, George,	Eyeman, Christopher,	Smith, Robert,

Bell, Isaac,
Bell, James,
Bell, John sr.,
Bell, John jr.,
Bell, William, jr.,
Bell, William,
Bell, William, sr.,
Boyce, John,
Boyce, William,
Brown, John,

Eyeman, Jacob (1),
Eyeman, Jacob, (2),
Gallacher, Thomas,
Gartner, George Adam,
Goudey, John,
Goudey, Robert,
Hilton, William,
Hoane, Anthony,
Johnston, Richard,
Lafferty, Patrick,

Smith, William,
Sturgeon, Samuel,
Sturgeon, Thomas,
Thomas, John,
Thompson, Thomas
Tinturf, Jacob,
Tinturf, Philip,
Vincent, William,
Yanelet, Michael,

JAMES BURD,
Col. 4th Battalion, Lancaster County.

CONTRIBUTIONS TO DAUPHIN COUNTY HISTORY.

Recently the library of the Pennsylvania Historical Society has been enriched by a collection of the papers of John and Isaac Taylor, who were surveyors of Chester county, when Lancaster and Dauphin were integral parts of that locality, comprising in the thirty odd folio volumes of manuscript a great mass of material relating to the days of the pioneer settlers, and as occasion offers we shall make such selections as may possibly be of interest, and especially of value to the future historian of our county.

James Steel, writing to Isaac Taylor under date of "4th, 11 mo., 1726," after mentioning various matters, says:

"The bearer, John Harris, has seen his warrants, which are now at James Logan's to be signed, which I expect will be done this day, there being now no objections, the original deeds being produced.

"Thee knows the warrants had been twice drawn over, but what I received from thee for it cannot tell, but J. Harris has paid me 12 shillings, which, if too much, I have told him it shall be returned.

"I have no more to add at present, but kind love and respects to thyself, spouse and family. Thy affectionate loving friend,
"JAMES STEEL."

Peter Bizalion, the first Indian trader in these parts, and who had located at Paxtang previous to John Harris, and concerning whom a very interesting sketch was written by Mr. Hamilton several years ago, receipts to James Logan, under date of "20th, 6 mo., 1703," for "fifteen pounds in full for a score of bear skins sold him at 15 sh. per skin."

Benjamin Eastburn, who was Surveyor General of the Province many years, of the date of "April the 20th, 1736," after noticing the appointment of Samuel Blunston as "Deputy Surveyor of the townships of Derry, Hempfield, Dunnegal and Lebanon," at the same time alluding to "a scheme of his (Blunston) for appeasing the tumults and animosities among the inhabitants thereof," writes:

"*April, the 20th, 1736.*

"*My Friend John Taylor:* Thine of the 3d inst. with several Returns I rec'd, but have not heard anything of the persons in Caln thou expectest to complain because thou refusedst to lay out to them land already surveyed to the Proprietor.

"Samuel Blunston is deputed surveyor of the Townships of Derry, Hempfield, Dunnegal & Lebanon, and upon a representation of Samuel Blunston in behalf of the inhabitants thereof, and a scheme of his for appeasing the tumults & Animosities among them, there was sent up to him a bundle of blank warr'ts by him to be filled up at discretion w'ch after the same manner I suppose he executes the warr'ts are only directed to me & his Deputation is only to execute such warr'ts as are by me directed to him.

"One William Skillirn a late settler at Pextang on part of tract of 300a sd. to have been formerly settled by one Jno Miller by leave of James Logan obtained a warrant for 150a dated the 23d of March last, and Esther Harris, John Harris's wife, tells me there is a man at Pextang (she had forgot his name) had lately got a Warrt. and is now making sad havock of the Timber on thy Land there. I take it to be the same man: she says he is a dancing master. Thou wilt take proper measures with him, he has a copy of ye Warrt. directed to Sam'l Blunston, but I then understood nothing of his intent nor am I yet sure that is the man E. H. spoke of, but no other has had any wart. lately here.

"Andreas Scroop (alias Krobff), a settler on Cocalico & Hans Shinover his neighb'r each had a warr't for 250a dated the first of Mar. 1733. Thou hast made a Return of 165a laid out to Scroop, who says that he & a widow woman both live on the land & expected and agreed for 125a each he has long since paid for about 200a & brought the rem'd of the money y't would compleat the pay for 250a. Shinover has paid nothing nor intends to pay, his settlem't being now offered to sale at £200 the Buy'r being also to pay the Proprit'r. I suppose Krobf ought first to have his 250a before Shinover's Return be made who has not yet applied for a copy or order.

" I am thy real fr'd

"BENJA EASTBURN."

[The Esther Harris here alluded to was a most estimable lady. She was a native of England; of the family of Say, and related to the Shippens of Philadelphia, where John Harris met her, and in 1722 married her. He was her senior some fifteen or twenty years.

After the death of the pioneer she married William Chesney, or McChesney, who resided on the opposite side of the Susquehanna, below the mouth of the Yellow Breeches. She died in 1757, but where buried is not known. She may possibly have been interred at Paxtang graveyard, but there is no stone to mark her grave.]

NOTES AND QUERIES.—III.

"SNAKETOWN" (N. and Q. No. i.)—It is possible that this trading point was at or between Burd's run and the mill run north of it, at the present town of Highspire, in Swatara township, Dauphin county. It was not at Paxtang creek where Bizalion established himself in 1707. Burt seems to have commenced his career as trader about 1719. His name is found on the assessment of West Conestogue, Chester county, in 1721, rated at twenty shillings. The locality designated is famous for its water snakes to this day, and is about thirty-nine miles, by the Susquehanna, from the mouth of the Conestoga creek. Evans, of Columbia, states that Burt "was a troublesome trader, living in continual violation of the provincial laws" regulating trade with the Indians. In 1726, Burt, Wright and some Muncy Indians had a drunken frolic at Snaketown, in which Wright and an Indian were killed by Burt, and the latter with his wife Esther, "forced out of the inhabited parts of this province" by order of "Gov. Gordon and ye council."

THE N. W. CORNER SECOND STREET AND CHERRY ALLEY.—The two houses now on the northwest corner of Second street and Cherry alley were built by John Downey, Esq., in the year 1812, and owned by him. George Loyer was the brick-layer. Mr. Downey, who was the first cashier of the Harrisburg Bank, resided in the upper house and rented the lower one, which was occupied by some of the first families of the town.

One of the earliest occupants, if not the first, was Moses McClean, a distinguished lawyer of his day. He removed to Lewistown, from thence to Huntingdon, where he died.

The next tenant was Mrs. Snyder, widow of Gov. Snyder, who kept a boarding house. Mrs. Snyder, whose maiden name was Slough, was a sister of Mrs. Clendennin and also of the first wife of James Peacock.

Mrs. Rebecca Orth resided there subsequently and kept boarders. Her family consitted of four sons, Henry, William, Adam and

Edward L., and three daughters, Rebecca, Elizabeth and Caroline It was here that young Dr. Luther Reily made a beginning in his profession, which proved so eminently useful and successful. He boarded with Mrs. Orth, and had for his office the one recently occupied by Dr. Ross Roberts. Dr. Reily married Rebecca Orth. Elizabeth Orth married John Whitehill, who lived and died on what is now known as the "Reily farm," above now Reily street. Caroline Orth married Dr. Witman, who resided at Halifax. Adam Orth married Miss Elizabeth Cox and resided near Coxestown, where he died. Edward L. read medicine with Dr. Reily, and after graduation became one of the firm of Reily & Orth. He was an eminent physician, dying April 15, 1861, aged 47 years.

Succeeding Mrs. Orth came James Maginnis, who taught a grammar school for boys. He was an Irishman, a fine mathematician and was considered one of Harrisburg's best teachers. He was a large, burly-looking man, a strict disciplinarian, who was feared and respected by his scholars, many of whom in after life occupying good positions. James W. Weir and others of our prominent men were his scholars. Mr. Maginnis was the author of an arithmetic, which was the standard book of that day. Frederick W. Leopold, who was a clerk in the bank while Mr. Downey was cashier, and Thomas Smith, once county surveyor, were brothers-in-law, having married sisters. Mr. Maginnis had three children—Edmund, who was a druggist, Mary and James B. Mrs. Maginnis was a Roman Catholic. If her husband was one be did not live up to the rules of the church. Mr. Leopold belonged to the same persuasion.

Mr. William LeBarron, one of Harrisburg's first and most enterprising men, purchased, improved and resided there some years. He built the first steam grist mill and warehouse, &c., in the borough. He was unfortunate, however, in business, and removed to Pittsburgh where he died.

Mr. Henry Alward, formerly a teller in the Harrisburg Bank, resided there a short time. Mr. Alward and General John Forster were brothers-in-law, having married daughters of Samuel Elder, son of Rev. John Elder, of Paxtang. Mr. Alward and family removed to Pittsburgh where he died.

The building was then purchased for a young ladies' seminary and boarding school. The principal was Mrs. Kingsford, wife of the Rev. E. Kingsford, pastor of the Baptist church here. The school was well sustained for several years, but closed about the year 1842, the Rev. K. and family leaving town. They were from England and were much liked by our citizens. Many of the young ladies who boarded with Mrs. Kingsford were the daughters of prominent famlies living in Juniata, Cumberland and York counties, and this sketch will be read by some of them and their children.

The Rev. William R. DeWitt, D. D., purchased the property from the Trustees of the Seminary, and resided there many years and until he moved to the present residence on Front street. Mr. M. Einstein succeeded him, and he was succeeded by the present owner and occupant, Mr. Charles S. Segelbaum. The number is now 120 South Second street.

The house occupied by Mr. Downey was purchased by Dr. James Roberts, who came from Cannonsburg, Washington county, Pa. He married Miss Emily Goldsmith, of this place, and had a good share of the practice of the town. In 1832 Edmond W. came from Cannonsburg, a young man, and read medicine with his brother, who removed to Illinois about 1835, and disposed of the property to Dr. E. W. The latter married Miss Caroline Ross, and had two children, Robert and Mary, who married the Rev. B. B. Leacock, D. D., pastor of St. Stephen's church. Dr. E. W. Roberts died October 10, 1865, aged 58 years. He was succeeded by Dr. R. Ross Roberts, who married Miss Mary Foote, and resided there practicing medicine until April 4, 1875, when he died, leaving two sons, Edmond and Leacock Roberts. The Rev. B. B. Leacock became owner, and disposed of it to Mr. A. M. Cleveland in March, 1879.   A. BURNETT.

ANDREW STEWART OF PAXTANG.

In the graveyard at Paxtang church are the following tombstone inscriptions:

In | memory of | Andrew Stewart | who departed | this life March | the 31st 1774 | Aged 75 years.

In | memory of | Mary Stewart | who departed | this life April | 30th 1772 | aged 65 years.

Andrew Stewart and Mary his wife came from Scotland prior to 1740. Owing to the destruction of the assessment lists immediately subsequent to the formation of Lancaster county, of which the townships of Paxtang, Derry and Hanover were an integral part upon its organization, it is very difficult to ascertain the precise year when the early settlers located here. Of the family of Stewart there were at least three distinct heads. The name is indifferently spelled Stuart and Stewart, but rarely Steward in the old records. The origin of the patronymic—Stewart—is from *ward*, to guard, to care for. The first syllable *ste* is of doubtful origin, but is supposed to mean a place, a corner, a quarter. Stuart, Stewart and Steward have all the same origin, although those who use the Stuart claim to have the bluer blood in their veins, which, of course, is a fallacy. The *u* was substituted for the *w* because of there being no *w* in the F ench alphabet, the Stewarts having retired to France, or perhaps during the reign of Queen Mary Stuart, the French courtiers having introduced or persisted in the French mode of spelling the name Stuart.

Andrew Stewart was a Covenanter of the most rigid faith, and the earliest Reformed Presbyterian minister in America, the Rev. John Cuthbertson, frequently tarried at his house while on his missionary tours. In his diary, under date of 20th of August, 1751, he notes the baptism of Eliza (Elizabeth), daughter of Andrew Stewart. On the organization of the Covenanter Church at Paxtang Mr. Stewart and his wife became members. But little is known of this hardy pioneer, save that in his day and generation he was ever loyal to the "Solemn League and Covenant."

Of the family of Andrew Stewart, his eldest son John, born in Paxtang, on the 24th of February, 1740, was educated for the ministry. While in England he was ordained in the established church, returned to Pennsylvania, where he was received with aught but favor by his strict old covenanter father. He went as a missionary among the Indians in the Mohawk valley, and made a translation of the New Testament into the Mohawk language. Refusing allegiance to the Colonies, in 1781 he went to Canada, where he became chaplain to a Provincial regiment, and subsequently as a missionary traveled through the upper province of Canada, where he labored with energy and success. In 1786 he settled at Kingston, and for some time previous to his death was chaplain to the Legislative Council. He died on the 15th of August, 1811.

Of the children of the Rev. John Stewart, or Stuart, as our Canadian friends prefer to write it, we have been able to glean the following data, hoping, however, that some member of the Literary and Historical Society of Quebec will furnish us with fuller, if not more accurate information. James Stewart, the eldest son, was born at Fort Hunter, New York, March 2, 1780, became an eminent Canadian jurist and chief justice of Lower Canada. He was called to the bar in 1801; appointed Solicitor General, 1805-9; Attorney General, 1822-32: Chief Justice, 1838-53. He was created a baronet in 1840, and died at Quebec, July 14, 1853. His son, Sir Charles Stuart, now resides in England during the summer season, and in Italy during the winter.

The second son, Andrew was also a distinguished jurist and solicitor general of Lower Canada—decidedly one of the most talented men of Canada—many years president of the Literary and

Historical Society of Quebec, was born at Kingston, U. C., in 1786, and died at Quebec February 21, 1840. He was the author of a number of valuable historical works. A son of Andrew Stuart is at present a judge—a gentleman of ability and ardent mind.

George O'Kill Stuart, another son, became an arch deacon. He married a daughter of Gen. John Brooks, a soldier of the Revolution and Governor of Massachusetts from 1816 to 1823. His son, of the same name, is Judge of the Vice Admiralty Court at Quebec.

John Stewart, sheriff, of Leeds and Greenville, who resided at Brockville, on the British side of the St. Lawrence, was also a son of the Rev. John first named.

We have given the forgoing to show the connection between the Stewarts of Paxtang and those of Canada.

The other children of Andrew Stewart, the pioneer, were James, Mary, Elizabeth, previously named, who died May 1, 1773, aged twenty-three years; Charles, Andrew and Eleanor. Of none of these do we know the history save that of Eleanor, the others probably removing from this locality after the death of their father and mother. Eleanor married Richard DeYarmond, second son of James and Mary DeYarmond. She was born May 4, 1753, and died February 19, 1830. Her husband, born in Hanover, September 1, 1743, died November 17, 1802. They are both interred in the old Hanover church graveyard. Their children were—James, born October 2, 1782, died January 7, 1812; Mary, born in 1784, who married James McCreight, junior; Eleanor, born in 1788; Andrew Stewart, born in 1791, and Margaret, born March 1, 1793, died May 6, 1824.

NOTES AND QUERIES.—IV.

ALWARD—ELDER.—"A. B." in his account of the three-story brick houses on the northwest corner of Second street and Cherry alley, mentions that Henry Alward, one of the occupants, married a daughter of Samuel Elder, as did also General John Forster. They both married the daughters of John Elder, brother of Samuel. The present Mrs. Sarah Doll is a daughter of the latter.

"THE INDIAN TOWN.—In the Records of Donegal Presbytery, in 1732, allusion is made to the Congregation of Paxtang and Derry having been made over to Mr. Bertram and his heirs their right and title to the plantation commonly called "The Indian Town, purchased from the Indians, over and above their subscriptions," and promising "to deliver him all papers relating thereto." Who can tell us whether Paxtang or Derry church is located on the site of "The Indian Town," or where was Mr. Bertram's land?

THE HISTORICAL SOCIETY OF THE CUMBERLAND VALLEY.—The organization of this body was affected at Doubling Gap Springs on the 10th of July by the adoption of a constitution and the election of officers. The Hon. M. C. Herman, of Carlisle, was chosen President, and J. B. Morrow, editor of *The Star of the Valley*, Newville, Secretary. It was decided to hold its next annual meeting on the third Tuesday of July, 1880, which occurs on the 150th anniversary of the settlement of the valley, at such place as the committee shall arrange therefor. The society has our best wishes. It can and we believe will accomplish all its industrious members essay to do.

THE OLD PETER'S MOUNTAIN ROAD.

Having at various times seen it claimed that such an one "made the road over Peter's mountain," &c., in the interest of historical accuracy I would like to take advantage of the opportunity afforded by *Notes and Queries* to discuss this question, taking it for granted that all who can will throw upon it what light they are able.

At some future time I hope to publish the story of the Ayres family in Dauphin county—as it was one of the very first in the Upper End—but at present will suffice to note that William Ayres located at the eastern base of Peter's mountain in October, 1773. One reason for doing so was the very impracticable road by which he would have to cross the mountain, and which to the female portion of his family (already exhausted by a long journey) was terrible to contemplate. It was simply the "Indian Path to Shamokin" (Sunbury), and instead of winding around the end of the mountain at the river, ran due north and led straight up the mountain, and over it. [See Scull's map.] This path was partly on William Ayres' land, and as he must need have a road up and over the mountain, he—so the family tradition saith—labored betimes at this path until it was reduced to an angle of easier ascent, and otherwise made practicable. He died in 1785, but it appears that his son John Ayres, took up the work of making the road still better. I have in my possession "the Petition of the Subscribers, Inhabitants of the Township of Middle Paxtang," to "the Honorable William Augustus Atlee and his Associate Judges of the Court," &c., &c., " now sitting at Harrisburg for the county of Dauphin, at their March term, a. d.

1792," signed by thirty-one persons, some of them German, stating: "That your Petitioners being highly pleased with the improvement made by John Heirs [Ayres] of the said Township on that part of the road leading from Harrisburg to Sunbury, which lays between the south end of the meadow of said Heirs and the first offset in the old Road which was opened by order of Court a few years since over Peter's mountain. . . . We pray that Heirs' road be confirmed."

The ancient document is the indisputable evidence that John Ayres made what might be termed the *second* improvement. The reference of this petition to "the old road which was opened by order of court a few years since," I take to mean the road, or the old Indian Path, as improved by William Ayres, his father, and accepted ["opened"] by the county, from him as a public highway. This, of course, was *the first* "road," so to speak. The road in time became a regular turnpike, and passed into the control of a turnpike company.

In my father's cash-receipt book I find an item under date of April 7, 1831, viz: "Turnpike company, pay as manager, $50;" and again "May 3, 1831, turnpike company in full, $29.50."

These entries do not *name* the company for which he was "Manager," but under the circumstances I assume it to be the turnpike over Peter's mountain. During his term as manager he made additional improvements upon the mountain division.

Documentary evidence in the possession of our family goes to show that William Ayres made the first *road*, John Ayres the second and William Ayres (my father) the third and present one. That is, they (or through their instrumentality) altered the grades, changing the old Indian Path into the turnpike road. But I would not make any undue assumption in this matter, and hence I invite others to assist in establishing the true facts of the case. I am disposed to believe, however, that the claim of the family to this honor is assured to a large degree, at least, by the evidence alluded to, as well as by the circumstances of the case, until disproven.   G. B. AYRES.

"PAXTANG & DERRY'S CALL TO MR. JNO. ELDER."

[The history of Paxtang and Derry churches has yet to be written, and no person is better fitted for this labor of love than the author of the history of Old Hanover. The minutes of Donegal Presbytery, although not complete, throw considerable light on the history of the congregations which until June, 1764, formed an integral part of that body. Unfortunately here and there are gaps in the minutes of the Presbytery, and especially is this the case from October 9,

1750, to June 5, 1759. The church records were not regularly kept, or if they were have been lost. But little light can be thrown, therefore, upon the following document, which we find endorsed as follows: "*Paxtang & Derry's Call to Mr. Jno. Elder, Sept. 26th,* 1754—128 —*Call Unanimously.*" The Rev. John Elder came into the Presbytery of Donegal as a licentiate October 5, 1737, and was ordained and installed pastor of Paxtang on the 22d of December, 1738. The cause which occasioned the following call is difficult to explain, without entering into the history of the churches in question and the many troubles and dissensions which existed. Of the names attached to the call, those marked * were written by the individuals themselves. The duplicating of signatures is perchance owing to the fact that the call was adopted at a congregational meeting, and some one who acted as clerk directed to append the names of those present. Its interest lies not only in the peculiarity of the document, but in the full list of members of Old Paxtang church one hundred and twenty-five years ago.]

To the Reverend Mr. Jno. Elder: SIR—We the Inhabitants in the Township & Congregation of Paxtang & Derry, Being now Destitute of a settled Gospel Minister amongst us; Being also Deeply Sensible of the great loss & Disadvantage we & ours may sustain In regard of our souls & spiritual Concerns by our living in such a Condition in this Wilderness; & having had Sufficient Proof of, & being well pleased & satisfied with the ministerial abilities & qualifications of y'u, the Revd. Jno. Elder, Do unanimously Invite & Call y'u to take the Pastoral Care & oversight of us, Promising all due subjection, submission & obedience to the Doctrine, Discipline & Government & Ordinances Exercised & administered By y'u as our Pastor in the Lord. And that y'u may be the Better Enabled to attend upon y'r Pastoral & ministerial work amongst us, without Anxious & Distracting Cares about y'r worldly Concerns, WE Do hereby Cheerfully Promise & Engage to take Care of y'r Support and maintenance for an Honourable & Creditable manner Suitable to & befitting y'r Honourable Function & office as a Minister of the Gospel of Jesus Christ amongst us; Knowing that the Lord hath ordained that they who Preach the Gospel should live by the Gospel." In testimony of all w'h we have hereunto Subscribed our Names This 26th of September, 1754.

*Thos. fforster,
*Wm. Armstrong,
*John Harris,
*Thomas McArthur,
*James Wallace,
David Walker,

John Cavit,
William Harris,
Robert Gilchrist,
John Gilchrist,
William McAlevey,
John Foster,

Stephen Gamble,
Alex'r Mahon,
James Galbraith,
Robert Wallace,
*John Harris,
James Foster,

*Robert Chambers,
*Moses Dickey,
William Stoe,
*Thomas Simpson,
James Collier,
Thomas Dougan,
Henry McKinney,
Andrew Stephen,
John Bell,
John Morrow,
Henry Renick,
John Johnson,
Oliver Wyllie,
Samuel Simpson,
Thomas Renick,
Patrick Montgomery,
Richard Cavit,
William Bell,
Thomas King,
Edward King,
Robert Montgomery,
John Wiggins, jr.,
James Gilchrist,
James Mitcheltree,
John Neal,
William Hannah,
John Carson,
James Drummond,
Samuel Hunter,
Alex. Johnson,
George Gillespy,
Patrick Gillespy,
David Patton,
James Potts,
Joseph Wilson,
John McCormick.
Robert Walker.

David McClanochan,
David Reaney,
John Craig,
John Wyllie,
Thomas Mays,
Hugh Hays,
Andrew Moore,
David Foster,
John Hays,
Henry Walker,
John Walker,
John Walker,
James Walker,
Hugh Carothers,
James Carothers,
James Williamson,
Samuel Galbraith,
Hugh McKillip,
Matthew Cowden,
James Houston,
James Tom.
John Starling,
Andrew Hannah,
Peter Corbit,
Wm. Kerr,
Joseph Kerr,
John Gray,
William Wilson.
Michael Whitley,
Thomas Alexander,
Valentine Stern,
Andrew Houston,
Alex. Johnson,
Samuel Stephenson,
Thomas Rutherford,
Mathias Taylor,

James Freeland,
Robert Armstrong.
Haugh Wilson,
James Wilson,
Robert Chambers, jr,
Arthur Chambers,
William Reney,
Robert McCallen,
John Hutchinson,
Charles McClure,
Hugh Black,
Robert Snodgrass,
Thomas Black,
Jean Black,
Wm. Laird,
Matthew Laird,
Elizabeth Park,
Chas. Clarke.
Mary M'Ilvain,
James Harris,
Samuel Shaw,
Thomas Aikens,
Th. Strean,
Thomas McClalen,
William Brison,
John McClintock,
James Davis,
James Rodgers,
Hugh Rodgers,
Joe McNot,
Widow Rodgers,
Seth Rodgers,
Joe Snoddy,
Robert Harris,
Wm. Galbraith,
David Jamison,

NOTES AND QUERIES.—V.

"CINQUAS."—John Sloan, who died in September, 1741, in his will mentions a daughter Cinquas. Can any one inform us what this means, or could it possibly be a mistake in transcribing the will in the office at Lancaster? If correct, it is at least a very singular name.

BROWN, JOHN, OF UPPER PAXTANG.—He died in 1786, leaving wife Rebecca and children, Audley, John, George, William. Mary married Wm. Smith; Elizabeth m. William Glover; Jane m. Robert Boyd; Rebecca m. Peter Smith. Can any one give an account of this family of Browns. It is probable that the Rev. Audley Brown, who was a candidate on the Prohibition State ticket several years ago, was a descendant.

LIND, REV. MATTHEW.—Was born at Cairn Castle, county Antrim, Ireland, in the year 1732. He was educated at the University of Glasgow, and was ordained by the Reformed (Covenanter) Presbytery of Scotland. For thirteen years he was pastor of the Reformed Presbyterian church, of Aghadowey, county of Londonderry, Ireland. In 1773, at the earnest solicitation of William Brown, of Paxtang, who went to Ireland for the purpose, he, in company with the Rev. Alex. Dobbins, came to America, arriving at New Castle, Delaware, in December of that year. In the spring of 1774 he became the first and only pastor of the Covenanter church of Paxtang, also officiating at Stony Ridge, now New Kingston, Cumberland county. When the Seceder and Covenanter churches united in 1782 and formed the Associate Reformed church, he and his two churches went into that union. By this time German immigration had largely pressed out his Irish families, so that in 1783 he felt compelled to resign and take the pastorate of the Associate Reformed congregations of Greencastle, Chambersburg, Mercersburg and the Great Cove. Here he died on the 21st of April, 1800, and was buried at Brown's Mill, six miles south of Chambersburg, near which he lived. The Rev. Mr. Lind married Jennie Fulton, of Paxtang, born in 1746, and dying April 1, 1819. She, too, is buried at Brown's Mill. Their son, John, subsequently succeeded his father to the ministry. He died at Hagerstown, Md., in 1824. The Rev. Matthew Lind was universally regarded by his associates as being both an able preacher and a zealous Christian.

WHERE WAS SNAKETOWN LOCATED?

Under the head of "Notes and Queries," in the *Telegraph* of July 12, 1879, **** undertakes to locate "Snaketown" at a point 35 miles above Conestoga creek, and charges Burt with killing Wright and an Indian. Both these statements are incorrect.

In the proceedings of Council, Mr. Logan quotes John Wright, Esq., who resided at Wright's Ferry, now Columbia, as locating "Snaketown" forty miles above Conestoga. See Col. Records, vol. iii, page 285. By the route traveled from the mouth of the Conestoga creek to the site of Harrisburg in Colonial times and at present is just forty miles. Harrisburg was always computed to be twenty-nine miles above Columbia and Conestoga creek ten miles below, the town of Columbia being one mile wide.

Burt, whatever his faults might have been was not guilty of murder. Wright was killed by an Indian, a full account of which is given by Jonas Davenport, in same volume and page. The principal objection to Burt was that he persisted to sell rum to the Indians, and neglected very often to take out a license to trade with the Indians. Could you not find room for Davenport's statement, and the list of jurors at the inquest?

Inquiry has also been made as to the location of Rev. William Bertram's farm. James Galbraith (the younger), who married Elizabeth, the only daughter of Rev. B., owned the adjoining farm of Rev. B. on the banks of the Swatara. There was a grist mill upon one of the farms. There is probably a mill there to-day, which may lead to the location of the Indian town. SAM'L EVANS.

COLUMBIA, PA., *July 22, 1879.*

EARLY COVENANTERS IN PAXTANG.

As early as 1720 six brothers of the name of Brown came from the north of Ireland and settled in Paxtang. They were Reformed Presbyterians or Covenanters, whose grandfather had been martyred in Scotland by the infamous Claverhouse for his attachment to the Scotch Covenants. The Browns were soon after joined by other families of Irish Covenanters, and within twenty years we find such names as Graham, Stuart, Williams, Taylor, Hains, McKnight, Chambers, Means, McCormick, Finney, Swan, Thorn and Mitchell. According to the rules of their Church they formed themselves into a religious society, and met in each others' houses on the Sabbath for prayer and praise, and the reading of the Scripture and religious conversation. Occasionally a sermon was read, which was generally selected from those of Cameron, or Cargill, or Paden, or Renwick, or some other Covenanting worthy.

At this time there was no Covenanter minister in America, but the Rev. Alexander Craighead, of the Presbytery of Donegal, strongly sympathized with them in their peculiar views, and was in the habit of frequently preaching to the little Covenanter societies at Paxtang, and at Pequea, and Octoraro, and Muddy Run, in Lancaster county.

The Rev. John Cuthbertson, a Scotch Covenanter, after missionating four years in Ireland, landed at New Castle, Delaware, on the 5th of August, 1751, and for 22 years made a visitation almost every year to all the little Covenanter societies in what are now the counties of Lancaster, Dauphin, York, Adams, Cumberland, Franklin and Fulton. He preached his first sermon in Paxtang at the house of William Brown on the 18th of August, 1751. He held one communion per year at some central place, to which the members of all these societies came, making a total number of about 250 communicants. His first communion was held at Stony Ridge, Cumberland county, on the 23d of July, 1752. The services on the Sabbath lasted about NINE hours. The next communion was on October 14, 1753, in Paxtang. These arrangements continued till December, 1773, when two more Covenanter ministers arrived from Ireland, the Rev. Alexander Dobbins who settled at Gettysburg and remained there until his death in 1809, and the Rev. Matthew Lind, who settled at Paxtang and Stony Ridge. These three—Cuthbertson, Lind and Dobbins—met in Paxtang on the 10th of March, 1774, and constituted the Reformed Presbytery of America.

On the 24th of February, 1771, William Brown, Benjamin Brown, Henry McCormick and Thomas Mitchell were ordained by Rev. Mr. Cuthbertson as ruling elders in Paxtang. It is possible there were no subsequent additions.

The Rev. Mr. Lind resigned in 1783 and removed to Franklin county. The few families left either identified themselves with neighboring Presbyterian churches or soon followed their migrated friends, so that in four or five years the entire organization had melted away.

WICONISCO IN 1775.

[The following is the earliest list we have been able to obtain of the "Taxables of Wisconisky, Paxtang Township." The names are given as spelled in the original document. Here and there is a surname familiar to the "Upper End," but the descendants of the majority of these early settlers have their homes in the Far West:]

Benjamin Buffington,
John Chester, jr.,
George Cooper,
Albright Diveler,
Anthony Fielich,
Peter Hoffman,
Henry Hanes,
Abe Jury,
Adam King,
Stophel Lark,
John Motter,
Abe Neighbour,
Jacob Newbacker,
Richard Peters, (?)
George Seal,

B. Stone,
Stophel Snyder,
Mike Sallady,
Ludwick Shotts,
Jacob Shotts,
George Supes,
Daniel Wolf,
James Woodside,
Felty Brough,
William Cline,
Mathias Diveler,
George Fight,
Jacob Herman,
Hansel Hoffman,
Mathias Hunter,

Samuel Jury,
Francis Lera,
John Miller,
Jacob Meets,
George Niggla,
John Powell,
George Riddle,
Joseph Staver,
Christ. Snokes,
Henry Wolf,
Robert Walker,
Adam Wertz,
Martin Weaver,
Jacob Weaver,
Mike Yetrack.

Located Unimproved Lands.

Abe Riggy,	John Walder,	Lazarts Winger,
Simon Levy,	Mike Roscolp,	Isaac Heeler,
Stephen Martin,	John Cline,	George Ekord,
Andrew Boggs,	James Beeham,	Isaac Haller,
Nick Miller,	Daniel Conn,	Simon Snyder,
Pat Work.	R. J. Enderline,	Philip D. Horst.
John Shock,	Anther Ticker,	Christ. Lauer.

LONDONDERRY IN 1775.

Within forty-eight hours of the receipt of the news of the battle of Lexington the able-bodied men of this entire region were organized for the defense of their liberties. The performance of military duty was no new thing to men who had been cradled amidst the clash of arms in the protection of the frontiers made desolate so many years by the ruthless savages—the merciless Delawares and the perfidious Shawanese. The document we publish herewith gives the names of the first company of the Associators we have yet seen. Almost the entire company were residents of Londonderry township. Its commanding officer, Capt. Jacob Cook, was prominent in organizing the troops throughout the war, at the same time being one of the Provincial magistrates, and as such continued by the convention of July 15, 1776. First Lieutenant William Hay rose to be a lieutenant colonel in the Flying Camp, in 1776-7, doing gallant service in the Jerseys and at Brandywine and Germantown. The McQueens, Robert and David, were subsequently connected with the Flying Camp, and if we mistake not were at Fort Washington at its capture. Of these officers we hope soon to obtain fuller information. Of the men who composed this first Londonderry company, several served through the war from Quebec to Yorktown, while others fell martyrs to the cause of Independence. The articles of association to which the men all subscribed are worthy of preservation.

The Association of the Liberty Company in Lancaster County.

In order to make ourselves perfect in the art of Military, &c., We, the subscribers, have associated, and severally Agree, Promise, and Resolve as follows, viz:

1st. That Jacob Cook be the Captain, Wm. Hay the first lieutenant, Robert McQueen the second Lieutenant, and David McQueen the Ensign of the Company in London Derry called the Liberty Company, which said Officers, according to their respective stations to have the Command of said Company, whilst under Arms, Mustering, or in actual Service, and that the said Officers shall remain till altered by a Majority of the Officers and two-thirds of the Company.

2d. That none of the subscribers or Company shall disobey the Orders of either of the said Officers, whilst under Arms or Mustering, or in actual Service, under the Penalty of paying a sum not exceeding Twenty shillings for every disobedience to be inflicted, and judged of, by a Majority of the Officers.

3d. That each Person of the Company shall (if not already done) as soon as possible, provide himself with a good Gun or Musket, in good order and repair, with a Cartouch-Box or Shot-Bag, and Powder-Horn, a half a Pound of Powder and two Pounds of Lead.

4th. That each of the said company shall attend weekly on Saturday, and on such other Times as the officers or a majority of them shall appoint, in the town of Lancaster, or in the county of Lancaster, at such places as the said officers shall deem necessary, under the Penalty of forfeiting and paying the sum of One Shilling, for every absence, Sickness of the person or Business out of the Town or Townships, to excuse. This is to be judged of by a majority of the Officers; but in case of absence at any Meeting, the Party so absenting to show Cause to the Officers against the next succeeding meeting, or the Fine to be absolute; every Person is to appear at such Meeting with his Arms and Ammunition as aforesaid under the Penalty of forfeiting the said Sum of One Shilling, for every default, unless a Majority of the Officers shall remit such Fine.

5th. That no Person of the said Company shall appear drunk, or curse or swear whilst under Arms Mustering, or in actual service, under the penalty of paying Three Shillings for the first offence; Five Shillings for the second offence, and for the third offence to be expelled the Company, a Majority of the Officers are also to judge of these offences.

6th. That should any of the Soldiers, by their Conduct render themselves unworthy of being a Member of said Company, a Majority of the Officers and Company may expel him; and in such case the Party expelled shall yet be obliged to pay off all arrearages of Fines.

7th. All Fines to be paid or exacted in consequence of the Resolutions or Regulations of this Company, are to be paid to the Captain for the time being, or the person appointed by him for that purpose, and are to be laid out for use of the said Company.

8th. That the said Company shall be increased to any number, not exceeding One Hundred Men.

9th. That the said Company shall not be obliged to march out of this Province, without the Direction of a Majority of the officers, with the consent of a Majority of the soldiers.

10th. That in case it be thought expedient the Companies of this County should form themselves into Battalions or regiments, we do hereby impower the Officers aforesaid, to join with the other officers of the County, in choosing Field Officers to command such Battalion or Regiment.

11th. That this Association to continue for the space of Eight Months next following, unless the time be enlarged by a Majority of the subscribers, or the Association dissolved by two-thirds of the Subscribers.

12th. That this Company and every member thereof shall also comply with any other Resolutions that shall be entered into by a majority of the officers and a majority of the Company for the Regulation, Government or Support of this Company.

13th. That a majority of the officers shall appoint the Sergeants, Corporals, and Drum for the Company.

14th. That the officers are to be fined for offences equal with ye privates.

In Testimony whereof we have hereunto set our Hands, the seventeenth day of May, 1775.

Privates.

Allemen, John,
Bratton John,
Bishop, Stophel,
Black, James,
Boyd, Samuel,
Brehm, Peter,
Brown, James,
Buck, Robert,
Buck, Thomas,
Campbell, John,
Campbell, William,
Carnahan, Robert,
Chambers, Robert,
Cook, Jacob,
Creed, James,
Davis, John,
Dixon, John,
Donaldson, James,
Dougherty, Hugh,
Duncan, John,
Elliot, Archibald,
Faulkner, Joseph,
Farmer, John,
Farmer. William,
Flack, James,
Foster, Andrew,
Foster, David,

Foster, James,
Fulton Alexander,
Fureman, Daniel,
Grimm, Dewalt,
Hall, William,
Hamilton, Charles,
Hay, James,
Hay, John,
Hay, Matthew,
Hay, William,
Henry, Adam,
Hoover, John,
Hostater, John,
Hunter, Robert,
Hunter, William,
Johnson, John,
Johnson, William,
Kelley, James,
Kelley, Patrick,
Kelley, Thomas,
Kennedy, John,
Keyner, Adam,
Lawser, Michael,
Logan, John,
Lynch, Patrick,
McCleary, Robert,
McClintick, Alexander,

McClintock, Joseph,
McDougal, Duncan,
McQueen, David,
McQueen, Jonas,
McQueen, Robert,
Moore, William,
Moore, Edward,
Morrison, James,
Morrison, Alexander,
Notemurr. James,
Null, Christopher,
Null, George,
Poorman, Peter,
Rheas, Robert,
Roan, John,
Shank, Stophel,
Sheeley, Michael,
Shier. Jacob,
Stauffer, Christian,
Stauffer, Jacob,
Steel, Dennis,
Stevick, John,
Thompson, John,
Walker, Archibald,
Weir, John,
Wolf, Michael.

A true Copy, Certified by JACOB COOK, Chairman of Committee, and James Sullivan, Clk.

NOTES AND QUERIES.—VI.

"Long Bullets" (N. & Q. ii.) was a past-time amusement fifty years ago. My father had three or four balls weighing from a pound and a half to two and a half (cast for artillery purposes). My brother was fond of athletic amusements, and exceeded all others I have ever seen throw them.　　　　　　　　　　　　　　H. R.

"Jumping the Bullies" was another old-time sport, which expired about fifty years ago. It was often practiced at "singing-school." Sides being chosen, four or five stood up against the wall in a leaning posture, one behind the other. The game was for the other side, of an equal number, to jump up on their shoulders, and the last man jumping had to clap his hands three times together. Quite a difficult feat, by the way.　　　　　　　　　H. R.

A Hanover Man.—The most remarkable man present at the last General Assembly of the Presbyterian Church at Saratoga is a native of Dauphin county—William Davis Snodgrass. He is the son of the last pastor of the Hanover (or "Manada") church on Bow creek, in East Hanover township, and was born there before the beginning of the present century. He has been pastor of a congregation at Goshen, New York, for forty or fifty years, nearly as long as that of his father James at Hanover, which extended over fifty six years. Rev. Dr. Prime, in his description of some of the Assembly, says of Rev. Dr. Snodgrass:

"I cannot see that the signs of old age appear on him any more than of fire on Abednego. Fresh, active, firm and strong, he preaches twice or three times on a Sabbath without weariness to himself *or his hearers.* Yet two full generations have passed away since he began to preach the word, and it would not be more strange if he should survive another, his bow abiding in strength. His usefulness is undiminished, and his hold on the affections of his people increases from year to year."

First Page to the House of Representatives.—A notice of the death of the late John A. Smull, Esq., says: "but his elder brother who filled the office of one of the first pages in the House of Representatives dying, he was appointed to fill the vacancy." This "elder brother" was my old playmate, Abram Levan Smull, who died April 21, 1849. He was *the first* Page employed in the Pennsylvania Legislature. Through the intercession of his mother, whose application was advocated by a member named Ford—who boarded at Mrs. Stehley's, then on Market street near Front—the office of Page was created for young Mr. A. L. Smull.

In those days, when "Pappy Hovis" was considered fully able to carry all the mails to and from the postoffice, and carry all the wood to the big fire-place beside, and do other things too, it was deemed a tremendous piece of extravagance to think of a page; each member having been accustomed to do his own errands.

[This same Ford, too, was the man who instigated the obligation that members should burn their spermaceti candles to the socket, before getting another; in order to break up a villainous practice which many had of "going through the motion" of burning, whilst they were simply stowing them away to take home at the end of the session!]

Indeed, I think that the office of page was not pluralized until many years after John A. Smull was promoted from it; and I make the correction for history's sake. A. Levan Smull was very competent in penmanship; he made beautiful designs for autograph albums, many of which are doubtless still extant. He was a noble boy and a worthy predecessor to his equally meritorious brother.

GEORGE B. AYRES.

SOME HEROES OF 1776.

Recently in looking over some court records we came upon the following detached accounts of soldiers of the Revolution from this locality who "bravely fought and bravely fell" for independence:

Simon Twoey, private, Captain Wm. Brown's Co., taken prisoner at Fort Washington and died on prison ship, December 8, 1776.

Jacob Neveland and John Dunlap, privates, Capt. James Crouch's Co., killed at Chestnut Hill.

Capt. John Reily, of the 3d Penna., wounded at Bonhamtown, in N. J.; shot through the body.

William Hall, private, Capt. Green's Battalion of the Flying Camp, killed at Fort Washington, certified to by Lieut.-Col. Wm. Hay and Lieut. Wm. McCullough of the Battalion.

Jacob Loeser, private of Capt. Peter Berry's company of Col. Greenawalt's Battalion, taken prisoner at Fort Washington and died on board prison ship.

Lieut. John Dunlap, of Capt. Crouch's company, killed at Chestnut Hill, Dec. 6, 1777.

Historical and Genealogical. 27

Capt. Michael Whitley, of Col. Robert Elder's Battalion, wounded and taken prisoner at Chestnut Hill, Dec. 6, 1777, and died a few days afterwards in Philadelphia, aged forty-seven years.

Lieut. John Gilchrist, of Capt. John Reed's company of the Flying Camp, wounded in right arm near Elizabethtown, N. J., August 14, 1776.

Henry Slotterbeck, private of Captain Oldenbuck's company, Col. Philip Greenawalt's Battalion, wounded in the thigh at Chestnut Hill, December 6, 1777.

Peter Boal, private of Capt. Collier's company, Col. Elder's Battalion, under the command of Col. Thomas Hartley, wounded in the attack on Fort Muncy, in Northumberland county, August 20, 1778.

William Campbell, private of Captain Robert Clark's company of Flying Camp, wounded and taken prisoner at Delancy's Mill, October, 1776.

William Johnston, corporal of Captain John Reed's company, wounded and taken prisoner at Delancy's Mill, October, 1776.

Patrick Lusk, sergeant, Capt. John Murray's company, wounded in right wrist at Princeton.

Joseph Wood, of Bethel township, now Lebanon county, in 1786, at the age of 65 years, certifies that while lieutenant colonel of Second Pennsylvania, Col. Arthur St. Clair, he received a dangerous wound in the left leg, and subsequently wounded in the left arm at Lake Champlain.

LINDLEY MURRAY, THE GRAMMARIAN.

In Derry township, Dauphin county, Pa., about one mile south of the old Derry Presbyterian church, on the 7th day of June, 1745, was born Lindley Murray. His father, Robert Murray, was of Scotch-Irish birth, had settled some ten years previously in Derry township, as did also one or two of his brothers. They were related to the Dixons, of Dixon's Ford, through inter-marriage, and that circumstance accounts for William Darby, in one of his letters, alluding to Lindley Murray as the cousin of Robert Dixon. The maiden name of Lindley Murray's mother has not come down to us, although biographers have ventured the opinion that she was a Lindley. There was a family of Lindleys settled at an early period on the Swatara, but whether Robert Murray's wife bore that surname there is no authority for saying. Singularly enough, Lindley Murray, in his autobiography published at York, England, in 1826, gives neither the Christian name of his father or mother. Of them, however, he writes:

"My parents were of respectable characters and in the middle station of life. My father possessed a good flour mill at Swatara, but being of an enterprising spirit, and anxious to provide handsomely for his family, he made several voyages to the West Indies, in the way of trade, by which he considerably augmented his property. Pursuing his inclinations, he, in time, acquired large possessions, and became one of the most respectable merchants in America. * * *
* * * My mother was a woman of an amiable disposition, and remarkable for mildness, humanity and liberality of sentiment. She was, indeed, a faithful and affectionate wife, a tender mother and a kind mistress."

Robert Murray moved to North Carolina about 1750, when the immigration thither was in full tide. Two or three years sufficed, however, when he turned his face northward and settled in the city of New York, where he entered into mercantile pursuits. Although brought up in the Westminister Confession and members of old Derry church, whatever may have been the cause we know not, Robert Murray and his wife joined the Society of Friends in New York, and it was therefore in the tenets of this persuasion that his large family of children were instructed. He died in the city of New York, July 22, 1786, at the age of sixty-five.

Lindley Murray, the eldest son, received, a good education, but having a dislike to mercantile pursuits studied law and was admitted to the bar at the age of twenty-one. The year after he married. His limited practice was temporarily interrupted by a visit to England, whither his father had preceded him in the hope of benefitting his health. He returned to New York in 1771, and renewed the practice of law with marked success, tiring of it, however, when the Revolution broke out and New York was occupied by the British army, or having no sympathy with the cause of Independence, he removed to Islip on Long Island, and entered a mercantile life. We have always given Lindley Murray credit for his religious principles as having precluded him from taking part in the struggle between the Colonies and the mother country, but in a letter in our possession, written by William Darby, to his friend, Mrs. Anna Dixon, the true incentive is perchance given. Mr. Darby was well acquainted with the men of his time—he was intimate with the patriots of the Revolution, and learned much of the inward history of the people concerning whom it is to be regretted, he did not give his reminiscences. As for Murray, William Darby was born in the same neighborhood, was intimate with the Dixons and Roans, to whom the former was related, and through whom he learned more of Lindley Murray than biographers choose to tell. Unfortunately in the success and greatness of a man we lose sight of the grave errors into which he may have fallen, and the defects in his principles and character. Nor would we dispel the bright halo which glimmers around the life of the celebrated grammarian. Sabine, it is true, classes him among the Loyalists of the Revolution, but Darby in contrasting him with Robert Dixon, whose blood was the first Pennsylvania offering to the cause of Independence, speaks of Murray's taking sides with the enemies of his country. This we can easily understand. Surrounded by his religious friends whose peace principles would not allow them to take up arms—although many hundreds did, who were subsequently disowned for it—and in a city occupied by the King's troops, he himself says he had little faith in the successful resistance of the Colonies. It was thus he became a loyalist. His father's business and his own thrived, and the rule of England was sufficient for him. We venture the opinion that there were really few instances when religious principles made men tories. Mercenary motives were generally at the bottom of it. Still, without doubting the sincerity of Lindley Murray, it is to be regretted that his influence should have been on the side of British oppression and tyranny. As it was, at the close of the war he had amassed a fortune, and when peace had dawned he sailed away from the land of his nativity and the home of liberty.

His attachment to the home of his fathers, he said, "was founded on many pleasing associations. In particular I had strong prepossessions in favor of a residence in England, because I was ever partial to its political constitution, and the mildness and wisdom of its general laws." * * * * "On leaving my native country, there was not, therefore, any land in which I could cast my eyes with so much pleasure, nor is there any which could have afforded me so much real satisfaction as I have found in Great Britain. May its political fabric, which has stood the test of ages, and long attracted the admiration of the world, be supported and perpetuated by Divine Providence."

In 1784, he went to England, and after visiting several localities purchased a small estate at Holdgate, about a mile from York, upon which he resided until his death.

Living in ease and retirement, he entered upon a literary life which proved a successful one and has inscribed his name high upon fame's portals.

In 1787 he published a small work entitled "The Power of Religion on the Mind," which passed through seventeen editions. His next work, and that by which he was principally known, was his "English Grammar," first published in 1795, and such was the unexpected demand for it that several editions were published during the same year. Following this appeared "English Exercises" and a "Key," an abridgement of which treatises were published in one volume in 1797.

Lindley Murray's other writings are, "The English Reader," with an "Introduction and Sequel;" "The English Spelling Book;" a new edition of his Grammar, Exercises and Key in two octavo volumes; a selection from Horne's "Commentary on the Psalms;" and "The Duty and Benefit of Reading the Scriptures."

Those who were scholars as late as thirty or forty years ago remember with great pleasure Murray's Grammar and "The English Reader." Many an old chest or drawer containing the old-time school books have recently been ransacked, bringing to light much of the school literature of other days, and none bears reading over so well as the admirable selections in Lindley Murray's "English Reader." Indeed so much interest in the work has been taken of late, that its reproduction under the auspices of that veteran scholar and editor, O. N. Worden, of Susquehanna county, Pa., is as eagerly looked for, as it will be highly appreciated. As Murray himself said, "that whilst they contain many selections which present the moral virtues, religion, and the Christian religion in particular, in very amiable points of view, not a sentiment has been admitted into any of them which can pain the most virtuous mind, or give the least offense to the eye or ear of modesty."

Lindley Murray's educational publications were not alone confined to his mother tongue. He prepared two French works, "Introduction au Lecteur Francois" and "Lecteur Francois," which soon came into general use, were highly commended, and passed through a large number of editions.

Lindley Murray's life in England was a busy one, as it was an eventful one. No American who made a European tour failed to visit Holdgate. His personal appearance, his unassuming demeanor and his conversational powers excited in the minds of all visitors an agreeable surprise.

On Thursday morning, the 16th of February, 1826, at the ripe old age of eighty-one, Lindley Murray died at his residence near York, England, sincerely lamented, not only in the land of his adoption, but in the land of his nativity, which latter has always claimed him and classed him among the eminent and distinguished men of America. And we who reside within a few miles of the place where he was born, cannot do better than to recall the main facts of his life, and honor ourselves by claiming Lindley Murray as belonging to Dauphin county and to Pennsylvania.

THE STEWARTS OF HANOVER.

The first Lazarus Stewart, of Hanover, died possessed of a valuable estate. When he died is not on record, but in the distribution of his property, in 1785, mention is made of the following heirs:

I. LAZARUS STEWART, d. 1745, wife d. 1754, m. and had issue:
  2.   *i. John*, b. 1714, died April 8, 1777.
  3.   *ii. Margaret*, m. James Stewart.
  4.   *iii. Margery*, m. John Young, bro. of Wm., of Han.
        iv. Lazarus.
        v. Peter; in 1784, resided in N. C.
        vi. James; "   "
        vii. David; "   "

II. JOHN STEWART, m., in 1736, Francis, b. 1716, d. in 1761, and had issue:
  5.   *i. William*, b. 1737, d. July 14, 1803.
        ii. Lazarus, m. and left issue.
        iii. George.
        iv. James.
        v. John.
        vi. Mary, m. George Espy.
        vii. Jane.

III. MARGARET STEWART, who married James Stewart, had issue:
  6.   *i. Charles.*
  7.   *ii. Lazarus.*
  8.   *iii. James.*
  9.   *iv. Jane*, m. John Campbell.

IV. MARGERY STEWART, who m. John Young, had issue:
        i. William, d. 1795.

V. WILLIAM STEWART, son of John Stewart, m. 1st. Mary ——, b. 1736, d. Feb. 22, 1780; 2d. Martha Stewart, b. 1743, d. Aug. 9, 1796.

VI. CHARLES STEWART, son of Margaret and James Stewart, m. and had issue:
        i. James.
        ii. Lazarus.
        iii. John.
        iv. Margaret.
        v. Charles.
        vi. George.

VII. LAZARUS STEWART, son of Margaret Stewart and James Stewart, m. and had issue:
        i. James, d. 1823 (?).
        ii. Josiah.
        iii. Margaret.

iv. *Priscilla.*
v. *Mary.*
vi. *Elizabeth.*
vii. *Martha.*

VIII. JAMES STEWART, son of Margaret Stewart and James Stewart, m. and had issue:
  i. *James*, d. s. p.
  ii. *Lazarus.*

IX. JANE STEWART, who m. James Campbell, b. 1732, d. June 1, 1781, had issue:
  i. *William*, d. July 3, 1804. William Campbell m. Margaret ———, and had issue—
    a. *James*, b. Sept. 14, 1789.
    b. *Martha*, bap. Nov. 9, 1791.

NOTES AND QUERIES.—VII.

STOPHEL AND CHRISTLY.—These Christian names so frequently met with in Pennsylvania assessment and other lists of inhabitants, stand —*Stophel* for Christopher and *Christly* for Christian.

"TIT-FOR-TAT."—*The Richmond (Va.) Standard*, although not even a yearling, is evidence how valuable a weekly newspaper can be made. It reminds us of the "Home Journal" of New York in its Morris and Willis palmy days, by its clean make up, its dash and vivacity, with this addition, however, that it deals not alone with the Present, but the Historic Past. The contributions of R. A. Brock, Esq., the industrious Librarian of the Virginia Historical Society, are of such a marked character, for interest, value and research, that not only the citizens of the Old Dominion but all lovers of literature, wheresoever dispersed, highly appreciate. His biographical sketches and historical "bric-a-brac," we hope to see reproduced in a more permanent form. In fine, the yearly volume of the *Standard* with a good index would make a capital annual encyclopedia.

GEN. JOHN HARRISON.—" T. S. McN." calls our attention to the egregious blunder made in the Report of the Superintendent of Public Instruction for 1877 by the County Superintendent of Lebanon (*vide* p. 354), in which he makes Gen. John Harrison, of Hanover, identical with Gen. William Henry Harrison, President of the United

States. The error alluded to being such a palpable one, that no ten year old scholar could be mislead by it, is the very reason little attention was paid to its correction. It may be true that President Harrison's ancestors originally settled in this locality, but it is doubtful if Gen. John Harrison was a relative. The latter was a native of Hanover township, the son of Isaac and Sarah Harrison, born January 8, 1775, and died February 28, 1837. His remains, as do those of his parents, rest in old Hanover graveyard. Gen. Harrison was one of the representative men of this locality sixty or seventy years ago. He was in public office a long time, and was an enterprising business man.

EARLY SCHOOLS.—" The historian of the Lebanon county schools makes a statement" says T. S. McN., " in the School Report for 1877, page 349, that the school begun by the German settlers in Annville township was the first within the county limits. You know, that if there was no other motive to induce the old Presbyterian stock to keep alive the rudiments of education, the importance they attached to their children being posted in the Catechism of their church, and the ability to read the Bible, and the authors who were regarded by them as defenders of the faith, required it. All would and did compel the Scotch-Irish to provide means for the education of their children." "T. S. McN." is correct. Wherever the Scotch-Irish settlers located, the church and the school were at once organized, and our researches among the old records prove that it was a rare thing for either man or woman to be unable to write his or her name or read the Confession of Faith. while among the German settlers it was also the exception, we are glad to say.

AUTOBIOGRAPHICAL LETTER OF WILLIAM DARBY.

[The following letter has been forwarded to us from Alabama, by a descendant of Dr. M. L. Dixon, of Winchester, Tenn., and as it contains so much additional information, not only concerning the great geographer himself, but the Dixons, Roans and other families of Derry, we believe its publication will be as appreciatingly welcomed as the former letters on the Dixons of Dixon's Ford.]

SANDY SPRING, *Montgomery County, Md., April 18, 1834.*

DEAR SIR: Your truly kind and welcome favor of the 19th inst. reached me on the 4th inst., and was read with deep interest. Before I received your letter I supposed that you must be the son of Sankey

Dixon. Though your father left Swatara when I was only seven months old, his name is as familiar to my ear as is that of my own father. Your father received his name, as I was informed by my parents, as a testimony of respect from his father and mother to the Rev. Mr. Sankey. I was so early in life removed from Swatara to the western part of Pennsylvania that I lost sight of your father, and by his removal from our native place to situations so totally unconnected with any section I ever visited, I never again received any knowledge of him until I received your valued communication.

I have an indistinct, though to myself satisfactory, recollection of the origin of the *prenomen* of Flavel Roan. He was named after the Rev. John Flavel, of Dartmouth, England. Will you do me the favor, when you write again, to state the fate of the very interesting Flavel Roan. With your uncle, Mr. John Cochran, I have a slight acquaintance, but have not seen or heard of him for some years past. With the Slaymakers, of Lancaster, Jesse and Isaac, I am acquainted, as I was with a family of the name of Cochran, who removed from the eastern to the western part of Pennsylvania, a little over forty years past.

The reason I particularly inquired of your mother whether or not she remembered the Pettigrew family, was because I knew that John Pettigrew was a particular friend and companion of all the sons of John Dixon, and of course with her husband. Old Mrs. Elizabeth Pettigrew and three of her daughters removed to the neighborhood where I was bred. Two of the daughters were married women when they crossed the mountains; one to Samuel McCullough, and the other to Sampson Nickle; a third, Betsey, never married that I know. Your mother must distinctly remember the death of your grandfather, and the marriage of your Aunt Nancy, or Mrs. Carson, with Patrick Campbell, which took place about the same time in the fall of 1780. And, by the way, how could I for a moment have forgotten what I so well knew, Mrs. Pettigrew had another daughter, Rosanna, who married Duncan Campbell, brother of Patrick Campbell. The latter fell in Crawford's defeat in 1772, leaving an only child, a son. Duncan Campbell was living not long since at a very advanced age, without children.

I can conceive of no other circumstance which could happen to me, which would give me such heartfelt satisfaction as would an interview with your mother, and strongly do I doubt if there remains now in existence any other two persons retaining in common the little, but soul-pleasing history of the society along Swatara from fifty to sixty or seventy years ago, those rich recollections of early days, which return as a balm to our hearts in the down-hill of life.

Thomas Elder, of Harrisburg, is still more advanced in life than your mother; and, when I saw him last, retained all his faculties in full vigor, but his mind has been so long employed on things of the world *as they are*, that he neither remembers or much cares for the things of the world *as they were*.

When I returned to Hanover and Derry in 1815, old John and Jane Robinson were the only old people who remembered the days of my infancy. Of those who were born about or near the time I was myself, I found, alas! not one. Eight years afterwards I found your Uncle James Dixon—who in a few more years followed his brothers. The Wilsons, Wallaces, Campbells, Mayers, Bells, Dixons, Murrays, Lindleys, Rodgers, Roans, Greens, and many more, where are they? Many names even echo does not repeat, of those who remain how scattered. But if your mother and myself could meet, what an immense period compared with individual human life, would we have to draw against of past pleasing yet melancholy recollections. Just say to your mother that though this letter is addressed to the son, every word is as much or more addressed to the mother. Sincerely as I would rejoice to meet either of you or both, and indeed any one of your kindred—such a happiness I dare not promise myself. There is but one contingency, *and a contingency it is*, the happening of which would lead to my visiting Tennessee. Since my return from Louisiana, I have at times delivered lectures on *Astronomy, Geography* and *History*, in New York, Philadelphia, Baltimore and other places, and I can assert with flattering approbation. Sometimes I think of making a *Grand Tour* in that way, but advancing age and a family, small as it is, but who *must go wheresoever I go*, as also an old Lady of the name of Prudence, all say, "*sit still, old man, you have already paid away your best days in traveling.*" Prudence, you know, if she *has* much of "old maid" about her, is to us all a maiden sister, and gives her advice from affection and a wise regard to our welfare. "Fine Spun Philosophy," it is likely you will say if you have patience to get through this *farrago* in the mouth of a man who has never in his life been at the end of any ten years, where probability would have pointed out at the beginning of those periods." Well! well! no matter, there is one thing I will dare and that is to consider your mother and her children as my cherished acquaintances and friends, though I have not even seen one of the number or may ever have that pleasure. Now to your generous confidence, and to me truly interesting sketches of your life, and the situation of your connections and family, I send you the inadequate but only return in my power; similar sketches of my own chequered existence.

You are accurate in your conjectures in regard to me as to my family. I was the eldest, and when you acquainted with him, Patrick H. Darby was the youngest surviving son of Patrick Darby. As I before mentioned, I was born on your Grandfather's farm, and in Hanover township, August 14, 1775, but Patrick H. was born west of the mountains, in Washington county, February 23d, 1783. With the Breading and Campbell families P. H. D. was acquainted, but with the earlier and far more interesting family history, he knew nothing except as you do yourself from tradition. The Juda Rice mentioned by your mother was no connection of ours, and from the age of your mother, she could never have known mine by maiden name. My father was a second husband, and my eldest, but maternal, brother only was born in April, 1770. My father began and ended by being poor, and his children had to find education where and as they could. What little I possess, was truly picked up along the Lanes, Highways and Commons of human life.

Before leaving Swatara I had learned to read a little, though only about two months turned of *six years of age.* Plunged into the West amid savage war and almost unbroken woods, the dangers and imperative wants of life would seem to preclude all thought of improving the mind. Happily for me, my desire of knowledge, even so situated, grew with my growth, and mental hunger was sharpened by food. Every book I could procure I read, and was aided by a tolerable good memory. Books were, however, rare, and when found mostly confined to school books. Before I was twelve years of age I had read the Jewish Scriptures five times, and many parts ten times over. Up to that age Sewell's "History of the Quakers" was the only work on any branch of general history I obtained. Without making much more intellectual advances, I was, from the poverty of my parents, compelled to labor more as my bodily strength increased.

I completed my eighteenth year; then by permission of my parents I commenced teaching—don't laugh at the attempt—since, if I was ignorant, I can say without boast that I had outstript most of my neighbor boys, of course could teach them. Tho' in many respects very irksome business, teaching was of invaluable benefit to me. I had the mornings, evenings and spare days to myself, and as far as other means offered, this leisure was used to effect.

At Wheeling, in 1793–4, on the then outer border of civilized life, I procured the reading of several very valuable works, among which were Rollin's Ancient History, Ward's Mathematics and Johnson's Lives of English Poets. From Wheeling, in my twenty-first year, I removed to Fayette county, Pennsylvania, and there obtained the perusal of The Universal History from Judge Nathaniel Breading. This immense work occupied my every leisure moments whilst I remained in the vicinity of Red Stone, now Brownsville. In my twenty-second year I removed to Westmoreland county, Pennsylvania, and there became acquainted with a man of the name of Benjamin Gilbert, belonging to the Society of Friends, like your cousin Lindley Murray. With Mr. Gilbert's books an entirely new species of reading was opened to my mind. From this man I procured the reading of *Montesquieu's Spirit of Laws, Locke's Essay on the Human Understanding, Reed on the Mind, Blair's Lectures on Elocution, Elements on Criticism*, by Henry Home Lord Kaimes, and perhaps the deepest metaphysical work ever written, *Edwards on Free Will.*

The latter course of reading produced on my mind a change and course of thinking, which, if I had remained in Pennsylvania, would, it is probable, have led me into the clerical profession, but the death of my father, in 1799, and some other circumstances of greatly less importance, induced me to travel, and I went to Natchez, where, very contrary to my expectations, I married, like your brother, a widow with a family of children, and quite handsome property. What led me into this connexion was a similarity of tastes. Like myself, Mrs. Boardman had been her own teacher, and had acquired a fine stock of information. As a wife she was everything I or any man could wish for, but her family involved us in litigation. I was compelled to quit the pursuits, which habit had endeared to me, to attend to affairs which were, to say the least, to me very repugnant. Out of this troublesome state we would have finally extricated ourselves, it is most likely, but in the spring of 1804 a large and well-filled cotton gin belonging to the estate was consumed by fire, and again, by a strange unity of misfortune, two months afterward, another house also full of cotton and belonging to the estate was lost by a similar accident. This double loss involved me in debt, to which I was compelled to yield. I have said these accidents happened by "*a strange unity of misfortune*," but I recall the words. Had I not lost this property, and been thrown once more on my own resources, I would no doubt have vegetated a Mississippi cotton planter. I speak this in full respect to cotton planters, and only because the business demanded what I did not possess.

And, in brief, availing myself of what mathematical knowledge I possessed, I entered on the surveying business, in the service of the United States. In that employment I continued until the middle of 1809, when I conceived the plan of " A Map and Statistical Account of Louisiana," and which I subsequently executed and published. Well for me when I commenced this task that its difficulties were not to be foreseen, for though not much disposed to yield to slight obstacles, yet in that case I must have shrank, had the whole issue been before my mind. But I went on and soon found that all the surveys made under the Government produced documents falling far short of what was requisite to the completion of my plan. I then relinquished the office of Deputy Surveyor, and commenced the extensive exploration to which you allude in your letter.

All these operations brought the middle of 1814, when, with my projection and manuscripts, I was ready to set out from Louisiana to the cities of New York and Philadelphia in search of a publisher. I had actually departed from my home, at Opelousas, and was on my way to New Orleans, when the news met me that Washington had been taken and burned by the British. This so dispirited my friends that I was advised to postpone my attempt, and did so. In the meantime I made an extensive tour in Florida and Southern Alabama.

On my return to Baton Rouge, I learned two distressing articles of intelligence almost at the same moment. One was the death of my wife, October 23d, 1814, and the other the great probability that Louisiana would be invaded. Before I could proceed to Opelousas and make arrangements for the care of my little daughter and only child, and again return to New Orleans, Louisiana was invaded. I hastened to the camp of our army, below New Orleans, volunteered my services as engineer, and in that capacity made that campaign which humbled the British army and eventually gave the crown to our general. As general or monarch, I never made of him but two requests. As general I demanded and received the office of engineer, and when candidate for sceptre I asked for and received the following:

"*William Darby, Esqr.:* Be it remembered, that during the late war, and whilst the enemy was before New Orleans, William Darby, Esqr., acted as one of my topographical staff, performed his duty much to the satisfaction of the commanding general, and at the close of the war I gave him a written testimonial that his service had obtained for him my full approbation.   ANDREW JACKSON."

The campaign over and without a family or much else to impede my motions, I returned to Pennsylvania in the summer of 1815. Poor in purse, but rich in the accumulated experience gained from near sixteen years of almost incessant motion—experience which I had reaped with the briars in my fingers; and now in my fortieth year commenced my life as an author. The first edition of my Louisiana was published in 1816 and the second in 1818. In 1819 I wrote for Kirk & Mercain, of New York, "The Emigrant's Guide." In 1821 I was employed to prepare for publication "Brooks' Gazeteer," which I found in many things relating to America so very defective as to induce me to advise a substitute. My advice was taken, and early in 1823 came out the first and early in 1827 the second edition of "Darby's Geographical Dictionary." In 1833 issued the first and in 1835 the second edition of "Darby and Dwight's United States Gazeteer." Mr. Dwight's name is united with mine in the later work, he furnished all beyond New Jersey and New York inclusive, and I the residue. In the second edition Mr. Dwight had no concern. Since 1820 and from the letters M I C H I have supplied nearly all the geographical articles for Philadelphia edition of "Brewster's Encyclopedia."

In 1829 I commenced supplying tales for "Atkinson's Casket," and have written all that species of writing which has appeared under the signature of Mark Bancroft. Recently I have made a regular engagement with Mr. Atkinson for a long series of border tales, and I may note here as peculiarly remarkable in our joint case, that the incident of the capture and recapture of your mother-in-law and Boone's daughter has been long since fixed in my eye as a chosen subject, and this added to the extraordinary fact of my having connected in the same tale the families of both your parents, gives true interest to the series of circumstances.

In a life so full of changes and in most part of it but scantly supplied with means of procuring books or securing leisure, most persons would suppose any chance of general reading was out of the question; but I must say I went far to render such a conclusion doubtful, at least to anything approaching the usual extent given in such cases. My reading has been desultory, I confess, and far indeed from that of many, but it has been beyond what is commonly attempted by persons of straitened means, and not professionally engaged. You see, I am laying my heart naked to you, and hope no charge of mere vanity will be made when I go a step farther in the dissection, and do so to demonstrate that a tolerable education is within the reach of every free white in the United States.

I was in my thirty-second year when I undertook to study the French language, and long years past, full one-half if not more, of all my reading is in that language. The learned languages I never have studied, but in their modern dress, in English and French, have read every one of the most eminent classics. In the "National Intelligencer" of November 13, 1833, as an editorial preface to my notes on Switzerland, over the signature of *Tacitus*, it is observed:

"To those who have been long readers of the 'National Intelligencer' we need not say that a gentleman who, under this signature occasionally enriches our columns with his communications is a person of great intelligence. We can add that he is probably better versed in History 'than any other individual in the Union.'" Under any other circumstances I should not dare enclosing such extracts, but take them as given.

The man you saw in Mobile, and who was passing there under my name, was an impudent imposter. The circumstances were these: When I left Opelousas in the Summer of 1814, a very particular friend of mine, Dr. Moses Little, gave me letters of introduction to his parents, residing in the city of New York. Detained for many months, as I have stated, a fact the doctor well knew, and wished also to write by me to his parents and sister, at the time of my really leaving Louisiana, he in January, 1815, made out a new set of letters, closed them in one to me, directed to Orleans, and entrusted to a young man of the name of William Garrett, a nephew of Governor Garrett, of Kentucky, and as unprincipled a scoundrel, as matters proved, as was ever nephew to any one. In place of coming to New Orleans, by some means, he found his way to Mobile, gave himself out as William Darby, who had explored Louisiana and Texas, told a long story of shipwreck, &c. Then found his way to the city of New York, actually delivered my letters to Captain Little and family, and repeated his shipwreck tale, lived on that family, bearing my name until he was detected by some person who knew me, and the bubble burst. I learned only a few weeks since that his father, Judge William Garrett, was still living at Opelousas. I believe the worthless son is dead. This was the man you saw at Mobile. I was in the United States army at New Orleans from the end of December, 1814, to the 7th of May, 1815, as an engineer.

In February, 1816, the year after my return from Louisiana, I intermarried with Elizabeth Tanner, a sister of the well known engravers of that name in Philadelphia. My daughter, left in Louisiana with her half-sisters, died in 1821. By my second wife I have but one surviving child, a young woman in her seventeenth year, so my entire family consists of my wife, child and myself. We live in a fine healthy country, twenty miles north of Washington city, and on a rented farm in a country place, I may repeat, possessing most of the essential advantages without the enormous expense of a city. We keep our own cows, and make their feed from the fields. Our source of living is, however, my pen, which is kept commonly busy. In summer I give courses of lectures, and the rank of intelligence of the people around us may be estimated to advantage by the fact that last summer I had a class of about fifty on general geography.

My father and mother had eight children, four sons and four daughters; my eldest sister, Arabella, called for your grandmother and one of your aunts, died on the Swatara, and was buried at the

Derry meeting house. Two more children died in Washington county, Pennsylvania. One brother, Robert, called for Robert Dixon, died also in the same county, as did my father in 1799. My brother Thomas was drowned in the Ohio river, and your acquaintance, Patrick H., you know died in Kentucky, at Brandenbury, Meade county. My mother died in Tennessee, and her eldest son, and my half brother in Louisiana. My dear sister Nancy, called for your Aunt Campbell, when I last heard from her, was living in Stewart county, Tennessee, near Dover. Her husband's name is Hugh Barr. They have several sons. I wrote to them upwards of a year ago, but have received no answer. If Nancy is gone, then I am alone of all my family. None of my brothers ever married or had children, and with my father's name expires in his own offspring.

Give my sincere respects and regards to your mother and all the residue of your family and connections, and receive for yourself expression of my unfeigned good wishes. WILLIAM DARBY.

P. S.—On reading the within to my wife and daughter, they both desire me to add their respects and good wishes to you all. Should you ever come this way, if you come via Washington, if you inquire of Mr. Peshey Thompson, book seller, he will direct you to where you will find a hearty welcome.

WHERE WAS SNAKETOWN?

"Samuel Evans, Columbia, Pa., July 26, 1879," is as certainly mistaken in locating "Snaketown" at the present Harrisburg, as I was in carelessly stating that John Burt had killed an Indian there, September 11, 1727.

On the tax assessment of Conestoga, Chester county, 1718, a John Harris is noted as a "single freeman," subject to a tax of "twelve shillings."

On the list of West Conestoga, for 1721, the same John Harris appears rated at £26, tax 6 and 6 pence.

On the list for 1722, he again appears. Mr. Evans notes of him: "Indian trader, first settled in the neighborhood of Conoytown, and afterward removed to the vicinity of the Paxtang Indians. * * Lived many years where Harrisburg is located."

In 1724, on the Donegal list, the name of the same John Harris appears.

In 1725 he is again noted as in the same township, which then comprised within its limits the whole of the present Dauphin county. By this time, however, he seems to have had neighbors: Rowland

Chambers, of Chambers' ferry; Peter Allen, at Hunter's Falls, foot of Kittatinny mountain, certainly, and possibly, the brothers Chambers at Fishing Creek (Fort Hunter).

In 1721, John Harris married. He was then forty-five years of age, permanently settled at Harrisburg. Mrs. Finley and Mrs. Plunket, daughters, were born in 1722 and 1724. In 1726, John Harris, the younger, founder of Harrisburg, was born. It appears that the Harris of 1718, had quite a family about him at Paxtang, as early as 1726.

Rowland Chambers was well established three miles below him. Robert Chambers and his brothers five miles above. Peter Allen eleven miles. The Duncans, Campbells and others on the east, and Andersons, Means, &c., south, on the Swatara.

It is well known these early Indian traders never established stations nearer each other than three to ten miles. It therefore follows that John and Esther Burt did not sell liquor to Indians at any point upon Harris' 1,000 acres tract of land "at the mouth of Paxtang creek"—or upon Rowland Chambers' 400 acres, where the present Steel Works are.

From this series of dates and the practices of the pioneers, it is as certain as can be that Snaketown *was not* at the present Harrisburg in 1727, or at Chambers' Ferry, but where the writer of this located it in his statement of July 12, 1879, at or near the present Highspire, which is about thirty-seven miles above Conestoga, not at the mouth of that crooked stream, but quite near enough forty miles to satisfy the not very accurate ideas of distances entertained by Davenport, Wright and Logan, so long ago as 1727.   ****

NOTES AND QUERIES.—VIII.

"FRENCH JACOB."—Is anything known of "French Jacob," a contemporary of Andrew Lycans, about whom old men, when I lived in the Valley, told marvelous stories. I think he lived near the mouth of the Wiconisco; and further, was supposed to possess supernatural powers, &c. Waifs and myths of early settlements are particularly interesting.   H. R.

HARRIS—FINDLEY—WIRTZ.—Elizabeth, eldest daughter of the first John Harris, married John Findley, or Finley, by whom she had two daughters—Esther m. William Patterson and Margaret m. William Wirtz. The latter was evidently from the neighborhood of Lancaster and had children—Margaret, Elizabeth, Esther, Christian, Hannah and William. Can Squire Evans give us any information as to the descendants of these Wirtz families?

BOWMAN—BAUMAN.—A correspondent says his parents who are of German descent write their names *Bauman*, and asks whether it would be proper to change his to *Bowman*. By no means, if you desire to preserve your family name. The English name Bowman has an entirely different meaning from the Teutonic, Bauman. The first relates to archery—an archer; the other either from *baum*, a tree, or *bau*, to build. So from this signification of names, it will be seen that Black has as much right to change his name to White, or *vice versa*, as Bauman to Bowman.

STEWART, ANDREW (N. & Q. vi).—Was this Andrew Stewart any connection of the Stewarts who owned the old Rickart place in the valley? James Stewart who lived there was physically a remarkable man. I have heard my father and uncle Sam say that he was in bodily strength more than the equal of two common men—that he could run as fast as a horse—that he could outstrip any man on his hands and feet, and that he could spring over a ten-rail fence without touching. I saw this man in his old age—a large fleshy man—on a visit to Paxtang. He lived at or near Springfield, O., and was there killed by the fall of a tree. H. R.

FIRE-PROOF BUILDINGS AND ELECTRICITY IN 1810.—Jacob Bucher, of Harrisburg, Edward Crouch, of Dauphin county, and John Dorsey, of Philadelphia, were appointed the commissioners for the construction of the State offices, prior to the removal of the Legislature from Lancaster, for the safe-keeping of the records and papers; and we quote from a document in our possession, under date of April 9, 1810, to show what were their ideas of what is " fire-proof," and some curious beliefs about " electricity." It appears that Messrs. Bucher and Crouch were of opinion " that *the heighth of the stories* would be itself nearly a security against an accident happening in any of the lower rooms, from communicating with the upper apartments, if the ceiling was put up in the ordinary way; and with the addition of *sheet iron lining*, we thought there could be no doubt of its safety. *
* * * We had derived assurances that the *iron ceiling would not attract lightning*, or endanger anything near it, as the electric fluid *it might attract* could be conveyed to the ground by means of rods, to be placed at the outer ends of said buildings." The Italics are ours.

But this plan was too hazardous for Mr. Dorsey, and his colleagues continue—" We now think strange to find *the doubts* suggested by him, whether rods placed at the ends of the buildings would not INCREASE rather than *abate* the electric fluid," and they offer to meet Mr. Dorsey in presence of the Governor (Snyder) and the officers of the Government, " if, upon further inquiry and reflection, it should appear that an alteration in part from the plan agreed on would be better." Since then, the world has made some advance in science!

PARSON ELDER'S FAMILY RECORD.

On the blank leaves of a volume of Bishop Atterbury's Sermons, in the possession of the Dauphin County Historical Society, is the following Family Record of the Rev. John Elder, the long-revered minister of Paxtang and Derry. It is in the handwriting of his son Thomas, but, with the exception of that enclosed in brackets, is a verbatim copy of the original memoranda made by Parson Elder himself. We have in preparation a genealogy of this family, and in the hope that further information may be gained relating thereto, we give the Record as originally preserved.

Deaths.

My D'r Mother departed this life Oct. 25th, at 8 o'Clock at night, 1742.

My D'r Father departed this life July 28th, at 7 o'Clock at night, 1746.

My D'r Wife departed this life June 12th at 2 o'Clock in the morning, 1749.

My daughter Jane died the 6th day of August, 1763.

My daughter Grizell died Sept'r 18th at 10 o'Clock afternoon, 1769.

My daughter Eleanor died Dec'r 12th at 4 o'Clock in the morn'g, 1775.

My daughter-in-law, Joshua's Polly, died the 21st day of November, 1782.

My D'r Wife died Oct. 3rd, 6 o'Clock in the morning, 1786.

[The Rev'd John Elder died the 17th day of July, 1792, in the 84th year of his age.

[David Elder died 22d May, 1809, at 11 o'Clock P. M., aged 40 yrs.

[John Elder died Ap'l 27th, 1811, in the 54th year of his age.

[Sam'l Elder died 26th Sept'r, 1815, aged 43 years.

[Rob't Elder died on Tuesday morning, 29th Sept'r, 1818, in the 77th year of his age.]

Marriages.

I was married again Nov'r 5th, 1751.
My Daughter Eleanor was married on Thursday, 11th of Dec'r, 1766.
My Son Robert was married on Tuesday, 7th Feb'y, 1769.
My Son Joshua was married Sept. 16, 1773.
My Son John was married Dec. 16, 1778.
My Daughter Ann went off Sept. 23, 1779.
My Son Joshua again May 27, 1783.
My Daughter Mary was married May 18th, 1784.
My Daughter Sarah was married June 19th, 1787.

Births.

Robert was born on Friday, June 11th, half an hour after 3 in the morn'g, 1742.

Joshua was born Mar. 9th, twenty minutes after 5 o'Clock in the morn'g, 1744-5.

My Daughter Eleanor was born May 21st, 1749, at 9 o'Clock, afternoon of the Sabbath.

My Daughter Sarah was born Saturday, Octr. 19th, 1752, at 9 o'Cl'k afternoon.

My Daughter Ann was born Oct. 8th, 1754, at half an hour after 10 at night.

My son John was born Wednesday, 3rd Augt., 1757, $\frac{3}{4}$ of an hour before 1 in the morning.

My daughter Mary was born Saturday, 12th Jany, 1760, $\frac{3}{4}$ of an hour after 9 A. M.

My daughter Jane was born on Friday, 21st May, 1762, $\frac{1}{4}$ after 1 o'Cl'k P. M.

My son James was born on Friday, 15 June, 1764, at 3 o'Cl'k in the morning.

My son Thomas was born on Friday, 30th January, 1767, 40 min. after 6 P. M.

My son David was born on Wed'y, 7th May, 1769, half an hour after 3 A. M.

My Son Sam'l was born on Thursday, 27 Feb'y, 1772, 10 min. after 3 A. M.

My son Michael was born Monday, 9th Augt., 1773, 20 min. after 7 A. M.

My Daughter Rebecca was born on Wednesday, fifty min. after 9 P. M., 1st Mar. 1775.

THE POSTMASTERS OF HARRISBURG AND WHERE THE OFFICES WERE HELD.

From 1789 to 1791 the mails for Harrisburg were served from Lancaster, and possibly those from the West at Carlisle. During the latter year an office was established at Harrisburg, and John Montgomery, son of the Rev. Joseph Montgomery, of Paxtang, appointed postmaster. Mr. Montgomery continued in office until the spring of 1793, when he resigned and John W. Allen, one of the proprietors of the *Oracle of Dauphin,* was either appointed or held the office *ad interim* until superseded by John Wyeth. Originally, says Mr. Hamilton, the post-office was "next opposite" the Register's office, which then was in Mulberry street. When Mr. Wyeth was appointed the office was in the building now owned by Frederick Gohl, No. 219 South Second street. In 1799, the *Oracle* notices the removal of the office to the residence of Mr. Wyeth, "adjoining the Rev. Mr. Snowden, being nearly opposite to where it has been kept for several years." As the Rev. Mr. Snowden then occupied the brick house, southwest corner of Mulberry and Second streets, the "building adjoining" is easily recognized.

Mr. Wyeth's successor was John Wright, who was appointed by President John Adams about the year 1799, and resided and kept the office in a two-story frame house located on South Second street below Chestnut street, now No. 112, owned by Jacob F. Haehnlen. The salary of the postmaster then was only fifty dollars per annum. Mr. Wright taught a school in connection with the office. He only resided here one year and then removed to South Front street below Chestnut, in the house now J. Brisben Boyd's, and is No. 111. For some reason he changed his residence the next year to Mulberry street near Second, upper side, where he resided eleven years, continuing his school, and where some of our older citizens now living received their preliminary education. This property was purchased by William Root about the year 1840, who removed the original house and erected a three-story brick building on the street and a large tinware and stove manufactory on the rear of the lot.

At this time the stage stables were located on the corner of River and Cherry alleys, the site being occupied by the bakery and spice mill of Mr. Haehnlen at the present time. These stables were subsequently removed to the east corner of Fourth and Walnut streets, as they were there many years, and the river was mainly crossed by them at the Upper, or Maclay's, ferry. These changes may have induced Mr. Wright again to move, for in 1812 his residence and office were at the corner of Front and Walnut streets, where he resided but one year. James McCormick's residence occupies the ground at the present. The next location was on Walnut street near Raspberry alley, in the house now occupied by Robert Bryson, No. 215. The post-office was kept here eleven years, and it was probably here that Mr. Wright died.

As the State Legislature and the public offices were now located here, the business of the office greatly increased and of course more laborious, the salary was made $500 per annum. During the year 1822, or in 1823, Mrs. Wright, who was continued in office, removed from Walnut street to the southeast corner of Market square, next door above George Zeigler's tavern. The salary was then raised to $900. Mrs. Wright died here during the year. Mr. Wright and family were from New Jersey. He came to Harrisburg at a very early day and lived and died greatly esteemed by the citizens of the place. Mrs. Jennette Forster is the only living member of the family.

Mrs. Wright was succeeded by James Peacock, who printed a newspaper called the *Pennsylvania Republican*. He was appointed by President Monroe about 1823. The Zollinger Brothers now own and occupy the place. Mr. Peacock did not remain in that location long, but removed the office to the house of Mr. Stine, north corner of Locust and Third streets, and the year following his office and residence to Front street above Market, now Mrs. John Haldeman's. It was here that the late James W. Weir served as Mr. Peacock's clerk. Subsequently the office was transferred to the two-story brick house next to Mrs. Mary Hanna's, now A. J. Herr's residence, where Mr. Peacock lived many years.

The first time the post-office was separated from the residence of the postmaster was in 1832 or 1833, when Mr. Peacock removed the office from his residence to a room in Mr. Keller's house, on Second street near Walnut, now occupied by Charles Smith, where it remained several years, when he purchased from the heirs of Henry Miller the three-story brick house now No. 7 North Market Square, occupied by Charles A. Boas and Dr. Seiler.

Mr. Peacock was superseded by Isaac G. McKinley, who was appointed by President Polk in 1845. The office remained there until the appointment of Andrew J. Jones, by President Taylor, in 1849, who changed it to the old Pennsylvania Bank house, on the south corner of Market square, now the site of the Presbyterian church. Here the office remained during Mr. Jones' term, and also during the four years John H. Brant was postmaster. The latter was appointed in 1853 by President Pierce. In 1857 Dr. George W. Porter was appointed Mr. Brant's successor by President Buchanan. He removed the office to his residence, on Market street, near Fourth street, now No. 336, where it was continued until the appointment of George Bergner by President Lincoln in 1861, who removed the office to his residence on Market street, near Third, and next door to the Lochiel Hotel, now 225, where it remained several years, when it was taken to its present location, at No. 314 Market street.

During the incumbency of President Johnson, General Joseph F. Knipe was honored with the appointment. On the accession, however, of General Grant to the Presidency, Mr. Bergner was reinstated in his old position, which he filled until his death, which occurred on the 5th of August, 1874, having held the office about eleven years.

M. W. McAlarney was shortly after appointed his successor by President Grant, reappointed by President Hayes, and retains the place at this date, August 1, 1879.

Five who held the position of postmaster were printers or editors, three were merchants, one a teacher, one a physician, one a shoemaker and one a lawyer. Four are living of the twelve, namely, Dr. Porter, Col. Brant, Gen. Knipe and Mr. McAlarney, and of Mr. Peacock's clerks Col. F. K. Boas alone remains. [1879.]

NOTES ON LINDLEY MURRAY.

The New York *Observer* of 8th May last has the following in answer to an inquiry:

"Lindley Murray, the grammarian, married Hannah Dobson, an American lady. His grandfather, John Murray, came from Perthshire to this country in 1723. While on his way his father, Robert Murray, was born. His mother, Mary Lindley Murray, was an American, I think of Philadelphia."

The name of the writer of that statement is not given, but the character of the *Observer* makes it certain that they are supposed to be reliable and authentic. Lindley Murray is a thorough Scotch name, and the current opinion as to his mother's family is here confirmed. The connection between Swatara and Philadelphia is indicated in the fact that Lindley, when six or seven years old, was sent to Philadelphia to school (we may presume, living with some of his mother's family). His tutor was Prof. Ebenezer Kinnersly, a Baptist minister (noted for his connection with Dr. Benjamin Franklin in electrical discoveries), of whom as a teacher Lindley Murray wrote in the highest terms of praise.

In this paper of the 2d inst., Dr. Egle has an interesting sketch of Mr. Murray, and also discusses his position during the American Revolution, intimating that he was positively hostile to the Whigs in that period. We must bear in mind that differences among relatives and families are sometimes especially unreasonable and unjust, and that there are radical extremes in each direction. Dr. E.'s Whig blood boils (as does mine) with the remembrance of Tory atrocities and Royal injustice of that period. But we must bear in mind how differently men are constituted, and how circumstances alter cases, *especially when viewed in the light of the past.* When a Scotch Presbyterian of the spirit of a Murray, came to be a Friend or Quaker, the change was indeed great. Resolved upon a strict neutrality, he would act accordingly. He obeyed *the powers that be,* paid taxes as they were assessed, sought to mitigate the horrors of war, and, as much as in him lay, to live peaceably with all men. While some Friends became Whigs and some Tories, and each side had men who went to the death for their opinions, thousands sided with neither, and had the respect and esteem of the best men of both extremes.

Lindley Murray states that when his prosperous law business was broken up in New York city, he removed forty miles east, hoping to remain "until the political storm blew over." So far from being in any way an enemy to the country, when Congress urged the establishment of salt works he and a friend laid out a large sum of money for means and men to manufacture that needed staple. "When the British forces took possession of Long Island," he says the work was abandoned at considerable loss. After living four years at Islip, the British holding New York, and seeming "likely to be established," Mr. Murray there removed. Aided by his father, he next went into mercantile business (doubtless protected by the party in possession), and was largely prospered, as he seems always to have been except in the salt venture.

Dr. E. is hardly just in failing to give the *reason* of Murray's removing into England. In his own sketch he devotes several pages to statements of his failing health. After traveling in New York, New Jersey and Pennsylvania for some time, a leading physician recommended the climate of Yorkshire as best suited to his case. Accordingly, in 1784, Murray and his wife determined to make a "short residence in England. Dear as were our relatives and friends, we determined to forego the enjoyment of them" for a season. "Four years was the utmost boundary" anticipated for absence from home. But the hoped-for boon of health came not; literary exercises were engaged in, and abundantly encouraged, and he remained until released by death.

I find no intimation that the change was made from choice, or that, on the whole, he preferred England to America, which he always considered *home.* It was his second choice, doubtless. He had seen the worst portions of the American Revolution—he read the horrors of the French Revolution—and, on looking over the history of the past few centuries, who, of English birth and speech, does not incline to the "Fast-anchored Isle," where substantial legal liberty has been so long enjoyed?

Chief Justice John Jay, who was Mr. Murray's fellow-student at law, was his correspondent in after years. Professor Silliman and Professor Griscom are named among the Americans admitted to the sick-room of Murray when mere visitors from the Continent were necessarily excluded. The abundant honors he enjoyed, and the high esteem in which he was held by the best men in America, are satisfactory proof that Mr. Murray was not regarded as anything but his country's friend by the more candid and judicious men who knew him best and who rightly appreciated his whole career.

Mr. Murray's will, written by himself some years before his death, is the final proof of the reality of his professed ardent love for his native land and his devotion to her best interests. Having no children, he provided that on his wife's decease, after certain specific gifts to friends, and distributing about three thousand dollars to nine charitable institutions, all his property—supposed to be several thousand more—should be taken to New York city to be used by trustees for the benefit of the colored people, the aborigines, and worthy poor, and in the distribution of good books.

No one can tell, reading Murray's works, what his religious profession was, but he was, from all accounts, a true Christian. He has left nothing to indicate what might have been his judgment—if he formed any—as to which side was nearest right in the terrible conflict through which he passed—1775 to 1782. But it is evident he was a useful citizen, although no partisan. He tried to do good unto all men as he had opportunity. And if his works were more read and his amiable, wise and kind spirit prevailed everywhere ours would be a much happier, far better world.   O. N. WORDEN.

[In connection with the foregoing communication of O. N. W. we are in receipt of a number of letters relative to the biographical sketch of Lindley Murray, nearly all thanking us for the sketch and offering additional biographical data concerning that great and good man. O. N. W., it seems, takes such exceptions to our remarks relative to the disloyalty of Lindley Murray that for their interest and warmth of expression we give his views. It was with the utmost candor, and yet with a strong love and high appreciation of the character of the individual that we attempted to give in brief detail the events of his life, nor did we allude to his course in the war of the Revolution with a fault-finding spirit. We did not even give all the facts in our possession relative to his disloyalty, as it was not our desire to provoke a discussion. We did not wish to infer that Lindley Murray "took sides with the enemies of his country" by shouldering a musket and going into the field, but that *his influence was on the side of the Mother Country as against the land of his nativity.* We refer O. N. W. to William Darby: "Dixon and Murray followed the irresistible current of their souls. Dixon rushed to the battle-field; Murray retired from the strife, not to do as many others done, join the standard of the enemies of his country, but *join the Society of Friends* and pass quietly along the stream of life."

[In regard to the name of the mother of Lindley Murray, one of the descendants of the Dixons writing from Nashville, Tennessee, under date of August 5, 1879, says: "Now the impression in my mind is, that the mother of Lindley Murray's father was a Lindley; that Robert Murray married a Henry, that John Dixon married a Henry and that John Roan married a Henry. I may be wrong, but it seems to me that is the way it has been handed down to me from our parents and grand-parents." This may be correct, but of one thing we are certain, that Lindley Murray's mother was *not* a Lindley. As Robert Murray's brother John married a Dixon, sister of John Dixon, we do think that was the only relationship existing between the Murrays and Dixons, but Mr. Robinson's traditional account is in all probability correct.]

NOTES AND QUERIES—IX.

PUGLIA, JAMES PHILIP.—This gentleman resided in Harrisburg about 1800 for a number of years. He was Worshipful Master of Perseverance Lodge No. 21, and was quite active in political affairs. He was appointed health officer of Philadelphia, and removing thither it is supposed died there. He was the author of several works in English and Spanish. Who can give any information concerning him?

HARRISBURG POSTMASTERS (N. and Q. viii.)—One or two errors occurred in this article which require correction. The stage stables were removed to Fourth and Walnut streets, instead of Fifth and Walnut. The second location of the postoffice, under Mr. Peacock, was on the site now occupied by the Rev. Dr. Robinson's residence. Where Col. Herr resides was then a vacant lot, subsequently built upon by the late John H. Briggs. Previous to the occupancy of the house by Mr. Peacock it had been the residence, if we mistake not of several of the Governors—Snyder, Hiester and Wolf. Governor Findlay resided in the adjoining house, afterwards occupied by his son-in-law, Gov. Shunk. We believe that two of Mr. Peacock's clerks are living—Mr. Mahon, of Washington city, and Mrs. Mary Clendenin Beatty, of Harrisburg.

HUTCHISON, JOSEPH.—In old Derry Church graveyard rest the remains of perhaps the first school teacher of Derry, Joseph Hutchison, and to whom frequent reference is made in the early records relating to this locality. Joseph Hutchison was a native of the county of Antrim, Ireland, born in 1711, received a classical education, came to Pennsylvania while a young man, and settled in Derry, where he conducted one of the earliest if not the first regularly established school in the Scotch-Irish settlement. He died in February, 1785. His son John, born in Derry, 1733, followed the profession of his father, whose death he survived by a few months, dying the 6th of September, 1785. His daughter Mary became the wife of Robert Moody, Esq., and was one of the most amiable of women. She died May 18, 1825, at the age of seventy-seven.

CHAMBERS.—Randel or Rowland Chambers died in the winter of 1747-8. He left a wife, Elizabeth, and among other children, sons John, Arthur, James and Robert. The executors, Elizabeth and John Chambers, filed their account July 29, 1748, in £385. They paid James Letort £8; Nathaniel Little, £10; and for gravestone and carriage, £5. John Riddle was auctioneer. Justice Hodge qualified the appraisers.

James Chambers died in Derry twp., March 13, 1758. He left a wife Sarah and children—Ann, Elizabeth, Rowland, James, Benjamin and Joseph. Arthur Chambers and Robert Boyd were the executors, Rev. John Roan and Robert Huston witnesses.

Arthur Chambers died in November, 1762. He left a wife Jean, and children as follows:
 i. *Arthur*, b. 1740; d. Sept. 29, 1784.
 ii. *Rowland*, b. 1743.
 iii. *Robert*, b. 1746.
 iv. *Maxwell*, b. 1748; d. July 4, 1785.
 v. *John*, b. 1750; d. Jan. 6, 1785.

Can any one give information relating to Rowland and Robert Chambers.

HERALDIC ARMS OF SOME PENNSYLVANIA FAMILIES.

[We are indebted to the courtesy of a gentleman, late of the Ulster College of Arms, who was recently sojourning in our city, for the following heraldic descriptions of the arms of a number of Pennsylvania families. To take an interest in these matters is nothing more than what our ancestors did long ago—and the distinction which arms may make is only that made by difference of surname. Neither is it following in the wake of aristocracy or titled nobility of foreign countries; for the arms of many a family in humble circumstances are more ancient and more honorable than that emblazoned and heralded by those who lord it over lands and realms. The arms of those which follow were earned by the bravery and valor of gallant men afore-time, and none of their descendants need be ashamed of their arms—the insignia of honorable services rendered their country or their King. We shall not attempt, save upon inquiry, to give an interpretation to the heraldic terms used, referring our readers to Webster or Worcester.]

HARRIS.—Sa. three crescents, within a bordure arg . . . *Crest*—on the stump of a tree raguly lying fesseways vert a falcon rising erm. beaked and legged or. [Ancient Motto of the Family, "Pro res pub. tra."]

BARNETT.—Sa. a Saltier or.

DIXON—Gu. a fleur-de-lis or, a chief erm . . . *Crest*—A demi-lion rampant ar.

ROAN.—Ar. three stags tripping ppr . . . *Crest*—A stag's head erased ppr. attired or holding in his mouth an acorn of the last leaved vert.

RUTHERFORD.—Arg. an orle engrailed gu. in chief three martlets sa. . . . *Crest*—a martlet sa.

SIMPSON.—Per bend wavy sa. and or. a lion rampant counterchanged . . . *Crest.*—Out of a tower az. a demi-lion rampant guardant per pale or. and sa. holding in his dexter paw a sword arg. hilt and pomel of the second.

NISLEY.—Az. a stag's head cabossed or.

STEWART.—Or. a fesse chequy or. and az.

IRWIN.—Arg. three bunches of holly leaves, three in a bunch vert tied gu. the strings flotant . . . *Crest*—An arm couped above the wrist in armor ppr. lying fesseways holding in the guantlet a bunch of holly as in the arms.

BRERETON.—Arg. two bars sa . . . *Crest.*—A bear's head ppr. issuing out of a ducal coronet.

HILL.—Erm. on a fesse sa. a castle triple-towered arg. . . . *Crest.* A tower arg. surmounted by a garland of laurel app.

MACLAY.—Az. three wolves heads erased arg. langued gu.
BERGNER.—Az. in base a rock or.
SWAN.—Az. three swans arg. two and one a chief or. . . . Crest.—a cockatrice's head erased ppr. ducally gorged, ringed and lined arg.
SNYDER.—Gu. a lion rampant arg. debruised by a chevron or. charged with three escallops sa. . . . Crest.—From the top of a tower ppr. a black-bird volunt of the last.
DOWNEY.—Az, a fesse engrailed between three boars' heads erased or [a branch of the Clan Gordon.]
HANNA.—Arg. three stags' heads erased az., ducally gorged or.
MURRAY.—Az. three mullets ar. within a double tressure flory counter-flory or. . . . Crest.—a demi man wreathed about the middle and temples vert, holding in his dexter hand a dagger arg. pomel or. hilt or. in the sinister a key ppr.
BOMBERGER.—Quarterly, 1st and 4th arg. on a mount vert. a tree ppr. 2d and 3d gu., a rocky mountain or.
KUNKEL.—Az. two chains in saltire or.
MOORHEAD.—Az. a cross crosslet arg. between 4 martlets or. on a chief of the 2d 3 escallops gu. . . . Crest.—A demi wivern vert. holding in the class an escutcheon arg.
ELDER.—Per chev. az. and arg. a bordure engrailed gu.
HUMMEL.—Sa. a cross arg.
MUMMA.—Az. a fesse fretty arg.
BUEHLER.—Gu. a lion rampant or ensigned with a ducal coronet.

THE CHARACTERS IN "THE SOLDIER'S TALE."

In my early life I had been an interested reader of the *Casket*, and of course an admirer of "Mark Bancroft's" tales. I had learned who he was, and when "The Soldier's Tale" appeared in 1833, I showed it to my father, and inquired what he knew of the characters therein described. Old men don't have much taste for fiction, but in this story he was greatly interested. Ellery Truman he regarded as a "make-up"—a myth, except the broken skull. That was probably founded upon the following incident: Two brothers whose names I think were Felty enlisted in the war. A British cavalry charge was made upon their company on one occasion. In the melee a stalwart dragoon drew up in front of one of the brothers, and raising in his stirrups, prepared to deliver a dreadful blow. As the sabre was suspended high overhead the other brother saw the peril and instantly raised his rifle and shot him down. But the blow was on its downward course, and though weakened somewhat was true to its mark—

both fell together. Felty recovered; the outer table only, it is probable, was injured, and he carried for the balance of his life a large sliver of his skull as a memento of the incident.

Sergeant Bertram was a character well known in Paxtang, Derry and Hanover. He belonged to the Pennsylvania line of the Revolution and was known as "Jimmy the Rover." By that name he is mentioned in one of Gen. Wayne's letters—see the *Casket* for 1829.

Of course you are familiar with Henry's "Campaign against Quebec," in which Robert Dixon is so often mentioned, with a detail of his tragic end.

Of the subordinate characters I would state that Emily Raymond, too, was a myth, very unlike the most notable girl of that day in Hanover, Mattie Crawford—and concerning whom I may write again.

The elder John Hutchison emigrated from Ireland in 1732. His father had as a defender participated in the siege of Londonderry, but the most interesting person connected with the story is the author of it and your sketch of William Darby is valuable and entertaining.

HIRAM RUTHERFORD.

INTERESTING LETTERS OF JOHN HARRIS.

We are indebted to the Rev. Dr. Murray, of Carlisle, for copies of the letters written by the Founder or Harrisburg to "Coll. Robt. McGaw, Esquire," of Carlisle. They contain several points of interest, and will bear perusal:

PAXTANG, *March 27th, 1784.*

"SIR: I am just Returned from Philada. Inclosed is the act of Assembly for the consideration of the people ab't my town. I miss'd Two Votes only of gett'g the law Inacted at this Session on Acco't of the Constitution ab't the law lying over for consideration, &c., till the next Meeting of the house, w'ch my Enemys & fr'ds made use of. I carry'd everything else with ease, & make no Doubt of Having the County. I am, Sir.

Y'r Most Humble Servant,
JOHN HARRIS.

"P. S.—The trustees of y'r College is to meet at Carlisle the 6th day of April next.

S'r y'rs, &c.,   J. H.

The next letter is dated not Paxtang but

HARRISBURG, *Oct. 14th, 1786.*

"SIR: Wee carry'd every member of Assembly in this county, the Sheriff & Commissioner; has, therefore, gave our antagonists a mortal defeat. Please to send me by the Bearer, Mr. George Page, a White Sword Belt for my son Robert, as ab't 20 or near 30 young men have agreed with the Lebanon Troop of Light-horsemen yesterday to meet them at Lebanon on next Saturday to choose the Officers; therefore our men will Equip themselves by next Fryday, (If Possible). The Lebanon Gentlemen, with Colo'l Gloninger paid us a visit & were completely Equipt ab't 12 file of them, Behaved with the Greatest decorum. spent ab't 24 hours with us, and returned yesterday. It's Expected that the Greatest Unanimity will hereafter take place, in future (in this county), and party spirit decrease. If you please to take the trouble to provide the Sword Belt, If to be got, shall be Oblidged to you. Underneath a list of our Ticket that Carry'd. I Expect a few lines from you, with a list of y'r Members & York County, If you have heard from them.

"I am, sir, yours most respectfully,
"JOHN HARRIS.

"Robert Clarke, ⎫
"Jacob Mylye,   ⎬ *Assembly men.*
"John Carson,   ⎭
"Sheriffs, Kelker & Berryhill.
"Commissioner, Captn James Wilson, only one to be choose, or we cou'd carry'd them. J. H.
"P.S. We are Well pleas'd at our election for the year, and the prospects of meeting all partys in a few years, or perhaps less time.
J. H.

Under date of "Harrisburg, January, 1787," after alluding to some business matters for which Col. Magaw was his attorney, he says. " . . . I have made free to trouble you to receive and forward to Baltimore some letters for me to my son David Harris and Mr. Crocket. I hope they are sent safe (ere this arrives). If any letters from them come to y'r care, be pleas'd to forward them by safe conveyances only, as my s'd son has wrote me several letters from France and other parts of Europe, and will contrive to write frequently till his return. I depend upon your particular care of them if any shou'd happen to arrive.

"I am, sir, your most Humble serv't,
"JOHN HARRIS."

In this connection we reprint, by request, a letter written one year to the day prior to the Declaration of Independence by John Harris to Col. James Wilson, a member of the Continental Congress, and one of the Immortal Signers, which is characteristic of the man and the times. The inhabitants of this section of the then Province of Pennsylvania were ripe for revolution, and it came not too soon for them. This letter was procured from a Philadelphia collector of autographs a few years ago. As the times are eventful, and it behooves us all to be loyal and true to our country and our God, its perusal will be interesting as it is *appropos:*

"PAXTANG, *July 4th, 1775.*

"SIR: Should it appear necessary to raise more troops for the Defence of American Liberty, I have a son now living in Baltimore, David Harris, who I gave a good Education to. He is a Competent Marksman, Used to the woods, as Surveyor, &c., & I think Every way fit for the army. You know him. If you please to speak in his favor, to the Hon'ble Congress for a Company, I hope he will never disgrace y'r Recommendation, should it succeed, Messrs. Dickeson & Ross, I make no doubt of their interest.

"If an Indian Warr breaks out against us I shall let my other son Johnny goe cheerfully in the service, any where in America. Our all is at stake—and wee must act with spirit on the present occasion. My son David has Interest and Influence Enough to raise a company of suitable men in a short time in this or the Maryland Province, I hope.

"To-morrow the Inhabitants of Paxtang Township will pay abt £130 cash, at least, to be forwarded Immediately to the Relief of the distressed People of Boston. You shall hear the number of Riflemen our Township turns out, w'ch I hope will be ab't or near 50 men; abt. 30 of them marches this day for Lancaster, to be equipped for the Expedition of Capt. Patterson's Company.

"I shall take it as a particular favor to get a line from you ye first safe opportunity.

"I am, sir, with the greatest Esteem and respect, y'r most obt Humble servant,

JOHN HARRIS.

"P. S. Excuse Haste.
To James Wilson, Esq."

In a subsequent letter, written the same day to Col. Wilson, John Harris says:

* * "You see I am willing to send all the sons I have to serve their country with the greatest cheerfulness, let the consequences be to them what Providence turns uppermost." * * * "My sons will not Presume to Disobey my Directions. I expect therefore in such a case advising with them I think not necessary."

The sons alluded to both served in the war of the revolution. "Johnny," a member of Capt. Matthew Smith's Paxtang company, fell in front of Quebec. David subsequently became a captain in the 1st Pennsylvania regiment of the Line. At the close of the war, with the exception of two or three years subsequent to the death of his venerable father, he resided in Baltimore, where he died, much respected and beloved, November 16, 1809.

NOTES AND QUERIES.—X.

MURRAY.—John Murray, supposed to be the grandfather of Lindley Murray, on the 10th January, 1737, obtained a land warrant from the Proprietary of the Province, and on "the 14th of ye 9th month," 1739, had the same located upon two hundred acres and 12 perches of land adjoining the north-west side of "Swahatawro" creek, then in Hanover township, Lancaster county. Adam Reed then held an adjoining tract on the north by improvement. On the 1st March, 1744, he obtained another warrant which was located about a year afterward, east of the other tract and between it and land of James Stewart. These tracts are now in East Hanover township, Dauphin county. The name of Murray does not occur in the tax list for either East or West Hanover for 1750, but in that year we find *John Morrow* (as Murray was often corruptly written) among the taxables of Paxtang township, South end.   J. S. A.

[CALL TO THE REV. WILLIAM KERR.—Below will be found a copy of a call made seventy-two years ago by the congregation of Donegal to the Rev. William Kerr to become their pastor. It possesses a double interest, because of the place and man. Donegal, though the oldest of congregations in this region, dating back beyond 1720, still survives in a small remnant of worshipers of probably the sixth generation. Mr. Kerr was the ancestor of some of our honored families. William M. Kerr, Esq., late president of the Harrisburg National Bank, was a son of his. Two children are still surviving, the widow of Dr. E. L. Orth and Dr. James W. Kerr, of York, Pa.]

T. H. R.

CALL.

"The congregation of Donegal, being on sufficient grounds, well satisfied of the ministerial qualifications of you, Mr. William Kerr, and having good hopes from our past experience of your labors, that your ministrations in the gospel will be profitable to our spiritual interests, do earnestly call and desire you to undertake the pastoral office in said congregation, promising you, in the discharge of your duty, all proper support and obedience in the Lord. And that you may be free from worldly cares and avocations, we hereby promise and oblige ourselves to pay to you, the sum of one hundred and fifty pounds in regularly yearly payments, for the three-fourths of your labors during the time of your being and continuing the regular pastor of this church. In testimony whereof we have respectively subscribed our names this 20th day of April, A. D. 1807.

We appoint Mr. Brice Clark commissioner to attend the Reverend Presbytery of New Castle with this our call, requesting them to present the same to the Reverend William Kerr, and for transacting in our name and behalf whatever may be necessary respecting said call.

John Hays,	John Watson,	James Galbraith,
Ephraim Moore,	Joseph Lytle,	Brice Clark,
Francis Little,	John Dinsmore,	Randle McClure,
James Sterret,	Thos. Bayley,	Adam Tate,
Alex. Boggs,	James Whiteside,	Jno. Pedan.
Robert Spear.	Samuel Galbraith,	

Attest:—That the congregation within mentioned, had proper previous notice, met at Donegal church, agreed in approving and subscribing the within call, is certified this twentieth day of April, one thousand eight hundred and seven, by

COLIN McFARQUHAR.

[Mr. Kerr was "highly esteemed by his brethren" of the Presbytery for his excellent Christian character and his worth as a preacher of the Gospel. He died in the pastorate of the Donegal church September 22, 1821, being still a young man.

Rev. Colin McFarquhar was his predecessor in the pulpit, and served the church with great acceptance and ability for about a quarter of a century.

Rev. Orson Douglass succeeded Mr. Kerr. T. H. R.]

FINLEY—WIRTZ—PATTERSON (N. & Q., viii).—I have the signature of Margaret Finley, daughter of John Finley and Elizabeth Harris, daughter of the first John Harris. It is a subscribing witness to a deed conveying lands on D. O. run, which empties into the Juniata river at Mexico, Juniata county. The tract was warranted to Thomas Evans, No. 1862, November 10, 1766, and sold to Capt. James Patterson, and in the deed conveyed by him to Wm. Curran, of Lancaster county, October 29, 1767. The other witnesses are Asher Clayton (in those days well-known in military circles) and Susanna Patterson (a daughter of said Captain James, and afterwards married to a Moore.)

There has of later years been a family of Wirtz's living near Mexico, who are probably descendants of the Margaret referred to. James Patterson lived at Mexico. It was his son William who married Esther Finley. He lived until about 1772 across the river from his father, where the Mexico station now is. He then removed to Pfoutz Valley, near Millerstown. This is the "Young Captain" Patterson spoken of in the Colonial Records of 1767, who arrested Stump and Ironcutter near Middleburg, Snyder county, and lodged them in Carlisle jail for the murder of the White Mingo and two other Indians, and whose rescue from the jail created a great sensation in the Province, and for which arrest Patterson was made a justice of the peace February 19, 1768, the first justice west of the Tuscarora mountains. It is certain he had a son called William A. Patterson. Many circumstances convince me that the Galbraith Patterson, who was an attorney-at-law in Harrisburg, was a son of this William Patterson. Galbraith swears to the signatures of William and Esther, January 21, 1794. He was admitted to the bar at Carlisle in July, 1787. He left Harrisburg about 1800, and lived near Williamsport and died there. He was the father of Mrs. Judge Hayes, of Lancaster, and Dr. Edward B. Patterson, of Lewistown, Pa. Can any one give us more particulars of William and his family? I might add that William Patterson's sister Mary married General Potter, and another, Elizabeth, marriage unknown. James married Jane Harris, daughter of the John Harris that laid out Mifflintown. George married Jane Burd, daughter of Colonel James Burd. These, with Susanna, above named, comprised the children of Capt. James Patterson—three sons and three daughters. Mary Patterson was the great-grandmother of Gov. Curtin. The second James Patterson had sons, John and William. John married a Hays, by whom he had a daughter, Ellen; then married Mary Irwin, by whom he had Jackson, Grizell, Eliza, Samuel (living at Spruce creek), John (married a Wallace, Clearfield), James (living at Yellow Springs), George (died at Spruce creek, married Sarah Cunningham), Juliann, Jane (married Wm. Hutchison), Calvin (Superintendent State Agricultural College) married a Mattern. William married Mary Riddle, by whom he had Riddle (married Evaline Scott—these are the parents of Capt. Wm. H. Patterson, of Harrisburg), Mary (married Gen. Buchanan, of Bellefonte), Eliza (married a Smith), Jane and Martha.

George Patterson had a son, Burd Patterson, who removed to Pottsville, where descendants still reside; a daughter, Eliza, who married Peale, the artist; another daughter, Charlotte, married William Thompson, who laid out Thompsontown, Juniata county, where descendants still reside.

Letters testamentary to the estate of Captain James Patterson were taken out on January 22, 1772. He was one of the very first settlers west of the Tuscarora mountains, even prior to the purchase of the Juniata region from the Indians, July 6, 1754. He was a leading man and able officer in the French and Indian war. See his letter to Col. John Armstrong, March 27, 1759, where he expresses a fear of losing the use of his limbs, and wishes to be placed in a fort, where he humbly conceives he could be useful to his country, as he is acquainted with the ways and humors of the Indians. (Pa. Arch, N. S., Vol. ii, page 722.) The story told of him defying the Proprietary Government, in Jones' History of the Juniata Valley, does him great injustice. His place at Mexico was marked on some maps as *Patterson's*, and he had a block house which is known in Provincial records as *Patterson's Fort*.

Can any one tell where this old captain came from? Who his wife, Mary, was? Or any additional details of the family?

A. L. GUSS.

PARTRIDGE'S MILITARY SCHOOL AT HARRISBURG— 1845-7.—I.

A full generation has passed since the institution of which I propose to write had "a local habitation and a name" at Harrisburg Whilst it is only remembered as among the things that were, many of its children—shall I say *alumni?*—remain among the foremost citizens of their native town. Some have loomed up conspicuously in law, theology, medicine, literature and the practical arts; many also perfected their military education amid scenes of deadly strife little dreamed of in their school-boy years!

As was the case respecting the introduction of water and gas into Harrisburg many years in advance of the times, I must be pardoned in claiming for my father, William Ayres, the leadership of the movement which resulted in establishing the "Pennsylvania Literary, Scientific and Military Institute"—who subscribed my name as the first one offered to make up its roll.

From his correspondence with Captain Partridge and other gentlemen of military proclivities, I glean that the matter was first proposed during the winter 1844-5. Captain Alden Partridge, who had been Superintendent of the United States Military Academy at West Point, having resigned, conceived the idea of associating military instruction and discipline with the usual collegiate education, and had made a successful test of this course at Norwich, Vermont, and Middletown, Ct., where his military schools had attained great popularity. He brought his system to Pennsylvania and opened an institution at Bristol, Bucks county, in 1843, but which was discontinued upon the opening of the one at Harrisburg in 1845. While there he first corresponded with my father upon the expediency of trying his system at the Capital. "I have no doubt," he wrote Jan. 31, 1845, "that Harrisburg is the best location in the State for an institution on this plan, and that if once established there it would flourish, if it was properly conducted."

A public meeting was shortly afterwards held in the old court house, the voice of which was highly favorable, and a committee appointed to invite Captain P. to visit Harrisburg, in order that he might personally explain his scheme.

Saturday evening, February 8th, was fixed upon, and Captain P. went from Bristol to Philadelphia *en route* for Harrisburg, but a snow storm "prevented the running of the cars for several days" (!) and the meeting did not occur until the 18th.

General Adam Diller, who was then the Adjutant General of the State, was also much interested in the project, promising to lend the necessary arms and equipments, and General (Dr.) Seiler espoused the matter also with a zeal worthy of record.

The all-important item of a roll of student's names was next in order, and was secured as follows:

[This roster of the cadets has been collated from various sources, and especially from a memoranda roll made during the first term, which is perhaps the only one in existence. Only the last name of the cadet was used at school and the Christian names have been added from memory. In addition, the residence of those who are living and the dates of death of those deceased have been affixed, while those of whom no information can be obtained, the names are printed in *italics*.]

ROLL OF CADETS—1845-6-7.

*Adams, John Quincy (fifer), Philadelphia.
Antes, John Forster, Missouri.
Arnold, Levi.
Ayres, George Bucher, Philadelphia.
*Baker, Napoleon Bonaparte, d. May, 1863, at Marietta, Ga.
Barrett, James, d. July, 1863, at Harrisburg.
Barrett, Charles, d. August, 1849, at Harrisburg.
Barrett, George, Weston, Lewis co., W. Va.
Berryhill, James Buchanan, Iowa.

*Black, Thomas Jefferson (fifer), d. Mar. 3, 1872, Harrisburg.
*Blattenberger, Julius, d. Mar. 14, 1875, at Osceola, Pa.
*Bombaugh, Charles Carroll, Balt., Md.
*Bomgardner, Cornelius (bass drummer), Harrisburg.
*Boyd, Robert Sloan, Harrisburg.
*Buffington, Thomas W., Md.
Burke, John Michael, d. June 15, 1849, at Harrisburg.
*Bush, John William (drummer), d. 1867, at Harrisburg.
Cadwallader, Iredell, d. May 19, 1849, at Milton, Pa.
*Camp, William Edwin, d. at Washington City.
*Castle, Theodore Butler, Glassboro, N. J.
Cunningham, Francis Robinson, Washington City.
*Dean, Richard Crain, Surg. U. S. N., Camden, N. J.
De Forrest, Thomas.
*De Witt, Louis Beviere, U. S. A., Fortress Monroe.
Dock, William, d. Feb. 29, 1864, at Harrisburg.
Doll, Samuel Elder, d. Feb. 15, 1853, at Callao, S. A.
*Dougherty, James Dennis, d. April 3, 1878, at Harrisburg.
*Egle, William Henry, Harrisburg.
Elmore, Charles A.
*Evans, William C., Erie, Pa.
Faunce, Eli, d. at Philadelphia.
Feltenberger, ——.
*Foster, Andrew Jackson, Harrisburg.
*Forster, Benjamin Law, Harrisburg.
Forster, John Elder, Erie, Pa.
*Frazer, Christian Selzer, Texas.
*Hackley, Charles Edward, New York City.
Haehnlen, William, Harrisburg.
Hallabach, Jacob Martin, d. at Rockville, Pa.
Haldeman, Richard Jacobs, Cumberland county, Pa.
**Haines, Philip D.*, of Chester county, Pa.
*Hammond, Lafayette, U. S. A., d. Sept. 6, 1873, at Fort Yuma, Arizona.
*Harris, William Hall, d. April 8, 1867, at Harrisburg.
*Holman, Samuel Augustus, West Philadelphia.
Irwin, William Bryson, Harrisburg.
*Jennings, Elmer, d. Dec. 22, 1876, at Philadelphia.
*Johnson, William Young, Portsmouth, Va.
*Johnson, Andrew Jackson, Dallas county, Texas.
*Johnson, John Bucher, U. S. A., d. June 24, 1871, at Harrisburg.
*Jones, John Andrew Williamson, Terre Haute, Ind.
*Keefer, John Brua, Paymaster U. S. A., Portland, Oregon.

*Kemble, James R., U. S. A., d. in New Mexico.
Klein, Theodore Berghaus, Lebanon, Pa.
Kramis, Amos, of Schuylkill county.
*Kunkel, John A. (drummer), Hannibal, Mo.
Landis, Jeremiah.
*Lawrence, James Kennedy, Brookville, Pa.
Leamy, James Crozier, d. April, 1875, at Baltimore, Md.
*Lescure, Edward Porter, d. Dec. 26, 1869, at Harrisburg.
Logan, James Jackson, of Dillsburg, York county, Pa.
Lombard, Frank, Springfield, Mass.
*Markley, Arthur Donaldson, Montgomery county, Pa.
*Maglaughlin, William J., Harrisburg.
McAllister, John Boas Cox, d. March 7, 1858, at Fort Hunter, Pa.
McAllister, John Carson, d. May 3, 1859, at Fort Hunter, Pa.
*McCormick, Henry, Harrisburg.
McCormick, James, Harrisburg.
McGee, John.
*McGowan, Alexander, Lebanon, Pa.
Miller, Charles Adam, d. May, 1875, at Philadelphia.
*Miller, James Madison, d. in Perry county, Pa.
Montgomery, Robert, Turbotville, Pa.
*Mowry, Sylvester, U. S. A., d. October 17, 1871, at London, Eng.
*Partridge, Frank, Burlington, Kansas.
Parke, William, of Parkesburg, Chester county.
*Parker, Gilbert Lafayette, Philadelphia.
*Piper, Alexander, U. S. A., West Point.
*Piper, James Wilson, U. S. A., d. Oct. 30, 1876, at Carlisle.
*Rehrer, Erasmus Godfrey, Florida.
Reily, John Whitehill, d. March 20, 1860, at Harrisburg.
Seiler, Herman Alricks, Harrisburg.
Shunk, James Findlay, d. Jan. 20, 1874, at Harrisburg.
*Shunk, Francis John, U. S. A., d. Dec. 15, 1867, at Richmond, Va.
Simon, Luther Melancthon, Harrisburg.
*Sees, Egbert Taylor (bass-drummer), Philadelphia.
*Snyder, Edward, Harrisburg.
Snyder, George (drummer).
Sterrett, Thomas W., of Sterrett's Gap, Cumberland county.
Storm, George Washington, Wheeling, W. Va.
Strong, Henry Knox, Dixon, Ill.
Strong, Nelson, Dixon, Ill.
Stehley, Edward, d. May, 1875, in King William county, Va.
Tait, Joseph LeCony (drummer), Harrisburg.
Visscher, Simeon G., Rome, N. Y.

Wallower, John, Harrisburg.
Wilson, Henry Stewart, W. Va.
Wilson, William Kennon, Washington Territory.
*Witman, Henry Orth, Harrisburg.
*Wright, Thomas Forster.
Wyeth, William Maxwell, St. Joseph, Mo.
Wyeth, John, Philadelphia.
*Zollinger, Elias Stecher, Harrisburg.

Of the foregoing cadets those marked (*) were in service during the Rebellion, being nearly one-half of the cadets then living.

Cadet Baker was a gallant officer in the Confederate army, and lost his life in a charge of Federal cavalry, May, 1863, near Marietta, Georgia . . . Cadet Frazer, residing in the South at the breaking out of the war, entered the Confederate service as an officer, but resigning, was allowed to return North, where he remained until the close of the civil strife . . . Cadet Johnson (A. J.) was a volunteer surgeon in the Russian army during the Crimean war and received the Imperial decoration. On returning home he studied for the ministry, subsequently went South, and at the outset of the Rebellion entered the Confederate service as surgeon . . . Cadet McGee, we are informed, was residing in southern Missouri at the opening of the civil conflict, entered the Confederate service as an officer, and it is supposed lost his life in the war.

Cadets Hammond, Johnson (J. B.), Kemble, Mowry, Piper (J. W.) and Shunk (F. J.) were officers of the regular army and died as such . . . Cadet Hammond entered the service as Captain in the 1st California infantry, transferred as Major of 2d Ohio heavy artillery, and for meritorious services appointed from California July 28, 1866, as 1st Lieut. 23d inf., U. S. A. . . . Cadet Johnson (J. B.) was appointed 1st Lieut. and died as Captain in the 6th cavalry, U. S. A., having been brevet major and lieutenant colonel during the war . . . Cadet Kemble entered the volunteer service in 1861 and was appointed therefrom to the regular army. He was 1st Lieut. U. S. A. at his death . . . Cadet Mowry, of R. I., graduated at West Point July 1, 1852, appointed 1st Lieut. 3d artillery March 3, 1855, resigned July 31, 1858 . . . Cadet Piper (J. W.) was an officer in the volunteer force and appointed therefrom. He died as 1st Lieut. 5th artillery, U. S. A. . . . Cadet Shunk (F. J.) was a graduate of West Point, was promoted Major of Ordnance March 7, 1867, and at the time of his death was chief of ordnance First Military district of Virginia.

Cadet Lawrence was Captain of the 11th U. S. infantry, received extraordinary wounds at Fredericksburg, Virginia, and at the close of the war he resigned.

Cadet Dean entered the U. S. N. as assistant surgeon April 17, 1856; commissioned as surgeon August 1, 1871; in 1870 attached to the Bureau of Medicine, and June 8, 1873, commissioned medical inspector.

Cadet Piper (Alex.) graduated at West Point July 1, 1851; commissioned Captain 3d artillery, May 14, 1861; brevet Major August 30, 1862, for gallant and meritorious services; brevet Lieutenant Colonel June 15, 1864, for gallant and meritorious services at the siege at Petersburg, being chief of artillery, 18th Army Corps; at present principal assistant instructor of artillery tactics at West Point.

Cadet DeWitt is in the engineer service, U. S. A.

Cadets Bombaugh, Egle, Evans, Hackley and Markley were surgeons in the Federal Army 1861-5.

Cadets Blattenberger, Dougherty (Capt. Ind. artillery co. 1862), Foster, A. J. (Qr. Mr. Sergeant. 25th Penna V.), Haines (Lieut. 124th Penna. V.), Harris (Capt. 9th Penna. Cav.), Jennings (Capt. 12th Penna. Cav.) Keefer, McCormick (Capt. 25th Penna. V., and Col. 1st Penna. V. M.), Parker (Lieut. Col. 28th P. V.), Partridge (Capt. — Ill. V.), Rehrer, and Witman (Lt. 6th Penna. V. M. and Capt. 36th Penna. V. M.) served their country faithfully as officers of the volunteer service.

Holman, Samuel Augustus, was chaplain of the 48th regiment, P. V.

Rehrer, Erasmus Godfrey, captain of Company E, 129th regiment, P. V., was wounded at the battle of Fredericksburg.

Cadets Holman and Rehrer, upon Captain Partridge's resignation, attended the Institution at Norwich one year.

Kemble, James Robinson, captain 3d U. S. Cavalry and Brevet Major U. S. A., died at Fort Wingate (of which he was in command at the time), Territory of New Mexico, April 3, 1867.

Castle, Theodore Butler, studied medicine and was in service as surgeon in the rebellion. Subsequently studied theology, and is now a clergyman of the M. E. Church.

Cadets Bombaugh, Dean, Egle, Evans, Harris, Johnson (A. J.,) Markley, Parker and Witman became physicians . . . Cadets Holman, Castle and Visscher, clergymen . . . Cadets Dougherty, Forster (B. L.,) Haldeman, Johnson (W. Y.,) Jones, McCormick (J.,) and Shunk (J. F.,) lawyers.

Cadets Irwin, Markley and Montgomery have been members of the Pennsylvania House of Representatives.

Cadet Haldeman was a member of the House of Representatives, Forty-first and Forty-second Congresses.

Cadets Ayres and Storm are artists, and Cadet Simon an architect. Cadets Barrett (C.), Burke, Cadwallader, McAllister (J. B. C.), McAllister (J. C.) and Reily died previous to the civil war.

Cadet Mowry was elected delegate to the United States House of Representatives from the proposed Territory of Arizona in 1857 and 1859. United States Commissioner to run and mark the boundary line between the State of California and the Territories of the United States, 1860–61, and superseded by President Lincoln in 1861. Was arrested and imprisoned at Fort Yuma on charge of disloyalty, but established his innocence; went abroad for his health and died at London. Author of the "Geography and Resources of Arizona and Sonora," 1865.

Cadet Shunk (J. F.) afterwards graduated at the University of Virginia, where he fitted himself for the legal profession, and was admitted to the Pennsylvania bar. He married a daughter of the distinguished Judge Black and became prominent among the leaders of the Democratic press. As a journalist he was racy and incisive, upholding the reputation of his honored ancestry.

Cadet Ayres is the author of "*How to Paint Photographs,*" now in its fifth edition, published by Appleton & Co, . . . Cadet Bombaugh is editor and proprietor of the *Baltimore Underwriter,* and compiler of several literary collections, among which is "*Gleanings for the Curious,*" the finest work extant of its kind. All his comrades doubtless remember him for his beautiful penmanship, and the graceful ease and purity of his literary composition. . . . Cadet Egle is so thoroughly identified with historical matters in his native State that his name has become an authority. As associated with the editing of the "*Pennsylvania Archives,*" (second series), and author of the latest and best "*History of Pennsylvania,*" he has developed a talent for research that only rivals his eminence in Masonry. I am indebted to him for kind and most valuable assistance in the preparation of this history.

By way of co-incidence, it may be noted that the foregoing roll of young soldiers contains the names of Washington, Lafayette and Napoleon; of Presidents Jefferson, Madison, Adams, Jackson and Buchanan, and Governors Findlay and Shunk.

A sufficient number of these names had been subscribed by the middle of March to indicate that the proposed school would surely open. The name of Charles Edward Partridge, a graduate of Dartmouth College, as professor of the classical department, and Jabez C. Crooker, a graduate of the Norwich Military Institute, as professor of the English department and military instruction, were sent on by the superintendent, Captain A. Partridge, and the gentlemen themselves appeared in due time. Mr. Otis S. Tenney, a graduate of Gen. Ransom's at Norwich, was also engaged, after a few months, as professor of penmanship, and assistant to Mr. Crooker.

Meanwhile the local committee secured the old Temperance Hotel building, on the northeast corner of State and Second streets, for the use of the school; it being intended that State street—which was then not macadamized, grass-covered and little used—should serve as our drill and parade ground ; and the neighborhood being quiet and retired it was a really excellent location.

The institution was formally opened here with brief exercises on April 15th, 1845. The season was not sufficiently advanced and the ground dry enough to allow of military drill out doors. Our military instruction was therefore begun in a third-story room of the old Exchange building, on Walnut street, near Third. But the vibration of the floor, caused by our marching, was deemed injurious to the building, and our quarters were changed to the old Shakespeare Hotel, the floor of hall there being more stable. Our instruction was limited, however, to facing and marching, as we did not receive arms until we drilled on State street.

The cadets appeared in uniform as fast as the town tailors were able to make them—and it was no doubt the biggest job they ever had! (I wonder whether a single one of those one hundred uniforms exists to-day!) [Yes; cadet Simon has his—W. H. E.] It consisted of a hussar jacket of dark blue cloth, with standing collar; a single row of silver bullet buttons in front; single buttons at cuffs and sides of the collar. The breast was heavily padded, and the jackets of the larger boys were made with small tails. In winter the pantaloons were blue cloth, and in summer—especially on dress parade—white. The cap was blue, encircled with a broad gold band.

Every cadet was expected to provide his own desk, provided with storing room for his books and a chair or stool. For a term of twelve weeks the tuition was $8 00, with no restriction of studies except for music and fencing, which were extra. These branches and broadsword exercises were taught by Mr. Edwin S. Perkins, a native of Vermont, who also kept the boarding students and led our military band.

This martial music consisted of Mr. Perkins' bugle; two fifers, cadets Adams and Black; two tenor drummers, cadets Bush and Tait, and base drummer cadet Sees and subsequently cadet Bomgardner—all of whom were given free tuition in exchange for their musical services.

The military institute was thus auspicuously begun, and was a very conspicuous feature at Harrisburg in the summer of 1845. The staid old Academy on the river bank at first sneered at its upstart rival on Second street and thought it was only fuss and feathers. But in a few months our military eclat became irresistible, and many of its scholars were enrolled with us. The classical attainments of Charles E. Partridge were not least among the attracting influences.

The *Democratic Union*, of April 23, 1845, alluding to the establishment of the school says: "Capt. Partridge so favorably known to the community as a gentleman preeminent in his profession, has opened a military school in our borough; and we are happy to learn, has already obtained a large class of scholars. The acknowledged ability of Capt. P. is a sure guaranty to those who may place their sons under his protection, that when they leave the Captain's quarters they are qualified for the counting house, the work-shop and the 'tented field.'"

Our military drill was had in summer at 5 o'clock a. m., and in winter at 4 p. m.—weather permitting. In good weather during the summer-time, we always had a number of spectators, especially of the fair sex, at morning drill.

> "Girls will follow when they hear the drum,
> To view the tassel and the waving plume
> That decks his hat;"

And the old song was verified in our case. The fair ones of the old borough were our *early* friends and admirers; and the dilapidated board-walk which preceded the east-side pavement on State street, was the gallery from which the fair beheld the brave—and the brave got too often "out of line" beholding the fair!

Among our regular visitors all will remember Capt. R. B. Marcy, U. S. A., then detailed on recruiting service at Harrisburg, who bent his morning walk toward our drill-ground. Tall, straight as an arrow, quiet, with fatigue cap, and cane, he would watch our drill with interest, and when we heard of an occasional word of praise from him we were highly pleased. Sometimes his attractive brunette daughter Helen — now Mrs. Gen. McClellan — accompanied her father.

In the military exercises, musket and rifle (or light infantry) drill were used on alternate days. Forming in line just opposite the Catholic church, the roll was called, and we started off invariably with a slow march toward Third street; then changing to quick step through various evolutions, how we *did* sweat on the hot morning! We drilled two hours, and there were few boys who went home lacking appetites for breakfast! We were also instructed in guard duty and the forms of military review, reception of officers, inspection and fortification. The latter science was a speciality with Captain Partridge, who delivered regular lectures to the whole school, which were illustrated by diagrams and the black-board.

Our collegiate progress after all was the principal thing. The daily work was always opened after roll-call by reading of the Scriptures by Prof. Partridge, who was a member of the Congregational church. One of the cadets was appointed "Officer of the Day,' whose duty it was to order the drum-beats for assembling, report absentees, misconduct, &c. Students of the classical department had their own room upstairs, whither they retired after the morning exercises or Capt. P's. lectures before the whole school.

Only few mornings after school had begun, Prof. Crooker handed me a note which (having been preserved) reads:

Squad No. 1 : Detailed and command given to Cadet Ayres,
Bush, Camp, Haehnlen, Haldeman, Castle.
(Signed) J. C. CROOKER.

I was too greatly surprised to appreciate the honor, or comprehend *what* I was expected to do; but it was explained to me that, inasmuch as the young gentlemen herein named had been lately received into the institution, *I* was to put them through the military rudiments privately, in the yard, before they could appear with the company in public. This was the first so-called " awkward squad," but I don't remember that they were any more awkward than the rest of us at the beginning. GEORGE B. AYRES.

NOTES AND QUERIES.—XI.

"WHERE IS SNAKETOWN?"

(N. & Q. vii.)—*** Persists in locating "Snaketown" at a point which he does not establish by any proof whatever, but relies entirely upon guess work, which is dangerous ground for any historian to stand upon. Although John Harris settled upon land at the mouth of Paxtang creek, on the north side, between the years 1720 and 1730, I doubt very much whether he took out a warrant for the land previous to 1733.

I also call in question the amount of land he is said to have owned at that time. On the 27th of May, 1733, John Harris took out a patent for 800 acres of land in the rear of the place he was then settled. This is the earliest date of any of his patents of which I can find a record.

The land upon which Harrisburg is laid out was surveyed for the

Proprietary *June* 4, 1733, by virtue of a warrant dated May 12, 1732. It contained one thousand acres and allowance. By reference to the draft of this tract of land, I find upon the north side marked "Barrens," upon the east side, the line at the north corner starts a considerable distance east of Paxtang creek, and runs south and crosses Paxtang creek to the west side, and from thence it runs a few hundred feet to the line of John Harris' land.

It appears from the draft that two streams of water flow from this tract of land into the river, another one flows through the south end, thence through John Harris' land to the river. Paxtang creek flows through the eastern side and empties into the river below Harris' land. The thousand acre tract owned by Mr. Harris was probably this tract surveyed by the Proprietary, which he purchased, if at all, after 1733.

From this draft it does not appear that Bizalion or any other trader, except Harris, settled upon or adjoined this land.

Subsequent research may establish the proprietor's tract as the site of "Snaketown."

Some other statements are made which I am inclined to think are not in accordance with historical truth. It is a well known fact and can easily be established from the county records, that several Indian traders had trading posts around Conoy Town, not a fourth of a mile apart. There were several traders, also, who lived close to Conestoga Town, and I presume the same rule applies to Paxtang. I could name a dozen traders who resided in Donegal who owned adjoining farms. There was no rule establishing Indian posts, although some made a special application to trade with a particular tribe. A few traders were especially favored in this way. As to Rowland Chambers, the records seem to locate him along Conewago creek. David McClure, who married his daughter Margaret, owned a farm adjoining Randel Chambers.

* will have to try again, but I hope he will not shorten his line to suit some preconceived idea of a fact.   SAMUEL EVANS.

[Such industrious antiquaries as "S. E." and *** should have no difficulty in locating Snaketown—or at least in settling the question whether it was at *this* point or not. Our early pioneers, and especially Indian traders, only *guessed* as a matter of course at distances. Burt's forty miles might just as well have been ten miles above or ten miles below as *at* Harrisburg, and hence no reliance can be placed on his statement. As to where the classic Indian locality of Snaketown was located, neither "S. E." or *** really have proven. In this controversy, however, there seems to be some difference as to the locating of John Harris, or rather to his taking up of land. John Harris was first commissioned a trader on the Susquehanna with permission to cultivate fifty acres of land in 1707. He established his trading post at the best ford on the Susquehanna river, near the mouth of Paxtang creek. Near him were Bizalion, Burt and Charter, but how near no one knoweth. By reference to N. & Q. (*No. iv*,) it will be seen that prior to 1726 he was in possession of a large quantity of land. Under date of Jan. 4th of that year James Steel writes to Isaac Taylor: "John Harris has seen his warrants which are now at James Logan's to be signed . . thee knows the warrants have been twice drawn over." It is true the land was not surveyed for six or seven years subsequent thereto. There was a ferry, as early as the incident narrated, at the point stated by ****, where Burt may have located, but even of this we are not certain; for we are inclined to the opinion that he was *not* a permanent but an itinerant Indian trader.]

PARTRIDGE'S MILITARY SCHOOL AT HARRISBURG— 1845-7.—II.

May 27th, 1845.—Capt. P. appointed a "committee of visitation, advice, and general supervision," consisting of William Ayres, chairman; Dr. Luther Reily, Gen. C. Seiler, James McCormick, Esq., and Francis Wyeth, Esq. This committee received instructions in detail from the superintendent, and the professors were directed to refer all important matters to its judgment.

May 28th.—Captain P. writes that Prof. Crooker complains that "the muskets received from the Arsenal are too heavy and too long for many of the cadets. Would it not be well for the committee to ascertain from Adjutant General Diller whether he would feel authorized to have them cut off to such length as Mr. Crooker may suggest." The fact here referred to was uncomfortably true.

I shall never forget the first morning we attempted to handle those muskets—the old-fashioned, superseded, Springfield flint-lock arm, and weighing pounds enough to sprain our young muscles. Such a squirming and writhing as it required for us boys—especially those at the smaller end of the line—to "carry" those ancient blunderbusses was a sight that would have conciliated Falstaff, or at this day would originate a suit for the prevention of cruelty to children. By daily practice, however, they grew lighter, but were always very unwieldly for the smaller boys. Cadets Dougherty and Hackley, who were the smallest boys, had miniature muskets of their own.

In the location of the military institute at Harrisburg, Captain Partridge not only looked forward to a permanent establishment there, but his plan embraced also the founding of similar auxiliary schools throughout the State; the *alma mater* being the central one at the Capital. To this end he desired an act of incorporation, and special buildings to accommodate 150 students, &c. He writes June 21, 1845:

"I perceive there is at this time a great rage for opening military schools at different places. This is all very well in principle if it does not run wild in practice. I believe, indeed have no doubt, that combining a correct knowledge of military science and of practical military duty with all the other branches of useful knowledge, much better prepares American youth to make his way independently through the world, and to move in a more elevated sphere than has been done by the old collegiate system; and that it is also in perfect accordance with the principles of our civil and political institutions. I consequently wish to see the system pursued generally throughout the United States, but I wish to see it pursued (prevail) on the same broad, liberal and elevated principles on which it was first established by me at this place in 1820 (Norwich, Vermont), and on which it has ever been conducted under my superintendence. I have consequently a strong aversion to seeing it under-estimated."

On Thursday, July 24th, by invitation the Cadet company participated in the obsequies solemnized at Harrisburg on the death of General Jackson, ex-President, which had occurred on the 8th June preceding. The eulogy was delivered in the hall of the House of Representatives by Governor Shunk. The procession of citizens was headed by the military companies—Dauphin Guards, Capt. E. W. Roberts; Harrisburg Rifles, Capt. C. Seiler; Cadets of Captain Partridge's Military School, the Junior Guards, Capt. J. M. Eyster—together with a number of society organizations. It is remembered that the cadets made a fine appearance, marched unexceptionably, and were a conspicuous feature of that imposing procession.

On Friday, the 8th of August following, the school made an excursion to Middletown, where we astonished the natives by our appearance and drill—for *boy soldiers* were a novelty in those days. The father of your honored townsman, Mr. William Calder, generously sent us there by canal packet-boat, under command of Capt. Henry Lyne. We were hospitably entertained there, and we recollect one prominent citizen of that locality to whom we were indebted for many kindly courtesies; that was Major Brua Cameron, son of Gen. Cameron. At Highspire, *en route*, we were taken good ca e of by Mr. Robert Wilson, whose sons were among us. Cadets Piper (Alex.), Bombaugh and McAllister (J. B. C.), committee of arrangements, in a card published, returned thanks to "the citizens of Middletown and Portsmouth for their elegant entertainment and untiring attention," to Mr. Wilson, of Highspire, Mr. Calder, and Captain Lyne.

At another time, in the fall, we made a "grand" excursion by canal to Columbia, and thence by railroad to Lancaster. Whilst in Columbia, we stopped at Black's Hotel (I think it was,) and in Lancaster, at Hubley's. Among the sights shown us at Lancaster was the bloody spot in the old jail where some of our historic ancestors among the "Paxtang Boys" had slaughtered the Conestoga Indian scoundrels in 1763.

The magnificence and importance of this tour (!) cannot be appreciated by the boys of to-day. It was a greater event for us to be taken to Lancaster *then* than for an excursion of juveniles *now* to Boston or Cincinnati.

The first public examination took place in the latter part of July, 1845, at the close of the first term. Professors Crooker and Partridge made a vacation trip to Norwich, Vermont, taking with them the committee's report, dated August 8th, and in response to which, the Superintendent writes on the 25th: "I have been much gratified reading the account of the examination, and in the respectable manner in which the cadets, as well as their instructors, have acquitted themselves. Under all the circumstances of the case, I do not apprehend that the institution has sustained any injury in consequence of my absence. The cadets are generally young, and not very far advanced in the higher departments of knowledge; and to all the branches to which they have, and probably will attend for the succeeding quarters, they can be as correctly taught by Messrs. Crooker and Partridge as by me. When they are further advanced, both my instructions and my lectures will be of more importance to them. I shall spend the winter with you; instruct in such branches as may be most necessary, and give my regular course of lectures, which will probably be of more importance to the welfare of the institution than my other instructions. I shall be in Harrisburg during the whole session of the Legislature, and we will ascertain what it will do in regard to act of incorporation," &c.

In the absence of record I presume the institution resumed operations in September. Captain Partridge came on, as he intended, and gave daily morning lectures chiefly on fortification and military affairs, but varied with some on History, Engineering and Moral Science.

During this winter a number of the cadets, mostly those of the classical department, organized *The Philomathean*—a literary and debating society—the cadets belonging to which were designated by the Greek letter *phi*, in brass, worn upon the cap. [I have mine yet]. Prof. Partridge was President; I was Secretary.

In addition to the usual debates, we had a (so-called) newspaper, the *Philomathean*, of which cadet Piper was the accomplished "editor and publisher" (reader), at the first. Cadets Bombaugh and Egle edited several numbers. Many interesting, profitable and memorable evenings were thus spent.

An out door item of this winter's experience is worth recalling. Once, during a night infantry drill, and being in sections of four, we were ordered to the "trail arms—close order—double quick—march!" The day was a cold one, and down the street we went; breast to back, a solid mass, when, in an instant, we were tumbled pell-mell into an indistinguishable conglomeration. Fortunately no one was injured, but of course *such* an evolution was *not* "according to Cooper's tactics," and the cause of the disgraceful melee was sought out on the spot. It so happened that cadet Burke had trailed his musket too low for the free locomotion of his neighbors—and hence the result.

But here was an unexpected opportunity to increase our military knowledge by the practical institution of a *Court Martial*. Poor Burke was duly "arrested,' the requisite number of cadets were detailed to *try* him according to the rules of war, and the investigation proceeded with decorum and solemnity. I presume he proved himself innocent—at least he was not shot.

During the summer of 1846 our school was at the heighth of its glory. The war with Mexico being then the absorbing public theme, its progress and our army's achievements were also of the most special interest to us military students. I remember that as soon as school was dismissed we lost no time at noon in getting down to Dan. Robinson's newspaper agency, opposite Herr's hotel, where the *Public Ledger*—the chief source of news—would be received by the morning train. As might be expected, each battle received its due share of comment; but how meager was the data, how poor the facilities for news, how limited the sinews of war, when compared to the opportunities during 1861–5!

I may add here that Gen. T. B. Ransom, who afterwards fell at the capture of the city of Mexico, had been one of Captain Partridge's pupils, and a superintendent of his school at Norwich, Connecticut.

It was during this summer that, reducing Captain Partridge's instructions to practice, we cadets built a miniature fortification of earth and stones in the then vacant lot bounded by State, North, Third streets and Willow alley. It was laid out "according to Partridge," with its rampart, bastions, ditch, covert-way, glacis, &c., &c., the waters of the run which flowed through the lot being turned into the ditch surrounding the "fortified" space. It was really complete.

Sometime in 1846, under circumstances not remembered, the administration of the school was changed. Prof. Charles E. Partridge assumed the superintendency in addition to his duties as classical instructor. Prof. Crooker bade us farewell, and his place was filled by Mr. Frederick W. Partridge, a graduate of Hanover, N. H., and brother of Charles E.—a tall, handsome man of military bearing. The labor and responsibilities of the position, however, proved too great for the delicate constitution of Charles E., and by mid-winter of 1846-7, the fortune of the school began to wane. At any rate it was passing out of the hands of the Partridge brothers, as will be seen.

Captain Partridge, writing from Norwich, February 9, 1847, says: "Mr. Charles E. Partridge is now here. His health is delicate, so much so that he thinks he shall be obliged to give up teaching; also that his brother will probably engage in some other pursuit. Under these circumstances it appears that the institution must stop unless measures are taken to continue after their year expires. As I first established it, I feel unwilling it should thus cease, and am disposed to continue it if there is any fair prospect of success. I have now arranged my business here so that I could probably give more of my *personal* attention to it, and would be enabled to furnish it with good teachers. * * * * * I think H. a good location, and should be pleased to see a permanent institution on this plan established there. * * * * * Will you inform me of the state of the institution at the present time, with such other information as you and the committee may think useful. In case I should again take the superintendence of it, I think, should it succeed well another year, that a proper act of incorporation might be obtained and other arrangements adopted to make it rank with any other seminary in the State."

This extract closes the data upon which I have based these reminiscenses of the Pennsylvania Literary, Scientific and Military Institute at Harrisburg. The loss sustained by the death of Prof. Charles E. Partridge and the resignation of Prof. Fred. W. Partridge was irreparable. The prospects for a successful continuation of the school were far from flattering. In August Captain P. announced that the fall term would commence on Monday, the 6th of September, but no allusion was made to the instructors. In the meantime the trustees of the Harrisburg Academy having secured the Rev. Mr. Long as Principal of that institution, strenuous efforts were made and nearly all the boys of academic age were obtained as scholars. Everything

Historical and Genealogical. 77

was uncertain about the military school, and not until the day of opening was it positively known who were the teachers, or even who would attend as scholars.

Capt. Partridge sent on as Principal Mr. James W. Phillips, a graduate of the Norwich institution, with an assistant, whose name is not now remembered. The class of students was very small, but the indefatigable committee—or rather trustees of the institute—were determined, if possible, to establish it upon a firm basis.

On Saturday evening, October, 16, 1847, a public meeting of the citizens of Harrisburg, favorable to the establishment of a *State* military and scientific college, agreeably to the plan of Capt. Partridge, was held at the Court House. The assemblage was a large one. Judge Dock was chairman, and after a number of brief addresses by Messrs. Ayers, R. J. Fleming, McCormick, Dr. Seiler and others, a preamble and resolutions were adopted providing for placing the institution on a firm basis. One committee was appointed to draft a memorial to the Legislature asking its aid to the measure, and another committee to obtain subscriptions, which were to be applied to the erection of proper buildings. The object was a noble one, but the enthusiasm had passed away. The first measure failed, and the citizens unaided by the State, lost heart in the enterprise. Under these discouraging circumstances Capt. Partridge withdrew all connection from the institution. Without his management it became a complete failure, and ere the third term had ended, that fine school—which at one time seemed strong with hope for an auspicious future—was brought to an unfortunate close. *Requiescat in pace.*

During the autumn of 1847 there were several excursions to Dauphin and again to Middletown, and the cadets acquitted themselves well. The last public notice we have of the school was on the occasion of a drill in front of the Capitol, and " the firing of a national salute of twenty-nine guns " in front of the State arsenal, on the celebration of Washington's birthday, February 22, 1848.

I may add, however, for the information of those who have lost the track of events, that our able superintendent, Captain Alden Partridge, died at his native home, Norwich, Vermont, January 17th, 1854, after one day's illness. He was sixty-nine years of age, and had been throughout his long life distinguished for good health, much of which he attributed to the habit of walking, which exercise he kept up almost to the last. He had been an instructor for nearly fifty years, and had taught over twelve hundred pupils! He was especially skilled in mathematics and the art of war, and was a high-toned man of generous impulses.

Prof. Charles Edward Partridge, whom to know was to love, was a second cousin of Capt. P.'s, and died also at Norwich, April 6, 1847, at the early age of twenty-five. Looking back from this point of time, it seems scarcely possible that his intellectual capabilities and manly character had not exceeded this period of life. He will be remembered as a most capable and thorough instructor; quiet and gentle but firm in his discipline; genial and kind in manners, very companionable, appreciative of fun at the right moment, and a consistent Christian, void of sectarianism. No occupant of a teacher's chair ever elicited greater respect and love, and his memory is affectionately cherished by all.

Professor Crooker was a New Englander, and graduate of the Norwich institution. He was the *locum tenens* during Capt. Partridge's absence, a good military instructor, and had special charge of mathematics and the English branches. Although not large, he was a man of great physical strength; could twirl one of those heavy muskets as if it were a rattan cane. On one occasion when two of his cadets (who shall be nameless) thought proper to "pitch into" each other, and became locked for a tussel, he caught each one by the coat collar and had the strength to pull them apart; and then to their mutual surprise, he brought them into uncomfortable collision with each other several times until both cried enough! They got more than they were contending for. Prof. C. is now a successful lawyer at Mendota, Ill.

Prof. Fred. W. Partridge became a lawyer, resident of Sycamore, Illinois. As might have been expected by his old students, he entered his country's service during the rebellion, and rose to a brigadier generalship. After the war he was sent as consul to Bankok, Siam, and returned from that post about two years ago. He was a man of native dignity, energetic character and highly respected.

Prof. Tenney was quite a favorite, genial and boyish—the youngest of our "faculty." He served his country's cause also, and was last heard of at Mt. Sterling, Ky., as a teacher.

Prof. Edwin Sturtivant Perkins, the music teacher, was born at Woodstock, Vermont, January 18, 1805. He was a man of cheerful disposition, and a good, practical musician. He was also very expert in fencing and sword exercises. He remained at Harrisburg after the close of the school, and was engaged in the Pennsylvania railroad service at the time of his death, which occurred June 18, 1876.

The arms and military equipments of the cadets were kept in a room known as "The Armory." Here each one had a niche for his musket and hanging places for his cap and belt, which supported the cartridge-box and bayonet-case. He was required to keep his arms and accoutrements bright and clean, and a periodical inspection was had to this effect. This was done in public, but I do not know of any one being ordered off in disgrace; on the contrary, the cadets were generally ambitious to present a clean and unexceptional appearance.

The cadets, as a rule, felt a degree of pride in their appearance and conduct. When not on military duty, the cap alone indicated that the wearer was one of "Captain Partridge's boys." But it was the talisman of general good conduct. Although it was the duty of "Officer of the Day" to report misconduct at any time or place, the necessity of so doing was very infrequent. At one time some of the smaller boys were found playing marbles—"boys will be boys"—but it was only necessary to remind them that *soldiers* were not expected to play in the dirt, and thereafter amusement was sought for at a higher grade.

I wish I could recall better than I can, the various qualities which distinguished many of my old comrades. It must necessarily follow that there be "some bright particular stars"—and there were. Bombaugh, Piper (A. M.), the McCormicks, Haldeman, Egle and Witman were good linguists. Johnson (W. Y.) and Visscher were the walking dictionaries; catch them using an ordinary word if they could lug in one of thundering sound! Haldeman would not study arithmetic; nothing short of algebra! Arnold thought that "compositions" selected from standard authors were always preferable to one's own; and on one occasion, after Professor Chas. E. had listened significantly to one whose authorship we all detected, he suggestively remarked: "I hope you have the *punctuation* correct!"

But the two crowning specialties of the school were Egle and Henry McCormick, in mathematics. When these two—as it would sometimes happen in reciting geometry or algebra—were *both* at the blackboard, the figures walked chalk in rapid style, I declare. No *pons asinorum* impeded their course, no problem seemed too difficult for these young mathematical ogres. It was music, figure-atively speaking, to hear those boys crack problems out of chalk.

I wish that space did not forbid many other personal recollections. One of my valued fellow-students, now a prominent iron-master at Harrisburg, only a few years after our school-days, wrote some lines for me which are so much more forcible after the lapse of thirty years, that I beg his leave to quote them in conclusion:

"If e'er this page arrest your eye, pause for a moment; lend a thought to days numbered with the past, when we proudly trod to music of the soul-stirring drum—in *bullets* all arrayed; and oft in the stormy debate, made the ancient walls of that old society hall resound with thrilling eloquence and argument unanswerable! But our comrades, where are they? What wondrous changes hath old Time wrought—and not yet has he ceased; for in dark futurity, to us unfathomable lie, awaiting development, the germs of many unlooked-for haps! Still let us ever cherish with kindliest feeling the memories of men and things of yore, and may the bonds of friendship wax stronger so long as we are exposed to the vicissitudes of this uncertain existence."

Our comrades! Yes, where are they? View the list and see how many are known to have answered the roll call of death, and are now "present" in eternity! Superintendent, professors, cadets, have met again, and await that Great Day of Review, when it will be revealed who among us all studied best the all-important lesson of life, how to die as well as how to live—"the knowledge of the glory of God"— and became "good soldiers of Jesus Christ."

GEORGE B. AYRES.

NOTES AND QUERIES.—XII.

CHAMBERS (N. & Q., ix.)—Maxwell Chambers, son of Arthur Chambers, b. 1748; d. July 4, 1785. He left issue as follows:
  i. Arthur, b. Dec. 5, 1772.
  ii. Elizabeth, b. April 14, 1777.
  iii. Jeremiah, b. Nov. 16, 1779.
  vi. Maxwell, b. Sept. 7, 1782.

Elizabeth, wife of Maxwell Chambers, b. 1751, d. Oct. 3, 1784, and with her husband lie interred in Derry church yard. Who can give additional information concerning this family?

AN OLD TIME DEBATING SOCIETY.—In the *Oracle* for January, 1797, "a Friend of Society" who was no less a personage than John Downey, Esq., proposed the formation of a "Lyceum for Free Debate." Acting upon this suggestion "the Patrons" held their first meeting shortly after at Montgomery's tavern, and organized "The Harrisburg Free Debating Society." Its officers were Stacy Potts, president; John Browne, secretary. Stacy Potts, Rev. Henry Moeller, John Browne, John Wyeth, John Downey, Lancelot Armstrong and Stacy Potts, jr. Among some of the (to us) amusing questions publicly debated by the learned men of our staid borough were " Which is the most preferable for a wife, an old maid or a widow." . . . "Is jealousy a proof of love?"

LINDLEY MURRAY'S POSITION (N. & Q. vi.)—Mr. Darby's words as quoted by Dr. E., recently, carry the impression that Mr. Murray joined the Society of Friends to escape responsibility during the trying period of the American Revolution. I think there is abundant evidence that the elder Murray and his family, Lindley included, conscientiously embraced the creed of opposition to all war some years *before* the Revolution. They were people of great *moral* courage. I wrote that L. M. was "no partizan," but the types made me say "a partizan." O. N. W.

DIXON.—Robert Strain, a native of Hanover, and until his removal to Ohio, about the commencement of the present century, member of Rev. Snodgrass' church, under date of " Dayton, Ohio, November 24th, 1835," gives this record of Richard Dixon:

"A statement of facts with regard to the services of Richard Dixon in the War of the Revolution:

"Richard Dixon, of Lancaster county, Penn'a, enlisted in Lancaster, Penn'a, in the early part of the year 1775, under Matthew Smith, a Captain, and remained under Capt. Smith until his term of enlistment was ended. He then enlisted for and during the war, and said Dixon was promoted to the rank of either Quartermaster Sergeant or Sergeant Major. I am very distinct in my recollection of Richard Dixon. When he first enlisted I made a shot pouch for him and stamped on the cover thereof the motto of "Liberty or Death!" The whole of the four brothers of the Dixon family were in the service until the war was ended, and were of the truest kind of Whigs and Patriots. "ROBERT STRAIN."

BOYD.—William Boyd, a native of Paxtang, b. in 1733, d. May 17, 1808. He was a soldier of the Revolution, an officer of one of the Lancaster county battalions, wounded and taken prisoner at the battle of Long Island, August 27, 1776. For a number of years he was the Master of Lodge No. 21. At his death he left a wife, Jennet, and children as follows:

 i. James.
 ii. John.
 iii. Jennet, m. ——— Moore.
 iv. Mary, m. ——— Strawbridge.
 v. Margaret, m. ——— Williams.
 vi. William.

From his will, of which James Cowden and James Rutherford were the executors, we copy the following: "I bequeath to the Lodge No. 21 in Harrisburg Five pound to be put to interest forever if the

Brethren thinks proper, for the charity fund of said Lodge." The minutes of the Lodge from the year 1804 to 1819 being lost, it is not known to any of "the Brethren" what disposition was made of this bequest. Are there any documents among the Cowden or Rutherford papers which would give the desired information?

PAXTANG CHURCH, 1808.—[In the year 1808 the following persons subscribed the sums opposite their names for "the repairing of Paxtang meeting house." Are any of them now living?]

Name	£	s.	d.	Name	£	s.	d.
Robert Elder	3	15	0	Sarah Wilson	1	2	6
James Cowden	3	15	0	John Forster	1	10	0
Edward Crouch	3	15	6	Charles Chamberlain	0	15	0
Elizabeth Gray	1	2	0	John Ross	0	9	4½
John Gray	1	5	0	Michael Simpson	1	10	0
John Wiggins	1	17	6	Jean Carson	0	7	6
James Rutherford	2	5	0	Joseph Burd	2	5	0
Samuel Sherer	1	17	6	Robert Gray	1	10	0
John Gilchrist	1	10	0	Thomas Walker	0	17	6
Samuel Rutherford	1	10	0	William Caldhoon	1	0	0
William Rutherford	1	10	0	John Rutherford	0	15	0
Robert McClure	1	10	0	Michael Simpson	6	0	0
John Ritchey	1	17	6	James Awl	0	7	6
Thomas Smith	3	5	0	Joseph Burd	2	5	0
Susanah Rutherford	0	11	8	David Patton	1	2	6
Thomas Elder	1	10	0	Robert Gray	1	10	0
John Carson	0	10	0	Thomas Walker	0	17	6
Josiah Espy	1	10	0	John Walker	0	17	6
James Awl	1	2	6	Jacob Richards	1	10	0
John Allison	0	17	6	Jean Wilson	1	5	0
James Cochran	0	15	0	Frederick Hatton	0	11	3
Ann Stephen	0	15	0	William Caldhoon	1	0	0
John McCammon	0	15	0	John Finney	0	10	0
Mary Fulton	1	17	6	Joseph Wilson	1	2	6
Mary Rutherford	0	7	6	Michael Whitley	0	12	6
William Larned	1	0	0	David Stewart	0	15	0
James Stewart	0	15	0	Thomas McCord	0	15	0
Joshua Elder	3	0	0	Elizabeth Wills	1	10	0
Thomas Buffington	0	15	0	Hugh Stephen	0	15	0
John Elder	1	10	0	John Rutherford	0	15	0

YE ANCIENT INHABITANTS.—I.

The assessment lists of this section of Lancaster county, prior to the formation of the county of Dauphin in 1785, are very few, owing no doubt to the destruction by fire of the court house at Lancaster in 1782. We have in our possession, however, copies of quite a number, and as they are of value, not alone to show who dwelt in this locality a century ago, but important in a genealogical point of view, we propose, from time to time, giving the lists as found, *verbatim*. This will be the means of preserving them for future reference.

EAST END OF HANOVER, 1769.

James Andrew,
Robert Bell,
John Baker,
Fredrick Bezore,
Wm. Brown,
John Brown,
Mathias Bezore,
And. Brown,
James Baird,
John Brightble,
David Braught,
George Countz,
James Crawford,
Philip Consleman,
William Clark,
William Clark, jr.,
Benjamin Clark,
Thos. Clark,
Adam Cleinan,
Thos. Copenhefer,
Wm. Craig,
Arnold Chearheart,
Christian Couch,
Andrew Carver,
John Campble,
Ambrose Crean,
Andrew Cooper,
John Cunningham,
James Carrethers,
James Dixon,
Robert Dixon,
Henry Dowdy,
John Evert,
Andrew Ensworth,
John Ensworth,
Josiah Espy,
Nicholas Earhart,
Robert Even,
Peter Felty,
John Foster,
Wm. G. Grenlie,
Nicholas Gerrah,
John Grenlie,
John Graham,
James Graham,
Wm. Gray,
John Gilliland,
Mathias Hiss,
Thos. Hume,
Robert Hill,

John Hollenback,
Martin Hiss,
Rudy Hook,
Christian Henry,
John Hume,
Adam Harper,
Abraham Hubler,
Peter Hendrick,
George Hendrick,
Brice Ines,
James Ines,
And. Kellender,
Mike Kitch,
Alex. Kidd,
Philip Kister,
Fite Livergood,
Alex. Laughlan,
Daniel Leady,
Henry Lowmiller,
Anthony McCreight,
Henry Miller,
Kellean Mark,
Charles Mire,
Daniel Muser,
Alex. Martin,
Walter McFarland,
Wm. McCullough,
John Miller,
Robert Misleby,
Adam P. Miley,
Fred. Pickel,
John Pruner,
David Preast,
Vendel Rattle,
Peter Potz,
Jacob Pruner,
Porgart Poor,
Mathias Poor,
Mathias Poor, jr.,
Joseph Perkey,
James Petecrew,
John Rough,
And. Reed,
Casper Reader,
Peter River,
Jacob Riegart,
Wm. Robison,
Peter Road,
Christian Rumberger,

Jacob Stover,
David Streain,
Henry Segler,
Ulery Seorger,
James Sloan,
Mike Straw,
Nicholas Simon,
Alex. Swann,
Archibald Slowan,
Charles Stewart,
William Stewart,
James Stewart,
Lazarus Stewart,
John Shaver,
Alex. Slowan,
Isaac Sharp,
John Strain,
Simon Tuce,
John Tiller,
John Tibbens,
John Tibbens, jr.,
Jacob Tups,
Edward Tate,
George Title,
John Todd,
John Toons,
John Thomson,
Moses Vance,
George Woolf,
Hugh Watson,
Adam White,
Hugh Watt,
George Willy,
John Weaver,
Jacob Woolf,
Daniel Weaver,
Samuel White,
Peter Walmor,
Abe Wingart,
John Winter,
Henry White,
Wm. Wreck,
John Weaver, jr.,
Widow Graham,
Peter Wolf,
Jacob Wolf,
William Young,
James Young,
Robert Young.

Freemen.

Robt. Billens,
Samuel Brown,
Alex. Greenlee,
Cauplen Gourdain,
Samuel Irwin,
John Lard,

John Linch,
Christ. Long,
Patrick McNay,
John Moor,
Henry Prunner,
Alexander Robinson,

John Toops,
Henry Tups,
Peter Wyrick,
Alex. Young,
Robert Young,

Inmates.

Robert White,
Wm. White,
David Tibbens,
Andrew Karson,
James Grain,

John Baumgardner,
Wm. Moreland,
Jacob Pickel,
Henry Fensler,
And. Thompson,

Jacob Weaver.
Christ. Baumgardner,
Sam'l Holliday,
Patrick Cunningham.

JOHN BRUNNER, *Collector.*

NOTES AND QUERIES.—XIII.

REMINISCENCES OF THE MILITARY ACADEMY AT HARRISBURG.

One of the professors of this institution, upon the receipt of Mr. Ayres' valuable sketch, writes:

"After a lapse of more than thirty-three years, I received the roll of the Pennsylvania Military Institute, of 1845. I was more than pleased in looking over the names of the young soldiers of that day. Their bright faces came up before my mind's eye as if but yesterday. Those morning drills on State street, the visitors on the broad board-walk under the locust trees, Mr. Perkins with his E flat bugle, the fifers and drummers, and the suits we all had on those cheerful June and July mornings. Do you remember the mischievous boys who used to come and disturb our studies at the windows, and the detail of cadets Zollinger, Maglaughlin and two more whose names I now disremember, who were ordered to bring them in on one Saturday morning?

"The fourth company of bright lads, the smallest of all in the school—Baker, Dock, Dougherty, Egle, Elmore, Hackley, Jones, Jennings, James McCormick, Rehrer and John Wyeth—who could execute all manual exercises, marchings and firings more accurate and better than any of the other companies. Every one was an epitome of a real soldier."

Jones, John Andrew Williamson, was an officer of the celebrated "Berdan's Sharpshooters," and served through the war.

Miller, James Madison, went out as an officer of a Pennsylvania regiment, and served as a staff officer. He died at Montrose, Pa.

Wright, Thomas Forster, was a graduate of West Point, served as colonel of a California regiment, made with his command the celebrated march through Arizona in 1861, was subsequently promoted in the regular army, and fell in the Modoc war.

PETITION OF THE INHABITANTS OF HANOVER TOWNSHIP AGAINST THE DIVISION OF THE SAID TOWNSHIP, FEBRUARY SESSIONS, 1769.

[In connection with the tax list of "East End of Hanover township 1769," recently published (N. & Q. xii.), we present the following petition to the court at Lancaster protesting against the division of the township. The signatures are originals, and although it confirms a statement repeatedly made that our Scotch-Irish ancestors, with scarcely an exception, were able to read and write—we cannot say much for their orthography, as will be seen, quite a number did not know how to spell their names. Adam Reed, Esq, in affixing his signature, adds: "As I don't Expect to be at next Court I doe not agree to any division of said township."]

To the Honorable Court of Common Pleas, to meet at Lancaster the seventh February, 1769:

GREETING: Whereas it has been reported that a Plan is now intended in order to have Hanover Township divided, in which the undernamed Persons do reside, which, if done, must necessarily prove to the Disadvantage and dissatisfaction of the Inhabitants thereof, and Consequently be attended with fatal Consequences.

We therefore beseech your Honors to put a stop to such proceedings and we will forever pray as in duty bound.

Timothy Green,
Sam'l Patterson,
Danel Shaw,
James Hutchison,
James Low,
Patrick Machan,
David Forgusson,
Samuel Fergusson,
William Fergusson,
William Cooper,
John Cooper,
John Stewart,
James Finney,
James Irwen,

James McCreight,
Samuel Sturgeon,
John Thomson,
Richard Dearmond,
John McQuown,
Joseph Allen,
William Crain,
Anthony McCreight,
Lazarus Stewart,
Jas. Pettycrew,
Jas. Robinson,
Robert Sturgeon,
Alexr. McCoy,
Jno. Campbell,

Thos. Kenedy,
Robert Kenedy,
Willm. Brown,
Jos. Barnet,
Wm. McCluer,
Wm. Brandon,
Thos. Finney,
Joseph Wilson,
Andrew Walles,
Thomas McCluer,
James Rogers,
William Rogers,
William Young,
John Crawford,

Thomas McMillan,
George McMillan,
James McMillan,
John Shaw,
Richard Johnson,
Matthew Snody,
James Johnson,
John M. Cory,
Wm. Wright,
James Robertson,
Robt. Hume,
Thos. Finney,
Martin Barnett,
William Moorehead,
William Cathcart,
Robert Porterfield,
Thomas Strain,
Jos. Thompson,
John Thompson,
Thomas Meen,
Thomas McElhinney,

Richard Crawford,
John Star,
Adam Reed,
John Grame,
James Willson,
James Wilson,
Samuel Allen,
Isaac Hannah,
Matthew Hannah,
William Repet,
Samuel Hutchison,
Thomas Scott,
John Woods.
Robert Hutchison,
Joseph Hutchison,
Jno. Hutchison,
James Hamilton,
Alexdr. Robinson,
Jas. McClanachan,
Joseph Hutchison, jr.

James Crawford,
James Wilson,
Robt. Wallace,
Robert Parks,
Joseph Parks,
Joseph Snodgrass,
Michael Vanlear,
Willm. McCullouch,
James Dixon,
Samuel Brown,
Andrew Endsworth,
John Gilkeson,
Brice Innes,
Alexander Sloan,
Mathew Thornton,
John Andrew,
John Todd,
James McCreight, jr.
Robt. Kirkwood,
Anthony McCreight.

HOW THEY FORMERLY EXTINGUISHED FIRES IN HARRISBURG.

One of the early ordinances of the borough required every householder to have one fire bucket for each story of the house. These buckets were made of heavy leather, long and narrow in size, and were painted different colors as the owner chose, with his or her name on them, and were kept hanging in some convenient place—frequently in the hall or entry—and it was the occupants duty, in case of an alarm, to carry or send them to the fire. Double lines were formed to the nearest pumps, and sometimes to the river; men and often women and children joined in these lines, the latter being in the empty bucket line. The buckets were passed from one to another filled with water and emptied into the side of the engines, which were worked by hand, the empty buckets then passed back by those on the opposite line. Often the buckets were not more than half full when reaching the engines, the water being spilled by passing them along the line. There were separate lines for each engine.

Balthaser Sees, who built the old Union, the first fire engine in the town, also made about fifty feet of leather-sewed hose, which was intended to have water conveyed from the pumps through them. As sewed hose was not water tight they never could be used. It was a difficult matter to maintain the lines at a distance from and out of sight of the fire, as everyone wished to see it. It was hard, laborious work to pump water for the buckets and to work the engines. When the pumps failed, as they often did, lines were then formed to the river.

This primitive means of putting out fires was continued until 1836, when to the great relief and joy of the people the Citizen engine was purchased. It was built by Agnew, of Philadelphia, and sucked the water and forced it through hose. Hose enough was bought to reach from either the river or the canal to the center of the town, and by that means the engines at the fire were supplied, but not in sufficient quantity without the bucket lines. This continued until the water works were completed in 1840, and fire plugs and hose took the place of primitive means.

The Citizen should be No. 4 instead of No. 3 in succession, as the third company was called the Harrisburg, and was an organized company for some years. They had the most modern as well the handsomest engine in the borough. It was made by Bates, of Philadelphia, but was not considered efficient in throwing water, and was finally sold and the company disbanded. The engine house was located on Second street above Locust, east side. Alderman Kepner was one of the original members.

The hard work of the firemen, at a conflagration, at the engine brakes, continued until the present steam engines were adopted. The Friendship being the first one, all the hand engines were gradually replaced by steam until the whole five companies were supplied with steamers. The laborious work of the firemen was only partially relieved by the change, as they were compelled to draw the heavy steamers to the fires until horses were substituted. The council and the citizens should always be liberal with our firemen, as there is no better and more efficient department in the country.

The first mode of giving the alarm of fire was by the ringing the old Court House bell, followed by the different church bells as the engine houses then were small frame buildings without bells. Subsequently the direction was struck by the bells on the different engine houses. The old Philadelphia system was then adopted, viz: One stroke for North, two for South, three for East and four for West; the other divisions of the compass were also struck. This alarm continued in both cities until the fire alarm was erected in 1874. This was adopted by council over much opposition, as all new enterprises mostly are, at an extent of ten thousand dollars. Our present Mayor, John D. Patterson, when in council was greatly censured for the course he took in advocating the passage of the ordinance. It has, however, proved so greatly beneficial in preventing extensive conflagrations that it could not be dispensed with.

A. BURNETT.

NOTES AND QUERIES.—XIV.

THE SAWYER FAMILY.

In the fond hope of unraveling the tangled threads of Scotch-Irish Genealogy, we shall from time to time print such records as we have in our possession, with the request, however, that whatever additional information can be given will be sent us, so that if possible they can be made complete:

I. WILLIAM SAWYER, a native of Ireland settled with his parents on the Kennebec in Maine in the fall of 1717. Whether his father ever came to Pennsylvania is doubtful—but William located in Londonderry township prior to 1735. He was born in 1703 and died October 18, 1784. In old Derry Church grave-yard is this inscription:

In memory of | WILLIAM SAW- | YER, who dep- | arted this Life | Octo'r the 18, 1784, | in the 81st year | of his age.

His wife Sophia (her maiden name we know not), b. in 1705, d. Sept. 9, 1788, and is buried by his side. They had issue, all b. in Londonderry township, among others:

  2.   *i.* John, b. 1735, m. Jane Allen.
      ii. Thomas, b. 1737; d. May 5, 1768.
  3. *iii.* William, b. 1739, m.
  4. *iv.* Benjamin, b. 1748, m.

II. JOHN SAWYER, b. 1735, m. Jane Allen of Hanover township. They had issue:

  i. Joseph, d. in Preble co., O.
  ii. John, m. Mary Bell of Hanover.
  iii. William.
  iv. Jane, b. 1764; d. Nov. 29, 1803, m. Robert Geddes.

And five other daughters—one of whom m. James Johnston, removed in 1827, to Fountain co., Ind., and died there. One m. John McCord, in 1827 removed to Preble co., O., and died there. One m. John Allen; one John Boal, and the fifth William Sawyer, a cousin. Concerning the last we have the following information: Some years after their marriage William Sawyer and his wife became thoroughly convinced that their marriage was wrong and agreed finally to separate. Accordingly their farm was sold and the proceeds divided. Both loved each other dearly, and when the time came for separation the ordeal was a severe one. After embracing his wife, he would go but a short distance, then return, and so continued for some time, when at last, amid tears, he passed out of view. William Sawyer went to the then far West, engaged in boating on the Ohio, and was subsequently drowned in the Kanawha river while taking down a boat load of salt. His widow married Joseph Clokey. By this marriage there were three children. A daughter Mary married Rev. Mr. Wilson, of Canonsburg, Pa.

III. WILLIAM SAWYER, b. 1739, d. August 20, 1785. He m. in 1763, and had issue:
   i. Jane, b. 1765, m. David Miskimins.
   ii. Mary, b. 1767, m. William Crain.
   iii. Margaret, b. 1769.
   iv. Joseph, b. 1771; d. Feb. 28, 1789.
   v. William, b. 1773.
   vi. Elizabeth, b. 1776.

IV. BENJAMIN SAWYER, b. 1748; d. Feb. 5, 1792. His wife was Margaret ———. They had issue:
   i. Thomas.
   ii. William.
   iii. James.
   iv. Hannah.

A WEDGEWOOD MASONIC PITCHER.

We have in our possession an artistic example of the celebrated Wedgewood ware, which is not only interesting to those who appreciate Ceramic art, but it is a valuable memorial of Free Masonry. The article was recently sent us from Ohio, by a descendant of Samuel Hill, a native of England, but who came early to America and resided for years in Harrisburg, where he died in the year 1809. Mr. Hill was made a Mason in Perseverance Lodge, No. 21, and during the years 1795–6, visited England. On his return he brought home the Masonic souvenir, which after the lapse of eighty odd years is still in existence. It is a pitcher of graceful form, of white ware, measuring eleven and a half inches in height, with a capacity of one and a half gallons. Beneath the spout, within a circular garland, composed of a grape vine in fruitage on one side, and blades of wheat with roses intertwined on the other, linked together by a cluster of roses, appears the monogram "S. H."

On the left cheek of the pitcher, resting on a Masonic pavement, there are two Corinthian columns bearing spirally respectively the inscription: "Vide, Aude, Tace," and "Sit Lux, et Lux Fuit," and surmounted by the figures of Faith and Charity. Within the columns are three candles, the coffin and sprig of acacia, the letter G within the center of a five-pointed irradiated star, the cock and bee hive, the motto on scroll "Memento Mori," the mallet, crossed keys, ashler, hour-glass, pick and spade crossed, crossed quills, the open Bible bearing the square and compasses, plumb, trowel and level, the All-Seeing Eye irradiated, the sun and moon and stars in firmament, and in ethereal space the figure of Hope seated upon the ark with the anchor. The whole is gracefully garlanded with acacia, roses and wheat blades.

On right cheek of the pitcher appears an oval wreath formed of acacia and roses. Below are the various emblems of agriculture, the arts and literature, with the word "Independence" in a scroll. Above the center is the cap of Liberty with the word thereon, surrounded by a wreath of acacia, the whole irradiated. On either side of the Liberty cap are the U. S. flag containing fifteen stars, a U. S. pennant. and a lighted torch. Within the oval are these lines:

"As he toils your rich glebe, the old peasant shall tell,
  While his bosom with liberty glows,
How your Warren expired—how Montgomery fell,
  And how WASHINGTON humbled your foes."

On the eve of the celebration of the centenary of Lodge 21 such relics of the old-time are more greatly appreciated and highly prized, *Sept. 27, 1879.*

ROBERT HARRIS—MEMBER OF CONGRESS, 1823-7.

A true representative of the Harris family in the third generation was Robert Harris, son of the Founder, John Harris, and of Mary Reed, daughter of Adam Reed, Esq., of Hanover. He was born at Harris' Ferry on the 5th of September, 1768. He was brought up as a farmer, and resided in the early part of his life in the log and frame building on Paxton street, now used as a public school. His farm extended from the dwelling house down the river to about the present location of Hanna street, and thence out over the bluff, including the ground occupied by the Catholic cemetery, containing about one hundred acres.

By the death of his father in 1791 much of the business affairs of the family was early entrusted to him. He was possessed of considerable public spirit, aiding in the establishment of various enterprises, including the bridge over the Susquehanna, the Harrisburg Bank and the Harrisburg and Middletown turnpike road. In the first two of which he was a director, and perhaps also in the last. Mr. Harris was appointed to various public trusts. He was one of the State Commissioners to survey and lay out a route for the turnpike from Chambersburg to Pittsburgh; also for improving the Susquehanna, in the course of which the commissioners descended the river below McCall's Ferry. When the Assembly of the State decided to remove the seat of Government to Harrisburg, Mr. Harris was selected as one of the Commissioners for fixing the location of the Capitol buildings, preparatory to the removal.

During the Mill-Dam troubles in 1795, Mr. H. was one of the party of prominent citizens who finally tore down the Landis dam, the site of which was in the lower part of the city, and to which was attributed much of the sickness then prevailing here. He was one of the first to rush into the water; and it was said that he was then laboring under an ague chill, but never afterwards had a return of it.

During the war of 1812-14 Mr. Harris was appointed paymaster of the troops which marched to Baltimore and acted as such at York where the soldiers were discharged.

He was elected to Congress, and took his seat in 1823, and by a re-election served therein until the 4th of March, 1827. On one of the occasions he brought home with him a picture, made before the days of daguerreotyping, of the celebrated John Randolph, of Virginia, representing him on the floor of the House of Representatives, enveloped in a large coat, extending his long, lank arms and his bony finger as he pointed it at Henry Clay and others, in the course of his impassioned and sarcastic harangue.

Mr. Harris served in Congress during the Presidency of John Quincy Adams, and of course knew him. When General Taylor, as President was in Harrisburg, Mr. Harris was appointed to deliver the address of welcome on the part of the citizens. During the subsequent intercourse with General Taylor, he observed to him that he had dined with all of the preceding Presidents. He was married in Philadelphia in the spring of 1791, during the Presidency of General Washington; and dined at his table, and there or elsewhere with Adams, Jefferson, Madison, and probably Mr. Monroe. He was intimately acquainted with Gen. Harrison when a lieutenant in the army, had entertained him at his house in Harrisburg, and was invited to dine with him during his brief term as President. He was on friendly terms with John C. Calhoun, and well acquainted with General Jackson.

After the State Capitol was removed to Harrisburg the residence of Mr. Harris, who had in 1805 purchased the Harris mansion from his brother David, and from that period occupied it, was the center of attraction at the seat of Government. He entertained many of the prominent men of the State and of the Legislature. At his house might have been seen Governor Findlay, Samuel D. Ingham, Thomas Sergeant, Wm. J. Duane, Gov. Wolf, and many other persons of distinction, including Isaac Weaver, of Greene county, Speaker of the Senate from 1817 to 1821, a gentleman of marked presence, and who Mr. Harris said more resembled Gen. Washington than any other man he had ever seen. During the Presidency of Gen. Washington, Mr. Harris, then a young man, accompanied the party on board the Clermont, the steamboat of John Fitch, when that vessel made its trial trip on the Delaware.

The first Prothonotary of Dauphin county was Alexander Graydon, and the first register Andrew Forrest, both sent from Philadelphia, by Governor Mifflin, with whom they had served as fellow-officers in the war of the Revolution. Gov. McKean for some reason refused to re-appoint Mr. Forrest and tendered the appointment to Mr. Harris. He however recommended the retention of Mr. Forrest. But Gov. McKean informed him that if he did not accept the office he would appoint some one else. He accordingly accepted it, but it is said divided the fees with Mr. Forrest for some time, and perhaps until his death.

Mr. Harris was not grasping in the acquisition of property, or he might have left a fortune. He suffered in his pecuniary circumstances through building operations, the enterprises of the day in which he invested, and the depreciation of real estate. He managed his farming operations with discretion. He had at his lower or farm house and also at the mansion, horses, cows, pigs and poultry in abundance, and laid up for the winter stores of fruit, vegetables, etc., and in the yards and cellars thirty or forty cords of wood, with back logs for the kitchen fire-place. In the room adjoining was a ten plate stove of a primitive pattern, weighing hundreds of pounds, with plates near half an inch thick—coal was not then in use here. He kept a carriage and pair of grey horses and lived like a gentleman of the old school. He was fond of cider either sweet or somewhat sour, and one of his children has the silver pint mug devised to him by his father, out of which he was accustomed frequently to drink it. When young, it is said, he played well on the violin, and could sing agreeably. He sent his children to dancing school and allowed dancing at his house. He was a good shot, and was expert in the management of a canoe. He kept a canoe, as did many of his neighbors, and had a sail-boat built for his children by a Canadian who came here at the breaking out of the war. He was kind to his neighbors, freely lending his horse, or cart, or wheelbarrow, and other utensils, and was liberal in disposing of the fruit of his lot and farm. He had a famous garden during his whole life, and enjoyed the cultivation of it.

Until the close of his long life Mr. Harris was quite active in body and mind. He died at Harrisburg on the 3d day of September 1851, being within two days of four score and three years of age. His remains repose in the beautiful cemetery now within the bounds of our City by the Susquehanna. His warm and life-long friend, Rev. William R. DeWitt, D. D., delivered the funeral discourse, which we recollect well of hearing, in which he paid a most glowing tribute to the memory of Robert Harris. He was a man of genial manners, hospitable, obliging, honest and honorable. He died, not unwillingly, in the faith and hope of a Christian, and in the respect and kind regard of his fellow-citizens.

In person Mr. Harris was almost six feet in height and of tolerably robust form. His portrait, by Eicholtz, presents a favorable countenance. His son, Thomas J., recently deceased, very much resembled his father in appearance, although the latter was taller.

Mr. Harris married in Philadelphia, May 12, 1791, Elizabeth Ewing, daughter of the Rev. John Ewing, D. D., provost of the University of Pennsylvania. They had issue as follows:

i. John Ewing, d. June 22, 1846.
ii. Hannah, d. in infancy.
iii. David.
iv. George Washington.
v. Thomas Jefferson.
vi. Robert, d. in infancy.
vii. Robert.
viii. William Augustus.
ix. Mary.

Mrs. Harris, b. in Philadelphia, Dec. 2, 1772; died at Harrisburg, April 27, 1835, and there buried.

NOTES AND QUERIES.—XV.

CHAMBERS (N. & Q. ix. xii.)—John Chambers, son of Roland Chambers, who died in the winter of 1747–8, resided in Paxtang at the time of his death, which occurred in March, 1770. He bequeathed to his wife his farm on the west side of the Susquehanna. Who can inform us as to the location of this farm? He left children as follows:

i. Samuel.
ii. Robert.

iii. Elizabeth.
v. Isabel.
iv. Esther.
vi. Mary.

STEWART.—Robert Stewart, a native of Glasgow, Scotland, removed to county Down, Ireland, 1720. He had two sons, Samuel and Hugh, who emigrated in 1735 and settled near Chestnut Level, Lancaster county. Hugh was then a youth of sixteen. Samuel had twelve sons and one daughter. After the eldest son, Samuel Templeton, became of age, land was purchased in Hanover township, where he settled, but *when* I am desirous of knowing. It is the tradition that at the same time his uncle Hugh located in Paxtang township. Hugh married and had nine children—the oldest, Jane, was born in Paxtang, Nov., 1751. The fifth was Robert, born 1765, who was the father of the late Robert Stewart who resided near Linglestown on the farm devised him by his grandfather Hugh. But it is with the other branch I desire information—especially the date of settlement.

JOHN MCCAMMON, of Middletown, was born in the county of Down, Ireland, about the year 1774, and emigrated to the United States when about 17 years of age. He resided a short time in Chester county, from whence he came to Middletown, where he followed his trade of stone mason. He married there, and afterward kept the principal hotel and stage office on Main street near Center square. When General Lafayette, on his visit to America in 1824-25, passed through Middletown on his way to Harrisburg, he and his escort dined at the house of Mr. McCammon. Mr. McCammon was appointed postmaster early in 1803, and continued to hold the office until December 24, 1829, a period of nearly twenty-seven years. He died July 24, 1838, aged 64 years, and is buried in the old Presbyterian graveyard in Middletown. Two of Mr. McCammon's daughters have served lengthened terms as postmistresses here—Mrs. Catharine A. Stouch, from February 17, 1849, to May 15, 1857, and Mrs. Rachel C. McKibbin, the present postmistress, who was first appointed April 5, 1867, and has received three appointments since, making in all a period of about 47 years for the family as postmasters. Mr. McCammon was a consistent member of the Paxtang Presbyterian church. Two children are still living, [1879] viz: Mrs. R. C. McKibbin, of Middletown, and David C. McCammon, Esq., of Gettysburg.

J. R.

Paxtang Church, in 1808, (N. & Q. xii.)—In reply to the query of T. H. R., we are able to give the dates of death of the following. There are none now living, the last worthy being Gen. John Forster.

Name.	Date of Death.	Age.
Robert Elder,	. . Sept. 29, 1818,	. 77
James Cowden,	. . Oct. 10, 1810,	. . 64
Edward Crouch,	. Jan. 2, 1826,	. . 66
Elizabeth Gray,	. . April 18, 1816,	. 72
John Gray,	. . . . May 30, 1819,	. . 66
John Wiggins,	. . June 12, 1794,	. . 82
James Rutherford,	March 6, 1809,	. 62
Samuel Sherer,	. . Dec. 26, 1821,	. . 66
John Gilchrist,		
Samuel Rutherford,	Nov. 26, 1833,	. 65
Wm. Rutherford,	. Jan. 17, 1850,	. . 74
Robert McClure,	July 21, 1839,	. . 76
John Ritchey,	. Dec. 3, 1831,	. . 56
Thomas Smith,		
Samuel Rutherford,	May 8, 1813,	. . 63
Thomas Elder,	. . April 29, 1853,	. 86
John Carson,	. . Oct. 10, 1817,	
Joshai Espy,	. . . July 26, 1813,	. . 71
James Awl,	. . . [removed in 1809]	
John Allison,	. . . March 17, 1816,	. 46
James Cochran,	. . July 16, 1822,	. . 80
Ann E. Stephen,	. Aug. 10, 1814,	. . 60
John McCammon,	. July 22, 1838,	. . 64
Mary Fulton,	. . Nov. 23, 1815,	. . 45
Mary Rutherford,		
Wm. Larned.		
James Stewart, [removed to Mifflin co.]		

Name.	Date of Death.	Age·
Joshua Elder,	. . . Dec. 5, 1820,	. . 76
Thomas Buffington,		
John Elder,	. . . . April 13, 1811,	. 54
Sarah Wilson,	. . Mar. 12, 1823,	. . 70
John Forster,	. . . May 28, 1862,	. . 86
Charles Chamberlain,		
John Ross,	. . . . [d. at Middletown.]	
Michael Simpson,	. June 1, 1813,	. . 73
Jean Carson,	*	
Joseph Burd,	. . . [removed]	
Robert Gray,	. . . April 27, 1848,	. 91
Thomas Walker,	. March 19, 1843,	. 54
William Calhoun,		
John Rutherford,	. May 1, 1832,	. . 59
David Patton,	. . Jan. 10, 1832,	. . 74
John Walker,		
Jacob Richards,		
Jean Wilson,		
Frederick Hatton,	. June 3, 1835,	. . 61
John Finney, [removed to Ohio in 1811]		
Joseph Wilson,	. . 1826*	
William Whitley,		
David Stewart, [removed to Mifflin co.]		
Thomas McCord,	. August 22, 1810,	
Elizabeth Wills,		
Hugh Stephen.		

* Date of either removal or of death. Who can supply those left blank?

YE ANCIENT INHABITANTS.—II.

The North End of Paxtang, 1749.

Lancaster, ss:

To Robert Wright, Collector of ye North End of Paxtang, These:
You being appointed Collector of ye within Tax are hereby Required to Demand of ye Persons within mentioned ye Several Sums where with they stand charged; But if any shall think Themselves agrieved with what they are here Rated against them the Day of Appeal is ye 25, 26 and 27 Days of this Instant, at ye Court house in the borough of Lancaster; But if you Cannot meet with ye Persons of whom demand is to be made Leave Notice in writing with some of ye family or at ye Place of their last abode signifying ye Day of

Appeal at which time you are to attend with this Duplicate and ye names of such Persons in your District as you find omitted herein. fail not at your Peril Dated ye Seventh Day of December Anno Domi 1749.

EDWIN COOPER,
WILLIAM WILSON,

Name	£	s	d	Name	£	s	d
John Hariss,	1	10	0	Jno. Thompson,	0	3	6
James Michael,	0	3	6	Jno. Caldwell,	0	4	0
Widow Foster,	0	3	0	James Toland,	0	2	6
James McNought,	0	2	0	Jno. Ross,	0	1	6
Moses Dickey,	0	4	0	Andrew Cochren,	0	3	0
Thos. McCarter,	0	2	0	Jno. McGumery,	0	4	0
Samll. Martin,	0	4	0	Joseph Ross,	0	2	0
Widow Karr,	0	3	0	Robt. Degan,	0	3	6
Thos. Simpson,	0	6	0	Andrew Stuart,	0	5	0
Robt. McGumere,	0	3	0	George Gillespy,	0	2	0
Edwd. Faride,	0	4	0	James Hains,	0	3	6
James Forgison,	0	1	6	Andrew Stone,	0	4	0
Jamel Alcorn,	0	4	0	Alexr. Johnston,	0	2	6
James Poak,	0	2	0	Robt. Chambers,	0	4	0
James Reed,	0	2	0	John Dougharty,	0	3	0
James Armstrong,	0	6	6	Jno. Seat,	0	4	0
Robt. Pots,	0	3	0	George Cochren,	0	3	0
Samll. Brice,	0	4	0	Samll. Coningham,	0	3	0
William Bell,	0	5	0	Jerh. Storgin,	0	1	6
Joseph Davis,	0	3	0	Francis Kah,	0	2	0
John Carson, Mer.,	7	0	0	Jno. Welley,	0	3	6
Thos. Foster, Esqr.,	0	10	0	Robt. Smith,	0	6	0
Widow Whiley,	0	4	6	Jno. Smith,	0	2	0
Samll. Simpson,	0	4	0	George Bell,	0	2	6
Arthur Foster,	0	6	0	Thos. Alexr,	0	2	0
Thos. Elder,	0	5	0	Thos. Larned,	0	2	6
Andrew Caldwell,	0	2	0	Noah Coply Smith,	0	2	0
Will'm Chambers,	0	3	6	Jno. Chambers,	0	3	6
William Chambers,	0	3	6	Hugh McCormack,	0	4	0
William Cochren,	0	3	0	David Deney,	0	1	6
William Brown,	0	4	0	William Thorn,	0	5	6
Francis Johnson,	0	3	6	Jno. Jno'son,	0	5	0
Alexr. Meharge,	0	4	0	Thos. Lee,	0	3	0
James Grahms,	0	4	0	Saml. Eaken,	0	3	0
Willm. Barnet,	0	2	0	*Freemen.*			
Widow Armstrong,	0	1	6	James Means,	0	9	0
Robt. Correy,	0	2	6	Jno. Cochren,	0	9	0
Stephen Gamble,	0	4	0	Willm. Cowden,	0	9	0
Willm. Barnet, Junr.,	0	2	9	George Ross,	0	9	0
John Wagons,	0	4	6	Thos. Armstrong,	0	9	0
David Paulin,	0	4	0	Jno. Martin,	0	9	0
Willm. McMullen,	0	4	0	Joseph Halley,	0	9	0
Hugh Inith,	0	1	0	Thos. Birney,	0	9	0
John Caffet,	0	4	0	Wm. Calhoun,	0	1	6
Iml. Gillcries,	0	9	0	Joseph Breden,	0	2	6
William Armstrong,	0	2	6	Alexd. Johnston,	0	2	6
Martha Cowden,	0	3	9	Jno. Barnett,	0	4	0
Jno. Neil,	0	4	6	Widow Wiley,	0	0	0
Richard Cavit,	0	4	0				

NOTES AND QUERIES.—XVI.

WILSON—STERRETT.—James Wilson came from Ireland with his parents, at the age of seven years, and settled in Derry township. He married first Martha Sterrett, and secondly Ann ———. They had issue as follows:
- *i. William*, m. Elizabeth Robinson.
- *ii. Hugh*, m. Isabella Fulton.
- *iii. Martha*, m. David Hayes.
- *iv. Joseph*, m. Margaret Boyd.
- *v. Mary*, m. James Todd.
- *vi. Andrew*, m. Martha McClure.
- *vii. James*, d., unm., at Reading.
- *viii. Elizabeth*, m. James Stewart.
- *ix. Samuel*, m. Eleanor Bell.

Information is desired as to the respective families of the foregoing. To which of them belonged James Wilson, who died in October, 1806?

OLD CONEWAGO CHURCH.

Rev. E. F. Rockwell, D. D., of Cool Spring, Iredell co., N. C., writes in reference to the account of this congregation as published by the Dauphin County Historical Society, as follows:

"It connects with a good deal of American history. George Davidson, father of Gen. William Lee Davidson, who fell at Cowan's Ford, February 1, 1781, came from your section in 1750, and settled in the lower end of this county. The ancestor of a large and influential connexion (Foote's Sketches of N. C., p. 433), Rev. John Thomson, came here about 1751, and died in 1753, near the same spot. He was the father-in-law of Rev. Richard Sankey, who, according to Webster's History of the Presbyterian Church (p. 356), seems to have come to Buffalo, Virginia, earlier than Dr. Robinson's History of Hanover church would allow.

"Some years ago I prepared a sketch of Rev. John Thomson, who was the first preacher that traversed this region, which was published in the 'Historical Magazine.' Mr. Thomson took up several tracts of land near here—one of which he conveyed to James Hall, on Fifth creek, near Bethany creek. I have the original deed, signed by him and witnessed by his daughter, Elizabeth Baker. In the sketch of Conewago church, p. 47, it appears the printing is wrong—this was

Anson county until 1753, when Rowan was set off; then in that county until Iredell was taken from it in 1788.

We have a map of the central part of Iredell, reaching ten or more miles from Statesville, drawn with a pen in 1773, within twenty years of the first settlement. Over one hundred names are on it. James Hall came in 1750. William Hall, said to be a cousin of his, about the same time settled on the same creek, a little higher up. I have the family tree of James Hall. He had five sons—Rev. James, Moderator General U. S. in 1803, and got D. D. same year; Rev. Robert Hall, Thomas, Hugh and Alexander;—five daughters, Margaret, Mary, Dorcas, Jane and Sarah, at least three granddaughters were named Prudence, and three great-granddaughters and probably a great many more; a grandson, James Roddy, another Hugh Roddy.

Rev. James Hall, D. D., was born in Carlisle, Penna., Aug. 22, 1744 (Foote, p. 316). I suppose, then, that your Hugh Hall (Hanover church, p. 54), who married a daughter of James Roddy, was the father of the first James Hall here, 1750, and grandfather of Dr. J. Hall, whose mother and grandmother both were named Roddy— that Hugh Hall son Hugh was the brother of our first James Hall, who had a son Hugh. He then would have named a son after the grandfather on both sides—James Hall after James Roddy—Hugh after Hugh Hall.

Rev. Thomas Espy (Foote, p. 363) was born August 1, 1800, in Cumberland county, Pa., and died near Beattie's Ford, on the Catawba, in 1833. His daughter, now the wife of Gov. Zeb. Vance, often visits in Bet any. She told a friend here that when she visits her father's connections in Pennsylvania, she finds the same names as in Bethany, and seemed to be at home. So Scotland, Ireland, your region in Pennsylvania, and western North Carolina, are directly connected. The Scotch-Irish and the Puritans did a great deal to resist tyranny and preserve religious liberty on both sides of the Atlantic.

John and James Murdoch are common names here—on old tombstones *Mordah*, on old map, *Mordoch*. Hugh Bowman is on the map, about five miles from where I write—one of John Thomson's tracts of land. It is surprising that Dr. James Hall, who graduated at Princeton college in 1774, went to General Assembly sixteen times, not married, traveled in sulky with clock work to measure distances, never visited—we never hear of his doing it.

Can you find out where the other branches of the Hall family went to? Are they all gone out of the region? I have heard of a Rev. Dr. Hall at the West somewhere, who was supposed to be of this family?

C. F. R.

INDIAN GEOGRAPHICAL NAMES.—I.

[Believing that a proper knowledge of Indian names of this locality, the only footprints which remain of the Red Man, we recently requested a gentleman, who has been paying especial attention to the subject, to prepare an article thereon, which we take pleasure in now presenting. Although few persons are aware of the great research which is required in the *proper* preparation of an historical sketch—biographical or genealogical—it is only the antiquary who can fully appreciate the great labor consequent upon the writing of an article, such as the one alluded to. It is exceedingly valuable—not only worthy of perusing, but preserving carefully for future reference.]

All names derived from the Indian languages have undergone many changes in orthography. At first every one spelled them to please himself. The English, Irish, German, French, Dutch and so on had each their peculiar way of representing the Indian sounds. This gave rise to many variations. The dialectical differences in the Indian tongue greatly increased these variations. The ignorance and carelessness of many men in the proper use of letters in their own language and of their sound in other languages increased these variations still further. Hence we find such a diversity of orthography that sometimes it takes an experienced person to recognize some of the forms.

At length these words, by common usage, have come to a settled orthography. This usage often destroyed or mutilated the original word. This process of Anglicising Indian words generally consulted ease of speech, and seldom correctness of original sounds. Most of them, right or wrong, are now established. A very few still remain unsettled.

One difficulty with Indian names along the Susquehanna river is that the region was inhabited by tribes of both the Huron-Iroquois and Algonquin stocks of Indians; and each of these families had tribes on its banks, whose dialectical variations were so great that they hardly understood each other a word. This was the case with the Shawanese and Delawares, though both Algonquins. One safe rule may be adopted, viz: All names requiring the use of the lips in pronunciation did not orginate from any of the tribes of the Huron-Iroquois family.

When the white people first began to settle on the Atlantic coast, the whole region of the Susquehanna and its branches was inhabited by tribes of the Huron-Iroquois family. The Algonquin tribes were along the coast and on the Delaware river. Each family had its own names for places in their own country, and also for parts adjoining.

All their geographical names were descriptive. They described the nature of the country, its people, or related to something that had happened there. These names formed a kind of national history, and some of them were associated with their sacred legends as to their origin and past experience. The names they gave themselves were always flattering; those applied to enemies always expressed their prejudices, contempt or fears.

When the Dutch in 1640 armed the Indians of the Five Nation confederacy in New York, they fell upon and exterminated a great many of the adjoining tribes, and, as has been said, "reared an empire on the ruins of extirpated nations." Among those destroyed were numerous tribes, or nations on the Susquehanna, who have been lost sight of and overlooked by historians. Among these were the *Carantowannais* about Waverly, Elmira and Towanda, and who numbered about 1,500 warriors in 1615. Stephen Brule is the only white man that visited them. At Wyoming were the *Scahentoar-ronon,* or people of the great flats. Our word Wyoming is derived torturously from the Delaware translation of the name of its original people. The West Branch from Shamokin (Sunbury) westward was inhabited by a nation whom the Iroquois formerly (before they were armed) feared, and whose stubborn defense they supposed could only emanate from the aid of demons who inhabited the rocky caves of that region. Hence the origin of *Otzinachson,* as applied to that river, and it expressed the Iroquois idea of the cave devils or people of the demon's dens. On the Juniata dwelt the *Onojutta-haga,* as given in the ancient maps from which the word Juniata itself is derived, and which signified the people of the Standing Stone, a name which clung to the locality of Huntingdon for a long time. It is a common thing to find the name of the nation or tribe given to the stream on which they resided. East of the mountains dwelt the original *Sasquesahanoughs,* as described by Captain John Smith in 1608, living in six towns. They were the last conquest southward by the Iroquois. The remnant of the Sasquehannocks, after their conquest in 1677, became known as the Conestogas, whose miserable remnant of impure blood were finally sent to the happy hunting grounds by the Paxtang Boys in 1763.

All these nations named above were of the Huron-Iroquois stock. The language of the Conestogas could be understood by the Iroquois. In fact we find it stated by Gov. Andros, as far back as 1675, that the Susquehannas were originally descended from the Mohawks. It is a significant fact that the Mohawks took no part in the final war against them, and never took any part in the sale of their lands, which the other four nations sold as a right of their conquest.

Historians tell us the Tuscaroras were an isolated body of the Huron-Iroquois family, living in North Carolina. This was not so originally. The inland country, from New York to the Tuscaroras, was at first covered with the Huron-Iroquois speaking tribes, all of whom were devastated by the Iroquois, except the Tuscaroras and a few other remnants, who assimilated to them. The Iroquois seem to have been especially hostile to these tribes of kindred blood, and speaking the dialect of the same language. They fared worse than the Algonquin tribes, who were only made tributary, while those of kindred blood were decimated and the remnants carried off and incorporated into the families of the Iroquois tribes. The Tuscaroras alone escaped the all-conquering grasp of the Northern confederates. Being far South and strong may have had something to do with their preservation, but more likely it was owing to the fact that the attention of the Iroquois was diverted to the conquest of the Illinois and other tribes as far West as the Mississippi. In after years, when the Tuscaroras got into trouble with the whites in Carolina, in 1713, the Iroquois took them to the Juniata, and thence to New York, and adopted them as a sixth member of the Confederacy. Hence the change of the term Five Nations to Six Nations.

After the Susquehanna was depopulated, and used only as an Iroquois hunting ground, the Shawanese in 1698, and later, were allowed to come from rambling over the South, and settle on some of the deserted posts of the lower Susquehanna, and in the Cumberland valley. Afterwards the Delawares, being crowded by the white settlers on their ancient river, began to cut loose and remove westward to the Susquehanna, and still later, 1727, passed over the Alleghenies, accompanied by the Shawanese, never to return except to plunder the border settlers.

The French who settled in Canada called all the tribes south of the Iroquois, and not of the Algonquin stock, by the generic name of *Andastes*. This, therefore, included the *Susquehannas*, which term the English in Virginia and Maryland sometimes employed much in the same way. Likewise, the Dutch and Swedes on the Delaware called all the tribes inland, who were not Algonquin speaking people, by the name of *Minquas*. This they especially applied to those on the lower part of the river called *Sasquesahanoughs* by Captain Smith. Hence, Minquas, Susquehannocks and Andastes were terms often used generically, but often specifically also, and applied to the same nation on the river below Harrisburg.

Geographical names are wonderful things to cling to the soil. Mountains repeat and rivers murmur the voices of nations denationalized and extirpated from their native land. In the unrecorded history of the past, a name glued to a mountain or stream often has perpetuated nearly all we know of the nation with whom the name originated. For this and many other reasons, which these remarks on Indian history will suggest, every Indian has connected with its origin and signification an interesting story. These names are not only beautiful in themselves, but serve as suggestive landmarks in the interesting, but too little cultivated field of aboriginal history. I am glad to see that a knowledge of them is being more cultivated.

A great difficulty attends their investigation. One and two hundred years ago, when it could have been easily done, and well done, no one took time to do a little work for posterity. Death has cut down both the white and red man that were once familiar with the names, about which we may now inquire in vain. Even "the last of the Mohegans" is gone, and we consult the liiving pale face in vain.

The regions of the lower Susquehanna, having been overrun by so many Indian races, and subdivisions of races, we may naturally look for remains of all these diversely speaking tribes, in the geographical vestiges that have come down to us. It is this that makes investigation so very difficult. To get at the meaning of a term we must first know the language or Indian nationality to which it belonged. To do this would involve a knowledge of several Indian tongues and many more almost equally difficult dialectical variations.

It is an interesting fact, also, that many of the names, given by the incoming tribe, were translations into their own tongue of the same names employed by the tribe that preceded them. Many terms used by the Delawares were only translations of Susquehanna or Iroquois terms previously used. Even the English, on their advent, often translated these names into the corresponding English terms. This is apt to be the case in all such cases as Fishing, Beaver and Stony creeks. The historical idea remains, clinging as with hooks of steel, even when given the new translated sound.

The only one, in the old days, that did posterity a great service in preserving the meaning of the Indian geographical names, was the Moravian missionary, Heckewelder. He lived long among the Delawares, and was quite familiar with their language and the dialectical of the sub-tribes. He has given us his opinion on many of these names, and he is in general, of course, good authority; but even he, in some cases, must be received with great caution. He was a great admirer of the Delawares and had strong prejudices against the Iroquois, which often warped his judgment. In his love for the Delawares he made all the names emanate from them that he possibly could. He made some undoubted Iroquois or Andastic words appear with far-fetched ideas of Delaware origin. We receive his statements with caution when they tend to disparage the Iroquois and extol the Delawares. Notwithstanding this, we must acknowledge him as having rendered a most valuable service in rescuing the origin of many words from oblivion.

We come now to notice the word *Susquehanna*. Our first knowledge of it is from the History of Virginia, by Captain John Smith, published in London in 1629. He describes his exploration of the Chesapeake Bay, at the head of which he found four rivers. He went up the largest one as far as his barge could pass for rocks. Here he awaited the arrival of some *Sasquesahannoughs*, for whom he had sent a couple of interpreters. The interpreters were of the people called *Tockwoghs*, one interpreted from Powhatten language to Tockwogh and Sasquesahanough. The chief town was "two days' journey higher than our barge could pass for rocks." They numbered "near 600 able men and are pallisadoed in their towns to defend them from the Massawomekes, their mortal enemies." "Three or four days we expected their return, then sixty of those giant-like people came down." Five of the chiefs came aboard and crossed over the bay. Smith took a picture of one of them, the calf of whose leg was 27 inches in circumference. They had five other towns belonging to their nation beside *Sasquesahanough*, the second *Quadroque* about 20 miles further up, beyond which there are two branches, on the western one is *Utchowig* and on the eastern one *Tesinigh*. Which branch is the main river cannot be told from the map. By the scale these towns would be about 60 miles from the bay. On a western branch, entering the river below Sasquesahanough, is *Attaock*, seemingly 16 miles from it. Smith drew this map from the representations of the Indians. The scale would place the first town only about 21 miles above the mouth of the river. But we know he was not very accurate, for he says he could not go two miles up the river for the falls, yet we know the first rocks at the head of tide are four miles; and the mark on his map of the distance penetrated along the river by the scale is some 12 miles, or more than half the distance from the bay to *Sasquesahanough*, to which it took the interpreters two days to travel. It is probable that at this time the chief town was at the Conestoga, Columbia, or even as high as Marietta; that Attaock was about York; Quadroque, at Middletown; Tesinigh, at Lebanon, and Utchowig about Harrisburg. The sixth town, *Cepawig*, was on the heads of the Patapsco, probably Westminister, Md.

Capt. Smith did not get the name *Sasquesahanoughs* from those Indians themselves. He does not tell us what they called themselves. He got his name for them from a tribe called *Tockwoghs*, who numbered only 100 men, and were probably of the Nanticoke family. The first part, *Sasquesa*, meant *Falls*, the second part, *Hanough*, is the Algonquin *hanne*, meaning *stream*. As applied to these people by their neighbors it signified very expressively *the people of the Falls-river*. Through time the word was gradually changed to Sasquehannock, and finally to Susquehanna. It is possible that *Sasquesa* was part of the name by which these people called themselves, and that they appended to it the Mohawk word *Haga*, for people or nation, as in the case of *Onojutta-Haga*. At all events Smith and his party well understood its meaning, for they translated it, as appears from the account given by his companion, who says "the Sasquesahanock's, river we called Smith's Falles." It is an interesting fact that the *Sasquesa* is the same word that still lingers in the creek, *Siccasa-rongo*, *Sicasa-lungo*, *Chickasa-lungo*, *Chiquesa-lungo*, now contracted into *Chickies* and *Chiques*, and applied to the stream entering the river above Columbia and below Marietta, on which there once was an Indian town of that name; and it strongly suggests that this may even have been the very location of Smith's chief town *Sasquesahanough*. The latter part of the word still remains in such names as Rappahannock, Loyal Hanna, etc.

Smith places the Susquehannas far above the Powhatan tribes in every respect. All the Huron-Iroquois were superior to the Algonquin races. Smith says their language sounded as a voice from a vault, which arose from their manner of speaking from the throat, as they discarded all labial sounds as undignified. The Swedish and Dutch authorities also accord to them the ruling power over the Delaware river tribes, whom Campanius says "dare not stir, much less go to war without the permission of *Minquas*. They had unmolested access to the Delaware river through the Minquaskill or creek, now White Clay, which empties at Wilmington, Del., and which was the shortest route to the Susquehanna river. Their trade in beaver and other peltry to the Swedes (1637 to 1655) and to the Dutch was tremendous. It was this that the Dutch so much begrudged and led to the conquest of the Swedes.

In 1660 to 1664, the Senecas and other Iroquois first attempted the subjugation of the Susquehannas. The English aided and armed them, by which means they successfully resisted the Northern invaders. In the war of 1673 to 1677, the Iroquois were at first not more successful, but the Susquehannas being finally deserted by the English and denied ammunition, were overthrown. They have a long, but exceedingly interesting history, and this interest is enhanced by their scattered geographical names which have come down to us. Most of those on the river called Iroquois names were really Susquehanna.

During the one hundred years that elapsed, from the conquest of the Minquas or Susquehannas, to the Revolutionary war, there were many changes in Indian affairs, but during the whole century the ruling power and control in Pennsylvania was with the Iroquois of New York. Because of their aid to the British, Washington sent General Sullivan into their country, just one century ago, who destroyed their towns, broke down their power, and split and demoralized their confederacy. A. L. GUSS.

MRS. KINGSFORD'S SCHOOL.

A contributor (N. & Q. iii.) to this interesting and valuable department having made reference to the young ladies' seminary of Mrs. Kingsford, at Harrisburg, I am reminded of one of its rolls. In the absence of date I fix it about 1839. It will be interesting to recall some of the names perhaps almost forgotten; to note those who are numbered among the silent dead of Kalmia; and to repeat the maiden-names of the majority who are to-day among the noble mothers (some may be grandmothers) of Harrisburg. G. B. AYRES.

Susun B. Ayres,
Mary Beatty,
Louisa Berryhill,
Julia Brooks,
Elizabeth De Pui,
Julia A. W. DeWitt,
Louisa Douglas,
Mary Dwight,
Ellen Dwight,
Margaret Espy,
Ellen Forster,
Mary Forster,
Susan Forster,
Caroline Heisly,
Elizabeth Harris,
Catharine Harris,
Elizabeth Hickok,

Susan Haldeman,
Catharine Hoyer,
Ann Holman,
Johanna Hale,
Eliza Jacobs,
Catharine Kunkel,
Sarah Lutz,
Catharine Mytinger,
Emily Nelson,
Agnes Nininger,
Margaret Piper,
Elizabeth Porter,
Mary A. Roberts,
Catharine Ramsey,
Clara Rehrer,
Sophia Sims,
Mary Stimmel,

Mary Sprigman,
Nancy Shunk,
Elizabeth Shunk,
Josephine Smith,
Susan Shoch,
Mary Small,
Ann Small,
Elizabeth Small,
Isabella Todd,
Anna Thompson,
Harriet Thompson,
Juliann Updegraff,
Mary Wiestling,
Fanny Wilson,
Margaret Wilson,
Emma Wilson,

Margaret Walters, Harrisburg.
Catharine Bowman, Cumberland co., Pa.
Margaret Brown, Hanover, Pa.
Susan Esworthy, Bainbridge, Pa.
Ann Elliott, Lewistown, Pa.
Ann Espy, Paxtang, Pa.
Rose Green, U. S. A.
Frances Green, U. S. A.
Hanna Glass, Philadelphia.
Mary Henry, Coxestown, Pa.
Margaret Jones, Harrisonburg, Va.
Ann Keller, Mechanicsburg, Pa.
Fanny Myers, Kingston, Pa.
Ellen Mitchell, Halifax, Pa.
Mary A. Owings, Owings' Mills, Md.
Mary Parke, Cumberland, Pa.

Clarissa Powers, Rochester, N. Y.
Cornelia Rogers, Little Falls, N. Y.
Mary Rogers, Little Falls, N. Y.
Frances S. Snyder, Philadelphia.
Ann Thompson, Jersey City, N. J.
Eleanor Updegraff, Coxestown, Pa.
Mary Wycoff, New York city.
Mary Waters, Northumberland, Pa.
Melinda Woodburn, Old Town, Md.
Amanda Woodburn, Old Town, Md.

Instructors.

Mrs. M. Kingsford, *Principal.*
Miss S. Sawyer, } *Associated Teachers.*
Miss A. Beebee, }
Mr. E. L. Walker, *Teacher of Piano.*
John H. Hickok, *Vocal Music.*

NOTES AND QUERIES.—XVII.

LOCAL POST ROUTES IN 1805.—From the Balloon Almanac for 1805, published at Lancaster, we learn that the post route from Philadelphia to Pittsburgh at that period gave Harrisburg the go-by. The Susquehanna was crossed at Chambers' Ferry, from thence via Silvers' Spring to Carlisle, The road from Reading to Harrisburg was as follows: To Reynolds, 4 miles; Conrad Weiser's, 9 miles; Benjamin Spyker's, 3 miles; F. Hatheroad's, 4 miles; John Gamble's, 8 miles; Galbraith's, 13 miles; Harris, by Swatara, 3 miles; Harrisburg, 9 miles. The cross posts from Philadelphia to Carlisle were through Pottsgrove, Reading, Lebanon and Harrisburg.

FERRIES OVER THE SUSQUEHANNA.

In early times there were quite a number of ferries over the Susquehanna from Middletown to Millersburg, all of which were named for their proprietor, and changed with the ownership.

HARRIS' was the oldest on the Susquehanna, and was known as such for one hundred and fifty years. In later years, say after 1780, the Cumberland side of the ferry was called *Kelso's*. This ceased to be a ferry upon the completion of the Harrisburg bridge. Both the Harris and Kelso ferry houses remain to this day.

CHAMBERS', three miles below, was also established at a very early period, and for many years was on "the great road from Philadelphia to Pittsburg" and Western Pennsylvania. In early maps (French) it is designated as "Guy de Carlisle." The west side of the ferry in later years became known as *Simpson's* Ferry, from the fact that Gen. Michael Simpson owned the landing on that side of the river.

SKEER's ferry [1790] was located two miles from Middletown and seven from Harrisburg, and at that period was kept by Nathan Skeer. Its location on the east side of the Susquehanna is what is now called the "White House."

MACLAY's ferry was across the Susquehanna, at the head of the Island, then named Maclay's Island, while Harris' ferry was at the lower end. The ferry house, adjoining the present water-house, was removed within a few years. The Cumberland side of this ferry was for many years named *Wormley's* and at one time *Montgomery's*.

Cox's ferry was at Estherton; on the west bank, at the foot of the first ridge of mountains, was *Wolf's,* from which ran a road leading to Carlisle.

GREEN'S ferry was at Dauphin, although, owing to the great difficulty in crossing the river at that point, seldom used.

CLARK'S Ferry, established by Daniel Clark about 1785, and previous to that period kept by a Mr. *Huling,* and also by Mr. *Baskin* on Duncan's island, and thus also called, still retains its old name. On the Cumberland side of the river, below the mouth of the Juniata, the ferry was named *Ellis'* being kept for a number of years by Francis Ellis.

CLEMSON'S Ferry was at Fort Halifax. It took in the largest island which to-day goes by the name of Clemson's island.

LYTLE'S Ferry, and subsequently *Montgomery's,* then *Moorehead's,* was one of the best fords on the Susquehanna between Harris Ferry and Fort Augusta. It was used as such at a very early period, and it was at this point just below Berry's mountain, where John Harris and a number of his Paxtang neighbors were attacked by the Indians —that a "doctor," whose name has never come down to us who had got on the horse behind Mr. Harris, was shot.

PFOUTZ' Ferry connected the east side of the Susquehanna at Millersburg, with the west, leading into the Pfoutz valley, now in Perry county. Upon the location of Miller at the mouth of the Wiconisco, the ferry on the Dauphin side was called for him.

There were undoubtedly other ferries, but at this writing we can not call them to mind.

THE PAXTANG BOYS.

Charles Miner, the impartial historian of Wyoming, during the preparation of his valuable work, opened up a correspondence with most of the historic students of his day. From one of his letters, written to a gentleman of this locality, whose information concerning the Paxtang Boys was superior to that of any one then living, we take the following extracts:

"The history in which my pen is engaged is confined to Wyoming. But a portion of the Paxtang Boys settled here and took a conspicuous part. I had read in early life, with unmitigated horror, the publications of the day reciting that crimson tragedy and not an alleviating circumstance mentioned. Whether to note their being here, their agency, etc., or to pass it over in silence as one of those dark occurrences of which the least said the better was a matter of doubt. But I resolved to investigate, and finally wrote a paper to be inserted or not, as should, on reflection and consultation, be thought best. That paper is, I believe in the hands of one who married a daughter of Stewart. I therefore, from memory, give the heads of my argument.

"On settling in Luzerne, I found *Hanover*, a valuable township, full of most worthy and respectable inhabitants, which had been specially allotted to and settled by the Paxtang Boys.

"1. Not only were they esteemed for humanity, integrity and virtue, but so also had those been who were gone to the grave, for Col. Denison, our most staid, soberminded, religious man, had named his oldest son for Lazarus Stewart. He could not have been ignorant of his true character. If he was the bloody minded demon who, without provocation had murdered women and children, he would not, he could not have done it.

"2. Conneticut—religious, moral, politic or cunning—in establishing a settlement at Wyoming would have gone counter to principles, policy and common-sense by engaging in their cause a set of men whom the moral sense of mankind had excommunicated from society for crimes involving cowardice and wanton cruelty. It could not be so. There must be some other version of the affair. So I looked as far as my vision could extend into the times, when, and immediately preceding the event, and found—

"3. That the preceding summer the Indians had murdered the Wyoming settlers. Massacre, conflagration and ruin, were driven like a whirlwind on the white settlements, from 30 to 40 miles west of the Susquehanna to the mountains. So audacious had the Indians become that they descended below the Blue mountains, and committing murders in the neighborhood of Bethlehem. The whole frontiers were aroused to despair and madness. Under these general provocations and that frenzy of excitement the deed seems to have been done, deeply to be deplored and the victims to be pitied.

"4. Fifty Paxtang Boys entered Lancaster in open day. It was known they were coming. If not welcome, why did not the people rise five hundred strong, as they might easily have done, and effectually expelled the assailants?

"5. But there was also a Highland company of regulars stationed at Lancaster. They neither pulled a trigger or presented a bayonet. It is evident that authorities and people did not look upon the deed as a cruel, unprovoked murder? but that they connived at it, if they did not participate; believing that the cruelties of the Indians justified their cutting off. Without such influence, the conduct of the troops and the people would be unaccountable."

The foregoing are the opinions of one whose research, intelligence

Historical and Genealogical. 109

and impartial judgment "puts," as he himself expresses it, "a very very different face upon it [the transaction at Conestoga and Lancaster] than has been given heretofore," and to those who have imbibed their ideas from historians warped in their judgment by partisan rancor and puritanical zeal, we commend Mr. Miner's conclusions. Our opinions we have from time to time given, not unsubstantiated, nor with the view of detracting from the fair fame of any class of people, but for the purpose of throwing aside the veil of obloquy which fanatical fury for over a century has covered the gallant frontiersmen of Paxtang, who loved their homes and their darling ones too well to tolerate a nest of copper-colored vipers in their midst.

INDIAN GEOGRAPHICAL NAMES.—II.

Our first knowledge of what was going on among the natives, on the Susquehanna after the days of Capt. Smith, comes to us from the *Relations* of the Jesuits, who had formed missions among various tribes surrounding their settlements in Canada. In 1647-49 the Iroquois were devastating the Hurons in Canada, among whom were several Jesuits. The tribes of Northern Pennsylvania had no doubt fallen prior to this date. The Susquehannas knew it was likely to come their term next. They offered to make common cause with the Hurons. They had at that time 1300 men trained by three Swedish soldiers to the use of firearms, and they were well provided. Either from apathy or some other cause, the Hurons did not receive this proffered aid. In 1602 the Susquehannas sold their territories on both sides of the bay to Maryland. There is an account in the Jesuits' Journal of a large town by the Iroquois called *Atra'kouaer* or *Andastoe*, in the Winter of 1651-2, the exact location of which is undetermined, but it must have been below Shamokin, and may have been down as far as Harrisburg. The identification and location of their town would be a signal service to our interior antiquities. It may have been the final struggle with the *Onojutta-Haga* or Juniata nation. At all events it opened the way for the restless Iroquois to the east of the Kittochtinny mountains, for in 1663 they formed a grand expedition of 860 men to attack the Susquahannas, and at a fort, which must have been located near Columbia, they were repulsed and driven back to New York with disaster. After a predatory warfare for some ten years, a terrible final conflict ensued, and the downfall of the ancient Susquehannas may be set down as terminating in 1677. The remnant were known for the next 87 years as Conestogas. Whether this was the name they gave themselves or what its origin is undetermined. In later days it was the name of the people, their town and the creek. The latter still bears the name. There is possibly a connection between Codestogues and the French Andostogues.

The Jesuits had no missionaries south of the Iroquois, and among these they commenced in 1656. Their journals, called *Relations*, yearly printed in Paris, make frequent reference to the wars with the Andastes, and relate the torture and burning of the captives brought in from the Andastes, many of whom the Jesuits baptized and sent to heaven. As they used this name generally for any and all nations south of the Iroquois, it is hard to tell at all times what tribe is intended. After the *Carantowannais*, whom they termed *Onnontigas*, were obliterated, the successive tribes that fell before the armed Iroquois were termed Andastes or Andastoques. Of some of these nations only the *name* has come down to us. Of others, we have reason to believe, not even this has survived the ruthless hand of the Iroquois devastator. In the Jesuit *relation* of 1647-8 we have some idea of the progress southward made by the conquerors. *Andastoe* is there described as a country beyond the *Neuter Nation* (which then lived about Niagara Falls), 150 leagues southeast, one fourth south from the Hurons (of Upper Canada), in a straight line, or 200 hundred leagues by the trails. This course and distance certainly locates their country from Harrisburg to the mouth of the river, and identifies the Andastes of the French, with the Minquas of the Dutch, the Mynquesses of the Swedes and the Susquehannas of the English. Further researches may throw some more light on the location of these ancient native villages. As a rule historians have taken no notice of these pre-Pennsylvania towns, and very little of those for 25 years later.

After the conquest of the Susquehannas, a new order of things began to prevail on the river. The little band of Conestogas were on the creek of that name. The whole country was a grand highway for the Iroquois in their incursions against the Indian tribes still further southward, through Virginia and as far as Georgia. Soon the remnant of Southern tribes were attracted by the friendly Penn, and began to form settlements on the deserted posts of the lower Susquehanna. Thus we read that in 1705 Logan visited "the Ganawese, settled some miles above Conestoga at a place called *Conejaghera*, above the fort." In 1707 Gov. Evans started from New Castle and came to the Susquehanna at *Otteraroe* [Octoraro,] and then came to a Shawanese town called *Pequehan*, located at Pequea, below Conestoga. He speaks also of going "to *Dekanoagah* upon the river Sasquehannagh, being about nine miles distance from Pequehan." He was visited by Nanticoke chiefs from seven towns in Maryland. They stated they had been conquered by the Iroquois in 1680, and wanted to settle on the river. From Conestoga the Governor went to *Peixtan* (Paxtang, Harrisburg), to arrest a Frenchman, named Nicole Godin, whom they took by stratagem, and conveyed to Philadelphia by way of *Turpyhockon.* Dekanoagah was a town of the Ganawese or Conoys, about the mouth of the creek still bearing the latter name, and near the site of Bainbridge. In 1727 we read of "*Snaketown,* forty miles above Conestoga," which was probably a translation of an Indian name. It will be observed that most of the above appellations have perished.

About this time we have some maps that give us some names now nowhere else found. In a new map of Virginia and Maryland and improved parts of Pennsylvania, by John Lenex, in 1719, revised in 1721, in atlas form, and printed in London, we have on the east side of the Susquehanna, from Maryland up, these towns marked: *Canoonawengh* [lat. 40° 5'] *Unondomeras, Ceskoe, Ocquandery* and *Skawaghkaha.* The latter is no doubt our modern Swatara. The map extends to lat. 40° 30'. The river forks at 40° 25'. The right branch is called *Onestega.* On the left branch [Juniata?] at 40° 12' is *Kahetnoge.* These are evidently Iroquois terms. The author says the natives are so much diminished by civil wars that they have not over 500 men, mostly on the eastern shore and employed by the English to hunt deer. Atlas Noveam, by Covens and Mortier, Amsterdam, no date—London, 1733, on back—gives, No. 69, part of a large Popple. Has on the Susquehanna river, from Maryland up—Conestoga, Indian Fort, Sicasarongo, Conewaga, *Swahadowri,* Ganadaguhet, Enwaga-Aratumquat, Chemegaide, Conahago, Codocoraren, Sionassi and Seawondaona (Towanda). De Annville's Amerique Septentrionale, French Atlas, smaller map, 1746, gives from Maryland up— Indian Fort, *Skahadowri,* Chemegaide, Canahoga, Juragen, Codocoraren, Sionassa, Juragen, Scawondaona.

It is said William Penn made two visits to the Susquehanna river, and was up as far as the Swatara creek, and contemplated founding a city somewhere on the river. His last visit was in the Spring of 1701, and it is believed the towns on the Popple map were all inhabited about this time and later. They differ from those given in the Colonial Records, probably because the French map makers got their names from the Iroquois who often gave their own names rather than that of the residents.

The Swahadowri will be recognized as Swatara ; Ganadaguhet as Conodoguinet, and Chemegaide, I think, should be Cheniegaide, and means the Juniata. I have found the word spelled Sogneijadie, Chuchniada, Choniata, Chinniotta, Joniady, Scokoonidy, and many other ways. The root of the word is the Iroquois term *Onəija* or *Onia*, meaning a *stone*. The first part, now written with a j, is only a breathing of some of the Iroquois dialects, which the English often designated by letters such as the above, but which the French seldom expressed, as for example the French made the Iroquois call the Governor of Canada "Onnontio," while the English mostly wrote it "Yonnondio." The Onojutta-Haga, or Juniata nation, were the people of the Standing Stone. There can be no doubt but that Indian towns were located on Duncan's Island, at the mouth of the river, at the different epochs in Indian history. Rev. David Brainerd visited the "pagans" on "Juneauta Island" in September of 1745. It may also have been the site of Atra'kouaer in 1654.

In the purchase of lands from the Iroquois, in 1736, it is said, that it was to extend westward as far as the mountains called in the Delaware language, *Kekkachtarin*, and in the Six Nation Language, *Tyannuntasachta*, both of which words it is stated mean *The Endless Hills*. In the deed of 1749, the mountains are again referred to, and the names spelled *Keckachtany* and *Tyannuntasachta*. In the deed of 1754, the Iroquois term is omitted, and the Delaware word is spelled *Kittochtinny*. While scholars seem to regard this as proper orthography, the word has been corrupted into *Kittatinny*. The name shows the Delaware, or Leni Lenape, idea of our geography, when they termed them the Endless Hills. In the deed of 1754, they are already termed the *Blue* mountains, a common name to this day. In the early days the settlers in the Cumberland valley called that portion adjoining them, the *North* mountain; and the one on the other side of the valley, *South* mountain. So we have Kittochtinny, Blue, and North, all meaning the same chain. The Indian name alone should be used; any mountain may be Blue at a distance, and any one is north of some place. Let us write it Kittochtinny all the time.

Mahantango, or Mohontongo is one of those words whose orthography is still unsettled. There are two creeks of this name. The one on the east side of the Susquehanna divides Dauphin and Northumberland, and the one on the west divides Juniata and Snyder. The oldest reference to this word is the one on the west side. In 1756, Gov. Morris ordered a fort to be built on this stream, at about the place where Richfield, Juniata county, is now located. It was on the Indian path that led from the river, at Shamokin, over land to the Juniata river. This path crossed, and probably forked, at Richfield. The building of it was entrusted to Major Burd and Captain James Patterson; but it is doubtful whether it was ever built. It seems certain that in some cases where Pomfort Castle is spoken as a fort, the reference was really to Patterson's fort at Mexico. However this may be, the letter of Gov. Morris, of Feb. 1, 1756, speaks of it as at a river called *Matchetongo*, about 12 miles from the Susquehanna." In two other letters he speaks of it as a *Matchitongo*. The Governor, I may say, was a careless and a poor speller.

The stream on the east was crossed and named by Count Zinzendorf in September, 1742, Benigna's creek, after his daughter, the Countess Benigna, but the name did not endure. Spangenberg, in 1745, mentions it by this name. Maps and other authorities have since that day given the present name in almost every conceivable variation.

The Post-office Department seem to spell it Mohontongo. Most map authorities now have it Mahantango; others have it Mahontongo, etc. The post-office is on the west side of the Susquehanna. I believe all writers now agree in spelling the names of both streams alike, whatever orthography they adopt. This is probably a mistake, and the cause of some of the variations.

If we wish to go to the bottom—to get at the merits of the case—to find the real Indian sound, there is but one authority of which we know. Heckewelder gives the origin and meaning of our Indian names grouping a number of counties together. If we understand him, the stream east of the river was, in his day, called *Mahantango*, and that this word is derived from a Delaware word *Mohantango*, which signifies, " where we had plenty of meat to eat;" and that the stream west of the river was, in his day, called *Mehantanga*, and that this was derived from a Delaware word *Meheentange*, which signifies " where we had been killing deer." I have no doubt the words are of Delaware origin, and that properly there should be a difference of pronunciation to denote a variation of meaning; but the words are so nearly alike and custom has so identified them that it would now be vain to establish a difference. Heckewelder understood the Delaware language well, and his spellings may be regarded as the real Indian pronunciation.

The Post-office Department has lately been making inquiries of the postmaster at Mifflintown as to the correct orthography of this word. From the above it is clear that in the official *Mohontongo* the second and third vowels should be changed from o to a. There is nothing in the original sounds to warrant the sound of o in either case. The final o, in a name for the east creek and in the official office name, might be retained, though not the true sound of the original western stream, from which the post-office got its name. It then remains to determine the first vowel. Local custom, maps and gazetteers incline to the use of the a, and the derivation seems to be violated in the long e. If, therefore, I were to give a uniform spelling for both these streams, and the mountain and the post-office, I would write it *Mahantango*, and the Department should so change the name of the office. This would make it conform to the best and latest maps, gazetteers and local authorities, and do much to settle the orthography of this word.

It is a shame that Pennsylvanians know so little of their own Indian history. In this respect the people of New York are far ahead of us. Their Archives and Colonial Records are much more complete than ours are. Local historical societies have worked up the matter to great perfection in the several counties. These antiquities have been written up and published. They are far in advance of us. So, too, of New England Indian history. Its books have found their way to our own State, and many of our people are more familiar with King Philip's war and all New England Indian history than they are with our own Pennsylvania. These things ought not so to be. But they will be so just as long as our own Indian history is not properly written.

We want bold scholars to take our Indian tribes, wars, migrations, names, locations, etc., in hand and elucidate their history as they have never been before. We need active historical societies in every county to rescue from oblivion the first land-marks of the white man, as well as the receding footsteps of the Indian.   A. L. GUSS.

NOTES AND QUERIES.—XVIII.

CHESNEY OR MACHESNEY.—In 1752 Wm. Chesney married Esther, widow of John Harris, the first, of Harrisburg. In 1771 he purchased of John Harris, the second, 420 acres of land, situated in Pennsboro, now Newberry township, for £1,100. In 1779 he was the agent for confiscated estates for York county. In 1782 he died, leaving a large estate. This he devised to the children of his sister, Isabel, the wife of Richard Fulton, and to his (Chesney's) niece, Nancy Chalmers, and his brother-in-law, William Chalmers. Can any one give me a further account of William Chesney, as to his coming to America, or of the descendants of William Chalmers or Nancy Chalmers.   J. C. A.

WILSON (N. & Q., xvi).—We have received communications giving the families of the following:
  i. *William Wilson*, m. Elizabeth Robinson.
  ii. *Hugh Wilson*, m. Isabella Fulton.
  v. *Mary Wilson*, m. James Todd.
In the hope of obtaining the others, we shall defer publishing these for a week or two.

REV. JOHN DIEDRICH PETERSON.—From 1803 to 1812 the Lutheran church of this city was under the pastorate of this able Minister of the Gospel. He was a native of the city of Bremen, Germany, where he was born on the 23d of November, 1756. He studied at the University of Halle, and was regularly ordained in 1783. On the 23d of November, 1791, he married a daughter of Gen. Van Borck, a nobleman of distinction of Prussia Minden,.with whom "he lived in great harmony upwards of 56 years." He came to America in 1795, and in 1803 took charge of the Lutheran church in this city. Despite his inability to speak English, he was, nevertheless, an efficient pastor—and he did what most ministers fail to do—kept a full record of his official duties. We have heard our old people speak of him in the kindliest terms and with filial reverence. In 1812 he resigned his pastorate here, and removed to Upper Canada, being one of the first pioneers if not *the* first, to the German churches in the wilderness of Markham and Vaughan, where he faithfully and zealously discharged the duties of pastor to his flock for many years, until compelled by age and infirmity to retire from active ministerial labor. He died at his residence, in the township of Markham, Home District, Canada West, on Tuesday, January 18, 1845, at the advanced age of 91 years. It can truthfully be said of the Rev. Peterson that he was a faithful minister of the Gospel of Christ.

YE ANCIENT INHABITANTS—III.

EAST END OF DERRY—1751.

	s.	d.		s.	d.
Joseph Galbreath, Esqr.,	9	6	Thos. Logan,	4	0
Jas. Willson,	4	6	George Miller,	2	6
Jas. Cample,	9	0	John McCallestar,	3	6
Jas. Walker,	5	0	Joseph White,	1	0
Jon. Walker,	4	6	John McCleland,	2	0
Jno. McCord,	2	0	Robert Mordah,	3	0
David McCord,	1	0	Moses Potts,	3	0
William Robinson,	1	0	David Jonson,	2	6

Notes and Queries.

	s.	d.		s.	d.
Archibald Walker,	4	0	Jacob Rife,	1	6
David Tyler,	5	0	Jacob Longneker,	1	6
John Over,	6	0	Andrew Rowan,	2	0
John Pinogel,	6	0	Hugh Hays,	7	6
William Willson,	4	6	Patrick Hays,	6	0
Jas. Miller,	3	0	John Kerr,	3	0
Wm. Boyd,	3	0	Duncan McDonnall,	1	6
Robt. Boyd,	3	0	Thos. Willison,	3	0
John Colp,	3	6	James Willison,	2	6
Wm. Syers,	6	0	John Cample,	4	0
George Esby,	5	0	Widow McClan,	3	0
David Mitichel,	5	0	Widow Sloan,	3	0
Leneard Dinie,	4	0	John Maben,	6	0
John McColech,	1	0	Patrick Kelley,	2	6
Charles Connoy,	1	6	James Duncan,	4	0
David Shank,	1	0	John Duncan,	4	0
fogal Haine,	1	0	William Hays,	4	0
David Clinn,	1	0	John foster,	3	6
Michael Hover,	3	0	Robt. foster,	2	6
Hannas Palmar,	2	0	David foster,	4	0
Hendry Peters,	2	6	Dison Cooper,	2	6
Hanes Ketrin,	4	0	John Strean,	2	0
Charles Clark,	3	0	John Cochran,	1	0
Thomas Make,	0	6	Hance Adem Nai,	2	0
Andrew More,	4	0	Jacob Sailer,	1	0
Jas. foster,	4	0	Hugh Miller,	2	6
Robt. McClire,	2	6	John Goarley,	1	0
Folti Fallopo,	2	6	Thomas Aken,	2	0
Hugh Hall,	6	0	Anthoney Hemple,	1	0
Vandall Row,	1	6	Christian Coughan,	1	6
Thos. Ritherford,	4	6	Aullbright Siglee,	3	6
Wilm. Rea,	4	0	Conrad Wisan,	1	6
John McQwin,	6	0	John McColouh,	1	0
John Ree.	4	0	John Kingre,	4	6
Neal McCallester,	5	0	William Miller,	3	0
Crisle Snidor,	4	0	John Moar,	3	0
Neal Daughtery,	1	0	John Hays,	3	0

free men.

	s.	d.		s.	d.
John Hover,	6	0	John Mordoch,	6	0
David Rea,	6	0	Thos. freeman,	6	0
Willm. Huston,	6	0			

Collector, JOHN HAYS,

WEST END OF DERRY—1751.

	s.	d.		s.	d.
James Semple,	8	6	John Tise,	1	0
James McKee,	6	0	John Leard,	4	0
Joseph Candor,	5	0	David Callwel,	2	0
Thos. Hall,	3	6	Andrew Morison,	4	0
Jas. Clark,	5	0	John Thomson,	4	0
Randle Boo,	2	6	Alexd. fley,	1	0

	s.	d.		s.	d.
John Allison,	2	0	Alexdr. Robison,	2	6
James Shaw,	5	0	John Nicom,	2	0
Robt. Ramsy,	3	0	John Keer,	7	0
Jas. Russell,	3	0	Wm. Blackburn,	2	6
Thos. Bowman,	3	6	Andrew Lockerd,	1	0
Jas. Chambers,	4	0	Widow Blackburn,	3	0
Hugh Carithers,	2	6	David McNear,	4	0
Robt. Bratehy,	1	6	Jas. Wiley,	1	0
Hugh Black,	4	6	Wm. Drennan,	2	0
Thos. Black,	3	0	Cristian Saddeler,	2	0
David Black,	4	6	William Mithel,	1	6
Robt. Chambrs,	4	6	Moses Wilson,	4	0
Jas. Long,	4	0	Micheal Hour,	2	6
David Cample,	2	0	Moses Patterson,	2	0
James Irland,	3	6	James Russel,	3	0
Patrick Down,	1	6	William Starrit,	2	0
John Vanlier,	3	0	Robt. Armstrong,	2	6
Robt. Carithers,	2	6	Valintin Clanninger,	4	0
John Harris,	4	0	Martin Brand,	4	6
Willm. Breeden,	2	6	John Singer,	1	6
Charles Nelie,	1	0	Jacob Jenan,	1	6
Arther Chambrs,	4	6	John Welsh,	1	0
the man on David Walkr place,	1	6			

free men.

	s.	d.		s.	d.
Hugh Leard,	6	0	Willm. Poar,	6	0
William Irland,	6	0	James Harris,	6	0

Collector, JAMES RUSSEL.

THROUGH DAUPHIN COUNTY IN 1745.

In 1745 that pious Moravian, Bishop Spangenberg, in company with two other members of the Mission board of the church, undertook a journey to Onondaga to treat with the Six Nations for permission for the Moravian Indians to remove to Wyoming. His notes of travel have recently appeared in the *Pennsylvania Magazine*, and as the route lay through the northern part of Dauphin county, we make such extracts as may be of local interest to us. The party set out from Bethlehem on the 24th of May. On the 30th, at Tulpehocken, Conrad Weiser and his two sons joined them. Spangenberg then continues:

" * * After traveling ten miles we came to the Kittatinny Hills (*a*), which are high and rocky, and difficult for horses to climb. On reaching the top we came to Pilger Ruh (*b*), where we dismounted and rested. After descending we entered Anton's Wilderness (*c*), where we pitched our first tents, built a fire, pastured our horses, partook of a light supper and retired to rest. Our course to-day was N. W.

"May 31. Arose early, looked up our horses, took a little breakfast and then continued our journey in the names of God our Savior. Bro. Meurer and Nicke returned to Tulpehocken with letters to Mary Spangenberg, at Bethlehem. After passing the Great Swatara we climbed the 'Thurnstein' (d), a high mountain, rocky and almost impassable for horses. On the high summit we refreshed ourselves at Erdmuth's spring (e), which flows through the valleys until it empties into the Susquehanna. We were four hours in crossing the mountain. At Ludwig's Ruh (f), at the foot of the mountain, we nooned. Here Laurel creek (g) flows past. After dinner our course was northwest. We passed through Anna's valley (h), beautiful and pleasing to the eyes, which lies in among the hills. At the Double Eagle (i), on Benigna's creek (k), we passed the night."

After their stay at Onondaga, about ten days, Spangenberg and his party began their return journey on the 29th of June. On the 10th of July they had reached the Double Eagle, on Mahantango creek.

" * * Here we found encamped a family of Indians, who, on learning from whence we had come, said we must be tired, and the man said to his wife, 'give them some spits full of venison.' In return Bro. Spangenberg gave them knives and thimbles. Nooned at Benigna's creek, and at night-fall came to the Thurnstein. As we were leading our horses down, Bro. Spangenburg, who was in advance, heard the rattle of a rattle snake, and called to us to come and kill it, but it could not be found. Encamped at the base of the Thurnstein on the Swatara.

"July 11. Our course was southeast. We early entered 'Anton's Wilderness," thence over the Kittatinny mountain, and nooned on Little Swatara. From thence we proceeded to Christopher Weiser's."

Notes.

a. Written also *Kechkachtany*, and *Kittochtinny*, in Delaware, signifying *endless hills.*

b. "Pilgrims Rest," a plain on the top of the mountain. The passage of the mountain was effected at the Great Swatara Gap, called *Toleheo* by the Indians, corrupted into "The Hole."

c. Anthony's Wilderness is noted on Lewis Evans' map of 1749. It included the valley through which runs Stony creek. It was named for Anthony Seyfert, one of the nine colonists whom Spangenberg led to Georgia in 1735, where the Moravians proposed establishing themselves with a view of commencing missions among the Creeks and Cherokees.

d. Peter's mountain. It has been stated that this name was given to it by Conrad Weiser in honor of Zinzendorf when guiding him to Shamokin in 1742. This is certainly a mistake. As early as 1725, Peter Allen was located at the foot of that mountain near the Susquehanna, and in 1729 it was thus named, and undoubtedly for him.

e. The head-waters of Wiconisco creek, named in honor of the Countess Erdmuth, the first wife of Zinzendorf.

f. Lewis' Rest, in Wiconisco township, Dauphin county. Zinzendorf was often familiarly called Brother Ludwig by the Moravians.

g. A branch of the Mohantango, noted on Lewis Evans' map of 1749.

h. Named in honor of Anna Nitschman, who accompanied Zinzendorf to Shamokin 1742. It is what is now so widely known as Lykens Valley.

i. The Spread Eagle is noted on Scull's map of 1759.

k. The Mahantango or Kind creek. Zinzendorf on his way to Shamokin gave this name in honor of his daughter, the Countess Benigna.

The foregoing notes are those of John W. Jordan, of Bethlehem, with the exception of certain interpolations in *c* and *d*.

Those familiar with the localities alluded to, no doubt have observed that but one of the names have been preserved. The desire of the early Moravian missionaries to perpetuate the names of their special friends and admirers has failed, and it is surprising that amid the many changes which have taken place only a few Indian names of the early times have been retained.

NOTES AND QUERIES.—XIX.

LUDINGTON.—James Ludington died September, 1742, leaving a wife Sarah, a son Thomas, and two daughters. As the witnesses to his will were William and Ann Barnett, and the executors named were John Morrow and John Guttry, all residents of Hanover, it is presumed he too resided in that township. What became of this family?

"CORMICK'S PLAINS."—James Allison, Sen., died in 1742, leaving a wife, Jean, and children, Isabel and James. He states that he is of "Cormick's Plains." Where was this plantation, and whence its name? The James spoken of was a brother of William Allison, of Derry, who died in 1739, and of whose estate he was one of the executors.

HARRISBURG IN 1787.—In July of this year the Rev. Manasseh Cutler, on his way to Ohio, passed through Harrisburg, and left this description of the place in his journal: "This is a beautiful town; it contains about one hundred houses, all built in less than three years, many of them brick, some of them three-story, built in the Philadelphia style, all appear very neat. A great number of taverns with handsome signs; houses all two-story; large windows. About one-half of the people are English. People were going to meeting; they meet in private houses; have no churches yet. People appear very well dressed; some gay." This was the second year from the founding of the town, and is a pretty good description of the place at that time. Middletown and Lebanon were larger towns—but the location of the county-seat at Harrisburg gave an impetus to its growth and prosperity, and it was in a few years ahead of its rivals, and has rapidly maintained its supremacy.

FRENCH.—James French, who died in Hanover, September, 1764, left a wife, Margaret, and children as follows:
  i. *May*, b. 1730.
  ii. *Thomas*, b. 1732.
  iii. *Isabel*, b. 1734.
  iv. *James*, b. 1736.
  v. *Agnes*, b. 1738.
  vi. *Elizabeth*, b. 1740.
  vii. *John*, b. 1742.
  viii. *Sarah*, b. 1744.
  ix. *Ruth*, b. 1746.
  x. *Margaret*. b. 1748.

John, b. 1742; d. August, 1783. He was the father of Captain James French, b. January 26, 1777; d. July 19, 1851. Both are buried in Hanover graveyard. Information is desired as to the other members of the family.

WALLACE.—Robert Wallace settled in Hanover township before 1738. He married Mary Clyde, who, with himself, is buried in Derry church burying ground—of which church Robert Wallace was one of the founders. They had issue :
  i. *Moses*, b. April 22, 1741; d. November 11, 1803; m. Jean Fulton.

ii. Isabel, b. 1744; d. 1755.
iii. Elizabeth, b. May 10, 1746; d. April 13, 1802; m. Joseph Boyd.
iv. Ann Maria, b. March 15, 1748; d. September 22, 1793; m. Thomas McNair.
v. James, b. August 18, 1751; d. December 15, 1823; m. Sarah Elder.
vi. Andrew, b. 1755; d. in infancy.
vii. Isabel, b. February 23, 1757; d. November 9, 1784; m. Moses Gillmor.
viii. Mary, b. Dec. 19, 1766; d. May 8, 1822; m. Hugh Graham.

Can any one give me the maiden name of Mrs. Wallace, or any information concerning Robert Wallace and his wife, previous to their settling in Hanover township?　　　　　　　　　　J. C. A.

RUTHERFORD.—FAMILY RECORD OF THE FIRST PIONEER.

From an old memorandum book in the possession of one of his descendents, on the fly-leaf of which is the inscription "Thomas Rutherford, his book. Bought in Cookstown upon 26 day of October, 1728, written at the house of Aggness Mordach," we take the following record "wonderfully complete and satisfactory of its kind." Little more is known of this first of the Rutherfords than what he details himself, from which it appears that he was born in the vicinity and had the honor to be baptized—as the old song has it—in "Fair Cookstown." The tradition in the family is that two of his brothers settled in New England, and we believe that we shall eventually, with the assistance of some friends in that locality, be able to substantiate the averment. He is described by one of his grandchildren as a person of five feet ten inches in height, heavy set, and of considerable force of character.

There is a spice of romance connected with his early manhood, which no doubt will prove as interesting to our readers as to his descendants. His attachment to Jean Mordah, whom he afterwards married, it is said was reciprocated, but her parents said no, and removed her with them to America, probably in the year 1728. On the cover of the memorandum book from which the record is taken is this note—"enquire for Dennygall." This was the location of the Mordahs, and Thomas Rutherford followed them either that or the following year. In 1730 they were married and it is probable they remained near the Mordah settlement until the death of John Mordah in December, 1744. The will of the latter was proved January 9, 1744–5, and from it we glean the fact that he left a wife Agnes, son James, a daughter Eleanor, unmarried; with two daughters, married respectively to Thomas Rutherford and Henry McKinney. The witnesses to this will were the Rev. Samuel Black, Presbyterian minister to the Conewago church, and his brother, Robert Mordah. Removing to Paxtang about 1750, Thomas Rutherford and his wife lived to advanced age, honored, beloved and respected by their neighbors, and revered by their numerous descendants. Thomas Rutherford died April 18, 1777, his wife Jean August 10, 1789. Both lie interred in old Paxtang church-yard.

Of the daughters of Thomas and Jean Mordah Rutherford, Eleanor married twice; first, William Wilson; second John Davidson. Jane married Thomas Mayes, and removed to South Carolina. Agnes m. William Gray, and removed to Buffalo Valley. Mary m. Andrew Mayes, brother of Thomas, and also removed to South Carolina. Elizabeth married first Patrick Gallaway or Calloway. He joined Captain Matthew Smith's company of Paxtang, and was in the expedition to Quebec in 1775, but never returned. His widow next married Patrick Harbison, and removed with him to the home of the Mayes' in Spartansburg district, South Carolina. The tories soon put an end to Harbison, and the times being too warm for him, Andrew Mayes removed his family together, with Mrs. H., to the settlement of the Mordahs in Iredell county, North Carolina. Here Mrs. Harbison married Thomas Archibald. Some of the descendants of these families reside in the South and West.

As to Thomas Rutherford's sons, they remained beside the paternal acres, and although the descendants in the female line are scattered over many States of the Union, but few of the male members of the family have gone out from the original settlement in Paxtang.

We shall endeavor ere long to obtain more information as to the descendants of Thomas Rutherford, at least for the third, fourth and fifth generations. They belong to one of the few families of the earlier settlers of this locality, who are in occupancy of the ancestral acres.

Record.

Thomas Rutherford, born the 24th day of June, A. D. 1707, and baptized by the Rev. John McClave, in the parish of Derry-lonsau, county of Tyrone, living in Cookstown.

Jean Mordah, my wife, the 9th day of April, A. D. 1712, and baptized by the Rev. John McClave in Gorty-Lowry.

Me and my wife was married the 7th day of September, A. D. 1730, by the Rev. James Anderson, in Donney Gall, America.

Our eldest daughter Agnes, the 9th day of July, 1731, and baptized by the Rev. James Anderson. Died when four years old.

Our second daughter, Ellenor, was born the 16th day of January, 1733, and baptized by Rev. James Anderson.

Our third daughter Jean, was born the 22d day of June, A. D. 1734; baptized by the Rev. Mr. Anderson.

Our son John was born the 16th day of February, A. D. 1737; baptized by Rev. Mr. Anderson.

Our son Thomas was born the 14th day of August, 1738. Died when about one year old.

Our fourth daughter, Agnes, was born the 14th day of September, 1740; baptized by the Rev. Mr. Richard Sankey.

Our son Thomas was born the 12th day of February, 1743; baptized by the Rev. Samuel Black.

Our two daughters, Mary and Elizabeth, born the 17th day of February, 1745. Elizabeth died when about eight months old; baptized by Mr. Black.

Our son James was born the 28th day of August, 1747, and baptized by the Rev. John Elder.

Our son Samuel was born 13th day of December, 1749, and baptized by the Rev. Richard Sankey.

Our daughter Elizabeth was born on the 27th of February, 1752, and baptized by the Rev. Richard Sankey.

CAPTAIN JOHN BRADY.

[In the Annals of Pennsylvania Pioneer Life, there are no more interesting scenes, no more stirring incidents than were participated in by the various members of the Brady family. From the earliest times they stood in defense of their homes and the frontiers. Among the most prominent of them was Captain John Brady, who located on the Susquehanna as early as 1769, and in whose memory the citizens of Muncy and the West Branch, through the indomitable energy and perseverance of J. M. Gernerd, Esq., having recently (October 15) erected a monument near the spot where, on the 11th of April, 1779, he fell a victim to Indian ferocity. The oration by the Hon. John Blair Linn, of Bellefonte, contains so much that is interesting and valuable relative to the old Warrior of the West Branch that we transfer to our column of " Notes and Queries " that portion especially entertaining. Mr. Linn recounts with powerful eloquence the services of the hardy pioneer, and we feel confident our readers will appreciate the narrative which follows.]

Captain John Brady was born in what is now the State of Delaware, in 1733. His father, Hugh Brady, was an emigrant from the North of Ireland; of that Godly Scotch-Irish ancestry who read their Bibles by the light of the camp fires of Oliver Cromwell's army, who were the first to cross the Boyne and engage the hosts of churchly despotism; and who at the siege of Londonderry slowly starved to death for the rights of conscience.

Captain Brady was as well educated as the circumstances of his father would allow, and taught an elementary school and singing school over in New Jersey, prior to the removal of his father and family to the banks of Conedoguinet, not far from Shippensburg, in Cumberland county, about the year 1750. In the quiet the Province had before the coming storm of the French and Indian war, he followed the usual avocations of frontier life; the primeval forest yearly bowing to the settler's axe. His personal appearance has come down to us by tradition; he was six feet high, well formed, had coal black hair, hazel eye and of rather dark complexion.

About the year 1755 he married Mary Quigley, who was also of of Scotch-Irish extraction, and in the year 1756 his eldest son, the celebrated Captain Samuel Brady, was born in the midst of the tempestuous waves of trouble that rolled in upon the settlements in the wake of Braddock's defeat. Armstrong's expedition against Kittanning was then organized and marched from Fort Shirley on the 30th of August three hundred strong. Brady going along as a private. General James Porter, his subsequent associate in the settlement of this valley, was a lieutenant in the command and was wounded at Kittanning. Kittanning was destroyed on the 8th of September, and the settlers returned in triumph. But this severe retaliation did not deter the savages. As late as the eighth of November, 1756, they entered the Kittatinny Valley, killed a number of inhabitants and carried away captives.

Forbes' expedition against Fort Duquesne followed in 1758. His troops were composed in part of the regular forces of the Province, but Brady does not seem to have been along, not at least as an officer, as there is a very circumstantial account extant of every officer who accompanied the expedition. On Forbes' approach the French burned Fort Duquesne and retired, thus terminating the struggle between the French and the English for the Ohio Valley, November 25, 1758. General Stanwix built Fort Pitt upon the ruins of Fort Duquesne, in 1759, and on the 13th of September, upon the plains of Abraham, rendered him immortal by the death of General Wolfe, Montcalm, with the "Lilies of France," went down before the Cross of St. George, virtually ending French dominion in North

America. This was followed by the peace of Paris, February 10, 1763.

But the end was not yet to blazing homes and border conflicts on the frontiers. Pontiac had secretly organized his noted conspiracy of the Indian tribes extending from the lakes of the lower Mississippi, and called upon them, in fiery eloquence, to save their race from slavery and ruin, and to drive the English into the Atlantic. About the 27th of April, 1763, he assembled a Council on the banks of the Excorces, a small stream not far from Detroit, and having aroused the chiefs in a speech of unparalleled fury to terrible earnestness, he let the tribes loose in vengeful wrath upon the frontiers. While nature was robing the forests of the West in the green mantle of May, they stole silently through them, seized most of the forts unawares and massacred the garrisons. They even surrounded Fort Pitt, and for five days threatened its capture, their scouting parties from the North penetrating nearly to Reading. Then John Brady sprang from the ranks apparently to the office of Captain. He was commissioned July 19, 1763, Captain of the Second Battalion of the Pennsylvania Regiment "commanded by Governor John Penn," Turbutt Francis and Asher Clayton, Lieutenant Colonels commandants. Then came Bouquet's expedition for the relief of Fort Pitt, the battle of Bushy Run beyond Fort Ligonier (August 5, 1763), a hard fought battle of two days, in which Bouquet's troops suffered severely, but he at last defeated the Indians by a bold stratagem—a victory which saved Fort Pitt, relieved the Western frontiers, and Provincials returned to battle with inroads from the North. Thus closed the year 1763.

With the return of spring in 1764, their incursions were renewed, and in the *Pennsylvania Gazette* of April 5, 1764, there is an account of "the Indian depredations in the Carlisle region on the 20th, 21st, and 22d of March; killing people, burning houses and making captives," adding "Captains Piper and Brady, with their companies, did all that lay in their power to protect the inhabitants. No man can go asleep within ten or fifteen miles of the border without being in danger of having his house burned and himself or family scalped or led into captivity before the next morning. The people along the North Mountain are moving farther in, especially about Shippensburg, which is crowded with families of the neighborhood."

Bouquet's second expedition followed, in which he was accompanied by the First and Second Battalions of the Pennsylvania Regiment. At Fort Loudoun (about twelve miles west of Chambersburg) he was met by a runner from Col. Bradstreet, who had penetrated with a force to Presqu' Isle (City of Erie now), who advised Col. Bouquet that he had granted a peace to all Indians between Lake Erie and the Ohio. Bouquet was at the head of the Provincial soldiery of Pennsylvania, and he and they were determined upon a conquered peace. He, therefore, forwarded the dispatch to Gov. Penn, with the remark, "that such a peace with no satisfaction insisted upon, would fix an indelible stain upon the Nation. I, therefore, take no notice of that pretended peace, and proceed forthwith upon the expedition, fully determined to treat as enemies any Delawares and Shawnees I shall find on my way." He accordingly penetrated the country of the Delawares to the Forks of the Muskingum (where Coshocton, Ohio, now stands) and upon the banks of that river dictated his own terms of peace; among these were the absolute return of about three hundred captives.

I come now to the connection of Bouquet's expedition with the history of the settlement of the West Branch Valley, On the 30th of November, 1764, the first Battalion of the Pennsylvania Regiment left Fort Pitt for home, and the Second followed the next day. When they reached Bedford the officers made an agreement with each other in writing, to apply to the Proprietaries for a tract of land sufficiently extensive and conveniently situated, whereon to erect a a compact and defensible town, and accommodate them with reasonable and commotious plantations, the same to be divided according to their several ranks, etc. John Brady was one of the officers who signed this agreement. In their application to the Proprietaries, dated April 30, 1765, they proposed to embody themselves into a compact settlement, at some distance from the inhabited part of the Province, where, by industry. they might procure a comfortable subsistence for themselves, and by their arms, union and increase, become a powerful barrier to the Province. They suggested the the confluence of the two branches of the Susquehanna at Shamokin as affording a situation convenient for their purpose, and asked the Proprietaries to make a purchase from the Indians to accommodate their application.

Meanwhile, urged by the restless, mysterious impulse that moulds the destiny of the pioneers of civilization, Captain Brady had removed from the Conedoguinet fifty miles further northwest to Standing Stone (now Huntingdon) Here, in 1768, his children, General Hugh Brady and twin sister Jennie, were born, and Captain Brady followed the occupation of surveyor. On the 5th of November, 1768, Thomas and Richard Penn purchased from the Six Nations at Fort Stanwix (now Rome, N. Y.), with other territory, all that portion of the West Branch Valley extending from the mouth of Mahanoy creek to the mouth of Pine creek, and on the 3d of

February, 1769, the officers of the First and Second Battalions met at the Governor's and obtained an order to take up twenty-four thousand acres. The surveys of 8,000 of it, in what is now Union county, were made by Samuel Maclay on the 1st, 2d and 3d of March, 1769, Captain Brady, with others of the officers being along. The surveys of the second 8,000 acres, at the mouth of the Chilisquaque creek were made at the same time, and the officers returned to Fort Augusta (now Sunbury), held a meeting and determined that the remaining 8,000 acres should be surveyed on Bald Eagle creek, and Captains Hunter, Brady and Piper were selected to oversee it. The latter surveys were made by Charles Lukens in April, 1769, Captain Brady accompanying him, and embrace the land from the city of Lock Haven up Bald Eagle creek to where Howard now stands, in Centre county.

During the summer of 1769 Captain Brady removed his family to the West Branch and cleared a place on the eastern side of the river, directly opposite Derr's Mill, now the site of Lewisburg. On the 21st of March, 1772, Northumberland county was created, and on the fourth Tuesday of May Captain John Brady was foreman of the first Grand Jury that ever sat in Northumberland county. But the air seemed to be full of trouble in those early days. The Connecticut people, who had settled at Wyoming, claimed under their charter the territory of the Province of Pennsylvania, as far south as the 41° of latitude, which would run a mile or so north of Lewisburg, and were determined to enforce it by adverse occupation. Between the 3d and 7th of July, 1772, a large party of them reached the river at Hulings, where Milton now stands, when Colonel Plunket summoned the Pennamites to arms and forcibly drove them off. This contest continued for some time after the trumpet of the Revolution summoned the combatants to fight a common foe. In December, 1775, Brady accompanied Col Plunket's force to Wyoming Valley as captain of a company, in which last encounter of the Pennamite war Jesse Lukens, son of the Surveyor General of the Province, lost his life.

Meanwhile the storm of war with the mother country broke upon the shores of New England, and when news of the Battle of Bunker Hill reached this valley, its heroic settlers promptly accepted the arbitrament of the sword, and Captain John Lowdon's company, one hundred strong, marched for Boston, Captain Samuel Brady, then a young man of twenty years, went along as a private, entering the trenches at Cambridge, with Lowdon, on the 31st of August, 1775.

Two Battalions of Associators were organized on the West Branch, one company by Colonel Hunter, the other by Colonel William

Plunket, in the latter Batalion Captain John Brady was commissioned First Major (March 13, 1776). On the 4th of July, 1776, he attended the Convention of Associators, at Lancaster, as one of the representatives of Plunket's Battalion, where Daniel Roberdeau and James Ewing were elected Brigadier Generals of the Associators of the Province. And now comes in order of time, August, 1776, the incident at Derr's trading house, when returning in haste from Sunbury (laid out in June, 1772, just below the site of Fort Augusta) he entered a canoe and shoved swiftly over to Derr's, to find the Indians in high carnival over a barrel of rum, with which Derr was standing treat. In the midst of their drunken orgies he kicked over a barrel. To this interference some attribute Captain Brady's sad fate, as the Indian appointed to be sober that day said, in effect, "He would rue the spilling of that rum some day."

Soon after this occurrence Capt. Brady moved to Muncy, having erected in the Spring of 1775, the semi-fortified residence which afterwards went by the name of Fort Brady. The day of associators was soon over with nine months and one year's service. It became imperative to raise regular regiments, enlisted for the war, if the independence of the States was to be maintained. Accordingly Colonel William Cook's Regiment, the Twelfth, was directed to be raised in the counties of Northampton and Northumberland. Among the last acts of the Convention which formed the first Constitution of this Commonwealth, September 28, 1776, was the election of the field officers of this Regiment. Col. William Cook, whose grandson, Jacob Cook, is with us to-day; Lieutenant Colonel Neigel Gray, then of Northampton county, but who after the war owned and died upon the place now known as Kelly's Mills, in Union county, and Major James Crawford, who died in Wayne township, Lycoming county, of which he was a Justice of the Peace in 1814, were elected. John Brady was commissioned one of its captains, October 14, 1786, and on the 18th of December, in mid-winter, it left Sunbury in boats for the battle fields of New Jersey. The regiment went immediately into active service. Being composed of good riflemen it was assigned to the same duties our "Bucktails" were in the late war, on picket, on the skirmish line, to commence the fighting, and to go through it. At Boundbrook, at Bonumtown, at Piscataway, it left its dead, and the green mounds that decked the purple heaths of New Jersey left their sorrow in many homes in the West Branch Valley.

When General Washington crossed the Delaware into Pennsylvania to await the development of General Howe's plans, he detached Captain Hawkins Boone, of the Twelfth to Morgan's Rifle Command, to assist in the capture of Burgoyne, and two at least (that I know of) of his wounded soldiers returned to this valley to tell that Timothy Murphy, a West Branch Rifleman, had shot Gen. Fraser at Saratoga, and how they, with Major James Parr, of Northumberland, and Lieutenant Colonel Richard Butler, of Westmoreland, stormed Breymand's camp, led by the lion-hearted Arnold. Within a few short months (July 26, 1779) after Capt. Brady's death, Capt. Boone bravely died in defence of this valley at Fort Freeland.

In due time Howe made his appearance at the Head of the Elk, and General Washington moved his army to the banks of the Brandywine to confront him. The Twelfth with the Third, the Ninth and the Sixth, was in Conway's Brigade, General Stirling's Division, in the right wing commanded by General Sullivan on the eventful 11th of September (battle of Brandywine). General Wayne, with the two other brigades of Pennsylvania, was left at Chadd's Ford to oppose Knyphausen while Sullivan's right wing was hurried on to Birmingham's Meeting House to attack the English left under Cornwallis. When the Twelfth Pennsylvania arrived on double quick upon the ground, "the cannon balls were ploughing up the ground, the trees cracking over their heads, the branches riven by the artillery, and the leaves were falling as in Autumn by the grape shot." Capt. Brady had two sons in the fight; Samuel, the eldest, was First Lieutenant, commissioned July 17, 1776, in Capt. John Doyle's company, then attached to the First Pennsylvania, Col. James Chambers, and was with General Wayne at Chadd's Ford. John (subsequently, 1795, Sheriff of Northumberland county), then a youth of fifteen years, who had gone to the army to ride the horses home, was with his father with a big rifle by his side.

They had scarcely time to obey the stentorian order of Col. Cook, "fall into line!" when the British made their appearance. The Twelfth fired sure and fast, and many an officer leaped forward in death after the sharp crack of its rifles. As the fight grew furious and the charge of gleaming bayonets came on, other troops that had not time to form reeled before "the burnished rows of steel." But the Twelfth stood firm, and Lieutenant William Boyd (of Northumberland) fell dead by his Captain. Little John was wounded and Captain Brady fell with a wound through his mouth. The day ended with disaster to our arms, and the Twelfth suddenly quit the field nearly cut to pieces.

The wound only loosened some of the Captain's teeth, but being disabled by a severe attack of pleurisy, caused by his exposures, which he never got entirely well of, he was sent home. On the invasion of Wyoming Valley, in 1778, he retired with his family to Sunbury, and it was there, on the 8th of August, 1778, his son, James, was sent to his parents, cruelly wounded and scalped by the Indians, to die. The circumstances of his death are very minutely detailed in a letter from Col. Hartley, to be found in the Pennsylvania Archives, vol. 6, O. S., page 689; also in Meginness' history, page 222, etc. I will only add General Hugh Brady's recollections of his brother. "James Brady was a remarkable man. His person was fine, he lacked but a quarter of an inch of six feet, and his mind was as well finished as his person. I have ever placed him by the side of Jonathan, son of Saul, for beauty of person and nobleness of soul, and like him, he fell by the hands of the Philistines. He was wounded and scalped on Saturday and was carried on a bier to Sunbury, where he died on Thursday following, after reviving sufficiently to relate everything that happened."

On the 1st of September, 1778, Captain Brady returned to the army. Meanwhile, under an arrangement of the army, which took place about the first day of July, the field officers had been mustered out and the companies and their officers distributed into the Third and Sixth Pennsylvania Regiments. Captain Brady was therefore sent home by General Washington's order, with Captain Boone, Lieutenants Samuel and John Dougherty, to assist Colonel Hartley in protecting the frontiers. He joined Colonel Hartley at Muncy on the 8th of September, and accompanied him on the expedition to Tioga. Colonel Hartley, in a letter to Congress (dated October 8th, 1778, describes the hardships of this march. "We waded or swam Lycoming creek upwards of twenty times, met great rains and prodigious swamps, mountain defiles and rocks impeded our course, and we had to open and clear the way as we passed. We carried two boxes of spare ammunition and twelve days' provision. I cannot help observing the difficulties in crossing the Alps or passing up the Kennebec could not have been greater than our men experienced for the time." On their return, after they left Wyalusing, the enemy made a heavy attack upon his rear and the rear guard gave way. "At the critical moment Captains Boone and Brady and Lieutenant King, with a few brave fellows, landed from the canoes and renewed the action. We advanced on the enemy on all sides, and the Indians, after a brave resistance, conceiving themselves surrounded, fled with the utmost haste, leaving ten dead."

During the whole of the fall of 1778 the savages ravaged the settlements, and Captain Brady was kept busy. He was one of those of whom Colonel Hunter wrote on the 13th of December, who told him, "They would rather die fighting than leave their homes again." With the opening spring of 1779 these inroads were renewed, and in such force that William Maclay wrote, "He believed the whole force of the Six Nations was being poured down upon the West Branch Valley."

Amid these scenes of terror and confusion Captain Brady stood manfully at his post, and died by it, at a time when his services could ill be spared. On the fatal 11th of April, 1779, in the golden light of morning, its sunlight reflected by the myriad rain drops lying on the bushes and the trees, with the songs of birds among the branches, in all the hope and glory of coming spring, going forth to the duties of the hour, the sharp summons came, and in the twinkling of an eye Captain John Brady stood before his God.

> "The car of victory, the plume, the wreath,
> Defend not from the bolt of fate the brave."

But—

> "Glory lights the soldier's tomb,
> And beauty weeps the brave."

After the death of her husband Mrs. Brady removed with her family to her father's place, in Cumberland county, where she arrived in May, 1779. She remained until October of that year, and then removed to Buffalo Valley, to what is now known as the Frederick place, three miles west of Lewisburg, where she died on the 20th of October, 1783, at the early age of forty-eight years. Over her remains in the beautiful cemetery at Lewisburg, in the same grave with those of the youthful hero of Brandywine (John Brady, who died on the 10th of December, 1809, at the same age—forty-eight), is a marble slab with the appropriate inscription, " All tears are wiped from her eyes."

NOTES AND QUERIES—XX.

BERRYHILL, ALEXANDER, was a native of Paxtang township, Dauphin county, Pa., where he was born in 1738. He became one of the first residents of Harrisburg, on its being laid out in 1785, and after its incorporation as a borough he was appointed one of its justices of the peace by Gov. Mifflin. He was one of the burgesses of the town in 1794, and signed the address to Gen. Washington then on his way westward to quell the so-called Whisky Insurrection. He died at Harrisburg, Sept. 7, 1798. Mr. Berryhill was an excellent penman, and many of his papers, still extant, are models of elegant penmanship.

BOMBAUGH, CONRAD, son of George Bombaugh, was born at Middletown, Pa., about 1750. He was a mill-wright by profession, and established the first mill at Standing Stone, now Huntingdon. About the commencement of the Revolution he located at Highspire, and when the county of Dauphin was organized in 1785, we find him a resident of the new town. He was a prominent citizen of Harrisburg; was the senior burgess of the borough during the Whisky Insurrection, and signed the address to Gen. Washington, on passing through Harrisburg westward. He died in April, 1821, aged seventy-one.

THE REDEEMED INDIAN CAPTIVES OF BOUQUET'S EXPEDITION OF 1764.

In order to confine the extracts from the oration of Hon. John B. Linn, to data concerning Capt. John Brady (N. & Q. xix.) several interesting portions were omitted, especially that relating to the redeemed Indian captives of 1764. As this has elicited the communications which follow, we give that to which the latter refer:

"Some of my hearers, the descendants of the Cummins, the Gambles, the Irvines, the McCormicks, the Montgomerys, the Robbs, and others, who with me trace their lineage to the dwellers under the shadow of the North mountain, will recall the traditions of Bouquet's return with the captives which were mingled with our grandmother's fireside tales, and haunt the memory of our infant years, like the cadence of some far distant music, or the words of a well-nigh forgotten song. It was on a wintry day, December 31, 1764, when Col. Bouquet, having advertised for those who had lost children to come to Carlisle and reclaim them, brought out the little band of captives for recognition. Many had been captured when very young and had grown up to boyhood and girlhood in the wigwam of the Indian, having learned the language of the savage and forgotten their own. One woman was unable to point out her daughter, and the captives could only talk in an unknown tongue. She told her sad lot to the Colonel, and mentioned that she used, many years before, sing to her daughter a hymn, of which the child was very fond. The Colonel told her to sing it, and she began—

> "Alone, yet not alone am I,
> Though in this solitude so drear,
> I feel my Saviour always nigh,
> He comes my dreary hours to cheer."

"She had not finished the first verse before her long lost daughter rushed into her arms."

The incident thus narrated elicited the following interesting letter to Mr. Linn, from the distinguished historian of Western Pennsylvania, Isaac Craig, Esq.:

ALLEGHENY, PA., *Oct. 28, 1879.*

DEAR SIR: I have received and read your address at the unveiling of the Brady monument with great interest. Your notice of the German mother finding her lost child by singing a favorite hymn, recalls an interesting sequel related to me about a year ago by the venerable and Rev. Samuel Williams.

In the old French war, two little girls who were on a peach tree in Tulpehocken were taken by the Indians. The youngest, Regina, was scalped without other injury by the Indian that first approached them, but another Indian approached who took a fancy to them, and instead of slaying them carried them into captivity. The scalped child was tenderly cared for and survived, to be returned in the manner related by you.

Mr. Williams, who is nearly eighty, told me that he was born and raised in Bedford county, where both his parents were born. He had often heard the story referred to. In 1825 or 1826, while yet a licentiate in the ministry, he served a small Presbyterian church in Schellsburgh and a small Baptist church in Somerset. About the close of 1826 Mr. Peter Schell, the son-in-law of Mrs. Statler, requested him to conduct the funeral services of his mother-in-law, on the top of the Allegheny mountains, not far from Stoyestown. When they arrived at the house, as it was customary among the Lutherans to give a sketch of the life of the deceased in connection with the service, Mr. Schell took him into the room where the corpse lay, to give him some particulars of her life. Approaching the corpse of a very aged woman, he drew back her cap and showed Mr. Williams that she had been scalped, and then narrated the story of her capture by the Indians seventy years before. It was the very Regina who recognized her mother by hearing her sing the once-familiar hymn. She had grown up and married Mr. Statler and raised a large family of most respectable character. The funeral services were at the house of a Mr. Lambert, another son-in-law.

Very truly yours,

ISAAC CRAIG.

[If I am not mistaken, the Peter Schell referred to in Mr. Craig's letter was the late Hon. Peter Schell, of Bedford, father of my friend, Hon. William P. Schell, present Auditor General of Pennsylvania. If so, the *bald* joke of our college days, which attributed Mr. Schell's premature venerable appearance to early piety, would, to express it in the language of our venerable President, John W. Nevin, D. D.,

"*have a far deeper meaning, historically considered.*" Since delivering my address, I have found the whole story of "Regina, the Captive Maid," in the *Friend*, a Quaker weekly, volume seven, 1834, page 244, translated from the Danish of Pastor Roane of Elsineur. Much of the early history of Pennsylvania will be found in letters of missionaries, transmitted to the societies that sent them from Europe and locked up in the German language in the Moravian archives at Bethlehem.
J. B. LINN.

THE FAMILY OF BROWNE.

BROWNE (N. & Q., v.)—Two brothers named Browne (baptismal names not known) settled in the county Tyrone, Ireland, previous to 1688. They were of the covenanting party in Scotland and left that country during "the persecutions." They settled near Maghry Lock. There the descendants of both seem to have lived for a century, and the descendants of one of these brothers are supposed to be there yet. The other brother was my ancestor, through a son named Andrew who was a man with a family of his own, say about 1720. This Andrew was father of my grandfather. He had two sons and nine (or eleven) daughters. His sons were Andrew (2d) and David. Andrew (2d) was my great-grandfather. David had two sons, David and John. John was drowned emigrating to America, and his widow, with three children, returned to the old neighborhood; beyond which up to 1812, nothing is known. The other son David, married, but left no children. The following table (I.) shows the family of Andrew (2d.) whose wife was *nee* Mitchell. The (II.) shows the family of his son James.

I. The Family of Andrew Browne (2d.)

   i. Audley * d. s. p.
   ii. James m. Eliz. Lyons.
   iii. Andrew m. ——— Woods; removed to Kentucky about 1800.
   iv. David, m. Esther McCreary; settled in Westmoreland county—left no issue.
   v. John, unm. settled in Ligonier valley.
   vi. Matthew, m. Jane McCoskey; settled in Ligonier valley and left eight children.
   vii. Joseph, m. ——— Orr; remained at the old home—Maghry Lock.
   viii. Rebecca, m. ——— Woods; removed to Kentucky about 1800.

ix. Jane, m. James White; settled in Western Pennsylvania.
x. Adam, m. —— Kerr; settled in County Connaught, Ireland.

II. Family of James Browne, son of Andrew.

i. Andrew, m. —— Gibson; settled in Chester county.
ii. Margaret, b. 1783, m. John Campbell.
iii. Audley; came to the United States about 1800, and d. at the age of 18 years.
iv. Jane, m. William Totten, U. S. A.; left one son James, who graduated at West Point and rose to be brigadier general in the rebellion.
v. Robert, m. Mary Steeser; had three sons, all deceased.
vi. David Lyons, b. 1793, m. in 1818, Sarah Miller; removed with her parents to the U. S. in 1812—and had issue—James M. of Pittsburg; Matthew, deceased; Robert Audley, New Castle, Pa.; George Greer, deceased; Margaret, deceased, first wife of A. Finkbine; Eliza Lyons, now Mrs.Finkbine, of Winchester, W. Va.; Andrew, deceased; Sarah Jane, d. s. p.; and David Lyons, d. s. p.
vii. John, d. s. p.
viii. James, d. s. p.

*Audley, the first on record marked (?) The doubt is whether the name belongs to the family of the first or second Andrew Browne. There is no doubt regarding the others who all lived to be men and women. Maghry Lock is probably in the parish of Ardstraw, county Tyrone, Ireland. My grandfather's residence was in the village of Ardstraw.

R. A. B.

[Our inquiry of July 26 has elicited the foregoing interesting reply, valuable for its genealogical data. The query as to the descendants of John Brown, of Upper Paxtang, whose eldest son was Audley, is yet unanswered. Our correspondent writes his name with a final *e*, and yet we are of the opinion he is of the same family and perchance of *the* Browns who settled in Paxtang in 1720.]

JOHN PENN'S VISIT TO HARRISBURG AND MIDDLETOWN IN 1788.

The *Pennsylvania Magazine,* a quarterly publication of the Penn'a Historical Society, is a periodical which should be more widely disseminated in our State, and which from its high character, its value and its interest to every Pennsylvanian, ought to number its subscribers by the tens of thousands. It is in the third year of its existence, and every number is rich with historical and genealogical information. It is little known beyond the membership of the society, and yet there are thousands who are not connected with the State Historical Society who would appreciate and value it. Its industrious editor, Mr. Frederick D. Stone, the Librarian also of the society, by his researches, and the material at his hands, is making it a most valuable repository for much that is worth preserving in the history of our State, and we have no hesitancy in saying that it has no superior as an historical publication.

We have been prompted in speaking thus of the *Pennsylvania Magazine* by way of some prefatory remarks concerning the following extracts from the journal of John Penn, who visited Harrisburg and Middletown in the year 1788. This John Penn was the eldest son of Thomas, who was the second son of William and Hannah Callowhill Penn, was born February 23, 1760, and died in 1834. His mother was Lady Juliana Penn, daughter of the Earl of Pomfret. He published several volumes of poems and to distinguish him from the John Penn who was Governor of the Province from 1763 to 1771 and again from 1773 to 1776, has been named John Penn, the poet. His portrait, through a mistake, occupies a place among the Governors in the Executive Department of the State, which should be filled by John, the son of Richard Penn. A portrait of the latter is in existence and efforts will be made to procure a copy of it. How the mistake occurred we shall not inquire into at present. John Penn, the poet, came to America to look after some of the proprietary estates, and it was this which brought him to this newly founded town on his way to Carlisle. He set out from Philadelphia on the 6th of April, 1788, on horseback, reached Reading the next day, where he tarried until the 9th, when he pursued his way towards the Susquehanna. We now quote from his journal.

"April 10. Rose by six o'clock, and after breakfast set out, in order to sleep at Harrisburg, the chief town of Dauphin county, and which was proposed to be the seat of Government. Passed some mills a few miles from thence at Tulpehocken creek, which afterwards meets the road somewhat farther in a very picturesque spot. On the eastern side of this is a most elegant new Lutheran church. On the western is a Calvinist's called here, by way of distinction, a Presbyterian church. After riding through a village I came to Lebanon, a handsome town containing some hundred inhabitants. This place is decorated by a spire, and the houses are well built; many of them stone or brick. It not being distant enough, the horses were baited at Millerstown, a small village half-way, and twenty miles from Harrisburg, or Harris's ferry. About sunset, I had a fine view of this town from an high part of the road, (*a*) the river Susquehanna flowing between its woody and cultivated banks close to the town. Mr. Harris (*b*), the owner and founder of this town informed me that three years ago there was but one house built, and seemed to possess that pride and pleasure which Æneas envied.

Feleces illi, quorum jam mænia surgunt !

Tho' the courts are held here generally, Lebanon is infinitely larger. The situation of this place is one of the finest I ever saw. One good point of view is the tavern, almost close to the river. This was the house which stood alone so many years. It is called the Compass (*c*), and is one of the first public houses in Pennsylvania. The room I had is 22 feet square, and high in proportion.

"*April 11.* After breakfasting about eight with Mr. Harris, we walked together to the ferry, when he gave me two pieces of information, one of an island he purchased of us, which the war prevented us from confirming to him ; and the other of the delinquency of one Litso, who wishes to detain the money due in part for a farm over the Susquehanna, tho' there is an encumbrance in our favor, on it, to the amount of six or seven hundred pounds going on upon interest. The waters being high, we ferried across with difficulty, and almost dropped down to a very rapid part below the landing place; but at length escaped a disagreeable situation. About two miles from the river passed the house of Whitehill the Assemblyman, (*d*) and arrived about three at Carlisle, seventeen miles off."

[Mr. Penn remained at Carlisle until the 13th, when he commenced his return to Philadelphia. He thus proceeds.]

"*April 13.* Rose early in order to see a cave near Conedogwinit creek, in which water petrifies, as it drops from the roof. Returned and pursued my route to a place called Lisburn, tho' it proved somewhat out of my way. Just at this spot the country is romantic. The name of the creek running thro' it, *Yellow-breeches creek*, may in deed be unworthy of it. From hence the road lay thro' woods till the Susquehanna and Harrisburg denoted that the ferry was at hand at a distance. I crossed the river about three and a half o'clock, surrounded by enchanting prospects. The ride to Middletown is along the eastern bank; and exhibits a striking sample of the *great*, in the opposite one, rising to a vast height, and wooded close to the water's edge for many miles. From this vast forest, and the expansive bed of the river navigable to its source to craft carrying two tons burdens, the idea of grandeur and immensity rush forcibly upon the mind, mixed with the desert wilderness of an uninhabited scene. The first particular object on this road is Simpson's (*e*) house, the owner of the ferry where I crossed. It is on a rock across the river. At Middletown I put up at one More's, who was teacher formerly at Philadelphia of Latin and Greek. He talked very sensibly, chiefly on subjects which discovered him to be a warm tory, and friend of passive obedience. Unlike many tories he is an enemy of the new Constitution. Here the Great Swatara joins the Susquehanna, and a very fine mill is kept at their confluence by Mr. Frey, a Dutchman, to whom I carried a letter from Mr. D. Clymer.

"Several trees, before I arrived at the Susquehanna ferry, had been girdled, as it is termed, that is cut all around thro' the bark, so as to prevent their continuing alive. This operation in a country so abounding in timber, saves the too great trouble of cutting down every tree whose leaves might obstruct the men's operation upon the corn.

"*April 14.* Before my departure, Mr. Frey showed me his excellent mill, and still more extraordinary mill-stream, running from one part of Swatara for above a mile till it rejoins it at the mouth. It was cut by himself, with great expense and trouble, and is the only work of the kind in Pennsylvania. Middletown is in a situation as beautiful as it is adapted to trade, and already of a respectable size. I left it threatened by rain, which came on rather violently soon after, and the roads proved the worst of the whole journey, till that time. I passed thro' Elizabethtown, eight miles off, and over the creeks (or small rivers) of Conewago and Chickesalunga. As you leave Dauphin for Lancaster county, the lands improve, and at a place half-way from Middletown, where I stopped for my horses, and to avoid the rain, it was said to be worth £15 per acre. There are some handsome farm-houses nearer Lancaster. The town itself has a far superior appearance to any I had passed thro'. The streets are regular, and the sides are paved with brick, like Philadelphia, or else stone; and separated by posts from the street."

NOTES.

a. This road was south of the present P. & R. R. R. It afforded an enchanting view of Kittatinny Gap, up and down the Susquehanna for about 10 miles, and some distance into the valley of Cumberland and York counties. The west side of the river was not wooded at that time, all the forest having been burned off twenty years before.

b. John Harris, the founder of Harrisburg, a man of great energy, and the owner of 1,000 acres of choice land about his fine residence, built in 1766—yet standing pretty much as he erected it—on Front street and Mary alley. His father is buried directly in front of it. Mr. Harris was "born at the ferry," 1726; died, 1791; buried in Paxtang church-yard.

c. The ferry house, now occupied as a public school-house—built of logs, weather-boarded, low ceilings, large rooms—just below the present Harris Park, on Paxtang place, about 200 yards below the Harris Mansion.

d. Robert Whitehill; he resided at the present village of Whitehill, where there is a large soldiers' orphans' school. He was born in Lancaster county, 1736, and died in Cumberland, 1813, and is buried in Silvers Spring church-yard. He was long in public service— assemblyman and congressman—for more than twenty years.

e. It was the residence of Gen. Michael Simpson, is yet standing, and is very spacious. It is directly opposite the Penna. Steel Works; they are at the "Chamber's ferry" of 1750. Simpson was a lieutenant at the storming of Quebec, and went through the Revolution with great credit. He was brother-in-law to Rev. Col. John Elder, had three wives, but left no issue. Born in Paxtang, 1748, died 1813, buried under a handsome monument in Paxtang church-yard. At his death he was Major-General of the Pennsylvania Militia. See, also, *Campaign against Quebec*, by John Joseph Henry, Albany, 1877, p. 30.

NOTES AND QUERIES.—XXI.

MORDAH (N. & Q. xix).—John Mordah, who died in December, 1744, left an unmarried daughter, Eleanor. On the sixth of November, 1746, she married James Brown, son of John Brown, of Paxtang, —of whose descendants we are in hope of obtaining full information.

ISENHOUR.—Casper Isenhour died prior to 1803, and left a wife, Mary, and children, John, Mary, Elizabeth and Catharine. Information is wanted as to the ancestor of this person, and also of John Isenhour, who died about the same period, and left children, Margaret, Michael, Benjamin, Eve, Ann Mary, and Frenoni. Were not John and Casper brothers?

SIMPSON (N. & Q. i.).—Samuel Simpson, of Paxtang, died in 1791. He left children as follows:
   i. Nathaniel.
   ii. Jane.

 iii. Margaret, m. William Harris (dec'd) who had John and Simpson, both dec'd.
 iv. Sarah, m. William Cook.
 v. Samuel.
 vi. Rebecca, m. Thomas Cavet.
 vii. Mary, m. Robert Taggart.
Samuel Simpson was a brother of the John Simpson referred to.

A HANOVER SPINSTER EIGHTY YEARS AGO.

 The heroine of the Soldier's Tale was not unlike Matty, the most notable girl in Hanover. Let me give you a sketch of her. A person of great force of character, quick witted, and a natural leader in her way. Like most uncultured persons, she used very plain language, spoke right out, and often used exceedingly rough expressions, a practice, by the way, more common seventy-five years ago than now. She associated with the young until fifty, and attended all the winter balls of the neighborhood; and further, as a matter of right and courtesy, led off the first dance. The contra dance was the fashion of those days, and when a particular difficult figure was to be "run," such as "the three merry dancers," or the "Jersey Hornpipe," *Matty* always led. Quadrilles she held as small game, but never could resist the fast and whirling mazes of the "Scotch Grounds."

 No funeral, wedding or other social gathering was complete without her presence and assistance Let me tell you as 'twas told to me, a few items of a wedding in Hanover eighty years ago.

 The elders and matrons of the neighborhood were patiently waiting in the great room of the house, disposed in a semi-circle converging towards the great "ten foot" fire-place, in which, on a block, sat an old lady smoking the old long clay pipe of that day. On a round turn-up tea-table stood a pitcher of water, a tumbler, a stem glass, and a decanter of whisky. In the great arm chair, with his massive hair plaited and clubbed, sat the Reverend Nathaniel Randolph Snowden. The youngsters were out of doors; but in a back bed-room might have been seen our old friend Matty preparing the bride for the floor. Around her and about her was a lot of young, giddy girls, of whom my mother was one, looking with intense interest upon the artistic performance.

 "Ah, Matty! why didn't *you* marry? didn't you never have any beaux?"

 "Well, dears, I never cared much about marrying; that thought always seemed to hamper me, and so I put it off, and off, and now of course I never will. But then as to beaux I had plenty, more than all of you will have put together. Why I never went to church but what one, and sometimes two, came to ride with me. Coming back home, I always managed to have a different one. There was plenty of nice young men, then."

" But, Matty, how happened it that you never fell in love, was'nt there some one amongst them that you liked well enough to marry?"

" Well no; but then there was one I liked better than the rest. He was very handsome, and what is more he dressed to perfection. His cocked beaver was of the finest quality, and then he wore broadcloth, think of that! You could see yourself in the buttons of his coat, beautiful shining brass. And then the frills at his shirt sleeves and bosom, were five inches long. His silver knee buckles and garters matched—wore gilded spurs on his fair topped boots, and then rode an elegant horse. Why you could have heard that horse snicker half a mile away, coming up the lane."

Here Mattie paused, lost in thought, and then slowly continued:

" He went to the army, and never came back—give me a pin, girls."

Such was Mattie—she lived all her long days, reaching beyond four-score—a maid—and died within my recollection. My father had so much respect for her, that he rode over to Hanover, ten miles, to attend her funeral. HIRAM RUTHERFORD.

OFFICERS OF THE REVOLUTION FROM PAXTANG AND HANOVER.

On the assessment lists of taxables, for the townships named, in 1780, we find the following persons who are designated by the titles prefixed:

Hanover for 1780.—Captain William Allen; Wm. Brown, Esq.; Sam'l Brown, jr., J. P.; Captain Daniel Bradley; Captain Ambrose Crain; Colonel Timothy Green; Captain Wm. Graham; Joseph Hutchison, J. P.; Major Abe Latcha; Wm. Montgomery, Esq.; Captain Wm. McCullough; Captain James McCreight; Col. John Rodgers; Wm. Stewart, quarter-master; Captain James Wilson; Lieutenant Wm. Young; Lieutenant James Rodgers; Second Lieutenant James Wilson; Second Lieutenant Henry Graham; Second Lieutenant Wm. Brandon; Second Lieutenant James Johnson; Second Lieutenant Baltzer Stone; First Lieutenant Mathew Gilchrist.

Paxtang for 1780.—Col. Robt. Elder; Major John Gilchrist; Captain

Hugh Robinson; Captain Andrew Stewart; Rev. Joseph Montgomery; Captain Jonathan McClure; Captain George McMullen; First Lieutenant John Mathews; Second Lieutenant William McMullen; Abner Wickersham; [was a brother of Elisha Wickersham, and a partner in business. They laid out the town at the mouth of Swatara.]

Dr. Robert Canady, of Middletown; First Lieutenant Wm. Montgomery; Second Lieutenant Geo. Tevebaugh; First Lieutenant John Hallebaugh; Captain Samuel Cochran; Abraham Eagley, Matthew Smith, Esq., Robert Rowland and John Chambers. Jacob Haldeman, 1779; Hugh Crocket, 1779; James Eaton, of Middletown, was a prisoner in 1779.

YE ANCIENT INHABITANTS—IV.

EAST END OF HANOVER—1751.

	s.	d.		s.	d.
Peter Hedrek,	9	6	Samuel Ensworth,		
Niclos Warner,	3	0	John Martin,	3	0
Milchor Hendrey,	3	0	Widow Brown,	3	6
Thomas Proner,	3	6	John Hums,	4	0
Hendrey Bachman,	3	6	Andrew McMeken,	1	0
Conrad Clett,	3	6	Tomas Preast,	4	0
Anthony Rosbom,	4	0	John Tomson,	2	6
Jacob Madgher,	3	6	Jams Graham,	3	0
Philap Mosear,	4	0	Jacob Bicer,	3	0
Isac Pickhar,	3	6	Lasares Stewart,	3	0
Jacob Pickhar,	3	6	John Coningham,	3	0
William Clark,	2	6	William Coningham,	4	0
John Tibbins,	3	0	Stufal Seas,	2	6
John Sheaner,	3	6	John Mires,	3	0
James Young,	2	6	Tomas Shiralo,	2	6
John Gilleland,	3	6	Patrick Broon,	2	0
Petter Halmer,	3	6	John Andrew,	3	0
Widow Werek,	3	6	John Stran,	3	6
Fredrek Hoak,	3	6	David Strain,	2	6
Jams Sloan,	2	6	Georg Shekley,	3	0
Widow Gilaland,	2	6	Anthony McCreight,	3	0
Jacob Sops,	3	6	Walter Bell,	3	9
John Sops,	3	6	Leonard Long,	3	0
Rudey Hoke,	3	0	Adam McKelvry,	2	6
Joseph Hufe,	4	0	John Henderson,	2	0
Benjamen Clark,	3	6	John McClure,	4	0
Kilen Mark,	3	6	William Woods,	2	6
Georg Tittel,	3	6	John Porterfield,	2	0
Isac Williams,	3	6	Robert Hestlet,	2	0
John Wearer,	3	0	John Crafart,	4	0
Adam Cleman,	3	0	William Watson,	3	9
Adam Casnet,	2	6	Hendrey Conts,	3	0

Historical and Genealogical. 143

	s.	d.		s.	d.
Jams Williams,	3	0	Jams Greler,	2	0
Anthony Tittel,	3	0	John Crage,	2	6
Dinis Keril,	2	6	Thomas Strain,	1	6
Mattis Poor,	3	0	Hugh McKoun,	3	6
John Sloan,	3	0	John Dikson,	3	6
Samuel Sloan,	3	0	Joseph Willson,	3	6
Danil Ankel,	3	6	Adam Millar,	3	9
William Young,	4	6	Edward McMurey,	3	0
Abraham Williams,	4	5	Jacob McCormick,	2	6
James Clark,	3	0	John Ramsey,	1	6
Martin Light,	4	0	Jams Stewart,	4	0
Adam Reed,	4	0	Petter Stewart,	1	6
Lodwick Sheets,	4	0	Humphrey Coningham,	1	6
John Stewart,	3	0	Robart Kirkwood,	2	0
John Foster,	3	6	Jams McCoorey,	2	6
John Andrew,	3	6	William Tomson,	2	6
Walter McFarland,	3	0	Tomas Strain,	1	6
Lorz Brightbill,	4	6	Mathis Plants,	3	0
William Robison,	3	0	Jacob Stoner,	3	0
Philap Coulp,	3	6	William Stoner,	3	0
Onwalt Iagle,	2	6	Bris Innis,	4	0
Thomas Croil,	2	6	Jams Tode,	3	0
Alexander Swan,	3	6	John Young,	4	0
Alexander Tomson,	2	0	Jams Dixon,	3	0
John Graham,	3	0	Barnet McNite,	1	6

freemen.

	s.	d.		s.	d.
Robert Bricon,	6	0	Willm. Kithcart,	6	0
Wlllm. Brison,	6	0	Willm. Crosbey,	6	0
David Andrews,	6	0	Benjamon Enswarth,	6	0
David Stephenson,	6	0	Patrick Brown,	6	0

Collector, JACOB MUSER.

WEST END OF HANOVER—1751.

	s.	d.		s.	d.
Jas. Rodgers,	3	6	Widow McDeormand,	2	0
Seth Rodgers,	4	6	Michial Neal,	2	0
Hugh Rodgers,	3	0	Henry Hart,	2	0
Sam'l Starat,	3	0	Robt. Humes,	3	6
Widow Rodgers,	9	0	James Roboson,	3	0
Jos. McKnit,	3	0	James Ripet,	1	6
Jas. Beard,	3	6	Mathew Snodey,	2	6
Robt. Porterfield,	2	0	Hanal Martin,	2	0
Matthew Thornton,	3	6	John McCormick,	3	0
Wm. Rodger,	3	6	Jos. Willson,	3	6
Wm. Thompson,	2	6	John Stream,	2	5
Sam'l Todd,	2	6	Gain Stream,	2	6
George Jonson,	2	6	Robt. Park,	3	6
John Brown,	3	0	Jas. Park,	3	6
John McCavit,	3	0	Hugh Willson,	2	0
James McCavit,	3	0	Jas. Willson,	3	6
Thos. french,	2	6	Robt. Wallace,	3	6

144   *Notes and Queries.*

	s.	d.		s.	d.
Jas. french,	2	6	Robt. Snodgres,	4	0
Jas. finney,	3	0	Wm. McClenahan,	2	5
Thos. Sharp,	3	0	Dutchman in Jno. Harris's place,	2	0
John Sharp,	3	0	Jos. Ripet,	1	0
John Dobins,	2	6	David McClennaihan, sr.,	3	6
Widow McKoun,	2	0	Alexd. Banot,	4	6
John Hill,	2	6	David McClennaihan, jr.,	3	6
Philip Roboson,	2	6	Daniel Shaw,	2	6
Jas. Brown,	2	6	Samuel Stuart,	3	6
Sam'l Brown,	12	6	Robt. Love,	3	0
Willim Erwen,	2	6	Wm. Lurd,	2	0
Sam. Barnat,	2	6	John Hutchison,	3	6
Alex. Mungumrey,	2	6	Samuel Young,	1	0
Thos. Bell,	1	6	John McNealey,	2	6
Samu'l Robison,	5	0	Jas. McConnel,	1	0
Jas. Ridell,	2	0	Thos. Russel,	1	0
Thos. McQuire,	2	6	Charles McClure,	3	6
John McCord,	3	0	John Woods,	3	0
Robt. Houston,	2	6	Andrew Woods,	4	6
John Gamble,	2	6	Mathew Tylor,	2	0
John Henry,	3	0	Andrew Walker,	2	0
Gain Jonston,	2	0	Robt Martin,	2	6
Thos. McClure,	3	0	James Willson,	2	6
Wm. Barnett,	3	0	George Miller,	2	6
And'r. Wallace,	3	0	John McClure,	4	6
Richard Jonston,	2	6	Pattrick Greacy,	4	6
Josias Whyte,	2	6	Wm. Cooper,	3	0
John Snoddy,	2	6	Thos. Martin,	3	0
John Cooper,	2	6	John Stueart,	3	0
Thos. Cooper,	2	6	Thomas Robinson,	4	0
Francis McClure,	2	6	Dutchman in John Brown's place,	3	0
John Knox,	2	6			

freemen.

James Wallace,	6	0	Michael Wallace,	6	0

Colector, SAMUEL ROBOSON.

NOTES AND QUERIES.—XXII.

ETTLEY.—David Ettley, of Middletown, died in 1781, and left children as follows:
    i. John Philip.
    ii. Conrad.
    iii. David.
    iv. Christina, m. Michael Conrad.
    v. Catherina, m. Christopher Heppeth, [Heppick.]

PENNSYLVANIA GENEALOGIES.—While the descendants of the Puritans and of the Dutch of New York have carefully preserved their family memorials, there have not been, until recently, any efforts made by Pennsylvanians, especially those of the German and Scotch-Irish, towards the compilation of family genealogies. In our own locality but few have been prepared, yet we are glad to learn that quite a number of our families are looking up the records of their ancestors for permanent preservation. This is a duty we all owe to the memory of a revered and pious ancestry, and even though the records be meagre, there is no one who cannot assist in the performance of this noble work—nor is it too late to begin. Those to come after us will honor the labors thus bestowed, even if we do not receive while living, the reward for well-doing.

Several years ago, the Rev. Dr. Robinson prepared the Robinson Memorial; A. Boyd Hamilton, Esq., the Hamilton Record, and J. R. Hoffer, a Genealogy of the Hoffer family. With the exception of families to which Dauphin county families may perchance be allied, and printed elsewhere, no other published genealogies are known to us. Recently, however, A. K. Fahnestock, Esq., has had printed in very neat form, a record of the Fahnestocks, and it is this work which has prompted these remarks upon the subject of Family Genealogies. It is a matter worthy of our most earnest and filial consideration—for he who cares nothing about his ancestry, is only "fit for treason, stratagem, and spoils."

CORRESPONDENCE OF THE REVOLUTION.

We have been favored with a portion of the correspondence of General Henry Miller, some of which is very interesting, and as opportunity will allow, will print an occasional letter or document. The one herewith given is valuable in so far as it relates to the news of an engagement between the British and American forces at or near Guilford Court House, North Carolina.

The battle of Guilford Court House, North Carolina, to which this letter relates, took place on the 15th of March, 1781, concerning full particulars of which we must refer our readers to Ramsey, Marshall and Lossing. It was a battle, in its effects highly beneficial to the cause of the patriots, though resulting in a nominal victory for the British army. Both of the belligerents displayed consummate courage and skill, and the flight of the North Carolina militia from a very strong position, is the only reproach which either army deserved. It doubtless caused the loss of victory to the Americans. Marshall justly observed "that no battle in the course of the war reflects more honor on the courage of the British troops than that of Guilford." The number of the Americans engaged in the action was quite double that of the British—though it must be borne in mind that two-thirds of these troops were raw militia; and not as Lossing observes "a much superior force"—beside the advantage of the position. The battle lasted almost two hours and many brave men fell upon that field of carnage.

WILLIAM AUGUSTUS ATLEE, the writer of this letter, was the eldest son of John Atlee and Jane Alcock, born in Philadelphia, July 1, 1735. Removing with his parents to Lancaster at an early day, he studied law under Edward Shippen, Esq. He was admitted to the bar August 3, 1756, and soon became prominent in his profession as one of the leading lawyers of his day. He was elected chief burgess of the borough of Lancaster, Sept. 15, 1770, to which position he was thrice subsequently chosen, and administered the duties of said office up to Sept., 1774. At the breaking out of the Revolution, he became active in the cause of the Colonies and was chosen chairman of the Committee of Safety for Lancaster county. On the 16th of August, 1777, he was appointed by the Supreme Executive Council second Judge of the Supreme Court of the State, his associates being Thomas McKean and John Evans. During the years 1777 and 1778 in addition, he held the position of commissary to the British prisoners confined at Lancaster. On the 9th of August, 1784, he was re-appointed Judge of the Supreme Court, and under the Constitution of 1790, appointed by Gov. Mifflin, August 17, 1791, President Judge of the district, composed of the counties of Dauphin, Lancaster, York and Chester, which he filled up to his death, September 9, 1793. As a member of the Supreme bench of Pennsylvania, he rendered efficient service; and it is somewhat noteworthy, says Mr. Harris, that a remarkable uniformity of opinion is observed in the proceedings of the Supreme Court at that early day. Lord Mansfield, speaking of Dallas' Reports in 1791, used the following language: "They do credit to the court, the bar, and the reporter. They show readiness in practice, liberality in principle, strong reason, and legal learning." Judge Atlee was a gentleman noted for his high-toned integrity and strong adherence to his sense of right.

HENRY MILLER, to whom the letter was written, was a native of Lancaster county, Penna., born Feb. 13, 1751. Brought up on the paternal farm, he was, nevertheless, well educated, and pursuing the bent of his inclination, he began the study of law and conveyancing with Colinson Read, of Reading. Before completing his studies he removed to Yorktown, where he pursued his law course under the direction of Samuel Johnston, then prothonotary of York county, young Miller acting as his clerk. He was appointed collector of the excise for York county in 1772, 1773 and 1774, in which latter year he became a clerk in the office of Charles Lukens, then sheriff of the county. In 1775 he went out as first lieutenant of Captain Michael Doudle's company, one of the earliest military companies which reached Boston after the battle of Bunker Hill. Owing to Captain Doudle's impaired health, that officer subsequently resigned, and Lieutenant Miller was appointed to the command of the company.

On March 12, 1777, Capt. Miller was promoted by Congress to major of the First Pennsylvania regiment, and in the following year he was appointed lieutenant-colonel of the Second regiment. Col. Miller took an active and gallant part in the several battles of Long Island, White Plains, Trenton, Princeton, Head of Elk, Brandywine, Germantown, Monmouth, and a considerable number of other, but less important, conflicts. Owing to pecuniary circumstances—financial embarrassments at home—in the spring of 1779, he resigned his commission in the army and returned to his family at York. In October, 1780, he was elected sheriff of the county, and as such continued in office until November, 1783. From 1782 to 1786 he served as a member of the General Assembly of the State. In May of the latter year he was commissioned prothonotary of York county, and in August subsequent appointed a justice of the court of common pleas. He was a member of the constitutional convention of 1789-90, and under that constitution was re-appointed prothonotary, serving until 1794.

During the so-called Whisky Insurrection he served as quartermaster general. The same year he was appointed by President Washington supervisor of the revenue for the district of Pennsylvania, serving until 1801, when he was removed by President Jefferson.

In November of the latter year (1801), General Miller removed to Baltimore, where he entered mercantile pursuits. The war of 1812, however, re-kindled the fires of his youthful feeling and, relinquishing the cares of business, he accepted the appointment of brigadier general of the militia of the United States, stationed at Baltimore, and charged with the defense of Fort McHenry and its dependencies. Upon the enemy's leaving the Chesapeake bay the troops were discharged, and he again retired to private life.

In the spring of 1813 General Miller returned to Pennsylvania. He purchased a farm at the mouth of the Juniata river, in Perry county, and devoted himself to agricultural pursuits. In 1814, however, he was again called from his retirement, and he marched out with the Pennsylvania troops to Baltimore in the capacity of quartermaster general. Until the spring of 1821 he continued to reside on his farm. At that time he received and accepted the appointment by Governor Hiester of prothonotary of Perry county, when he removed to Landisburg, then the county seat, where he resided until he was retired from office by Governor Shulze, in March, 1824.

The Legislature of Pennsylvania, determined to show their high appreciation of the great services of General Miller to his State and country, although at a late period, in March, 1824, passed an act directing that the State Treasurer pay him immediately $240 and an annuity of the same sum during the remainder of his life. But the old warrior did not live long enough to enjoy this righteous provision. He removed about the same time with his family to Carlisle, where he was soon after taken suddenly ill, and died on Monday, the 5th of April, 1824, at the age of seventy-three. On the day following he was buried with military and Masonic honors at Carlisle. One of the most genial of men, General Miller, in public life, was brave, energetic and spirited. His biography, as of many another Pennsylvania worthy, deserves to be fully written, as a bright example to the youth of the present day.

The following is the text of the letter in full:

William A. Atlee to Henry Miller.

LANCASTER, *ye 29th March, 1781.*

SIR: I have just now received the enclosed Letter & Warrant from the Chief Justice with a request to forward it to you by Express.

He writes me that they have a Letter from Governor Jefferson informing that Gen. Green with 4,000, chiefly militia, has had an engagement with Lord Cornwallis and about 2,500 regulars, about a mile and a half from Guilford Court House, on Thursday, the 15th instant. The action continued an hour & a half & was very bloody. General Green thought proper to retire about a mile & a half in good order, & Cornwallis was so crippled that he did not attempt to follow. The engagement would have been renewed the next day, but it proved rainy, & Captain Singleton who was in the action & brought the intelligence from camp to Governor Jefferson, then came away; he supposes there must have been another action as soon as the weather cleared up, as Gen'l Green's army were in high spirits and resolved upon it. It is conjectured (the returns not being made) that we have had about 300 killed & wounded, among the former Major Anderson & Captain Barrett, of the Maryland Line; and among the latter, General Stevens, shot in the thigh & brought off, & Captain Fontleroy shot also in the thigh & left on the field. The enemy are said to have between 500 & 700 killed & wounded.

Also, that on the same a battle was fought between the French and British fleets near the Capes of Virginia; it continued an hour & 45 minutes. The British were considerably superior in number & force, haviug 12 ships to 9, and the consequence was that the British got into Chesapeak & the French returned to Rhode Island, without a vessel being taken or lost on either side.

You will oblige me if you will mention to Mr. Zachary Shugart of your town, that I shou'd be very glad to see him here, if he cou'd make it suit him to take a ride this far—the Council having requested me to make some inquiry of him respecting some transactions of some of our people while on Long Island.

Please my compliments to Col. Hartley & your Family.

I am, sir, with esteem,

Your most obedt. Servt.

WILLI'M A. ATLEE.

HENRY MILLER, Esquire.

Indorsed: To Henry Miller, Esquire, High Sheriff of York County —p. Mr. Killar, Express.

The letter and warrant enclosed, to which reference is made in the correspondence, relates to the arrest of one of the Rankin brothers for treason. Concerning this family of tories we hope to obtain additional data and information, in order that the citizens of our State may learn the more of the justice meted out to them, and for which their descendants seek to claim damages from the Commonwealth.

PATRIOTIC HANOVER.

On the 7th of November, 1782, John Dickinson, the author of the "Farmer's Letters," and at the outset of the Revolution, one of the most energetic in the cause of American Rights, was elected by the Assembly of the State, and the Supreme Executive Council, President of the State of Pennsylvania, under the Constitution of 1776. Although Mr. Dickinson was formost in the defense of the liberties of the Colonies, when the resolutions for Independence came before the Continental Congress, he believed, and no doubt sincerely, too, that the "Declaration" was premature, and was one of the members who was not returned to Congress by the Convention of July 15, 1776. There is no doubt that had he been chosen, his name would have been affixed to that instrument. His course during the debates on Mr. Lee's resolve, made him unpopular, and for several years he was not in active life. Nevertheless he was not an idle spectator, and in October, 1777, he was made a brigadier-general in the Pennsylvania militia, having previously been in command of a Philadelphia battalion doing active service in the Jerseys during Washington's campaign there. It was during this period that the officers of the Lancaster battalion became acquainted with the statesman Dickinson. General Williamson in 1779, was chosen by Delaware as one of her representatives in the Confederated Congress, and in 1781 he was President of that State. In obedience to the call from Pennsylvania, he accepted its Presidency, when at once it was maliciously reported that he was inimical to the Independence of the States. At this juncture his compatriots in arms sought his defence.

HANOVER, *November 28th, 1782.*
To the Colonels of the Lancaster county Militia:

DEAR SIR: The officers and representatives of the ninth battalion of Lancaster county Militia, upon consultation have concluded from the complexion of the present House of Assembly, that the Constitution and Liberty of the State are at stake in some measure; and sensible of the importance of what has cost us so much blood and treasure, we have thought it incumbent upon us to exert ourselves for their preservation as far as our influence extends, and to warn all who would wish to be free from the dangers that seem to impend, not doubting at the same time, but you are ready to take the alarm, as you must be sensible of the same danger. We do not think it necessary to multiply words, tending to inspire your spirit, for we are of opinion that you possess the same, and have been only waiting to know the sentiments of your fellow friends to *Liberty.* Let us not then cooly and simply suffer any of our rights to be taken from us by any men, especially as our Constitution invests us with full power to oppose any such attempt. Perhaps our fears are groundless; but in case of apparent danger, which undoubtedly is our present case, a wise man will be on his guard; and therefore let such a number of persons as you will please to appoint meet us at Manheim, on the 15th day of January next, in order that we may mutually contrive such measures as may have a tendency to preserve our good and estimable Constitution and our dear Independence and sweet Liberty. Be active and do not fail to fulfill our request. By order of the whole. JOHN RODGERS, *Colonel.*

In pursuance of the foregoing circular, the deputies from the different battalions met at Manheim, on the 15th of January following. There were present at that meeting the following:

Colonels—Thomas Edwards, Ziegler, Alexander Lowrey, George Ross, John Rodgers and Robert Elder.

Majors—Jacob Cook, Kelly, Hays and Herr.

Captains—Ewing, Joseph Hubley and Laird.

Mr. Clark and Mr. Chambers.

On motion, Colonel Rodgers was unanimously chosen Chairman, and Captain Joseph Hubley, Secretary.

Colonel Rodgers made a neat and appropriate speech explaining the objects of the meeting, that a rumor was in circulation calculated to do much injury, "that the President of the State of Pennsylvania was hostile to the Independence of America."

On motion, this question was put to each battalion:

Is it the opinion of the members present that they approve of the appointment of John Dickinson, Esq., as President of the State of Pennsylvania, or not?

Answer. The members of the Second Battalion are unanimously of the opinion that a better choice of a President could not be made.

Colonel Zeigler—Same opinion.

Seventh Battalion—Same.

Eighth Battalion—Same.

Ninth Battalion—We hope the Assembly have made a good choice, and if they have we thank them.

Colonel Elder agrees in opinion with the Ninth.

The following resolves, after being duly prepared and unanimously agreed to, were ordered to be forthwith communicated to the Assembly, the Supreme Executive Council, and to every battalion in the State.

Resolved, unanimously, That the people have a right to assemble together for their common good, to instruct our Representatives, and to apply to the Legislature for redress of grievances, by address, petition, or remonstrance.

Resolved, unanimously. That in the opinion of the deputies from the different battalions now met, that the complexion of the present House of Assembly is such that we have no reason to doubt that the Independence and Constitution of this State are safe, and that we highly approve of the appointment of his Excellency John Dickinson, Esq., as President.

Resolved, unanimously, That we approve of Colonel Rodgers' calling this meeting, as it has tended to remove doubts and unjust charges that were in circulation to the disadvantage of his Excellency the President of this State, and two of our Members of Congress, James Wilson and John Montgomery, Esquires; and we conceive such meetings have a tendency to suppress false and malicious reports, and that thereby virtue may meet with its just reward and vice be depicted in its true deformity.

(Signed)   JOHN RODGERS, *Chairman.*

J. HUBLEY, *Secretary.*

Of the Col. Rodgers, whose motion instigated this meeting, which speaks so well for the intelligent patriotism of not only then Lancaster county but the township of Hanover, we hope ere long to give further particulars.

NOTES AND QUERIES.—XXIII.

THE "INDIAN TOWN." (N. & Q. iv.)—Neither Paxtang nor Derry church were located on this tract of land. The plantation in question was "scituate in Hannover Township, upon the north side of Suetara creek, adjoyning to David Wilson;" so reads the survey which was made August 9, 1737. It also gives this important information, "whereon he, the Rev. William Bartrem, minister, has been five years settled." The original tract contained three hundred and fifty acres—considerable more land than any minister would like to cultivate now-a-days.

REV. JOSEPH MONTGOMERY.—A correspondent calls our attention to the fact that in Harris Biographical History of Lancaster county, is the statement that Joseph Montgomery, member of the Assembly from Lancaster county, in 1782, was from the city of Lancaster, and the ancestor of John R. Montgomery, a lawyer of that place, etc. We do not know how such an egregious blunder could have been made. The Joseph Montgomery who represented the county at that period, was the Rev. Joseph Montgomery, of Paxtang —one of the most noted men in central Pennsylvania at that day, and of whom, we hope to present a full and interesting biographical sketch ere long.

THE ANTI-MASONIC INVESTIGATION OF 1836.—I see my venerable friend "C. F. M." is fighting his old battles over again and appears determined at least to convince the old ghost of Anti-Masonry, that there is "a punishment after death." And poor old Thad., who lies so quietly in his grave at Lancaster, will no doubt feel bad about it if he can. "C. F. M." tells of one scene in his subject which it is probable he did not see at all, and that is the appearance of the Rev. Mr. Sproule, before Mr. Stevens' committee. "C. F. M." says Mr. Sproule stood fifty feet from the committee when he read his "protest." The only time I ever saw that committee in session was on that particular occasion. It was in the Supreme Court room. The committee sat in front of the judge's stand. The witnesses were on their right, and the spectators were outside the "bar." I was a few feet from Mr. Sproule and he perhaps a dozen from the committee. If he bandied words with chairman Stevens, I have no remembrance of it; certainly Mr. Stevens was not a meek nor a patient man enough to tolerate it. Mr. Sproule's protest was read in a low tone, out was remarkable for the superior character of its composition. His climacteric sentence was, to my recollection, much as "C. F. M." states—"If it is your purpose [the committee's] to constitute yourselves into a political 'Car of Juggernaut, ROLL ON! But remember, that the cry of your crushed and bleeding victims will ascend to HIM who hath declared, that it were better for *you* that a mill-stone were hanged about *your* necks, and '——.'" Mr. Stevens stopped him and would not permit him to utter the closing words."

PETER BIZALLION'S WILL.

A very interesting sketch of perchance the first "squatter" in this locality, Peter Bizallion, was prepared several years ago by Mr. A. Boyd Hamilton. Since then, however, additional information has been obtained relative to Bizallion, and what is interesting—his Will, which is herewith given. From this it will be seen that he died in Chester county, and not on the Ohio, as was then supposed. For these records we are indebted to our venerable friend, Gilbert Cope, of West Chester.

"I Peter Bizallion of East Caln in the County of Chester and Province of Pennsylvania, yeoman, being Antient and weak in Body but of sound mind and memory, thanks be given unto God, But Calling to mind the uncertainty of this Life do therefore make this pressent writing my Last will and Testament, hereby annulling and making void all other wills and Testaments heretofore by me made, Either by word or Writing, and as touching such worldly Eastate as it hath pleased God to bless me in this Life, I give. Devise, and Dispose of the same in the following manner & form: first, it is my will and I do order that in the first place all my Just Debts and Funeral Charges be paid and satisfied. Item, my will is and I give and bequeath the sum of five Pounds to such poor people as my Executrix shall think fit. Item, I give to my well Beloved wife Martha Bizallion (whom I likewise Constitute and Ordain my only and sole Executrix of this my last will and Testament) all and singular my Real Estate, Lands and Tenements, to her, her heirs, and assigns forever, as also all the residue & Remainder of my Personal Estate, money, Goods, Chattels, and all of my negroes, viz: Betty, Ned, Jo, Nanny, Su, Judy, Prudence and Abigail. In witness whereof I have hereunto voluntarily & sensibly set my hand and seal this Ninth day of January in the year of our Lord one Thousand seven hundred and forty one two. PIERRE BIZALLION. [L. S.]

"*Witnesses*—William Pim, Robert Miller, George Larow, Wm. Harlan.

"Proved Aug. 31, 1742. Letters to Martha."

The signature is in a very trembling hand, almost illegible. The following additional record is given in connection with the foregoing:

An Invitary of The Goods and Chattels of Peter Bezellon, Discesed viz:

	£	S.	P.		£	S.	P.
To his waring a Perril and Cash,	5	0	0	To ten horses and mairs,	50	0	0
To Books	1	0	0	To thirty-two shepe,	7	10	0
To four beds and fornitour	20	0	0	To Whete, Ry, otes, in ye stack and Barne,	50	0	0
To two Pare of draws and two tabels, one chest	6	10	0	To two Plows one harrah,	2	0	0
To twelve Chears and three spining wheels	2	0	0	To one Wagin and Ceart,	12	10	0
To Pots, Puter and Brace	2	10	6	To Gears for six horseses,	3	10	6
To a sarvent Boye	5	0	0	To axes, hose, and other working Toules,	1	15	6
To negros	120	0	0	To Bonds,	182	10	0
To Eaight Cows and six stears,	36	0	0	To Bills,	45	19	5
To three yearlings and seven Calves,	9	0	0	To Book Depts,	0	10	0
					£573	05	11

"Appraised by us this ninth day August one Thousand seven hundred and forty-two.   ROBERT MILLER,

[Filed August 31, 1742.]   JAMES LOVE.

"Dec. 22, 1762.—Martha Bizallion, widow of Peter Bizallion late of East Caln. Deed to her nephew John Hartt of East Caln for 158 acres and allowance in East Caln in consideration of love and natural affection and the sum of £5." This was patented Feb. 5, 1740, to Peter and Martha Bizalion (A vol. 9, p. 421) and became vested in the latter by right of survivorship as well as by the will of Peter. It was adjoining other land of Peter and Martha, perhaps a mile or more east of the present Coatesville.

SWAN FAMILY RECORD.

In the *New England Historical and Genealogical Register* for October, 1879, Dr. William B. Lapham, of Augusta, Me., contributes a genealogy of the Swan family of New England. As the surnames of the family correspond or rather are identical with those of the family who settled in this locality, we have been induced to give so much as we have been able to glean from the court and other records relating to them, with the hope that some of the descendants will fill up the gaps which occur.

The family of Swan is of English origin, but the ancestor of the Swans, who settled in Hanover and Paxtang townships, was one of the one hundred English families whom King James of England placed in possession of an equal number of Irish confiscated estates. At what time Richard Swan came with his family to America we have no record—nor of all his children, save the names of six sons.

Upon an examination of the records of the Land Department of the State, we have the following data:

"Alexander Swan had surveyed to him on the 23d of January, 1743, one hundred and fifty acres in Hanover township, adjoining land of Andrew Lachin and others."

"On the 25th of August, 1767, there was surveyed to Hugh Swan, two hundred and eighty-three acres of land, adjoining land of James Wallace, John Carson and the Blue Mountain, in Paxtang township."

"To Moses Swan there was surveyed, on the 8th of November, 1774, one hundred and fifty acres, adjoining land of William McRoberts on the north, Andrew Carson on the east, John Jameson on the south, and Alexander Johnson on the west, in Paxtang township."

Record of the Family of Richard Swan.

I. Richard Swan settled in Hanover township, Lancaster county, Penn'a, prior to 1738. His children were:
  2. *i. James*, b. 1711; m. Mary ———.
  3. *ii. Moses*, b. 1713; m. Jean Barnett.
       iii. Joseph, b. 1715; resided in Letterkenny township, Franklin county.
  4. *iv. William*, b. 1719; m. Jennett Shields.
  5. *v. Richard*, b. 1725.
  6. *vi. Alexander*, b. 1727; m. Martha Gilchrist.

II. James Swan, b. 1711 in Ireland, d. December, 1741, settled in Hanover township, Lancaster county, m. Mary ————, and had issue:
    i. James.
    ii. Alexander.
    iii. Margaret.
    iv. Mary.
    v. Jean.
    vi. Sarah, m. Robert Bill.

III. Moses Swan, b. 1713; settled in Paxtang township about 1730 m., in 1737, Jean Barnett, and had issue:
    i. Hugh, b. 1738.
  7. *ii. John*, b. 1740; m.
    iii. Isaac, b. 1742; d. unm.
    iv. Catharine, b. 1743; m. Thomas Porter, and had issue.

8.   *v. William*, b. 1743; m. Martha Renick.
  vi. Joseph, b. 1747.
  vii. Moses, b. 1749.
  viii. Jean, b. 1751.
  ix. Margaret, b. 1753.
9. *x. Richard*, b. 1757, m. Catharine Boggs.

IV. William Swan, b. 1719 in Ireland; settled in Hamilton township, Franklin county, and there d. Jan. 1773, m. Jennett Shields, and had:
 i. William.
 ii. Margaret.
 iii. Jennett.
 iv. Robert.

V. Richard Swan, b. 1725, settled in Philadelphia, a merchant, and was one of the signers to the non-importation revolutions of 1765.

VI. Alexander Swan b. 1727, in Ireland, settled in Hanover township, Dauphin county, d. March 1778; m. Martha Gilchrist, and had issue:
 i. Samuel.
 ii. Alexander.
 iii. Jean, m. James Taylor.
 iv. Mary, m. Wm. Owens.
10. *v. Margaret*, m. Thomas Finney.
 vi. Agnes, m. Andrew Armstrong.

VII. John Swan b. 1740, in Paxtang, removed to now Washington county, Penna., prior to 1771, and had issue among others,:
 i. John.
 ii. Thomas.

VIII. William Swan, b. 1745, in Paxtang; d. prior to 1787; m. in 1775, Martha Renick, and had issue:
 i. Margaret, b. 1776; m. James Ingram.
 ii. Sarah, b. 1779, m. Wm. Rutherford.
 iii. Moses, b. 1781; d. at Harrisburg, Sept. 11, 1822.
 iv. William, b. 1783.

IX. Richard Swan, b. in Paxtang, 1757; removed to Erie county in 1802, and d. there in April, 1808; m. Catharine Boggs, b. in Donegal, Feb. 8, 1759; and d. in Erie county, April, 1843. Had issue—all b. in Paxtang except viii:
 i. Lydia, b. Sept. 15, 1789, m. Joseph McCreary, d. April, 1867.
 ii. William-Boggs, b. Feb. 27, 1791; d. Feb. 10, 1792.
 iii. John-Joseph, b. Mar. 14, 1793; m. Eunice Ann White, d. July 22, 1878.

 iv. William, b. Nov. 25, 1794; removed to the West, and d. there about 1832, unm.
 v. Richard, b. Dec. 4, 1796, m. Margaret Boal Sturgeon, d. Sept. 11, 1811.
 vi. Moses, b. Dec. 9, 1798; d. June 30, 1833, at Galena, Ill.; m. Virginia Bates.
 vii. Andrew-Cavet, b. July 20, 1802; d. July, 1867, at Galena, Ill.; m. Angeline Mitchell.

X. Margaret Swan, dau. of Alexander, b. in Hanover, m. Thomas Finney and had issue:
 i. James.
 ii. Sarah.
 iii. Jennett.

XI. Margaret Swan, dau. of William, b. 1776; d. ——; m. Nov. 26, 1799, by Rev. Mr. Snowden, Major James Ingram, b. 1761; d. Aug. 12, 1811; and had issue—
 i. William.
 ii. Martha–Smith, m. William D. Boas.
 iii. Sarah.
 iv. James.
 v. Maria, m. Nathaniel Henry.

XII. Sarah Swan, b. 1779; d. June 17, 1852; m. William Rutherford, b. 1775; d. Jan. 17, 1850; and had issue.

Further information will be gladly received.

NOTES AND QUERIES.—XXIV.

ANTI-MASONIC INVESTIGATION IN 1836.—(N. & Q. xxiii.)—In a court of justice the jury are quietly obliged to listen to contradictory evidence, In your issue of Saturday evening, "H. R," gives his recollection of what Rev. Mr. Sproule said on that occasion. I happened to be present at the same time, in the north corner room over the Senate Chamber, and I am sorry to give a different version from "H. R.s" recollection. When Rev. Mr. Sproule was called, he was standing near the door, he advanced a pace or two and complained of the harsh treatment of the committee in tearing him away from his study, where he was preparing for the services of the sanctuary on the approaching Sabbath. "If you intend to become political oppressors *roll on your car of Juggernaut*," at this point and as quick as lightning Mr. Steven's hand came down on the table like a clap of thunder, at the same time crying *silence*. Mr. Sproule wanted to explain, but Stevens replied, "Not a word, you have insulted the Legislature already;" and he did not allow him to say another word.

ANOTHER WITNESS.

HOPE FIRE COMPANY IN 1814 AND 1816.—The following "List of the Hope Fire Company of Harrisburg who have been furnished with Badges," is furnished us by a gentleman who has been much interested in *Notes and Queries*. Those marked with a (*) were members in 1814. Only one on the roll survives—the genial and scholarly gentleman that he is—Samuel Shoch, Esq., of Columbia.

John Lyne,	*John H. Candor,	Thomas Martin,
Henry Antis,	John Whitehill,	—— Snyder,
John C. Bucher,	Samuel Sees,	John Williams,
William Smith,	*John M. Forster,	Samuel Shoch,
Alexander Graydon,	Jacob Bogler,	Andrew Krause,
Joseph Wallace,	Luther Reily,	Jacob Kimmel,
John Peacock,	J. Lindermuth,	—— Kurtz,
Henry Colestock,	—— Kroberger,	*Moses Musgrave,
Jacob Zollinger,	Charles Shaffer,	*David Gregg,
John Smith,	James Wright,	*Ezekiel Gregg,
Henry Smith,	Andrew Graydon,	*Zeno Fenn,
John A. Fisher,	W. Crist,	*John Wilson,
Jacob Hoyer.	James Scull,	*G. W. Hollis.
Wm. Roberts,	—— Hughes,	*G. Taylor,
James R. Boyd,	*John Kunkel,	*F. Scheaffer,
John Buffington,	Jacob Baughman,	*Hugh Roland,
Samuel Weistling,	Thomas Buffington,	*George Horter,
Joseph Youse,	*James Mitchel,	*George Mish,
Wm. Burns,		

REMINISCENCES OF THE OLD HOME.—Those who were familiar or on terms of intimacy with the late Robert Gillnor, Esq., will remember with what pleasure he related incidents connected with the Grahams and Fergusons, especially after his return from one of his visits to some of the descendants of those families resident in Kentucky. These are forcibly brought to our mind, as we peruse a letter written by the venerable John Graham of Hardin county, Kentucky, under date of September 27, 1867. He was then upwards of eighty-five years of age, and the letter written in lead pencil, betokens neither age or tremulousness. He thus alludes to events of the by-gone, being a native of Hanover.

. . . "You allude to the massacre of the Conestoga Indians near Lancaster. I have often heard my grandmother seak of that affair, and of the Paxtang boys or rangers. It was something like the tea party at Boston. The men who had done it were not known. Old Parson Elder was the Colonel of the regiment; the rank and file who were engaged in that affair were the most respectable of men. I had an old uncle, Thomas Bell (he was married to my grandfather's sister), he was an Elder in Hanover Church when I can recollect him first, and died an Elder in 1815. My grandmother always said that Uncle Bell was one of the squad who were at Conestoga, but was not an Elder in the church at the time. The reason for killing those Indians was that then and long before, there were a great many murders committed, and the friendly Indians harbored the strange Indians, who were the guilty parties. It was the only thing to do, and every person on the frontiers approved of the act.

THE LOCATION OF THE NATIONAL CAPITOL.

The following letters of WILLIAM MACLAY, of Harrisburg, one of the first Senators from Pennsylvania in the U. S. Congress, and of JASPER YEATES, the eminent lawyer of Lancaster, are, perhaps, sufficiently explanatory. However, it may not be generally known that had an earnest and energetic effort been made by the citizens of Lancaster and Pennsylvania, the Capitol of the United States would have been located on or near the Susquehanna. The defeat of the movement is due to the citizens and representatives of the metropolis, who, because the seat of Government was not permanently established at Philadelphia, opposed every other location. Perhaps it is is just as well; and viewing it from the present standpoint, had the National Capitol been located on the banks of the Ohio, it would have been a wiser selection on the part of the then representatives of the people.

NEW YORK, *March 13, 1789.*

SIR: I consider it as almost certain that the permanent residence of Congress will be agitated at the ensuing session. Desirous as I am to bring forward information from every part of Pennsylvania, to throw light on this important subject, you may guess my mortification at receiving no answers to my letters on this Head, from Lancaster. Let it suffice to say that you have been wrong, and be no longer so, but send me the Information which I requested. But you should not stop here. Mr. Hamilton should be spoke to, and he should furnish some Member of Congress with proposals under his Hand, relating to the terms on which he will give grounds for the public buildings and sell out-lots for private Persons. With all the pains you may take, it is possible you may not succeed, but without pains you need not expect it.

      I am, Sir, your most Obed.
        & very Hum. Servt.,
         Wm. Maclay.

To Jasper Yeates, Esq.

      Lancaster, *23d March, 1789.*

Dear Sir: Within this hour I have rec'd a letter from Mr. Maclay, a copy of which is subjoined; the Propriety of being peculiarly active at this Period strikes me very forcibly, I shall answer this letter immediately. I beg you will wait on Messrs. Clymer & Fitzsimons as soon as possible & inform them of yr. Intentions & Dispositions. A Letter from you to our friends in Congress, and particularly to some if not all our Representatives, should express the same matter fully and at large. In one word, My Dear Sir, I would almost, if not quite, give them a cart blanche.

Mr. John Hubley tells me this moment, that by a Letter which Parson Muhlenburg has received from his brother Frederick he is informed that Congress will in all probability settle at some place between the Delaware & Susquehanna. This is very encouraging. Do ask Clymer & Fitzsimons to see our map forwarded to them, and let me know yr. Sentiments.

     I am Dr., Sir,
      Very Affectionately Yrs.,
        J. Yeates.

Wm. Hamilton, Esq.

PARSON ELDER'S MARRIAGE RECORD FROM 1733 TO 1791.

At the request of a number of correspondents, at the same time in order to furnish to our readers with everything relating to the history and genealogy of this locality, we herewith present such marriage records of the Rev. John Elder as have been preserved to us. The record is one of great value, and being the earliest, is one of more than passing interest. The data within brackets have been added, not being on the original entry:

       1744.

June 14.—Richard Fulton and Isabella McChesney.
Sept. 16.—John Findlay and Elizabeth Harris.

1745.
April 3.—James Wilson and Martha Sterrett.
1748.
June 3.—William Plunket and Esther Harris.
1749.
May 3.—John Harris and Elizabeth McClure.
1751.
Nov. 5.—Rev. John Elder and Mary Simpson.
1752.
Oct. 4.—William Augustus Harris and Margaret Simpson.
June 1.—William McChesney and Esther (Say) Harris.
1757.
May 24.—William Kelso and ——— Simpson.
Feb. 11.—Samuel Allen and Rebecca Smith.
1766.
Dec.—John Hays and Eleanor Elder.
1768.
June 2.—James Harris and Mary Laird.
1769.
Feb 7.—Robert Elder [son of Rev. John] and Mary J. Thompson.
Feb. 16.—John Reid.
April 27.—James Cavet.
May 15.—William Smith.
Sept 12.—James Robinson and Martha Cochran.
Oct. 19.—William Brown and Sarah Semple.
Dec. 14.—William Christy.
1770.
Moses Wallace and Jean Fulton.
James Monteith and Margaret Maxwell.
1771.
Jan. 24.—Alexander Hetherington.
Jan. 31.—Thomas Simpson.
May 9.—Thomas McNair and Ann Maria Wallace.
May 30.—James Montgomery.
June 27.—Robert Rea [Wray].
July 15.—James Johnson.
Aug. 22.—John Gilchrist.

Sept 34.—Elijah Buck.
Nov. 4.—Benjamin Fulton.
Dec. 4.—Maxwell Chambers and Elizabeth ———
Dec. 12.—Benjamin Galbraith.

1772.

Jan. 2—James Rutherford and Margaret Brisban.
Feb. 6.—William Rodgers.
March —.—James Anderson and Margaret Chambers.
April 30.—Hugh Wilson and Isabella Fulton.
May 7.—James McFadden.
May 11.—James Shaw.
May 18.—James Thompson.
June 16.—Andrew Young.
Dec. 1.—William Dickey.

1773.

John Graham, of Allen township, and Sarah Brown, of Hanover.
William Wilson and Elizabeth Robinson.
Alex. McCullom and Mary Calhoun, both of East Pennsboro'.
Sept. 15.—Joshua Elder and Mary McAllister.
Oct. 14.—John Bell, of Cumberland co., and Martha Gilchrist.
Nov. 1.—William Forster and Margaret Ayres, both of Upper Paxtang.
Nov. 10.—Samuel Maclay and Elizabeth Plunket.

1774.

Jan. 9.—Mr. Dougal and Sarah Wilson.
Feb. 10.—Matthias Simpson.
March 15.—James McCormick and Isabella Dixon of Hanover.
March 31.—Alexander Johnson.
April 14.—William Curry and Agnes Curry.
April 21.—David Ramsey.
June 15.—John Gowdie and Abigail Ryan.
June 16—Alexander Wilson and Grizel Fulton.
June 24.—Samuel Bell and Ann Berryhill.
Aug. 13.—John Ryan and Jane Gowdie.
Aug. 25.—John Trousdale.
Sept. 15.—William Maclay and Mary Harris.
Sept. 29.—John Lerkin.

1775.

Jan. 17.—David Kennedy.
Jan. 31.—Andrew McClure.
March 7.—Daniel Curry.

April 13.—William Clark.
April 18.—Robert Moody and Margaret Hutchinson.
Sept. 19.—William Wallace.
Nov. 16.—Andrew Robinson and Jane Wilson.
Dec. 19.—William Swan and Martha Renick.

1776.

Jan. 12.—John Snodgrass.
Jan. 25.—James Walker and Barbara McArthur.
Feb. 13.—James Wilson.
March 14.—Samuel Rutherford and Susan Collier.
April 9.—Samuel Thompson.
April 14.—James Wylie.
April 25.—Thomas Miller.
May 7.—James McNamara.
May 7.—John Simpson and Margaret Murray, dau. of Capt. James Murray.
June 25.—John Templeton.
July 3.—Walter Jenkins.
Oct. 15.—Samuel Patton.
Nov. 28.—John Gourly.
Dec. 10.—Isaac Hodge and Margaret Wilson, both of Hanover.

1777.

Jan. 23.—David Wray of Derry and Mary Cowden of Paxtang.
March 23.—Richard McClure.
March 20.—James Cowden and Mary Crouch.
April 8.—Joseph Wilson and Margaret Boyd, both of Derry.
April 22.—David Pinkerton.
June 19.—John Thompson.
July 31.—Thomas Wylie.
Nov. 4.—Thomas Foster, of Buffalo, and Jane Young, of Hanover.
Dec. 4.—George Dixon.
Dec. 23.—James Kyle and Eleanor Carothers.

1778.

Jan. 13.—John Dickey.
Jan. 22.—George Crain.
April 9.—Archibald McAllister and ——— Hayes, of Derry.
April 30.—James Todd and Mary Wilson.
June 4.—William McHadden.
June 22.—Samuel Weir.
Sept. 10.—Hugh Robinson.
Sept. 10.—Jane Laird.
Dec. 10.—James McKinzie and Mary King.

1779.

April 12.—John McQuown [McEwen].
April 15.—Adam Means.
May 27.—James Harris.
Aug. 3.—Joseph McClure.
Sept. 14.—William Moore and ——— Boyd.
Sept. 23.—Samuel McTeer and ——— Quigley.
Sept. 23.—Ann Elder, daughter of Rev. John and Andrew Stephen.
Oct. 5.—Andrew Duncan.
Nov. 11.—John Gray and Mary Robinson.
Nov. 15.—David Watson.
Dec. 14.—James Donaldson.
Dec. 23.—William Sterrett, jr.

1780.

Jan. 13.—John Chesney.
Jan. 25.—Joseph Fulton.
June 29.—Samuel Hutchinson and Jane Rutherford.
July 13.—James Dickey.
July 20.—John Lyttle.

1781.

Feb. 27.—Richard McGuire and Eleanor Gilchrist.
March 1.—James Robinson and ——— Boyce.
March 6.—John Fleming and Nancy Neill.
March 8.—John Shearl and Margaret Thom.
April 3.—John Patterson and Jane Johnston.
April 12.—John Maxwell and Mary Houston.
May 10.—William Young and Martha Wilson.
June 21.—William Trousdale and Elizabeth Glen.
Nov. 13.—Matthew Gilchrist and Elizabeth Crouch.
Dec. 11.—Samuel McCord and Martha McCormick.
Dec. 18.—William Sawyers and Mary Sawyers.

1782.

Jan. 31.—Thomas Smiley and Ann Tucker.
March 31.—James Reid.
April 1.—Hugh Swan.
April 8.—Hugh Ramsey and Margaret McHargue.
May 6.—John Lewis.
May 9.—James Spence.
May 14.—Samuel Russell.
Aug. 8.—Francis McClure.

Aug. 19.—Lambert Van Dyke.
Dec. 31.—Richard King and Mary Wylie, both of Paxtang.

1783.

Jan. 23.—James McCleester and Sarah Roan.
Feb. 25.—Joseph Green, of Hanover, and Sarah Awl, of Paxtang.
Feb. 27.—Matthew Caldwell, of Sewickly, and Mary Pinkerton.
March 11.—Joseph Wilson and Margaret Boyd.
May 12.—Edward Jackson and Margaret Lewis.
May 27.—Joshua Elder and Sarah McAllister.
Aug. 7.—John Clark and Mary Smith.

1784.

March 2.—Robert Boal and Mary Wilson.
March 20.—William McCormick and Grizel Porter, both of Derry.
April 15.—George Williams and Ann Meley.
May 18.—James Wilson and Mary Elder.
June 3.—John McDonald and Lydia Sturgeon.
June 7.—Christopher Irwin and Mary Fulk, both of Londonderry.
Oct. 21.—Robert Keys and Elizabeth Cowden.
Nov. 9.—Duncan Sinclair and Hannah Templeton.
Nov. 9.—Moses Gilmore and Isabella Wallace.
Dec. 14.—Robert Foster and Esther Rennick.

1785.

Jan. 3.—William Buck and Margaret Elliott, both of Derry.
March 7.—James Smith Polk and Jean Fullion.
March 15.—Robert Templeton and Mary Boyd.
April 28.—Alexander Wilson and Elizabeth Carson.

1786.

April 11.—David Calhoun and Eleanor King.
April 13.—Joseph Hutchinson, of Paxtang, and Sarah Cathcart, of Hanover.
Dec. 19.—John Wylie and Sarah Whitley.
Dec. 19.—Patrick Murray and Mary Brereton Beatty.

1788.

March 13.—David Ramsey and Martha Graham.
April 3.—David Mitchel and Susanna Wilson, both of Derry.
May 1.—William McIlhenny and Elizabeth McNeal.
June 19.—James Wallace and Sarah Elder.
Nov. 20.—James Henderson and Margaret Wiggins.
Nov. 20.—John Culbertson and Mary Augeer.

1788.

Jan. 18.—John Elder and Sarah Kennedy.
Jan. 13.—Thomas White and Jane Spence.
Feb. 12.—James Laird and Mary McFarland.
March 11.—Joseph Sawyers and Elizabeth McFarland.
    James Anderson and Esther Thom.
Sept. 27.—Thomas Hamilton and Mary Kyle.

1789.

March 3.—Samuel Sloan and Prudence Walker.

1790.

Feb. 5.—Samuel Hill and Nancy Beatty.
Oct. 14.—Charles Clark and Elizabeth Robinson.

1791.

April 4.—John Laird and Rachel ———

NOTES AND QUERIES.—XXV.

HARRIS—SIMPSON.—By the records at Lancaster I find that Simpson Harris, a soldier of the First Pennsylvania Regiment of the Revolution, died in hospital at Ashley Hill, near Charleston, S. C., on the 2nd of November, 1782. He was the nephew of John Harris and Nathaniel Simpson, to whom he left his personal property. John Hilsdorph, the surgeon's mate of the First Pennsylvania Regiment, was with him when he died.   S. E.

MORDAH—BROWN (N. & Q. xix., xxii.)—You stated that when John Mordah died in 1744, he left an unmarried daughter, Eleanor. This same Eleanor, who was born in 1724, married, November 6, 1746, James Brown, one of the oldest of the seven sons of John Brown, of Paxtang. She died in 1752. In due time James Brown married Mary McClellan, and removed to the Conedoguinet, between Carlisle and Newville. From this last marriage sprang some of the Browns of Kentucky, and those of Brown's Mills, Mercer county, Pa., and Surgeon General Finley, who died last summer in Philadelphia, &c. The first wife, Eleanor, left four children, two of whom died young. The third, Agnes, married a Mr. Boyd, of Juniata county, who has left descendants named Boyd and Patterson. The fourth was John, born in 1752; married Margaret Truesdell in 1778

Of their six children, James is still represented in Cumberland county by one son and two daughters, and the family of a deceased son. John, born in 1780, by four granddaughters. Jane, born in 1782, married John Scouller, near Newville, and left four sons and one daughter, still living. William, born in 1784, left one son and one daughter in Clermont county, Ohio. Eleanor and Mary left no descendants. J. B. S.

CAPT. ANDREW LEE OF PAXTANG.

Interesting Reminiscences of the Revolution.

Capt. Andrew Lee, concerning whom the following incidents relate, was the son of Thomas Lee, born in Paxtang, now Dauphin county, on the 17th of December, 1742. He was brought up on his father's farm, but received a fair education under the instruction of that old schoolmaster Joseph Hutchinson of Derry. During the French and Indian war, he served towards its close in Col. John Elder's regiment on the frontiers. He was probably one of the celebrated "Paxtang Boys," although we have only tradition for the authority. At the breaking out of the Revolution, as did every man, woman and child in Paxtang, he espoused the cause of Independence, and enrolled himself among the first associators. He subsequently rose to be captain in Col. Hazen's "Congress' Own" regiment, and was in active service during the whole period of the war.

Captain Lee accompanied Sullivan's expedition to Staten Island in August, 1777, and a portion of which force, including Captain Lee's, after a hard-fought engagement, surrendered to the enemy. From his diary, recently published, he thus speaks of his captivity:

"The enemy acknowledged we made a brave defense, and were surprised at the smallness of our party when they saw us come in. * * * * * * Our usage was rather cruel than otherwise from this [Aug. 22d] to the 28th inst., having never eaten but four times in seven days, and lodging two nights in the open field. On Saturday the 23d we were delivered to the Hanspac [Anspach] guard, the officers of whom behaved with the utmost politeness to us, and showed a tenderness which the British seemed strangers to. On Sunday we were put on board a ship and transported to New York, where we were landed the next morning, and conducted to the City Hall through a multitude of insulting spectators. We remained in this place until the 28th inst., when we removed to Frankfort street on parol, with the liberty of said street, being 200 yards in length. Here we continued upon two-thirds allowance until the 4th of November when we were removed to Long Island to Flatlands, on condition that we would pay our board.

"Nothing material happened until the 27th of November, when the appearance of part of the American army on Staten Island carried such fears into the General commanding New York as to determine him for our better safety to remove us on board a ship. Accordingly two transports being ready we were the next day put on board under guard, being in number about 255. Here we expected a greater hardship than we had yet undergone, having a scant allowance of provisions, and badly cooked as might reasonably be supposed, for the want of materials to do it with, there being but one fire and one kettle to a ship, which being fixed to the deck, rendered it very difficult to cook at all. On Wednesday, which happened very often at this season of the year, on account of bannard [banyan], days, as they term it, we drew musty oaten meal. When we could spare time from the cittel, we used to pass the evenings in walking the deck, and playing a game at whist, and sometimes with dancing on the quarter-deck, as some of the gentlemen were performers on the violin. Our evenings were generally ended in singing, which always began upon blowing out the light, immediately after turning into our berths. Our situation was truly pitiable on many accounts, but more especially of provisions, which being altogether salt, without any kind of vegetables, must infallibly have brought on sickness and disorder had we stayed long on board. But the General's fears in regard to the prisoners having subsided, on the 12th day of our confinement he issued orders that we should return to Long Island, and accordingly on December 10th we re-landed at Brooklyn." We are not informed as to the date of Capt. Lee's release, but believe it was in the spring of 1778.

It was during the year 1778–9 that Captain Lee was sent home to Paxtang to recruit for the army. At Lancaster were yet confined the prisoners of war taken at Burgoyne's surrender at Trenton, and at Princeton, of whom there had been a large number on hand, owing to the difficulties encountered in the negotiations for a proper exchange. As a result the American authorities found much difficulty in disposing of them. They had no posts regularly fitted for the purpose, and they could suggest no better means for securing them than to place them under guard in a thickly settled part of the country, where the inhabitants were most decidedly hostile to the English. The town of Lancaster in Pennsylvania was of those selected for this purpose. The prisoners were confined in barracks, enclosed with a stockade and vigilantly guarded. But, in spite of all precaution, they often disappeared in an unaccountable manner, and nothing was heard of them till they had resumed their places in the British army. Many and various were the conjectures as to the means of their escape; the officers inquired and investigated in vain; the country was explored to no purpose; the soldiers shook their heads and told of fortune-tellers, peddlers, and such characters, who had been seen at intervals; and sundry of the more credulous could think of nothing but supernatural agency; but whether man or spirit was the conspirator, the mystery remained unbroken.

When this became known to Washington, he sent Gen. Hazen to take this responsible charge. This energetic officer, after exhausting all resources, resorted to stratagem. He was convinced that, as the nearest post was more than a hundred miles distant, the prisoners must be aided by Americans; but where the suspicion should fall, he could not even conjecture—the reproach of toryism being almost unknown in that region. Having been trained to meet exigencies of this kind in a distinguished career, as colonel in the British army, his plan was formed at once, and communicated to an officer of his own, upon whose talent he relied for its successful execution. This was Capt. Andrew Lee, whose courage and ability fully justified the selection.

The secret plan concerted between them was this: It was to be given out that Capt. Lee was absent on furlough or command. He, meantime, was to assume the dress of a British prisoner, and having provided himself with information and a story of his capture, was to be thrown into the barracks, where he might gain the confidence of the soldiers, and join them in a plan of escape. How well Capt. Lee sustained his part may be inferred from the fact that, when he had disappeared and placed himself among the prisoners, his own officers and soldiers saw him every day without the least suspicion. The person to whom we are indebted for most of these particulars was the Intendant of the prisoners, and familiar with Lee; but, though compelled to see him often in the discharge of his duty, he never penetrated the disguise. Well it was for Capt. Lee that his disguise was so complete. Had his associates suspected his purpose to betray them, his history would have been embraced in the proverb, "dead men tell no tales."

For many days he remained in this situation, making no discoveries whatever. He thought he perceived at times signs of intelligence between the prisoners and an old woman who was allowed to bring fruit for sale within the enclosure. She was known to be deaf and half-witted, and was therefore no object of suspicion. It was known that her son had been disgraced and punished in the American army, but she had never betrayed any malice on that account, and no one dreamed that she could have the power to do injury if she possessed the will. Lee watched her closely, but saw nothing to confirm his suspicions. Her dwelling was about a mile distant, in a wild retreat, where she shared her miserable quarters with a dog and cat, the former of which mounted guard over the mansion, while the latter occasioned superstitious fears, which were equally effectual in keeping visitors away.

One dark stormy night in Autumn, Capt. Lee was lying awake at midnight, meditating on the enterprise he had undertaken, which though in the beginning it had recommended itself to his romantic disposition, had now lost all its charms. It was one of these tempests which in our climate so often hang upon the path of the departing year. His companions slept soundly, but the wind which shook the building to its foundation, and threw heavy splashes of rain against the window, conspired with the state of his mind to keep him wakeful. All at once the door was gently opened, and a figure moved silently into the room. It was too dark to observe its motions narrowly, but he could see that it stooped towards one of the sleepers, who immediately rose; next it approached and touched him on the shoulder. Capt. Lee immediately started up; the figure then allowed a slight gleam from a dark lantern to pass over his face, as he did so, whispered, impatiently, "not the man—but come!" It then occurred to Lee that it was the opportunity he desired. The unknown whispered to him to keep his place till another man was called; but just at that moment something disturbed him, and making a signal to Capt. Lee, to follow, he moved silently out of the room.

They found the door of the house unbarred, and a small part of the fence removed, where they passed out without molestation; the sentry had retired to a shelter where he thought he could guard his post without suffering from the rain; but Lee saw his conductors put themselves in preparation to silence him if he should happen to address them. Just without the fence appeared a stooping figure, wrapped in a red cloak, and supporting itself with a large stick, which Lee at once perceived could be no other than the old fruit woman. But the most profound silence was observed; a man came out from a thicket a little distance and joined them, and the whole party moved onward by the guidance of the old woman. At first they frequently stopped to listen, but having heard the sentinel cry, "all's well," they seemed re-assured, and moved with more confidence than before.

They soon came near to her cottage under an overhanging bank, where a bright light was shining out from a little window upon the wet and drooping boughs that hung near it. The dog received them graciously, and they entered. A table was spread with some coarse provisions upon it and a large jug, which one of the soldiers was about to seize, when the man who conducted them withheld him. "No," said he, "we must first proceed to business." He then went to a small closet, from which he returned with what seemed to have been originally a Bible, though now it was worn to a mahogany color and a spherical form. While they were doing this, Lee had time to examine his companions; one of them was a large quiet-looking soldier, the other a short stout man with much of the aspect of a villian. They examined him in turn, and as the Captain had been obliged formerly to punish the shorter soldier severely, he felt some misgivings when the fellow's eyes rested upon him. The conductor was a middle-aged, harsh-looking man, whom Captain Lee had never seen before.

As no time was to be lost, their guide explained to them in few words, that before he should undertake his dangerous enterprise, he should require of them to swear upon the Scriptures not to make the least attempt to escape, and never to reveal the circumstances or agents in the proceeding, whatever might befall them. The soldiers however insisted on deferring this measure till they had formed some slight acquaintance with the contents of the jug, and expressed their sentiments on the subject rather by actions than words. In this they were joined by Captain Lee, who by this time had begun to contemplate the danger of his enterprise in a new and unpleasant point of view. If he were to be compelled to accompany his party to New York, his disguise would at once be detected, and it was certain he would be hanged as a spy. He had supposed beforehand that he should find no difficulty in escaping at any moment, but he saw that their conductor had prepared arms for them, which they were to use in taking the life of any one who should attempt to leave them—and then the oath. He might possibly have released himself from its obligations, when it became necessary, for the interests of his country, but no honorable man could well bear to be driven to an emergency, in which he must violate an oath, however reluctantly it was taken. He felt that there was no retreating, when there came a heavy shock as of something falling against the sides of the house; their practiced ears at once detected the sound of the alarm gun, and their conductor, throwing down the old Bible which he had held all the while impatiently in his hand, directed the party to follow him in close order, and immediately quitted the house, taking with him his dark lantern.

They went on with great dispatch, but not without difficulty.

Sometimes their footing would give way on some sandy bank or slippery field; and when their path led through the woods, the wet boughs dashed heavily in their faces. Captain Lee felt that he might have deserted his precious companions while they were in this hurry and alarm; but he felt that as yet he had made no discoveries, and however dangerous his situation was he could not bear to confess that he had not nerve to carry him through. On he went, therefore, for two or three hours, and was beginning to sink with fatigue, when the barking of a dog brought the party to a stand. Their conductor gave a low whistle, which was answered at no great distance, and a figure came forward in the darkness, who whispered to their guide and then led the way up to a building which seemed by the shadowy outline to be a large stone barn. They entered it and were severally placed in small nooks where they could feel that the hay was all around them except on the side of the wall. Shortly after some provisions were brought to them with the same silence, and it was signified to them that they were to remain concealed the whole of the coming day. Through a crevice in the wall, Lee could discover as the day came on that the barn was attached to a small farm house. He was so near the house that he could hear the conversation which was carried on about the door. The morning rose clear, and it was evident from the inquiries of horsemen, who occasionally galloped up to the door, that the country was alarmed. The farmer gave short and surly replies, as if unwilling to be taken off from his work, but the other inmates of the house were eager in their questions, and from the answers Captain Lee gathered that the means by which he and his companions had escaped were as mysterious as ever.

The next night, when all was quiet, they resumed their march, and explained to Captain Lee that, as he was not with them in their conspiracy, and was accidentally associated with them in their escape, they should take the precaution to keep him before them, just behind the guide. He submitted without opposition, though the arrangement considerably lessened his chances of escape. He observed, from the direction of the stars, that they did not move in a direct line towards the Delaware, but they changed their courses so often that he could not conjecture at what point they intended to strike the river. He endeavored, whenever any peculiar object appeared, to fix it in his memory as well as the darkness would permit, and succeeded better than could have been expected, considering the agitated state in which he traveled.

For several nights they went on in this manner, being delivered over to different persons, from time to time; and as Capt. Lee could gather from their whispered conversations, they were regularly employed on occasions like the present, and well rewarded by the British for their services. Their employment was full of danger, and though they seemed like desperate men, he could observe that they never remitted their precautions. They were concealed days in barns—cellars—caves made for the purpose, and similar retreats, and one day was passed in a tomb, the dimensions of which had been enlarged, and the inmates, if there had been any, banished to make room for the living. The burying grounds were a favorite retreat, and on more occasions than one they were obliged to resort to superstitious alarms to remove intruders upon their path; their success fully justified the experiment and, unpleasantly situated as he was, in the prospect of soon being a ghost himself, he could not avoid laughing at the expedition with which old and young fled from the fancied apparitions under clouds of night, wishing to meet such enemies, like Ajax, in the face of day.

Though the distance to the Delaware was not great, they had now been twelve days on the road, and such was the vigilance and suspicion prevailing throughout the country, that they almost despaired of effecting their object. The conductor grew impatient, and Lee's companions, at least one of them, became ferocious. There was, as we have said, something unpleasant to him in the glances of this fellow towards him, which became more and more fierce as they went on; but it did not appear, whether it was owing to circumstance or actual suspicion. It so happened that on the twelfth night Captain Lee was placed in a barn, while the rest of the party sheltered themselves in a cellar of a little stone church, where they could talk and act with more freedom, both because the solitude of the church was not often disturbed even on the Sabbath—and because even the proprietors did not know that illegal hands had added a cellar to the conveniences of the building.

The party was seated as the day broke, and the light, which struggled in through the crevices, opened for the purpose, showed a low room about twelve feet square, with a damp floor and large patches of white mould on the walls. Finding, probably, that the pavement afforded no accommodations for sleeping, the worthies were seated each upon a little cask, which seemed like those used for gunpowder. Here they were smoking pipes wtth great diligence, and, at intervals not distant, applying a huge canteen to their mouths, from which they drank with upturned faces, expressive of solemn satisfaction. While they were thus engaged, the short soldier asked them in a careless way if they knew whom they had in their party. The others started, and took their pipes from their mouths to ask them what he ment. "I mean," said he, "that we are honored with the company of Captain Andrew Lee, of the rebel army. The rascal once punished me, and I never mistook my man when I had a debt of that kind to pay. Now, I shall have my revenge."

The others hastened to express their disgust at his ferocity, saying that if, as he said, their companion was an American officer, all they had to do was to watch him closely. They said that, as he had come among them uninvited, he must go with them to New York, and take the consequences, but meantime, it was their interest not to seem to suspect him, otherwise he might give an alarm, whereas it was evidently his intentions to go with them till they were ready to embark for New York. The other person persisted in saying that he would have his revenge with his own hand, upon which the conductor, drawing a pistol, declared to him that if he saw the least attempt to injure Captain Lee, or any conduct which would lead him to suspect that his disguise was discovered, he would that moment shoot him through the head. The soldier put his hand upon his knife, with an ominous scowl upon his conductor, but seeing that he had to do with one who was likely to be as good as his word, he restrained himself, and began to arrange some rubbish to serve him for a bed. The other soldier followed his example, and their guide withdrew, locking the door after him.

The next night they went on as usual, but the manner of their conductor showed that there was more danger than before; in fact, he explained to the party that they were now not far from the Delaware, and hoped to reach it before midnight. They occasionally heard the report of a musket, which seemed to indicate that some movement was going on in the country. Thus warned, they quickened their steps, and it was not long before they saw the gleam of the broad clear light before them, such as if reflected upon the calm waters, even in the darkest night. They moved up to it in deep silence; there were various emotions in their breasts; Captain Lee was hoping for an opportunity to escape from an enterprise which was growing too serious, and the principal objects of which were already answered; the others were anxious lest some accident might have happened to the boat on which they depended for crossing the stream.

When they came to the bank there were no traces of a boat on the waters. Their conductor stood still for a moment in dismay; but recollecting himself, he said it was possible it might have been secured lower down the stream, and forgetting everything else, he directed the larger soldier to accompany him, and giving a pistol to the other, he whispered, "if the rebel officer attempts to betray us, shoot him; if not, you will not for your own sake, make any noise to show where we are." In the same instant they departed, and Captain Lee was alone with the ruffian.

He had before suspected that the fellow knew him, and now doubts were changed to certainty at once. Dark as it was, it seemed as if fire flashed from his eye, now he felt that revenge was within his power. Captain Lee was as brave as any officer in the army; but he was unarmed, and though he was strong, his adversary was still more powerful. While he stood uncertain what to do, the fellow seemed enjoying the prospect of revenge, as he looked on him with a steady eye. Though the officer stood to appearance unmoved, the sweat rolled in heavy drops from his brow. He soon took his resolution, and sprang upon his adversary with the intention of wrestling the pistol from his hand; but the other was upon his guard and aimed with such precision that had the pistol been charged with a bullet that moment would have been his last. But it seemed that the conductor had trusted to the sight of his weapons to render them unnecessary, and therefore had only loaded them with powder; as it was, the shock threw Captain Lee upon the ground; but fortunately the fellow dropped the pistol, it fell where the Captain could reach it, and as his adversary stooped and drew his knife from his bosom Capt. Lee was able to give him a stunning blow. He immediately threw himself upon the assassin, and a long and bloody struggle began; they were so nearly matched in strength and advantage that neither dared unclench his hold for the sake of grasping the knife; the blood gushed from their mouths and the conflict would have probably ended in favor of the assassin, when steps and voices were heard advancing and they found themselves in the hands of a party of countrymen, who were armed for the occasion, and were scouring the banks of the river. They were forcibly torn apart, but so exhausted and breathless, that neither could made any explanation, and they submitted quietly to their captors.

The party of armed countrymen, though they had succeeded in their attempt, and were sufficiently triumphant on the occasion, were sorely perplexed how to dispose of their prisoners. After some discussion, one of them proposed to throw the decision upon the wisdom of the nearest magistrate. They accordingly proceeded with their prisoners to his mansion, about two miles distant, and called upon him to arise and attend to business. A window was hastily thrown up and the justice put forth his night-capped head and, with more wrath than became his dignity, ordered them off; and, in requital for their calling him out of bed in the cold, generously wished them in the warmest place. However, resistance was vain; he was compelled to rise; and, as soon as the prisoners were brought before him, he ordered them to be taken in irons to the prison at Philadelphia. Lee improved the opportunity to take the old gentleman aside and told him who he was and why he was thus disguised; the justice only interrupted him with the occasional inquiry, "Most done?" When he had finished the magistrate told him that his story was very well made, and told in a manner very creditable to his address, and that he should give it all the weight it seemed to require. And Captain Lee's remonstrances were unavailing.

As soon as they were fairly lodged in prison Captain Lee prevailed on the jailer to carry a note to General Lincoln, informing him of his condition. The General received it as he was dressing in the morning, immediately sent one of his aids to the jail. That officer could not believe his eyes that he saw Captain Andrew Lee. His uniform, worn out when he assumed it, was now hanging in rags about him, and he had not been shaved for a fortnight; he wished, very naturally, to improve his appearance before presenting himself before the Secretary of War, but the orders were peremptory to bring him as he was. The General loved a joke full well; his laughter was hardly exceeded by the report of his own cannon, and long and loud did he laugh that day.

When Captain Lee returned to Lancaster, he immediately attempted to retrace the ground; and so accurate, under the unfavorable circumstances, had been his investigation, that he brought to justice fifteen persons who had aided in the escape of the British prisoners.

Captain Lee, like many of the bravest of the officers of the Revolution, never received any reward for his hazardous and valuable services. He was subsequently ordered back to Paxtang, where he was on the recruiting service until the close of the war. There of course he remained, but like other patriots, the prime of his life had passed, and with broken constitution—shattered health—was unable to undergo hard labor, and resorted to keeping a public tavern or inn at Harrisburg, shortly after that town was laid out. Here he remained a number of years, honored and respected. He was one of the earliest members of the Ancient Masonic Lodge at Paxtang, having received the honors of that fraternity in one of the army lodges, became its master, and for many years its treasurer.

Prior to the war of 1812-14, Captain Lee removed to Hanover township, Luzerne county, where he closed his eventful life at the age of 80 years, on Friday the 22d of June, 1821. He was buried with military and masonic honors.

Capt. Lee's son, Washington Lee, entered the regular army, and rose to be a colonel in that service.

NOTES AND QUERIES.—XXVI.

A HANOVER SPINSTER EIGHTY YEARS AGO. [N. & Q. xxi].—I wish "H. R." would tell us something more of that wonderful character in Hanover. Of course it is Matty Crawford, who had a sister Violet. Once when Major John Barnett was returning home on horseback with his son Joseph from Hanover Church, Joseph looked back and said: "Put the spurs in your horse, father, Mattie Crawford, is after you." That was enough to make any fellow feel as though the de'il was after him. "Oh," said he to me, "how father did fly."
I. M.

WHO IS BURIED THERE?—On the farm now belonging to Rev. Simon Mower, about one mile this side of Linglestown, there were some graves on a knoll in the field, behind the barn and across the road. Recently the traces were obliterated and the ground is now cultivated as the rest of the field. Who can tell who were there buried and when? This farm was owned once by one of my ancestors and the possibility of it being their family burying ground annoys me.
A. L. G.

"LAUREL HILL."—A correspondent makes inquiry as to the location of this place where, 80 years ago, the Fourth of July celebrations were held. We are of the opinion that Laurel Hill was the ground partly occupied by the Harrisburg cemetery, and which is appropriately named by many Mt. Kalmia—this word being the botanical name for laurel and so designated by the great Linneus, in honor of Kalm, who first sent a description of the shrub to that botanist.

UPPER PAXTANG IN THE REVOLUTION.

[We herewith present two rolls of companies formed during the Revolution in the northern part of Dauphin county—then known as Upper Paxtang. The company of Captain Deibler was in active service for nearly a year, returning home in January, 1777. A portion of the command was captured at the battle of Long Island, and were not released from captivity until the year 1778. During that and the following year, the company was commanded by Captain John Hoffman, and under him they were on the frontiers protecting the defenseless inhabitants from the encroachments of the Indians and Tories who had their headquarters in Southern New

York, and against whom General Sullivan's army was successfully sent in 1779. The little company from Upper Paxtang did valiant service, and all through the Revolution were a well-disciplined body of men. Capt. Martin Weaver, who commanded the detachment in 1781 was connected with Captain Matthew Smith's company of 1775, and probably was among those who returned home sick from Boston, as he seems to have been second lieutenant in Captain Deibler's company in the Spring of 1776. We regret we are unable to give the roll of the company as organized in 1778-9. The descendants of the Hoffmans, Deiblers, Sallada, Steever, Seal, and others whose names are enrolled among these heroes of the "times which tried men's souls," will no doubt be gratified to learn of the valor, the bravery and undying courage of their ancestors. As they read over these names, let their hearts be imbued with the lofty spirit of patriotism which fired the souls of their forefathers, and cherish in faithful remembrance the glorious deeds of a century ago, in behalf, not of themselves, but of posterity.]

A true return of Capt. Albright Deibler's Company of Associators of the 4th Battalion commanded by Col. James Burd, Esqr., March 14th, 1776.

Captain.
Albright Deibler.
 First Lieutenant.
John Hoffman.
 Second Lieutenant.
Martin Weaver.
 Ensign.
Abraham Neighbor.
 Privates.
Bretz Lodwick,
Cline, Sen., William,
Cline, Jr., William,
Conway, Francis,
Deibler, Mathias,
Deibler, Michael,
Fonderback, Henry,
Harman, Jacob,

Harman, David,
Hoffman, John Nicholas,
Jury, Samuel,
Klinger, Philip,
Keadley [Keayler], Michael,
Keller, Jacob,
Kench, John,
Larue, Francis,
Lark, Stophel,
Meetch, Bastian,
Meetch, Jacob,
Meetch, Peter,
Minich, George,
Motter, John,
Neevling, Jacob,
Normier, Henry,

Reigel, George,
Rouscoulp, Philip,
Sallade, Michael,
Shesley, Christopher,
Shesley, Jacob,
Shesley, John,
Shott, Jacob,
Smith, Peter,
Snider, Leonard,
Snokes, Christly,
Steever, Leonard,
Stonebraker, Bast'n,
Work, Adam,
Wolf, Adam,
Wolf, Henry,
Yeager, Andrew,
Yeager, Matthew.

Return of Captain Martin Weaver's Company, of Upper Paxtang, April 23, 1881.

Captain.
Martin Weaver.
 Lieutenant.
John Sheesley.
 Ensign.
Daniel Steever,
 Sergeants.
Mathias Deibler,

Ludwig Bretz,
John Harman.
 Corporals.
John Motter,
George Reigel,
Christian Lark.
 Drummer.
William Cline.

Privates.
 First class—
Edward Wheelock,
Jacob Sheesly,
Frederick Paul,
William Ingram,
George Paul,
George Ream,

James Miley,
John Moyer.
Second class—
John Motter,
Abraham Jury,
John Miller,
Lawrence Kortz,
Henry Warfel,
John Ditty,
John Richter,
George Klinger.
Third class.
Michael Sallade,
Leonard Snyder,
Andrew Yeager,
Henry Ults,
Michael Shadel,
Abraham Neighbour,
Frederick Bender,
Andrew Spangle.
Fourth class—
John Hoffman,
Deidrick Stonebreaker,
"Sartify'd,

George Deibler,
Jere Berger,
Zacheus Spanaberger,
Peter Metz,
Adam Cooper,
George Shoop,
Christopher Yeager.
Fifth class—
Francis Conway,
Sebastian Metz,
Henry Umholtz,
Michael Melcher,
Leonard Steever,
Henry Henn,
Ludwig Shott,
Leonard Kauffman.
Sixth class—
Philip Rauskolb,
Jacob Harman,
Adam King.
Christopher Sheesly,
William Armengost,
Peter Miller,

John Woodside,
John Wirtz,
Jonathan Woodside.
Seventh class—
David Harman,
George Seal,
John Nicholas Hoffman,
Christian Wirtz,
Thomas Korts,
Anthony Fraley,
Adam Wirtz,
George Minnich,
Henry Moyer.
Eighth class—
Michael Deibler,
Christian Hoffman,
Henry Woof,
George Lark,
Samuel Jury,
George Buffington,
Michael Shott,
Stephen Bender.

Capt. MARTIN WEAVER.

YE ANCIENT INHABITANTS.

PAXTANG ASSESSMENT FOR 1770.

[The following list seems to be a full one, and probably takes in all the sub-divisions of the township. Among the inmates and freemen are, perchance, some who resided at Middletown. We are in hopes that in time we shall be able to gather up the assessment lists for all the years, from the formation of the different townships up to the organization of the county of Dauphin. If this is possible, it will enable us to give the almost precise year when our early settlers came to America, a desiderata earnestly wished for by all who take any interest in history or genealogy. As regards the spelling, we give that as found in the original, not venturing to correct it. Our readers must do this for themselves, although now and then this is a difficult matter, as many names are written as probably pronounced.]

Henry Antas,
Jacob Aull,
James Burd, Esq.,
Michael Bumbarger,
William Brown,
Casper Byerly,
Thomas Bell,
William Boyd,
John Barnet,

John Gray,
Mike Graham,
Geo. Gross,
John Gillaspy,
George Gray,
John Harris,
James Harris,
Bartholomew Hannes,
Robt. Heazlet,

Stephen Poorman,
Criley Poorman,
David Patton,
Peter Patterson,
Wm. Patterson,
John Postlewight,
Sarah Potts,
Peter Pether,
George Baye,

John Barnet, Jr.,
Andrew Berryhill,
James Swift,
John Buzard.
William Bell,
John Bell,
John Bumberger,
Jacob Bumberger,
Jean Boyd,
Joseph Brand,
Henry Boal,
William Boggs,
Benjamin Brown,
John Cox,
George Carson,
Fred. Castle,
James Calhoun,
William Calhoun,
John Cavet,
Christ. Crall
James Collier,
Hugh Cunningham,
William Cochran,
Walter Clark,
Robert Clark,
James Carson,
John Chambers,
Andrew Caldwell,
John Caldwell,
John Carpenter,
John Cline,
John Carver.
James Cowden,
William Curray,
James Chamber,
Samuel Cocheran,
John Dunkan,
Wm. Dickey,
John Dickey,
John Davidson,
Abe. Eagley,
Rev. John Elder,
Robert Elder,
John Elder, jr.,
James Espy.
Joseph Erewen,
Thomas Forester,
Joseph Flora,
George Fisher,
Richard Fulton,
John Forester,
John Fleckener,
Adam Fackeler,
Fred. Foster,
Robt. Frute.
Philip Fisher,
Thos. Finney,
John Gilchrist,

John Hearsha,
Patrick Hoagan,
John Hilton,
Patrick Heanney,
And. Huston,
Martin Houser,
Joseph Hutchison,
Alexander Johnson,
John Jameson,
James Johnson,
John Johnson,
David Jones,
Thomas King,
Edward King,
Margaret Kirkpatrick,
William Kerr,
Jacob Kerr.
John Kneel,
John Knopp,
Abe. Kneidick,
Geo. Kneeveling,
John Kiesener,
Jacob Lane,
Stoppil Laficaur,
Mary Lusic,
Henry Larue,
Jean Lamb,
Elizabeth Martin,
William McClure,
John Means,
Henry McKinney,
Jacob Miller,
James McKnight,
Wm. M. Roberts,
Wm. M. McClenahan,
Alex. M. Harg.
David Montgomery,
Wm. McKnight,
Robt. Montgomery,
Michael Miers,
Alex. McKee,
Thomas McCormick.
Robert McCormick.
James McCord,
Hugh McKillip,
Wm. Mayes,
John Muma,
Richard McClure,
Thos. Mayes,
Alex. McClure,
Thomas McArthur,
Hugh Montgomery,
George McMullen,
William McClay,
Thos. Miller,
William McMullen,
Hugh Martain,
Pat McGranahan,

Peter Pancake,
Henry Renick,
Thos. Renick,
James Renick,
Thomas Rutherford,
Jacob Roop,
James Robinson,
John Steel,
Robt. Starratt.
John Steel,
John Shoemaker,
Albert Sighely,
Jos. Shearer,
John Shaleberger,
Benj. Starrat,
George Sheets,
Leonard Sheets,
Jacob Snyder,
William Swan,
Matthew Smith,
Andrew Stewart,
Rebecca Simpson,
Hugh Stephen,
Ann Stephen,
Jean Sloan,
John Smith,
William Sloan,
Jeremiah Sturgeon,
Mike Shearer,
James Smith,
Joseph Shaw,
Sam'l Steel,
Edward Sharp,
Stophel Soop,
Henry Stoner,
Elijah Steward,
John Simpson,
Thomas Simpson,
Michael Simpson,
William Smith,
Hugh Steward,
James Thom,
George Tevelbaugh,
Robert Taylor,
Daniel Voshel,
James Wallace,
Robt. Wright,
Eliz. Weiley,
John Wiggens,
Hugh Wray,
Joseph White,
James Walker,
Leonard Wallow,
James Wilson,
Joseph Wilson,
Michael Whittly,
Matthias Winagle,
Adam Wagganer,

Robt. Gilchrist,
James Gilchrist,
Robert Gray,
John Gallacher,

Wm. Montgomery,
John Medders,
Jonathan McClure,
Jacob Poorman,

John Winderly,
Alex. Wilson,
Thos. Willy,
John Willson.

Freemen.

John McCulloch,
John Freeman,
Geo. Miller,
John Hatfield,
John Patton,
Joseph Patton,
John McGlugadge,
Moses Ramsey,
William Curry (weaver),
Francis Larue,
Barney Raferty,
Jacob Brand,
Francis Owens,
Eirs Frenck,
Robert Ramsey,
William Bell, jr.,
John Carson,
William Cowden,
James McFadden,
John Shaw,

Robt. Smith,
William Calhoun,
William Wilson,
George Shanklin,
John Leany,
Thos. Robinson,
George Dickson,
Cornelius Cox,
Benj. Fulton,
James Mordock,
George Temple,
James Finney,
William Thom,
George Williams,
Samuel Smith,
Henry Shearer.
Wm. Gray,
Thos. Murray,
Vendal Frackner,
Jacob King,

James Kennedy,
Abe. Money,
Fred. Dingar,
John Lively,
John Brown,
Philip Miller,
Mike Gross,
Christy Seabough,
James Ketch (Eastertown),
George Bennet,
Thos. Leman,
Philip Davis,
Robt. Conn,
Thos. Leman,
John Mitcheltree,
David Ellis,
Aquila Richard.

Inmates.

John Hutchison,
John McKinney,
Dan'l McLeese,
William McWhorter, sr.
John Coulter,
Jonas Foak,
John Robinson,
William Cristie,
John Barr,
Jacob Eaten,
Samuel Harris,
William Plunket,
Henry Flemen,

John Henderson,
Philty Snyder,
George Avernier,
Peter Brown,
Jacob Strecker,
Michael Troy,
Matthew Lard,
William Clark,
Samuel Beaty,
Robt. Smith,
William Bell,
Jacob Buckart,
Stophel Amalong,

Ed. Betts,
James Cochran,
Joseph Gray,
John Cragė,
John Teadle,
George Reist,
Matthew McKinney,
Ludwick Couts,
William McClintock,
John Lenan,
Daniel Double,
Thos. Norris.

Middletown.

Albright Swinefort,
John Bakesto,
John Metzgar,
George Loughman,
Fred Zebernick,
Jacob Spade,
Jacob Walter,
George Fry,
Christ. Roads,
John Myers,
Anthony Wierick,

Ludwick Hemperly,
Christ. Spade,
Philip Craft,
Peter Money,
Nick. Castle,
George Dougherty,
Conrad Wolfly,
George Shoeken,
William Mills,
Godfried Catchman,
Robt. Humel,

Henry McCann,
Abe Flora,
Jacob Gross,
Sampson Leadle,
David Etlin,
Fred. Bickener,
Thos. Bralman,
Wm. Walls,
Henry Davis,
Philip Parthmore,
Mike Fisher.

NOTES AND QUERIES.—XXVII.

ACHE OR ACHEY.—In 1774, John Ache (Achey, etc., now Aughey), removed from Tulpehocken township, Berks county, to a place a mile south of Linglestown, where he is on the tax lists up to 1791, and from which his son Henry removed to Juniata county in 1803. Can any one tell when said John Ache died, and at what age, or give any other particulars? Henry's wife, my grandmother, is buried in a marked grave at Wenrich's Lutheran church in 1803.   A. L. G.

DAUPHIN COUNTY MARRIAGES EIGHTY YEARS AGO.—I.

[Believing that a record of early marriages will be acceptable to the genealogist and those of the descendants of the contracting parties of the old time, we transcribe the following for better preservation. The major portion were copied from the *Oracle of Dauphin* prior to the removal of the files of that paper; the others from the *Morgenrothe* and the *Guardian*. The expressions used are those employed in the original newspaper notices. Some are quite personal, others extremely funny:]

ALRICKS—HAMILTON.—On July 21, 1793, by Rev. Mr. Snowden, James Alricks, of Maytown, to Miss Patty Hamilton, of this borough.

ALDEN—CARVER.—On Wednesday, Feb. 11, 1801, at Mr. Andrew Berryhill's, by the Rev. Mr. Snowden, Major Roger Alden, of Presqu' Isle, to the lovely Miss Eliza Carver, of Paxtang.

AUGHENBERG—FAHNESTOCK.—In this town, on December 19, 1802, by Rev. Mr. Snowden, Miss Christina, daughter of Benjamin Fahnestock, to Peter Aughenberg, of Adams county.

ALBRIGHT—ATKINSON.—"In this town last week [December 9, 1802,] my dear Doctor Frederick Albright, late from Germany, via. Lancaster and Hummelstown, but now of this town, to Miss Sally Atkinson, daughter of the late Mrs. Atkinson, now ycleped the consort of Mr. Benjamin Mayer, printer, of this borough.

ATKINSON—SOMMERS.—On Saturday, March 24, 1804, by the Rev. Mr. Peterson, Thomas Atkinson, printer, to the agreeable Miss Sally Sommers, all of this borough.

ARMSTRONG—HATFIELD.—On Thursday, April 5, 1804, by Rev. Mr. Snowden, James Armstrong to Miss Jane Hatfield, both of Middle Paxtang.

BEATTY—GREER.—On the 6th of May, 1799, by the Rev. N. R.

Snowden, Gawin Irwin Beatty and Letitia Greer, both of this borough.

BRUNSON—WHITE.—On March 27, 1800, Hugh Brunson, hatter of this town, to Miss Polly White, of Northumberland county.

BEADER—FISHER.—On May 13, 1802, Peter Beader, hatter, to Miss Jane Fisher, both of this borough.

BUCHANAN—HATFIELD.—On Thursday, March 10, 1803, by Rev. Mr. Snowden, John Buchanan to Miss Sarah Hatfield, daughter of John Hatfield, of Middle Paxtang.

BRADLEY—ROBINSON.—On April 5, 1804, Mr. Bradley to Mrs. Jenny Robinson, late co-partner of Mr. John Robinson, both of this borough.

BURNETT—WALLACE.—On Saturday, April 22, 1804, in this town, by Rev. Mr. Snowden, Gilbert Burnett, of Baltimore, to Miss Elizabeth Wallace, of Cumberland county.

BELL—WATT.—On Thursday, February 14, 1805, by Rev. Mr. Snowden, Samuel Bell, to Miss Isabella Watt, all of Middle Paxtang.

CRABB—KENDRICK.—At Sunbury, March 17, 1800, William Crabb, of Middletown, to Miss Kendrick, formerly of Lancaster.

CRAIN—COCHRAN.—On November 3, 1803, by Rev. Mr. Snowden, Jeremiah Crain, of Hanover, to Miss Ann Cochran, of Middle Paxtang.

COCHRAN—HART.—On March 3, 1804, by Rev. Mr. Snowden, John Cochran to Miss Mary Hart, both of Middle Paxtang.

DOWNEY—BEATTY.—On June 5, 1798, by the Rev. Nathaniel R. Snowden, John Downey, Esq., to Alice Ann Beatty, both of this town.

DUGAL—HILTON.—On April 21, 1795, by Rev. Mr. Snowden, Mr. Dugal, eldest son of Rev. Dugal, of Path Valley, to Miss Jennie Hilton, of Paxtang.

DOUGHERTY—GRAYBILL.—On June 4, 1794, by Rev. Mr. Snowden, William Dougherty to Mrs. Jane Graybill, both of Harrisburg.

DENTZELL—GILCHRIST.—On Friday, February 10, 1799, John Dentzell, Esq., to Miss Jane Gilchrist, both of this town.

DINDORFF—HOSTER.—On Tuesday, February 19, 1799, by Rev. Mr. Moeller, Jacob Dindorf to Miss Catharine Hoster, both of West Hanover.

ELDER—McKINNEY.—On June 4, 1795, by Rev. Mr. Snowden, Michael Elder to Miss Nancy McKinney, both of Middletown.

ELDER—COX.—On Thursday evening, March 23, 1799, by Rev. Mr. Snowden, Thomas Elder, Esq., of this town, to the beautiful and accomplished Miss Catharine Cox, of Cox's town.

EICHOLTZ—SNIDER.—On Thursday evening, April 7, 1803, by Rev. Mr. Peterson, George Eicholtz, of Lancaster, to the beautiful Miss Polly Snider, daughter of Mr. Simon Snider, innkeeper, of this borough.

FISHER—MINSHALL.—On Wednesday, November 9, 1795, Major George Fisher, attorney, to Miss Betsy Minshall, both of Harrisburg.

FORSTER—ELDER.—On Tuesday, September 25, 1798, John Forster to Miss Polly Elder.

FORREST—PATTERSON.—On Monday evening, May 12, 1800, by Rev. Mr. Snowden, Andrew Forrest, Esq., to Miss Fanny, second daughter of Robert Patterson.

GALBRAITH—HULING.—On February 15, 1798, at Hanover, Bartrem Galbraith to Miss Harriet Huling.

GRAYDON—PETTIT.—At Philadelphia, on Monday, December 16, 1799, Alexander Graydon, Esq., of Harrisburg, to Miss Pettit, daughter of Charles Pettit, Esq., of Philadelphia.

GREEN—MURRAY.—On Thursday, April 19, 1804, by Rev. Mr. Snowden, Captain Innis Green to Miss Rebecca Murray, daughter of the late Colonel John Murray, both of Middle Paxtang.

HAMILTON—BOYD.—On June 11, 1795, by Rev. Mr. Snowden, William Hamilton to Rachel Boyd, both of Derry.

HARBISON—FINNEY.—On April 14, 1796, by Rev. Mr. Snowden, Adam Harbison to Miss Martha Finney, both of Hanover.

HALL—MACLAY.—On Saturday evening, April 26, 1800, by Rev. Mr. Snowden, Dr. Henry Hall to the amiable Miss Hetty Maclay, daughter, of William Maclay, Esq., both of this town.

HENNING—RENNEL.—On Friday evening, June 11, 1802, by Jacob Bucher, Esq.. Jacob Henning, hatter, of this town, to the amiable Miss Magdalena Rennel, of York.

HEHL—HENNING.—On Sunday, October 10, 1802, Michael Hehl, of Hummelstown, to Miss Elizabeth Henning, daughter of Jacob Henning, innkeeper, of this town.

HORTER—FEDDER.—On Thursday evening, February 10, 1803, by Rev. Mr. Snowden, John Horter, to Miss Mary Fedder, both of this borough.

HARRISON—CRAIN.—On Wednesday, April 27, 1803, Isaac Harrison, Jr., to Miss Nancy Crain, both of Hanover.

HINES—CLARK.—On Wednesday, August 10, 1803, by Rev. Mr. Snowden, James Hines to Miss Love Clark, both of Middle Paxtang.

HILL—TODD.—On Thursday, February 20, 1804, by Rev. Mr. Snowden, Robert Hill to Miss Polly Todd, both of Hanover.

HAMILTON—HAYS.—On Thursday, March 15, 1804, by Rev. Mr. Snowden, Mr. Hamilton, of Lancaster, to Miss Jane Hays, daughter of David Hays, of Derry.

HARRISON—RODGERS.—On Thursday, April 26, 1804, by Rev. Mr. Snodgrass, John Harrison to Miss Frances Rodgers, all of Hanover.

HOUSEMAN—BEATTY.—On the evening of December 12, 1809, by the Rev. Mr. Buchanan, Daniel Houseman, of Cumberland county, and Miss Rebecca Beatty, of this borough.

ISETT—RODGERS.—On April 14, 1796, by Rev. Mr. Snowden, Henry Isett, of this town, to Miss Frances Rodgers, of Hanover.

IRWIN—MONTGOMERY.—On Thursday, December 1, 1803, Jared Irwin, merchant, of this place, to Miss Nancy Montgomery, second daughter of Hugh Montgomery, innkeeper, of Milton, Northumberland county.

ISENHAUER.—MCDONALD.—On Thursday, June 9, 1803, Jacob Isenhauer, shoemaker and dealer in boot legs, to Miss Nancy McDonald, both of Dauphin county.

IRWIN—WEAVER.—In Virginia, April, 1797, Major John Irwin, of Harrisburg, to the much admired Miss Kitty Weaver, daughter of Adam Weaver, formerly of Cumberland county.

INGRAM—SWAN.—On Tuesday, November 26, 1799, by Rev. Mr. Snowden, James Ingram to Miss Margaret Swan, both of this town.

IRWIN—MACLAY.—On Saturday, March 10, 1804, by Rev. Mr. Snowden, Major John Irwin to the amiable Miss Sarah Maclay, daughter of William Maclay, Esq., of this place.

THE BUCKSHOT WAR.

GEN. ROBERT PATTERSON'S RECOLLECTIONS OF THAT EVENT.

A reporter of the Philadelphia *Press* recently interviewed General Robert Patterson on the subject of General Grant's conduct in the Mexican war. In the course of the interview General Patterson gave his recollection of the Buckshot War in the following language:

"At the time of the Buckshot War I was in command of the troops that marched from the city to restore order and quell the riot. The difficulty arose from a few of the leaders of the party then in power trying to treat the election as a nullity and to retain possession of the government for three years longer. Governor Ritner, a perfectly honest and well-meaning man, was persuaded to co-operate in the matter. The friends of David R. Porter, who had received a decided majority of the votes, the Democratic candidate, were determined not to submit, and assembled in Harrisburg in immense numbers. They were led and commanded by about 25 officers of the old regular army of the war of 1812. The mob, if I may use the word, surrounded the Capitol and entered the Senate chamber and took possession, the Speaker and some of the Senators jumping out of a back window to save themselves from the fury of the rioters. Whereupon an order was sent to me by the Governor of the State to proceed with my division of 1,500 men to Harrisburg. I, of course, wished to go prepared for emergencies, and obtained from the United States Arsenal, at Frankford, a full supply of ammunition. For the infantry mainly buck-shot cartridges, which consisted of a cartridge with twelve buck-shot, each as good as a bullet. I did this certainly not from any desire to kill many of those then in possession of the Senate chamber, many of whom were personal friends and old associates in the army. Instead, I was prompted by a desire to save my own people, in the event of a conflict at close quarters, by rapidly laying over a few and dispersing the remainder. I had good reasons for this, as my command consisted in the main of the flower of Philadelphia—the best young men in it in fact. The exceeding good conduct of the officers and men of that command prevented a conflict between the troops and the mob. If blood had been shed the whole State would have been involved in a civil war. On my arrival at Harrisburg, I, with my staff, reported to the Governor at his residence. Such was the panic at that time in Harrisburg that the Governor deemed it expedient to have his door locked and barred, and we could not get in until, after repeated knockings, a second-story front window was opened, raised and the Governor in person leaned out and asked who was there and what was wanted. I looked up, gave him my name, told him I was there with my division in obedience to his orders and had taken possession of the arsenal and put my command in a good position. He at once came down, opened the door and asked us in. After we were seated I asked for his instructions, and desired to know what he wanted me to do. He said he wished to have his Cabinet about him, and sent for them. Four or five responded, and he and they asked a variety of questions, among others, if I would obey the order of the Speaker of the Senate. I replied I would not, as that would be sustaining a party, who, in my judgment, had acted very improperly and who ought not to be sustained. I said that I had not come for any political purpose and would not sustain any party in the wrong; that my command was composed of both parties, nearly as many of the one as the other, who would obey any command I gave, because they knew me well enough to know that I would not give an improper one. I was also asked if I would obey an order from the Speaker of the House. I said I would not, for two reasons: First, they had organized themselves into two houses, a Democratic House and a Whig House, and that I then did not know which was the right one. But if there was a regular Speaker I would not obey him, as he had no right to give me orders. I was there in obedience to the commands of the Governor, and would obey no one else, but that I would protect the Capitol and the public property and preserve order.

"I was then asked, and pressed for an answer by some of the council or Cabinet, if I would obey the orders of the Governor. I replied that I would obey all orders that the Governor had a right to give. One of the questions following was, 'What would you consider a proper order?' I replied, I will consider that when the order is given. If ordered to clear the capitol and install in the chair either or both of the Speakers I would not do it. That must be settled by the Senators and Representatives themselves. If ordered to fire upon those they chose to call rebels I would not do it, nor would I permit a single shot to be fired, except in self-defense, if assailed by the rebels or in the protection of public property.'

"The result was the entire restoration of order in a few days, both houses recognizing and electing their Speakers and David R. Porter being installed as Governor, as he ought to have been.

"I desire to exonerate Governor Ritner from all that was wrong in this matter, and it was altogether wrong, because I believed then and believe now that he was forced into it by a set of unscrupulous officials who had surrounded him.

"I heard afterward that some of the so-called rebels had given as high as five dollars for buck-shot cartridges to take home with them to show the savage disposition of the soldiery and the terrible dangers they had gone through."

THE PROTECTION OF FISH IN 1792.

They had fish pirates "in those days," and our staid ancestors were as much interested in the protection of fish in the Susquehanna as we are, if we may judge from the following records, collected from the papers of Capt. John Rutherford. It is to be regretted that the good work then begun was not continued. However, their example is worthy of being followed even to-day. The first paper is the "Warrant to the Supervisors of the Highways," from the Judges of our court, which reads as follows:

"*To James Cochran and John Rutherford, Supervisors of the Highways in the Township of Paxtang in the County of Dauphin:*

"WHEREAS, The Constable of the said Township of Paxtang hath presented to the Justices of the County Court of Quarter Sessions of the peace now held for the said County of Dauphin, That a number of Wears, Racks, Dams, Baskets, Pounds and other Devices and obstructions are erected in the River Susquehanna, adjacent to the said Township of Paxtang, whereby the navigation of the said River is impeded, and the Spawn, Fry and Brood of Fish in the same River are injured and destroyed; These are, therefore, to require and command you and each of you forthwith to remove or cause to be removed every such Wear, Rack, Basket, Dam, Pound or other Device and obstruction aforesaid, and for that purpose to summon the Inhabitants of your said Township, giving them three Days notice to repair to, throw down, remove and destroy such Wears, Racks, Baskets, Dams, Pounds & other Devices and obstructions so erected, built or set up; and That you make return of your proceedings to the Justices at the next Court of Quarter Sessions of the peace to be held for the said county; And that you also make return of the names of all Persons who, being so by you summoned shall refuse or neglect to attend in person, or to send an able Person in his room to assist in the throwing down, removing and destroying the obstructions aforesaid, that they may be dealt with according to law—together with the names of every Person or Persons, who shall assault, hinder or obstruct any persons in pulling down, breaking, removing or destroying any of the aforesaid Devices or Obstructions, that they may be dealt with as the Laws direct.

"Given under our hands and seals at Dauphin, the eleventh Day of September, in the year of Our Lord One thousand seven hundred & ninety-two.

"WIL'M. A. ATLEE,
"JAMES CLUNIE,
"JOHN KEAN."

From the notes of Capt. Rutherford, which follow, we have this account of the action of the supervisors:

"Sept. 11th, 1892.

Warned by the constable to attend the Judges at Harrisburg on account of the fish dams.

"Sept. 20th, 1792.

Attended at Harrisburg, and then warned the following hands to throw Down the fish dams—
Robert Harris,
Landis, the miller,
Richard Fulton,
John Fleckiner,
Jacob Knoop,
"September ye 24th, 1792.

Met the following hands at Richard Fulton's and threw Down the Baskets and Dams in the River.
Jacob Knoop,
John Fleckiner,
Robert Harris,
Richard Fulton."
The gentlemen who composed this band of fish-wardens done their duty well, and not an obstruction was left in the Susquehanna, at least within their jurisdiction. We give the foregoing as a portion of the history of fish protection in our Commonwealth.

NOTES AND QUERIES.—XXVIII.

PENNSYLVANIA QUAKERS IN THE REVOLUTION.—From *The Richmond (Va.) Standard* of Dec. 13th we have the following extract of a letter dated "New York, December 20, 1779.—The friends to Government in North Carolina have taken up arms in favor of the King. The Quakers in Philadelphia, to avoid being thought ambiguous in their proceedings, have declared in favor of the King, and have raised subscriptions in order to purchase provisions, which they cook and send regularly to the British prisoners. Numbers of violent Whigs have got their eyes opened by d'Estaing's conduct, and demand of the surrender of Savannah in the King of France's name, which, with the reports of the Germans [sic] rising against Congress, seem to speak a general disaffection, and an abhorrence of French and Congressional tyranny."

CHAMBERS (N. & Q. ix, xii, xv.)—On the tax lists of Milford township, formerly embracing the lower half of the west end of Juniata county, I find the following:
Thomas Chambers, 1763.
James Chambers, 1767 to 1795.
Randle Chambers, 1769 to 1793.
John Chambers, 1769 to 1776.
Margaret Chambers, 1796.
This year (1796) is the last list on which the name appears. James Chambers received a warrant for a tract of land at Thompsontown, Sept. 8, 1755. A few years ago I visited an old lady named Milliken, near Academia, in Juniata county, who told me her mother was a *Chambers* whose father's name was *James*, and that *William Chambers*

was the brother of her mother. Her mother married Wm. Barclay, that is as I understand it—James Chambers' daughter married Wm. Barclay, and their daughter married Milliken. I can find no trace on tax lists of William Chambers. So far as I know the old lady is still living, and if these Chambers are of the family you are inquiring after, she no doubt could tell you all about them. Can this James be Capt. James of the Revolutionary War?   A. L. G.

WILLIAM DENNING, THE BLACKSMITH OF THE REVOLUTION.

That our citizens may take inspiration from the subject, and also to present the matter to those of our readers who may be interested therein, we present the following, relative to one of those brave souls of the Revolution, whose name and fame our friends "across the Susquehanna," (of Cumberland county), seek, after the lapse of a century, to honor, by erecting a monument. Who Denning was and what were his services, we condense from the interesting address of Mr. J. B. Morrow, at the meeting inaugurating the movement recently held at Carlisle. One hundred years ago, spoke Mr. M., "a sturdy blacksmith as he was, became fired with the loftiest spirit of patriotism and undertook to make *wrought iron cannon*, so that he could teach his brother blacksmiths how to perform the work with a view of supplying the patriot army, then struggling with a foe rich in resources if not the most powerful nation on the globe. At Middlesex he succeeded in completing two—*two wrought iron cannon*, gentlemen blacksmiths, a feat (considering the meager appliance of the day) which required the most heroic endurance, indomitable will and highest skill. Blacksmiths now tell us, considering the mass of iron he was compelled to handle and the amount of heat he must endure, they cannot see how it was accomplished. As has been said, two were completed, but were subsequently captured at Brandywine, and one is now in the Tower of London. What became of the other is not known. Stimulated by his success, Wm. Denning commenced another and larger one at Holly Forge, but the undertaking was too large for a single blacksmith to perform, for so great was the heat and so toilsome the work he could get no one to assist him, and finally was compelled to abandon it, it is supposed, at the close of the war. In attempting this last feat, so intense was the heat, that it is handed down as a veritable fact that the pewter buttons on his coat melted. The remains of this unfinished piece lay for many years at the Carlisle Barracks, but finally disappeared and no one knows where it is. . . . William Denning spent the remaining part of his years in Mifflin township, on the banks of the Conedoguinet creek, about one and a half miles north of Newville. Here he lived quite a number of years in extreme poverty, and died on Sunday, Dec. 16. 1830, in the 94th year of his age. Many of the older residents were well acquainted with him, he being a frequent visitor to the town, and doubtless there are some living who heard him relate the *modus operandi* and difficulties he encountered when constructing his wrought iron cannon. While he probably possessed as much pluck and spirit as any other man of revolutionary times, he was always known there simply as the quiet and unobtrusive William Denning. The British government offered a large sum, and a stated annuity to the person who would instruct them in the manufacture of that article; but the patriotic blacksmith preferred obscurity and poverty in his own country, to that of wealth and affluence in that of his oppressors; although that country, for which he did so much, kept her purse closed from the veteran soldier till near the close of his long life. And it often required the whole weight of his well known character for honesty to save him from the severest pangs of poverty."

THE CONEWAGO FALLS CANAL.

The history of this daring enterprise in the annals of internal improvements would form an exceedingly entertaining chapter. It was one which shipwrecked a number of private fortunes, besides sinking a large sum of money appropriated by the State. With the active business and representative men in the early days of the Commonwealth the improving of the navigation at the Susquehanna river was a great desideratum. As in the present day, trade was sought for, and every avenue was opened which could assist in developing the resources of the State. In the navigation of the Susquehanna the greatest impediment was the falls at Conewago. The passage of this watery ordeal was a terror to the rafting community, and hence the almost superhuman efforts three-quarters of a century ago to render the passage down the river less perilous. The following letter, written by the Rev. William Smith, D. D., Provost of the University of Pennsylvania, to General Henry Miller, of York, forms a part of the history of that enterprise which we hope at some not far distant period to give an account. Without further comment we print the letter which has recently come into our possession.

LANCASTER, *July 8th, 1792.*

Henry Miller, Esqr.:

DEAR SIR: A Number of your Friends in Philadelphia, who are Friends also to the Improvement of our Roads & inland Navigation, and interested in the Direction of the Works now on Foot for that Purpose—having taken into their Consideration that the Plan proposed by Mr. Whitmer for opening the Conewago Falls, by a Sluice-Navigation within Shore, was not only dangerous in the Descent of Boats, but almost impracticable in the Ascent, and that the Reports of all the Commissioners were for a Canal Navigation along the Bank, with two Locks, there being 19 feet Fall—& considering further that the public money, viz: £5,250, was granted by the Legislature upon the Estimate made by the Commissioners for a Canal & Lock Navigation, and that applying the money to open any other kind of Navigation, would in a great Degree be losing the Money to the Public—it was therefore resolved to make Proposals to the Governor for opening a Canal & Lock Navigation for the Money granted by Law, & take the Risk of purchasing the Ground & upholding the Canal, for the Benefit of the immense water works, which with 19 feet fall, the Company may erect adjoining the Locks, with a never-failing and abundant Supply of the waste waters of the Canal not necessary for the Supply of the Locks, the Canal being proposed 40 feet width and 4 feet Depth of Water.—The following are the Names of the Persons concern'd in the Contract, viz:

Robert Morris, Wm. Smith, John Nicholson, Walter Stewart, Samuel Meredith, Timothy Matlack, Tench Francis, Samuel Miles, Samuel Powel, John Steinmetz, David Rittenhouse, William Bingham, John Donaldson, A. J. Dallas, Robert Harris, Henry Miller, of Yorktown, & Abram Whitmer, of Lancaster—being 17 Names in the Whole. Mr. Nicholson, the Comptroller, signed the Contract on your Behalf, and I signed in Behalf of Abram Whitmer, of Lancaster, wishing that the Houses of York & Lancaster might be connected in the Execution of the Work, as they are greatly interested in the Success. We have purchased the whole of Robt. Harris's Property, w'ch he describes as 240 Acres on the York Side and 100 Acres on the Lancaster Side of the River; and you are requested to search your Books and to give us an Account what Judgments, Claims or Suits of any Kind may be against Harris' Estate, that may bind the same, so that we may discharge them.

Mr. Matlack & myself, who are at present marking off the Ground for the Quitipahilla Canal, are directed also to view the Conewaga Falls, & to see what other Ground, besides Harris' may be necessary for our projected Plan of Navigation & Water Works, &c. We are to meet at the Ferry House on the Lancaster Side, formerly Rankin's (now R. Harris' w'ch we have purchased), on Monday Morning the 16th Instant; Mr. Whitmer & some Gentlemen from Lancaster are to be with us, and we request your Attendance, that we may consult you on this Important Plan. Until we meet, I wish that nothing may be said, as if more Land than Harris' would be necessary, as it might set the Enemies to the work, about purchasing the same, in order to make a Market of the Company afterwards.

I beg you not to fail meeting us at the Ferry, on Monday the 16th early—& remain your most obed'-Serv't—in Haste.

WILLIAM SMITH.

P. S.—I go to-morrow from this Place to Lebanon.

DAUPHIN COUNTY MARRIAGES EIGHTY YEARS AGO.—II.

JOHNSON—JOHNSON.—On Thursday, August 23, 1804, by Rev. Mr. Snowden, James Johnson and Miss Polly Johnson, both of Derry.

JOHNSTON—PHILSON.—On Tuesday, April 3, 1810, by Rev. Mr. Buchanan, Isaac Johnston and Miss Lydia Philson, both of Halifax township.

JOHNSTON—BRADLEY.—On Tuesday, November 2, 1807, by Rev. Mr. Sharon, John Johnston and Miss Ann Bradley, all of Hanover.

KELSO—MORTON.—On February 4, 1796, by Rev. Mr. Snowden, John Kelso and the amiable Mrs. Sally Morton.

KUNKEL—WELSAUER.—On May 25, 1797, Christian Kunkel, of this town, merchant, and Miss Elizabeth Welsauer, of York county.

KUCHER—WRAY.—In Philadelphia, May 24, 1808, Jacob Kucher, son of the late Colonel Kucher, and Miss Jane Wray, daughter of the late Wm. Wray, formerly of this borough.

KNORR—EBRIGHT.—On April 12, 1803, John Knorr and Miss Carry Ebright, both of this town.

KAPP—SHAFFER.—On Tuesday, February 4, 1804, Michael Kapp, jr., merchant, of this town, and Miss Catharine Shaffer, of Lancaster.

KERR—WILSON.—On Thursday, April 28, 1808, Rev. William Kerr, of Donegal, and Miss Mary Wilson, only daughter of James Wilson, Esq., of Derry.

KETTERELL—WILSON.—On Sunday, November 6, 1808, by Rev. Mr. Buchanan, William Ketterell and Miss Letitia Wilson, all of this town.

KOOVER—BESHORE.—On Sunday, December 11, 1805, by Rev. Mr. Gloninger, Adam Koover and Miss Magdalene Beshore, daughter of Frederick Beshore, all of this borough.

KAUFFMAN—GROVE.—On Sunday, Mar. 26, 1809, by Rev. Mr. Gloninger, Jacob Kauffman, of Manor township, Lancaster county, and Miss Barbara Grove, daughter of Peter Grove, of this borugh.

KNEPLEY—BESHORE.—On November 21, 1809, by Rev. Mr. Gloninger, John Knepley, shoemaker, and Miss Mary Beshore, daughter of Frederick Beshore, all of this place.

KREMER—SHERIG.—On December 19, 1809, by Rev. Mr. Gloninger, Jacob Kremer and Miss Molly Sherig, both of Londonderry township.

KEITER—REID.—On Monday, December 15, 1808, by Rev. Mr. Petersen, John Keiter and Mrs. Elizabeth Reid, both of Halifax township.

LAIRD—MONTGOMERY.—In this town, on Friday, April 22, 1796, by Rev. Snowden, Samuel Laird, Attorney-at-law, and Miss Betsy Montgomery, daughter of the late Joseph Montgomery, Esq., of this place.

LYTLE—ROBINSON.—On Thursday, Sept. 22, 1796, by Rev. Mr. Snowden, Samuel Lytle of Derry township, and Miss Nancy Robinson, daughter of Thomas Robinson, Esq., of Lancaster county.

LANNING—VOUGHT.—On March 9, 1799, John Lanning and Catherine Vought, both of Paxtang.

LITTLE—CONNOR.—On Tuesday, June 24, 1800, "after a courtship of three weeks," J. Little and Miss Sarah Connor.

LECHNER—ORTH.—On June 27, 1804, by Rev. Mr. Petersen, John Lechner and Miss Mary Orth, all of this town.

LYTLE—GREEN.—On Thursday, Jan. 10, 1805, by Rev. Mr. Snowden, Major John Lytle and the agreeable and lovely Miss Elizabeth Green, daughter of Timothy Green, Esq., all of Middle Paxtang.

LYON—MACLAY.—On Thursday evening, April 28, 1808, by Rev. Mr. Sharon, John Lyon and Miss Jane Maclay, youngest daughter of the late William Maclay, Esq., dec'd.

LONG—MOSER.—On Thursday, September 22, 1805, by Rev. Mr. Petersen, John Long and Christiana Moser.

LEININGER—EISENHAUER.—On Tuesday, October 4, 1808, by Rev. Philip Gloninger, George Leininger and Margaret Eisenhauer, both of Lower Paxtang township.

LORENTZ—SHERK.—On Wednesday, February 22, 1809, by Rev. Mr. Gloninger, Peter Lorentz, of Lower Paxtang, and Miss Barbara Sherk, of the same place.

LEOPOLD—BRANDON.—On Thursday, May 17, 1810, by Rev. Mr. Buchanan, Frederick W. Leopold, merchant of this town, and Miss Harriet Brandon, daughter of Charles Brandon, Esq., of Middletown.

MCKINNEY—CHAMBERS.—On June 18, 1795, Mordecai McKinney, of Middletown, and Miss Polly Chambers, of Cumberland county.

McEwen—Boal.—In East Hanover, on April 20, 1796, by Rev. James Snodgrass, James McEwen and Miss Frances Boal. "An entertainment was provided on this occasion, at which about 120 partook."

Morrison—McCord.—On April 6, 1797, by Rev. Mr. Snowden, John Morrison, Esq., of Sherman's Valley, and Miss Flora McCord, of Middle Paxtang.

McCreight—Rowan.—On Wednesday evening, January 1, 1800, by Rev. Mr. Snowden, John McCreight and Miss Peggy Rowan, both of this borough.

Montgomery—Fedder.—On Thursday evening, April 23, 1801, by Rev. Mr. Moeller, James Montgomery and Miss Susan Fedder, both of this borough.

Moody—Crawford.—On the 30th of March, 1802, by Rev. Mr. Snodgrass, Rev. John Moody and Miss Elizabeth Crawford, both of Hanover.

Moorhead—Wilson.—On March 30, 1802, by Rev. Mr. Snodgrass, Mr. Moorhead and Miss Ann Wilson, both of Hanover.

McKinley—Dougherty.—On July 18, 1802, George McKinley and Mrs. Dougherty.

Moody—Montgomery.—At Milton, August 3, 1802, by the Rev. Mr. Brison, James Moody and Miss Jane Montgomery, daughter of Mr. Hugh Montgomery, formerly of this county.

McCallen—Johnson.—On Thursday, December 23, 1802, by Rev. Mr. Snowden, Thomas McCallen, of Adams county, and Miss Elizabeth Johnson, of Derry township.

Marsh—Philson.—On Thursday, March 10, 1803, by Rev. Mr. Snowden, Peter Marsh and Miss Ann Philson.

McAllister—MacLeod.—At Savannah, Georgia, on March 11, 1804, George Washington McAllister, son of Captain A. McAllister, of Fort Hunter, and Miss Catherine MacLeod, daughter of the late Dr. Donald MacLeod, of that place.

McCreight—DeYarmond.—On Thursday, November 15, 1804, John McCreight, son of James McCreight, Esq., and Miss Polly DeYarmond, daughter of the late Richard DeYarmond, deceased, all of Hanover.

McCullough—Robinson.—On December 24, 1806, by James Reed, Esq., Alexander McCullough, widower, and Miss Jane Robinson, spinster, all of Halifax. "Sing tantarara, wives all, wives all!"

McElrath — McCabe.— In this town, on Thursday, August 21, 1807, by Rev. James Snodgrass, John McElrath and the amiable and accomplished Miss Mary McCabe, both of Londonderry township.

Moorhead—Wilson.—On Monday, April 4, 1808, by Rev. Mr.

Sharon, Col. Thomas Moorhead, of Northumberland county, and Mrs. Jane Wilson, late consort of John Wilson, deceased, of Swatara township.

McFARLAND—MITCHELL.—On Friday, May 13, 1808, by Rev. Mr. Peterson, John McFarland, wheelwright, and Miss Nancy Mitchell, all of this town.

MITCHELL—ARMSTRONG.—On Monday, August 29, 1808, by Rev. Mr. Petersen, Nathan Mitchell and Mrs. Catherine Armstrong, all of this town.

MILLER—HOUSER.—On Tuesday, October 18, 1808, Andrew Miller and Miss Annie Houser, both of Lower Paxtang.

McCLINTOCK—BUFFINGTON.—On Friday, January 20, 1809, by Thomas Smith, Esq., Samuel McClintock and Miss Margaret Buffington, daughter of Thomas Buffington.

McCLEAN—HAMILTON.—In Mifflin county, on Thursday, April 18, 1809, by Rev. Mr. Hutchison, Moses McClean, Esq., and Miss Margaret Hamilton, daughter of the late John Hamilton, deceased.

NEISLEY—LANDIS.—On Tuesday, December 15, 1807, by the Rev. Mr. Petersen, Martin Neisley and Mrs. Landis, widow of the late Abraham Landis, deceased, all of Swatara township.

PRIESTLY—FOULKE.—On Wednesday, February 3, 1796, by Rev. Mr. Snowden, William Priestly, second son of the celebrated Dr. Joseph Priestly, and the agreeable Miss Peggy Foulke, a young lady possessed with every quality to render the marriage state happy.

POTTS—BOYD.—On Thursday evening, March 11, 1801, by Rev. Mr. Snowden, Stacy Potts, Esq., member of the House of Representatives of this State, and Mrs. Mary Boyd, late consort of John Boyd, deceased.

POTTS—SOMMERS.—On Sunday evening, March 22, 1801, by Jacob Bucher, Esq., Stacy Potts, Jun., and Miss Polly Sommers, eldest daughter of Mr. Leonard Sommers, all of this town.

NOTES AND QUERIES.—XXIX.

"LAUREL HILL" (N. & Q. xxvi).—If the location and naming of the Harrisburg cemetery, "Mount Kalmia," antedated the vivid recollections of my boyhood, I might easily concur with your inference that Mt. Kalmia and "Laurel Hill" were identical. Nor would I presume to a positive assertion in regard to its locality; but I remember, as if but yesterday, that the hill upon which John H. Brant's

building stands was thickly covered with laurel bushes along its top edges and sides; the tableland being under cultivation. The boys and girls of the North Ward went there frequently for laurel flowers, and one of my sisters was a victim to their poisonous qualities. Mount Kalmia was previously known as "Hare's Hill," and its ravine was called "Fairy Valley"—a beautiful and shady spot for picnics. This hill was thickly wooded and along the swamp side (toward the town) was impenetrably overgrown with vines, and with underbrush throughout. The other hill—then owned by Wm. Allison—was more favorable to the growth of the laurel, and was thickly covered with it, as mentioned. Whilst I have only an impression that it was *called* "Laurel Hill" in those days, I have certain knowledge that it *was* a laurel hill; and more so than any of the adjacent ones.
G. B. A.

THE TWO BURRS AND GEN. HANNA.—It is stated in a "romantic legend," published in the regular edition of the *Telegraph*, of January 7th, 1880, that Aaron Burr visited Theodore Burr, the original constructor of the Harrisburg bridge, while he was Vice-President. He might have done so, but not at Harrisburg. Theodore Burr was not at this place as a resident until 1811, and Aaron was out of office in March, 1805. Aaron Burr went down the Ohio in November of the same year, and was tried at Richmond in September, 1807, so he could not have met Hanna here, as the latter died in July, 1805. Whatever correspondence was had between these gentlemen must have been during the Vice-Presidency of the former, while Hanna was in Congress, and his duties in that position ceased before any charge of treason was made against Burr. The first intimation of any criminality was in Wilkinson's letter to Jefferson late in the year 1805. It is a loss, to be sure, that Gen. Hanna's papers were carelessly scattered or destroyed after his death, yet if there was any constructive treason in them, it could not have affected himself or his family, as he was in his grave three years before Burr was arrested. He was a great friend of Jefferson, and it is not believed that there was a line of Hanna's correspondence, calculated to cast a shadow upon his political purity, or his friendship for the political institutions of his country. He was not a great man, but he was an upright one, or he could not have maintained his high public station, from 1788, to the time of his death, in 1805. We hope the statement commented upon will not be taken as an historic fact.
* * *

[We have been credibly informed that about the close of the year 1813, Col. Aaron Burr visited Theodore Burr, who was then engaged in erecting the bridge over the Susquehanna. The latter had built a house on the island and resided there at the time. Colonel Burr traveled in a gig, and was met somewhere on the road by Theodore. As to the relationship existing between the Burrs we have no reliable information, although the author of the Burr Genealogy, recently published, writes us that they were possibly full cousins.

Since the foregoing was written Colonel Shoch, of Columbia, a native of this city, verifies the foregoing statement.]

DAUPHIN COUNTY MARRIAGES EIGHTY YEARS AGO—III.

PORTER—DUGAL.—On Thursday, May 13, 1802, by Rev. Mr. Snowden, George Porter, of this town, and Miss Mary Dugal, of Lancaster county.

PEACOCK—ORTH.—On May 10, 1804, Thomas Peacock and Miss Peggy Orth, of Paxtang.

POTTS—SHERMAN.—At Trenton, N. J., on Monday evening, April 6, 1807, by James Ewing, Esq., Miss Rebecca Potts, daughter of Stacy Potts, Esq., formerly of this town, and George Sherman, editor of the Trenton *Federalist.*

PORTER—FACKLER.—On Tuesday, June 16, 1807, by Rev. Mr. Petersen, John Porter, mason, aged 20, and Miss Elizabeth Fackler, aged 14, all of Paxtang. "These children deserve praise."

PHILIPS—FOX.—On Thursday, August 20, 1807, John Philips and the accomplished Miss Margaret Fox, daughter of John Fox, inn keeper of Hummelstown.

PECK—STAUFFER.—On Sunday, October 23, 1808, by Rev. Mr. Gloninger, Jacob Peck and Miss Feronica Stauffer, both of Lower Paxtang.

PIERSOL—MAYER.—On Thursday, May 18, 1809, by Rev. Mr. Gloninger, Jacob Piersol, of Honeybrook township, Chester county, and Miss Magdalena Mayer, of Swatara township, this county.

PORTER—STEEL.—On Thursday, Dec. 12, 1809, by Rev. Buchanan, Robert Porter, of Lewistown, Mifflin county, and Mrs. Ann Steel, of this town.

RUSSELL—MOORE.—On Tuesday, June 7, 1796, by Rev. Mr. Snowden, James Russell, merchant, and Miss Frances Moore, both of Middletown.

ROBINSON—POLLOCK.—On Thursday, July 9, 1799, at Silvers Spring, by Rev. Snowden, Dr. Samuel Robinson and Miss Mary Pollock, eldest daughter of Oliver Pollock, Esq.

RUTHERFORD—SWAN.—On March 17, 1801, by Rev. Mr. Snowden,

Lieutenant William Rutherford and Miss Sallie Swan, both of Paxtang.

RUTHERFORD—SHULZE.—On Tuesday, June 28, 1803, by Thomas Smith, Esq., Thomas Rutherford and the beautiful Miss Mary Shulze, daughter of Mr. Jacob Shulze, both of Swatara.

ROGERS—ALLEN.—On Thursday evening, February 16, 1804, by Rev. Mr. Snodgrass, Robert Rodgers and Effy Allen, all of Hanover.

RAMSEY—CLARK.—On Thursday, July 5, 1804, William Ramsey Esq., deputy surveyor of Cumberland county, and Miss Clark, of Clark's Ferry.

ROBINSON—CLENDENIN.—On June 23, 1807, Samuel Robinson, of Hanover, and Miss Rachel Clendenin, of Paxtang.

RODGERS—CARSON.—On Saturday, October 31, 1807, by Rev. Mr. Sharon, John Rodgers and Miss Dinah Carson, of Paxtang.

RYAN—STEWART.—On Thursday, November 24, 1808, by Rev. Snodgrass, John Ryan, of Middle Paxtang, and Miss Lydia Stewart, daughter of James Stewart, of Lower Paxtang.

REES—SMITH.—On Monday, May 2, 1808, by Rev. Snodgrass, Jeremiah Rees and Miss Margaret Smith, both of this town.

REES—POWDERS—On Thursday, June 26, 1810, by Rev. Mr. Buchanan, Jeremiah Rees, innkeeper, and Miss Lydia Powers, both of this town.

SMITH—MOORE.—On March 7, 1793, Thomas Smith and Miss Anna Moore, both of Middletown.

STURGEON—RITCHEY.—On March 7, 1793, by Rev. Mr. Snodgrass, Jeremiah Sturgeon and Miss Anna Ritchey.

SINGER—NORTON.—On February 17, 1796, by Rev. Moeller, Jacob Singer, merchant, and Nancy Norton, both of this town

SMITH—BRUCE.—On Thursday, April 24, 1800, by Rev. Mr. Snowden, John Smith and Miss Frances Bruce.

SOMMERS—FEDDER.—On Thursday evening, June 2, 1801, by Rev. Snowden, John Sommers and Miss Barbara Fedder, both of this borough.

SOMMERS—CHAMBERLAIN.—On Saturday, May 1, 1802, Henry Sommers, printer, and Miss Peggy Chamberlain, both of this town.

SMITH—ROBINSON.—On Thursday evening, January 20, 1803, by the Rev. James Johnston, Mr. Smith, son of William Smith, late of Derry township, and Miss Peggy Robinson, daughter of William Robinson, of Wayne township, Mifflin county.

STUBBS—TAYLOR.—On May 25, 1803, Thomas Stubbs, merchant, and steel manufacturer, of Middletown, and Miss Mary Taylor, of Chester county.

SELLNER—HEFFLEY.—On September 18, 1803, Ulrich Sellner and Miss Betsey Heffley, both of this town.

SEES—RUPPLEY.—On Thursday, December 8, 1803, John Sees, carpenter, of this town, and Miss Polly Ruppley, daughter of Col. Jacob Ruppley, of Cumberland county.

SOMMERS—SHAEFFER.—On January 14, 1804, Jacob Sommers and Miss Catharine Shaeffer, both of this town.

SEYFERT—SHEILY.—On Monday, October 29, 1804, by Rev. Mr. Petersen, Mr. Anthony Seyfert, of this borough, and Miss Jane Sheily, of Paxtang.

SESSAMAN—BUCK.—On Thursday, December 20, 1804, Mathias Sessaman and Miss Esther Buck, all of Hummelstown.

SPAYD—DEYARMOND.—On Thursday, October 10, 1806, Christian Spayd, merchant, of Middletown, and Miss Betsy DeYarmond, daughter of Joseph DeYarmond, Esq., of Palmstown.

SELLER—KRIEG.—On Tuesday, March 24, 1807, John Frederick Seller and Miss Mary Krieg.

SIMONTON—CLARK.—On April 9, 1807, Miss Jane Simonton, daughter of the late Dr. William Simonton, and Mr. John Clark, both of Hanover.

SIMONTON—BELL.—On Monday, April 9, 1807, by Rev. Snodgrass, James Simonton and Miss Ann Bell, all of Hanover.

SMITH—TOOT.—On December 10, 1807, by Rev. Petersen, John Smith and Miss Magdalena Toot, both of Middletown.

SHOEMAKER—RHOADS.—On Sunday, April 17, 1809, Jacob Shoemaker, hatter, and Miss Anna Rhoads, both of this town.

STEWART—ELDER.—On Tuesday, October 11, 1808, by Rev. Snodgrass, Samuel Stewart, of the State of Ohio, and Miss Elizabeth Elder eldest daughter of Robert Elder, merchant, of Hanover.

SHARP—WEISS.—On Sunday evening, November 6, 1808, by Rev. Buchanan, Michael Sharp and Elizabeth Weiss, daughter of Adam Weiss, Esq., both of Upper Paxtang.

SHRENK—MACHEN.—On Tuesday, March 7, 1809, by Rev. Gloninger, Martin Shrenk and Miss Ann Machen, both of Swatara.

STEWART—BUCHANAN.—On Thursday, July 5, 1810, by Rev. Johnston, David Stewart, of Paxtang, and the worthy Miss Molly Buchanan, of Lewistown.

TOOT—SHULZE.—On Sunday, March 22, 1807, by Rev. Petersen, Col. George Toot and Mrs. Catharine Shulze.

THOME—ROBINSON.—On Thursday, April 16, 1807, by Rev. Snodgrass, John Thome and Miss Nancy Robinson, all of Hanover.

TAYLOR—WENTZ.—On Thursday evening, May 26, 1808, by Charles Brandon, Esq., Samuel Taylor, of Ontario county, N. Y., and Mrs. Elizabeth Wentz, of Middletown.

TAYLOR—HOOVER,—On Thursday, October 13, 1808, by Rev. Petersen, Jacob Taylor and Miss Eve Hoover, all of this town.

UPDEGRAFF—NORTON.—On Thursday, November 17, 1809, by Rev. Petersen, Jacob Updegraff and Miss Sarah Norton, daughter of John Norton, both of this town.

ULRICH—WEIDMAN.—On Thursday, October 4, 1810, by Rev. Hiester, Daniel Ulrich, of Sunbury, and Miss Elizabeth Weidman, daughter of John Weidman, of Union Forge, this county.

WEIR—WALLACE.—On May 4, 1797, Samuel Weir, of this town, and Miss Mary Wallace, of Cumberland county.

WILLIS—LAWYER.—On Monday, November 20, 1797, by Rev. Moeller, Henry Willis and the amiable Mary Lawyer, both of this town.

WATSON—LYTLE.—On January 24, 1797, by Rev. Snowden, David Watson and Elizabeth Lytle.

WATSON—MITCHELL.—On Thursday evening, February 10, 1803, by Rev. Snowden, Thomas Watson and Miss Mary Mitchell, both of Derry.

WILSON—WALLACE.—On Thursday April 21, 1803, James Wilson, jr., and Miss Polly Wallace, both of Hanover.

WALLACE—FORREST.—On Thursday, April 27, 1803, in Lycoming county, William Wallace, Esq., attorney-at-law at Presqui' Isle, son of Benjamin Wallace, Esq., of Hanover, this county, and Miss Rachael Forrest, daughter of Dr. Andrew Forrest, formerly of this town.

WHITALL—TICE.—On November 14, 1803, by Rev. Snowden, John Whitall and Miss Mary Tice, both of Middle Paxtang.

WILLIAMS—NEIL.—On Thursday, March 5, 1804, by Rev. Snowden, Daniel Williams, of York, and Miss Jane Neil, of this town.

WOLFERT—SHAFFER.—On Thursday, March 5, 1807, by Rev. Petersen, Leonard Wolfert, near Hummelstown, and Catharine Shaffer, of Hanover.

WETHERHOLT—MOSER.—On Tuesday, August 4, 1807, by John Capp, Esq., Geo. Wetherholt, of this borough, and Miss Betsy Moser daughter of Mr. Moser, formerly of Carlisle.

WAETH—SHREIT.—On May 19, 1808, by Rev. Petersen, Richard Waeth and Miss Barbara Shreit, all of Fishing Creek Valley, Dauphin county.

WELTMER—WEISER.—On Thursday, September 29, 1808, by Rev. Philip Gloninger, Abraham Weltmer, Jr., and the amiable Miss Margaret Weiser, both of Londonderry.

WENERICK—WONNEMACHER.—On Tuesday, November 12, 1808, by Rev. Gloninger, Joseph Wenerick, of West Hanover, and Miss Maria Wonnemacher, of Lower Paxtang.

WILHELM—KOCH.—On March 2, 1809, Jacob Wilhelm and Miss Mary Koch, both of this place.

WHITE—MAYER.—On Tuesday, May 16, 1809, by Rev. Gloninger, James White, of Lower Paxtang, and Miss Elizabeth Mayer, of the same place.

WEAVER—KLINE.—On Tuesday, July 18, 1809, Philip Weaver and Miss Louisa Kline, daughter of George Kline, Esq., all of Carlisle.

WELSH—HARDY.—On Saturday, Sept. 17, 1809, by Rev. Gloninger, James Welsh and Miss Eliza Hardy, both of Middletown.

WELTMER—MINSKER.—On Thursday, March 13, 1810, by Rev. Petersen, Jacob Weltmer and Miss Catharine Minsker, both of Upper Paxtang.

ELDER—ESPY.—On March 7, 1793, by Rev. Snodgrass, Samuel Elder and Miss Margaret Espy.

BRICE—KEARSLEY.—On May 19, 1796, by Rev. Mr. Snowden, Alexander Brice and Miss Peggy Kearsley, daughter of Capt. Samuel Kearsley.

HALDEMAN—JACOBS.—On Thursday, May 17, 1810, by Rev. Lochman, Jacob M. Haldeman, of Cumberland county, and Miss Eliza Ewing Jacobs, daughter of Samuel Jacobs, of Colebrook Furnace.

NOTES AND QUERIES.—XXX.

HOFFMAN'S CREEK.—In the old deeds we find a stream thus named. It was, we are credibly informed, what is now called Little Wiconisco. In early warrants and surveys the smaller streams were named for the first settlers or owners of land along them, and that was no doubt the case in this instance.

HUGUENOT SETTLEMENT IN THE UPPER END.—It may not be generally known, but many of the earlier settlers of the Wiconisco Valley were of French Huguenot descent. The Jury, Larue, Sallade and other families are all of French extraction. Although coming among the German immigrants, they were a part and a parcel of that great influx of French Protestants into the German and Swiss Provinces, which followed the Revocation of the Edict of Nantes. It is the only section of our county which appears to have been settled by the descendants of the Huguenot refugees. As a people, they have all the peculiar characteristics of our Scotch-Irish pioneers.

FERREE'S GUNPOWDER MILL.—About 1812-13, Isaac Ferree commenced the manufacture of gunpowder, at his mill on Wiconisco creek, which was located some distance below Oakdale forge, at the place where the old pioneer, Andrew Lycan or Lykens settled. As to the quality of the powder manufactured we have more knowledge than as to the quantity. It was considered *equal to any made in this country*, and during the war of 1812-14 was in considerable demand. It is not known how long Mr. Ferree continued the manufacture, but probably until the Dupont mills established at Wilmington crushed out of existence all similar enterprises. Mr. Ferree was a native of Lancaster county, son of Isaac Ferree, an early settler on the Pequa, and of French Huguenot descent. He was an enterprising business man, and it is to be regretted that our biographical details are so meagre.

GREEN — MURRAY.— In N. & Q., xxvii, the publication of the marriage of Innis Green and a daughter of Col. John Murray reminds me of the following data, copied from tombstones in the cemetery at Dauphin.

TIMOTHY GREEN, departed this life February 27th, 1812, aged 77 years.

COL. JOHN MURRAY, departed this life February 3d, 1798, aged 68 years.

MARGARET MURRAY, departed this life June 22d, 1807, aged 74 years.

HON. INNIS GREEN, who departed this life August 4th, 1839, aged 63 years, 14 months and ten days.

REBECCA, consort of Hon. Innis Green, who departed this life January 6th, 1837, aged 60 years.

I have transcribed the foregoing for reference.   J. S. A.

BIOGRAPHICAL SKETCHES.

DR. ROBERT AUCHMUTY.—Dr. Robert Auchmuty, the son of Samuel Auchmuty, was born near Sunbury, Northumberland county, Penna., in the year 1785. He was descended from an old Celtic family of Scotland. Robert Auchmuty, the first of the American family of that name, an eminent lawyer, was in practice at Boston, Mass., as early as 1719. He died in 1750, leaving several children. Among these, Robert, who in 1767 became Judge of the Court of Admiralty at Boston; Samuel, who was rector of Trinity Church, New York city, and Arthur Gates. The latter came to Pennsylvania as early as 1765, and located in then Lancaster county. In that year we find him commissioned as an Indian trader, with permission to trade with the natives at Penn's creek, Shamokin and such other forts as may by his majesty or the Provincial authorities be established. He first settled at the mouth of Penn's creek, on the Isle of Que, and from thence removed to the opposite side of the Susquehanna, a few miles below Fort Augusta, in what is now Lower Augusta township, Northumberland county. During the war of the Revolution Samuel Auchmuty, one of his sons, and father of the Doctor, entered the patriot army, and was in service from the winter at Valley Forge until the close of the war. The veteran's remains rest in the old burial ground at Millersburg, unmarked and the spot unknown. Dr. Robert Auchmuty received a good education, studied medicine and began the practice of his profession at Millersburg about 1830–31. Apart from the duties of his profession he served many years as a justice of the peace, being first commissioned by Governor Ritner. He was an enterprising, active citizen, and a warm advocate of the common school system when that noble measure was adopted, and was a gentleman beloved and respected by his fellow citizens. He died at Millersburg in 1849, at the age of 64, and is buried in the new cemetery at that place. He was the father of S. P. Auchmuty, Esq., of Millersburg.

JOHN F. BOWMAN.—John F. Bowman was born in Lancaster county, Penna., May 10, 1771. His father was a farmer, residing on Pequea creek, not far from Strasburg. John F. was brought up as a millwright, but subsequently entered mercantile pursuits. In 1809 he removed to Halifax, where he was a merchant from that period to 1830, when, believing a larger sphere of trade was opened for him, he went to Millersburg, where he successfully continued in business until his death, which occurred on the 6th of November, 1835. Mr. Bowman first married in 1794 a daughter of Isaac Ferree, whose farm adjoined that of his father. By this marriage they had the following children:

 i. Eliza.
 ii. Maria.
 iii. George.
 iv. Josiah, m. Elizabeth Rutter.

Mr. Bowman married, secondly, in 1805, Frances Crossen, daughter of John Crossen. They had issue as follows:

 v. John J., m. Margaret Sallade.
 vi. Levi.
 vii. Louisa.

viii. Isaac.
ix. Mary E., m. Rev. C. W. Jackson.
x. Lucinda, m. Dr. Hiram Rutherford.
xi. Jacob.
xii. Emeline.
xiii. Benjamin.

John F. Bowman was one of the representative men of the "Upper End," enjoyed a reputation for uprightness and honesty, and highly esteemed by those who knew him. Genial, yet quiet and unobtrusive, he never sought or would accept any local or public office. His second wife, Frances Crossen, b. August 13, 1786; d. September 30, 1846, and lies interred beside her husband in the old Methodist graveyard at Millersburg.

ABRAHAM JURY.—Among the earliest settlers on the Wiconisco was Abraham Jury, or, as it is sometimes written, Shora. He was of French Huguenot descent, and emigrated from Switzerland about 1755. He located within the Valley not far from the town of Millersburg. He was a farmer and took up a large tract of land. In the Revolution he served during the campaign in the Jerseys, and subsequently on the frontiers, as did also his eldest son, Samuel. He died in August, 1785, leaving a wife, Catharine, and the following children:

i. Samuel.
ii. Abraham.
iii. Mary.
iv. Magdalena.
v. Margaret.
vi. Catharine.
vii. Susanna.
viii. Salome.

Samuel, we presume, either removed from the valley or died early, for Abraham, junior, seems to have come into possession of the old homestead. The latter died in November, 1805, leaving John, who was of age, and Jacob, Hannah and Sally, minors.

REV. CHARLES EDWARD MUENCH.—Any historic record of the Upper End would fail of completeness without some mention of the distinguished "Dominie" of Hoffman church. We refer to the Rev. Charles Edward Muench, a native of Mettenheim, Wartenburg, in the Palatinate of Chur Pfaltz on the Rhine, Germany, born January 7, 1769. He was of Huguenot-French descent, his grandfather, Charles Frederick Beauvoir, fleeing France during the religious persecutions,

and purchasing the "Muench Hoff," took his surname therefrom.
Charles Frederick, the younger, was early sent to Heidelberg, where
he completed his theological studies. It was just at the commencement of the general war in Europe, when on the occasion of his
home being invaded by the French army he received and accepted a
commission as captain of a company of huzzars in the Allied armies,
in which service he was severely wounded by a pistol ball in the leg,
and a sabre cut on the left hand. He commanded the guard that
conducted Lafayette to the prison at Olmutz. On the 8th of July,
1794, he was promoted quartermaster under Sir Francis of Wiedlungen. On the very day of his promotion he married Margaretha
Bieser. In 1798 he came to America, where he taught a German
school successively at Shaefferstown, Lebanon county, and Rehrersburg, Berks county. In 1804 he removed to Lykens Valley, at the
Hoffman church school property; but discouraged somewhat at the
wild appearance of the land, he went to Union county. Subsequently,
in 1806, the congregation at Hoffman church requested his return,
when yielding thereto, he once more entered upon the duties of his
station. For a period of twenty-eight years he was a faithful teacher,
and although not the ordained minister, yet very frequently conducted the religious services in Hoffman church, and officiated on
funeral occasions. He was greatly beloved by the people, and his
death, which occurred on the 8th of January, 1833, occasioned sorrow
in many a household. His beloved wife, Margaretha, died in the
following year, 1834, and their remains lie interred side by side in
the graveyard of old Hoffman church. The Rev. Muench was exceedingly expert with the pen—had a refined artistic taste as to
drawing and designing—and in the ornamentation of books and inlaying of furniture. He was a musician of no ordinary ability, and
was an adept in all those essentials characteristic of the home culture
of the Germans of the better class.

Mr. Muench's children were:
  i. Juliana, m. Jacob Wolf.
  ii. William Henry, m. Eliz. Reed, of Northumberland county.
  iii. Susanna Louisa, m. Jacob Riegel.
  iv. Charles Frederick, m. Grace Leyburn, of Carlisle.
  v. Daniel Augustus, of Halifax, m. Lydia Smith.
  vi. Jacob Dewalt, m. Salome Moyer.
  vii. Margaret, m. Peter Miller, of Halifax.

SIMON SALLADE.—There are few citizens of the county of Dauphin
who are not familiar with the name and valuable services of SIMON
SALLADE, one of the representative men of this district forty years ago,

and concerning whom we have been able to glean the biographical data which herewith follows.

Simon Sallade was born near Gratz, Dauphin county, Pa., on the 7th of March, 1785. His father, John Sallade, of French Huguenot descent, was a native of Bosel on the Rhine, born in March, 1739, emigrated, with other members of his family, to America at an early period, and was among the first settlers on the Wiconisco. He died at the age of 88 years, in November 1827, being blind about 10 years before his death. He married on the 8th of February, 1771, Margaret Everhart, daughter of George Everhart, born in Berks county in 1747, and concerning whom we have the following incident. Upon the Indian incursions on the East side of the Susquehanna, subsequent to the defeat of Braddock, in the Fall of 1755, she was taken captive by the savage marauders, near what is now Pine Grove, Schuylkill county. She was an unwilling witness to the scenes of murder and atrocity, when the merciless Indians tomahawked and scalped her parents, brothers and sisters, and beheld the home of her birth illuminating by its red glare the midnight sky, while only she of all her friends was left—and she a prisoner with the cruel and blood-thirsty savage. Doubtless there was some attractiveness of person or piteousness of appeal which saved her life. Of the wearisome years of her captivity among the Indians, West of the Ohio, we have little knowledge. It was not, however, until the power of the French on the Beautiful River was broken by the courage and skill of Gen. Forbes, that the little prisoner was rescued and returned to her friends in Berks county. She lived to a ripe old age. John Sallade had five sons and two daughters, Simon being next to the youngest. Simon Sallade, owing to the want of schools in those early days in the Valley, was obliged to depend upon the educational instruction given by his parents, but being an apt scholar, it was not long before he mastered the main branches in a good education. He was a great reader, and, although books were few in those days, he read and re-read those falling into his hands. Later in life, towards manhood's years, he acquired considerable knowledge by the aid of a teacher, whom he and some of the young men of his neighborhood employed for that purpose. He was quite a performer on the violin and being of a social nature, he was often the center and life of the many winter evening gatherings of that time.

Mr. Sallade was a mill-wright by trade, acquiring much of his proficiency in that vocation from an apprenticeship to Jacob Berkstresser, of Bellefonte. Many of the old mills within 30 or 40 miles of his home, were of his designing, and in fact the workmanship of his hands. A self-made man, energetic, social and industrious, he became in time one of the most popular men of the Upper End.

His constant contact with the people of all classes in social life or business relations resulted in his taking a warm interest in political affairs. Although a politician. he was such for the advancement of the public good. He was a Democrat of the old school, and when named for office, he appealed to the people instead of the party for support. He was four times elected to the Penn'a House of Representatives. First, in the years 1819 and 1820, at the age of 34; next in 1836–7, at the age of 51 years; and again in 1853, when he was in his 69th year. Each time the Whigs were largely in the majority in Dauphin county, yet always when put in nomination by the Democratic party, Mr. Sallade, save in one instance, was elected. This defeat was due in part to a letter written at the time to Charles C. Rawn, Esq., chairman of the temperance committee, in which he announced his opposition to the passage of the Maine liquor law. His letter was bold and outspoken. He did not conceal his opinions for the purpose of sailing into office under false colors. He might have done as latter-day politicians do, or as did his opponents at that time—evaded the question and deceived the voter. Simon Sallade prefered defeat to deception—that the honorable career that he had made and sustained for political integrity and honesty should lose nothing of its lustre in his declining years.

During his term in the Legislature he was the author of what was generally known as "Wiconisco Feeder Bill." To his zeal and tact, that important legislation for the Upper End of Dauphin county, owes its passage. Through this outlet the Lykens Valley coal fields were first developed. He was the superintendent for the construction of the Wiconisco canal, and held the appointment through the Canal Commissioners.

Simon Sallade died at the old homestead, near Elizabethville, on the 8th of November, 1854, and is interred in the village graveyard at that place. His wife was Jane Woodside, daughter of John Woodside of Lykens Valley. She died September 3d, 1854, and is buried in the same graveyard. They had issue as follows:

    i. Margaret, m. John J. Bowman, of Millersburg.
    ii. Ann, m. Edward Bickel.
    iii. Jane, m. Daniel K. Smith.
    iv. Simon.
    v. Jacob.
    vi. John.
    vii. George.
    viii. Joseph.

There are many hearth-stones, writes one who knew Simon Sallade well, and to whom we are greatly indebted for much of the information herewith given, in Lykens Valley, where the story of his sociability, hospitality, humor, honesty and his many deeds of charity are rehearsed by those of the fathers of the present generation who never saw or knew him, except from the traditionary history, which is part and parcel of every family and community.

JOHN PETER WILLARD.—John Peter Willard was a native of Switzerland, born in 1745. He came to America as a soldier in the British service, but shortly after landing effected his escape. He then volunteered in the cause of the Colonies, and was with other deserters stationed on the Indian frontier or as guard of prisoners of war. At the close of the Revolution he took up a tract of land in Lykens township, called "Amsterdam," where he settled, began farming, and subsequently married. He died in 1821, at the age of seventy-six. His wife died the following year (1822) aged seventy-seven. They left the following family:

    i. Adam, who came into possession of the homestead. His children, Joseph, John A., Henry B., and Adam, Jr., then divided the farm. Part of it yet remains in possession of the descendants.

    ii. Samuel remained in the valley, a farmer, and had a large family.

    iii. Anna Maria married John Philip Umholtz.

THE UMHOLTZ FAMILY.

We are not entirely satisfied as to the orthography of this surname. Many of the old records have it Imholtz, some Omholtz, and others Umholtz. We are of the opinion that the former is the correct orthography. As the present members of the family adhere to the latter, it is this nomenclature we also shall employ.

Henry Umholtz, with a younger brother, came to this country from Switzerland, prior to the Revolution, and located in what is now Lykens township, Dauphin county, along the base of Short mountain, about two miles from Gratztown, where John Umholtz now resides. Here they took up quite a large tract of land and commenced farming. The brother entered the army at the outset of the war of the Revolution, in Capt. William Hendricks' company, and fell in the assault on Quebec. Henry was also in service during the war, as appears by the rolls of Captains Hoffman and Weaver's companies.

Henry Umholtz married about 1769 his first wife, who was a Miss Rouch. Sometime after her death he married Magdalena Seidensticker, daughter of Philip Seidensticker, of Bethel township, now Lebanon county. Mr. Umholtz died at an advanced age, and with his two wives are buried at Hoffman's church. His children as follows:

 i. John, born August 11th, 1770, was a farmer, and resided near Berrysburg. He married Catharine Harman and had a large family.

 ii. Barnhart, born October 22d, 1772, was a farmer, and resided above Gratztown. He married Catharine Rissinger, and had Michael and Solomon, who resides on or near his father's place; Philip; Susan, married Jacob Walborn; Anna Margaret, married George Hollobach; Catharine, married Michael Fisher; and Esther, married Daniel Emanuel.

 iii. Michael, born August 31st, 1776, removed to what is now Perry county, where he married and raised a family.

 iv. John Philip, born September 14th, 1779. He purchased his father's farm, following farming, and died in 1837. He married Anna Maria Willard, daughter of Peter Willard, and had:—Matthias, who settled in Starke county Ohio; John married Molly Shoffstall, and resides on the old homestead; Samuel resides near Gratz; Christian removed to Mercer county, Pa.; Susan married Daniel Loudenslager; Catharine married Isaac Henninger, of Starke county, Ohio; and Elizabeth married John P. Hoffman.

 v. Henry, b. September 17, 1783; was a soldier of the war of 1812, followed farming and owned a farm near Isaac Zitlinger. He married Susan Hoover, daughter of Jacob Hoover, of Hoover's Mill. They had Rebecca, m. Benjamin Gise, father of Captain Joseph D.; Leah, m. George W. Ferree; Polly, m. John Henninger, and Henry, jr., who for many years was a distinguished teacher in the "Upper End."

 vi. Anna Maria, b. July 12, 1781; m. Peter Yorty.

The family of Umholtz have all been substantial and representative farmers of the Valley, and we present the foregoing to show how faithfully they have preserved their geneological record, as an incentive to many others to do likewise.

HOFFMAN FAMILY, OF LYKENS VALLEY.

Among the earliest settlers of the Wiconisco valley was John Peter Hoffman, a native of Germany, born in 1709. With others of his family and friends he came to America in 1739 in the ship Robert and Alice, Captain Walter Goodman, arriving at Philadelphia in September of that year. He first located in Berks county, where he worked at his trade, that of a carpenter. During the early Indian troubles on the frontiers he served some time as a soldier in the Provincial forces. About the year 1750 he came to the end of Short mountain, in Lykens Valley, where he built a small log house, just across the road from the present residence of Daniel Romberger. Sixty years ago ago this was used as a blacksmith shop. John Peter Hoffman the contemporary of Andrew and John Lycan, or Lykens, Ludwig Shott, John Rewalt, and others, and with them driven off by the Indians in their marauds of 1756. It was subsequent to this period that he brought his family to the Valley. Here he followed farming and died in 1798 at the age of eighty-nine years. His remains with those of his wife, who had deceased previously, were interred in the field near the the present house on the old farm now owned by Mr. Romberger, before named. He left issue, among others, as follows:

  i. Catherine, m. Andrew Reigle, the head of a large family of that name in the "Upper End." They both reached the age of four score years.

  ii. Barbara, m. George Buffington, a soldier of the Revolution, and the head of the family of that name.

  iii. Elizabeth, m. Ludwig Sheetz, the head of the large family by that name.

1. *iv. John*, b. 1746, m. Miss Kauffman.
2. *v. John Nicholas*, b. 1749; m. Margaret Harman.
3. *vi. Christian*, b. 1752; m. Miss Deibler.

I. JOHN HOFFMAN (John-Peter), eldest son of John Peter Hoffman, was a native of Berks county, born in 1746. He served in the war of the Revolution, and commanded the Upper Paxtang company, in its expedition up the West Branch in 1778, and participated in the battle of Muncy Hill. He resided near Hoffman's church on the farm now owned by George Willard. He was a farmer, and served as a justice of the peace from 1771 until 1831, the year of his death. He and his wife, a Miss Kauffman, are buried in Hoffman's church grave-yard. They had issue as follows:

  i. Elizabeth, m. John Hoffman, a farmer. They resided near Hoffman's church, on the farm now owned by George Row.

ii. Mary, m. Joseph Neagley, a farmer, who resided in the lower part of the Valley. They had a large family, and lived to advanced ages.

iii. Magdalena, m. Thomas Koppenheffer. He was a Captain in Col. Timothy Green's Battalion, and was at the battle of Long Island. Mrs. Koppenheffer lived to be over four score years of age.

iv. Catharine, m. John Buffington, a farmer, who resided on the farm adjoining Robert Elder's, now owned by Jacob Hartman. Mr. Buffington was County Commissioner from 1822 to 1824.

v. Barbara, b. 1800; m. John N. Specht. She d. in 1879.

vi. John, m. Miss Diebler.

vii. Jacob, married and removed to Schuylkill county, where some of his descendants yet reside.

viii. Daniel, m. Miss Snyder.

II. JOHN NICHOLAS HOFFMAN (John-Peter) was born in Tulpehocken township, Berks county, in the year 1749. He settled on the farm now owned by Benjamin Rickert, near Short Mountain. He was the owner of a large tract of land, at present divided into a number of farms. He deeded land to the congregation of Hoffman's church, for church, school and burial purposes. He was a soldier of the Revolution, and participated in the battles of Brandywine and Germantown. His life was an active, busy and useful one. He was married April 22, 1772, by pastor Kurtz, of the Lutheran church, to Margaret Harman, also a native of Berks county. They had issue as follows:

i. Catharine, b. 1775; m. Peter Shoffstall. They resided near Gratztown, and died at advanced ages, leaving a large family.

ii. Susanna, m. Levi Buffington, a carpenter. He built the Hoffman church.

iii. Sarah, m. Jonathan Snyder. They removed to Starke county, Ohio, near Canton, where they were both living about eight years ago, upwards of ninety years of age.

iv. Margaret, m. Alexander Klinger, and removed to Crawford county, Pa. She died a few years ago at the age of 98.

6. *v. Peter*, b. September 22, 1778; m. Miss Lubold.
7. *vi. Jacob*, b. 1782; m. Catharine Ferree.
8. *vii. Daniel*, b. 1784; m. Hannah Ferree.
9. *viii. Nicholas*, b. 1784; m.
10. *ix. John*, b. 1780; m.

x. George, b. 1798; resides in Gratztown; was appointed justice of the peace in 1834, and at present holds that office.

III. CHRISTIAN HOFFMAN (John-Peter), resided on the old homestead at the end of Short Mountain. He died in Powell's Valley. He was a soldier of the Revolution, and an active citizen in the "Upper End." He married a Miss Deibler, sister of John's wife, and they had issue:
    i. Anna Mary, married John Pres, and left a large family. They resided at Sand Spring, in the upper end of Powell's Valley.
    ii. Susanna, married Philip Shott, and raised a numerous family.
    iii. Catharine, married Jonathan Novinger.
11. *iv. John B.*, born 1790, married Margaret Bowman.
    v. Jonas was a farmer, and resided at the foot of Peter's mountain, where he died.
    vi. Peter was a farmer, married and resided near Fisherville, where he died, leaving a large family.
    vii. Christian was a farmer, resided near Snyder's mill, Lykens Valley.
    viii. Daniel G., born 1795, was a farmer, and resides near Fisherville. Was a long time justice of the peace, and held other offices.
    ix. Philip, born about 1800, is justice of the peace for Jefferson township.

IV. JOHN HOFFMAN (John, John-Peter) resided near his father; was a farmer, and held the office of justice of the peace until he received the appointment of steward of the county almshouse in 1824, a position he held until 1838, when he was elected register, serving until 1841. He was married four times, his first wife being a Miss Deibler, sister to Daniel Deibler, senior, and left a large family.

V. DANIEL HOFFMAN (John, John-Peter), m. Miss Snyder and had one son, Daniel, jr., a distinguished civil engineer, residing in Philadelphia. John R., a son of the latter, also a civil engineer in the employ of the Summit Branch Railroad and Coal Company, resides at Pottsville. Daniel Hoffman, senior, died young, in Lyken's Valley, and his widow subsequently married John Hoke.

VI. PETER HOFFMAN (John-Nicholas, John-Peter) was born on the 22d of September, 1778. He was a farmer and owned the farm now in the occupancy of William Hawk; was a soldier of the War of 1812 and died in 1864, aged 86 years. He married a Miss Lubold, sister of Frederick Lubold. They are both buried in the Hoffman church graveyard. They left issue as follows:
    i. Daniel, m. Miss Rissinger and removed to Crawford county, Penn'a., where his son Josiah now resides. Another son,

Jonas, a carpenter resides at Lykens. Daniel died a few years ago aged 73 years.

ii. Jacob Peter, was quite a politician and died a few years ago in Lykens, where his widow and children now reside.

iii. John Peter, b. 1806, m. Elizabeth Umholtz, daughter of J. Philip Umholtz; is a farmer residing near Short Mountain. Their son, Henry B. was an aid on the staff of Gov. Pollock with the rank of Colonel, and represented Dauphin county in the Legislature, sessions of 1866, 1867 and 1869; resides at Harrisburg. Another son, John P., resides in Powell's Valley.

iv. Catharine, married Daniel Reigle. Mr. R. was County Commissioner, 1852–4.

v. Elizabeth, married Philip Keiser. Their son Daniel was a member of the Legislature, 1863–4.

vii. Hannah, m. Samuel Thomas.

VII. JACOB HOFFMAN (John-Nicholas, John-Peter), b. in 1782, purchased his father's farm. He was a well-informed farmer, and was exceedingly popular. He filled several local offices, and in 1833 and 1834 served in the Legislature. He was quite prominent in the church, and a zealous christian. He married Catharine Ferree. They had issue:

i. Amos, b. 1809; m. Amanda, daughter of the late Gen. Thomas Harper; was for a number of years steward of the almshouse, and at present resides at Berrysburg. At one time he had five sons in the Union army, Col. Thomas W., Capt. Jacob F., John H., Edwin A., and Henry.

ii. Jacob B., resides near Williamstown.

iii. Hannah, m. John Romberger.

iv. Sarah, m. Michael Forney.

v. Catharine, m. Abram Hess.

VII. DANIEL HOFFMAN (John-Nicholas, John-Peter), was born in 1784; was a farmer, and served as a soldier in the War of 1812. He died in 1830 at the age of 46 years. He married Hannah Ferree, and had issue:

i. David Ferree, was a merchant and justice of the peace. He died and is buried at Berrysburg. His son, Daniel C., became superintendent of a Kentucky and Tennessee railroad, and died of yellow fever in 1878, at Louisville, Ky.

ii. Jacob D., was a county commissioner and twice sheriff; resides at Harrisburg.

iii. Daniel, is a miner, and resides at Lykens.
iv. Joseph, resides at Hummelstown.
v. Hannah, m. Isaac Uhler, a miller.
vi. Elmira, m. John S. Musser, who was county commissioner, 1860–62; resides at Millersburg.

IX. NICHOLAS HOFFMAN (John-Nicholas, John-Peter), was born in 1790—a farmer, and served in the War of 1812. He died in 1874, at the age of 84. He had issue:
i. John Nicholas; was director of the poor; resides in Washington township.
ii. Isaac; was county commissioner 1867–70.
iii. Sarah, m. ——— Sheaffer; their daughter Mary married William B. Meetch, present register of the county.
iv. James, resides on the old homestead.

X. JOHN B. HOFFMAN (John-Nicholas, John-Peter), born in 1794, was a soldier in the War of 1812; a tailor by trade, and resided near Berrysburg, where he died. He left a large family. George, Daniel and Henry Hoffman severally married daughters of John Katterman.

XI. JOHN B. HOFFMAN (Christian, John-Peter), born in 1790, was a blacksmith by trade; served in the War of 1812, in which he was promoted a Lieut. Colonel. He filled a number of responsible official positions, and died in 1875, aged 85 years. He married Margaret Bowman, and left a large family, most of whom reside in Powell's Valley.

What is remarkable in the foregoing Record is the great age the heads of the different families reached—few dying under four score. Several who are yet living have passed that finger board of time, and are as hale and hearty as many who have not passed their sixtieth birthday. Industry, sobriety and pure morals no doubt have produced this extraordinary general longevity.

NOTES AND QUERIES—XXXI.

CIDER A CURE FOR RHEUMATISM.—The following letter of Hon. William Maclay, one of the first Senators from Pennsylvania, to Joshua Elder, Esq.. another prominent man at the time in this State, is perchance explanatory in itself. The allusion to a "Companion of the Compass," refers to the tavern which was so called, kept at that period by Robert Harris, son of the founder, and now used as a school-house, opposite the Harris Park, on Paxtang street. The letter will bear reading:

"SUNBURY, *11th April, 1791.*

"DEAR SIR: I am told that Cider is a good remedy against the Rheumatism, and have some reason to believe that it has been of some service to me. I have, however, experienced a severe disappointment in my arrangements to provide myself with this medicine, and instead of Two Barrels of fine racked Cider which I expected, Two have been delivered that cannot be used. As you live near where Cider is often sold, I want you to help an old lame Companion of the Compass. I have not a Barrel left, and I send you a Quarter Cask, which in better times contained better liquor. We have endeavored to season it as well as we could, and hope it will be true to its Trust both as to Quantity and Quality. This I hope you will have both leisure and opportunity to get filled with the best racked Cider. I have sent you Two Dollars to discharge the pecuniary expense; as to the Trouble, I know not how you will devise ways and means to be reimbursed. Until that happens, I consent to be your grateful Debtor, and in the meanwhile, am with best compliments to Mrs. Elder,

Your sincere Friend,
& most H'ble Serv't,
WM. MACLAY.

"To Joshua Elder, Esq."

HERALDIC ARMS OF SOME PENNSLYVANIANS.

When the previous article (N. &. Q. ix.) was printed, we had in our possession the following additional descriptions of the arms of Dauphin county families, but retained them in the hope of securing other information. The gentleman to whom we were indebted for them leaving the city, we have not been able to obtain such data, and hence give those which follow:

PORTER.—Sa. a chevron between three church bells arg. . . *Crest* —A church bell between two columns, with pyramidal tops arg.

VON TREUPEL.—Arg. on a mount a Moor wreathed around the middle with feathers or., in the dexter hand a bow, in the sinister a quiver. . . *Crest*—a demi-Moor as in the arms.

THOMAS.—Quarterly—1st & 4th Arg. on a chev. engrailled az 2 griffins rencoutrant of the field gorged with 2 bars gu. on a chief of the 2d. 3 cincquefoils pierced or; 2d and 3d ar. a lion rampant ppr. . . *Crests*—Out of a ducal coronet a demi-sea horse sal. Second a lion rampant ppr.

McIlhenny.—Ar. six horses head erased, sa. bridled ar. . . *Crest* —A horse's head, as in the arms.

Cowden.—Azure on a fesse argent between three annulets, or a lion passant sable. . . *Crest*—A demi-lion sable, charged with an annulet or.

Boyd.—Azure a fesse cheequey ar., and gu in base a cross moline or. . . *Crest*—A cross moline sable.

Hoffman.—Ermine, three lozenges gu. . . *Crest*—Out of the top of a tower, a demi-man, attired in a chain mail, pro the dex-hand brandishing a battle axe or.

Haldeman.—Sa. a chev ermine between three cats passant argent. . . *Crest*—A cat passant argent.

Buehler.—Gules, a lion rampant or. ensigned with a ducal coronet.

While on this subject we may state that George W. Harris, Esq., at the time Mr. De Courcy was here, handed us an engraved book-mark of the Rev. John Ewing, D. D., his grandfather, that a description might be obtained from Mr. De Courcy. On showing it to the latter he at once said it was the arms of the Ewing and Sargent family impaled. After inquiry we ascertained that the Rev. Dr. Ewing married a daughter of Jonathan Dickinson Sargent, of Philadelphia, and hence the description was correct. It is herewith appended:

Ewing.—Arg. a chev. embattled az. consigned with a banner gu. thereon a canton of the second, charged with a saltire arg. between two mullets in chief and a sun in base of the third . . *Crest*—A demilion arg. holding in his dexter paw mullet gu.

Sargent.—Arg. a chev. between three dolphins embowed sa.— Motto—" Audaciter."

LYTLE'S FERRY.

Joseph Lytle removed from Marietta to the spot which was afterwards known as "Lytle's Ferry" in the fall of 1773. The property was obtained by warrents issued severally to John Krocker, Samuel Hunter and Joseph Lytle, and comprised about two hundred acres in all.

Geographically, the location was about four miles north of Halifax, two miles south of Millersburg, and about a half mile below Berry's mountain—which was then a formidable barrier to journeying along the river.

Here Joseph Lytle established a ferry, which became the most important crossing on the river between Harris' Ferry and Sunbury (Fort Augusta). The property was surveyed by Bartrem Galbraith and styled "Fairview," in December of 1773. Joseph Lytle continued in this occupation until his death, about 1790. The ferry property was then purchased by his only son, John Lytle, and Michael Bauer. At the end of about sixteen years they sold the ferry to William Moorehead, father of the Moorehead brothers (J. Kennedy, of Pittsburgh, J. Barlow, of Philadelphia, &c.), well known through Pennsylvania, in April, 1806. Mr. Moorehead came from Soudersburg, Lancaster county, and after some time also tried to start up a town—"Williamsville"—but I don't think it was successful. He changed the name to "Moorehead's Ferry," and at the expiration of his ownership he removed to Harrisburg in 1814, and died there in 1817. After Moorehead it was called "Montgomery's Ferry," and is only remembered as such at this day.

I am under the impression that Joseph Lytle was connected with or had experience at, the ferries at Columbia, Marietta and the lower Susquehanna, and that, seeing a good opening above, he seized the opportunity. When he arrived at Lytle's ferry he had a wife and three children. Concerning him we hope to have additional information.

G. B. A.

A POLITICAL POEM IN LATIN OF 1800.

[The author of the following poem in Latin doggerel was JOHN DOWNEY, ESQ., one of the representative men of this locality seventy or eighty years ago, and as a fitting preface to its production it may be of some interest to know more of the gentleman who figured so conspicuously in political affairs from 1795 to 1826, the year of his death.

[JOHN DOWNEY, the son of John and Sarah Downey, was born at Germantown, Pennsylvania, in the year 1770. He received a classical education in the old academy there, and in 1795 located at Harrisburg, where he opened a Latin and a Grammar school. At this period in a letter to Governor Thomas Mifflin he proposed a "Plan of Education," remarkably forshadowing the present common school system, and which has placed him in the front rank of early American Educators. The Hon. Henry Barnard, of Connecticut, whose numerous works on education demand respect for his opinion pronounces the "Plan" of Mr. Downey, as being "far in advance of of the age in which he lived." As one of the representative men of this section of the State, Mr. Downey was in correspondence with the leaders of public opinion at the commencement of the century, and it is a serious loss that his papers were destroyed. He was for many years a justice of the peace, and served as town clerk for a long time. He was the first cashier of the Harrisburg Bank, largely instrumental in securing the erection of the bridge over the Susquehanna, and one of the corporators of the Harrisburg and Middletown turnpike company. Was a member of the Legislature 1817-18 and filled other positions of honor and profit. He died at Harrisburg on the 21st of July, 1827, and the *Oracle* speaks of him as "a useful magistrate and a pious man." Mr. Downey married June 5th, 1798, Alice Ann Beatty, daughter of James Beatty, Esq., one of the first settlers at Harrisburg. She died in Ashland county, Ohio, May 14, 1841. Their adopted daughter, Ellen Downey, married Hon. Daniel Kilgore, of Ohio.]

A Republican Caucus or Democratic Assembly.

PRÆSES.

Savantissimi Doctores
Republicanæ Professors
Qui hic assemblat estis ;
Et vos altri Messiores
Fidelis Executores
Mendaces, Mimæ et Scriptores,
Atqua tota Campania aussi
Libertas et Egalite
Salut, et Fraternite.

Non possum, docti Confreri,
En moi satis admirari
Qua is bona Inventio
Est REPUBLICANA PROFESSIO :
Quam bella chosa est, et bene trovata,
Resublicansin illa benedicta ;
Quæ suo homine solo
Suprenanti miraculo,
Depuis Revolutione,
Fait a gogo vivere
Tant de Gens omni genere.

Per totam terram videmus
Grandam vogam ubi sumus ;
Et quod grandes et petiti
Sunt de nobis in atuti,
Totus mundus currens ad nostra Exempla,
Nos regardat sicut Deos,
Et nostris Ordinanciis
Principes et Reges soumissos videtis.

Donque il est nostræ Sapientiæ,
Boni sensus, atqua Prudentiæ,
De fortement travillare
A nos bene conservare

In tali Credito, Voga et Honore ;
Et prendere Gardam a non recevere
In Sedious Congress : nec Presidentiæ,
Quam personas capabiles
Et totas dignas ramplire
Has placas honorabiles.

C'est pour cela, que nunc convocati estis,
Et crede quod trovabitis
Dignam Materiam Jacobino,
In excelsum erigere velle
Le Philosophe de Monticelli;
Et facere Amicum Mazzei
Directorem Publicæ Rei
Donque roulantes
Sur libertat is Pelagi Æstus,
Pour jamais submergitis,
Jacobinico Felle
"Tutos nimium, timidosque Procellæ,"*

Primus Citoyen.

Si mihi Licentiam dat Citoyen Præses
Et tanti Illuminati et Homines de Talens,
Damandabo,
Ut Quidam Methodum voluit dare
Per quem Electionem speramus portare.

Jacobinus.

Nobis a docto Illuminato
Demandatur Methodum optimum
Electionem portandi ;
A quo respondeo :
   Vulgum adorare,
   Classem formidare,
   Exercitum reprobare,
   Les Federalists vituperare,
   Tyrannidem imputare,
   Ensuitta Scandalizare, Royalizare,
   Robbins-are, calumniare.

Chorus.

   Bene, Bene, Bene, respondere
   Dignus, Dignus est Methodus
   De nostro Docto Corpore,
   Bene, Bene, respondere.

Un Simple Citoyen.

Mais si Oppositio
Opiniatra,
Non vult se succumbre ;
Si les Federalists nos probent Mendaces ;
Et nomen Parati,
Nashum non Robbins, suisse,
Et Hiberniam non Danb'ry, Homicidam dedisse,
Quid illi facere ?

---

*Who prefer the calm of Despotism, to the "tumultuous sea of liberty."

JACOBINUS.

Vulgum adorare,
Classem formidare,
Exercitum reprobare,
Les Federalists vituperare,
Tyrannidem imputare,
Ensuitta Scandalizare
Re-Royalizare, re-Robbins-are, et re-Calumniare.

CHORUS.

Bene, Bene, Bene, respondere
Dignus, dignus est Methodus
De nostro Docto Corpore.
Bene, Bene, respondere.

A SERMON OF PARSON ELDER.

The following are the heads of one of the Sermons of the Rev. John Elder, the original of which is in the possession of the Dauphin County Historical Society. It is written on one side of a piece of paper about three by six inches, in remarkably fine penmanship, and is endorsed as follows:

"Donegal—Action Sermon, October, 31, 1779.
Paxtang—Action Sermon, October 3, 1784.
Donegal—June 2d, 1787, on Psalm xxxvi: 8.
Paxtang—Action Sermon, October 11, 1789, on Psalm lxv: 4.

"*They shall be abundantly satisfied*," &c.: *Psalm, xxxii: 28.*

DOCT.—God provides in his Church the most rich and satisfying delicacies for his people.

In speaking of this I shall show—
1. That Christ in his ordinances provides richly for his people.
2. That the Lord's Supper is one principal feast he prepares for them.
3. Why he provides such a feast. And apply it.

As to the *first* this is evident.
1. From his promises, as in the text and Isaiah xxv: 6.
2. From his faithfulness, Ps. xxxvi: 5; lxxxix: 33, and xcii: 2, and Num. xxiii: 19.

Second. I'm to show that the Lord's Supper is one feast—a rich and satisfying feast—where the most delicate provision is made. For here it is—
1. A pardon of sin sealed to the believer. Matt. ix: 2; 2 Sam. xii: 13.
2. Peace and friendship with God. Rom. viii: 33, 34.

3. Adoption into the family of heaven. Gal. iv: 6, 7.
4. Peace of conscience. John xiv: 27; Luke xxiv: 36, 37, 38, 39.
5. Plentiful supplies to our weak graces.
6. Christ's gracious presence. Ps. xvi : 11.
7. The comforts of the Spirit. 2 Cor. i : 4.
8. Full assurance of faith. Job. xix : 25; 2 Tim. i : 12.
Here everything necessary is provided, as—
1. Here is a laver for you to wash in. Zach. xiii : 1.
2. Here is music to delight you. Is. lvi : 7 ; Luke xv : 23, 24.
3. Here is the master of the feast to bid you welcome.
4. Here servants to attend you.
5. Here is a blessing by the Master.
6. Here is delightful company.
Thirdly. Why does God provide such a feast?
Answer:
1. To be a solemn memorial of his love to sinners.
2. To express his infinite riches and goodness. Esth. i : 3, 4.
3. To discover the joy and satisfaction he feels on the sinner's coming.
4. To afford the believers fuller communion with him.
2. To ratify and confirm the covenant with us. It was usual in the Eastern countries to confirm their contracts by eating and drinking together. Thus did Isaac and Abimelech, Gen. xxvi : 28, 30 ; thus Laban and Jacob, Gen. xxxi : 54 ; so did David and Abner, 2 Sam. iii : 20.
6. To be a cordial to his children, to strengthen them by the way.
7. To fortify and encourage them against all difficulties and trials.
8. To wean them from the vanities of this world, and to give them a relish for heaven.
APPLICATION. Hence I infer—
1. What a reproach they cast upon religion who carry with them a sour and melancholy aspect.
2. Infer the amazing condescension of God in providing such a feast for poor guilty worms. 2 Sam. ix : 7, 8.
3. How inexcusable they are who slight this feast.
O, be exhorted then, to come to this feast. But some may object. How shall I dare to approach this solemnly ? Now, for your encouragement, I would recommend to you—
1. To employ Christ to introduce you.
2. Get your robes washed in his blood.
3. Put on the wedding garment of righteousness.
4. Plead for the drawings of his spirit. But with these following dispositions, as

1. With an holy awe and reverence of God.
2. With pure hearts and clean hands.
3. With an holy fear and jealousy.
4. With broken and bleeding hearts.
5. With lively faith.
6. [Obliterated.]
7. With strong desires after Christ.
8. With admiration and praise.

NOTES AND QUERIES.—XXXII.

MORDAH—MCKINNEY (N. & Q. xix. xxii. xxv.)—Agnes Mordah, daughter of John and Agnes Mordah, b. 1715, d. August, 1753, m. Henry McKinney, b. 1714, d. March 11, 1777. Their remains lie in Paxtang church-yard.

LEE (N. & Q., xxv).— From a memoranda found among the Yeates papers we learn that William Lee, of Paxtang, "died in April, 1748 or '49," leaving a wife and children. On the back of the paper is the following endorsement: "William Lee, dec'd—qu. also on the estate of John Lee, dec'd—(Mr. Andrew Lee, in Colonel Hazen's reg't)." Could this William Lee have been the father of the celebrated Captain Andrew Lee? It would seem so, yet we assumed the statement made by another writer that Thomas Lee was the father of the hero of the Revolution. Can any one give us the correct name, as also further information?

WARD, THE SCULPTOR.—Perhaps it would interest the readers of *Notes and Queries* to know that J. Q. A. Ward, the sculptor, of No. 9 West Forty-ninth street, New York, who modeled the equestrian statute recently unveiled at Washington City, was a great grandson of Hon. Robert Whitehill, whose mansion still stands two miles west of Harrisburg, and who lies interred in the churchyard at Silvers Spring. His daughter, Rachel Whitehill, was married, July 8, 1790, by Rev. Robert Davidson, D. D., to Alexander Macbeth. They removed to Ohio in the early part of this century, where Mr. Macbeth became prominent, politically, as Associate Judge, &c. (Mrs. Rachel Macbeth, *nee* Whitehill, died at Urbana, Ohio, Feb. 13, 1846, aged 82). Their daughter, Eleanor, married John A. Ward, father of the sculptor. Their great grandson, Edgar M. Ward, is an artist of considerable ability, who spent some time last summer sketching scenery about Harrisburg.   J. B. L.

MEANS.—Samuel Means took up a trac^t of land in Paxtang previous to 1736. He died February 25, 1746–7, leaving a widow, Grizel Means, who died in November following. They had issue—
  i. *Samuel.*
  ii. *Margaret.*
  iii. *Nelly.*
  iv. *Andrew.*
  v. *Jean.*
  vi. *Isabella.*
  vii. *John.* b. 1745, d. Oct. 3, 1795.
  viii. *Mary.*

From a memoranda in the hand-writing of Judge Yeates, of Lancaster, we have this data—
  i. *Samuel,* d. umn. at twenty-five years of age.
  ii. *Francis,* d. at eleven years of age.
  iii. *Catharine,* m. James Dickey; removed to Carolina.
  iv. *Agnes,* m. Israel Holcup, and had issue—Anna m. Edward Dunn; Jonas; Israel, who went aboard a privateer and was never heard of afterward.
  v. *Robert,* removed to Cumberland county, twenty miles from Carlisle.
  vi. *Grizel,* m. William Little, and removed to Maryland.

This memoranda was made about the year 1780. Can any one unravel it, or rather reconcile it with the data obtained from the original will.

ITINERARY OF PRESIDENT WASHINGTON DURING THE WHISKY INSURRECTION.

[Recently the Shippensburg *News* published an article from the pen of one of the historians of the Cumberland Valley relative to Washington remaining over night at Shippensburg, while on his journey to the Western part of Pennsylvania, in the fall of 1794, to quell the so-called Whisky Insurrection. Impressed with the idea that an Itinerary of the same would be interesting, as well as valuable, in a historic point of view, we essayed to prepare one, but found it a labor we were unable to successfully complete. What was found, after considerable research, we forwarded to the *News,* and which we transfer to the column of *Notes and Queries,* feeling confident that it will prove interesting to the readers thereof.

Wednesday, Oct. 1.—President Washington, accompanied by his escort, left Philadelphia for the westward, via Reading, reaching Harrisburg on the afternoon of Friday, October 3, where he remained over night. We have not yet been able to ascertain where General Washington passed Wednesday and Thursday evenings. At Harrisburg, on the evening of the 3d, he was presented with the address of the burgesses, to which he replied next morning.

Saturday, Oct. 4.—General W. left Harrisburg in the morning, reaching Carlisle about twelve o'clock noon. This point was the rendezvous of the Pennsylvania and New Jersey troops, who turned out to receive him. The address of the inhabitants of Carlisle was presented on the 6th (Monday), and not on the 17th, as dated in the Archives. The latter date is the endorsement on the copy, and was evidently a mistake of the copyist at the time. In the Philadelphia newspapers no date is given, but as the heading to the address is in these words, it is presumed to be the correct date: "Carlisle, Oct. 7, 1794. The following address of the Inhabitants of Carlisle was yesterday presented to the President."

From Saturday, Oct. 4, to Saturday, Oct. 11, the President remained at Carlisle, reviewing the troops, etc.

Saturday, Oct. 11.—General W. left Carlisle, dined at Shippensburg, reaching Chambersburg the same evening.

Sunday, Oct. 12, was probably spent with Dr. Robert Johnson, who was a surgeon of the Pennsylvania Line during the Revolution, and a warm personal friend of the President. This is merely traditionary, but as he met Dr. Johnson, either going or returning at this time, it is presumed that it was the 12th.

Monday, Oct. 13.—In a letter dated "Oct. 14, 1794," at Hargerstown, published in the Philadelphia papers, it is stated: "The President reached Williamsport last evening from Chambersburg. He starts for Fort Cumberland this morning." A letter also dated Chambersburg, Oct. 12, says: "The President arrived in this town last evening. On Monday morning he will proceed on his journey to the westward by way of Williamsport and Fort Cumberland."

Tuesday, Oct. 14.—"Early this morning General Washington set out for Fort Cumberland."—*Letter from Williamsport, Md.*

Thursday, Oct. 16.—General Washington reached Fort Cumberland. Next day (17th) he reviewed the Virginia and Maryland troops under the command of General Lee.

Sunday, Oct. 19.—General Washington arrived at Bedford from Fort Cumberland. Here he remained until Tuesday, Oct. 21, when he set out on his return by way of "Strasburg and Burnt Cabins." It was on his return he remained over night at Shippensburg, which was probably Friday, Oct. 24. The next night he stopped with General Michael Simpson, who resided on the Cumberland side of the Susquehanna at Chambers', or, as sometimes called, Carlisle Ferry. It is not definitely known where Washington passed Sunday and Monday nights, but he reached Philadelphia early on the morning of Tuesday, October 28. Owing to the exigency of affairs, his return to the Capital admitted of no delay.

It is somewhat surprising that not one of the vast number of biographers of Washington ever attempted to give an "Itinerary" of this expedition to the westward in 1794, and it is wonderful, notwithstanding the commotion and excitement relating thereto, that the newspapers of that period are so meagre in their details of this episode in the history of Western Pennsylvania.

NAMES OF PERSONS WHO TOOK THE OATH OF ALLEGIANCE TO THE STATE OF PENNSYLVANIA IN PAXTANG TOWNSHIP, 1778-79.

A history of the Test Oath in Pennsylvania is an interesting subject, but we can only refer our readers to Vol. III. 2d Series Pennsylvania Archives, for a summary thereof. Suffice it to say that owing to the large number of Tories in and around Philadelphia during the Revolution, it was decided necessary by the Convention of July 15, 1776, which adopted the first Constitution of the State, and by the first Assembly acting under it, to adopt an oath of allegiance, a measure which was absolutely requisite to restrain the insolence of the Tories.

To this measure of self-protection the Quakers of Chester, Bucks and Philadelphia made stern resistance, and a number of the more prominent of them were exiled to Virginia, as an example to others of the fate which awaited those persisting in a refusal to take the oath. In the interior counties there was little or no objection. The people were patriotic from the first, and had an inborn hatred to British oppression and British tyranny.

Through the kindness of that indefatigable antiquary, SAMUEL EVANS, ESQ., of Columbia, we have in our possession the list of persons who took the oaths in Paxtang, Hanover and Derry townships, the first of which we propose to give in this number. They are valuable contributions to the history of our county. The indorsement on the following is in these words: "The within is a list of Person's Names who took the Oath of Allegiance before Joshua Elder, one of the Justices for Lancaster county, from the 28th of January, 1778, to the 7th of January, 1779."

Historical and Genealogical.

"We, the subscribers, do swear (or affirm), that we renounce and refuse all allegiance to George the Third, King of Great Britain, his heirs and successors, and that we will be faithfnl and bear true allegiance to the Commonwealth of Pennsylvania, as a free and independent State, and that we will not, at any time, do, or cause to be done, any matter or thing that will be prejudicial or injurious to the freedom and independence thereof, as declared by Congress, and, also, that we will discover, and make known to some justice of the peace of the said State, all treasons and traitorous conspiracies which we now know, or hereafter shall know, to be formed against this or any of the United States of America."

Jacob Springer,
John Sprouls,
Felix McCaskey,
John Spilenburg,
Christian Myer,
Valentine Hummel,

Fred. Hummel, Jr.,
Abel Morgan,
Robert Brodie,
John Graham,
Samuel McFadden,
James Curry,

George Louer,
John Eversol,
James Barber,
Peter Pancake,
Robert Chambers.

Before the 26th of March, 1778.

Abner Wickersham,
Thomas Thompson,
John Donley,
William Ashcraft,
John Hinds,
Joseph McElrath,
Michael Shaver,
Jacob Noss,
Conrad Yonce,
Rowland Chambers,
John Millegan,
George Williams,
Jacob Derigh,
Hugh Crockett,
John Darby,
John Thompson,
Jeremiah Sullivan,
Frederick Hummel,
Michael Spade,
David Ritchey,
James Kyle,
Joseph Smith,
Robert Crawford.
William Glover,
John Brown,
Peter Duffey,
Alexander Reynolds,
John Garber,
Hugh Cunningham,
Colonel Matthew Smith,
Marcus Huling,
Hugh Stuart,
Hugh Jones,

James Burd, Esqr.,
Edward Burd, Attorney,
John Foh,
William Sawyer,
Adam Shelly,
Henry Foght,
Frederick Cundrum,
Matthias Strean,
Arch'd. McAllister, Captain,
John Mitchel,
James Finey,
Ludwick Hemperly,
George Philip Shocken,
William Wall,
John Steel,
Richard McClure,
James McCord,
Samuel Smith,
William Steel,
Thomas Crab,
Peter Shuster,
John Steel,
John Brown,
John Boland,
John Larkey,
Mungo Lindsey,
William McClenaghan,
James Means,
Jacob Youngman,
Barney Shoop,
Howard Moore,
John Means,

Thomas King,
Thomas Johnston,
John Adam Wertz,
John Wertz,
Daniel Steever,
Adam Deem,
James Work, Esq.,
Philip Ettele,
John Ryan, Jun'r,
Christian Gross,
George Minsker,
Nicholas Cassel,
Lary Smith,
Conrad Tate,
John Seibert,
Joseph Flora, Jr.,
John Lanning, Sr.,
David Tate, Jr.,
George Carson,
Michael Lewis,
Peter Flora,
William Lindsey,
Gottlieb David Ettelin,
Anthony Plesson,
John Moore,
Robert McGill,
Henry Davis,
Abram Holmes,
Daniel Dowdle,
Conrad Derr,
Michael Wolf,
Simon Raredon.

George Wood,
John King,
Adam Kitchmiller,
William Palm,
Thomas Murray, Col.; a prisoner,
Joseph Fearer,
David McCausland,
Thomas Beard,
John Maxwell,
Jacob King,
James Robertson,
John Cline,
Francis Conway,
George Fouts,
Francis Burleigh,
Robert Neel,
Samuel Barnett,
Philip Conser,
John Richmond,
John Wilson,
James Johnston,
John Forster,
James Walker,
William Dickey,
James Bell,
John Cochran,
James Watt,
Robert Armstrong,
Sam'l Pollock,
George Neagle,
Robert Wilson,
Alexander Wilson,
John Wilson,
John Parker,
John Kisner,
Aquilla Richard,
James Burney,
David Shaw,
Patrick Heany,
John Brown,
Thomas McArthur,
Casper Byerly,
James Boggs,
Patrick Lafferty,
Adam Means,
James Wilson,
Arthur Brisbin,
Thomas Moore,
Joseph Wilson, Jr.,
Fred'k. Forster,
George Fridley,
Jacob Fridley,
Jacob Poorman,
Joseph Wilson,
David Rose,
Henry Noramire,
John Renick,
John Elder,
George Gray,
James Veech,
Edward McAtee,
John Thomas,
Ludwig Bretz,
Thomas Wiley,
Jacob Kerr,
John Wonderleigh,
John Burrowe,
Hugh Montgomery,
John Dyce,
Philip Tinturf,
Abraham Mooney,
John Peter Vee,
John Cavet,
William Forster,
Joseph Colligan,
James Leonard,
William Ayers,
Robert Armstrong,
Moses Lockhart,
Daniel McKoy,
John Melone,
John McFaddin,
Robert Smith,
Jacob Tinturf,
Anthony Hoan,
William Bell,
Robert Gowdy,
John Bell,
Stophel Lark,
Jacob Sheesly,
Michael Yonrell,
George Adam Gardner,
Peter Corbett,
Thomas Gallagher,
Andrew Bell,
John Bell,
William Fulton,
Joseph Fulton,
Arthur Chambers,
Mich'l Smith,
James DeFrance,
John Bowman,
John Barnett,
Thomas Nichols,
Thomas Murray,
Elisha Chambers,
George Simmons,
Paul Randolph,
George Weatherhold,
John Litle,
Abraham Brunson,
Maurice Sullivan,
Benjamin Brown,
Joseph Litle,
Laurence Hatten,
Edward Wilcox,
Charles McCoy,
Robert Boyd,
Jacob Miller,
Abraham Edgar,
Michael Cassel,
Frederick Cassel,
Jacob Cryder,
Martin Hemperley,
Jno. Wonderleigh, Jr.,
John Sadler,
George Pancake,
John O'Neal,
Andrew Smith,
George Wreddle,
Peter Patterson,
John Whitehill,
John Cochran,
Michael Ault,
Elijah Stuart,
Alex'r. McCompsey,
Sam'l Cochran,
Rich'd Carson,
John Murray,
William Wilson,
John Bell,
John Miller,
John Raredon.

N. B. One hundred and forty-three of the last-mentioned names on this list, beginning at George Wood under the black line, were sworn and subscribed since the first day of June, 1778.

A true copy from the original.
Given under my hand and seal,

JOSHUA ELDER, [L. S.]

NOTES AND QUERIES.—XXXIII.

CATHEY—MOORHEAD.—John Cathey, of Paxtang, died in the month of February, 1742-3. By his will, proved October 1st, he left his estate to his wife, Ann Cathey; his children, Alexander, George and Jean Cathey; his grandchildren, Alice Cathey, John Cathey, Jean Trindell and John Graham, and his daughter, Eleanor Moorhead, "if she comes to this country." Who was this Moorhead whom Eleanor Cathey married, and did she come to America?

MONTGOMERY—LEE.—Robert Montgomery, of Paxtang, died in October, 1748, leaving his estate to his wife, Elizabeth, his son John and grandson Robert, daughter Jean, who married James Toland; Robert, the son of his daughter, who married George Clark; and daughter Rebecca, who married ———— Lee. Could this latter have been the ancestor of Capt. Andrew Lee? (N. & Q., xxv.)

JUSTICE EIGHTY YEARS AGO.—One of the early dispensers of justice in Millersburg was 'Squire Weaver, grandfather of the late Martin Weaver. Old 'Squire Seal used to describe Weaver's courts to me. He always effected a compromise agreement between parties in suit. To this end he used two pursuasives. He placed on his table a bottle of whisky and a heavy stick. Parties litigant had first to drink, then to talk it over and drink again. If they did not agree by the time the third drink was taken the 'Squire used the club argument, and that never failed. I may add that Mr. Weaver was a very popular justice of the peace. H. R.

['Squire Martin Weaver, of whom the foregoing is related, was an early settler near Millersburg. He was a soldier of Captain Matthew Smith's company of Paxtang—was left ill at Cambridge and returning home, assisting in raising a company of associators, of which he was a lieutenant, and in active service during the campaign in the Jerseys during the summer of 1776. He subsequently became captain of the Upper Paxtang company of Colonel Murray's battalion, employed during the remainder of the Revolution on the frontier, in defending it from the marauds of the Indians and their hardly less savage allies, the Tories. Under the Constitution of 1790, Captain Weaver was commissioned a justice of the peace, and held the office at the time of his death, which occurred the 29th of August, 1803, at an advanced age.]

CARSON.—Readers of *Notes and Queries* will have noticed obituaries of John Carson in late newspapers. All that we have observed are inaccurate. It is here proposed to tell something of that gentleman, his family and his official services. Mr. Carson was appointed an officer in the revenue service as long ago as 1844 by the Secretary of the Treasury under President Polk, Robert J. Walker, who was a connexion of his family through the Duncans of Carlisle. At the time of his decease, Captain Carson was one of the oldest and highest in rank of the revenue officers. He served thirty-six years with integrity and distinction. During the civil war his duties were very active and his labor great. With other commanders of the revenue navy, he participated in several of the enterprises undertaken to obtain command of the Atlantic seaboard, led, of course, by officers of the regular navy. As the men of the revenue service are not recognized as part of the military establishment, it may be that his family will not be able to secure a pension, yet he is as much entitled to it as the survivors of any other officer, whilst technically unable to secure it. He came of good Dauphin county stock. His great-grandfather, John Carson, came to the spot, now the residence of Leander N. Ott, known as "Carson Hall," as early as 1740, possibly a few years previously. He was a successful trader, a soldier in the Braddock campaign and a useful frontier magistrate. He married a Berryhill, of Paxtang, near Fort Hunter. One of his daughters married Captain Archibald McAllister, hence the connexion between the family of Cox at Estherton, McAllister of Fort Hunter, and many other families of the early residents of the upper part of the then county of Lancaster. His son, Judge John Carson, upon the death of his father, took the substantial residence and farm as his share, where he resided all his life, a representative in the Legislature, a judge of the county courts, a soldier of 1776, one of the most esteemed and hospitable of gentlemen. He married a Duncan, of Cumberland county, sister of Judge Thomas Duncan. His son, Charles Carson, born at "Carson Hall," was both a merchant and farmer, a soldier of 1812, keeping up the reputation of the race for patriotism and activity. He married a Campbell, of Cumberland, whose mother was a Duncan. His son, Captain John Carson, was born in 1819 at "Carson Hall," was for a time a clerk in the office of the Secretary of the Commonwealth, then a clerk with Daniel D. Boas and David W. Mahon in the postoffice in Harrisburg under James Peacock. Jonas Rudy was the messenger—a "carrier" was not then known in coaching circles. After his appointment under the treasury, as he rose in grade, he married Susan Rinney, of New London, Conn., by whom he leaves a family of four children.

Historical and Genealogical.

In his youth, when best known at Harrisburg, he was beloved by a large circle of social friends for his genial and frank demeanor. He was not a frequent visitor to the land of his nativity for the last ten or fifteen years. When he came he was heartily welcomed by the friends of his youth, now grey-beards and grandfathers. He always expressed the greatest attachment to and pride in the prosperity and growth of Dauphin county.

At the time of his death, Monday, January 26, 1880, he was stationed at Oswego, New York, in command of the Revenue Steamer Manhattan. He is buried at Oswego.   A. B. H.

NAMES OF PERSONS WHO TOOK THE OATH OF ALLEGIANCE TO THE STATE OF PENNSYLVANIA, IN HANOVER TOWNSHIP, 1777–1779.

" *We, the subscribers, do swear (or affirm) that we renounce and refuse all allegiance to George the third, King of Great Britain, his heirs and successors, and that we will be faithful and bear true allegiance to the Commonweath of Pennsylvania, as a free and independent State, and that we will not, at any time, do, or cause to be done, any matter or thing that will be prejudicial or injurious to the freedom and independence thereof, as declared by Congress, and, also, that we will discover, and make known to some justice of the peace of said State, all treasons and traitorous conspiracies which we now know, or hereafter shall know, to be formed against this or any of the United States of America.*"

July 1, 1777.
Willm. McCullough,
William Young,
John Armstrong,
Robert Clark,
William Brown,
William McClure,
John Hume,
James Stewart,
George Boal,
John Dupes,
Daniel Musser,
Andrew Young,
Charles Barr,
Patrick Nattan,
Hugh Calhoun,
Henry Laughlin,
John Carter,
Joshua Magus,
Robt Freckelton,
James Young,
Leonard Brisben,
James Connor,

Joseph Riddle,
Colon Campbell,
William Watt,
John Torrance,
William Glen,
Neal McColigan,
Charles McElroy,
John Morison,
Chas Dougherty,
James Ripeth,
William Moore,
William Cunningham,
Robert Hervey,
Robt Alexander,
William McCormick,
James McMillan,
David Hoeney.
Thos. McCullough,
Daniel Valeney,
Robert Barr,
Robert Bedford,
Daniel Smith,
John Nowlan.

John Johnson,
Randal McDonel,
Samuel Starret,
David Davis,
William Hume,
Robert Dickey,
Moses Swan,
Jacob Musser,
James Hambel.
John Thompson,
Robert Craig,
Edward Tate,
James Webster,
John Kirkpatrick,
William Allen, Sr.,
Conrad Helam,
John Templeton,
July 9.
Philip Pleasly,
Adam Fierbaugh,
Milkey Rahm,
Peter Eversole,
Jacob Brunner,

July 16.
Valentine Conson,
Peter Perah,
Henry Newfer,
John Plesent,
Henry Fritz,
July 19.
Martin Miller,
John McNaughton,
Richard Johnson,
Conrad Smith,
Jacob Besoer,
July 20.
James Sloan,
William Vance,
Nicholas Brunner,
Jacob Cleaman,
William Hedrick,
July 21.
John McFarland,
Thomas Rowland,
William Miskimins,
Patrick Connor,
July 22.
James Low,
James Long,
July 23.
Andrew Berryhill,
James Taylor,
July 24.
Andrew Berryhill, Jr.,
Conrad Rhodes,
July 25.
William McRoberts,
John Templeton,
July 26.
James McEwen,
Alex. Berryhill,
William Carson,
July 27.
Joshua Elder, Esq.,
August 1.
William Brandon,
Abraham Ellis,
Robert Kenedy,
August 2.
Leonard Umbarger,
John Hewey,
August 3.
Alex. McIlhenny,
Andrew Kerr,
August 4.
John Miseeley,
Richard Deyermand,
James Willson,
Christly Bomberger,
Absalom Charles,
Abraham Ellis,

Thomas Robinson,
August 5.
Thomas Hume,
William Swan,
Richard Swan,
Robert Dalton,
John Rogers,
Henry Umbarger,
John Pleasant,
William Allen, Jr.,
August 6.
John Gowdey,
Martin McClure,
James Boyle,
Thomas McClure,
August 7.
John Barnett,
William Barnett,
William Allison,
George McMillan,
Robert Allen,
John McIlhenny,
Thomas Lintow,
Richard Crawford,
August 9.
James Johnson,
Joseph McClure,
James Johnson,
August 10.
David McCrokan,
August 11.
James Young,
George Nord,
John McCord,
John Petoric,
August 12.
John Poe,
William Hill,
August 14.
Albord Bowman,
William Sterrett,
David Maffrot,
Samuel Stewart,
James Porter,
Isaac Hody,
Joseph Wilson,
Robert Dunn,
Robert McColey,
James McCreight,
August 15.
James Blackburn,
Joseph McGuire,
August 18.
Hugh Gower,
Robert McCulley,
Robert Gilchrist,
August 19.
James McClure,

Joseph Hutchinson,
Francis McClure,
William Snodgrass,
August 22.
Joseph Wilson,
James Wallace,
August 28.
William Kithcart,
William Cowden,
James Alcorn,
Conrad Myer,
George Peters,
David Ramsey,
August 29.
Jacob Smith,
William Clark,
David Young,
John Barnett,
August 30.
John Ripeth,
William Mitchell,
Samuel Robinson,
Sept. 1.
Mical VanLear,
Stophel Heany,
Andrew Rogers,
John Miller,
William Crabb,
George Fleming,
Bernard Fridley,
Alexander Young,
Sept. 3.
John Deyermond,
Robert Cooper,
George Gilbarts,
Josias White,
John McClellan,
John McQuown,
James McNamara,
David Kindau,
Amos Thatcher,
Sept. 12.
Thomas Sturgeon,
George McMahan,
Francis Carson,
David Watson,
Sept. 17.
William Brown,
James Wilson,
David McGuire,
John Breaur,
Peter Brown,
John McMullan,
John Afford,
James Beard,
Thomas Srain,
Michael Whitley
John Snoddy,

William Snoddy,
Henry McCormick,
   Sept. 28.
Thomas Cook,

John Adams,
James Robinson,
James Rogers,
Hugh Ripeth,

Robert Hill,
John Trousdale,
Joseph Park,
Thomas McNair.

   The aforegoing names is the persons who have taken the oath of Aledgiance and fidelity to the State, agreeable to an Act of Assembly of Pennsylvania, sertified this 1st day of October, 1777.

Tim'y Green.

1778.

Henry Bucher,
John Cummins,
Robert Lusk,
Duncan Campbell,
John Campbell,
David Peticrue,
Henery Schrivar,
Robert Henery,
John Thompson,
Michael Salser,
Peter Stone,
James Philips,

George Tittle,
Samuel Ferguson,
Daniel NcBride,
William Wilkinson.
Benj. Sayers,
Barnard Fridley,
Henry Miller,
Daniel Till,
Ludwig Sherrat,
Jacob Heroff,
Peter Grasleas,
John Sayer,

Robert Boal,
James Stewart,
Thomas McMillan,
Alexander Johnston,
James Patterson,
John Fisher,
William Romage,
John Shissy,
David Caldwell,
James Clendenin,
Joseph Archer,
William Crain.

   I hereby certify that the above named persons have been sworn and affirmed before me, agreeable to an act of General Assembly of Pennsylvania, past June last.

Certify'd 6th May, 1778.
Tim'y Green

Jacob Keaplar,
Matthias Keaplar,
Hugh Ramsay,
Rob't Sturgeon,
Adam Harbison,
John Duncan,
John Ensworth,
James Andrew,
Eman'l Twoey,
Sam'l Sturgeon,
David Ramsay,
Thos. Strain, Jr.,
Michael Wallace,
Sam'l McCollough,
Jacob Rahm,
Thos. McCord,

John Brown,
Thomas Walker,
Joseph Barnet,
And'w Rogers,
Wm. Smith,
James Long,
Will'm Bright,
Thos. Finney,
John Calins,
Francis Colter,
Thos. Bell,
Will'm Thom,
Jacob Awl,
Thos. McElhenny,
George Wolf,

Michaes Myer,
Jas. Peticrue,
Will'm Wilson,
William Wilson,
John Reed,
Jacob Gray,
Nicholas Yont,
Abram Brubaker,
John Yont,
Nicholas Brubaker,
Emos Smither,
John Dunlap,
John Wiggins,
Mathew Crowser,
John Henry.

Lancaster County, ss:

   I do hereby certify that the above mentioned persons have been sworn and affirmed by me agreeable to the act of Assembly of Pennsylvania, pased June last obliging the inhabitants to pay allegiance to the same.   Sertify'd the 4th March, 1777.

Tim'y Green.

Henry Miller,
Wm. Trousdale,
Christopher Capp,
Henry Miller,
William Wallace,
Rob't McCallen,
Christ Kichwine,
Michael Mulver,
Michael Mulver, jr.,
John Wiggins,
Hugh Ray,
Abraham Jurey,
Samuel Jurey,
John Campbell,
Wm. Donaldson,
James Todd,
Michael Umberger,
John Todd,
David Todd,
Wendel Bartholemew,
Michael Mower,
Gilbert Graham,
Wm. McCauley,
John Miller,
Conrad Bombach,

Wm. Whitner,
John Ashbough,
Wm. Bollinger,
Dan'l Hoffman,
Wm. Carpenter,
John Francis Fox,
David Strain,
Wm. Strain,
James McMillen,
Alex. Kidd,
Arch. McCullough,
Christ. Fox,
Christ. Brown,
Matthias Beaker,
John Miller,
John Beaker,
John Umberger,
Peter Stone,
Geo. Crain,
Wm. Boys,
Jacob Miller,
James Dixon,
Jacob Kitsmiller,
John Hoover,
Christ. Forrer,

Philip Peter,
Geo. Stricker,
Alex. Sloan,
Wm. Ripeth,
Thos. Wallace,
Jacob Grove,
Fred. Pickle,
And. Cooper,
Michael Ryan,
Rob't Hill,
Dan'l Miller,
George Haine,
John Carvery,
Adam Poor,
Peter Fitting,
John Carvery,
Henry Fitting,
John Poor,
John Bruner, Sr.,
John Bruner, Jr,
Robt. Porterfield, sr.,
James Cavet,
James Breden,
Peter Killinger.

Lancaster County, ss:

The within is a just and true account of the persons' names, to whom the oath of allegiance has been administered to, agreeable to act of General Assembly, since my last return as made.

Certified March, 1, 1779, by
TIM'Y GREEN, [L. S.]

NOTES AND QUERIES.—XXXIV.

DUNCAN'S ISLAND.—It may not generally be known, for a number of years prior to 1819, strenuous efforts were made by interested parties to annex Duncan's Island to Cumberland county. Upon the formation of Perry county no doubt the opportunity would have been afforded the secessionists to be annexed to the new county, but that did not please them, and the excitement which agitated that fussy island was allayed, the inhabitants concluding to remain with their first love.

PALMSTOWN.—This town, now Palmyra, Lebanon county, was laid out by William Palm about the commencement of the century.

Quite a number of people were attracted to the new place, owing to inducements held out by the proprietor, but it suddenly came to "a stand still" by a water famine. As to the cause of this we are not credibly informed, yet it was probably due to the want of proper depth of the wells. All water had to be hauled a distance of two miles, and in 1807 the Legislature was petitioned for aid to build works for supplying the town. The citizens, however, were left to their own resources, and in due time the evil was remedied.

EARLY EFFORTS TO SUPPLY HARRISBURG WITH WATER.—In 1792 petitions were presented to the Legislature, asking for the passage of an act authorizing a company to open a canal from Hunter's Falls, on the Susquehanna, to the borough of Harrisburg, and a bill for this purpose was introduced in the Senate therefor. The main object was to afford not only mill power, but also to supply the town with an abundance of water. It was proposed to erect a wing dam in the Susquehanna, but the fear of obstructing the navigation of the river caused the defeat of the measure. A number of years subsequent, the celebrated bridge builder, and mechanic, Theodore Burr, proposed a similar improvement, but in his plan the bed of Paxtang creek was to be used for the projected canal. Mr. Burr and his colleagues gave such a wide scope in the privileges asked for, that for similar reasons it also failed. Beside the authority petitioned for, the aid of the State was invoked.

THE RANKIN TRAITORS.

The following document was recently found among the papers of General Henry Miller, who, during a portion of the dark period of the Revolution, was high sheriff of the county of York. The order was issued at a time when it was absolutely necessary to make treason odious, and the patriots of that day had determined to get rid of all persons who were inimical to the cause of independence. The order speaks for itself, and gives the charge on which it is based. Col. Rankin was one of three brothers, who, having at the outset of the Revolution sympathized with the Whigs, in a short time became the most virulent and disaffected of the Tories in Pennsylvania. Their arrest being imminent, they escaped to the British lines, sought the protection of the enemies of their country, and were all handsomely compensated by British gold for the loss of their property, which, as a matter of course, was righteously confiscated by the authorities of Pennsylvania. As efforts are constantly being made

236 *Notes and Queries.*

to compensate the descendants of the Rankins for the confiscation of the estate of their ancestors, the following paper will be a valuable document in connection with these memorials. It will bear reading:

Pennsylvania, ss:

The Commonwealth of Pennsylvania to the Sheriffs of the Counties of Chester, Lancaster, York and Cumberland, and to all and singular, Bailiffs, Constables and Ministers of Justice of the said Counties, and to every of the said officers, Greeting—

Inasmuch as the Chief Justice of our Supreme Court is given to understand, and be informed, that William Rankin, late of the aforesaid county of York, yeoman, commonly called Colonel William Rankin, John Jackson, the younger, late of the aforesaid county of Chester, and ——— McLaughlin, late of the said county of Chester, yeoman, hold a traitorous correspondence with the enemies of the United States of America, have given them intelligence, and traitorously engaged to join the armies of the King of Great Britain, together with one hundred troops, by them or some of them raised and enlisted for that purpose, and that they are guilty of other acts of treason. You, or one or more of you are therefore hereby commanded to apprehend them, the said William Rankin, John Jackson, the younger, and ——— McLaughlin, and them, or such of them, as shall be taken, to bring forthwith before our said Chief Justice, or some one of the other Justices of our said Supreme Court, to answer the premises and to be further dealt withal according to law. Hereof fail not at your peril.

Witness the Honorable Thomas McKean, Esquire, our said Chief Justice at Philadelphia, the twenty-fourth day of March, in the year of our Lord, one thousand seven hundred and eighty-one, and in the fifth year of our Government. THOS. MCKEAN.

PERSONS WHO TOOK THE OATH OF ALLEGIANCE IN LONDONDERRY TOWNSHIP, 1777–1778.

We herewith present the remaining list of persons who took the oath of allegiance as prescribed by the Assembly of Pennsylvania. As to the orthography of the names, we are not responsible. The unfamiliarity of the copyist with them no doubt accounts for the many blunders, and we have preferred that everyone should make the proper reading.

In connection therewith we give the following copy of the certificate given each person subscribing to the oath or affirmation of allegiance:

> I DO hereby CERTIFY, That *John Simpson* hath voluntarily taken and subscribed the Oath or Affirmation of Allegiance and Fidelity, as directed by an Act of General Assembly of Pennsylvania, passed the 13th day of June, A. D. 1777. Witness my hand and seal, the 14th day of October A. D. 1778.
> [L. S.] JOSHUA ELDER.

Printed by JOHN DUNLAP.

"*I do swear (or affirm), that I renounce and refuse all allegiance to George the Third, King of Great Britain, his heirs and successors, and that I will be faithful and bear true allegiance to the Commonwealth of Pennsylvania, as a free and independent State, and that I will not, at any time, do or cause to be done, any matter or thing that will be prejudicial or injurious to the freedom and independence thereof, as declared by Congress, and, also, that I will discover, and make known to some justice of the peace of the said State, all treasons and traitorous conspiracies which I now or hereafter shall know, to be formed against this or any of the United States of America.*

July 3.
James Bailey,
Alex'd Barnet.
July 19.
Darby Cassedy.
July 21.
James Kernachan,
John Kernachan.
July 22.
David Chambers.
July 29.
Michael Dermolt,
James Scott,
William Jamison,
Andw. Gross.
July 31.
Wm. Harvey.
Aug. 1.
Henry McGee.
Aug. 2.
Arch'd Walker,
Robert Allison,
Syms Chambers,
David Ramsey,
Sam'l Fenton,
William Campbell,
John Dean,
Thomas Ogle,
Sam'l Hannah,
Thomas Ramsey,
Barney Queen,
James Noble,
Moses Campbell,
John Campbell,
Samuel Bell,
Joseph Chambers,
Hugh Hall,
William Buck.
Aug. 4.
John Hay,
John Campbell,
James Russell,
John Logan,
James Riden.
Aug. 11.
Anth'y Bisman.
John Blair.
Aug. 12.
John Kimper,
Sam'l Sherrer,
George Bell,
John Jamison,
William Hay,
Joseph McQueen,
John Johnston,
David McQueen,
John Hagon.
Aug. 22.
David Jamison.
Aug. 28.
David Watson,
David Hays,
Patrick Hays,
John Weir,
Benjamin Boyd.
Oct. 27.
David Wray,
John Smith.
Nov. 1.
Joseph Shearer.
Nov. 14.
John Morrow.
Nov. 17.
John Kain.
Nov. 30.
Robert Jamison.
Dec. 8.
David McIntire.
Dec. 16.
Flavel Roan.

Jan. 3.
Henry Duey.
Feb. 10.
James Candour,
Rob't Rhea,
John Ritzel,
Joseph McClintoch.
Feb. 12.
David Mitchel.
Feb. 16.
James Smith,
Sam'l Hineman.
Mar. 17.
James Wilson.
Mar. 21.
Adam Henry.
Mar. 28.
Thomas Seaton.
Mar. 30.
John Thornton.
May 10.
Philip Ruard.
May 13.
David Johnston.
May 15.
James Hineman.
May 18.
John Black.
May 19.
Thomas McAllen,
Rich'd Allison,
William Allison.
May 23.
Jacob Shaffner,
James Clunie.
May 25.
Andrew Shill,
Robert McQueen,
Nicholas Hite,
Robert Moorhead,
Thomas Clyde,
William Boal,

1778.
Samuel Willson,
Robert Willson.
May 26.
James McCan,
Edward Brison,
Thomas Foot,
William Hineman.
May 27.
George Allison,
John Myer.
May 28.
John Drubingstoltz,
Peter Sheffer,
John Black.
May 30.
Henry Hine,
Robert Bradon,
Frederick Sellers,
William McKain,
John Wilson,
Christley Eater,
Valentine Weirick,
George Lauman,
Christian Spade,
Jacob Eater,
James Kyle,
William Braden,
Matthew Gray,
William Gray,
Christopher Kelly,
Samuel Campbel,
Andrew Hunter,
James Morrison,
Alexander Long,
James Notman,
Timothy Conner,
Melchoir Rahm,
John Byers,
Jacob Zeiter.
June 1.
Henry Eager,
Nicholas Redsecker,

Conrad Meyer,
James Donaldson,
Anthony Buck,
James Kirkpatrick,
Christian Pfisgar,
Thomas Buck,
Daniel Ulwehee,
Robert Cunningham,
Jacob Sheafer,
Peter Capp,
Baltzar Stotz,
Charles Imhoff,
John Town,
Henry Metzler,
John Shana,
June 11.
John Huffman,
William Stewart.
June 12.
Adam Miller,
Christian Shearts,
George Wood,
Jacob Holtz.
Patrick Kelly.
August 10.
Matthew Dewlar,
Edward Jackson,
John McDonald,
David Hunter,
David McDonald.
August 17.
Michael Keiser,
Matthias Blaner,
John Guilford.
October 29.
George Nuky,
James Kenady,
George Segrist,
Peter Hiltzemer,
Nicholas Stout,
John Keller.

I do hereby certify that the above and within contents is a true copy from the original, certified by me November 4th, 1778. Given under my hand and seal, JACOB COOK. [L. S.]

BADGES OF THE CLANS OF SCOTLAND.

A correspondent furnishes us with the following list of the badges of the Highland Clans, and as there are so many of the descendants of these Scots among our readers, it will no doubt be a gratification to them to see it. It may here be remarked that the chief of each respective clan wore two eagle feathers in his bonnet in addition to the distinguishing badge of his clan:

Names.	Badges.	Names.	Badges.
Buchanan,	Birch.	McKay,	Bullrush.
Cameron,	Oak.	McKenzie,	Deer grass.
Campbell,	Myrtle.	McKinnon,	St. John's wort.
Chisholm,	Alder.	McLachlan,	Mountain ash.
Colquhoun,	Hazel.	McLean,	Blackberry Heath.
Cuming,	Common Sallow.	McLeod,	Red Whortleberries.
Drummond,	Holly.	McNab,	Rose Buckberries.
Farquarson,	Purple Foxglove.	McNeil,	Sea wave.
Ferguson,	Poplar.	McPherson,	Variegated boxwood.
Forbes,	Broom.	McQuarrie,	Blackthorn.
Frazer,	Yew.	McRae,	Fir club moss.
Gordon,	Ivy.	Munro,	Eagle's feathers.
Graham,	Laurel.	Menzies,	Ash.
Grant,	Cranberry Heath.	Murray,	Juniper.
Gunn,	Rosewort.	Ogilvie,	Hawthorn.
Lamont,	Crab apple tree.	Oliphant,	The great maple.
McAllister,	Five leaved heath.	Robertson,	Fern or brechins.
McDonald,	Bell heath.	Rose,	Brier rose.
McDonnell,	Mountain heath.	Ross,	Bear berries.
McDougal,	Cypress.	Sinclair,	Cloves.
McFarland,	Clodberry bush.	Stewart,	Thistle.
McGregor,	Pine.	Sutherland,	Cat tail grass.
McIntosh,	Boxwood.		

WILLIAM CARROLL TOBEY.

[William C. Tobey, the author of the following poem, was well known in Harrisburg thirty years ago, having served a portion of his apprenticeship here, in the office of the *Keystone,* published by Packer, Barrett and & Parke. He came to this (then borough) city from Towanda, Bradford county. He was born about 1818 at Caroline Center, a small town in Tompkins county, within a few miles from Ithaca, New York. His father was a man of little note, dying while William was very young; his mother, of French-Canadian extraction, was a woman of more than ordinary mental force, vivacity and beauty, which were inherited by her son, whose volatile and imaginative disposition directed all his actions in life, infusing the poetic to the rejection of the practical, giving a rose tint to that which in other men's observation presented the surface of the commonplace. How young Tobey got to Bradford county, Pa., the writer has no knowledge, but from Towanda he was brought to Harrisburg by John C. Cantine, who was at that time foreman of the *Keystone* office, in which the State printing was then done and in which office Tobey worked a short time. This was in 1837. The

Keystone was published by Packer, Barrett & Parke—Cantine was foreman of the *Keystone* office during the time Packer, Barrett & Parke had the State printing. Subsequently Hickok & Cantine started a book store and bindery. Hutter & Cantine published a campaign paper at the *Keystone* office. For some article published in that sheet Thad. Stevens sued the firm for libel. When the case came up for trial a previous pardon was produced, signed by Gov. Porter, and "that settled it." Tobey early developed a taste for literature and music, and in the inspirations of the composing room took to the pen as naturally as he did to the composing stick. He became the Harrisburg correspondent of the *Pennsylvanian*, the old Democratic organ of Philadelphia, printed for years by Mifflin & Parry, and on which James Gordon Bennett, sr., began his editorial career in the United States, and where Joseph C. Neal was nursed into literary life. From the *Pennsylvanian* Tobey went to the *Spirit of the Times* (also a Democratic organ), edited by John S. DuSolle, at the period of which we speak (1839) one of the most brilliant writers in the country. During this period Tobey spent the winter in Harrisburg, regularly corresponding with the *Times*, over his favorite signature of *John of York*. Mingled with the matter of fact of which his letters were necessarily composed, were many graphic sketches of individuals, and vivid descriptions of scenes in the Legislature, which made him famous as a journalist and personally popular. To this he added a love of poetry and music, which was intense, absorbing and often interfering with his more practical duties. At the close of a legislative session, he spent the time principally in Philadelphia, during which he held a situation on the *Public Ledger*, on its city staff, when Swain, Abel & Simmons were its publishers, and a correspondent of such New York papers as he could make engagements.

While on the *Ledger* (about 1840) he made a trip by sea to Boston, in company with the captain of a coaster whom he knew, and while at the "Hub" was attracted by a portrait of Daniel Webster (then in the zenith of his fame), which hung in a window. Then and there, on the edge of the window frame, Tobey wrote a poem on Webster, which was published in the *Ledger* on his return and attracted great attention, being copied widely by northern journals.

Though a practical printer, he did not work at case very long after his majority. His love of men was unbounded and his friendships numerous and sincere. In Philadelphia he was welcome among men of letters and the literary coterie of the Quaker City, having for his companions such men as George Lippard, Edgar Poe, Mayne Ried, James Reese (the dramatic critic), Bayard Taylor, John

S. DuSolle, and others whose names have passed out of memory, but who were of the Bohemian tribe, many of them wayward, reckless, but light hearted and honorable men of the quill, who devoted themselves to letters, leaving the more sordid pursuits to take care of themselves.

At the breaking out of the Mexican war Tobey went as a war correspondent. He was one of the first war correspondents of the country, writing for a number of Northern journals and maintaining his identity as *John of York* until the end of that war, when he returned to Washington city, where he remained in very reduced circumstances, broken down in health, impoverished and neglected. The poet and journalist could not withstand the fierce fires of temptation. Lured by vice and tainted in passion and appetite, the sweet singer of other days became a wreck, in which condition General Cameron found and succored him, and by whom he was sent to Harrisburg, in the hope of his recovery. Several years before, General Cameron offered to defray his expenses if Tobey would study law, and had made arrangements for him with a well-known lawyer of Harrisburg to do so, but the gay Bohemian could not bring himself down to the stern studies of the law, preferring the more fascinating paths of journalism. From the winter of 1853 to the spring of 1854, Tobey lived an invalid in Harrisburg, at the Washington House, where Gen. Cameron paid his board, his fatherly care never having ceased for his young craftsman until he was decently interred in the graveyard of the Catholic church, State street.

William C. Tobey was naturally a poet. His songs were the result of those flashes of the mind produced when the heart is warmed by generous emotion. Like Samuel Woodworth, the printer author of the "Old Oaken Bucket," and J. Howard Payne, the author of "Home, Sweet Home," Tobey published no productions except those of a fugitive character, but these were scattered like the golden grains found in the sands of a gently flowing river, to glitter awhile beneath its translucent wave, until time's flood washed them out into a broader surge, when they were lost beneath its fiercest billows. His was a blithe voice, while its music lasted—the flashes of his wit and the cadence of his merriment never ceasing until Death darkened the one and chilled the other.

We essay no biography of the printer, journalist, singer, soldier and poet. And although his life was full of noble incidents and holy friendship, he had no record as the world goes. He now sleeps beneath the shadow of the cross of the pro-cathedral, having only embraced the Catholic faith a few days before his death. But it was the faith of his mother, and that endeared it to him. We, the old craftsmen of the dead poet, still love his memory. There are those living who followed his remains to their interment, and helped to bear them to their last resting place. There are still others, now old, with the shadows growing darker in their path, who will feel a glow of the past, and see a flicker of its light, when memories of Tobey, the sweet singer and poet, are once more called up. Then arise the mystic shadows of a glorious company in the neighborhood of Second and Chestnut streets, where the Seven Stars shed their typical light on the paths of the old, old typos who trod the same road with Tobey.

WEIN FORNEY.

A CONFAB WITH A STRAW JACKET.

"That **warm** champaigny, old particular brandy punchy feeling."—*O. Wendell Holmes.*

Last night while dozing in my chair, at "No. Seventeen,"
A-looking at the coal grate, with its blaze of red and green,
And r*u*m-inating future hopes, and sighing for the past,
That, like the weather out of doors, was all a wintry blast,
A huge "Straw Jacket," fat and plump, stole from beneath my bed,
With looks half stupid and half queer, and a nid-in-nod-in-head—
Hoped he did not intrude at all, with a Pry-ish sort of air,
Then took a toll of old eighteen and my only rocking-chair.
"Friend," said the jacket, "I have come to have a little chat:
I saw that you were all alone—not even had a cat—
And I thought the time hung heavily, the way your winkers wagged,
Like tales of slimy, speckled trout just after they are bagged.
How go the *Times* of late, my boy, you do not seem to 'swell'
As you did a month ago, sir, on that virgin snow that fell:
Has fortune cheated you again, the fickle jade: then kick her—
Or have your 'spirits' fallen with a fall in *Harry's* liquor?
There must be something in the wind, now your's is getting low,
And you cannot raise a merry breeze when you used to have a blow."
"Sir John," said I, "for you're a sir, though but a demi-john,
I was thinking of the chequered past, its joys, its griefs, its fun,
An old-time failing such as comes when one gets tired of rout,
And begins to scent the symptoms of the asthma or the gout.
I was thinking of a home—no more—and those I loved while there,
Who used to gather flowers with me in the early summer air,
And of one who now is sleeping beneath the orange trees,
Whose mellow fruits are ripening, and whose blossoms kiss the breeze—
Where the skies are always bright and pure, and whose flowers ever bloom
Above the little simple stone that guards my brother's tomb.
A single name is on that slab, but oh! 'tis dear to me,
For he and I were all alone in that land beyond the sea.
God keep his soldier spirit and guard it with his care,
For it had its trials in this land, and they were not lighter there,
But he always bore them gaily, with a trusting hope and heart,
And bravely he commenced his march when he found orders to depart.
And I thought of one—no matter who—you wouldn't know the name,
For she who wore it never sought of such as you for fame;

But lighted with her joyous smiles, and soul of love and truth
Alike the fireside of her home and the heart-wreath formed by youth.
And then one won her from me, though he was not half as true,
And so I took, my glorious friend, to soldiering, and you
And I was thinking, also, as I pulled at my moustache,
Of the many chances let go by for piling up the cash—
Of the thousand slighted offerings for building up a name—
But they are over—here, let's drink—I s'pose it's all the same."
"No, sir," said Jack, "though I drink a monstrous deal of spirit,
My constitution's not the sort of one that you inherit.
My stomach was for liquor formed, but your's was not, my lad,
For it gives you gout and headache, and cheats you of your bed—
It numbs your mind and strings your nerves, and keeps you up at night,
And while it burns the candle, it is burning out your light.
Just take my word, old fellow, and turn me out of doors,
Leave wine and wassail to your friends, and whisky to the boors,
The past is past—well let it go, at least the squandered end,
Start out anew, and fortune will again her favors lend.
The world is just as bright for you as when you saw it first.
And the sight of life, all May-morn like, into your eyelids burst,
Your heart's as green as ever, and your brain as bright and quick,
As when you played convivial and let him win the trick.
ONWARD should be your *trump*, my boy, the word is full of power,
FRUGALITY should be your *left* and HONOR your *right bower*."
The jacket rose, another drink, another nod of head,
Then clumsily crawled back again to sleep beneath the bed.
I found I had been dreaming a good long hour or more,
The candle in the socket, my segar stump on the floor.
But I sat and thought the matter o'er another hour it seems,
'Till I made my mind up that there was philosophy in dreams.
                                              JOHN OF YORK.

NOTES AND QUERIES.—XXXV.

WILLIAMSBURG ON SWATARA is Jonestown, Lebanon county. It was laid out by William Jones about 1761, on a tract of land conveyed to him by a Mr. Kline, to whom had granted the warrant therefor, bearing date December 13, 1753. It was located in or near the forks of the Big and Little Swatara, at that time on the main road from Harris' Ferry to Easton. William Jones died in 1771, leaving the following children:

    i. Samuel, who was a man of considerable prominence and a Justice of the Peace many years.

    ii. Jane, m. Jacob Shelly.

    iii. John, d. s. p.

    iv. Margaret, m. George Dollinger.

    v. Robert.

    vi. Charles.

vii. Mary, m. Abraham Witter.
viii. Thomas.

For several years Williamsburg, or Jonestown, seemed to prosper, but with the dawn of international improvements, trade was diverted, and until recent years the town was at a stand. It is now becoming quite a prosperous little town, and with the development of the coal and iron resources, it may yet realize the dream of the founder.

IMPRESSIONS OF HARRISBURG IN 1828.

[In the autumn of 1828, a lady who had traveled extensively throughout the United States, visited the Capital of Pennsylvania, and in a volume published at Washington City in 1829, devoted wholly to her tour in this State, gives her impressions of our town and its citizens. The author was Mrs. Anna Royall. She was a native of Virginia, where she was born on the 11th of June, 1769. In her childhood she was taken captive by the marauding Indians, and for the period of fifteen years was detained as a prisoner among them. Some time after her restoration to her friends she married Captain Royall, an officer of the Revolution, and resided many years in Alabama. In 1826 she published her first volume, "Sketches;" in 1827 "The Tennesseeans;" in 1828 "The Black-Book," a narrative of travels in the United States, containing criticisms of persons and places, which was supplemented by two other volumes, one of which was confined to Pennsylvania, as before remarked. She promised a second volume, but her venture on the first was not properly appreciated, and the continuation never appeared. In 1830 she published "Letters from Alabama," and in 1835, establishing herself in the city of Washington, began the publication of a series of papers under the titles of "Paul Pry," and "The Huntress." Mrs. Royall died in that city on the 1st of October, 1854, well advanced in years. She was a short, dumpy little woman, and very talkative. She wielded a sarcastic, and often a bitter pen, and for the truth of this statement we need only refer our readers to her sketch of Carlisle, which is full of invective. That relating to our own town will no doubt be interesting to all who peruse *Notes and Queries*. The notes which follow are from the pen of a gentleman who was personally acquainted with those of whom he writes.]

We saw the mill (*a*) which was burnt the previous night, smoking, as we drove on through the finest country in the world, to Harrisburg. Harrisburg, the capital of Pennsylvania, is seated on the banks of the Susquehanna, in one of the most charming spots on the globe. Nothing could add to its beauty, if we except ships and steamboats. The land here, and the whole distance from Middletown, equals any of the rich bottom land on the Western rivers. Large grape vines, black walnut, locust, and level as a die. But the straight fence! the green wheat, the green meadows, the great barns, the bursting apple trees, the profusion of gardens and summer houses, (I never saw gardens before), the neat, white palings and net work round the doors, the smooth columns, the massy mansions, the droves of cattle, while

> "The groaning cider press is busy heard,
> The fowls loud cackling, swarm about the yard,
> The snowy geese harrangue their numerous brood,
> And flapping flails re-echo through the wood."

And the broad, smooth river astounds the ravished eye.

The Susquehanna flows in a smooth but quick current at Harrisburg, and is about a mile in breadth. At this place it is very much like the Ohio, and to add to the beauty of the picture it has a most superb bridge. The bridges I have already seen in Penn'a, without going further, surpass in number and beauty those of the whole of my travels in other States; their roads and bridges seem to attract all their pride, to say nothing of their farms and barns.

Intending to return from Pittsburgh to Harrisburg, about the meeting of the Legislature, I hurried on to Carlisle, a place where I was much wanted. Having made this arrangement, I merely rested one day at Harrisburg and resumed my tour.

It was quite late in the evening when I arrived, and leaving a card at my booksellers, Messrs. Wyeths, (*b*) a very friendly, pleasant young man called on me during the evening. He was the principal bookseller, and very politely tendered his services during my visit.

Being desirous of seeing his excellency, Governor Shulze, Mr. W. said he would attend me to his house next day. I had more than common curiosity to see Gov. Shulze (*c*), hearing, as I had, a thousand remarks and anecdotes of the man. My visit to Lancaster, to say nothing of the rest of Pennsylvania, had effectually cured me of prejudice. and I set off next day to see the Governor, perfectly convinced that I had never heard a word of truth respecting him. Such as "great, awkward Dutchman, bigoted priest, Federalist, Jew, a Gentile," "did not know a spit-box from a tea-pot," and again, "a good-natured fool, a tory, a Whig, a gentleman, a clown,"—but tongues, like wheels. were made to run.

The Governor lives in the town, on the river bank, in a very plain, common brick house, and the door being opened by the Governor himself, Mr. Wyeth introduced me and withdrew. I walked before the Governor into his parlor. It was just the kind of a parlor I like, and just in my favorite point on the north of the building. I do not like a parlor or chamber on the south, east or west; give me the north at all seasons. A small, simple furnished parlor, and a large chamber;—I detest a pigeon-box to sleep in. But you all want to hear about Governor Shulze. Then you shall hear.

I said I had discarded that fiend prejudice. Not exactly as I expected to find Governor Shulze, a rough, black-faced old man at least. But to return; Gov. S. is about 45 or 50 years of age, though he might well pass for 40, and in a Southern clime for 30. He is over six feet in heighth, remarkably straight and erect. He is athletic, with muscular, handsome limbs, and rather of the two inclined to corpulency. Now, if you can imagine as much ease of manner and grace as not to spoil the thing—just as much as you would incorporate, were you to mix the ingredients yourself, and one of the fairest faces in nature, with fine features, and a lovely black eye, you have the exact portrait of Governor Shulze. His face could not be altered for the better, if anything is too fair and smooth for a man—rather too effeminate, otherwise it is without a fault. His countenance is open and gay; and though he does not wear a barbarous brogue, you might perceive, by a certain lisp, that he was a German —so much for his person and manners. Nor is Governor Shulze at all that ignorant man he is represented by some; he is a man, not only of a good mind, but well informed in the common affairs of life, and gave me some very judicious instruction on the subject of my tour, and pointed out the objects most worthy of notice. He was very affable, and conversed freely on various topics, and laughed at the description I had received of him. He was a Lutheran preacher, it is said, but this ought rather to enhance his character, as it will be seen they are the most honest, upright men we have. Such is Governor Shulze, a good, honest German, who doubtless, like all public men, has his friends and his enemies.

I understood there was a den of blueskins in the place, but I had not time to look after them; they may prepare for battle against I return, as they wish to retain their acquired glory, and so do I.

Having received several marks of politeness from Mr. Peacock (*d*), the postmaster, through the postoffice, and a letter of introduction to Mr. Stambaugh, the editor of the *Reporter*, I called to pay my respects to them. Mr. Peacock is amongst the best men of our country, and Stambaugh (*e*) excels him. To say more of these gentlemen would only mar their fame, but I shall see them again, when I shall have more leisure to notice Harrisburg, a very beautiful, flourishing place. Dr. Keagy (*f*), Mr. Buehler (*g*), and several other gentlemen will also receive particular notice. But I must proceed, as "my purse is light and I have far to gang." About two o'clock in the morning I was called to get up, but the stage did not arrive for an hour, when, with a stage full as it could stow, we left Mr. Wilson's (*h*) tavern, a very good house.

(*a*) Whose mill this was we are not informed. Could it have been McCallen's, now Lochiel?

(*b*) This was *Mr. Francis Wyeth*, whose modesty "will mantle his cheeks with blushes" as he peruses this estimate of his polish fifty years ago. He then was fresh from college, and his suavity of so long ago, like old wine, has not lost its flavor. It becomes him now, as when he was a lively youngster in the generation whose virtues will be rehearsed, let us hope, for "generations following."

(*c*) *Gov. Shulze*, at this time and during his whole administration, resided in the house now occupied by the venerable Mrs. Haldeman, on the south corner of Walnut and Front streets. This house was erected by Stephen Hill, the architect of the State House and buildings. He died there. Its exterior presents pretty much the same aspect at present, as it did in 1828. Mrs. Royall was a profuse conversationalist, and embraced so excellent an opportunity to hold forth. Her victim was not a talker, but a good listener; a perfectly civil gentleman withal.

(*d*) *Mr. James Peacock* was the postmaster; a hospitable, polite and liberal gentleman. His residence and the office was in the building, erected by Robert Harris on Front street, torn down by and now occupied by Rev. Dr. Robinson. Mr. Peacock was the postmaster for about a quarter of a century.

(*e*) *Samuel C. Stambaugh*, a Lancaster printer, editor of the *Reporter*, a small, wiry man, at the moment a power in the State. Positive, polite, talkative and gay. As a politician, decided—one of the very first to advocate Jackson and to believe that no one could be a good patriot who was opposed to him. On this account Governor Shulze was one of his antipathies. Mr. Stambaugh's office was on Market street, opposite the court house, now the McCormick estate, then a two story frame house, with a deep back building. He resided next door to Governor Shulze on Front street.

Dr. John M. Keagy, principal of the Harrisburg academy, an intelligent and popular gentleman. He resigned that position about the close of the year 1828, and kept a private school for some years, when he removed from Harrisburg.

(*g*) *Mr. Buehler* was Col. Henry Buehler who kept the house at the corner of Market Square and Second Street, "The Golden Eagle." He was one of the most affable young gentleman of the town, intelligent, active and public spirited. His house was the headquarters of the Calder lines, west by Chambersburg to Pittsburgh, and north by Lewistown to the same point. Mrs Royal journeyed west by the former line, which had a trick of leaving Harrisburg at any hour between two o'clock a. m. and two or three hours later. It was not unusual for passengers for the west, to wait for the "Slaymaker lines" in bad weather, just in the most disagreeable part of the twenty-four hours.

(*h*) *Matthew Wilson* kept the house at the corner of Third and Walnut streets, where the post office is at present in course of construction. It had then a great reputation for the excellence of its administration. It was the headquarters of the "Slaymaker line" of coaches from Philadelphia to Harrisburg.

CAPT. JAMES COWDEN OF PAXTANG.

James Cowden, the fourth child of Matthew Cowden and Martha Johnson, was born in Paxtang township, Lancaster, now Dauphin county, Pa., on the 16th of June, 1737. James was brought up on his father's farm, enjoying, however, the advantages of that early education of those pioneer times, which among the Scotch-Irish settlers was remarkably comprehensive and ample. Apart from this, he was well-grounded in the tenets of the Westminister Confession, which among our pious ancestry formed a part of the instruction given to all.

Until the thunders of the Revolution rolled toward the Susquehanna Mr. Cowden remained on the paternal acres, busily engaged in farming. At the outset he was a strong advocate for active defensive measures, and in favor of independence. He was one of the leading spirits at the meeting at Middletown, June 9, 1774, of which Col. James Burd was chairman, and whose action, in conjunction with those of Hanover, nerved the people of Lancaster in their patriotic resolves. Suiting the action to the word, Mr. Cowden, and the young men of his neighborhood, took measures towards raising a battalion of Associators, of which Col. James Burd was in command, and a company of which was entrusted to Capt. Cowden. His company, although not belonging to the Pennsylvania Line, was, nevertheless, in several campaigns, and did faithful service at Fort Washington, in the Jerseys, at Brandywine and Germantown—and in the war on the Northern and Western frontiers, defending them from the attacks of the savage Indian and treacherous Tory.

At the close of the war, Capt. Cowden returned to his farm. Under the Constitution of 1790 he was appointed the Justice of the Peace for the district of Lower Paxtang, April 10, 1793, which he held up to the time he was commissioned by Gov. Thomas Mifflin, one of the Associate Judges of the county of Dauphin, on the 2d of October, 1795, an office he filled acceptably and creditably. He was chosen a Presidential elector in 1809.

Capt. Cowden married, in 1777, Mary Crouch, a daughter of Col. James Crouch, of the Revolution, a native of Virginia. She outlived her husband many years, and is buried in the graveyard of Paxtang church. They had issue:

 i. Hannah; m. John Cochran.
 ii. Martha; m. William Boyer.
 iii. Margaret; d, unm.
 iv. Elizabeth; m. William Gillmor.
 v. Matthew Benjamin.
 vi. James.
 vii. Mary; m. Joseph Jordan.

Concerning some of whom we propose to refer at another time.

Judge Cowden died at his farm in Paxtang very suddenly on Wednesday evening, October 10, 1810, in the seventy-fourth year of his age. The *Oracle* of Saturday, Oct. 13, 1810, in noticing his death alluded to him as follows:

"It is a tribute, but justly due to the memory of Mr. Cowden, to observe that he died universally regretted by all who had the happiness of his acquaintance. The services which he rendered his country during the Revolutionary struggle, will ever entitle him to the grateful remembrance of his countrymen; and the many important offices which he has subsequently filled, fully evinces the confidence reposed in his integrity by his fellow citizens. His private virtues have been but rarely transcended. In his disposition he was naturally social, mild and obliging—in his friendship, sincere—and in his duties as a Christian and believer, firm, unshaken and inflexible. He has left a number of friends, and an afflicted family, deeply to lament their irreparable loss; but, not, however, without the consoling hope, that a long life of exemplary virtue and piety will, *in another and a better world*, meet its just reward. His remains were yesterday interred in the graveyard in Paxtang, attended by a very numerous concourse of people.

" ' —— Feeble nature drops perhaps a tear,
While reason and religion, better taught,
Congratulate the dead, and crown his tomb
With wreath triumphant.' "

NOTES AND QUERIES.—XXXVI.

DICKEY—CARSON—FORSTER.—Moses Dickey was one of the first settlers in Paxtang. With others of his family he emigrated from the North of Ireland. He was a mill-wright by trade, and erected a mill on Spring Creek which subsequently became Elder's mill, now Walker's. He died on the 1st of June, 1766, and was buried in the graveyard "belonging to Mr. Elder's meeting-house." By his will, proved on the 12th of June following, he left a wife Agnes and children:
   i. William.
   ii. John.
   iii. Sarah, m. John Carson.
   iv. Catharine, m. John Forster.
   v. Agnes, m. Robert Dickey.
   vi. Moses.
His daughter Agnes, having, "it is said, run away with her cousin Robert Dickey," was cut off with "one shilling."

LONDONDERRY, N. H.—In perusing a history of this New England town, one is reminded on every page of our own Paxtang, Hanover and Derry. The early settlers were natives of the North of Ireland, Scotch-Irish Presbyterians. The surnames are so familiar to us that if some one else were reading the volume, we would imagine it was historical or genealogical data relating to this locality. There are the names of Wilson, Moor, Green, Clark, Barnett, Allen, Gregg, Montgomery, Gray, Ritchey, Weir, Allison, Rogers, Cochran, Wallace, Todd, Bell, Duncan, Dickey, Boyd and others, so prominent in our early annals. It is not alone in the surnames, but in the Christian prefix that the resemblance is the stronger—Hugh Montgomery, John, William and Hugh Wilson, Robert Rogers, Moses and John Barnett, Archibald McAllister, James and Thomas Wallace, Hugh Alexander, William Ayres, and a host of others. Like our own ancestors, they were a God-fearing, liberty-loving people, and the settlement of Londonderry has left its impress on many portions of Puritanical New England.

GREGG.—William Gregg, of Paxtang, died in July, 1744. By his will, his estate went to his uncle, Andrew Gregg, his sister, Elizabeth Lang, of Belly-nagallah, near Londonderry, Ireland, and his Father, John Gregg, of Belly-arnat, near Londonderry, Ireland. The

Andrew Gregg mentioned was the father of Hon. Andrew Gregg, one of the most eminent statesmen of Pennsylvania. The Greggs were originally from Ayrshire, Scotland, who emigrated to Ireland about 1670, settling near Londonderry. John Gregg, of Belly-arnat, had four children, John, who remained in Ireland, above alluded to, Daniel and Rachael, who came to America in 1722 and settled in Londonderry, N. H., and Andrew, who came to Pennsylvania at the same time. David married in 1713 Mary Evans, of Londonderry, Ireland, their descendants, many of them, remaining in New Hampshire. Andrew Gregg married Jean Scott, an emigrant from the county Armagh, Ireland. Their descendants, through their son, Hon. Andrew Gregg, have been prominent among the representative people of Pennsylvania. As to Rachael Gregg we have little or no information. She married and thus lost her identity with the Gregg family.

BAZILLION (N. & Q. xxiii).—The following is a copy of a letter of instruction from James Logan to Isaac Taylor, which may possibly lead to the location of Martha Bazillion's land;

ISAAC TAYLOR—*Loving Friend:* I wrote to thee lately by George Pearce to which I hoped for thy answer, but I doubt thou spoken to him about it, which I wish thou hadst not done. The bearer *Jonah Davenport* is recommended to me for an honest man. He wants two hundred acres of land to be laid out next to *Moses Combs*, lately Jno. Combs, where N. Christopher lived, and Anne Letort desires some at the same place. If it can be laid out regularly with a reasonable proportion of front to the several quantities, it may be done, but not otherwise. They are all concerned in the Indian trade, but I desire the Proprietor's interest may chiefly be considered . . . Thy assured loving ff'd. JAMES LOGAN.

Philada., 21,—5 mo. 1719.

I suppose thou understands what I mean by J. Combs' land from former directions, though thou hast not a warr't, for I think I wrote to thee about it. They desire 2 or 300 acres there, but ye front must be proportioned to ye quantity. I would have Jonah accommodated. J. L.

The latter part of the letter refers to another party on the Pequea

S. E.

PAXTANG OR PAXTON.—With the view of preserving the Indian nomenclature of this word, the Dauphin County Historical Society, and those most interested in historic lore among us, adhere to the original name. The word Paxtang, which is the approved way of spelling it, *has a meaning*—and one, too, characteristic of the stream to which it refers. It means, according to Heckewelder, whose authority on this subject is not to be questioned, " where the waters stand —the place of dead water, whether in a stream, or pool, or lake." Everyone knows that this signification holds good, for there is no stream as sluggish—" dead water "—as that of Paxtang creek. The word Paxton is an English surname, and even if it was thus written by many of our early settlers, it is not to be inferred that they were correct. We know they were wrong, and although we would not in publishing old documents change the orthography, even in proper names, we prefer in our own articles to employ Paxtang, which means something, in preference to Paxton which is void of significance. In this connection we may state that the Founder of our Commonwealth wrote the name Pensilvania, whereas the word is a combination the surname of *Penn* and that of the word *Sylvania*, and hence we are correct in the present orthography—Pennsylvania.— Proper names during the lapse of several generations become tortured out of all recognition, and hence there should be a uniformity of nomenclature; and that is the reason we adhere to the original in this instance.

THE MAGNETIC TELEGRAPH OFFICE AT HARRISBURG.

" *What hath God wrought !*"

" This sentence was written from Washington by me at Baltimore terminus, at 8:45 A. M., on Friday, May 24th, 1844; being the first ever transmitted from Washington to Baltimore by telegraph, and was indited by my much loved friend, Annie G. Ellsworth, now Mrs. Roswell Smith, of New York." SAM. F. B. MORSE.

I copied the above from the original slip of paper containing the dispatch written in three parallel lines of telegraphic characters, and attested in the handwriting of Prof. Morse. It was only a scrap of paper, but it was the practical evidence of the accomplishment of a momentous victory of mind over time and space. Looking back in imagination, to the Empress Helena, and her towers erected along her pathway toward Calvary, how feebly her signal-telegraph compares with the lightning course of Morse; and yet how little the Professor, himself, dreamed of the illimitable fact he had produced.

I have a copy of the *Mechanics' Register*, a journal published in 1837–8, in which notices are made of Morse's attempt to complete his invention; but I can only quote briefly here:

" The Telegraph now exhibited (in New York) is calculated to convey the most minute information to a distance of *ten* miles, a wire of that length being disposed, coiled upon reels. . . . . The experiment was performed several times with perfect accuracy. . . . . . . We wish some useful national purpose may be found to which it may be applied. . . . . Reflecting as it does so much honor on the inventor and his country, we should be sorry if it were any longer kept back from the world."—*Vol. i., p. 174.*

How strange that sounds, and stranger too, that "the message to be transmitted is first translated into numbers by the telegraphic dictionary—giving a number to every word in the English language—and received in the same numbers at the other end of the line, where it is re-translated by another dictionary, and the operation is completed."

Wouldn't that be a pretty "operation" to undergo in these times! and *when* would it be "completed?" But happily, my readers are familiar with the perfected apparatus, and the advanced system of operations; and I come now to that topic for which the foregoing is but an introduction, viz: the Electric Telegraph Office at Harrisburg.

We have seen that the telegraph was inaugurated in May, 1844. From Baltimore, its natural extension would be toward Philadelphia and New York, and from Philadelphia to Pittsburgh and the West. This latter extension was accomplished by the Atlantic and Ohio Telegraph Company, whose first officers I have any recollection of, were Hon. J. Kennedy Moorhead, of Pittsburgh, *President*, and James D. Reid, *Superintendent*. Mr. Reid, whose official duties brought him into personal relations with the operators and employees, was a man of quiet demeanor, always gentlemanly and kind, but no less positive than courteous, and was greatly respected. From Philadelphia to Harrisburg the wire followed the railroad, but thence it crossed the river to Carlisle, Chambersburg, Bedford, Greensburg and Pittsburgh. At that time the Pennsylvania Railroad route was a thing of the future, the company having only been incorporated in April, 1846.

In the absence of exact date, I think I may safely record that it was in the fall of 1845 when the office was first opened at Harrisburg. It was located in the second story of the old railroad depot, whither the ancient burghers wended their venerable steps to see the extraordinary machine. I remember one old gentleman, who expected to see something like the water-house engine—then "the biggest thing" in that section—who, after looking all round the office, turned to a man who *seemed* to be amusing himself by pulling a long strip of paper out of the works of a clock on a table, and said, "I've come to see what they call the *telegraph*, and they said it was *here*, but *where is it?*" He had looked for something like the interior of a machine shop, or Edison's laboratory. But he was not singular, it *was*, indeed, a great curiosity to everybody, and I could relate many amusing instances of my subsequent experience when opening offices in other towns of the State.

The operations at Harrisburg were, for convenience—especially so to the Philadelphia reporters in the Legislature, and for the State officers—soon transferred from the depot to the Democratic Union building to the office now No. 15 North Third street. The completion of the line from Baltimore, under the superintendence of Mr. George C. Penniman, rendered it necessary to provide further accommodations; and two windows were cut in the south wall of the office, looking out upon what was then my father's vegetable garden, now Nos. 11 and 13.

Samuel Hubert Brooks— a gentleman of sterling character, whose merit was only equaled by his real modesty—came as an operator to the Harrisburg office, I think, in the spring of 1846. His brother, David Brooks, Esq.—now very prominent in telegraphic enterprises, and one of the original builders of the line—was manager of the Pittsburgh office, and the most legible of telegraphic writers; not rapid, but true and distinct, and seldom asked to repeat.

I became very intimate with Samuel, my father's residence being at the corner of Third and Market; and in August of '46 I took charge of the office during a visit of Mr. Brooks to his home at Cheshire, Conn. I was not then an operator, but Mr. B. had instructed a very bright lad named Oliver W. Sees, who was his messenger boy. I need not pause here to allude to one who in time became so distinguished in his profession, and whom I remember with affection; his career as an operator during the war only fulfilled the promise of his earlier years—and I shall allude to him anon. By degrees I came to be a sort of extra clerk, and always assisted Mr. Brooks when business required it—during election time, and in the transmission of Governor's messages and legislative proceedings.

What dry old times they were in that office, particularly in Summer! The messages consisted mostly of those sent by warehouse men along the canal, and those of the Harrisburg and Lancaster R. R. Co., which were "dead-head;" but those of the town were limited to the banks, deaths, and very important matters. In the Winter there was a synopsis of the Legislative proceedings telegraphed (but the bulk was sent by train to Philadelphia) and messages incident to the State offices.

After the line from Baltimore was finished, it added considerably to the labors of the office, as the lottery-drawings sent westward were copied off at one instrument and rewritten at the other; a proceeding, the senselessness of which would be more than trying in these days of through connections.

In the Winter of 1848-9, I engaged there permanently, and in March we received the first Presidential message (Zachary Taylor's) ever sent to Harrisburg—or perhaps anywhere else—by telegraph!—
—I well remember the immense pile of paper required for this purpose; how often it was run through the machine, and what ado when it happened to catch or get torn. This is a strange story to tell to modern operators, and although there were even those on the line who *could* read *by sound*—in addition to understanding the ordinary calls and signals—the matter of *depending upon* the hearing instead of sight and paper, had not yet entered the mind of man, and would not have been tolerated "officially" in conducting the work of the company. At this very time, back in a corner of our office, sat a mere boy, our messenger Oliver, whose sensitive ears we knew to be as reliable as the paper we read from; and sometimes when the paper tore we would get him to *tell* us the words of the dispatch until the paper was made to work again. When we think of it, the fact is astonishing, even after the conceded ability of the operators to receive *by sound, how long* it was before sound-reading became adopted as a proper and official method, and sufficient confidence was given it to lay the interminable paper aside.

Passing over a year's absence (during which I was engaged on the Philadelphia and Wilkes-Barre telegraph line) I accepted an offer from Mr. Brooks to resume at Harrisburg, in January, 1851. By this time the telegraph business had become of considerable bulk and importance; and the character of the dispatches, instead of conveying exceptional intelligences, had become of practical necessity in the daily transactions of life. The town afforded quite a business, and the telegraph communications of the State officials and the members of the Legislature had become a very large item. Indeed, we were glad of the assistance of Mr. Silas Ward, who had come to Harrisburg upon Mr. Brooks' recommendation. Primarily, Mr. Ward was needed as a music teacher and chorister, and his advent was like a glorious sunrise upon the benighted condition of music there. But his fine clerical abilities were also engaged for the telegraph office during the heavier work of the Winter.

In August, 1851, I was sent to begin telegraphic operations at Johnstown, Pa., where the instrument was put up in the Canal Collector's office. Returning to the Harrisburg office, I remained until November, '51, when I resigned, to become the assistant of Lewis L.

Houpt, Esq., General Ticket Agent, Pennsylvania Railroad company. How long Mr. Brooks remained as manager of the Harrisburg office I cannot recall. He was succeeded by John P. McLear, of Wilmington, Del., who was in turn succeeded by Oliver W. Sees, one of the most rapid writers and accomplished hands at the operating table.

Like the weaving of the spider's web, the wires have multiplied from one, solitary and alone, until they have become innumerable—"their line is gone out through all the earth, and their words to the end of the world." But little do the operators of the present comprehend of the day of small beginnings in the past. The telegraph having become one of the indispensable necessities of the times, the men now at Harrisburg don't know what it is to go to sleep between dispatches or wait until the big offices choose to give them a chance to send one!

Here's an instance of the "way-business" of the olden time. Mr. E. M. Pollock being in Philadelphia, left at the office a message to his family that he *would be* at home for dinner. When Oliver delivered the dispatch at Harrisburg, he found Mr. Pollock *at home*, eating said dinner; but Oliver did not wait to learn Mr. P.'s idea of that kind of telegraphing!

It may not be irrelevant to note, in connection with a reminiscence of the telegraph office, the organization of the Harrisburg female seminary. Mrs. Anna Leconte, its accomplished principal, was a widowed sister of Mr. S. H. Brooks, and was brought to Harrisburg through his instrumentality. From a small private school her endeavor increased to such proportions as induced the procuring of an act of incorporation, and it became permanently domiciled in the old Shakespeare hotel, on Locust street. Mrs. Leconte was the means of bringing a number of accomplished teachers to Harrisburg, was energetic and successful, and left her impress upon the character of many of Pennsylvania's fair daughters. She married Rev. Daniel March, D. D., and is now deceased.　　　GEORGE B. AYRES.

NOTES AND QUERIES—XXXVII.

MASONRY IN DAUPHIN, PRIOR TO THE REVOLUTION.—So far as I have seen it published nothing is named concerning it prior to the organization of Perseverance Lodge. Tradition tells that previous to the War of the Revolution, a schoolmaster, Francis Kerr, taught in a cabin a little southwest of Paxtang church (perhaps three hundred yards), and there organized a clandestine lodge. He took in the neighboring rustics, amongst whom was "Uncle Jimmy," as my father called him. George Gray was tyler, and sat on the top poles which weighted down the roof. My father went there to Martha Allen, a character ninety years ago. Betty Gray, wife of George, was a character amongst women, spoke in broad Scotch-Irish dialect, and was remarkable for her candor. She was sister of Robin Foster, and the maternal grandmother of Josiah Espy. Perseverance Lodge was held for years in "Uncle Jimmy's" garrett, a place I have slept in school-days many a night. The house was burned many years ago, and the old log cabin by the little spring where Francis Kerr taught has departed as though it had never been. I may state that my father told me the cabin was built by Tommy McArthur. It was of round logs and had a stick chimney. Its occupants were various. I remember Black Bill and Black Peter—the latter a slave of the Awl family. Peter lived alone, and so died in his chair. My brother, the doctor, desired to place a memorial stone over him, but could not find his grave. H. R.

[We do not like to dispel the tradition which our esteemed correspondent "H. R." no doubt learned at his mother's knee in old Paxtang, nor of the old story when some good dame, whose curiosity was excited, became an "eavesdropper," saw all the "ancient ceremonies," but when urged by her neighbors to tell said "No, my husband is a mason"—and kept the secret all her life. "Uncle Jimmy" was not a "clandestine" mason—but received the degrees in an army lodge, and uniting with Lodge 21, was his whole life-time a member thereof. We have no record of the lodge ever being held in that school house—although it *was* convened now and then at "Uncle Jimmy's." We concluded to publish the foregoing to set at rest the many unfounded ridiculous stories concerning Masonry in its early days. James and Matthew Gray were early members of No. 21, but George Gray was not.]

"THE MAGNETIC TELEGRAPH OFFICE AT HARRISBURG."—*Notes and Queries of March 6, 1880*, contained a very interesting and sketchy article under the above caption from the pen of George B. Ayres. Time seems, however, to have obliterated from the recollections of Mr. Ayres some facts which I cull from corroborated data in my possession. He says that he thinks Samuel H. Brooks took charge of the telegraph office in Harrisburg in the spring of 1846, and claims to have taken charge of the office himself during a temporary absence of Mr. Brooks, in August of 1846. He is manifestly mistaken in his dates, for in the spring of 1846, as well as in August of that year, there was no wire running into, and consequently no use for an office in Harrisburg. In November, 1845, the line from Lancaster to Harrisburg was completed, and James D. Reid and O. Courtney Hughes were stationed at Harrisburg. November 27, 1845, David Brooks arrived in Lancaster, found the wire up, but no instruments. The instruments arrived on or about January 1st, 1846, and were put up by James D. Reid, but it was not until January 8, 1846, that an intelligible message passed over the wire. In February, 1846, James D. Reid and Henry C. Hepburn (the latter had been associated with David Brooks at Lancaster) left the line, and joined O'Reilly in constructing the line from Baltimore to Philadelphia. James M. Lindsey came from Baltimore and took Reid's place at Harrisburg. The line was kept open for a few weeks after Lindsey's arrival, when no revenues coming in, he was ordered to Philadelphia, and David Brooks was ordered to take the wire down and sell it for old copper, which he did before the 1st of March, 1846. David Brooks remained in Lancaster, awaiting orders, until August, 1846, when he received orders to assist in the construction of the line from Philadelphia to Lancaster. The line was completed to Lancaster in September, 1846, and on Monday, the 5th of October, 1846, was extended to Harrisburg by Henry O'Reilly, under his contracts with the patentees. *From March 1, 1846, to October 5, 1846, there was no telegraph wire running into Harrisburg.* WM. B. WILSON.

LETTER FROM JOHN HARRIS TO COL. BURD.

We are indebted to a descendant of the Founder, John Harris, for the following characteristic letter. It gives some important facts, and will no doubt prove interesting to readers of *Notes and Queries*. We have in our possession a number of unpublished letters of John Harris, which we hope from time to time to give. The orthography of the original is preserved.

PAXTON, *April 30th, 1757.*

SIR: I sent your crock of butter with Capt. Hambright's last command, w'ch I hope you Rec'd safe. I shall endeavor to procure another crock for you against next trip. I forwarded all the letters you sent me by Lee to Lancaster immediately, and Capt. McKee was going to Philad'a, so that there was not the least delay.

Mr. West wrote me this week that there was an English Packet arrived at Antigua, which left Spithead the 26th Feb'ry, and that there were laying there 200 Transports, storeships, &c., with 16 sail of the line, commanded by Adm'l Knowles, w'ch were to sail in a few days for No. America. (God send them a Quick & safe passage.) There is actually arrived at Ft. Cumberl'd 126 Cutawba warriors, & 50 or 60 other Indians, & a number more Expected, who seems Heartily in our cause. I expect they'l pay our cruel Enemys in their own Coin this Summer.

I am, sir, in Haste, your most obed't Humble serv't,

JOHN HARRIS.

To Major JAMES BURD at Fort Augusta.

CAPT. JAMES COWDEN'S COMPANY OF THE REVOLUTION.

In connection with the biographical sketch of Capt. Cowden in *Notes and Queries* (No. xxxv.) we herewith present a muster-roll of his company. It contains one hundred and fourteen names, officers and privates. During the campaign of the year 1776, they were in active service—quite a number were captured at Fort Washington, and several lost their lives. Many of the younger portion subsequently enlisted in the Pennsylvania Line, remaining in the patriot army until its close. By reference to the names of these departed heroes of a century ago, it will be seen how many of their descendants remain in our midst. It is one of the most valuable rolls of the men of the Revolution we have come across.]

A true return of Capt. James Cowden's company of the Fourth Batallion of Lancaster county, commanded by Col. James Burd, Esq., March 13, 1776.

Captain.
Cowden, James.

First Lieutenant.
Gilchrist, John.

Second Lieutenant.
Cochran, William.

Ensign.
McArthur, Thomas.

Sergeants.
Berryhill, Andrew,
Swan, William,
James, Derrick,
Cochran, Samuel.

Court Martial.
Bell, Thomas,
Hilton, John.

Clerk.
Montgomery, Robert.

Privates.
Allison, David,
Allison, William,
Askens, Thomas.
Barnett John, Jr.,
Barr, Samuel,
Cavet, Andrew,
Chambers, James.
Cochran, Andrew,
Cochran, James,
Cook, James,
Crabb, William,
Cummens, John,
Davis, John,
Duncan, James, Jr.,
Duncan, John,
Duncan, William,
Elder, John.
Farrier, Robert,
Finney, James,
Gamble, Andrew,
Gilchrist, John, Jr.,
Gilchrist, Matthew,
Gilchrist, Robert,
Gilchrist, Thomas,
Glen, William,
Graham, Michael,
Hatfield, John,
Harbeson, Patrick,
Hogan, William,
McRoberts, William,
Miller, John,
Milligan, John,
Montgomery, William,
Neel, Robert,
Patterson, James,
Patterson, Peter,
Patterson, William,
Patton, David,
Peden, John,
Peterson, Thomas,
Potts, Robert,
Ranken, William,
Richardson, Andrew,
Ritchey, David,
Scott, John,
Shaw, Joseph,
Smith, Andrew,
Smith, George,
Smith, Peter,
Smith, Robert,
Spence, James,
Stephen, Andrew,
Stephen, Hugh,

Barnett, Samuel,
Berryhill, Samuel,
Berryhill, Andrew, Jr.,
Boggs, James,
Boggs, William,
Boyd, William,
Brann, John,
Brisben, William,
Byers, James,
Caldwell, David,
Caldwell, James,
Caddow, George, Jr.,
Caddow, Thomas,
Calhoun, Matthew,
Campbell, Colin,
Carson, John,
Carson, Richard,
Ingram, William,
Jamison, John,
Johnston, Joseph,
Jones, Benjamin,
Jones, William,
Linton, Thomas,
Lochary, William,
Marshall, Joseph,
McClanachan, Wm.,
McClure, William,
McConnell, Matthew,
McElhenny, John,
McGaw, William,
McMath, James,
McMullen, George,
McMullen, William,
McNamara, James,
Stephen, Zachary,
Stuart, Elijah,
Swan, Richard,
Taggart, James,
Thompson, Samuel,
Twoey, Hugh,
Wallace, Samuel,
Warnick, Robert,
Wylie, Robert,
Wiggins, James,
Wilson, Abraham,
Wilson, Alexander,
Wilson, James,
Wilson, John,
Wilson, Joseph,
Wilson, William.

"THE MOURNFUL TRAGEDY OF JAMES BIRD."

It is a very easy matter to get wrong, while on the contrary it is only by inquiry and research that one may become accurate. We are led to this conclusion, especially concerning not only the subject of the ballad referred to, but the author thereof. We have before us a "broad sheet," containing a brief sketch of James Bird, from the Wilkes-Barre *Gleaner* of March 5, 1815, his last letter to his parents and the ballad. We have also a copy of the original roll of Capt. Samuel Thomas' company, and venture to give the facts as therein set forth.

In the spring of 1813 a number of the citizens of Kingston, Luzerne county, volunteered under command of Captain Samuel Thomas for service in the Western Department under Gen. Harrison. Thirty-one, beside the officers, were from Luzerne county; twenty-seven were recruited in Fayette county, and thirty-five in Bedford county. Among the number was James Bird. He was the son of John Bird, of Luzerne county. Arriving at Erie, it has been stated, on a call for volunteers for the fleet under Perry, Bird "enlisted June 6, on board the fleet," so reads Captain Thomas' roll, and certified by him on the 5th of November, 1813, with this addition: "*Now at Erie, wounded.*" On the 10th of September previous, during an engagement, a canister shot struck him on the shoulder while stooping at his gun. But not until victory was proclaimed did Bird go below deck.

Upon his partial recovery, Bird asked permission to go home, which was refused. Absent from the smiles of his sweetheart for over a year, he took "French leave," went to Kingston, and on returning was arrested for desertion, tried and sentenced to be shot.

The motives given for Bird's desertion, are only such as tradition have brought down to us, but the probabilities are that it was some very serious insubordination, or other overt act, which seemed to demand the severe punishment. For years after, it was a matter of common belief that Bird was prematurely executed at the instigation of an officer who afterwards committed suicide, and that Commodore Perry, of whom Bird was a special favorite, hearing of his condemnation, hastened to pardon him, but arriving a few hours too late could only lament the fate of the poor fellow.

On the 9th of November, 1814, Bird wrote the letter to his parents alluded to in the ballad, and a very sad letter it is—but its length prevents us from making extracts therefrom. He gives no excuse for his "deserting from the United States brig Niagara," and we presume he felt at the time that his sentence was just. On the day following, November 10th, 1814, he was executed.

The author of the ballad was Charles Miner, editor of the *Gleaner*. He was an early settler from Connecticut, was a member of Congress, and in 1844 published a history of Wyoming. He died in 1865 at an advanced age.

We may as well state that the information given in our note to the ballad was obtained from a little volume published at Pittsburgh several years ago, entitled, "South-Western Pennsylvania, in Ballad and Song," as a matter of course presuming it was correct.

The family of John Bird were from New Jersey, and some of the descendants remain in the Wyoming Valley. A sister of James Bird, Mrs. Sally Bird Harding, resided at Tunkhannock, a woman of great energy and force of character. Her son, Captain James Bird Harding, was recently sheriff of the county. The late Captain Brady, of the State Senate, was at Erie at the time and knew Bird well.

Captain Samuel Thomas "became a general," and died in Illinois last year, aged ninety-four years. Ziba Hoyt, who was a lieutenant in his company, was father of Gov. Hoyt.

NOTES AND QUERIES.—XXXVIII.

THE BURNING MILL (N. & Q. xxxv.), alluded to in Anna Royall's Travels in Pennsylvania, we have been informed by Jerome K. Boyer, Esq., was the distillery of Robert Wilson, at Highspire, which was consumed by fire in the fall of 1828, about the time Mrs. Royall was making her trip. So lurid were the flames the night of its destruction that for many miles distant the conflagration was seen.

THE TOWN OF NEWVILLE.—In the autumn of 1809, Daniel Ferree issued proposals to lay out " the scite of a town on the pleasant and fertile boundary which connects Williams' to Lichen's Valley, in Upper Paxton township, Dauphin county." We quote the balance of his advertisement: "Newville being situated so as to engross the trade of the great Wiconisco creek, and laying on the great road from the Susquehanna and its branches to the borough of Reading, and from thence to Philadelphia, which route is clearly the nearest way to the marts aforesaid. And as another public road has been lately opened from that noted ferry on the Susquehanna called *Moorhead's Ferry*, through the said town, it bids fair to become a place equal in convenience to any other in Dauphin county. Add to this its perfect salubrity, the convenience for building, and its present public situation, at once offer an opportunity of advancing the merchant, the mechanic, and every other useful description of men. No pecuniary interest has induced the laying out this town, further than to make a useful addition to the means which nature has pointed out on the spot. Preference of the lots will be drawn for in the usual way, of which public notice will soon be given. Indisputable title in fee simple will be made to purchasers, the deeds to whom shall not exceed the sum of one dollar. Tickets may be had of the subscriber, and at other places where plans of the town may be seen." The price of lots was fixed at eighteen dollars, and quite a number were sold, but Mr. Ferree subsequently withdrew the lots from sale and refunded the money to those who had purchased. The site of this proposed town is now owned by Dr. Beshler, and the postoffice of Loyalton there established.

MILLERSBURG.—In August, 1807, Daniel Miller, who owned the land at the mouth of the Wiconisco, on the north side, issued the following proposals for laying out a town. This was the only one of the four towns projected at the time in the " Upper End," which was a successful venture. Of its location, etc., we need say but little. At present it is the second town in the county, outside of the city of Harrisburg. It is the terminus of the Lykens' Valley railroad, and the shipping point for the coal and produce of the Wiconisco Valley. The plan of the town was surveyed by Peter Williamson, in July, 1807, and is recorded at Harrisburg. Daniel Miller, to whom the town of Millersburg is indebted for its name and origin, was the son of John Miller, an early settler on the Wiconisco, and probably born there about 1770. He died in December, 1828, and is buried at Millersburg.

"The Town of Millersburg, situate on the East Bank of Susquehanna River, in the county of Dauphin, being laid out in Lots, the subscriber now offers them for sale at the moderate price of *Thirty-Three Dollars* per lot;—preference to be drawn in the usual way.

"Millersburg, from its elegant and public situation, bids fair to become a place of very great trade and business. On its southern boundary floats the great Wickoniska, and in its front the Susquehanna. Its harbor is safe and convenient, while the extensive and fertile country in its rear, producing all kind of Lumber and Grain, will at all times furnish its public ground with the means of trade in abundance—add to these the conveniency to Mills, the public Roads, the healthy and delightful situation, and above all, the fair prospect of its soon becoming a county town, furnish advantages incalculable.

"The Lots are generally a Quarter of an Acre each, exclusive of Streets and Alleys, and a large Area for a Market Square. Indisputable titles will be made to purchasers, free from ground rent or other incumbrance. Ferry right reserved generally, and the Shad Fishery along its Banks. A Plan of the Town may be seen at the places where Tickets may be obtained. Tickets may now be had of the subscriber. "DANIEL MILLER."

WILLIAMSVILLE (N. & Q. xxxi.)—William Moorhead, who at the time was the owner of Lytle's Ferry, issued, under date of June 9, 1805, the following proposals for laying out this town. At this period there were a number of these projected towns in the county of Dauphin, only one of which ever resulted successfully—that was Millersburg. As a part of the history of the time we give Mr. Moorhead's plans as found in his advertisement. He sold quite a number of tickets to citizens of Harrisburg, but like all schemes of the kind, there was much disappointment at the result. One or two law suits grew out of the failure, but Mr. Moorhead succeeded in compromising the affair. Williamsville never existed save on paper.

"Williamsville, situate on the east bank of Susquehanna river, about 21 miles above the borough of Harrisburg, in the county of Dauphin, being laid out in town lots of 66 feet in front and 165 feet in depth, excepting a few lots, whose vicinity to the river has rendered them a few feet shorter. The plan is elegant and convenient.

"The subscriber now offers the said lots for sale, at the moderate sum of 40 dollars per lot, preference to be drawn by lottery in the usual way. He has reserved but 4 lots out of 180, of the whole number; and has attached in place of them to lot No. 22, an Island containing about 2 acres—and a Fishery nearly opposite; to lot No. 13, the sum of 150 dollars; to lot No. 164, the sum of 100 dollars; and to lot No. 1, the sum of 50 dollars, to be paid and conveyed to the fortunate drawers respectively, in addition to the lots so drawed. Indisputable titles will be made, free from ground rent, or other incumberances. Ferry right reserved generally.

"Williamsville, from its peculiar convenient situation, and salubrious air, offers an encouragement to merchants, mechanics, and almost every other industrious class of men; lying on the bank of the finest rivers, surrounded by a fertile and healthy country. The very great trade, passing as it were in profile before it, at once bespeaks its opulence, while the state road leading to the extensive branches of the Susquehanna, the western parts of the state of New York, and the extensive country of Niagara passing thro' Williamsville, and whose portage expedites the route, evidently points out to the active mind, the means of plenty and happiness. Building will be cheap and easy, as the best timber and stones are as convenient as may be wished for. From all which, and the very great probability of its being the seat of justice of a contemplated county, it is expected that the sale of tickets will be rapid.

"The plan may be seen at the subscriber's house. Tickets may be had, by calling on George Brenizer, Daniel Stine, Jacob Fridley, or Andrew Berryhill, in Harrisburgh—where also the plan may be seen. "WILLIAM MOORHEAD.

"LYTLE'S FERRY, *June 7, 1807.*"

ANDREW LYCANS, THE PIONEER OF THE WICONISCO VALLEY;

In 1723 Andrew Lycans (not Lycan) settled on the Swatara creek, where he took up two hundred and fifty acres of land adjoining lands of Robert Young and Lazarus Stewart, and which was surveyed to him on the 4th of April, 1737. About 1740 he seems to have sold out, and removed, with a number of others, to the west side of the Susquehanna, where he settled and made some improvements on a tract of land between Shearman's creek and the Juniata, in then Cumberland county. This not being included in the last Indian purchase, the Shawanese, who had a few scattered villages on the Juniata, complained of the encroachments of these settlers and demanded their removal. To pacify the Indians, the Provincial authorities sent, in 1748, the sheriff of Lancaster county, with three magistrates, accompanied by Conrad Weiser, to warn the people to leave at once. But, notwithstanding all this, the settlers remained, determined not to be driven away at least by threats.

On the 22d of May, 1740, after more decisive measures had been decided upon by the Provincial Government, a number of high dignitaries who had been appointed by the Lieutenant Governor, held a conference at the house of George Croghan in Pennsboro' township Cumberland county. Subsequently, accompanied by the under-sheriff of that county, they went to the place where Lycans and others lived, and after taking the settlers into custody burned their cabins to the number of five or six.*

They were subsequently released by order of the Governor of the Province, when Andrew Lycans removed with his family to the east side of the Susquehanna beyond the Kittatinny mountains, and by permission of the authorities, settled on a tract of about two hundred acres, situated on the northerly side of Whiconescong creek." Here he made "considerable improvements," which we learn from a document in our possession.

Until the spring of 1756 these pioneers on the Wiconisco were not disturbed in their homes, but following the defeat of Braddock, everywhere along the frontier the savages began their work of devastation and death. Their implacable cruelty was stimulated by the promise of reward for scalps on the part of the French, beside the further one of being put into possession of their lands. On the morning of the 7th of March, 1756, Andrew Lycans and John Rewalt went out early to fodder their cattle, when two guns were fired at them. Neither being harmed, they ran into the house, and prepared themselves for defense in case of an attack. The Indians then got under cover of a hog house near the dwelling house, when John Lycans, a son of Andrew, John Rewalt and Ludwig Shott, a neighbor, crept out of the house in order to get a shot at them, but were fired upon by the savages, and all wounded, the latter (Shott), in the abdomen. At this moment Andrew Lycans saw one of the Indians over the hog house, and also two white men running out of the same, and get a little distance therefrom. Upon this, Lycans and his party attempted to escape, but were pursued by the Indians to the number of sixteen or

---

*NOTE.—We have before us the "account of Andrew Work, Sheriff of Lancaster, for removal of trespassers at Juniata," which is as follows:

"Dr. Province of Pennsylvania to Andrew Work, Sheriff of the County of Lancaster and Cumberland.

"To ten days attendance on the Secretary Magistrates of Cumberland, by his Hon'r, the Governor's command to remove sundry persons settled to the northward of the Kichitania mountains :
"To paid the Messenger sent from Lancaster at my own expenses, ... 3:7:0
" To the Under-Sheriff's Attendance on the like service, eight days, . .
" To his Expenses in taking down Andrew Lycan to Prison to Lancaster
other Expenses on the Journey, ... 2:10:0
" Augt., 1650. AND. WORK, Sher.

upwards. John Lycans and Rewalt, being badly wounded and not able to do anything, with a negro, who was with them, made off, leaving Andrew Lycans, Shott and a boy engaged with the Indians. The savages pursued them so closely that one of them coming up to the boy was going to strike his tomahawk into him, when Ludwig Shott turned and shot him dead, while Lycans killed two more and wounded several in addition. At last, being exhausted and wounded, they sat down on a log to rest themselves; but the Indians were somewhat cautious and stood some distance from them, and consequently returned to look after their own wounded. Lycans and all his party managed to get over the mountain into Hanover township, where they were properly cared for. Here Andrew Lycans died, leaving a wife, Jane Lycans, and children, John, Susanna, Rebecca, Elizabeth, Mary and Margaret. It is not known when Lycans' family, with the other settlers, returned to their homes in the Wiconisco Valley—but not until all danger was over; and although on a subsequent occasion they were obliged to leave all and flee before the marauding savages, yet the one alluded to was the only instance where they so narrowly escaped with their lives. Besides, the erection of the forts at Shamokin (Sunbury) and at Armstrong's (Halifax) and at McKee's, at the foot of Berry's mountain, was perchance ample protection from the annual marauds of the Indians, which up to the year 1764 kept the frontier inhabitants in a terrible state of apprehension and fear.

John Lycans, son of Andrew, became an officer of the Provincial service, commissioned July 12, 1762. In June, 1764, he was stationed at Manada Gap. It is probable he removed from the valley prior to the Revolution. His mother, Jane Lycans, in February, 1765, had a patent issued to her, for the land on which her husband had located. The Lycans' cabin stood until about twenty years ago on McClure's farm, owned at present by H. L. Lark. Ludwig Shott died about 1790, and left a large family; some of his descendants remain in the Valley. Rewalt subsequently removed to the now thickly settled portion of the Province.

Andrew Lycans has given his name to this beautiful valley of the Wiconisco, owing perchance to the terrible encounter with the Indians as narrated. The orthopraphy has been changed within the last fifty years, but we have not learned the reason therefore. Whether Lykens, or Lycans, we trust that no attempt may ever be made to deprive the first pioneer of the name which has been appropriately given to it.

NOTES AND QUERIES.—XXXIX.

DAUPHIN.—The establishment of a post-office at Green's Mills required a change of name, as there was then one office so called, the county town of Westmoreland county, and thence the appellation, Dauphin, was given to it on the first of October, 1826, when John Peter Miller was appointed postmaster. This post-office name has been retained, and the town gradually ceased to be called after its founder, Hon. Innis Green.

McCOSH—BOYD.—John McCosh, of Derry, died in November, 1754, bequeathing his estate to his wife Jennet or Janet. The latter died in October, 1757, leaving considerable property, which she disposed of as follows: To her brothers William, John, Alexander and Robert Boyd; her niece Margaret, daughter of John Boyd; to Alexander, Robert, William and Margaret, children of Alexander Boyd; to Benjamin, Joseph and William, children of William Boyd; niece Catherine Boyd, who, we presume, was a daughter of William Boyd; to her sister-in-law Jean Boyd; to her nieces Elizabeth, Catherine and Mary, daughters, we suppose, of Robert Boyd; to Rev. John Roan; and "the sum of twenty shillings to Derry congregation." The witnesses to the will were Mary and Margaret McCord. The executors were Robert Boyd, her brother, and Andrew Roan, son of the Rev. John Roan. Concerning the foregoing, we desire further information. Joseph Boyd, son of William Boyd, b. 1740, d. Sept. 20, 1781; his wife Elizabeth, b. 1746, d. April 13, 1802. Benjamin Boyd, son of William Boyd, b. 1738, d. May 8, 1803; wife Jennett, b. 1737, d. November 21, 1820. They are all buried at Derry graveyard.

CAPTAIN ADAM BOYD.

THE FIRST BURGESS OF THE BOROUGH OF HARRISBURG.

Adam Boyd, the son of John Boyd and Elizabeth Young, was a native of Northampton county, Pa., born in 1746. His ancestors were of that sturdy and fearless race who, after winning religious liberty at home, braved the perils of the ocean and a life in the wilds of America that they might establish civil and religious freedom in the New World. Early in the year 1714 John Boyd and a younger brother, Rev. Adam Boyd, Sr., left Scotland and landed in

Philadelphia. John married there the year following, Jane Craig, the daughter of Thomas Craig, and subsequently came [1728] one of the first immigrants to the "Irish Settlement," now Northampton county. His son John, born in Philadelphia in 1716, married in 1744, Elizabeth, daughter of Sir William Young, "an Ulster baronet." Their eldest son was Adam Boyd, the subject of this sketch.

Of Mr. Boyd's early education we know but little, save that from his papers, and documents extant, we should judge him to have been well grounded in the rudiments of a thorough English education. He learned the trade of a carpenter, and was following that avocation when the war of the Revolution called to arms. He was an early associator, and when the State of Pennsylvania had formed its little navy for the protection of the ports on the Delaware, Lieutenant Boyd received a commission therein. During the year 1776, and the early part of 1777, he was most of the time in command of the armed sloop "Burke," and rendered efficient service in the conflict between the Pennsylvania navy and the British ships Roebuck and Liverpool in May, 1776. Growing tired of that branch of the service, Lieutenant Boyd requested to be discharged, that he might volunteer in the land forces. Being honorably dismissed from the navy, he at once entered the army proper, holding the same rank therein. He was at the battles of Brandywine and Germantown, with two of his brothers, one of whom was killed in the latter engagement. Subsequently, Lieutenant Boyd acted as "Master of Wagons," and as such remained with the army until after the surrender at Yorktown.

Returning to the home of his mother, near Newville, he married and came to Harrisburg. While passing through Harris' Ferry, in the spring of 1782, Mr. Boyd was struck with the immense advantages offered by the location of the proposed town, and subsequently purchased of the proprietor a lot on the corner of Second and Mulberry streets. In 1784 he became a permanent resident. The dwelling house erected by him in 1792, on lots 210 and 212 of the original plan of the borough, on Second below Mulberry, is yet in the ownership of his descendants.

Upon the incorporation of the borough of Harrisburg, in 1791, he was chosen a burgess, Dr. John Luther being the other. In 1792 he was elected treasurer of the county and held the office until 1806, when he declined a re-election. In 1809 Mr. Boyd was elected a director of the poor, and during his term of office a county poor house was erected; the mill having been built before the purchase of the farm by the county.

Upon the founding of the Presbyterian congregation in 1787, Mr.

Boyd was chosen its treasurer for one year, and at its organization in 1794, one of its Ruling Elders, his colleagues being Moses Gilmor and Samuel Weir, the latter a fellow patriot in Revolutionary days—venerated citizens, all of them. Henry Fulton and John Kean were the treasurers of the church from 1789 to 1793, when Mr. Boyd again assumed it, and filled the position as long as he lived.

Mr. Boyd died on the 14th of May, 1814; was interred in the Presbyterian graveyard, but subsequently his remains were removed to the Harrisburg cemetery. The *Oracle* speaks of him as "an inhabitant of this town from its first formation—a man of truth and integrity, and an eminently useful citizen, both as to church and State. His character was without blot or stain—benevolent to every one. He was a firm friend to his country when men's souls were tried, and never ceased to be such; of a noble and masculine piety, trusting in God for future happiness, through the merits of a crucified Redeemer. His remains were followed to their last resting place by a great assemblage of neighbors and weeping friends."

In private trusts Mr. Boyd was very frequently employed. His correspondence and accounts show precision and method, particularly the case with which he managed the estate of the younger William Maclay. In person he was five feet eight inches in height, a stout, healthy, florid man, dark brown hair and eyes. At fifty-two years of age he had no gray hairs. He is rated on the "Mill Purchase" at £23:2, being the fourth highest assessment upon that curious record.

Mr. Boyd married, in 1784, Jeannette Macfarlane, of Big Spring, Cumberland dounty, daughter of Patrick and granddaughter of James Macfarlane, who came from Ireland to Penn'a in 1717. Mrs. Boyd died in early life at Harrisburg, leaving one child, a daughter, Rosanna, who married Hugh Hamilton in 1807. This estimable lady lived until 1872, when she died, the oldest inhabitant of Harrisburg, having been born here in 1786.

DR. JOHN LUTHER.

The Second Burgess of the Borough of Harrisburg.

John Luther was a native of Freuhlingen, Germany, born on the 1st of April, 1756. In his youth he came to America, and with either his parents or friends located in Virginia. He studied medicine, and married in that State, coming to Harrisburg in 1785, the year it was laid out, purchasing the lot now occupied by the Harrisburg Nation al Bank and the house adjoining, the latter of which he erected. Here he at once began his profession, which proved a successful one. He was chosen, at the first election held under the charter given the borough, one of the burgesses, and subsequently served as a member of the Town Council, of which body he was at one time president.

From the "Reminiscences of an Octogenarian," we have this description of Dr. Luther: "He was a man somewhat resembling the Great Reformer, Martin Luther, if I dare judge from the printed representation I have seen of the latter. He was of medium height and proportionably stout. He was a very pleasant man, and agreeably received when he entered company. He carried a snuff box and made frequent use of its contents. He wore black cloth, coat, vest and breeches, with buckles on his shoes. He was popular as a physician and esteemed highly for his skill. He wore his hair in a cue, as was common in the early days of Harrisburg, but wherever he went there was healing in the creak of his shoes. When he felt your pulse, told you to put out your tongue, and smelled the ivory on the top of his cane, you might be sure he was hunting for a fever, or something direful, that might require a dose of calomel and jalap . . . Dr. Luther was of a jovial disposition, and it was said, as was the custom of those days when anti-fogmatics was necessary to keep off fever and ague, that he 'didn't object to his patients taking a little tanzy bitters in the morning.' His practice was extensive.

Dr. Luther died at Harrisburg on Monday, January 28, 1811, in his fifty-fourth year. The *Oracle* of the 30th thus speaks of him: "For many years Dr. Luther was a useful, humane, and fortunate practitioner in the science of physic and surgery in this borough. The many first-rate virtues which adorned the character of the deceased, had endeared him to as many friends as few can boast. Very few are exempt from the envious shaft of malice, but if he had any enemies we know them not. Many, whose pecuniary situations were straitened, will long deplore the loss of a benevolent friend. His remains were deposited on Tuesday last with Masonic honors, to which fraternity he was a distinguished and valuable member, attended by as large a concourse of neighbors as has ever been witnessed on a similar occasion in this borough."

Previous to coming to Harrisburg, (in 1779), Dr. Luther had married. His wife, Eve Hisser, b. in 1766, died at Harrisburg, Wednesday, August 15, 1804. They left four children who survived their parents, *Catharine, Cornelius, Martin* and *John*. All of Dr. Luther's sons became physicians. Drs. Cornelius and Martin remained at Harrisburg, and succeeded in a great measure to their father's practice. Cornelius died quite young, and Martin, April 29, 1829, aged forty-five years. Dr. John Luther settled in New Holland, Lancaster county, married Elizabeth, daughter of Peter Diller, and raised a large family. Catharine Luther married Dr. King of Hummelstown, and on becoming a widow, married Judge William Lyon, of Cumberland county. The remains of Dr. Luther, his wife and two sons are interred in the Harrisburg cemetery.

YE ANCIENT INHABITANTS—VI.

UPPER PAXTANG, WICONISCO DISTRICT, 1778.

[We present herewith the earliest list of the inhabitants of the Wiconisco Valley, as separate from the assessment list of Upper Paxtang, which previously included the former. The paper is endorsed "Apeal Doblicate, 1778, Peter Hoffman, Upper Paxtang, Wikiniski District," and the orthography of the surnames given as in the original. It will be seen by the large number of "Located Lands," that much of the valley had been taken up by outside parties for speculation or as investments. Levy Aaron, Michael Miller, John Cline and Henry Wails, from the amount of taxes assessed seem to have been very large land owners. The latter portion of the list refers to the age of persons who were not liable to military duty.]

Upper Paxton Wiconisco District, Continental Tax.

Buffington, Benj.,
Bretz, Ludwick,
Conaway, Francis,
Con, Daniel,
Cline, Widow,
Divler, Michael,
Divler, Mathias,
Fritz, George,
Frelick, Anthony,
Grub's Land,
Huffman, Peter,
Huffman, Hanicle,
Huffman, John,
Huffman, Jacob,
Herman, David,
Hains, Henry,
Jury, Abraham.
King, Adam,
Kooper, George,

Lerue, Francis,
Lark, Stopher,
Leman, Daniel,
Meck, Nicholas,
Metz, Jacob,
Miller, John,
Matter, John,
Myers, John,
Nighbour, Abraham,
Nigla, George,
Peter, Richard,
Paul, John,
Regel, Andrew,
Rither, William,
Ridle, George,
Seal, George,
Stiver, Yost,
Snoak, Christian,
Saladay, Michael,

Saladay, John,
Stonebreaker, Nitter,
Shesley, Stophel,
Shotz, Jacob,
Shesley, John,
Shesley, Jacob,
Smith, Jacob,
Snider, Leonard,
Shotz, Ludwick,
Sheadel, George,
Walker, Robert,
Woodside, James,
Weaver, Martin,
Wolf, Daniel,
Worz, Adam,
Weaver, Jacob,
Wersel, Henry,
Yeager, Andrew.

Freemen.

Jonathan Woodsides,
Samuel Kessler,

John Philips,
Adam Nartz,

John Herman,
Godlep Kline.

Located Lands.

Aaron Levy,
Bartrem Galbraith,
Lattis Winger,
Isaac Heeler,
Simon Snyder,
Daniel Williams,
Felty Overlady,
—— Lauman,
Michael Miller,
Jacob Whitmore,
Caleb Way,
William Poore,
George Fry,

Abraham Reggy,
John Cline,
James Beeham,
Stephen Martin,
And'w Boggs,
Rev'd Anderline,
Nicholas Miller,
Patrick Work,
John Shock,
George Muckland,
Philip Dehause,
Martin Cryder,
Arthur Niger,

Christian Snyder,
Michael Grosculp,
Simon Brand,
Frederick Height,
Henry Wails,
Samuel Sleight,
George Harris,
Levy Simeons,
Doctor Leight,
John Clandining,
—— Teeker,
George Ferree,
John Didde.

Above 53 Years.

Richard Peter,
Peter Huffman,
John Coulman,
William Rider,

Jacob Weaver,
Chrisley Snoak,
Jacob Shot,
George Nigley,

Philip Glinger,
John Gilman.

NOTES AND QUERIES.—XL.

LUTHER, DR. JOHN (N. & Q., xxxix.)—We have from our "Octogenarian," the following: "The Doctor had a gray horse that he highly prized and provided for in his will, directing that he should 'do no work, be shod and fed.' I recollect the horse well and saw him after the Doctor's death, roving over the Capitol Hill, before it was built upon, and was an open common. The Doctor had ridden the gray one evening into Cumberland county, and on returning after night, being too late for the ferry, undertook to ford the river, but lost his way, got into deep water and paddled about until daylight, when he found himself approaching a sand bar. He was so grateful to the horse, that he would not part with him."

CAMPBELL—GILBERT—PATTERSON—WIRTZ.—I was very much interested in Darby's letter (N. & Q. vii.)

The Patrick Campbell he mentions was not the constable of Donegal, but belonged to another family in Dauphin county, who were large landholders.

Benjamin Gilbert was a Quaker, and was taken prisoner with his father and family, by the Indians, on the 25th day of April, 1780.

You will find a full and interesting narrative of the captivity of the Gilbert family in the Archives and State histories. Some of their descendants now reside in Lancaster county. There is a long line of school teachers running through this family. Although they were men of talent, there was a vein of eccentricity running through them.

Col. William Patterson moved from Donegal to Cumberland county, and from thence to Juniata Valley. Hon. A. L. Hayes married his granddaughter.

Wirtz was a very prominent patriot. S. E.

FAMILY RECORD.—Hon. Marshal P. Wilder, president of the New England Historic-Genealogical Society, in his annual address for 1879, thus alludes to the preparation and preservation of family records: " The first institution established by our benevolent Creator was the family, and it has been the chief school of human virtue. No influence for good is so great. From it have emanated the principles, piety and patriotism, on which must forever rest the prosperity and strength of nations. 'The records of families,' says Dr. Alexander Wilder, ' constitute the frame work of history, and are invaluable auxilaries to science, religion, and especially to civilization.' The ties of kindred are the golden links of that chain which binds families, States and Nations together in one great bond of humanity. Everything, therefore, which pertains to our families should be carefully recorded and preserved for the benefit of those who are to follow us. He who collects and preserves his own family history is not only a benefactor in his way, but will deserve and receive the grateful thanks of all future generations. ' He confers a priceless boon upon those whose names and achievements are thus rescued from oblivion, and preserves the experience and wisdom of ages for the emulation and admonition of posterity.' It is therefore a matter of special gratification that so many of our wealthy and influential citizens have aided in publishing the history of their towns and the genealogies of their families. These praiseworthy examples are highly commendable, and permit me to say, that I have no sympathy with those who care not from whence they came, or have no interest in the generations which are to succeed them." [No greater truths than the foregoing have ever been uttered, and we commend them to the earnest and serious consideration of every one of our readers. Every family should carefully preserve not only its own immediate record, but those preceding them, and if possible these should be gathered in time together, and printed so that they may be permanently preserved. We are glad to note the increased interest taken everywhere in this particular subject. Within the past week we have received numerous inquiries concerning the ancestors of the writers, to some of whom we were able to furnish interesting data. Unfortunately there are no church records of any account until recent years—and no public registry of marriages, births and deaths—so the genealogist must confine his researches to tombstone inscriptions and records of the courts. Alas, how much is lost; but again, how much there is left to collate and preserve. We can only close with this advice to our readers : *See that your own Family Record is complete.*]

REV. DAVID BRAINERD'S VISIT TO JUNIATA ISLAND IN 1745.

[The Rev. David Brainerd, missionary to the Indians, was a native of Haddam, Conn., where he was born on the 20th of April, 1718. He entered Yale College in 1739, but for some trivial offense was expelled therefrom in 1742. In July of that year, however, he was licensed to preach, and having expressed a strong desire to spread the Gospel among the heathen, the Society for Propagating Christian Knowledge, sent him as a missionary to the Indians. He was first stationed at Kaunamuk, an Indian village situated between Stockbridge and Albany. In 1744 these were removed to the former town, when his attention was called to the Delaware Indians. In June of that year he was ordained by the Presbytery of Newark, N. J., and took up his habitation near the Forks of the Delaware in Northampton county, Pa. During this period he made two visits to the Indians on the Susquehanna. His mission here was not a successful one. He subsequently missionated among the Indians at Crossweeksung, N. J., and was very successful, and nearly one hundred of the savages were baptized within the year. His health which was always delicate, completely broke down, and he returned to New England, dying at Northampton, Mass., on the 9th of October, 1747. His biography was written by Rev. Jonathan Edwards, who also edited his journals. President Edwards proved an unfortunate biographer, and from the full diary of the devoted missionary he eradicated everything save his religious experience, and hence very much relating to affairs on the Susquehanna, narrated by an intelligent missionary, has been lost to us. It was a period of which we know but little of either the natives or pioneer settlers. The original journals are lost, or destroyed, and, perchance, some may say we ought to be thankful for what remains. Brainerd's first visit was made in May, 1745, when he passed down the river from a visit to the

Shawanese on Juniata, now Duncan's Island. In September, 1745, he was at Shamokin (Sunbury) and traveled " down the river southwestward." We give such extracts from his diary as may be interesting to the readers of *Notes and Queries.*

Sept. 19, 1745.—Visited an Indian town, called Juneauta, situate on an island in the Susquehanna. Was much discouraged with the temper and behavior of the Indians here: although they appeared friendly when I was with them the last spring, and then gave me encouragement to come and see them again. But they now seemed resolved to retain their pagan notions and persist in their idolatrous practices.

Sept. 20.—Visited the Indians again at Juneauta island, and found them almost universally very busy in making preparations for a great sacrifice and dance. Had no opportunity to get them together, in order to discourse with them about Christianity, by reason of their being so much engaged about their sacrifice. My spirits were much sunk with a prospect so very discouraging; and especially seeing I had this day no interpreter but a pagan, who was as much attached to idolatry as any of them, and who could neither speak nor understand the language of these Indians; so that I was under the greatest disadvantages imaginable. However, I attempted to discourse privately with some of them, but without any appearance of success; notwithstanding, I still tarried with them.

In the evening they met together, nearly one hundred of them, and danced around a large fire, having prepared ten fat deer for the sacrifice. The fat of the inwards they burn in the fire while they were dancing, which sometimes raised the flame to a prodigous height, at the same time yelling and shouting in such a manner that they might easily have been heard two miles or more. They continued their sacred dance nearly all night, after which they ate the flesh of the sacrifice, and so retired each one to his own lodging.

I enjoyed little satisfaction; being entirely alone on the island, as to any Christian company, and in the midst of this idolatrous revel; and walked to and fro till body and mind were pained and much oppressed. I at length crept into a little crib made for corn, and there slept on the poles.

Lord's day, Sept. 21.—Spent the day with the Indians on the island. As soon as they were well up in the morning I attempted to instruct them, and labored for that purpose to get them together; but soon found they had something else to do; for near noon they gathered together all their pow-wows or conjurers, and set about half a dozen of them playing their juggling tricks and acting their frantic, distracted postures, in order to find out why they were so sickly upon the island, numbers of them being at that time disordered with a fever and bloody flux. In this exercise they were engaged for several hours, making all the wild, ridiculous and distracted motions imaginable, sometimes singing, sometimes howling, sometimes extending their hands to the utmost stretch, and spreading all their fingers; they seemed to push with them as if they designed to push something away, or at least keep it off at arm's end; sometimes stroking their faces with their hands, then spurting water as fine as mist; sometimes sitting flat on the earth, then bowing down their faces to the ground; then wringing their sides as if in pain and anguish, twisting their faces, turning up their eyes, grunting, puffing, &c.

Their monstrous actions tended to excite ideas of horror, and seemed to have something in them, as I thought, peculiarly suited to raise the devil, if he could be raised by anything odd, ridiculous and frightful. Some of them, I could observe, were much more fervent and devout in the business than others, and seemed to chant, peep and mutter with a degree of warmth and vigor, as if determined to awaken and engage the powers below. I sat at a small distance, not more than thirty feet from them, though undiscovered, with my Bible in my hand, resolving, if possible, to spoil their sport, and prevent their receiving any answer from the infernal world, and there viewed the whole scene. They continued their hideous charms and incantations for more than three hours, until they had all wearied themselves out; although they had in that space of time taken several intervals of rest; and at length broke up, I apprehended, without receiving any answer at all.

After they had done pow-wowing I attempted to discourse with them about Christianity, but they soon scattered, and gave me no opportunity for anything of that nature. A view of these things, while I was entirely alone in the wilderness, destitute of the society of any one who so much as "named the name of Christ," greatly sunk my spirits and gave me the most gloomy turn of mind imaginable almost stripped me of all resolution and hope respecting further atttempts for propagating the gospel and converting the pagans, and rendered this the most burdensome and disagreeable Sabbath which I ever saw. But nothing, I can truly say, sunk and distressed me like the loss of my hope respecting their conversion. This concern appeared so great, and seemed to be so much my own, that I seemed to have nothing to do on earth if this failed. A prospect of the greatest success in the saving conversion of souls under gospel light would have done little or nothing towards compensating for the loss of my hope in this respect; and my spirits now were so damped and depressed, that I had not heart nor power to make any further attempts among them for that purpose, and could not possibly recover my hope, resolution and courage by the utmost of my endeavors.

The Indians of this island can, many of them, understand the English language considerably well, having formerly lived in some part of Maryland, among or near the white people; but are very drunken, vicious and profane, although not so savage as those who have less acquaintance with the English. Their customs, in various respects, differ from those of the other Indians up this river. They do not bury their dead in a common form, but let their flesh consume above the ground, in close cribs made for that purpose. At the end of a year, or sometimes a longer space of time, they take the bones, when the flesh is all consumed, and wash and scrape them, and afterwards bury them with some ceremony. Their method of charming or conjuring over the sick seems somewhat different from that of the other Indians, though in substance the same. The whole of it among these and others, perhaps, is an imitation of what seems, by Naaman's expression (II. Kings v. 11,) to have been the custom of the ancient heathen. It seems chiefly to consist in their "striking their hands over the diseased," repeatedly stroaking them, "and calling upon their god;" except the spurting of water like a mist, and some other frantic ceremonies common to the other conjurations which I have already mentioned.

When I was in this region in May last, I had an opportunity of learning many of the notions and customs of the Indians, as well as observing many of their practices. I then traveled more than one hundred and thirty miles upon the river, above the English settlements; and in that journey met with individuals of seven or eight distinct tribes, speaking as many different languages. But of all the sights I ever saw among them, or indeed anywhere else, none appeared so frightful, or so near akin to what is usually imagined of *infernal powers*, none ever excited such images of terror in my mind as the appearance of one who was a devout and zealous reformer, or rather restorer of what he supposed was the ancient religion of the Indians. He made his appearance in his *pontifical garb*, which was a coat of *bearskins*, dressed with the hair on, and hanging down to his toes; a pair of bear-skin stockings, with a great *wooden* face painted, the one-half black, the other half tawny, about the color of an Indian's skin, with an extravagant mouth, cut very much awry; the face fastened to a bear-skin cap, which was drawn over his head. He advanced towards me with the instrument in his hand which he used for music in his idolatrous worship; which was a dry tortoise-shell with some corn in it, and the neck of it drawn on to a piece of wood, which made a very convenient handle. As he came forward he beat his tune with the rattle, and danced with all his might, but did not suffer any part of his body, not so much as his fingers, to be seen. No one would have imagined from his appearance or actions, that he could have been a human creature, if they had not had some intimation of it otherwise. When he came near me I could not but shrink away from him, although it was then noonday, and I knew who it was; his appearance and gestures were so prodigously frightful. He had a house consecrated to religious uses, with divers images cut upon the several parts of it. I went in and found the ground beat almost as hard as a rock, with their frequent dancing upon it.

I discoursed with him about Christianity. Some of my discourse he seemed to like, but some of it he disliked extremely. He told me that God had taught him his religion, and that he would never turn from it, but wanted to find some who would join heartily with him in it; for the Indians, he said, were grown very degenerate and corrupt. He had thought, he said, of leaving all his friends, and traveling abroad, in order to find some who would join with him; for he believed that God had some good people somewhere, who felt as he did; but had formerly been like the rest of the Indians, until about four or five years before that time. Then, he said, his heart was very much distressed, so that he could not live among the Indians, but got away into the woods and lived alone for some months. At length, he said, God comforted his heart, and showed him what he should do; and since that time he had known God, and tried to serve him; and loved all men, be they who they would, so as he never did before. He treated me with uncommon courtesy, and seemed to be hearty in it. I was told by the Indians that he opposed their drinking strong liquor with all his power; and that, if at any time he could not dissuade them from it by all he could say, he would leave them, and go crying into the woods. It was manifest that he had a set of religious notions which he had examined for himself, and not taken for granted upon bare tradition; and he relished or disrelished whatever was spoken of a religious nature, as it either agreed or disagreed with his *standard*. While I was discoursing, he would sometimes say, "Now that I like; so God has taught me," &c.; and some of his sentiments seemed very just. Yet he utterly denied the existence of a devil, and declared there was no such creature known among the Indians of old times, whose religion he supposed he was attempting to revive. He likewise told me that departed souls went *southward*, and that the difference between the good and the bad was this: that the former were admitted into a beautiful town with spiritual walls, and that the latter would forever hover around these walls in vain attempts to get in. He seemed to be sincere, honest and conscientious in his own religious notions; which was more than I ever saw in any other pagan. I perceived that he was looked upon and derided among most of the Indians as a *precise zealot*, who made a needless noise about religious matters; but I must say that there was something in his temper and disposition which looked more like true religion than anything I ever observed among other heathens.

But, alas! how deplorable is the state of the Indians upon this river! The brief representation which I have here given of their notions and manners is sufficient to show that they are "led captive by Satan at his will," in the most eminent manner; and methinks might likewise be sufficient to excite the compassion and engage the prayers of God's children for these their fellow men, who "sit in the region of the shadow of death."

Sept. 22.—Made some further attempts to instruct and Christianize the Indians on this island, but all to no purpose. They live so near the white people that they are always in the way of strong liquor, as well as of the ill examples of nominal Christians, which renders it so unspeakably difficult to treat them about Christianity.

[In the summer of 1746 Brainerd, on his way to Shamokin, makes the following notes:]

Aug. 19.—Lodged by the side of the Susquehanna. Was weak and disordered both this and the preceding day, and found my spirits considerably dampened, meeting with none that I thought Godly people.

Aug. 20.—Rode this day to one Chambers, upon the Susquehanna, and there lodged. Was much afflicted in the evening with an ungodly crew, drinking, swearing, &c. Oh, what a *hell* would it be to be numbered among the ungodly.

Aug. 21.—Rode up the river about fifteen miles and there lodged in a family which appeared quite destitute of God. Labored to discourse with the man about the life of religion, but found him very artful in evading such conversation. O, what a death it is to some to hear of the things of God! Was out of my element, but was not so dejected as at some time.

Aug. 23.—Continued my course up the river, my people now being with me who before were parted from me. Traveled above all the English settlements; at night lodged in the open woods, and slept with more comfort than while among an ungodly company of white people. Enjoyed some liberty in secret prayer this evening, and was helped to remember dear friends, as well as my dear flock, and the church of God in general.

[The next month the missionary, enfeebled in health, passed down the river on his return home. He never came back.]

Sept. 9.—Rode down the river near thirty miles. Was extremely weak, much fatigued and wet with a thunder storm. Discoursed with some warmth and closeness to some poor, ignorant souls on the *life* and *power of religion*, what were and what were not the *evidences* of it. They seemed much astonished when they saw my Indians ask a blessing and give thanks at dinner, concluding *that* a very high evidence of grace in them; but were equally astonished when I insisted that neither that nor yet secret prayer was any sure evidence of grace. O the ignorance of the world! How are some empty outward forms, that may all be entirely selfish, mistaken for true religion, infallible evidences of it! The Lord pity a deluded world!

Sept. 11.—Rode homeward; but was very weak, and sometimes scarce able to ride. He had a very importunate invitation to preach at a meeting-house I came by, the people being then gathered; but could not by reason of weakness. Was resigned and composed under my weakness; but was much exercised with concern for my companions in travel, whom I had left with much regret, some lame, and some sick.

HARRISBURG VOLUNTEERS, 1812-14.

During the war with Great Britain, commencing in 1812, Pennsylvania was called upon by the United States Government for a quota of five thousand men for public service. After the destruction of the Capitol at Washington, in August or September, in 1814, four companies of volunteers marched from Harrisburg to Baltimore as part of the draft made, and remained there in service three months. The first and oldest company, called "The Harrisburg Infantry," was commanded by Captain Thomas Walker, numbering ninety-four men, all of whom at this date are dead, with the exception of Mr. George J. Heisly, the sole survivor, yet living in Harrisburg, enjoying good health. The next company, second in date of organization, called "The Harrisburg Artillerists," was commanded by Captain Richard M. Crain, numbering eighty-four men, all of whom, except Col. Samuel Shoch, of Columbia, have paid the debt of nature. He was born in Harrisburg on the 28th of May, 1797, and was the youngest man of all the four companies that volunteered on that occasion, if not the youngest man of the whole quota, as he was believed and said to be. He is yet in full health and vigor after a service of more than forty years as chief officer of the Columbia National Bank, the presidency of which he still holds. The third company numbered fifty-six men, was commanded by Captain John Carothers, and the fourth company, numbering sixty-six men, was at first commanded by Captain Jeremiah Rees, and afterward by Captain Philip Cline. It is uncertain whether there are any survivors of either of these two companies. The whole number of the four companies was three hundred and were part of the First Brigade, commanded by General John Forster, of Harrisburg, and of the First Regiment, commanded by Colonel Maxwell Kennedy, of Salisbury township, Lancaster county.

NOTES AND QUERIES—XLI.

MSS. FROM HERCULANEUM.—In 1820 the State of Pennsylvania purchased for the Library a valuable MSS. found in Herculaneum. What became of this curiosity?

CAPITOL OF THE STATE.—In 1808 strenuous efforts were made by the citizens of Middletown to have the seat of State Government fixed at that point. Had it not been for this division in the Councils by the representatives of Dauphin county, it is probable that Harrisburg would have been chosen several years before—but at last our good neighbors on the Swatara gracefully yielded, and were just as enthusiastic as our own citizens to locate the Capitol here.

BOYD—WALLACE, &c.—Joseph Boyd (N. & Q. xxxix), son of William Boyd, married Elizabeth Wallace, daughter of Robert and Mary Wallace, of Derry. She was born in 1745, d. April 13, 1802. They left issue—
  i. *William*, m. Martha Cowden.
  ii. *Mary*, m. William Baird.
  iii. *Margaret*, m. William McDonald.
  iv. *Ann*, d. unm.
  v. *Jane*, d. unm.   J. C. A.

[The Mary Wallace, wife of Robert Wallace, above mentioned, and of whom inquiry has been made, we are of the opinion was a daughter of Robert Rodgers, sr., of Hanover. He had a daughter Mary who married a Wallace, and as Robert Wallace, who resided in Derry, was at Hanover at the death bed of Robert Rodgers, jr., witnessing his will, the inference is very strong that there was such relationship existing.

CAMPBELL—BOWMAN—CLARK.—Samuel Campbell, of Derry, died in October, 1747. He left a wife, and children as follows:
  i. Hugh, who m. and had Elizabeth and Samuel.
  ii. Mary, m. Thomas Bowman, and had Jean and Elizabeth.
  iii. William.
  iv. Jean, m. James Clark, and had John, Samuel, Isabella and Jean.

The Campbells were early settlers in Derry. Among the oldest inscriptions in the graveyard there are those of members of that family:
  John Campbell d. February 20, 1734, aged 78 years.
  James Campbell, jun., d. August 25, 1757, in his 33d year.
  James Campbell, sen., d. May 31, 1771, aged 80 years; his second wife, Agnes, d. April 3, 175/, aged 50 years.
  James Campbell, the third in descent, d. June 10, 1783, aged 25 years.

Information, however, is especially requested concerning the children of Mary Bowman and Jean Clark.

THE OLD-TIME FAIRS.—" People have always had amusements and will patronize them." Some of the annual attractions in the interior of the State, sixty or seventy years ago, were fairs, which were legalized by acts of the Assembly. They were held on fixed days, at the different county seats, so that venders of eatables and drinks, as well as those who conducted amusements went from place to place.

The month of May was the time fixed, and two days were allowed; but as most of the men could only devote one day of time, the first was the most important. Here they were held in the market house, and innumerable booths were erected in the Square, where the tables were spread with cakes, beer, porter and ale. Most of the lads and lassies of the surrounding country attended—also the fighting men, who had regular set fights. The principal pugilist of Harrisburg was ———, while ———, a respectable farmer of Cumberland county, often came here to fight. They were large, athletic men and well matched. Others also engaged in the same brutal sport. At an early day the ———, of Cumberland county, were noted men for fighting. While the fair was going on in the Square, dancing was carried on with great spirit in the different taverns in town. This was kept up most of the day and night. Other amusements, the circus, puppet shows, flying horses, and games of various kinds, were in full blast all over the borough. So demoralizing, however, did these fairs become, that an act was subsequently passed abolishing and forbididg them.

FAMILY OF JAMES HALL AND PRUDENCE RODDY.

Among the first settlers along the Conewago were the Halls, Roddys, Mordahs, Bowmans, McQueen's, and other familiar Scotch-Irish names, but whose descendants have all gone out from the old locality and become prominent in the South and West, knowing but little of the pioneer life of their pious ancestors, and less of the locality where some of those ancestors were born. In searching among the records of "the days which are past," we come across facts relating to these hardy pioneers, and if it is possible to trace up their after history, we essay to do it. Of course, there are but few persons who care for records beyond their own families; and though there are none probably in this locality related or connected with the family whose genealogical details we present in this number of *Notes and Queries*, yet in the hope that the interest of some may be aroused in the gathering up of the scattered fragments of their own family history—we give that which follow. We have gleaned the facts from various fields, and as a record of one of our earliest families, it is worthy of preservation.

I. JAMES HALL, son of Hugh Hall, b. in Ireland, 1705; m. in 1730 Prudence Roddy, his cousin, daughter of James Roddy, b. 1710 in Ireland. Both emigrated to Pennsylvania in early life, as their parents' names appear on the first assessment list of Donegal township, Lancaster county, in 1723. They located in what was Derry, now Londonderry township, Dauphin county, where they were married by the Rev. James Anderson. Here all their children were born. They were in full communion with the "Church at Conewago," and in 1751 removed with their family to Iredell county, North Carolina, settling on Fifth Creek, near Bethany Church. There they died and are buried. Among their descendants were twenty-four or twenty-five ministers of the Gospel, and more than that number of the females married preachers.

They had issue as follows:
  i. Sarah, b. 1732; m. James King, and had a large family.
  ii. Jean, b. 1734; m. 1st, ———— Roseborough, and had one son; 2d, Rev. James McEwen, and left a daughter, Erixena, who m. Rev. James Adams, of South Carolina.
  iii. Margaret, b. 1736; m. Robert Woods; d. 1771.
  iv. Mary, b. 1738; m. John Archibald, brother of Rev. Robert Archibald; d. 1776.
2. *v. Alexander*, b. 1740; m. Ann Dobson.
3. *vi. Hugh*, b. 1742; m. Margaret King.
  vii. James, b. August 22, 1744.

[The Rev. James Hall just named was born in Derry township, Lancaster county, now Londonderry, Dauphin county, Pennsylvania, on the 22d of August, 1744. He was brought up on his father's farm, receiving a fair education, but it was not until he had attained his majority and decided to enter the ministerial field that he commenced the study of the classics. Having prepared himself for college, he entered at Princeton, and graduated under President Witherspoon in 1774, when he was in his thirty-first year. He was licensed to preach by the Presbytery of Orange sometime between the meeting of the Synod in 1775 and 1776. On the 8th of April he was installed pastor of the United Congregations of Fourth Creek, Concord and Bethany, in North Carolina. Here he remained until 1790, when he was released by the two former congregations, retaining his connection with Bethany during the remainder of his life.

[During the Revolution Dr. Hall was no idle spectator. With his heart fully in accord with the patriot cause, he accepted the command of a select company of cavalry and was in service several months. After the skirmish at Cowan's Ford, on the Cataba, between the forces of Cornwallis and the North Carolina militia, Gen. Greene offered him the commission of Brigadier General, to succeed General Davidson, who had fallen in that conflict, but he declined it, on the ground that others could fill that post, while he had pledged his life in defense of the gospel.

[Princeton honored him with the degree of Doctor of Divinity, and in 1810 the University of North Carolina complimented him by the same. Doctor Hall was a Commissioner at Philadelphia from the Presbytery of Orange sixteen times, and was moderator of that body in 1803. He died on the 25th of July, 1826, in his eighty-second year, and his remains are interred in Bethany churchyard. The prominent trait of Dr. Hall's character was his devoted piety. For forty years his ministry was one glowing scene of untiring activity.]

   viii. Dorcas, b. 1747; m. Wm. Roseborough; removed to Kentucky; d. 1773.
   ix. Rev. Robert, b. 1749; m. and had James Roddy, John and Prudence.
4. *x. Thomas*, b. 1751; m. Elizabeth Sloan.
 II. ALEXANDER HALL, b. 1740; m. Ann Dobson, and had issue:
   i. Prudence.
5. *ii. Joseph*, m. Dorcas Vandever.
6. *iii. Thomas*, m. Mary Collins.
7. *iv. Hugh Roddy*, m. Mary Nesbit.
8. *v. Rev. Robert James*, m. Nancy Turner.

III. HUGH HALL, b. 1742; m. Margaret King, and had issue:
[Hugh Hall was an ensign in Capt. Adam Read's company, of Colonel (afterwards General) Hugh Mercer's Third Pennsylvania Battalion, in the Forbes expedition, commissioned May 4th, 1758. On the rolls he is certified to as "of reputable and good family in Lancaster county." He went to North Carolina at the close of the French and Indian war.]

    i. Prudence, m. A. Hill.
9.   *ii. Margaret*, m. Rev. L. F. Wilson.
    iii. Mary, m. James Cowan.
    iv. Elizabeth, m. James McCord, M. D.
10. *v. James*, m. Elizabeth Nesbit.
11. *vi. Samuel*, m. Mary Gregg.
12. *vii. Richard*, m. Martha More.
    viii. Dorcas, m. 1st, A. Knox; 2d, Robert Johnston.
    ix. Sophia, m. Alexander Barr.
    x. Sarah, m. David Adams.
    xi. Jane, m. Moses Hague.

IV. THOMAS HALL, b. 1751, m. Elizabeth Sloan, and had issue :
    i. Prudence, m. William Stevenson.
13. *ii. James*, m. Rachel Johnston.
    iii. Fergus, m. Margaret Bell; removed very early to Tennessee.
14. *iv.* Rev. *Thomas J.*, m. Amy Wallace.
15. *v. Alexander*, m. Adaline Sharpe.
    vi. Margaret, m. James Hill.
    vii. Mary, m. William S. Johnston, and had Rev. T. P. and Prof. Mortimer Johnston.
    viii. Ann, m. Samuel Johnston.
    ix. Sarah, m. Benjamin Knox.
16. *x. William Davidson*, m. Elizabeth Gregg.
17. *xi. Hugh*, m. Matilda Crawford.
18. *xii. Robert Sloan*, m. Ann King.

V. JOSEPH HALL, m. Dorcas Vandever, and had—
    i. Mary.
    ii. Elizabeth.
    iii. William D., m. Ann Hoke, and had Julius, d. in war—Merrill, Adaline, Martha, Candace, Henry, William, John, and Laura, d. s. p.
    iv. Rufus Scott, a lawyer resident in Tennessee, m. Jemima ———, and had issue.
    v. Mariah R., m. James McLaughlin, and had Margaret, m. Rev. LeQuex, John F., William A., E. Irvin, Laura, d. s. p., and Walter.

  vi. Alexander.
  vii. Lorenzo.
  viii. Martha.
  ix. Hugh, m. 1st, —— Bolio, and had Julia and Betsey; 2d, —— Smith.
VI. THOMAS HALL, m. Mary Collins, and had:
  i. Prudence.
  ii. Emeline.
  iii. Emma.
  iv. Robert-Alexander, d. s. p.
  v. Mary-Ann, m. A. Garrison.
  vi. Robert-A., d. in the war of 1861-5.
  vii. Elizabeth, m. Richard Nesbit, and had Jasper and Udell.
  viii. Martha Clarissa.
VII. HUGH RODDY HALL, m. Mary Nesbit and had:
  i. Laura, m. C. W. Smith.
  ii. Eugenia, m. Wm. C. White, and had Hugh Ralph, Alvin Flake, Mary, Lizzie and Lavinnia.
  iii. Anthony, d. in the war of 1861-5.
  iv. Milroy Nisbet, m. Martha Adams, and had Mary C., Ashley and Eugenia Rockwell.
VIII. ROBERT JAMES HALL, m. Nancy Turner, and had issue:
  i. Sarah Ann, m. Samuel Adams, of Ohio.
IX. MARGARET HALL, m. Rev. L. F. Wilson, and had:
  i. Hugh, m. Ethlinda Hall.
  ii. Lewis F.
X. JAMES HALL, m. Elizabeth Nesbit, and had:
  i. Eliza, m. Sheldon Lemmons, M. D., (Yale, 1816).
  ii. John Nesbit, m. —— Alexander, and had John G., Hattie and Rose.
  iii. James W., m. Eliza Kearns, had Mary and John P.
XI. SAMUEL HALL, m Mary Gregg, and had:
  i. Ollvia, m. Rev. William A. Hall, of Tenn.
  ii. Mary, m. John G. Hall.
  iii. Sophia, m. William Garrison.
  iv. Elizabeth Gregg.
  v. Samuel P.
XII. RICHARD HALL, m. Martha Moore, and had:
  i. Mary.
  ii. Elizabeth.
  iii. Hugh Addison, m. and had Margaret, Samuel, Franklin, Mary, Elizabeth Constantine, John Ramsey, Wm. Penn, James Monroe and Ann H.
  iv. James K., m. Fanny Rank.

Historical and Genealogical. 287

XIII. JAMES HALL, m. Rachel Johnston, and had:
  i. *Jessie D.*, m. Rebecca McGracy; removed to Tennessee.
  ii. *Elizabeth*, m. Sloan Mathews.
  iii. *Ethlinda*, m. Rev. Hugh Wilson.
  iv. *Rev. William A.*, m. Olivia Hall, and had Emma C., Spencer H. and Julia.
  v. *Thomas*, m. 1st, E. Sharp; 2d, —— Sample, 3d, —— Perkins.
  vi. *Rev. James D.*, m. 1st, Isabella Scott, and had Rev. Wm., m. —— Witherspoon; 2d, —— Brandon; 3d, —— Neagle, and had Elva, m. Rev. Robert M. Hall.
  vii. *Nancy E.*, m. James B. Gracy.
  viii. *David J.*, m. Dorcas Sherrill.
  ix. *Fergus A.*, m. Catharine Sherrill.
  x. *John J.*, m. 1st, M. Sharpe; 2d, —— Sharpe.
XIV. REV. THOMAS J. HALL, m. Amy Wallace, and had:
  i. *Cedilla*, m. Rev. J. R. Wood.
  ii. *Emma*, m. Rev, —— Calvert, of Ky.
XV. ALEXANDER Hall, m. Adaline Sharpe, and had:
  i. *Mary*, m. Alexander McRae.
  ii. *Ethalinda Catharine*, m. Robert McLelland.
  iii. *John.*
  iv. *Matilda.*
  v. *Melissa*, d. s. p.
  vi. *Alphosa.*
XVI. WM. DAVIDSON HALL, m. Elizabeth Gregg, and had:
  i. *Thomas.*
  ii. *James.*
  iii. *Elias Gregg.*
  iv. *William.*
  v. *Sarah.*
  vi. *Richard.*
  vii. *Henry.*
  viii. *John.*
  ix. *Robert.*
  x. *Harriet.*
  xi. *Henrietta.*
  xii. *Ermina.*
XVII. HUGH HALL, m. Matilda Crawford, and had:
  i. *Elizabeth*, m. —— Baker.
  ii. *Pinckney.*
  iii. *Sarah.*
  iv. *David.*

  v. Sidney.
  vi. Jane.
  vii. Wilson.
  viii. Claudius.
XVIII. ROBERT SLOAN HALL, m. Ann King (of Illinois), and had:
  i. James.
  ii. Mary.
  iii. Chalmers.
  iv. Amanda.
  v. Elizabeth.
  vi. Matilda.
  vii. Martha.
  viii. Caroline.
  ix. Electa.
  x. Rev. Robert M., m. Elva Hall.

With the exception of the Rev. James Hall, D. D., we have little biographical details of those named in the foregoing record. We are remote from those connected, which will account for the lack of data.

ADAM WEISE.

Adam Weise was born in New Goshenhoppen, Philadelphia county, Pa., December 23, 1751. His parents were John George and Eve Weise. They moved from New Goshenhoppen to Heidelberg township, Berks county, Pa., where Adam was brought up in a Christianlike manner in the faith and doctrine of the Evangelical Lutheran Church.

The subject of this sketch was married on the 2d of February, A. D. 1772, to Margaret Elizabeth Wingard, who was born in Heidelberg township, Berks county, on the 15th of March, A. D. 1749. Her parents were Lazarus and Catharine Elizabeth Wingard. She belonged to the Evangelical Presbyterian (German Reformed) Church. By this marriage there were the following children:

  i. Catharine Elizabeth was born Nov. 21, A. D. 1772, in Heidelberg township, Berks county, and married to George Gundrum on the 7th of April, A. D. 1795, by Rev. William Hendel.

  ii. Ann Elizabeth was born April 28, A. D. 1774, in Hagerstown, Md. (the family having removed to that place the previous year), and married Philip Shaffer on the 5th of April, A. D. 1795. He died on the 23d of March, A. D. 1814, in Upper Paxtang township, Dauphin county.

iii. John was born August 13, A. D. 1776, in Hagerstown, and married Elizabeth Bordner, daughter of Michael Bordner, of Upper Paxtang township, Dauphin county, on the 7th of June, A. D. 1801.

iv. Anna-Mary was born June 28, A. D. 1778, in Hagerstown, and married Michael Shadel on the 7th of November, A. D. 1797, in Upper Paxtang township, Dauphin county.

v. John-Adam was born January 24, 1780, in Hagerstown, and married Eve Bordner, daughter of Peter Bordner, of Upper Paxtang township, Dauphin county, in the year A. D. 1801. His wife died the first year of their marriage, and he was married the second time to Elizabeth Lebo.

Adam Weise served as a sergeant in the Maryland cavalry in the Revolutionary war, enlisting at Hagerstown. He moved with his family from Hagerstown to Upper Paxtang township, in Lykens Valley, Dauphin county, Pa., in the year A. D. 1782. [He settled at this time on the north or south side of Wiconisco creek, on the road (as now known) leading from Cross-Roads to Berrysburg, formerly Hellerstown. According to the best information obtainable, he settled on the north of said creek, on what is generally known as the Elder farm, and very likely he owned the land on both sides of the creek, for he owned three hundred acres or over. When I (his youngest son) was ten or twelve years old, in passing along on that road in company with old men of the valley, I was shown the place where they said my father's blacksmith shop had stood, which was a little back in the field from the road, southwest from the old residence, which is still standing, but has been remodeled and repaired at different times. I was also shown where he had his coal-pit or hearth, which was about a hundred yards slightly northwest from where the shop stood, in the woods. Blacksmiths used nothing but charcoal in those days, and most of them burnt or charred their own coal. It should be remembered, also, that nearly all of what is now Washington and Mifflin townships to the Susquehanna river was included in Upper Paxtang township.]

vi. John-George was born January 7, A. D. 1786, in Upper Paxtang township, Dauphin county, and married Charlotte Moore A D. 1808.

The Indians were very troublesome, and from this and other causes the family removed to Bethel township, Berks county, Pa., A. D. 1788.

vii. Anna-Margaret was born February 14, A. D. 1789, in Bethel township, Berks county, and married Michael Shoop on the

6th of November, A. D. 1808, in Upper Paxtang township, Dauphin county.

viii. Anna-Maria was born on the 21st of July, A. D. 1791, in Bethel township, Berks county, and married Abraham Jury, A. D. 1811, in Upper Paxtang township, Dauphin county.

Mr. Weise moved back to Lykens Valley to the old place in the year 1796, and in 1802 took up his residence in Millersburg, erecting the third house in the town and a blacksmith shop, on the southwest corner of Union and Race streets (now owned by Levi Bowman, Sr.) His anvil was the town clock in the morning for a number of years, so the old people of Millersburg used to say. He was commissioned a justice of the peace by Governor Mifflin February 1, 1799. Remained in office over thirty-four years, or until his death in 1833.

His wife died on Sunday, March 29, A. D. 1818, and was buried on the following Tuesday, in the David's (German Reformed) graveyard, about three miles northeast of Millersburg. The funeral attendance was exceedingly large, and Revs. J. R. Reily and Nicholas Hemping were present. A very appropriate sermon was preached by Rev. J. R. Reily, from Psalms iv: 8. She reached the age of 69 years and 14 days. They lived together in matrimony 46 years, 1 month and 26 days.

Adam Weise entered into matrimony the second time on the 23d of August, A. D. 1818, with Mary Kuehly (Keely), widow of George Kuehly, of Swinefordstown, Union county, Pa., (now Middleburg, Snyder county.) Her parents were Jacob and Mary Bitterman, from Montgomery county, Pa. She was born March 20, A. D. 1765, in Montgomery county.

On Sunday evening, Sept. 10, 1820, his second wife died, and was buried the following Tuesday in the German Reformed burial ground, alongside his former partner. Her age was 55 years, 5 month and 15 days. Rev. Isaac Gearheart preached on the occasion, from the words recorded in Isaiah, xxxviii : 1.

Mr. Weise entered into matrimony the third time on the 10th of December, A. D. 1820, with Catharine Patton, widow of James Patton, of Swinefordstown, Union county, Pa., (now Middleburg, Snyder county.) Her maiden name was Catharine Neiman. She was born November, 10, A. D. 1785, in Montgomery county, Pa. Her parents were Conrad and Catharine Neiman. This union was blessed with the following issue :

ix. Abel was born on the 3d of October, A. D. 1821, in Millersburg, Dauphin county, Pa. He is still living, a resident of Lykens.

x. Hannah was born February 13, A. D. 1823, in Millersburg.

xi. Frederick-Neiman was born the 25th day of August, A. D. 1825, in Millersburg, and now resides in this borough.

Adam Weise died October 5, A. D. 1833, in Millersburg, after a long and useful life, and was buried by the side of his two deceased wives in the graveyard of David's Reformed Church, Upper Paxtang township. Rev. Isaac Gearheart officiated at the funeral. His age was 81 years, 9 months and 12 days.

Catharine Weise, surviving relict of Adam Weise, died in Berrysburg, Dauphin county, April 30, A. D. 1863, aged 77 years, 5 months and 20 days. She was buried in the cemetery of the Evangelical Lutheran and German Reformed Church at Berrysburg. Funeral services were held by Revs. Bosler and I. Gearheart.

At the death of Adam Weise there were 11 children, 63 grandchildren and 133 great-grandchildren. The descendants of the above record (which is made from a correct translation of the original German by Rev. Michael Lenker) are now scattered in nearly every State of the Union, especially in the West. F. N. W.

NOTES AND QUERIES.—XLII.

1001.—In 1810 there was a society in Harrisburg by this name. They held their meetings at the "Golden Eagle," Buehler's tavern, now Bolton's. What was the object of this association—and who composed it?

BRYAN, JOHN.—We have been favored with an Iowa paper giving an account of the death of a native of Harrisburg—John Bryan. He was the son of Samuel Bryan and Elizabeth Cleckner, born at Harrisburg, Penn., in April, 1808. His grandfather was a soldier of the revolution and an early inhabitant of this city; was a house carpenter by trade, as was also the son and grandson. The latter became a noted builder, and the court houses of three or four of the western counties of Pennsylvania attest the skill and fidelity which Mr. Bryan brought to his work. He subsequently removed to Iowa, and in May, 1856, settled in the city of Des Moines, then the capital of that State. In the following year, with a partner, his brother-in-law, Mr. Hyde, he took the contract for the construction of the now old State house at that place. In his adopted home he was well known and highly respected. He died on the 8th of October, 1879, in his seventy-second year, leaving a wife and three children.

APPRECIATED.—The April number of the *New England Historical and Genealogical Register*, in noticing the *Notes and Queries* which appear in the *Telegraph* supplement, makes the statement that three newspapers in the United States have a regular series of articles concerning the history and genealogy of their locality. The Richmond (Va.) *Standard*, in charge of that learned historian, R. A. Brock, Esq.; The Boston *Evening Transcript*, in care of Charles E. Hurd, Esq.; and the Harrisburg *Daily Telegraph*. We can only reciprocate the *Register's* notice by saying that although we are thoroughly Pensylvanian by birth and by affection, we highly prize the *Register*, and therefore believe that no one who has ever slept beneath the shadow of Bunker Hill ought to be without a copy of so interesting, and so valuable a quarterly—especially to all connected by blood or marriage to New England Pilgrim or New England Puritan. Like old wine, it becomes more precious by age.

LEGISLATORS IN THE LONG AGO.—I.

Paper read before the Dauphin County Historical Society.

Mr. President and Gentlemen: I have here some old papers which have accidentally fallen into my possession, and which our worthy President and Librarian have induced me to lay before you this evening. They are "old papers," doubtless, but I do not believe that the veriest tyro in historical research would place them in the category of rare documents bearing that impress of antiquity which invokes reverence. They have no intrinsic value, no import of subject matter grave enough to arrest the attention of the average reader; they are not specimens of the chirography either of dead patriots or living heroes, and it is a woful commentary upon the foresight and prudence of the State of Pennsylvania that these papers in their isolated, meagre condition should be worthy of even a passing consideration at the hands of the gleaner in the fields of her history. They are simply specimens of that flotsam and jetsam which the waves of Time occasionally wash up and expose to sight upon the shores of the Present, from that vast whirlpool of Chaos to which the carelessness of the earlier, and the downright vandalism of the later guardians of our State records have consigned them. Had our Commonwealth's archives been properly preserved at the right time, such papers as these would now be utterly worthless; but as it is, from the meagre tale they and kindred waifs may tell, must be woven the woof of much of Pennsylvania's early history.

If I shall succeed in interesting you in the story in part, which these papers will suggest to a careful examiner, and thereby quicken your appreciation of the importance of a more assiduous collation and preservation of records of like character, and impart in never so slight a degree to the general public a knowledge of the present value of such documents, something will have been accomplished for the good of history, more probably than this feeble effort deserves. I call attention first to these two papers:

A List of Members and Officers of the House of Representatives of the Commonwealth of Pennsylvania, with their places of Residence in Harrisburg, for the Session of 1813–14.

Philadelphia City.—William J. Duane, Robert Harris's, Front street; Thomas Sergeant, George Ziegler's, Second street; John Connelly, Robert Harris's, Front street; Jacob Mitchell, Frederick Hyneman's, Market street; Joseph McCoy, John Wright's, Walnut street.

Philadelphia County.—John Holmes, Frederick Hyneman's, Market street; Joseph Starne, Frederick Hyneman's, Market street; John Carter, Frederick Hyneman's, Market street; Joel B. Sutherland, John Wright's, Walnut street; Isaac Heston, John Shoch's, Front street; Charles Souder, Frederick Hyneman's, Market street.

Bucks.—Samuel Smith, John Shoch's, Front street; William H. Rowland, Mrs. McCreight's, Market street; Michael Fackenthall, John Shoch's, Front street; Joseph Clunn, John Shoch's, Front street.

Chester.—John Harris, John Shoch's, Front street; John Read, John Shoch's, Front street; James Brooke, Nicholas Schwoyer's, Walnut street; James Hindman, John Shoch's, Front street; Edward Darlington, John Shoch's, Front street.

Lancaster.—Emanual Reigart, Mrs. Scott's, Second street; Joel Lightner, Mrs. Scott's, Second street; Jacob Grosh, Andrew Berryhill's, Second street; John Graff, Mrs. Scott's, Second street; Henry Hambright, John Norton's, Second street; Robert Maxwell, Andrew Berryhill's, Second street.

York.—James S. Mitchell, Philip Youse's, Second street; Archibald S. Jordan, Frederick Beissel's, Second street; Jacob Heckert, Philip Youse's, Second street; George Frysinger, Nicholas Schwoyer's, Walnut street.

Cumberland.—John Maclay, Mrs. Scott's, Second street; Moses

Watson, George Ziegler's, Second street; George Metzger, Mrs. Scott's, Second street.

Berks and Schuylkill.—Jacob Krebs, Jacob Steinman's, Market street; Conrad Fager, John Fager's, Market street; George Marx, Peter Marx's, Market street; John Addams, Frederick Hyneman's, Market street; Jonathan Hudson, Frederick Hyneman's, Market street.

Northampton, Lehigh and Wayne.—Daniel W. Dingman, John Benjamin's, Market street; Henry Winters, John Benjamin's, Market street; John Hays, Frederick Beissel's, Second street; Philip Seller John Benjamin's, Market street; Abraham Rinker, Frederick Beissel's, Second street.

Northumberland, Union and Columbia.—Samuel Bond, Mrs. McCreight's, Market street; Leonard Rupert, Nicholas Schwoyer's, Walnut street; Thomas Murray, Mrs. McCreight's, Market street; George Kremer, Nicholas Schwoyer's, Walnut street.

Washington.—Joshua Dickerson, Thomas McCall, James Stevenson, and James Kerr, at Nicholas Schwoyer's, Walnut street.

Armstrong, Indiana and Jefferson.—James McComb, John Benjamin's, Market street.

Westmoreland.—George Plumer, Henry Allhouse and Peter Wallace, Melchior Rahm's, Second street.

Fafayette.—Henry Heaton, Nicholas Schwoyer's, Walnut street; John Shreve, Melchior Rahm's, Second street; John St. Clair, George Ziegler's, Second street.

Bedford.—Joseph S. Morrison and Jacob Hart, Philip Youse's, Second street.

Franklin.—Robert Smith, William Findlay's, Front street; David Maclay, John Shoch's, Front street; Jacob Dechert, George Ziegler's, Second street.

Montgomery.—Jesse Bean, Benjamin Reiff, Philip Reed and William Powell, Nicholas Schwoyer's, Walnut street.

Dauphin and Lebanon—Amos Ellmaker, George Ziegler's, Second street; Peter Shindel, Nicholas Schwoyer's; David Ferguson, Philip Youse's, Second street.

Luzerne and Susquehanna—Jabez Hyde and Joseph Pruner, George Ziegler's, Second street.

Huntingdon—R. James Law and John Crum, Mrs. McCreight's, Market street.

Beaver—John Lawrence, Melchior Rahm's, Second street.

Allegheny and Butler—John Potts, William Courtney, William Marks and Samuel Scott, John Shoch's, Front street.

Mifflin—Jonathan Rothrock, Melchior Rahm's, Second street; James Milliken, Mrs. McCreight's, Market street.

Delaware—William Cheyney and John Thomson, Mrs. Scott's, Second street.

Somerset and Cambria—James Mitchell, George Ziegler's, Second street; Daniel Stoy, John Benjamin's, Market street.

Lycoming, Bradford, Tioga and Potter—Henry Welles, Mrs. McCreight's, Market street; John Forster, Andrew Berryhill's, Market street.

Greene—William T. Hays, Nicholas Schowoyer's, Walnut street.

Adams—William Miller and James Robinette, Andrew Berryhill's, Market street.

Centre, Clearfield and McKean—Michael Bollinger, Frederick Beissel's, Second street.

Crawford, Erie and Warren—James Weston and James Burchfield, Melchior Rahm's, Second streeet.

Mercer and Venango—Samuel Hays and Jacob Herrington, Melchior Rahm's, Second street.

George Heckert, clerk, Philip Youse's, Second street.

Samuel D. Franks, ass't clerk, J. Downey's, Second street.

J. Benjamin, sergeant-at arms, corner Market and Third street.

James Taylor, door-keeper, G. Ziegler's, Market square.

James Peacock, printer of the English Journal, Mrs. Scott's; office, Market street.

J. Schnee, printer of the German Journal, Lebanon, Lebanon county.

Jacob Elder, printer of the bills, Chestnut street.

List of Members and Officers of the Senate of the Commonwealth of Pennsylvania, for the Session 1813–14, with their places of residence in the Borough of Harrisburg.

1. Composed of the city and county of *Philadelphia*—Charles Biddle, Mr. Kean's, Market street; Joseph Worrell, Mrs. Scott's, Second street; Jacob Shearer, Mr. Hyneman's, Market street; John Barclay, Mr. Berryhill's, Second street.

2. *Chester and Delaware*—John Gemmil, Mr. Ziegler's, Market street; John Newbold, Mrs. Scott's, Second street.

3. *Bucks*—William Erwin, Mrs. Berryhill's, Second street.

4. *Lancaster*—Nathaniel Watson, Mr. Ziegler's, Market square; William Hamilton, Mr. Buehler's, Market square.

5. *Berks and Schuylkill*—Peter Frailey and Charles Shoemaker, Mr. Steinman's, Market street.

6. *Dauphin and Lebanon*—Melchior Rahm, Second street.

7. *Montgomery*—Samuel Gross, Mr. Benjamin's, Market street.

8. *Northampton, Wayne and Lehigh*—Henry Jarrett, Mr. Beissel's, Second street; James Ralston, Mrs. Scott's, Second street.

9. *Northumberland and Luzerne*—James Laird, Mr. Laird's, Second street; William Ross, Mr. Ziegler's, Market square.

10. *Centre, Lycoming, &c.*—Thomas Burnside, Mr. Berryhill's, Second street.

11. *York and Adams*—John Stroman, Mr. Beissel's, Second street; James McSherry, Mr. Berryhill's, Second street.

12. *Mifflin and Huntingdon*—William Beale, Mr. Ziegler's, Market square.

13. *Cumberland*—Isaiah Graham, Mr. Ziegler's, Market square.

14. *Bedford, Somerset, &c.*—John Tod, Mr. Youse's, Market square.

15. *Franklin*—James Poe, Mr. Rahm's, Second street.

16. *Westmoreland, &c.*—James Brady, Mr. Youse's, Market square.

17. *Fayette*—P. C. Lane, speaker, Mr. Downey's, Second street.

18. *Washington and Greene*—Abel McFarland and Isaac Weaver, Mr. Schwoyer's, Walnut street.

19. *Allegheny, Beaver and Butler*—Thomas Baird and Walter Lowrie, Mrs. Shoch's, Front street.

20. *Erie, Crawford, &c.*—Joseph Shannon, Mr. Rahm's, Second street.

Joseph A. McJimsey, clerk, Market street.

George Harrison, assistant clerk, Mr. Zeigler's, Market square.

William Wilson, sergeant-at-arms, Mr. Benjamin's, Market street.

Henry Garloch, door-keeper, Dewberry alley.

Christian Gleim, printer of the Journal in the English language, Walnut street.

John Ritter & Co., printer of the Journal in the German language, at Reading.

William Gilmor, printer of the bills, Walnut street.

There is nothing significant in their general appearance, certainly. Upon a casual examination you would say that the "waste paper fiends" who infest the Capitol Hill during the present sessions of the Legislature, could doubtless make daily deposits in their capacious budgets of scores of documents just like them, gathered from the debris of Senate and House floors. But mark if you please the date their captions bear.

The paper on which they are printed is immaculate and the typography clear and legible, although it is now nearly seventy years since these broadsides dropped from the presses of James Peacock and Christian Gleim, printers at Harrisburg, and were laid damp upon the tables of Senate and House at the second meeting of the Legislature, held at the present State Capital, in a building which stood upon the site of this Court House where we meet this evening.

With what a familiar sound will the names upon these papers fall upon the ears of aged citizens of Harrisburg, and how their eyes will brighten at the suddenly recurring thoughts of boyhood which the mention of these old landmarks will cause. They are the names of men who were then well-known and honored throughout the Commonwealth, and of localities in the town prominent then, and around which pleasant memories still cling. These relics of the long ago may be looked upon as interesting by those of us who are young, but they are more than interesting, they are precious to the aged.

It is not within the scope of an article of so local a character as this must necessarily be, to attempt any biographical sketch of the Senators and members whose names appear in these lists, entertaining as in some respects it might prove. We trust, however, that your patience will brook a brief mention of a few characters in whom we are locally interested, together with some description of the old inns and taverns mentioned in these papers by the names of their landlords, which the kindness of Dr. Egle in furnishing data has enabled the writer to give.

The inns of old England have had a place in her literature from the days of Chaucer down. They have been imbued with a character as distinct as their nomenclature is unique. They have been made the scene of many a pleasing romance, many a heart-rending tragedy, and many a tale of grim hobgoblin and phantom strange. It may not, therefore, be difficult to account for the tendency of Americans, and especially we Pennsylvanians, to invest our early inns and taverns with a garb of romance. It is a legitimate inheritance. But if you be too democratic to subscribe to this theory, we may adopt another and less fanciful reason for the interest that is generally manifested in the history of these old landmarks. The taverns of the towns and the inns of the roadsides were the social, military and business centers of the community, as well as the news-depots, and as a consequence were the scenes of many an interesting event, the record of which, perhaps, is preserved only in the history of the inn or tavern where it transpired.

Harrisburg has had her full quota of these old temples of accommodation for man and beast, and at no period was the business more prosperous than in that to which we have reverted to-night. The Legislature then, as now, was an important factor in its success, and as a matter of course the establishments patronized by the members were the more important. It is the present purpose to describe these only.

"*The King of Prussia.*"—The inn most popular with the law-makers at this date seems to have been "The King of Prussia," Nicholas Schwoyer, landlord. This inn was located near the northwest corner of Second and Walnut streets, on Second street. It was a large, two-storied log and weather-boarded house, painted yellow. Its substantial stone stables stood beside it, facing on Second street and running nearly to Locust. A cobble-stone pavement secured passers-by a solid footing from the inn-door to the corner of Locust. Various persons figured as its landlords—Schwoyer, above mentioned, Melchior Rahm and David Doebler among them. The King of Prussia is said to have been famous for its gaiety. Shows and dances were common occurrences, and, if we may believe tradition, the study of science was prosecuted in one of its upper rooms, if not to the wholesale instruction, at least to the delight of a number of young gentlemen who frequently met together there and administered to each other that delightful anæsthetic nitrous oxide, or some other kindred vapor, for the extraction—not of teeth, but of amusement at each other's expense. The site of the King of Prussia is now occupied by the Heisley, Buehler, Fleming and Lamberton properties and the building of the Young Men's Christian Association. At this inn Mr. Schwoyer accommodated fifteen of our members.

The "Sheaf of Wheat."—This tavern was kept by John Shoch in the double brick house on Front street, next to the north corner of Front and Market. The corner house was prominently occupied as a tavern before the next house was built, Mr. Shoch being its last proprietor. "The Sheaf of Wheat" or the "Golden Sheaf," as it was sometimes called, accommodated thirteen members and two Senators, and is said to have always been quite a popular resort for the law-makers. Isaac Wills, of Cumberland county, brother of Alexander Wills, was a boarder at this house at the time he was murdered in the store of his brother, on the upper corner of Front street and Blackberry alley. In personal appearance "Mine Host" Shoch is represented as being tall and corpulent. He was a shoemaker by trade, one of the leading men of the town, and much esteemed.

The "Cross Keys."—Eight members, five Senators, the Assistant Clerk of the Senate and Doorkeeper of the House stopped with Colonel George Ziegler at the sign of the "Cross Keys." This was a three story brick building, with gable fronting the street, still standing at the northeast corner of Market Square and Blackberry alley (No. 15). It was built for a tavern and place of public amusement. It contained a large room on the second floor which was used for dancing and theatrical purposes. This tavern was abandoned at a comparatively early day. Mr. Ziegler quit the business of tavern keeping and opened what in time proved to be the principal liquor store in the town. He is described as a tall, slender man, with a decided German face, Quaker like stile of dress and sombre appearance. He live much respected through life and died at a good old age.

"The Sign of Dr. Franklin."—Senator Melchoir Rahm combined the business of law-making with that of tavern keeping. He was the representative in the Senate for the Dauphin and Lebanon district, and at the same time entertained at his house, on the S. E. corner of Second and Walnut, eleven members of the House and our fellow Senator. Mr. Rahm also kept tavern at other localities at different times, and it might as well here be mentioned that scarcely any of these bonifaces moved in fixed orbits. One year we find them at one stand and the next at another, and so it was a matter of no little difficulty to fix them all definitely for any one year.

Mrs. Scott's.—Mrs. Scott kept a popular private boarding house on Second Street below Chestnut. Seven members of the House, three Senators and James Peacock, printer of the English Journal, resided with her. Mrs. Scott subsequently married Gov. Snyder.

The " Union Hotel."—This tavern with the patriotic name was situated on the S. E. corner of Market Square and Blackberry alley, and was kept at this date by John Buffington, Geo. Nagle, Wells Coverly and others. It was one of the best hotels in the borough, and was patronized by the better classes of the community. President Van Buren stopped at this tavern during his visit here. General Z. Taylor, when a candidate for the Presidency, received the citizens of Harrisburg in its parlors. Governors Johnson and Pollock both boarded at the " Union " during their official terms. It was the stopping place of five members and four Senators of the Legislature of 1813–14. The " Union " was also a popular place of resort for the star actors of the day, in regard to whose comminglings with the community curious stories are told.

The " Harrisburg Inn."—This was one, and perhaps the most important of the four taverns which stood at the corner of Third and Market streets. It was situated on the Southwest corner of the intersection, upon the site now occupied by the Lochiel. There was nothing striking in its appearance, being a plain brick house, three stories in height. To the rear of it, on the corner of Third street and Blackberry alley, the site of the present Mayor's office, stood a frame building an adjunct of the tavern, adjoining which on the alley were the stables. The intervening space between the alley and Third street which was not occupied by the hotel proper, was a yard which for many years served as the place of exhibition for numerous menageries, circus performances and like entertainments. Theatrical performances also frequently took place inside the tavern building. It was in this house that Joseph Jefferson, the elder, died. The old building was removed in 1835 by Matthew Wilson, formerly of Franklin county, and the present Lochiel Hotel erected, of which Mr. Wilson took charge sometime in 1836. Various landlords of the old Harrisburg Inn are mentioned: Frederick Hyneman, Michael Krehl, John M. Eberman, Peter Wenrich, Sr., Thomas Wallace, Conrad Knepley. In our list of members, seven Representatives and one Senator are ticketed to Fred. Hyneman at the Harrisburg Inn.

The " Washington House."—By far the most pretentious hotel in Harrisburg at the period of which we are speaking was the Washington House. Attractive in appearance, and centrally located, it generally commanded a large business. It was a double three-storied brick house, fronting on Second street. For its sign it had a creditably executed painting of General Washington in citizen's dress, holding a roll of paper in his right hand. Its frame built and white washed stables were on Market street on the ground at present now occupied by the Dauphin Deposit Bank. The Jones House now graces the site of the old Washington. Among the subsequent landlords of the Washington were Philip Youse, Nicholas Schwoyer, Mr. Hensey, John Small, William E. Camp, Mr. Joslin P. Hughes, Major Sanders and his son William T. Sanders. Five Representatives, two Senators and the Clerk of the House were the guests of Mr. Philip Youse during the winter of 1813-14.

Mrs. McCreight's.—Mrs. McCreight kept a private boarding house on Market street and was favored with the patronage of seven members.

The " Ship."—Five Representatives, one Senator and the Sergeant-at-Arms of the Senate found a stopping place at the " sign of the ship," over which Major John Benjamin, an old-time military character, presided in the capacity of landlord. This tavern was situated on the Northwest corner of Third and Market streets, on the site now occupied by the TELEGRAPH building owned by the Bergner heirs. The house was of logs, weatherboarded and painted white. Under the proprietorship of Major James Emerson, who, also, at one time kept this hotel, it was quite a military center, all the brigade elections being held there.

The " Golden Lamb."—Was situated on the Southwest corner of Second and Locust streets, and was owned by George Boyer, Sr., and kept at the time we write of by Frederick Beissel, and accommodated four Representatives and two Senators. It was a large log and weatherboard house, with a brick stable adjoining it on Locust street. It was another popular place of resort for the showmen of the day, especially of circus performers, and, as a matter of course, was the center of attraction for the boys of town.

John Wright's.—John Wright kept a private house of entertainment on Walnut street next to the present Franklin House. He had boarding with him four Representatives. Mr. Wright was a schoolmaster, and for many years postmaster of Harrisburg. The postoffice was kept at his house on Walnut street from 1813 to 1822.

The " Red (or Golden) Lion."—This tavern stood on the S. E. corner of Third and Market streets, where the Mechanics' bank now is. It was a two-storied log building, rough-cast, and was well patronized by country people. Its proprietor in 1813 was Jacob Steinman, and one Representative and two Senators made it their abiding place during the session.

Robert Harris'.—Two members also boarded with Robert Harris, son of John Harris, the founder, in the old stone mansion on the river bank. Robert Harris was a member of Congress from this district from 1823 to 1827.

John Norton's.—The two-storied weatherboarded house on the west side of Market square, now occupied by William Calder, Esq., as a stage office, was in 1813 John Norton's tavern.

Mr. Norton was a carpenter by trade, and was once so unfortunate as to have his leg broken by the falling upon it of a boat which he was repairing upon the river bank. An accident such as this which would occur unheeded to-day, was the cause of no little excitement to the people of the town then. Mr. Norton was taken home in a cart, in which proceeding the populace evinced considerable interest. Mr. Norton's boarders in 1813 numbered among them one Senator.

The " Golden Eagle."—Kept by George Buehler, stood on the northeast corner of Market Square and Second street, now Bolton's. One Senator boarded here.

At John Downey's on Second street another member of the same body, and the Assistant Clerk of the House were found. Mr. Kean, on Market street and Mr. Laird on Second street, in the capacity of private boarding house keepers, accommodated two more Senators, while the Hon. Wm. Findlay, the then State Treasurer, played the host at his residence on Front street, for one member of the House, his friend and relative, Hon. Robert Smith, of Franklin county, a legislator and prominent man.

Besides the taverns above mentioned, which comprise all the stopping places of members at this period, there were many other inns and taverns in the town, of which much of interest could be told. We have space only for a notice of the names of several of them. On Second street could be found: "The Buck Inn," "Lindermuth's Tavern," "Sampson and the Lion," "The Sign of the Mermaid," "The Green Tree," "The Fountain Inn," "The Poplar Tavern," "The Golden Swan," "The Pennsylvania Inn" and "The Seven Stars." On the N. E. corner of Third and Market, "The Golden Cross Keys." On Front street, "The Blue Ball," "The White Swan," "Weitzel's Hotel," "The Rising Sun." On Market street, "The Green Bay Tavern." On Third street, "The Globe Inn" and "The Eagle Inn." On the old Harris Ferry road (Paxton street), "The Ship," subsequently the "General Jackson," "The Spread Eagle" and the Black Horse Inn." B. M. NEAD.

NOTES AND QUERIES.—XLIII.

MILITARY SPIRIT IN 1821.—An editorial in the *Intelligencer* of May 18, 1821, in alluding to a recent review of the military of the borough, under Col. Joel Bailey, which consisted of "four companies of militia and two of volunteers," says: "In Carlisle, we are told, are seven volunteer companies, and in the neighborhood of a little town in Cumberland county, called Mechanicsburg, are six companies of this description."

TEMPLETON.—Agnes Templeton, widow of Robert Templeton, of Derry, died at an advanced age in February, 1790, leaving children as follows:
    i. *Robert*, and had William and Robert.
    ii. *Jane*, m. ——— Henry.
    iii. *Mary*, m. ——— McAllcy.
    iv. *John*.
    v. *Ruth*, m. ——— Johnston and had Agnes.
    vi. ——— ———, m. ——— Stewart, and had Agnes and Mary.
    vii. *Sarah*, m. ——— Clark.
    viii. *Barbara*, m. ——— McCormick.
    ix. *Susanna*, m. ——— Hawthorn.
    x. *Hannah*, m. ——— Sinclair.

Can any one inform us as to the Christian name of No. vi. and also the full names of those intermarried.

WALLACE—CLYDE.—We have been informed, that our surmisings as to the maiden name of the wife of Robert Wallace (N. & Q. xlii), were not correct, that her name was Mary Clyde. She was a descendant, if not a daughter, of Michael and Bridget Clyde, of Scotch ancestry, who came from the north of Ireland and settled in the "Irish Settlement," Northampton county, Penna., prior to 1750. There was a strong intimacy existing between the "Settlement" on the Delaware and the Scotch-Irish of this section, and hence this information may probably be correct.

A BUNDLE OF BLUNDERS.—In the "Cyclopedia of Methodism" is an article on Harrisburg, which contains more errors in the first ten lines than we have ever seen in a similar article, and it is to be regretted that the individual who furnished the information did not obtain his data from those who knew somewhat about the history of this locality. "The Capitol of the state was not founded on the site of an Indian village of Paxton." "The first white settlement was *not* made by John Harris in 1785, and the grant of land was *not* obtained in 1753." We allude to these in the hope that in future editions of this valuable work these errors may be corrected.

THE MILITARY SPIRIT IN 1786.—We present herewith the petition of sundry inhabitants of Louisburgh (Harrisburg) in 1786, one year after its founding, requesting permission "to raise a troop of light horse" in part of the county of Dauphin. As the document was originally written on a whole sheet of paper, and one half has been torn off, we are of the opinion that other names than those here appended were affixed thereto. The company was formally organized under the command of Captain Archibald McAllister, and was in existence at least ten years.

To his Excellency, Benjamin Franklin, Esq., President, and the Supreme Executive Council of the Commonwealth of Pennsylvania:

The Remonstrance and Petition of a number of Inhabitants of Louisburgh and its vicinity in the County of Dauphin:

Respectfully Showeth—

That your Petitioners, together with divers others, have for sometime past been equiping themselves, and are now in compleat uniform to join a troop of light horse or Dragoons, provided they can obtain the approbation of your Honourable Council. They take leave to represent that the Idea of raising a troop was first suggested by themselves in the County Town, at which time they had no expectations that the people in the most remote end of the County would think of joining them; this, however, proved to be the case, and has unhappily created great dissentions amongst them, so much so that a large number have declined the troop, and are firmly resolved not to muster under the Officers who were appointed by fraud and chicane. The intention of your petitioners at first was to form a Company in and about the County Town, and to have their meeting there, but the nomination of men to the command who live at a great distance and who are unfriendy to the rising greatness of the place, has entirely frustrated our wishes, and creates the necessity of an application to your honors for liberty to raise another troop. Your Petitioners humbly apprehend that nothing gives greater security to a Republic than a well-trained Militia, and that with proper encouragement from government the militia of Pennsylvania, from the military spirit that now prevails, will in a short time be equal to any Troops in the world.

Your Petitioners, therefore, pray that Council will grant them license to embody themselves into a Troop, and commission those they shall hereafter return for their Officers; and they, as in duty bound, will ever pray.

ARCHIBALD McALLISTER,   JOHN A. HANNA,
WILLIAM SPIEGLE,   WILLIAM McCOSKRY,
THOMAS FORSTER,   JOHN McCLELLAND,
ROBERT HARRIS,   MALCOLM BOYCE,
JOHN TITSWORTH, JUN.,   JAMES STEVENSON,
JOHN GILCHRIST,   ROBERT McCLURE.

LEGISLATORS IN THE LONG AGO.—II.

WHERE THEY BOARDED AND WHAT THEY DID.

We have not been quite so fortunate in our rambles among the ruins of these, our ancient inns, as our friend Mark Twain was when he visited the Coliseum at Rome, or we might now place before you for examination the "bill of fare" with which some of the above-named "first-class" taverns served their guests. If, however, we can not thus determine definitely what our law-makers ate, we can, at least, tell you what they drank, and how much it and their boarding cost. We here present you the board bill for the session of an aristocratic Senator, lodging at the fashionable house of Philip Youse. I submit that the bill is thoroughly legislative from beginning to end.

Even the feelings of the landlord in getting his pay as evidenced in the curl of satisfaction that he imparts to his signature, are also thoroughly natural. However, Legislators then were not quite so erratic as they are nowadays. They were so foolishly honest, as to prefer a cold lunch, brought from home at the beginning of the week and eaten periodically on the Court House steps, to cheating a landlord out of a warm dinner:

Mr.———— (A Senator), To P. Youse,   *Dr.*

December 1, To Boarding and Lodging Till 29th March, 1813, 17 weeks,	$60 00	16, To 1 Pint B. wine,	00 75
		20, To 1 Bottle Best wine,	1 50
December 28th, To his Bill for Sundry Drinks to this day,	00 60	21, To 1 Gill Brandy,	0 12¼
		24, To Glass of wine with Mrs. Morgan,	1 10
23, to Paid for letters,	00 37½		$75 49¼
January 4th, To 1 quart Sider,	00 12½		
8, To ½ Gill Gin,	00 06	James Gallacher's bill,	6 00
17, To 1 Glass Beer,	00 06	To washing woman,	3 10
20, To 1 quart do	00 12½		
February 6. To Paid Maloner's Girl for washing,	00 60		$84 59½
		Credit for 2 weeks,*	06 00
6, To 1 quart Beer,	00 12½		
17, To 1 Pint Best Wine,	00 75		$78 59½
23, To ¼ Pint Brandy,	00 25		6 23
To this account Brought over from Small Book for Sundres,	00 55½		84 82¼
March 1st, To ¼ Pint Brandy,	00 20	Received the above in full,	
10, To 1 Gill Brandy,	00 12½	P. YOUSE.	

Having thus fixed the local habitations of the members of the Legislature in town, let us now take a brief glance at the personnel of the State Government, and as briefly note the character of the legislative work of this session. That staunch old Statesman, Simon Snyder, was Governor, just entering upon the closing term of his gubernatorial career. Nathaniel B. Boileau was Secretary of the Commonwealth; the trusted friend of the Governor then, but subsequently a bitter opponent. "Old Jimmy Trimble" was Deputy Secretary of the Commonwealth, plodding along doing the business of the State, whose faithful servant he had been for a quarter of a century—full measure—and was afterwards for nearly a quarter of a century longer. William Findlay (all honor to his memory) was State Treasurer, serving a last term before his election as Governor. He was Treasurer from 1807 to 1817. George Bryan, of whom it can be truthfully said that no man served the State more faithfully, was Auditor General, which position he held from May 2, 1809, to April

---

*A commentator says:
Such a custom as this, to wit, giving credit for time absent, would ruin a hotel keeper of to-day.

2, 1821, when he resigned. John Cochran was Secretary of the Land Office, serving from April 4, 1800, to May 11, 1818, and the noted lawyer, Jared Ingersoll, to whom Pennsylvania owes much, was in a second term as Attorney General, having served in that capacity before from 1791 to 1800, bringing to the discharge of his duties that large legal learning which proved such a benefit to the Commonwealth in its infancy.

The Legislature of 1813–14 was the thirty-eighth in the history of the Commonwealth, and the second which met at Harrisburg. The session continued from Dec. 7th, 1813, to March 22d, 1814. The meetings were held in the old Court House, which stood upon the site of the present one, but every vestige of which, at least to our knowledge, has disappeared, excepting the old dome, which fell into the possession of Mr. Brant, and now serves as the roof of a summer house in the yard attached to the property on Sylvan Heights. The Senate met upstairs in the Court House, and the House on the first floor. Pine desks, unpainted, and common chairs were the furniture of each chamber, and these became the property of the schools of the borough when the Legislature moved to more pretentious quarters. Presly C. Lane, of Fayette county, was Speaker of the Senate, and John St. Clair, of the same county, was Speaker of the House. Robert Smith, of Franklin, had been Speaker, but served only until February 14th, 1814, when he resigned, and St. Clair took his place.

The work of this Legislature, as it appears upon the statute books, was extended and important—one hundred and ninety-one laws were enacted, many of them necessarily pertaining to war measures.

Harrisburg and Dauphin county received some legislation. The commissioners were authorized to divide the county into six districts for the election of justices of the peace. The Harrisburg canal company was incorporated, and a company authorized to build a turnpike road from Harrisburg to Berlin, in Adams county. The Commonwealth's property, where the capital now stands, also claimed the attention of the Legislature. It was given in charge of the Secretary of the Commonwealth, and he was ordered to plant trees upon it, to have it leveled, and a substantial fence built around it. This was to be done at a total cost of $500. By a subsequent act, part of the Commonwealth's ground, situated on Walnut street, was granted to the Harrisburg Academy, but never used.

It was this Legislature also which did honor to Captain Perry (afterwards Commodore), and Captain Elliot, for the victory achieved by them over the British fleet on Lake Erie, by ordering a gold medal to be struck and presented to them. The original resolutions on this subject were presented in the Senate by Hon. Thomas Burnside, of the Centre and Lycoming district, and were seconded by Hon. Walter Lowrie, of the Allegheny, Beaver and Butler district. As originally presented they contained the names only of Captains Perry and Elliot, but the name of Lieut. Jno. J. Yarnell was added by the House. The resolutions were adopted finally Jan. 11th, 1814, and read partly as follows:

" The Legislature of Pennsylvania, believing that the gratitude and applause of a free people are the most acceptable and honorable rewards of great and glorious actions, do, in the name of the people of this State, hereby express the high sense which they entertain of the character and consequences of the victory achieved on the 10th of September last on Lake Erie, by the American fleet under command of O. H. Perry, over a British fleet of superior force, commanded by Captain Barclay; a victory not more distinguished by the bravery and skill displayed in the *achievement* than by the clemency with which it was *followed*, on the part of the illustrious conqueror. Be it therefore—

"*Resolved by the Senate and House of Representatives of the Commonwealth of Pennsylvania*, That the Governor be and he is hereby requested to convey the thanks of the Government of this Commonwealth to Captain *Oliver Hazard Perry*, for the brilliant action in which he succeeded in capturing his Brittanic Majesty's fleet on Lake Erie, and likewise to procure for and present to him, in compliment of the said victory, a gold medal of fine workmanship, emblematically finished with the flag of our country and noting him as Commander in Chief; with such other devices as the Governor shall direct."

A gold medal was likewise voted to Master Commandant Jesse Duncan Elliot and Lieutenant John J. Yarnall. To each of the volunteer soldiers on board the American squadron on Lake Erie on this occasion a silver medal of the value of two dollars was voted, in compliment of their patriotism and bravery.

The following correspondence in connection with the presentation of the gold medal to Commodore Perry, I do not think has ever been published. It may be interesting in this connection.

WEST CHESTER, *April 8, 1819.*

Dear Sir: I received from the Deputy Secretary of the Commonwealth a letter of the 1st inst., stating that the gold medals awarded by the Legislature to Captains Perry & Elliot were ready for delivery, and asking, at your request, whether it would suit me as your aid to deliver one of them. I have decided to present Captain Perry's, and shall immediately write and make all the due private arrangements with him on the subject. As soon as I get his answer and the time & place for prosenting the medal is known, I shall give yon immediate notice. I cannot find time to see Captain Perry before the latter end of May or the beginning of June, but this I presume will be sufficiently early.

With great respect,
Your ob't Serv't,
CROMWELL PEARCE.

William Findlay, Esq.

WEST CHESTER, PENNA., *April 27, 1819.*

Sir: The Legislature of Pennsylvania to shew their exalted sense of the Glorious and important victory atchieved on the memorable 10th of September by the Fleet under your command on Lake Erie, directed the governor of the state to procure a Gold medal emblematical of the event to be presented to you. This medal is now prepared for delivery, and I am instructed by his excellency Governor Findlay (as one of his aids) to apprise you of the fact and to make the necessary private arrangements with you for presentation.

I understand that you are at present at your Residence in Newport, Rhode Island, and shall direct this letter to that place. I propose, if you continue at Newport, to be there about the first of June next, to perform the very honorable duty assigned me; this time will suit me better than any other and I trust will equally suit your convenience. If you should not be at Newport at that time, you will be pleased to inform at what place I can have the pleasure of seeing you. It will afford me the greatest satisfaction to be selected to present this medal to you, as I have a full knowledge of the very great benefits that resulted to our country from your signal victory, and know how that Country is indebted to your skill and gallantry in atchieving it. I was at that time an officer of the army and stationed at Fort George.

You will be good enough to let me hear from you as soon as convenient.

With great regard and Esteem,
Your ob't Serv't,
CROMWELL PEARCE.

Capt. O. H. Perry.

NEWPORT, RHODE ISLAND, *May 17, 1810.*

Sir: I have the honour to acknowledg the rec't of your letter informing me that you had been appointed by his Excellency Governor Findlay to present a medal voted me by the Legislature of Penn'a. I regret extremely that it will not be in my power to receive you in Newport at this time, as I am on the eve of my departure from home, to be absent several months. I regret this because

it deprives me of the pleasure of testifying my respects for you at my own house, and forming an acquaintance which I promise myself great satisfaction. I shall pass through Philadelphia on Saturday or Sunday next on my way to Washington.
Very respectfully,
I have the honour,
to be your
ob't serv't,
O. H. PERRY.

Col. Cromwell Pearce.

There is no more interesting feature of a Legislature's work than the petitions presented to that body, which, alas, to-day receive but little attention from our lawmakers. At the period mentioned, however, such expressions of the popular will still continue to receive some attention. They were taken as indications of what the people desired, and the desires of the people and the wishes of the Legislature, however wide apart they may be to-day, were then in accord.

It is much to be regretted that the petitions to the Legislature prior to 1836 have nearly all been destroyed, some having served, as the writer is informed, as kindling wood for vandals in the uniform of soldiers during the late war, whilst others have gone the way which many documents in these days of utility are prone to traverse, the way that leads, via the waste paper man's bag, to the pulp tub of the paper mill.

With the presentation of one or two specimens of these petitions, which have been preserved not by our Commonwealth's care for them, but by private hands, I will close this already too lengthy paper.

The first is of a general character, so to speak. It is from one of those unfortunates who had lands in the "seventeen townships" of Luzerne county, over which Connecticut settlers and Pennsylvanians had such long continued and bitter disputes. This petitioner was one of the dissatisfied Pennsylvanians. A perusal of the petition will interest some.

SIR: The Petition of the Subscriber is before your honorable House, for relief. Decline of life is my excuse for this mode of stating my claim against the Commonwealth. The facts have been partially detailed in my Petitions of 1802 and 1809, and sundry Letters to the Executive.

Several acts of former Legislatures have been injurious to me. By granting to Connecticut Claimants my lands and improvements, and shutting the Courts of Justice against me, they have prevented myself or Assignee from recovering the property or compensation; which has compelled your Petitioner to assign his lands, for the use of his Creditors.

The Assignee refusing to act, where the Legislature interfered; and suits being brought, and failing to recover; he now has proven the value of his property by disinterested men of the neighborhood. Eight years have elapsed, and delays are oppressive. About 500 acres of land, with improvements, part of the town of Berwick, ferry, fishery, 3 springs, waterworks to water the town, and part of my wing-dam, for mill-works, have been taken from me; for which I have not received one cent.

It may be said, the Pennsylvania Purchasers, Settlers and Improvers knew there were Connecticut Claims in this State; and they must abide the consequence. They knew these disputes were settled by the Decree of Trenton, 1782, in favor of Pennsylvania; and could not know that the Agents of the Commonwealth would injure their titles and settlements, at the risk of the Government.

It must be presumed the passers of the laws knew that the Pennsylvania Owners, who lost their property, and had no provision for payment, must apply to future Legislatures to give them compensation, or open the Courts, that they might obtain their property and damages.

Though I was an early Settler in Northumberland county in 1773; and was compelled to abandon my home with a family in 1778, when the Savages laid waste that part of the State, and suffered a loss of about £1,500, and 8 years time, before I returned to the county; all this did not affect my family like my present loss.

EVAN OWEN.

The second and last petition is rather more local in its character, and the writer confesses to considerable hesitancy in submitting it, but will preface its presentation with this remark: That our Lutheran friends—and the writer is in the "*freund schaft*"—need take no offense at its contents, for many churches in the State (nearly all of every denomination in the Cumberland Valley) in early times had recourse to this method of raising money. It was a sort of embryonic system of incorporation, and it was only in later days that the system degenerated into improper uses.

HARRISBURG, Decbr. 30, 1815.

SIR: The vestry of the Evangelic Lutheran Congregation at Harrisburg, have ventured to petition your Honorable Body, for the liberty of raising a sum, by way of lottery, to pay their debts incurred by building a house of public worship. And they now take the liberty to state to you, the grounds, upon which they have had the boldness to apply:

1. They have built the said house not only for their own accommodation, but also with a view to accommodate the honorable members of the Legislature. It was very disagreeable to them, that during former sessions, many honorable members wishing to attend divine worship in their former small and old Church, were excluded for want of room—this induced them to attempt building a larger one—they certainly would not have attempted it, had it not been for this consideration.

2. The members of the Congregation have subscribed very generously & altho' not numerous, have already paid upwards of 5,000 dollars. They have, it is true, about 1,000 dollars outstanding debts; but owing to the scarcity of money and the badness of the times—they cannot get it in, and it would ruin such persons were they compelled to pay it.

3. The inhabitants of Harrisburg have expended large sums of money with a view to the accommodation of the State Legislature, which expenditures have incapacitated them from discharging the large debt incurred by the erection of the said house of public worship.

4. The petitioners will enter into any security that may be thought proper, that no immoral or illegal use shall be made of the confidence and indulgence of the legislature.

For the Vestry of the Congregation.

DANL STINE, *Pres.*

GEO. LOCHMAN, *Secr'y.*

NOTES AND QUERIES.—XLIV.

A "FAIR" AT HALIFAX.—Under date of "Halifax, August 1, 1809," we have before us the "Halifax invitation," which is interesting reading seventy years after. It is as follows: "A good market will be held in the town of Halifax on Thursday and Friday, the 24th and 25th days of August [1809] next, for the sale of all kinds of cattle, such as Horses, Cows, sheeb and Hogs, and all kind of merchandise. Halifax being seated on the bank of the Susquehanna river, open to an extensive trade, it is expected a great number will attend; the preparations for accommodating dealers of every description will be particularly attended to. Traveling merchants, drovers, lads and lasses, are particularly invited to come and make bargains. A great variety of music is expected to be there in order to exhilerate and enliven the spirits."

"THE FIRST FLAG.—In 1820 the executors of Capt. Gustavus Conyngham presented to the Legislature of Pennsylvania the first American flag that was raised in the British Channel. It was deposited at that time in the State Library. This flag was made under direction of Benjamin Franklin for the government vessel *Surprise*, commanded by Captain Conyngham in 1776. At the request of Rear Admiral Preble, who is preparing the second edition of the "History of the American Flag," I write to ask if that flag is yet in existence, if so, as to its condition and the number of its stars.
J. A. MCA.

PENNSYLVANIA IMMIGRATION INTO NEW YORK.

The people who came to Seneca county, N. Y., from Pennsylvania may be divided into two classes:

1. The Pennsylvania Germans, from Northumberland, Berks, Lehigh, Lancaster, York and Northumberland, who to a large extent settled the towns of Fayette and Varick, and whose descendants have almost forgotten the German language, at least greatly neglected it.

2. A number of Pennsylvanians, not German, chiefly from the Susquehanna, among whom were the Harris family, the Bennetts, Alexanders and Whites all from near Sunbury. A large Hood and Hayes family—four brothers of the former—came from near Turbutville and Milton. They came to this town [Varick] in 1797. There were a number of others, who, I think, must have been from the Wilkes-Barre region—the McKnights, Bainbridges, Barrs, Dunlaps and others—and a Flood family, from near McEwensville. I think some of these persons must have been in some way connected with the Wyoming Land Controversy, although I have not found their names in Miner's History of Wyoming.

It has always been asserted hereabouts that Andrew McKnight, William Chattim or Chatham, Robert Wilson, Michael Vreeland John Shay and Jonathan Pray, early residents of Seneca county, at some time had suffered Indian captivity—and it has occurred to me that they might have been carried off as children after the Massacre of Wyoming, although I do not know that they were actually Pennsylvanians except McKnight.

We have a number of descendants of Lancaster county people in this county (Seneca), among whom are Hon. Daniel S. Kendig, of Waterloo, a descendant of Martin Kendig, and a number of Baers, whose ancestry settled in Lancaster county in 1709, or soon afterwards. A few of our Pennsylvania Germans served in the Revolutionary war.
D. W.

JOHN JACOB BUCHER.

JOHN JACOB BUCHER—born January 1, 1764, at Carlisle—was the eldest child of Rev. John Conrad Bucher, an officer of the Provincial service, and stationed at Carlisle, Pa. The father had been successively promoted from ensign to lieutenant, adjutant and captain; but finally exchanging the military for the ecclesiastical, he became chaplain. In 1768, the father resigned and moved to Lebanon, Pa., where he accepted the pastorship of the German Reformed congregation. Here, at the age of fourteen, Jacob Bucher began to learn the trade of a hatter with Michael Krebbs, grandfather of the distinguished Rev. John Krebbs, lately of New York city: Whatever of education Jacob obtained must have been derived from his accomplished father, and by self-tuition—as evidenced by his "copy-book," still preserved and now ninety-six years old!

After his freedom from apprenticeship, he visited some maternal uncles "out West." Starting on this trip via Harrisburg, in 1785, John Harris wanted him, as a hatmaker, to locate in his "town," which was as yet no town. Jacob not being able to see it, went his way, and during his sojourn attended an Indian council on the spot where Cincinnati stands to-day. Having the ague during three out of four years on the lower Ohio, he returned to Lebanon in 1789. But his paternal relatives at Schaffhausen, Switzerland, induced him to visit them, and off he went, by packet from Philadelphia to Amsterdam. He was absent about a year, and returning, located at Harrisburg.

The present generation may be surprised to learn his whereabouts at this time. Sitting at the door of his "Bachelor's Hall" on River alley between Walnut and Locust streets, he looked down the ravine to the beautiful river and its magnificent islands. If Jacob ever saw "castles in the air," as he gazed toward the Cumberland hill on a summer evening, he certainly did not see the residence of William Calder, Esq., as he might to-day—but River alley was Front street then.

In March, 1792, Jacob married Susanna Horter, a maiden scarce eighteen, and he built No. 103 South Front street, as a home. His hatter shop stood at No. 3, near Market street. About 1802 they moved to the corner building, which the Bucher family still occupies, after three-fourths of a century—a longer time, perhaps, than any other continuous residence in the town. John Bucher had two sons, the late Judge John Conrad, of Harrisburg, and Hon. George H., now residing at Mechanicsburg. His daughters married, respectively—William Ayres, Esq., of Harrisburg; Robert Allen, Esq., of Philadelphia; Hon. Joseph Lawrence, of Washington co., Pa.; and Robert Bryson, Esq., of Harrisburg.

The public life of Jacob Bucher began with his election as Coroner in 1796; appointed by Gov. Mifflin a Justice of the Peace in 1798; elected to the House of Representatives in 1803, and re-elected for the sessions of 1805–6 and 1807–8. In 1810 he was appointed chairman of the commission to erect the State buildings, preparatory to to removal of the Capital from Lancaster to Harrisburg. Edward Crouch, of Dauphin county, and John Dorsey, of Phila., where his co-adjutors, but he being the resident commissioner, the bulk of superintendence naturally devolved upon him. The substantial character of the buildings fully attest that Jacob Bucher and his confreres had no idea of modern "bonus" structures, whilst their accounts show all that they had not yet learned "addition, division, and silence!"

In 1812 he was nominated by the Democratic party for Congress, but the Federalists carried the district comprising Dauphin, Lebanon and Lancaster. He was sent again to the Legislature in 1814 and the session following.

In 1818 Gov. Findlay appointed him an Associate Judge for Dauphin county, which position he held nine years, until his death, October 16, 1827, aged nearly sixty-four. It is a coincidence worth noting that his son, John Conrad, occupied the same office also for twelve years prior to his death, October 21, 1852.

The trusts which Jacob Bucher filled of a more private character, were those which designate him as a man enjoying the confidence of his fellow citizens, and in the church a member above reproach. From his judicious management of the State buildings, or some other reason, he became the common treasurer or financier of the town.

In 1795, when the public demanded the destruction of Landis' mill dam to allay the fever then epidemic, he was one of the committee of seven to indemnify the owners and abate the evil.

In 1803, when the Presbyterians sought a proper place to conduct the "Lottery"—then a legal procedure, and no worse than modern fairs—which obtained the funds to build their first church, Jacob Bucher, a German Reformed brother, was selected to handle the money.

In 1814 we find him as Treasurer for the company erecting the Harrisburg bridge. In 1821, he is both Treasurer of the fund and chairman of the building committee to erect the German Reformed church. He was one of the commissioners to locate the seat of justice for Perry county, a director of the branch Bank of Philadelphia at Harrisburg, and guardian and arbiter in many minor trusts.

His associates, personal and political, were always among the foremost and best in his county and State. Personally he was a man of extraordinary methods, systematic and correct in everything I can see, from his copy-book to his coffin; not given to display, and eminently sober and practical in all his concerns. And yet this man, with hereditary German instincts, was a great lover of music, played the flute, showed exhaustless patience in copying music for his children, and including a love for pictures and books. An example from which may be derived the fact that attention to business, public life and great responsibilities need not, and should not, necessarily, estrange a man from the pleasures that sweeten life. A worthy son of a reverend sire. GEORGE B. AYRES.

TRIAL FOR BLASPHEMY.

[Among the records of the Dauphin county court we find but one case of trial and conviction for blasphemy under an old Provincial law, and for the benefit of the "Liberal Leagues," which are organizing in the larger cities of our country, we present the following case to show these individuals that our ancestors treated such blasphemies as they are inculcating with proper severity. The founders of our Government, and our advancement in civilization rests upon the upholding of the revealed religion of the Christ of Nazareth, and if the law of God is of no avail, the civil law should stretch out its arms and check the head-long career of all blasphemers. We copy the following from the *Oracle* of September 17, 1799.]

"At the Court of Oyer & Terminer, held in this town on the 11th ult., one . . . . . . tobacconist and fiddler, a man who has a wife and several young children, was convicted on an indictment for BLASPHEMY. In order to give the reader a more perfect idea of the magnitude of the crime, we extract from the indictment the following:

"The Grand Inquest for the body of the county of Dauphin upon their oaths and affirmations respectively do present, that . . . . . tobacconist, not having the fear of God in his heart, but being moved and seduced by diabolical instigation, and contriving and intending Almighty God, and our blessed Savior Jesus Christ to blaspheme and dishonor, the first day of September, in the year of our Lord one thousand seven hundred and ninety-nine, at the county aforesaid, and within the jurisdiction of this Court, in the presence and hearing of divers liege subjects of the Commonwealth of Pennsylvania, well understanding the English and High Dutch languages, falsely, impiously and blasphemously did say, speak, and with a loud voice pronounce and publish in the High Dutch language, these false, impious and blasphemous words, to wit: "Christ (our blessed Saviour Jesus Christ meaning) is a . . . If Christ is the Son of God (meaning the Almighty God) then God hath . . . " To the great dishonor and contempt of Almighty God and our Saviour Jesus Christ—to the evil example of all others in like manner offending, contrary to the laws, and the act of General Assembly of this State in such case made and provided, and against the peace and dignity of the Commonwealth of Pennsylvania, &c.

"The prisoner being arraigned, plead not guilty, but afterwards retracted his plea and submitted to the Court. Whereupon the Court gave judgment that he pay a fine of £10, for the use of the poor of the county of Dauphin, suffer three months imprisonment in the jail of said county, and pay the costs of prosecution. The Court also directed that he be bound to keep the peace and be of good behavior to all the liege citizens of the United States for seven years, himself in 400 dls. and one surety in the like sum of 400 dls."

NOTES AND QUERIES.—XLV.

ESCAPE OF LUKENS (N. & Q., xlii).—In justice to the memory of Captain William Watson it may be stated that at the quarter sessions of Dauphin county, held November 16, 1846, Asahel Lukens was convicted of counterfeiting on two indictments and sentenced to the Dauphin county prison for two years at hard labor, &c. After being confined for a short time he escaped. A letter from him to one of his daughters disclosed his residence. A requisition was obtained from Governor Shunk upon the Governor of Iowa. The late Aaron Bombaugh and Captain Watson found him at his home ploughing in that far distant State. He had been elected a justice of the peace in the township in which he resided, was a sober, industrious and hardworking farmer, living with his family. Of course the people of that neighborhood knew nothing of his antecedants. He pledged his word to Messrs. B. and W. that he would accompany them to Harrisburg without any further trouble, and most faithfully kept his word. I remember seeing him walking from the depot with those gentlemen to our prison. Upon remaining in jail a short time, upon the petition of our leading citizens, Governor Shunk pardoned him. He then left for his home; and I doubt whether any of his neighbors or friends in

Iowa ever heard of his troubles here. Lukens told the writer of this article that he had assistance from some friends *outside* of the prison, but not from those *within*. This he at all times asserted, and the fact that one of our fire ladders was found standing against the prison at the corner of Strawberry and Raspberry avenues the morning of his escape, corroborated his statement, and those who knew him best believed him, for with all his faults he was truthful. When I reflect that Captain Watson and the Prison Inspectors pursued him for a long time, I cannot believe that the resignation of Mr. W. can be charged to the escape of Lukens. F. K. B.

BIOGRAPHICAL HISTORY OF DAUPHIN COUNTY.—I.

[The following biographical sketches have been compiled from data gleaned from various sources. There are, no doubt, errors, which it is desired those possessing information may at least interest themselves in correcting. In the hope that these contributions may be acceptable to the present citizens of the locality in which the individuals here named were prominent in their day and generation, they are earnestly submitted.]

SAMUEL AINSWORTH, the eldest son of John Ainsworth and Margaret Mayes, was born in Hanover township, Dauphin county, Pa., on the 11th of November, 1765. He was brought up on his father's farm in Hanover, receiving a year's education in Philadelphia, in addition to that acquired in the schools of the neighborhood. After the organization of the county he became quite prominent, and twice elected to the Legislature. He died while in attendance on this body, at Philadelphia, in February, 1798, aged thirty-three years. Mr. Ainsworth married May 10, 1792, Margaret McEwen, of Hanover, born in 1770. She died near Lancaster, Ohio, October 29, 1867. They had three children who married and removed to Ohio.

JAMES ALRICKS, captain in the Whiskey Insurrection, the youngest son of Hermanus Alricks and Ann West, was born at Carlisle, Pennsylvania, December 2, 1769. His ancestor, Peter Alricks, a prominent participant in the affairs of the Colony and Province on the Delaware. Wessels, the third in descent, was sheriff of Philadelphia under the Proprietary Government, while Hermanus, the father of James Alricks, was the prothonotary of Cumberland county. He married, in 1798, Martha, second daughter of John Hamilton and Margaret Alexander, of Harrisburg. Mr. Alricks then resided at Oakland Mills, on Lost creek, now in Juniata county, engaged in farming, but about 1815 removed to Harrisburg, where he entered mercantile pursuits. On March 10, 1821, he was appointed Clerk of the Orphans Court and Quarter Sessions, serving until January 17, 1824. He subsequently served as one of the magistrates of the borough. Mr. Alricks died at Harrisburg on the 28th of October, 1833, aged sixty-four years. His wife preceded him, dying on the 16th of March, 1830. He was highly esteemed as a citizen, honorable and upright in character. He was the father of Hermanus and Hamilton Alricks, Esquires, of this city.

WILLIAM BERTRAM was a native of Ireland, born February 2, 1674. He studied for the ministry, and was licensed by the Presbytery of Bangor, Ireland, who gave him "ample testimonials of his ordination, ministerial qualifications and regular Christian conversation." He married about 1706, and his wife dying in early life, he concluded to come to America, which he did in 1731, and the following year was unanimously received by Donegal Presbytery, which he joined. At the same time, George Renick presented him an invitation to settle at Paxtang and Derry, which he accepted. He was installed November 17, 1732, at the meeting-house on Swatara. The congregation then appointed representatives: "on this side, Thomas Forster, George Renick, William Cunningham and Thomas Mayes; on the other side, Rowland Chambers, Hugh Black, Robert Campbell, John Willson, William Willson, James Quigley, William McCord and John Sloan." They executed to Bertram the right and title to the "Indian town tract," situated in Hanover township, on the north side of the Swatara, containing three hundred and fifty acres. On the settlement of Rev. Bertram, the congregation in Swatara took the name of Derry, and the upper congregation on Spring creek was styled Paxtang. In 1735 Mr. Bertram complained of the "intolerable burden" he was under with the two congregations, and September 13, 1736, he was released from the care of Paxtang. The Rev. William Bertram died on the 2d of May, 1746, aged seventy-two, and his remains are interred in Derry church graveyard. He was a faithful minister of the gospel.

GEORGE BEATTY, youngest son of James Beatty and Alice Ann Irwin, was born in the townland of Bally-keel Ednagonnell, county Down, Ireland, January 4, 1781. His father emigrated to America in the summer of 1784, locating at Harrisburg the same year. The elder Beatty dying in 1794, the son, after receiving a regular school education, learned the watch and clock making with his brother-in-law, Samuel Hill, whose clocks are more or less celebrated to this day. In 1808 Mr. Beatty established himself in business, which he continued uninterruptedly for upwards of forty years. He was an ingenious mechanician, and constructed several clocks of peculiar and rare invention. In 1814 he was orderly sergeant of Capt. Thomas Walker's company, the "Harrisburg Volunteers," which marched to the defense of the city of Baltimore. Mr. Beatty in early life took a prominent part in local affairs, and as a consequence was frequently solicited to become a candidate for office, but he almost invariably declined. He, nevertheless, served a term as director of the poor, and also as county auditor. He was elected a burgess of the borough, and was a member of the town council several years, and, while serving in the latter capacity, was one of the prime movers in the efforts to supply the borough with water. Had his suggestions, however, been carried out, the water works and reservoir would have been located above the present city limits. Mr. Beatty retired from a successful business life about 1850. He died at Harrisburg on the 10th of March, 1862, aged eighty-one years, and is interred in the Harrisburg Cemetery. He was an active, enterprising citizen, and an upright Christian gentleman.

JOHN BRISBAN, a native of Ireland, was born Dec. 25, 1730. With an elder brother he came to America, just prior to the Revolution, and settled in Lancaster county. He early espoused the cause of the Colonies, and receiving a commission as captain in the Second (Colonel St. Clair's) Pennsylvania Battalion, January 5, 1776, raised a company, mostly in the upper part of then Lancaster county, now Dauphin and Lebanon, which was in active service in Canada. At the close of that arduous campaign, he was transferred to the Third Regiment of the Pennsylvania Line, serving almost to the close of the war. He then returned to his family and farm. Captain Brisban died at the residence of his son-in-law, Samuel Rutherford, near Harrisburg, Pa., March 13, 1822, aged ninety-one years. He lies buried in Paxtang church graveyard. Captain Brisban was an ardent patriot, a dutiful citizen and a gentleman of generous impulses. He lived an eventful life and died at a ripe old age, honored and respected by his fellow-citizens.

MERCER BROWN was born near West Chester, Chester county, Penna., April 22, 1795. After receiving a thorough academic education, he began the study of medicine under Dr. King, of Columbia. He graduated in 1816, and located at McCall's Ferry, at which point many persons at that time were being employed in the erection of the bridge over the Susquehanna, numbers of whom had been attacked by severe sickness. He subsequently removed to Wrightsville, where he remained several years, when he located in Middletown, and, until his death, which took place February 19, 1871, he was regarded as the head of the medical profession. Dr. Brown was long a prominent actor in local and State politics. He was a candidate for Congress at one time, but his party being in the minority in the district he was defeated. As a citizen he was highly respected and beloved. Dr. Brown married Rebecca Wolfly, daughter of Jacob Wolfly, an early settler at Middletown. She died April 2, 1861.

GEORGE BUEHLER, the son of Henry Buehler, a soldier of the Revolution, and Jane Trotter, was born near the town of Lebanon, Pa., in July, 1776. His parents were Moravians; they lie buried in Mount Hebron burying ground and were life-long members of old Hebron church. George received a good English and German education at the celebrated Moravian school at Lititz, and was subsequently brought up to mercantile pursuits. He was commissioned by Gov. Mifflin justice of the peace for Lebanon township, December 3, 1799. The year following, under the auspices of the Harrisburg and Presqu' Isle land company, he removed to Erie, and was appointed in August, 1801, by President Jefferson, collector of the 18th collection district of Pennsylvania. Mr. Buehler took a prominent part in the affairs connected with the early organization of Erie county. At his residence, on the 2d of April, 1803, that county was organized for judicial purposes. He was a member of the first council of the town of Erie in 1806, and in 1808 and 1809 was borough burgess. He was one of the first to aid in developing the Lake Erie trade, forseeing at that early day the advantages of that magnificent port of the lakes. In 1811-2 he was a member of the Erie Light Infantry, Captain Forster, which was in active service during a portion of that period. In 1812, owing probably to the war troubles on the frontiers, he came to Harrisburg, and took charge of the "Golden Eagle." He died at Harrisburg on the 5th of August, 1816, aged forty years. Mr. Buehler married, previous to removing to Erie, Maria, daughter of Peter Nagle, of Reading. She was born December 25, 1779, and died at Harrisburg July 27, 1843; a lady of great amiability of character. Mr. Buehler was a man of sterling integrity and his brief life was one of activity, enterprise and industry. At Erie he stood high in the esteem of its citizens, and at Harrisburg his appreciation was none the less.

JAMES CLUNIE, the son of James and Elizabeth Clunie, was a native of Scotland, born 1767. He was brought up a merchant, and towards the close of the Revolution seems to have been established in business with his father at Hummelstown. Some time after the death of his father he removed to Harrisburg. He was appointed Collector of Excise for Dauphin county October 3, 1785, at the same time holding the office of Agent for Forfeited Estates. He was elected Sheriff, commissioned 20th of October, 1788, and upon the resignation of David Harris, appointed by Gov. Mifflin February 23, 1792, one of the Associate Judges of the county. He died suddenly at Harrisburg September 14, 1793. Judge Clunie was an intelligent, high-minded gentleman, and very popular among the people. His appointment to the Bench was warmly pressed by them against the bitter opposition of the leading politicians of the county. The Governor did not hesitate in commissioning Mr. Clunie. In the Harrisburg cemetery, removed from the old graveyard, is a stone with this inscription: Under this stone | are deposited the Remains | of JAMES CLUNIE, ESQ., | who died 14th Sept, 1793, | Aged 82 Years.

WILLIAM COCHRAN was born in what is now Middle Paxtang township, Dauphin county, Penn'a, in 1780. He received a good English education, and was brought up on his father's farm. In 1814 he served as a volunteer and marched to the defense of Baltimore. He served as coroner of the county from 1818 to 1821; member of the House of Representatives from 1820 to 1824; county commissioner from 1830 to 1833; and sheriff from 1837 to 1839. He died at Harrisburg on Sunday, 26th of April, 1840, aged sixty years, and was interred in the family burying-ground in Middle Paxtang. The *Intelligencer* pays this tribute to his memory: "Mr. Cochran was a highly-respected citizen, a popular officer, and a kind and hospitable neighbor."

WILLIAM RADCLIFFE DE WITT, the son of John De Witt, was born at Paulding's Manor, Duchess county, N. Y., on the 25th of February, 1792. His ancestors were among the first immigrants from Holland to New Netherlands in 1623. His early years were spent in commercial pursuits, but about 1810, he turned his attention to the sacred ministry. He studied with Dr. Alexander Proudfit, of Salem N. Y., and entered Washington academy. The war of 1812 interrupting his studies, he volunteered in the regiment of Colonel Rice and was at Lake Champlain at the time of McDonough's victory, September 11, 1814. After the close of the war, he entered Nassau Hall, Princeton, as a sophomore, but subsequently entered the senior class of Union College, Schenectady, where he graduated, completing his theological studies under Rev. Dr. John M. Mason, of New York. He was licensed to preach by the Presbytery of New York April 23, 1818. In the fall of that year he came to Harrisburg by invitation, and was called to the pastorate of the Presbyterian church, October 5, 1818. He was received by the Presbytery of Carlisle, April 13, 1819, but not ordained until the 26th of October, that year. Though invited to settle elsewhere, he preferred not to change. "His ministry was highly successful, and the church under his care grew in numbers, efficiency and influence. For half a century he was a power in the surrounding region." Dr. De Witt received the degree of A. M. in course from Union College and in 1838 the University of Pennsylvania conferred on him the title of Doctor of Divinity. From 1854 to 1860 he held the office of State Librarian, appointed by Governors Bigler and Pollock. In 1854 he felt the necessity of taking a colleague—Rev. T. H. Robinson, D. D., the recent minister. He died at Harrisburg, December 23, 1867, in his seventy-sixth year. It may be here said of Dr. DeWitt that for a period of almost half a century he was intimate with and had the confidence of the different Executives of Pennsylvania.

SAMUEL DOUGLAS, the son of Henry Douglas and Jane Blair, was born near the town of Newton Limavady, county Derry, Ireland, in 1781. He received a classical education in Scotland, but came to America about the age of seventeen, and located at Pittsburgh with a brother, Rev. Joseph Douglas, who had preceded him. Here he studied law, was admitted to the bar in 1804, and began his profession there. In 1812 he volunteered as aid to Gen. Adamson Tannehill, and was with him in the expedition to Black Rock. In 1817 Mr. Douglas was nominated for Congress against Judge Henry Baldwin, but was defeated by a small majority. The same year he came to Harrisburg in the interests of securing proper legislation for a bridge across the Allegheny; and subsequently was induced to locate here. He was appointed Deputy Attorney General for Dauphin county, July 17, 1819, under Governor Findlay. Governor Wolf commissioned him February 10, 1830, Attorney General of the State, a position he held three years. Mr. Douglas died at Harrisburg July 8, 1833, aged fifty-two. He married in 1818, Louisa Wyeth, daughter of John Wyeth, of Harrisburg. He was a gentleman of fine classical attainments, of refined tastes, a good criminal lawyer and highly esteemed by the members of his profession.

NOTES AND QUERIES.—XLVI.

KYLE—MCARTHUR—GALBRAITH.—James Kyle was an early settler in Paxtang. He married —— McArthur, daughter of Mrs. Mary McArthur, who died in Paxtang on the 24th of October, 1742, her tombstone being one of the earliest in the old graveyard. Thomas McArthur, another Paxtang worthy, was the brother of Mrs. Kyle. James Peacock, of Paxtang, married a sister of McArthur's. James Kyle's sister Mary married Andrew Galbraith, of Cumberland county, brother of Bertram Galbraith. Their daughter was the mother of

Chief Justice Gibson. Of the children of James Kyle and Mary McArthur, Thomas Kyle, the eldest, became a minister, settled in Harrodsburg, Kentucky, in 1800, and died there about 1850, aged ninety years. Andrew married and went West, locating near his brother Thomas in Kentucky, and died there. James, another son, removed to Lycoming county, and thence to Lafayette, Indiana, where some of his descendants now reside. As to their daughter, we have no information.

BIOGRAPHICAL HISTORY OF DAUPHIN COUNTY—II.

JOSHUA ELDER, second son of Rev. John Elder and Mary Baker, was born in Paxtang township, now Dauphin county, Penn'a, on the 9th of March, 1744–45. He was a farmer by occupation. During the frontier troubles of 1763–4 he was in active military service. When the Revolution broke out he was a leader on the patriot side— and appointed one of the sub-Lieutenants of Lancaster county, as also a Justice of the Peace, serving until the close of the war. He was a prominent advocate for the formation of the county of Dauphin, and under the constitution of 1790 was commissioned by Gov. Mifflin one of the Associate Judges of the courts, August 17, 1791. The appointment, however, of Sheriff Clunie to the Bench on the resignation of David Harris, who had removed to Baltimore, so incensed him that he peremptorily resigned. He was appointed by Gov. McKean prothonotary Jan. 5, 1800, a position he filled by re-appointment until Feb. 6, 1809. In March, 1810, he was elected burgess of the borough of Harrisburg. He died at his residence in Paxtang on the 5th of December, 1820. Judge Elder was twice married, first to Mary McAllister, who died Nov. 21, 1792; secondly to Sarah McAllister, who died Dec. 6, 1807. They are all interred in Paxtang church graveyard. Mr. Elder left a large estate, which he carefully devised by will to the children of his deceased brothers and sisters. He was an influential and patriotic citizen, a kind neighbor and a gentleman of remarkable dignity of manners. He was a warm supporter of free education, and on the organization of the Harrisburg academy, was one of its first trustees.

AMOS ELLMAKER, the son of Nathaniel Ellmaker, was born in New Holland, Lancaster county, Penna., on the 2nd of February, 1787. He graduated at Yale College, and after completing his law studies at the celebrated law school under Judge Reeves, at Litchfield, Conn., he came to Harrisburg and began the practice of his profession, being admitted to the bar at the December term, 1808. He was commissioned Deputy Attorney General for the county of Dauphin,

January 13, 1809, serving until 1812, and represented Dauphin county in the Legislature 1812–14. He was appointed by Governor Snyder President Judge of this judicial district, July 3, 1815. In 1814 he accompanied the volunteers to Baltimore as an aid to Gen. Forster. On the 30th of December, 1816, he resigned, to accept the position of Attorney General of the State, serving to 1819. In June, 1821, he removed to Lancaster, resuming the practice of his profession. He was the anti-Masonic candidate for Vice-President of the United States in 1832. Judge Ellmaker died at Lancaster on the 28th of November, 1851. He married, June 13, 1816, Mary R., daughter of Thomas Elder and Catharine Cox, of Harrisburg, who survived. Mr. Ellmaker, says Mr. Harris in his reminiscences, "was reported to be a good lawyer, and his addresses to the jury, when at the bar, were clear, distinct and argumentative." As a gentleman, he possessed in an eminent degree those characteristics which distinguish men of rare endowment. He was well informed and of a lively social disposition, and in all the relations and positions of life was a model worthy of imitation.

OBED FAHNESTOCK, the son of Peter Fahnestock and Elizabeth Bolthouser, was born at Ephrata, Lancaster county, Pa., February 25, 1770. He came to Harrisburg with his brother, Conrad, who was a printer, and began merchandizing, in which he was quite successful. He served as coroner from 1802 to 1805, and Nov. 12, 1813, was appointed by Gov. Snyder one of the associate judges of the county; but July 30, 1818, upon the appointment of Samuel D. Franks as president of the courts, both he and his colleague, George Whitehill, resigned. January 17, 1824, Mr. Fahnestock was commissioned prothonotary and clerk of the court of quarter sessions, serving six years. He took an active and prominent part in local affairs, and was for a number of years a member of the town council and president thereof. He died at Harrisburg March 2, 1840, aged seventy years. Mr. Fahnestock married, April 19, 1796, Anna Maria Gessel, b. January 9, 1777. She survived her husband two years, dying on the 3d of December, 1842.

PHILIP FETTERHOFF, son of John Fetterhoff, was a native of Lancaster county, Penn'a, born Sept. 2, 1788. His father removed to Upper Paxtang township prior to 1806, and established a mill in what is now Jackson township. He was brought up to the occupation of his father. He commanded a company from his neighborhood which marched to the defense of Baltimore in 1814. After his return he was chosen colonel of one of the militia battalions. He was elected coroner of the county, serving from Oct. 24, 1821, to Nov.

20, 1824, and filled a number of local offices. Col. Fetterhoff died at his residence, in Jackson township, on the 4th of September, 1833. He was much esteemed socially, and courted for his political influence.

GEORGE FISHER, the son of John and Catharine Fisher, influential Quakers of Philadelphia, was born in that city in 1732. His father purchasing a large tract of land on the Swatara, conveyed it to the son in 1754, and on which he settled about the same year. Forseeing the advantages, George Fisher, in 1755, laid out a town on the highest portion of his farm, naming it Middletown. He married, in 1755, Hannah, daughter of Jonas Chamberlain, of Salisbury township, Lancaster county, Pa., by whom he had three children, John, George and Hannah. Mr. Fisher died in February, 1777. By will, he devised to his son John, the homestead, and to his son, George, the plantation at the mouth of the Swatara; his daughter receiving, in lieu of land, £800. John Fisher became a physician; and George Fisher, a lawyer of considerable reputation at the Dauphin county bar. The latter was the father of Judge Fisher, of York.

ROBERT FLEMING, the fourth son of Robert Fleming and Jane Jackson, was born in Chester county, Pa., June 6, 1756. His parents were natives of Argyleshire, Scotland, who subsequently removed to Ireland, and from thence emigrated to America, about 1746, settling near Flemington, Chester county. Prior to the Revolution they located within the limits of the "New Purchase," on the West Branch of the Susquehanna, but during the "Great Runaway," in 1778, they sought refuge among some friends in now Dauphin county. About 1784 they removed to Hanover township, Washington county, Pa., locating on Harmon's creek, where they resided at the time of their death, Robert Fleming at ninety-six and his wife ninety-four. Robert Fleming, the subject of this notice, remained in Dauphin county, purchased a large tract of land in Hanover township, on which he resided during his life time. On the 6th of February, 1783, he married Margaret, daughter of John Wright. In the early history of this locality, Mr. Fleming bore a prominent part. He was one of the founders of the Harrisburg bank, and largely instrumental in the erection of the Harrisburg bridge. He was an officer in the volunteer force of 1812, and filled acceptably various local offices. He was an elder in the Hanover church during the ministrations of Rev. James Snodgrass, and was an earnest, zealous Christian. He died February 4, 1817; his wife December 12, 1813, aged fifty-nine years. They are both interred in Hanover church graveyard.

THOMAS FORSTER (1st) was a native of county Antrim, Ireland, of Scotch parentage, born in 1696. He emigrated to America at an early period, and was among the first who took up land in what is now Paxtang township. He was a gentleman of means, had received a good education, and was for many years one of the Provincial magistrates. He was removed, late in life, on account of his refusal to oust some squatters on Proprietary lands. He was a prominent personage on the then frontiers of the Province in civil affairs, and much interested in the establishment of Paxtang church, to which he donated a valuable tract of land. During the Indian troubles he greatly assisted in preparing for the defense of the border settlements, and his name appears frequently in the voluminous correspondence preserved in the Archives of the State. He died in Paxtang, 25th of July, 1772, aged seventy-six years, and is buried in the old church grave-yard. Mr. Forster was never married; the principal part of his estate went to his brother John and nephew Thomas Forster, the latter named for him.

THOMAS FORSTER, (2d) the son of John Forster, brother of Thomas Forster, Esq., and Catharine Dickey, was born in Paxtang township, Dauphin county, Pa., on the 16th of May, 1762. He received a good education and was brought up as a surveyor. During the latter part of the Revolution he was in arms for the defense of the frontiers, in 1794, during the so-called Whiskey Insurrection, served as colonel of one of the volunteer regiments in that expedition. He was one of the associate judges of Dauphin county, appointed October 26, 1793, by Governor Mifflin, resigning December 3, 1798, having been elected one of the Representatives of the State Legislature that year. At the close of 1799 or early in 1800, as the agent of the Harrisburg and Presqu' Isle Land Company, he permanently removed to Erie. In the affairs incident to the early settlement of that town, and the organization of that county he took a prominent part. He was one of the first street commissioners of the town, president of the Erie and Waterford turnpike company, one of the directors of the first library company, and its librarian, and captain of the first military company formed at Erie, and which, in 1812, was in service at Buffalo, Captain Forster being promoted brigade inspector. In 1823 he was appointed by Gov. Shultz one of the commissioners to explore the route for the Erie extension of the Pennsylvania canal, and in 1827 was chairman of the meeting organizing St. Paul's Episcopal church. In 1823 he was appointed by President Adams collector of the port at Erie, and uccessively commissioned by Presidents Jefferson, Madison, J. Q. Adams and Jackson, filling the office until his death, which occurred at Erie, June 29, 1836. Col. Forster married October 5, 1786, Sarah Pettit Montgomery, daughter of the Rev. Joseph Montgomery, a member of the Confederated Congress. She died at Erie, July 27, 1808.

JOHN FORSTER, the son of John Forster and Catharine, daughter of Moses Dickey, was born in Paxtang township, Lancaster county, now Susquehanna township, Dauphin county, Penna, on the 17th of September, 1777. He received a good education, and was at Princeton when a call was made by President Washington for volunteers to march to Western Penn'a to put down the so-called " Whiskey Insurrection" of 1794, and was on that expedition as an aid to Gen. Murray. He subsequently read law with Gen. Hanna, but never applied for admission, turning his attention to mercantile pursuits, in which he was very successful. During the military era of the Government prior to the war of 1812, he was colonel of State militia, and in 1814, when the troops from Pennsylvania marched to the defense of the beleagured city of Baltimore, he was placed in command of a brigade of volunteers. For his gallant services in that campaign the thanks of the general commanding were tendered in special orders. He served in the State Senate from 1814 to 1818. Gen. Forster was cashier of the Harrisburg bank for a period of at least sixteen years, established the bank of Lewistown, and in 1840 was cashier of the Exchange bank of Pittsburgh. He subsequently became president of the Branch bank at Hollidaysburg, but in a few years retired from all business pursuits and returned to his home at Harrisburg. He died there on the 28th of May, 1863, at the advanced age of almost eighty-six years. Gen. Forster was faithful, honest and upright in all his business connections; as a citizen he was patriotic and enterprising; and in the social walks of life refined in his manners, amiable in disposition, humane and generous.

WALTER FRANKLIN was born in the city of New York, in February 1773. His father having during his minority removed to Philadelphia, he there read law, and was appointed by Governor Snyder, Attorney General of Pennsylvania, which position he held until 1810 when he resigned. In January, 1811, upon the resignation of Judge John Joseph Henry, Mr. Franklin was appointed President Judge of the Court of Common Pleas of the Second Judicial District which comprised at the time, Dauphin, Lancaster and York, to which was afterwards added the counties of Cumberland and Lebanon. His judicial administration did not prove satisfactory to the bar in Lancaster county, where he afterwards resided, and when acting as judge of that county, three attempts were made before the Legislature to effect his removal. He continued in office until death, which occurred February 7, 1838. Of Judge Franklin it may truly be said he was distinguished for clearness of conception, vigor of mind, and eminent integrity. As a jurist he seems not to have been successful.

CHRISTIAN GLEIM, fourth son of George Christian Gleim and Ann Maria Mathias, was born in Lancaster county, Pa., January 10, 1780. His grandfather, Rev. John Godfried Gleim, in 1753, was located at Wiesbaden, Germany, where he met Casper Fahnestock, the ancestor of the family of that name, who had been deputed by Drs. Muhlenberg, Passavant, and others, to induce Protestant divines to come to America. The following year he came to Pennsylvania, and preached at Germantown until his death in 1757. With Weiser, Mathias and others, he published a work entitled "The Inspired." His son George Christian Gleim was an active participant in the Revolution, and in one of the skirmishes around Philadelphia was severely wounded in his head and face by the sabre of a British dragoon. In 1779 he removed to Lancaster county, where he resided until his death, July 21, 1817, aged eighty-one years. Christian Gleim the subject of this sketch, received a fair education, and subsequently went to Philadelphia, where he entered the printing office of Ezra Baily, serving with Duane, Binns, Marshall, Wynkoop and others, who became men of note. He next went to Richmond, Va., and thence to Baltimore. There he married Martha Henry, daughter of John Henry. In 1812 Mr. Gleim settled in Harrisburg, and was appointed printer of the Senate Journal in English. He served as ensign in Capt. Thomas Walker's company, and returned as paymaster U. S. Volunteers. In October, 1821, he was elected sheriff of Dauphin county, serving three years. In 1830 Col. Gleim removed to Pittsburgh, where he resided until his death, which occurred September 21, 1864. Col. Gleim was an enterprising and prominent citizen of this locality sixty or seventy years ago. He was a highly cultivated Christian gentleman.

WILLIAM GRAHAM was born in Paxtang township, Lancaster county, Pa., December 19, 1745. His father came from the north of Ireland, as did his mother, Susannah Miller. His early years were spent on the farm, but by dint of hard labor and perseverance, so characteristic of the Scotch-Irish youth of that day, he prepared himself for admission to the college of New Jersey (now Princeton), where he graduated in 1773. He taught the grammar school connected with that institution, while studying theology under the tuition of the Rev. John Roan. On the 26th of October, 1775, he was licensed to preach by the Presbytery of Hanover, Virginia, to which locality his family had previously removed. When the Presbytery had determined to establish a school for the rearing of young men for the ministry, they applied to the Rev. Stanhope Smith, then itinerating in Virginia, to recommend a suitable person to take charge of their school, upon which he at once suggested Mr. Graham. Prior to this a classical school had been taught at a place called Mt. Pleasant, and there Mr. G. commenced his labors as a teacher, and there we find the germ whence sprung Washington College, and the now celebrated Washington and Lee University of Virginia. Mr. Graham died at Richmond, Va., June 8, 1799. He married Mary Kerr, of Carlisle, Pa., and by her had two sons and three daughters. His eldest son entered the ministry, but died young; the other studied medicine, settled in Georgia, and died about 1850.

RACHEL GRAYDON, was a native of the Island of Barbadoes and the eldest of four daughters. Her father, Mr. Marks—engaged in the West India trade—was of German birth; her mother a native of Glasgow, Scotland. At the age of seven years her parents removed to Philadelphia, where Rachel was educated. She formed the acquaintance, and married, about 1750, Alexander Graydon, a native of Longford, Ireland, doing business at that time in the old town of Bristol, Bucks county, Penna. At this period the celebrated Dr. Baird wrote of her that she was "the finest girl in Philadelphia, having the manners of a lady bred at court." At the opening of the War of the Revolution her oldest sons enlisted in the patriot army—one of whom Alexander has recorded in the "Memoirs of a Life Passed in Pennsylvania," much concerning the maternal affection, the fortitude and patriotic spirit of an American matron. Taken prisoner at the capture of Fort Washington, the devoted mother, accomplished by personal appeals, the parole of Captain Graydon. During the major part of the Revolution, Mrs. Graydon resided at Reading, and while there her house was "the seat of hospitality, and the resort of numerous guests of distinction, including officers of the British army, who were there detained as prisoners of war." The Baron de Kalb was often there; and between her own and General Mifflin's family there was a strong intimacy existing. When the county of Dauphin was organized, the appointment of her son, Alexander, as prothonotary, occasioned her removal to Harrisburg. She was a lady much devoted to her family, and yet in the early days of this city, she was prominent in deeds of love and charity. She died at Harrisburg at the residence of her son on the 23d of January, 1807, aged 73 years, and is buried in the Harrisburg cemetery.

NOTES AND QUERIES.—XLVII.

GRADUATES OF THE UNIVERSITY OF PENN'A.—In preparing a list of the Alumni of the University of Pennsylvania, the dates of birth and death of the following graduates of that institution are wanting. They were probably from the central part of the State. Any information will be gladly received:

Rev. William Edmeston, class of		1759
John Beard,	"	1759
John Porter,	"	1762
William Paxton,	"	1763
Steven Porter,	"	1763
Can. Hamilton,	"	1766
David Sample,	"	1766
Daniel Kuhn (Lancaster),	"	1768
Hamilton Bell,	"	1869
Patterson Bell,	"	1770
James Kelly (York),	"	1782
Cunningham Semple,	"	1791
Thos. M. Ross (Lancaster),	"	1811
Geo. W. Hopkins (Lan.),	"	1819
Samuel S. Cochran,	"	1820

BIOGRAPHICAL HISTORY OF DAUPHIN COUNTY.—III.

INNIS GREEN, the eldest son of Colonel Timothy Green and Mary Innis, was born in Hanover township, Dauphin county, Penn'a, March 25, 1776. His early years were spent on his father's farm, but he received a tolerable fair English education, an essential in the Scotch-Irish settlements. His father, who built a mill at the mouth of Stony creek about 1790, dying in 1812, Innis took charge of it. He was appointed one of the associate judges of Dauphin county by Governor Findlay, August 10, 1818, resigning October 23, 1827, having been elected to the National House of Representatives. He served during the twentieth and twenty-first Congresses. Gov. Wolf, January 26th, 1832, reappointed him associate judge, a position he held at the time of his death, which occurred on the 4th of August, 1839. His remains lie interred in the cemetery at Dauphin. Judge Green laid out the town (which for many years went by the names of

Port Lyon and Greensburg), about the year 1826. He married, in 1804, Rebecca Murray, daughter of Col. John Murray, of the Revolution. He is described as "a heavy set man, of medium height, with a fair, florid face, and little beard." He was a leading and influential man, and deservedly popular among the masses.

WILLIAM GRAYDON, the son of Alexander Graydon and Rachel Marks, was born near Bristol, Bucks county, Penn'a, September 4, 1759. He was educated in Philadelphia, and studied law under Edward Biddle, of that city. He came to Harrisburg upon the organization of the county of Dauphin, and began the practice of his profession, being admitted at the May term, 1786. He was the first notary public, commissioned September 2, 1791, and a leading man in the borough during the "Mill-Dam Troubles" of 1794-5. He was many years member of the Town Council and president thereof, and subsequently one of the burgesses. He was the author of "Forms of Conveyancing" (in two volumes), "The Judge's Assistant," and edited "An Abridgment of the Laws of the United States" in 1802. Mr. Graydon was prominent in the organization of the First Presbyterian church, and for many years an elder thereof. He died at Harrisburg on the 13th of October, 1840, in the eighty-second year of his age. "Mr. Graydon," says Rev. Dr. Robinson, "was a man of fine literary tastes; was highly esteemed as a gentleman of the old school, in his manners refined, courteous, of unblemished integrity in the many trusts committed to him, of high and honorable principles, and in the church and walks of Christian life a man of true piety and deep devotion." Mr. Harris in his *Reminiscences of the Bar* says, "he was a man of medium height, of very gentlemanly manners, of dark lively eyes, neat, if not precise, in dress, and of an intelligent countenance . . . His portrait painted by Francis is in existence, and is an excellent representation. He wore a cue tied with a ribbon, and had his hair powdered." We can add this additional testimony, that he was humane and benevolent, and in all charitable enterprises was the acknowledged leader. H. Murray Graydon, of this city, and Dr. William Graydon, of Dauphin, are his sons.

JACOB GRUBER was a native of Lancaster county, Pennsylvania, born on the 30th of February, 1778. He became a convert to Methodism in 1793, and for this act, it is stated, he was driven from his home by his parents, such was the aversion to that denomination at the period named. At the age of twenty-one, by advice of a minister of the church, he purchased a horse, and commenced missionating in a vacant circuit. In 1800 he was received by the Philadelphia Conference, and in subsequent years itinerated in New Jersey, Pennsylvania, Maryland and Virginia. He was stationed in Harrisburg in 1820 and 1821, and during his ministry, the church on Second street, now the Jewish Synagogue, was built and dedicated. During his appointment here, he did efficient service. He was original and eccentric as a preacher, and many are the ludicrous incidents treasured up in the memory of the older citizens, of his wit and sarcasm. He was a circuit preacher thirty-two years, presiding elder eleven years, and station minister seven years. He died at Lewistown, Pennsylvania, May 25, 1850. Notwithstanding his eccentricity, the Rev. Gruber was earnest and bold—a devoted preacher of the gospel of Christ.

JACOB M. HALDEMAN, the second son of John Haldeman and Maria Brenneman, was born in Donegal township, Lancaster county, March 4, 1781. His grandfather, Jacob Haldeman, a native of German Switzerland, emigrated at an early period. The former received a good English and German education, and, about 1806, purchasing the water power and forge at the mouth of Yellow Breeches creek, Cumberland county, established himself in the iron business. He added a rolling and slitting mill, and by his energy and industry soon became one of the foremost iron manufacturers in the State. His superior iron found a steady market, and upon the establishment of the arsenal at Harper's Ferry he supplied the Government for several years. About the year 1814, Mr. Haldeman laid out the town of New Cumberland. He greatly aided in the building of the bridge over the Susquehanna, and in the other enterprises of the day. He was a large stockholder of the Harrisburg Bank, and on the death of Mr. Elder, in 1853, chosen president thereof, a position he held at the time of his death. From the period when Mr. Haldeman made Harrisburg his permanent residence, he was largely interested in its local enterprises. He died at Harrisburg on the 15th of December, 1856, aged seventy-five years, and is interred in the cemetery there. He married, May 17th, 1810, Eliza Ewing Jacobs, daughter of Samuel Jacobs, of Colebrook Furnace, who survived. Mr. Haldeman was very successful in all his business transactions, and left a handsome estate. He was a leading citizen, and aided largely in the prosperity of our city.

HUGH HAMILTON, the son of John Hamilton and Margaret Alexander, was born at "Fermanagh," now in Juniata county, Pa., on the 30th of June, 1785. He received a careful preparatory education and with his brother John was sent to Dickinson College, where he graduated. He studied law under Thomas Elder, one of the most brilliant lawyers of his day, and was admitted to the Dauphin county bar at the June term, 1805. At the time of his admission to the bar,

Judge Henry had ordered the prothonotary to issue commissions on parchment; acordingly the descendants of the young lawyer have his commission "on parchment" issued 21 June, 1805, signed by "Joshua Elder, Pro'thy, by order of the Court," with the seal of the county attached. In 1808 Mr. Hamilton edited and published "*The Times*" at Lancaster, and upon the removal of the seat of Government to Harrisburg, with William Gillmor, "*The Harrisburg Chronicle*," the leading and influential newspaper at the State Capital for twenty years. The "*Chronicle*" was the first paper in Pennsylvania which gave full and systematic Legislative reports. He died at Harrisburg on the 3d of September, 1836, aged fifty-one years. Mr. Hamilton married, January 6, 1807, Rosanna, daughter of Adam Boyd and Jeannette Macfarlane, born December 1st, 1789; died April 17, 1872. They are both buried in the Harrisburg cemetery. Mr. Hamilton was a vigorous and polished writer, and his editorials were models of elegant composition. For a quarter of a century he wielded considerable political influence through his newspaper. He was an active and enterprising citizen, and highly esteemed.

DAVID HARRIS, youngest son of John Harris and Elizabeth McClure, was born at Harris' Ferry, February 24, 1754. He received a good education and was a student under the Rev. Dr. Alison. At the time of the breaking out of the Revolution, he was in Baltimore, but he volunteered in Col. William Thompson's Pennsylvania Batallion of Riflemen, and subsequently was commissioned paymaster thereof. He served in different positions until the close of the war, when he returned to Baltimore, and married Miss Crockett of that city. After the death of his father, being one of the executors of the estate, he came to Harrisburg, and was appointed by his old companion-in-arms, Gov. Mifflin, one of the associate judges of Dauphin county, August 17, 1791. This position he resigned on the 20th of February following, to accept an appointment in the Bank of the United States. Upon the establishment of the office of discount and deposit in Baltimore, he accepted the cashiership thereof. Major Harris died in that city on the 16th of November, 1809, at the age of fifty-five years. "He was a brave, active and useful officer," says the *Baltimore American*, "and in the private walks of life he was ever cheerful and hospitable, and an ornament to society. As a banking officer he was universally correct, just and obliging." Mr. Harris left no descendants save in the female line.

ELIZABETH HARRIS, the daughter of Richard McClure, was born in Paxtang township, Lancaster now Dauphin county, Penn'a, in 1729. In 1749 she married John Harris, the founder of Harrisburg. She was a woman of undoubted energy and courage, and at the same time being of refined taste and manners. Two incidents have come down to us which exemplify the former characteristics. The first Harris mansion was a log house surrounded by a stockade for the better security against the Indians. In 1758 an English officer was one night at the house, when by accident the gate of the enclosure was left unfastened. The officer was seated at the table with Mr. Harris and his wife. An Indian entered the gate of the stockade and thrust his rifle through one of the port holes of the house, and it is supposed pointed it at the officer. The night being damp, the gun simply flashed. Instantly Mrs. Harris blue out the candle to prevent the Indian aiming a second time, and he retreated. On another occasion the servant girl was sent upstairs by Mrs. Harris, who took with her a piece of lighted candle without a candlestick. The girl coming down without the candle, Mrs. Harris asked what she had done with it, who said she had stuck it into the barrel of *flaxseed*. This, however, happened to be a barrel of *powder*. Mrs. Harris ininstantly arose, and without saying a word, went upstairs, and advancing to the barrel, cautiously placed her hands under the candle and lifted it out—and then cooly reproved the girl for her stupidness. Mrs. Harris died at Harris' Ferry on the 20th of January, 1764, aged thirty-five years. She was buried in the Pantang church graveyard. It was her daughter Mary who married William Maclay.

FREDERICK HUMMEL was a native of the Pfalz, in Germany, born April 14, 1726. With some friends he came to America about 1738, and subsequently took up a large body of land where Hummelstown is located. In 1762, forseeing the advantages, he laid out on a portion of his tract a town, which he named Frederickstown, but was changed upon his death to that now bestowed upon it. He donated land for the erection of the Lutheran and German Reformed churches, and erected a school house, directing the English branches should be taught therein. He was an active participant in the French and Indian war, and when the frontiers were setting an example to the people of the three original counties to prepare for resistance to British injustice, he was chairman of the patriotic meeting at Derry, held at Hummelstown in June, 1774. Mr. Hummel, however, did not live to see the triumph of liberty in America. He died at his residence on the 24th of June, 1779, aged fifty-three years. He was the ancestor of a large family, who can look with pride to the high-born zeal, energy and patriotism of their progenitor. His remains, with those of his two wives and children, are interred in the Lutheran church graveyard at Hummelstown.

JOSEPH JEFFERSON was a native of England, born in 1776. He was the son of a distinguished actor, who was the contemporary of Garrick. He was educated for the stage, and in 1795 came to Boston, where, and in New York, he performed until about 1803, when he located in Philadelphia. Here he was quite a favorite, especially at the Chestnut Street Theater. From 1825 to 1832 he made Harrisburg his home, having a suite of apartments in the old Shakespeare building. He died here on the 4th of August, 1832, greatly lamented. His remains were interred in the burying ground attached to St. Stephen's Episcopal church, and from thence removed to the Harrisburg Cemetery. The inscription on his tomb was written by Chief Justice Gibson, and has often been quoted and admired for its diction. Mr. Jefferson possessed great taste and skill in the construction of intricate stage machinery, and was unrivaled in his peculiar personations. His favorite characters were Kit Cosey, Old D'Oiley and Admiral Cop. He is known as the elder Jefferson. His son and grandson were alike great actors—the father of the second Joseph bequeathing to him his genius and his aspirations, with all that polish which rendered each so popular in his day. And now comes a third Joseph Jefferson, who, since the days of Hackett, has made the character of Rip Van Winkle his own.

OVID FRAZER JOHNSON, son of Rev. Jehoida Pitt Johnson and Hannah Frazer, was born in the Valley of the Wyoming, near Wilkes-Barre, Pennsylvania, in 1807. His ancestor, Rev. Jacob Johnson, a graduate of Yale in 1740, removed from Connecticut in 1773. Mr. Johnson studied law under Judge Conyngham, of Wilkes-Barre, and subsequently admitted and entered upon the practice of his profession. In 1833 he came to Harrisburg, where he married Jane, daughter of James Alricks and Martha Hamilton. On January 15, 1839, he was appointed, by Governor Porter, Attorney General of Pennsylvania, a position he creditably filled during that administration. He died in the city of Washington, whither he had gone in the interest of a prominent legal claim, in February, 1854. As a political writer, orator and lawyer Mr. Johnson had a high reputation. He was the author of the celebrated "Governor's Letters," published during the administration of Governor Ritner, and which purported to give the ludicrous side to the political characters then figuring in the politics of the State.

JOHN M. KEAGY was born in Martic township, Lancaster county, Pennsylvania, about the year 1795. He was of German descent on the maternal side, the name of his mother's family being Litzenburg. He received a classical education, studied medicine and graduated in 1817. In 1819 he published a series of educational articles in the

Baltimore *Chronicle*, which were reprinted at Harrisburg in 1824, in an octavo pamphlet of thirty-eight pages. In 1827 Dr. Keagy became principal of the Harrisburg Academy, and during the same year published his "Pestallozian Primer," a work made up largely of the more modern object-lessons, but under the name of "Thinking Lessons, and Lessons in Generalization." By this method, as soon as the child knows a vowel and a consonant he is taught to spell and read the syllables which they form. In the introduction the author advocated the teaching of a child to read words, "as if they were Chinese syllables," and without a previous knowledge of the letters, a practicable mode which avoids the absurdity of telling a child that *see a tea* (which should spell *seat*) spells *cat*. He remained at Harrisburg about two years, when he went to Philadelphia to take charge of the Friends' High School. Shortly before his death, which occurred at Philadelphia in the winter of 1836–37, Dr. Keagy was elected Professor of the Languages in Dickinson College, but did not live to act. Besides being a classical scholar, the Doctor knew Hebrew, German and French; he knew the principles of mechanics, and insisted that steam boilers should have more fire surface. Had he been brought up as a machinist, he would have invented tubular boilers, having constructed a copper model composed partly of tubes.

ANTHONY KELKER, son of Henry Kelker and Regula Braetscher was a native of Herliberg, near Zurich, Switzerland, born on the 30th of December, 1733. At the age of ten years, in 1743, his parents emigrated to America and located in Lebanon township, Lancaster county, now Lebanon county, Pa., four miles north of the town of Lebanon. Anthony was brought up on his father's farm, receiving the meager advantages of the schools of that period. He was commissioned August 28, 1775, lieutenant in the second battalion of Lancaster county associators, and was in active service during the campaign of 1776. In 1777 he was an officer in the militia at Brandywine and Germantown. He was appointed Jan. 19th, 1778, wagon-master of Col. Greenawalt's battalion; and the same year was sent on a secret expedition to Virginia and Maryland. Until the close of the war, Capt. Kelker was an active participant. He was deputy sheriff of Lancaster county in 1781 and 1782; and upon the formation of the county of Dauphin was commissioned the first sheriff in 1785, and subsequently elected, serving until 1788. He was a member of the Pennsylvania House of Representatives 1793-4. Mr. Kelker died at Lebanon on the 10th of March, 1812. He married Mary Magdalene, daughter of George Meister, a Moravian. She died at Lebanon, December 30th, 1818. Mr. Kelker was a man of strict integrity, an unflinching patriot, and highly esteemed by his fellow citizens.

HOW SENECA G. SIMMONS DIED.

We are indebted to Mrs. Col. Seneca G. Simmons, of this city, for a copy of a letter recently received by her from the Confederate surgeon under whose care her gallant and lamented husband was placed after he received his death wound. This letter was written in reply to one from Mrs. Simmons requesting information concerning certain effects of her deceased husband, reported to have fallen into the possession of the Confederate surgeon, and throws some light on the manner of Col. Simmons' death. The letter is as follows:

Toccoa, Ga., *May 3, 1882.*

Mrs. Simmons, *Harrisburg, Pa.:* Yours of the 27th of March has been to hand a few days. Urgent business engagements have prevented me from replying until the present time. The impressions which you received are in the main correct, except the impression that I am in possession of some of your "husband's effects." That is an error you have been led into by some one in the correspondence on the subject.

At the time of the battle referred to I was regimental surgeon and, with others of the brigade, in charge of field hospital. I was told that Col. Simmons fell in front of our part of the line, and, as our line advanced, he was taken up and brought to the field hospital by my ambulance corps. He was wounded by a minnie ball, through the liver and lung, and died, I think, the second day. I treated him the best possible under the circumstances, and had him buried as decently as could be done there at such a time. He was reported by our officers and men as acting conspicuously brave on that sanguinary field, as being the cause, in their opinion, of that part of the Federal line standing as long as it did. That report did much towards stimulating a greater desire on our part to do all that was possible for a brave but fallen foe. Before death he thanked us sincerely for our attentions. He gave to some one of our party (I do not recollect in whose hand he placed them) a gold watch, a picture of his wife, and I think $60 in gold coin, with the request that the watch and picture (I do not think he included the coin) be sent to his wife. I have no knowledge or recollection of a masonic pin or badge. If I had seen one I am sure I would recollect it from my association with the order. These articles were placed in possession of Dr. Gaston, our brigade surgeon (now dead), with the request made by Col. Simmons (coin and all). A few days after this occurrence there was a Federal surgeon at our quarters, temporarily in our lines. We were all together, this surgeon, Dr. Gaston and myself, and Dr. Gaston stated to me that he had turned those articles of Col. Simmons over to this surgeon to be sent to his widow. I suppose I heard the name of the Federal surgeon, when I met him, but I have no recollection of what it was. Such is a hasty account of what I know of your husband's death.

Since the excitement and trouble incident to the war have passed, I have often felt an anxiety to learn if the articles belonging to a brave officer had ever reached his widow. The impression I got of the name of your husband at the time was "Simons," as if written with one m. I suppose the reason of that was the weakness of his voice at the time. Those articles were never in my personal possession, but, as I stated, with the hospital attendant, until handed Brigade Surgeon Gaston, as stated above.

Respectfully and truly,

O. M. DOYLE.

NOTES AND QUERIES.—XLVIII.

GIBSON (N. & Q. xlv.)—You err in saying that Judge Gibson was the son of Andrew Galbraith's daughter. The judge's wife, Sally Galbraith, as she was called, was the daughter of Andrew G. I forget who the Judge's mother was, but as the Gibsons of that family (the chief justice, General George, Francis, etc.) were born in that part of Cumberland which is now Perry county, she was probably a Cumberland county woman. The old homestead in Shearman's Valley is, I think, still owned by some of Francis Gibson's descendants.

G. P.

[The mother of Chief Justice Gibson was Ann West, daughter of Francis West, of Shearman's Valley.]

A CHURCH CENTENNIAL.—St. John's Lutheran church near Berrysburg, Dauphin county, was organized in 1780 by the Rev. Michael Enterline, a member of the first Ministerium and Synod of the Evangelical Lutheran Church organization of America, and on the 5th and 6th of June next celebrates its Centennial anniversary. The first deacons of the Church were Solomon Schnug and John Matter. The first building was a log school house, in which for eighteen or twenty years divine worship was held. In 1798 a church building proper was commenced, but not completed until 1802. It was consecrated on the 24th of October that year, by the Revs. George Lochman and John Herbst. For three-quarters of a century the congregation worshiped in that church. In 1876 it was decided to erect a more commodious edifice, and on the 11th day of November, 1877, the second building was dedicated. The Rev. Michael Enterline continued pastor of St. John's for a number of years, and after his discontinuance was followed by the Revs. Hinza, Moeller, Kramer, Walter, Daniel Ulrich, J P. Schindel, N. Hemping, C. F. Welden, N. Jaeger, F. Waltz, Jeremiah Schindel, T. Steck and R. S. Wagner, the present pastor. The church has an eventful and interesting history, and it is to be hoped that at least a complete biographical record of the ministry and leading men of the church be prepared by the present pastor of St. John's.

A MATRON OF THE REVOLUTION.

The biographical sketch of Mrs. Rachel Graydon (N. & Q., xlvi), brings to mind her strenuous exertions for the release of her son, Capt. Alexander Graydon, who was a prisoner of war at New York, and we present herewith such papers as have come before us relating thereto, the originals of which are in the possession of her grandson, H. Murray Graydon, Esq.

In the spring of 1777, having learned of the harsh treatment of the British prisoners, Mrs. Graydon determined to go to New York, notwithstanding the opposition of her friends on account of the difficulties of traveling at that date. She accordingly purchased a horse and chair and set out for Philadelphia, her residence being then at Reading. On her arrival in the city, a relative of her mother named Fisher was officious in tendering his services to drive her to New York, and the offer was accepted; but when they had nearly reached Princeton, they were overtaken, to their great astonishment, by a detachment of American cavalry—Fisher it seems being a loyalist. Mrs. Graydon, found in such evil company was taken also in custody, and after some delay was obliged to retrace her road to Philadelphia, under an escort of horse.

When they arrived at Bristol on their return, means were found for Mr. Fisher to go on without the chair, and at once proper measures were taken for Mrs. Graydon to proceed within the British lines. Col. McIlvaine, an old friend, agreed to accompany her—and the following passport was obtained from the President of Congress:

" *To all Continental Officers which it may concern:*
 "Permit Colonel Joseph McIlvaine and Mrs. Rachel Graydon to Pass Morris Town without the least hindrance or Interruption.

"Given under my hand at Philadelphia, this Twenty-sixth Day of May, 1777. JOHN HANCOCK, *Presid't.*"

"Mr. Gustavus Reisburgh attends Mrs. Graydon to Bristol, who is to pass unmolested. JOHN HANCOCK, *Presid't.*"

Proceeding under the escort of Colonel McIlvaine to the headquarters of the American army, General Washington gave the following:

"Mrs. Graydon, a Widow Lady of Philadelphia, has permission to pass the Guards of my Army in order to go into Brunswick, to endeavor to obtain liberty of the Commanding Officer there to go into New York to visit her Son, Captain Graydon, a prisoner of War.

"Given at Head Quarters, Camp at Middle Brook, this 30th day of May, 1777. GEO. WASHINGTON."

After being conducted to the lines, Mrs. Graydon was committed to the courtesy of some Hessian officers. It happened during the ceremony of the flag that a gun was somewhere discharged on the American side. This infringement of military etiquette was furiously resented by the German officers; and their vehement gestures and expressions of indignation, but imperfectly understood by Mrs. Graydon, alarmed her not a little. She supported herself as well as she could under this inauspicious introduction into the hostile territory, and had her horse led to the quarters of Gen. Cornwallis, who was in command in Brunswick, where she alighted and was shown into a parlor. Weary and faint from fatigue and agitation she partook of some refreshment offered her, and then went to deliver a letter of introduction she had received from Mr. VanHorn, of Boundbrook, to a gentleman in Brunswick. Five of the Misses VanHorn, his nieces, were staying at the house, and with them Mrs. Graydon became well acquainted, as they avowed Whig principles. Their uncle had been compelled to leave Flatbush on account of his attachment to the American cause; but was permitted not long afterwards to return to his house there, accompanied by Mrs. VanHorn and her daughters.

On presenting her passports to Gen. Cornwallis, that officer directed the following to be issued:

"BRUNSWICK, *May 31st, 1777.*

"It is Lord Cornwallis' order that Mrs. Graydon be permitted to go to New York in one of the Sloops. CHAS. EUSTICE, *Aid-de-Camp.*"

Being detained in Brunswick for several days, Mrs. Graydon at last embarked in a sloop or shallop for New York, where she arrived in due time. The vessel, however, was fired upon from the shore, but no one was injured. At New York she received, upon application, the following:

" *To all whom it may concern:*

"Mrs. Graydon has permission to pass & repass from hence to flat Bush to see her Son. "Jos. LORING,
Commissary Prisoners.

"NEW YORK, *3d June, 1777.*"

Reaching Flatbush, Mrs. Graydon, through the kindness of Mr. Bache, occupied his part of Mr. Suydam's house during her stay there. Here, in the society of her son, her accustomed flow of good spirits returned. She even gave one or two tea drinkings to the "rebel clan," and learned from Major Williams the art of making Johnny cakes in the true Maryland fashion. These recreations did not, however, interfere with the object of her expedition, nor could her son dissuade her from her purpose of proving the result of an application.

When Mrs. Graydon called on Mr. Galloway, in New York, whom she had known when he was a citizen of Philadelphia, and who was supposed to have much influence at British headquarters, he advised her to apply to Sir William Howe by memorial, and offered to draw one up for her. In a few minutes he produced what accorded with his ideas on the subject, and read to her what he had written, commencing with—

"*Whereas*, Mrs. Graydon has always been a true and faithful subject to his Majesty, George the Third; *And Whereas*, her son, an inexperienced youth, has been deluded by the arts of designing men——"

"Oh, sir," said Mrs. Graydon, "that will never do! my son cannot obtain his release on those terms."

"Then, madam," replied Mr. Galloway, somewhat peevishly, "I can do nothing for you."

Though depressed by the treatment she thus received at the hands of Mr. Galloway, Mrs. Graydon would not relinquish her object; but continued to advise with every one she thought able or willing to assist her. In accordance with the counsel received from a friend, she at length resolved upon a direct application to Sir William Howe.

After several weeks of delay, anxiety and disappointment, the design was put into execution. Without having informed her son of what she meant to do, lest he might prevent her, through the fear of improper concessions on her part, she went one evening into New York, and boldly waited upon General Howe. She was shown into a parlor and had a few moments to consider how she should address him who possessed the power to grant her request, or destroy her hopes. He entered the room, and was near her before she perceived him.

"Sir William Howe—I presume?" said Mrs. Graydon, rising. He bowed; she made known her business—a mother's feelings doubtless giving eloquence to her speech—and entreated permission for her son to go home with her on parole.

"And then immediately to take up arms against us, I suppose?" said Lord Howe.

"By no means, sir; I solicit his release upon parole; that will restrain him until exchanged; but on my own part I will go further, and say that if I have any influence over him he shall never take up arms again." Here the feelings of the patriot were wholly lost in those of the "war-detesting mother."

General Howe seemed to hesitate; but at the earnest renewal of her suit, gave the desired permission.

The mother's joy at her success was the prelude to a welcome summons to the prisoner to repair to New York for the purpose of being transported in a flag vessel to Elizabethtown.

After some further adventures the travelers reached Philadelphia, where they dined at President Hancock's. The latter had at first, it is said, opposed Mrs. Graydon's going to New York, but was gratified at her success. On all sides she was warmly congratulated for her endurance and heroism; and after the lapse of over a century the account as herewith given exemplifies, in a great measure, the hardships of a true American woman of the Revolution.

JOHN HOYT HICKOK.

[In *Notes and Queries* No. *xvi*, allusion was made to the services of Mr. Hickok, as connected with Mrs. Kingsford's school. The following biographical sketch of him will no doubt interest many of our readers who remember him well, and especially the sudden termination of his useful life.]

JOHN HOYT HICKOK, the eldest child of Jesse Hickok and Betsy Hoyt, was born at Wilton, Conn., November 27, 1792. He was brought up on his father's farm, receiving the usual educational advantages of the time, at the winter school and a few sessions at a neighboring academy. When about seventeen years of age he commenced teaching during the winter months, pursuing meanwhile, in connection therewith, his own studies, until finally, soon after attaining his majority, he selected and embarked in teaching as his life profession.

Mr. Hickok married, in 1814, Mary, daughter of Job Lockwood and Sarah Hickok, of Wilton. Mrs. Lockwood was a native of Wilton, and a daughter of Nathan Hickok and grand-daughter of Nathaniel Hickok, who was, as is supposed, a cousin of the father of Jesse Hickok, so that John H. Hickok and his wife were distantly related by blood.

He spent some years teaching in western New York, from whence he emigrated to Pennsylvania in 1823, teaching a select and boarding school in Union county until 1828, when he removed to Lewistown, Mifflin county, and took charge of the Academy there, at that time a largely patronized and well known institution, which, aided by a corps of teachers, he conducted successfully until 1836, Mrs. Hickok having the superintendence of the ladies' department of the school.

In 1836 he embarked in the book-publishing business at Chambersburg, continuing in it until the spring of 1839, when he removed to Harrisburg, where he engaged in teaching. He died there on January 14, 1841, his death resulting from injuries received on the preceding 12th of December, as he was attempting to step on the platform of a car on the Cumberland Valley railroad at Front and Mulberry streets, the train being in motion.

Mr. Hickok was a thorough scholar, an accomplished musician and widely known as a teacher of music. In the various places of his residence he generally conducted the choirs of the churches in which he held membership. He was the author of several books of church, and one of secular music, much used at the time, but now out of print. He was a man of indomitable energy, activity and decision of character, dignified and somewhat stern, yet withal, possessing great kindness.

Though naturally of high temper, he had acquired unusual self-control, and this was one marked element of his success as an educator. A strict disciplinarian; exacting and enforcing implicit obedience from his children and his pupils—in fact almost a martinet in discipline—he was, at the same time, kind and just; and possessed, in an eminent degree, the faculty of commanding the respect of the members of his schools and at the same time of winning their attachment.

It has, in later years, often been remarked by his former wards—and very many, far and near, have been under his care—that his eye seemed to keep within its scope all the proceedings of his own school room and to know, almost by intuition, all that was going on in the rooms of his subordinates. One of his sons—the wayward boy of the family—says he "never could look father in the eye and succeed in the slightest prevarication."

In manners he was "a gentleman of the old school;" and, perhaps, in the present day, might be considered somewhat punctilious in the observance of his own part, and the demanding from others the fulfillment of the "code of etiquette."

With all his positiveness, he was a good man, a sincere Christian, a warm friend, an affectionate husband, a kind father. All about him "knew just where to find him," and when he died he was deeply regretted by his acquaintances and in the community in which he lived. His wife survived him twenty-seven years. She deceased at Bedford, but her remains rest beside those of her husband in the Harrisburg cemetery.

The ancestor of the name in this country was William Hiccox, of ——— England, whence he emigrated to America, sometime between the years 1630 and 1640, consequently he was one of the very early settlers of New England. His name appears at about that date in the annals of Farmington, Conn., as one of the original proprietors of that town. His sons, Samuel and Joseph, were also on the list of proprietors of Farmington, in 1672, and Samuel was one of the earliest proprietors of Waterbury, Conn., in 1674. The records speak of Samuel as one of the leading men of the settlement, who died at his post when men of the right stamp could be poorly spared. His death occcured in 1694, the year after his youngest son, the youngest of eleven children, was born. The original name was Hiccox, but its orthography has become as diversified, almost, as the letters capable of producing the sound are susceptible of transposition. It was spelled Hickox generally as early as 1672, perhaps earlier, and such was, as far as can be learned, the more general rendering of it until 1722, when Ebenezer Hickox, the third in the line and the youngest child, above referred to, of Samuel, removed to Danbury, after which it is observable that the Danbury branch and their descendants uniformly write it Hickok, while the descendants of the Waterbury branch retain the early spelling—Hickox; and other branches have changed it in many ways. In 1724, Ebenezer Hickok, nephew of Ebenezer above mentioned, followed his uncle and namesake from Waterbury to Danbury. He was the great grandfather of Rev. Laurens P. Hickok, D. D., of Union College, N. Y.

The succession of names, in the direct line, from William Hiccox, of Farmington, to the subject of this biography, is as follows:

1. William Hiccox, date of birth and death not known.
2. Samuel Hickox, born in 1643, died in 1694.
3. Ebenezer Hickok, born in 1693, date of death uncertain.
4. John Hickok, son of Ebenezer Hickok and Abigail Stevens, his second wife, born in 1734, and died in 1811.

5. Jesse Hickok, son of John Hickok and Lidia Kellog, his wife, born in 1769, died in 1826.

6. John Hickok, son of Jesse Hickok and Betsey Hoyt, his wife, born in 1792, died in 1841. His baptismal name was John, but on becoming of age, he adopted, in addition, his mother's family name Hoyt. It will be observed that in the list of names above given, there were no "middle" names for mere euphony; simply William, Samuel, Ebenezer, John, Jessie, John. They were evidently people of hard, solid sense.

There are not, so far as is known to the American branches of the family, any of the name now living in England, although tradition has it that William left a brother living there on his emigration to America.

A gentlemen of Waterbury, Conn., a member of the connection by marriage, who visited England in 1877, wrote from London of a visit he made to the Church of the Holy Trinity, Stratford on Avon, for the purpose of seeing the tomb of Shakespeare. After describing the tomb of the poet and his feelings on perusing its epitaph, he goes on to say:

"I must give you a copy of an inscription I noted down for the purpose, from a tablet in the vestry of the same church, viz:

To the Memory of | Edward Hiccox, Gent., | who died March 23d, 1774. | Æt. 66.

He was pious, charitable and of the strictest integrity."

The only other reference to the name as existing, or having existed in England, is in the London edition, 1844, of Burke's Encyclopedia of Heraldy.

NOTES AND QUERIES.—XLIX.

THE FIRST CENSUS OF DAUPHIN COUNTY.—Under the authority of an act of Congress of the first day of March, 1790, a census of the inhabitants of Pennsylvania was taken, and to the county of Dauphin, which then embraced the whole of Lebanon, the total population was officially stated at 18,177. Harrisburg, which only became a borough a year later, appropriated 875 of this number, and the county at large, 17,302. Of the total census thus stated, 4,657 were white males of sixteen years and upwards; 4,437 white males under sixteen; 8,814 white females, whose ages were not given; 57 of no classification whatever [colored]; and 212 were slaves.   C. H. M.

PATTERSON—MCKNIGHT—TAYLOR—ELDER. — William Patterson, of Paxtang, died in October, 1745, leaving a wife and the following children:
  i. *Samuel*, m. —— Barnett.
  ii. *Francis*.
  iii. *Robert*.
  iv. *Ann*.
  v. *Catharine*, m. James McKnight.
  vi. *Jean*, m. Robert Taylor.
  vii. *Mary*, m. Thomas Elder.

The Thomas Elder who married Mary Patterson was a son of Robert Elder, and brother of Rev. John Elder, of Paxtang. Thomas Elder died in July, 1752, leaving a wife and children—John, Rachel and Robert. Information is desired as to the other children.

MANUFACTURING FACILITIES AT HARRISBURG.

On the 4th of February, 1792, the following preamble and resolution "was made and seconded by Mr. Potts and Mr. Hanna" in the General Assembly, looking towards the incorporation of a company for the establishing a manufactory in Harrisburg. More properly it was for affording facilities therefor by the construction of a canal from Hunter's Falls. The bed of this canal was to be Paxtang creek. The resolution passed, a bill was matured and presented, but the fear of impeding the navigation of the Susquehanna by a shot-wing dam, which was deemed necessary by the projectors of this scheme, occasioned its defeat. This plan was, nevertheless, considered for a long time a feasible one. Harrisburg was undoubtedly then, as it is now, a desirable point for the establishment of manufactories, and had any one of the numerous plans for supplying water-power to the town been carried out there can be no doubt that it would have added greatly to its wealth and prosperity:

"As the attention of the Citizens of the United States are now very properly engaged in promoting many useful improvements for increasing the wealth and happiness of the people of each particular State; and the recent report of the Secretary of the Treasury of the United States and others who have lately published their Sentiments on the subject have clearly demonstrated the great advantages which must result from establishing Manufactories in this Country; to engross the time of this House with Arguments in their favour, would be entirely superfluous. It is only necessary to suggest *some* of the many concurring circumstances which point out the Borough of Harrisburg, as a very eligible place for that purpose, not only, as being on the waters of an extensive inland navigation, where the raw materials for different kinds of Manufacturies may be obtained with great ease and plenty, and the reduced price of provisions, occasioned by the distance from foreign navigation, will always contribute to an equal reduction in the price of Labour; but also, the great ease with which the waters of Susquehanna may be brought out of that River at or near Hunter's falls, along Paxtang Creek, for the Accommodation of the Borough, and to provide a sufficient force in aid of manual Labour, in every branch of Manufactory which will admit of machinery assistance, in the most extensive manner.

"*Resolved*, that a Committee be appointed to enquire into the propriety, to bring in a Bill to be passed into a Law, to authorize the Governor to incorporate a Company for establishing a manufactory in the Borough of Harrisburg, and for opening a Canal between the River Susquehanna, at or near Hunter's falls, and Paxtang Creek; and for extending the said Manufactory, to Linen, Cotton, and such other branches, as they may hereafter find useful and advantageous."

THE HORTER FAMILY.

Prominent among the early families at Harrisburg, was that of Horter. Two brothers of this name had emigrated from the fatherland—the locality not definitely known, but believed to have been the city of Speyer, in Rhenish Bavaria—and settled at Germantown, Pa.

John Valentine Horter, my ancestor, sailed from Rotterdam in the ship "Brittania," and landed at Philadelphia, September 26, 1764. Born in 1739, he was consequently 25 years old when he arrived. About 1767, he married Magdalena Reis (Rice), third daughter of George Reis, of Germantown. The issue of this marriage was two sons and five daughters, whom I shall mention anon.

At Germantown the children attended school in what is now known as the "Academy" building, on School Lane; which ancient structure, now one hundred and twenty years old, is still in use as a public school.

The family was yet at Germantown when the memorable battle occurred, October 4, 1777, and always mentioned it as a thrilling episode in their history. Their home was in the line of the fight; the British not only occupied their grounds, but used their cooking utensils for the time being. When the battle opened a British officer advised the Horters to take refuge in their cellar, which they were soon glad to do; and the old vault where they stowed themselves was torn out only a few years ago, in the building of "Parker's Hall." In Watson's Annals mention is made of wounded soldiers having been found on Horter's lot. The elder children remembered seeing Washington at the time.

William Reis, uncle of Mrs. Horter, was Captain of a company of Pennsylvania Germans during the Revolution, and afterwards became a member of the distinguished "Order of the Cincinnati"— which hereditary honor is now held by Henry B. Wood, lately of Harrisburg.

In May, 1785, John Valentine Horter, leaving his brother Jacob at Germantown, removed his family to "Harris' Ferry" or "Louisburg," afterwards (1791) Harrisburg. It must have been a poor prospect for a "town," as the wife, no doubt remembering the better-settled place they had left (family tradition saith) lifted up her voice and wept when she beheld the sight of her future home. We have no record of the inducements that effected this change. Mr. Horter was doubtless needed in the young town as a victualler, just as John Harris told Jacob Bucher he was needed as a hatter.

The after life of the family includes the settlement of the children as follows: Anna Margaretta (1768–1847) married Henry Beader; Maria Magdalena (1769–1853) m. Conrad Horning; Catherine (1772–1833) m. Matthias Hutman; Susanna Margaret (1774–1838) m. Jacob Bucher; John Valentine (1777–1823) m. Mary Fedder; Elizabeth (1779–1852) m. Jacob Ziegler; and George Reis (1784–1830). This list embraces some of the "ancient and honorable" families of the old borough, whose descendants still remain, whilst some of the names have been erased in the march of time.

Mr. Horter's residence was eventually fixed on Second street, east of Mulberry, where his wife died in 1807, aged 58. He died at Mrs. Beader's (in the German house) on Chestnut street, in 1816, aged 77. George R. Horter never married; acted as deputy of Henry Beader, in the Register's office in 1809; was appointed major in the army and served during the war of 1812, but afterwards resigned. He served as Transcribing Clerk of the Senate for a number of years prior to his death in 1830. John V. Horter, jr., was a hatter with Jacob Zollinger, successor to Jacob Bucher. He was emphatically a good man, and pre-eminent for his interest in religious affairs. He was one of the first-chosen deacons in the German Reformed congregation in 1814, when it separated from the Lutherans, and was an active committee-man in the erection of the new church in 1821.

The Horter family was one of those not so much distinguished for public zeal as for private excellence. Quiet and unostentatious, it infused good blood and left its impress upon the character of other families that had the energy to develop what is meritorious. Consisting mostly of daughters, it was absorbed into other names, and its own thus disappeared with the generation to which it belonged.

GEORGE B. AYRES.

PAXTANG VOLUNTEERS ON THE FRONTIER IN 1779.

We are indebted to Mr. Silas Rutherford for the following, which is explanatory in itself:

PAXTANG, *19th April, 1779.*

"SIR: I have this Day Received a Letter from Coll. Galbraith calling on the Sixth Class of this Battalion to March to Bedford for the protection of the Inhabitants there, whilst Putting in there Spring Crops, Until a certain number of men can be Raised who are called Rangers. Therefore I Desire that you immediately warn the Sixth Class of Yr Comp'y to Parade at the House of —— on Monday next at Ten O'Clock forenoon, with all their accouterments in readiness to march; where an appeal will be held as presented by the Militia Law.

I am, sir,
Y'r Humble Serv't,

ROBT. ELDER, *Col.*

" *Capt. John Rutherford.*"

Pursuant to the foregoing order, the following persons comprised the company which, under the command of Capt. John Rutherford, marched to Bedford, where they remained about six weeks, until relieved by Ranging Companies recruited for the purpose. During this period the farmers of Bedford county finished their sping planting. Capt. Rutherford's command as will be observed consisted of detachments from the different companies comprising Col. Elder's Battalion:

Capt. Murray's Company.

John Cochran, Senr.,	Samuel Pollock,	William Forster,
Michael Steever,	Philip Tinturff,	Samuel Cochran.
John Bunnel, 4 Serg.,	John Grames,	

Capt. Collier's Company.

Stophel Earnest,	John Little,	Robert McWhorter,
John Smith,	John Brand,	Matthias Winagle,
James McCord,	Conrad Alleman,	Lodwick Dagon,
George Consor,	Philip Newhouse,	Abraham Brunson.

Capt. Rutherford's Company.

Martin Houser,
Jacob Miller,
Peter Pancake,
George Pancake,

Barnabas Shoop,
Benj. Jones,
George Sheets,

Frederick Castle,
George Carson,
James Gailey.

Capt. Crouch's Company.

Adam Ritter,
John Minsker,
Conrad Wolfley,
Dr. Robert Kennedy,
Albright Swineford,

Christian King,
John Ritter,
Jacob Miller,
John Swineford,
George Segance,

Robert Harron,
George Williams
Simon Rairdon,
Joseph Mark.

Capt. Clark's Company.

Robert Kennedy,
Samuel Kisler,
Andrew Richardson,

Samuel Barnet,
Richard Allison,

John Chambers,
Jesse Packer.

Capt. Weaver's Company.

Jonathan Woodside, Serg.,
Ludwick Light,
Frank Conway,

Lemuel Snyder,
Abraham Neighbour,

Andrew Yeager,
Michael Chattel.

Capt. Whitley's Company.

Christian Crawl,
Jacob Weiser,
Charles Grogan,

Thomas Miller (sick),
William Gamble,
Conrad Yountz,

John Bell,
James Doyle.

Capt. Gilchrist's Company.

James Cochran,
Samuel Cochran,
James Morrison,

Wm. Hogan,
Wm. Boyd,

John Hatfield,
·Dennis Dougherty.

YE ANCIENT INHABITANTS.—VII.

[The year 1756 witnessed a scene of terror on the frontiers of th Province which at this day would be difficult to imagine. The inroads of the treacherous Delawares and perfidious Shawanese— with tomahawk and scalping knife stained with the life-blood of their helpless victims—spread dismay and horror into the border settlements of Hanover. A silent witness of these terrible times is the original assessment lists of the East and West Ends of the Township for 1756 which are before us. On these herewith presented, those marked with an asterisk (*) have written before them "*fled.*" We give the orthography as in the original.]

West End of Hanover Assessment, Provincial Tax 1756.

Matthew Snoddy,
Joseph Wilson,
Jno. McCormick,
Henry McCormick,
Adam Hamaker,
Lorrance Rahlan,
John Gordon,*
Richard Johnston,*
David McClenaghan,
Alex. Barned,*
Jno. MacNeely,
Thos. Finny,
Philip Robinson,*
Robert Snodgrass,
Robert Love,
Sam'l Young,
Daniel Shaw,
Jno. Woods,
Andrew Wood,
Charles McClure,
Jno. Taylor,
Jno. Hutchinson,
Daniel Brown,
Wm. Loard,
Widow Rodger,
Seth Rodger,
Samuel Staret,
Hugh Roger,
Wm. Roger,
Thos. McClure,*
Wm. Wallis,*
John Johnston Kill'd & boy taken,
James Riddle,*
John Cooper,
David Fargison,*
John McClure,
James Wright,
Thos Robinson (miller),
Jas. Robinson,
Michael McNeely,
John Miller,
Jamuel Stuart,
James Park,*
James Rippett,
James Wilson,
Matthew Taylor,
Widow McCarvin,
Thos. Hill,*
Wm. Roger,
Jno. Brown,
James McCarver,*
Robert Porterfield,*
Widow Parker,
Alix. Muclehenny,
Samuel Robinson,
James Finney,
Thos. French,
Thos. Sharp,
Jas. French,
Jno. Sharp,
Jno. Hill,*
Thos. Bell,*
Hugh McNeet,
Jas. Beard,
Wm. Thompson,
Wm. Trousdell,
Matthew Thornton,
Francis McClure,
Thos. Maguire,
Wm. McCord,
Robert Huston,*
Benjamin Wallice,*
Wm. Barnett,*
Bartholomy Hain,*
John Swan,*
Jas. Bannon,*
Wm. McClure,*
Andrew Wallis,*
John Henry,*
Jas. Riddle, jr.,*
Wm. Coopper,
John Thomson,
Wm. Allen,
Wm. Galbreath,
Widow Dearmin,*
Henry Hart,
Robert Stuart,
John Stuart,
Thos. MacMullen,
Robert Martin,
James Wilson,*
Jyon Strean,
Robt. Wallis,
Samuel Barnett,*
James Brown, Kill'd,
Samuel Brown,
Hugh Wilson,
Henry Smith,
JOHN DIXON,
Coll'r of the West End of Hanover.

East End of Hanover Assessment for ye Provincial Tax, 1756.

Dorst Braghtbill,
John Foster,
Martin Light,
Andrew Berrihill, Kill'd,
Joseph Hoff,
Samuel Sloan,
Mathias Poor,
Isaac Williams,
John Gilliland,*
John MaCollogh,
Walter Magfarling,
Wm. Robinson,*
Adam Cleaman,*
Peter Walmor,*
James Rafter,*
John Brown,*
Andrew MacMaghen,
Thos. Strean,
John Kreag, kill'd, & wife & boy taken captive.
Henry Cuntz,*
John Crawford,
John Stuart,*
David Strean,*
Wm. Greams,
Alex. Martin,
Anthony MaCraight,*
Walter Bell,
Samuel Tod,
Brice Innis,
Wm. MaCullough,*
John Faurney,
Phillip Colp,*
Rudy Houk,
Anthony Rosenbom,
Geo. Sheffer,
Dayvolt Angony,
Casper Yost,
Conrad Kleck,*
Daniel Moser,*
Adam Harper,
Lazarus Stuart,
John Anderson,
John Coningham,
Henry Weever,

Adam Reed, Esq.,
Fredrick Noah, kill'd,
Phillip Mour,*
Jacob Bashore,
Benja. Clark,
Geo. Tittle,
John Tups,
John Weaver,
Jacob Toops,
John Dibbin, jun.,
John Dibbin, sen.,
Wm. Clark,
Peter Hedrick,
Christian Albert,*
Nicholas Winer,
James Stuart,
John McClure,*
Patrick Brown,
Widow Coningham,
Stophel Sees,
Samuel Graime,
Jacob Rigard,
Samuel Endworth's* son
  taken.
Barnett MacNett,*

Isaac Sharp,
Jno. Jacob Stover,
John Thompson,
Joseph Willson,
Conrad Rice.*
Alex. Swan,*
Andrew Karsnits,*
John Young,
Wm. Young,
James Williams,
Daniel Angst,
John Slone,
James Clark,
John Stuart,
James Young,
John Andrew,
Robt. Kirkwood,*
Valentine Stofelbain,*
Rud. Fry,*
John MaCollough,*
Moses Vance,*
Ike Brooner,*
Jacob Moser,*
Barned Bashore,*
Tyce Bashore,*

Thos. Shurly,*
Adam MacNeely,
James Grame,*
Andrew Brown,*
Wm. Brown,*
Thos. Hume,*
Christophel Henry,
Peter Wolf,*
John Gream,*
Wm. Watson,*
John Hume,*
John Porterfield,*
John Strean,*
Wm. Thomson,
John Mire,
James Dixon,*
Wm. Woods,
Christophel Plautz,
Geo. Miller,
Jacob Stover,
James MaCurry,*
John Dixon,
Wm. James,
Thos. Priece.

ISAAC SHARP,
Coll'r East End of Hanover.

NOTES AND QUERIES—L.

BRISBAN, CAPT. JOHN, (N. & Q. xlv.) "J. B. R." sends this additional information. "He was a soldier in the French and Indian war, and held a lieutenant's commission in the English army. He was a part of the time in Canada, and I think was with General Wolfe on the Plains of Abraham. For his services he received a grant from George III of two thousand acres of land in Virginia. * *
* * At the close of the Revolutionary war he settled on his farm near "Bird-in-Hand," Lancaster county, when he was appointed collector of military fines. He was however too kind-hearted to oppress the delinquents, consequently he became responsible to the Government for the amount, which resulted in Capt. Brisban becoming poor and penniless. All the papers pertaining to his military services were sent to Washington for the purpose of securing a pension, but unfortunately lost. * * * Capt. Brisban was twice married and left issue by both."

MACFARLANE.—In will book A, Dauphin county records, is the following:

"We do certify that Edward McFarlan was born and lived in the parish of Loughgully and county of Armagh—that his parents are honest, reputable people, and we do believe the bearer to be a sober, honest young man. We also certify that he has not left this country on acct. of any misconduct whatsoever.

"Dated this 21st of May, 1783.

WALTER SIPPIT,
High Sheriff Armagh.
JOHN HIGERS,
Pastor of Loughgully these
17 years past.

JOHN McCOMBE, Clk.

To these are also attached the following names:
 Robert Martin,
 John Reed,
 William Ham'l Hanna,
 John Caulfield,
 Morris Nclory,
 Hugh O'Hanlon.

Can any one give us information as to this Edward McFarlan, or Macfarlane, whose certificate of good character has thus been preserved?

INDIAN NAMES OF STREAMS IN DAUPHIN COUNTY.

Omitting the origin of Susquehanna, or rather its Indian meaning, we present herewith the derivation of the streams within, or contingent to the county of Dauphin. To that devoted Moravian missionary, Heckewelder, are we chiefly indebted for the meagre knowledge we have of Indian signification given in the names to mountains, rivers and localities by the Aborigines. It will be seen that we have not alluded to Powell's, Armstrong's and Clark's creeks. As yet we have no knowledge of the names conferred on them by the Indians, although we have no doubt they, too, were properly designated by the primeval race.

MAHANTANGO corrupted from *Mohantanga*, signifying *where we had plenty to eat.*

WICONISCO corrupted from *Wikenkniskeu*, signifying *a wet and muddy camp.* (Probably some Indians encamped along the creek where the bank was wet and muddy.)

SWATARA, written in old deeds LSTURARA and *Suataro;* in Susquehanna, *Swahadowry*, corrupted from *Schaha-dawa, i. e., where we fed on eels.*

CONEWAGO, or Conewaugha in Iroquois, *at the place of the rapids.* From this fact there are several streams emptying into the Susquehanna, so named.

MANADA, or Monody, corrupted from *Menatey*, signifying *an island.*

STONY CREEK. In Delaware, *Sinnehanne* or *Achsin-hanne, i. e., stony stream.*

FISHING CREEK. In Delaware, *Nameeshanne, i. e., fish stream.* There are six or seven streams of this name in Pennsylvania.

PAXTANG, Delaware, from *Peckstank* or *Peshtank*, signifying *where the waters stand*—the place of dead water, whether in a stream, or pool, or lake.

BEAVER CREEK. In Delaware, *Sangamochke, i. e., little beaver stream.*

RACCOON CREEK. In Delaware, *Nachenum-hanne, i. e., raccoon stream.*

COL. JOSEPH C. AUDENREID.

The death of an esteemed correspondent of *N. & Q.*, Col. Joseph C. Audenreid, has been announced, and we feel it a duty incumbent on us, to briefly allude to the main incidents of his useful life. Joseph Crain Audenreid, the son of William Audenreid and Jane Maria Wills, was born at Pottsville, Schuylkill county, Penn'a, on the 6th of November, 1839. His father was a member of the State Senate for several years, and one of the leaders in the establishment of the System of Public Education in Pennsylvania. His mother was a daughter of 'Squire Alexander Wills, who lived and died in the large stone house opposite the city of Harrisburg, some distance below the Cumberland Valley R. R. bridge. The son, after receiving a preliminary education at Dickinson College, was appointed to West Point in 1857, from which institution he graduated June 24th, 1861, and shortly after sent into the field as second lieutenant of the 4th, now the 1st, cavalry; afterwards commissioned as first lieutenant and adjutant of the 6th cavalry, with rank from date of graduating.

He immediately entered upon active duty and served in various capacities during the Rebellion of the seceding States, 1861–1865. He was successively on the staffs of Generals D. Tyler, E. V. Sumner, John E. Wool, U. S. Grant and W. T. Sherman. He was promoted in 1866 to the rank of captain of the 6th United States Cavalry, and in 1869 was breveted colonel and aid-de-camp to General Sherman.

Since 1869 Col. Audenreid has been stationed at Washington City, being chief of the staff of the Lieutenant General. During these years of relaxation from active military service, he became much interested in historical and genealogical research. Besides preparing material for a biography of his father, he had almost completed a Genealogical Record of his own and allied families. In this work he was largely aided by a few friends, and had gathered together considerable information relating to the Wallaces, Fultons, Gillmors, Boyds, Buffingtons, Clarkes, Grahams and other families identified with the history of this locality. After all his labor and research, it would be an unfortunate circumstance if the data thus gleaned should not be put into a shape for permanent preservation. Deeply interested in his own family history, Col. Audenreid was quite enthusiastic in the development of everything which related to the history of Paxtang, Hanover and Derry. He had a high veneration for the last resting-places of his ancestry, and several years ago the time-defaced tombstones which marked the spot of his honored dead in old Paxtang Church graveyard, were, by his direction, chiseled anew and reset. As an officer, he was brave and chivalric; as a citizen, honorable and upright; and as a friend, sincere and faithful. May the earth lie lightly over his breast. Col. Audenreid died at the city of Washington on the 3d of June, 1880, aged forty years, and was interred at West Point on the 6th.

NOTES AND QUERIES—LI.

PATTERSON—POTTER—MOORE.—Mary Patterson, widow of James Patterson, of "Fermanagh, Cumberland county," died in April, 1785. Her will was probated at Harrisburg on the 29th of April. In it she mentions the following children:
 i. William.
 ii. Margaret, m. Gen. James Potter.
 iii. Susanna, m. James Moore.
 iv. James.
Inquiry is made as to the maiden name of Mrs. Mary Patterson, and further information concerning William, James, and Susanna Patterson.

SEILER.—Henry Seiler, a native of the town of Weisenburg, old Alsace, Germany, came to this country with his brother Christopher prior to the Revolution. He died at Lebanon in June, 1785, his will being probated July 7, following. He left a wife Catharine, to whom, and to his brother Christopher, his estate was devised, save ten pounds to the Lutheran Church at Lebanon. Provision was made for his son Andrew, who remained at Weisenburg, should he come to America. Henry Buehler and Christopher Seiler were executors of the estate. Information is requested whether Andrew Seiler came to this country, and also as to the children of Christopher Seiler above named.

THE SWORD OF DERRY.—"The daughter of John Sawyer who married John McCord, Hanover, reminds me of a bit of history. John McCord's great grandfather was one of the Protestants who was at the siege of Londonderry when the Catholics determined to kill every Protestant in Ireland. Without referring to the siege of Derry, I believe it was about 1660 or 1666. I often had the sword in my hand which old Mr. McCord used in that siege. I got my son James to hunt up the family of John McCord in Preble county, O., and obtain possession of the sword, and have it placed among the curiosities of one of our colleges as a relic of the olden time. My son James, however, did not succeed in getting possession of the sword. It appears that Mr. McCord sometime previous to his decease removed from his old house, leaving the sword hang, when it was stolen."—*Samuel Barnett's Ms. Letter.*

CLOKEY.—"The widow of William Sawyer married Joseph Clokey, who left Ireland at the time of the Rebellion of '98, immediately after the battle of Belaney Hench. I was quite a boy at the time, but remember hearing all about the case. He escaped almost by miracle to this country. Mr. Clokey's daughter Eliza came subsequently to this country. She married a Mr. Hughes, near Canonsburg, Pa., and deceased there, leaving two or three children. Mrs. Clokey was a cousin of my mother's. She had by this second marriage two sons and one daughter. The daughter Mary married Rev. Mr. Wilson, of Canonsburg, and died about 1866. Mr. Clokey removed from where he lived near Hanover church to Canonsburg about 1813 or 1814. Mr. and Mrs. Clokey deceased there a number of years ago. Their son, John Clokey, married and had a family. His widow resides in Springfield, Ohio. Joseph Clokey, the other son, took a college course at Canonsburg, studied theology, joined the Associate Reformed Church at the time the union was consummated between the Associate and Associate Reformed Church, now the United Presbyterian Church. He afterwards became Professor of Pastoral Theology in the United Theological Seminary at Xenia, O. He has been twice married. His first wife was a Patterson, by whom he had a son and daughter. The former died at Springfield, Ohio; the daughter married a Mr. Henry, and removed to Illinois. Dr. Clokey married secondly a Miss Waddell, from near Wheeling, by whom he had three sons and two daughters. One son is preaching at Steubenville, Ohio, another at Indianapolis, and the third is a lawyer. The Rev. Dr. Clokey is the oldest minister in Springfield [1867] and an able divine."—*Samuel Barnett.*

NOTES AND QUERIES.—LII.

KLOPPEN CHURCH.—In the published list of "Letters remaining in the Postoffice, Harrisburg, October 14, 1799," is a letter for "Jacob Wenger, near Kloppen church." Can any one inform us of the location of this church?

HORTER (N. & Q. xlix).—In his reminiscences, our "Octogenarian,' furnishes the following: "George R. Horter, the son of John Valentine Horter and the brother of Mrs. Jacob Bucher and Mrs. Henry Beader, learned the hatting trade I presume, with Mr. Bucher, though I am not sure of that. He left Harrisburg when very young as a traveling 'jour,' and immortalized himself at that early day by going to Pittsburgh, thence down the Ohio and Mississippi to New Orleans, a most perilous adventure at that time—and returned somewhere about 1807 or 1808 as a wonderful traveler. To go to New Orleans then was to go out of the world; and while absent he was given up for lost, but when he returned he was like one that was found. In 1808 Simon Snyder was elected Governor over James Ross. Mr. Beader was appointed Register and Recorder of Dauphin county, and Mr. Horter being on hand, was appointed clerk and filled the post for many years. He was a very clever gentlemen—fond of gay life, and constantly spouting Shakespeare—" Now is the winter of our discontent," &c., was generally his beginning. During the war of 1812 he was an officer of the United States army, as a lieutenant; and I think was at the battle of Lundy's Lane. He was fond of the drum and fife, and of military display. He commenced to study law with Mr. Ellmaker, but did not wade through. A thorough Democrat, he was always on hand at elections—was Transcribing Clerk to the Senate or House a number of years. He was much loved and cherished by his immediate relatives, who thought there was nobody equal to Uncle George. He belonged to the Masonic order, and proud of its emblems. He never married and died a bachelor."

THE CUMBERLAND VALLEY HISTORICAL SOCIETY, organized one year ago, propose celebrating the settlement of the Cumberland Valley by a meeting at Doubling Gap Springs, beginning on the 1st of July. The place at which the society's meetings are held prevent the attendance of many who might otherwise be present. An out of the way place like Doubling Gap is not the proper point for these meetings, none save those whose leisure will allow being able to get there. Some central location along the line of the Cumberland Valley would have secured the attendance of many who take a deep interest in developing the abundant historical resources of the Valley. Judge Herman, of Carlisle, the president of the society, is to deliver the opening address; Gen. George Snowden, of Philadelphia, the patriotic address, and Prof. Wm. M. Nevin, of Lancaster, will read a paper on the "Romance of the Valley." No section of our glorious old State is so rich in historic lore as the beautiful Valley of Cumberland, and why the history and genealogy thereof should be supplanted by the *romantic*, we are at a loss to conceive. *History is truth*, and the sooner historical societies discard legendary, traditionary and romantic theories, and devote their time to the collection and collation of *facts*, the more good will they accomplish. If Prof. Nevin will take up the biographical records of Generals Wm. Irvine, Wm. Thompson, John Armstrong, Henry Miller and Robt. Magaw, Revolutionary patriots, every one of them; pursue the incidents in the life of Colonel George Croghan, Assistant Deputy of Indian Affairs, during the most trying period of the early history of the Valley; or the early settlements of the same, from the Susquehanna to the Conecocheague, without encroaching upon the last hundred years, and he will find that his "Romance" will not pass as "dry as dust," and he will be doing valiant services in the cause of history and add to the renown of the Cumberland Valley. The society has a wide field of usefulness before it, but where are the reapers?

BIOGRAPHICAL HISTORY OF DAUPHIN COUNTY—IV.

LAIRD, SAMUEL, the son of Samuel Laird, was born at Carlisle' Penn'a, on the 15th of February, 1769. His father was for many years one of the Provincial magistrates of Cumberland county, and, under the Constitution of 1776, one of the justices of the courts. Mr. Laird received a classical education, studied law at Carlisle, and was admitted to the Dauphin county bar at the September term, 1792. He located at Harrisburg, and soon secured a large and successful practice. In the early years of the borough he took an active part in its local affairs, and was a prominent actor in the first decade of its history. He died at Harrisburg, January 15, 1815, aged forty-five years. He married Elizabeth Montgomery, second daughter of Rev. Joseph Montgomery, who died October 12, 1814, aged forty-four. Their remains lie interred in the Harrisburg cemetery. Mr. Laird was a good lawyer, a pleasant speaker, and a courteous, honorable gentleman of the old school.

LAUMAN, WILLIAM, the son of George and Elizabeth Lauman, early settlers at Middletown, was born in that borough on the 18th of June, 1772. He learned the trade of a hatter in Philadelphia, where he became acquainted with Elizabeth Meyers and married her. He then returned to Middletown, where he carried on a successful business. He was chosen to the Legislature in 1827, serving two terms, having previously been County Auditor, 1822 to 1825. Mr. Lauman kept the "stage office" near Center Square, and on the 24th of December, 1829, succeeded John McCammon as postmaster, an office he held until his death, which occurred on the 13th of December, 1832. He was succeeded by his widow, who filled the position until June, 1834, when she removed from the borough. Mrs. Lauman died at Morgan's Corners, near Philadelphia, on the 4th of July, 1853. Her remains rest by those of her husband in the old Lutheran graveyard in Middletown. They had nine children, four of whom are living. The late Major George M. Lauman was one of their sons. Mr. Lauman was an industrious and enterprising citizen, hospitable, generous and social.

LEWIS, ELI, was a native of York county, Penn'a, born about 1750, and the first settler of the town of Lewisberry. He was a printer by profession, and has the honor of establishing the first newspaper in this city—the *Harrisburg Advertiser*, in 1789. This was purchased by Mr. Wyeth in 1792 and changed to "The Oracle of Dauphin and Harrisburg Advertiser." Major Lewis was a soldier of the Revolution, and a gentleman of considerable literary acquirements. He was the author of a poem, entitled "St. Clair's Defeat," printed in a small 32mo at his office, copies of which are exceedingly rare. He died at his residence at Lewisberry on Sunday, February 2, 1807, aged fifty-seven years. He was the father of Chief Justice Ellis Lewis of the Supreme Court of Penn'a.

McCAMMON, JAMES, of Scotch ancestry, was a native of the county Down, Ireland, born about 1778. He was educated at Edinburg, and received his degree of Doctor of Medicine at the University of that city. He subsequently served two years in the London Hospital under that celebrated physician Dr. Fordyce. He came to the United States about 1804, and located at Newville, in Cumberland county, where he had a very general and extensive practice. In September, 1811, he removed to Middletown, where his brother John resided and was postmaster, at that period a preferable field to the Cumberland Valley, and was very successful. He died at Middletown on the 7th of November, 1815, and was buried in the old Presbyterian graveyard on High street in that borough. He left a wife and three children, who afterwards removed to Zanesville, Ohio. Dr. McCammon was a skillful surgeon and ranked high in his profession. Socially, he was agreeable in conversation and of refined manners.

MAGINNIS, JAMES, was a native of Ireland, born about 1780. He was educated at Dublin, and at the age of twenty came to America, locating in Philadelphia, where he began the profession of teaching. In 1807 or 8 he was invited to take charge of the Harrisburg Academy, but in 1810 relinquished his position there and entered into mercantile business with his brother-in-law, Fred. W. Leopold. Subsequently, about 1814, he resumed school teaching, and all his energies for a number of years were devoted to that calling. It was during that period that he compiled his "System of Book-Keeping," and the "New Arithmetic," both published at Harrisburg, which for many years was extensively used as text books in Central Pennsylvania. In 1821, Mr. Maginnis was appointed Deputy Surveyor of Dauphin county. He had previously been surveyor for several State commissions authorized to lay out certain roads, as also county boundaries. He studied law at Harrisburg and was admitted at the March term, 1820. His wife, Ann Brandon, a woman of rare accomplishments and lovely disposition, to whom he was fondly devoted, dying March 18, 1828, so preyed upon his mind that he sank under the affliction, and died the 21st of May, 1829. Mr. Maginnis was a gentleman of undoubted integrity, an able teacher, and a good citizen.

MAHER, PIERCE, was a native of Ireland, born about 1813, where he received a classical education. He came to this country in 1836, and shortly after began the study of theology in Philadelphia; and subsequently appointed pastor of St. Patrick's church, Harrisburg. Until the establishment of the bishopric of Harrisburg, for a period of thirty-two years, the Rev. Maher was the beloved and revered pastor of that church, and the writer of this sketch holds in his affection and memory the most pleasing recollection and warm friendship of that pious and devoted minister of the Gospel of Christ. From Harrisburg Rev. Maher went to Norristown, where he remained unitl his death, which occurred on the 28th of December, 1873, at the age of sixty.

MELISH, JOHN, was born in Perthshire, Scotland, on the 13th of June, 1771. He was educated at Edinburg. He came to America in 1809, and traveled extensively through the United States and Canada, publishing in 1812, in two volumes, an account thereof. In 1814 he published "A Description of the Roads" described in his former volumes. This was followed by the "Traveler's Directory" in 1815; "Descriptions of the U. S.," 1816; "Universal School Geography and Atlas," 1817; "Necessity of Protecting Manufactures," 1818 "Maps of Penn'a and the U. S.," and "Information to Emigrants," in 1819; and "Statistical review of the U. S.," in 1822. He subsequently published a number of county maps of Pennsylvania by aid from the State, and projected others. He died at Harrisburg on the 30th of December, 1832, aged seventy-one. As a geographer and political economist Mr. Melish was highly esteemed, and numerous learned societies enrolled him among their membership.

MONTGOMERY, RACHEL, the eldest daughter of John and Rachel Rush, was born at Byberry, in Philadelphia county, Penn'a, in 1741. She was full sister of the celebrated Dr. Benjamin Rush, a signer of the Declaration of Independence. Rachel received an excellent education, and was a woman of refined taste and manners. She married, about 1761, Angus Boyce, a merchant of Philadelphia. He died a few years later, leaving one child, Malcolm. Mrs. Boyce married, about 1769, the Rev. Joseph Montgomery, then pastor of the Presbyterian congregations of New Castle and Christiana Bridge, Delaware, and subsequently member from Pennsylvania in Congress, 1781 to 1783. In 1785 Mr. Montgomery, having been appointed Recorder and Register of the new county of Dauphin, removed with his family to Harrisburg. Here he died, in 1794, leaving his wife with three children, one by his former marriage. Mrs. Montgomery died on Saturday, July 28 1798, at Harrisburg, and the *Oracle* gives this estimate of her character: "In her were united those virtues which beautify and adorn the Christian and human nature. She was invariably mild and affable, amiable and courteous to all. Her communicative and sweet disposition, her benevolent and beneficent heart, led her at least to attempt the character of our blessed Lord, to be going about doing good. In her friendship she was sincere, cordial and constant—in her domestic connections she was yet more amiable and unoffending—as a wife, she was endowed with all the tender sensibilities and kind attentions which can improve and complete matrimonial happiness. As a mother she was remarked by others, and loved by her children for the constant and engaging discharge of all those maternal offices which are generally seen to attract love and command respect—and as a mistress, humane and indulgent. In her tedious and distressing sickness (which lasted ever since the commencement of the past winter to her death) no complaint was heard from her lips. She supported with serenity and fortitude the approach of death, leaning upon the blessed Redeemer as upon the beloved of her soul—she slept in the arms of Jesus, with a cheerful and humble hope of a blessed immortality, aged about fifty-seven years."

MURRAY, JOHN, was a native of Scotland, born about 1731. His father emigrated to America the year following, and settled on Swatara creek, in Hanover township, then Lancaster, now Dauphin county. In 1766 John took up a tract of land lying on the Susquehanna, immediately above his brother James' farm, which adjoined the present town of Dauphin. He commanded a rifle company, which in March, 1776, was attached to Col. Samuel Miles' battalion, and participated in the battles of Long Island, White Plains, Trenton and Princeton. He was promoted to major, April 18, 1777, and lieutenant colonel of the Second Pennsylvania regiment in 1780, serving until the disbanding of the army in 1783. He then returned to his family and farm. Gov. Mifflin appointed him a justice of the peace August 29, 1791, the only political office he ever held. He died on the 3d of February, 1798, in his sixty-eighth year, and his remains rest in the cemetery near the borough of Dauphin. Col. Murray married, 29th of December, 1762, Margaret, daughter of Andrew and Rebecca Mayes. She died June 22d, 1807, aged seventy-four years. They had—*Margaret*, m. John, son of Capt. James Murray; *William*, who removed to Ohio; and *Rebecca*, m. Hon. Innis Green. Col. Murray was an ardent patriot and a gallant officer.

PEACOCK, JAMES, the eldest son of William Peacock and Mary Kyle, of Scotch-Irish ancestry, was born in Paxtang township, Dauphin county, Penn'a, April 8, 1788. His education was in a great measure due to his mother's care and tuition, with self-application in after years. At the age of fifteen he began to learn the printing business with Mr. Edward Cole, of Lewistown, where he remained until 1807, when he went to Lancaster to work on the *Intelligencer*. In 1809 he was employed by the celebrated John

Binns, of Philadelphia, on book work, and subsequently by Mr. Dinnie on the *Port Folio.* While in the latter establishment he became intimate with quite a number of the literati of that period, and concerning whom he has left some interesting "Reminiscences." In 1811 Mr. Peacock returned to Lancaster and from thence came to Harrisburg, where in December of that year he started the *Pennsylvania Republican,* which he continued to publish for about eight or nine years, in the meantime being one of the printers to the Senate and House. In December, 1821, he was employed as an assistant clerk of the Senate, and in March, 1822, received the appointment of postmaster at Harrisburg in place of Mrs. Wright, who had recently deceased, an office he held under different National administrations until the 15th of November, 1846. In December, 1847, he removed to Philadelphia, where he became identified with the publication of the *Evening Bulletin* (now being conducted by his son, Mr. Gibson Peacock), *The Sun,* and *Neal's Saturday Gazette,* which he managed with all the tact and skill of his earlier years, relinquishing his labors only a brief time prior to his death. He died in the city of Philadelphia, on the 23d of August, 1863, and is interred in the Harrisburg cemetery. Mr. Peacock was twice married—first, to Frances C., daughter of Matthias Slough and Mary Gibson, of Lancaster, who died Oct. 27, 1837; and, secondly, to Mrs. Louisa V. Sims, of Mount Holly, N. J., who died 1869. Mr. Peacock was ever held in high esteem by the citizens of Harrisburg, whether as journalist, or his occupancy of the post office for a quarter of a century. He always took an active part in public affairs, and was largely instrumental in organizing St. Stephen's Episcopal Church, in which there has been erected a tablet to his memory. He was a gentleman of dignified manners, of refined culture and a sincere Christian.

RAMSEY, THOMAS, was born near York, Pennsylvania, on the 15th of June, 1784. With a limited education, acquired during his early years, he learned the trade of blacksmithing, at that period an important occupation. About 1806 he located at Hummelstown, Dauphin county, and there carried on business. In 1814 he was a corporal of Capt. Moorhead's company, of the First Regiment, Col. Kennedy, which marched to the defense of Baltimore. Mr. Ramsey died at Hummelstown on the 4th of May, 1826, at the age of forty-two years. He married Elizabeth Kelker, daughter of Henry Kelker and Elizabeth Greenawalt, of Lebanon, born Sept. 8th, 1791, and died at Harrisburg, 5th of February, 1858. Hon. Alexander Ramsey, present Secretary of War, is their son. Mr. Ramsey was an industrious, enterprising citizen, patriotic, generous, and held in great esteem by his fellow citizens.

NOTES AND QUERIES.—LIII.

The First Communion of Covenanters observed in this country, and indeed outside of the British Isles, was on the 23d of August, 1752, at Stony Ridge, in Cumberland county, Pennsylvania, and although there was but a handful of people in that "society," yet more than two hundred and fifty persons communed. J. B. S.

Politics in 1799.—Harrisburg has for a long while been noted for the political proclivities of its citizens; eighty years of such reputation should give us good standing in that line. A long while ago many of them were keen politicians, and as at present, happy to take a hand in what was in reality, the first political contest in the State, as previously "Mifflin and the fathers" had it all in their own hands. When Governor Mifflin had finished his constitutional term this contest opened. In our own part of the State a circular was issued inviting the people of then Dauphin county, in favor of Thomas McKean for Governor, to a county meeting at the house of "Samuel Weir, in Harrisburg, on the Thursday of next court." The circular is dated August 24, 1799, signed by John Elder, chairman; Jacob Bucher, secretary. The committee appointed to circulate the document named in the MSS. are Robt. Harris, John Luther, Moses Gillmor, Henry Beader, Stacy Potts, William Wray, P. Brecker, David Rowland, William Connolly and George Peffer, of Harrisburg. The circular comes out boldly for McKean, who was elected. In turning over the newspaper containing an account of the meeting, it is curious to observe how many of the participants became, in after years, opponents of McKean and his policy. H.

Early Correspondence.—The following letter of John Harris, the founder, to Col. James Burd, has never been printed. It has really no local interest, but its reference to events then transpiring makes it nevertheless interesting:

Paxtang, *Nov. 15th, 1757.*

Dear Sir: I am just arrived from Philadelphia. No news of Importance; the Troops from the Northward are Part arrived in Philada., such as are to be quartered there this Winter; & three companies if not more of the first Battalion of y'r Royal American Regiment from Carlisle is to pass here next Thursday on their way to Winter Quarters in Philada. The 2d Battalion is to soon follow &

remain at Lancaster, excepting some who is by the General Report to be at York, Reading, etc., this Winter.

We have acc'ts of our Grand English Fleet sailing, in September last, on a secret Expedition, & good accounts soon expected from them.

No Battles lately in Europe, except skirmishing between us, the French, Prussians, Austrians, Russians, &c., tho' it's currently Reported, and Generally Believed, that ab't Seventy thousand Turks is actually on their march against the Queen of Hungary, & a Larger army of Turks & Tartars is also marching against the Russians, to make a Diversion on the side of Prussia. Good accounts are also expected from his Prussian majesty, tho' his Enemys is numerous, on all sides. The French seems to be yet too strong for the Turks in Hanover; but considering their Numbers, Greater Strokes might have been Expected from them.

We have been Tolerable Quiet on all the frontiers this long time (from Indian Incursions). The Barracks in Philada. in great Forwardness.

I am, Sir, your most obd't Humble Serv't,

JOHN HARRIS.

P. S. Mrs. Shippen and Mrs. Burd & familys well yesterday. I am, sir, yr., &c., &c.

To MAJOR JAMES BURD, at Fort Augusta.

BIOGRAPHICAL HISTORY OF DAUPHIN COUNTY.—V.

REILY, JOHN, was born at Leeds, England, on the 12th of April, 1752. His father, Benjamin Reily, emigrated soon after, and was a gentleman of some note in the Province of Pennsylvania. Receiving a classical education the former began the study of law, and was admitted to the bar on the eve of the Revolution. Accepting a commission as captain in the 12th regiment of the Pennsylvania Line, subsequently (1778) transferred to the Third regiment he served with valor and distinction, and was severely wounded at Bonhamton, New Jersey, being shot through the body. Returning home, he slowly recovered, when he resumed the practice of his profession. He was present and took part in the first term of the Dauphin county court, in May, 1785. In 1795, he published at Harrisburg, "A Compendium for Pennsylvania Justices of the Peace," the first work of that character printed in America. Capt. Reily died at Myerstown, May 2, 1810. He married at Lancaster by Rev. Thomas Barton, of the Episcopal Church, on May 20, 1773, Elizabeth Myer, the daughter of the founder of Myerstown, Lebanon county, born April 2, 1775; died April 2, 1800. They had a large family. Dr. Luther Reily, so well known to our oldest citizens, was their son. Capt. Reily was not a brilliant orator, but was perfectly reliable as a lawyer, and had an extensive practice at the Lancaster, Berks and Dauphin courts. He was a tall, courtly gentleman, and an ardent Whig, of the Revolutionary era. He was a polished writer, and a MSS. book of literary excerpts in the possession of his descendants show a refined and cultivated taste.

ROAN, JOHN, was born in Ireland in the year 1716. He was brought up as a weaver, and emigrated to Pennsylvania about 1740. He entered the "Log College," and taught school on the Neshaminy and in Chester county, while pursuing his theological studies. He was licensed by the "new-side" Presbytery of New Castle, and in the Winter of 1744 sent to Hanover, Virginia. The following year (1745) he was settled over the united congregations of Derry, Paxtang and Conewago, the latter having one-fifth of his time. The minutes of the synods placed Roan in Donegal Presbytery, and "points of difficulty," says Webster, "continually arose." Towards the latter days of his ministry Mr. Roan missionated frequently on the south branch of the Potomac. He died on the 3d of October, 1775, and is interred at Derry church graveyard. On his tombstone is this inscription:

"Beneath this stone | are deposited the Remains | of an able, faithful | courageous & successful | minister of Jesus Christ | The Rev'd John Roan | Pastor of Paxtang, Derry & Mount Joy | Congregations | from the year 1745 | till Oct. 3, 1775 | when he exchanged | a Militant for a triumphant | Life | in the 59th year of his Age."

The Rev. John Roan married Ann, daughter of James Cochran and Ann Rowan, of Chester county, born in 1722; she died in 1788.

JOHN SHOCH, of German ancestry, was born in the city of Philadelphia on the 27th of December, 1763. In 1792 he located at Harrisburg, engaging in active business pursuits. During the "mill dam troubles" in 1794-5, Mr. Shoch took a prominent part, and was on the committee to confer with the owners and abate the nuisance. For a long time he was a member of the town council, borough supervisor and one time burgess. He was director of the poor, and county commissioner, serving the usual terms, when he was chosen treasurer of the county, an office he filled acceptably from 1812 to 1815. In 1810 he was appointed one of the commissioners to survey what was then termed the Northern and Southern routes from Harrisburg to Pittsburgh, to ascertain the most practicable and preferable one for a turnpike. The commissioners reported in favor of the

Southern route, but when the Legislature met it was thought best to charter companies to turnpike both. Mr. Shoch labored hard and successfully for the removal of the seat of government to Harrisburg, for the erection of the bridge over the Susquehanna, the establishment of the Harrisburg Bank, of which he was one of its first directors, and the Harrisburg Academy, being a trustee for many years. Mr. Shoch retired from business about 1825. He died at Harrisburg, Tuesday, August 31, 1841. He married, in 1792, Salome Gilbert, of Philadelphia. She died at Harrisburg, October 13, 1828. They are both buried in the Harrisburg cemetery. Of their children one survived, Col. Samuel Shoch, of Columbia. Mr. Shoch always took a deep interest in the affairs of the town and county, and was highly esteemed by his fellow-citizens as a strictly honest and upright gentleman.

SENECA G. SIMMONS, was a native of Windsor, Vermont, where he was born December 27, 1808. He entered West Point, graduated therefrom in 1834, and was assigned to the Seventh U. S. Infantry. He served in the Florida and Mexican wars with marked credit, and properly promoted therefor. At the time of the breaking out of the Rebellion in 1861, Capt. Simmons was at his home at Harrisburg laboring under a severe injury. Upon the organization of the famous Reserve Corps, he was chosen Colonel of the Fifth Regiment. For his conduct in the Autumn campaign of 1861, he was promoted Major of the Fourth U. S. Infantry. During the Peninsular campaign of 1862, under General McClellan, while leading the first brigade of the Reserves, at Charles City X Roads, June 20th, he fell in the thickest of the fight, breathing his last upon the field of honor. His remains were buried beneath a large tree, but being unmarked, was not distinguished among the thousand who sleep their last sleep on the Chickahominy. The loss of Colonel Simmons was greatly lamented. He was a gallant and brave officer, and had he been spared, would have done valiant service in the cause of the Union.

WILLIAM SIMONTON, the elder, was born in county Antrim, Ireland, in 1755. He was brought to this country at the age of ten, by his uncle, the Rev. John Simonton, pastor of the Great Valley Presbyterian church, in Chester county, Penna. Under the direction of this uncle he received his academic and professional education. Soon after completing his medical course he entered upon the practice of his profession, but at what place is unknown. On the 17th of November, 1777, he was married to Jane Wiggins, daughter of John Wiggins, sr., of Paxtang, his uncle performing the ceremony. In 1784 he purchased a tract of land called "Antigua," containing one hundred and eighty-two acres, situated in West Hanover township, from Joseph Hutchison. Upon this farm he resided all his life. He had eight children, six of whom reached mature age, viz: *Jane, Thomas, James, William, John W.,* and *Elizabeth.* Dr. Simonton died on the 24th of April, 1800, at the early age of forty-five. All the traditions that have reached us concerning his standard as a physician, a man and a Christian, are highly favorable. A fitting testimonial to his life, labors and character, was prepared by the Rev. James Snodgrass, pastor of Hanover church, and delivered on the occasion of his funeral. His remains with those of his wife are interred in the old Hanover graveyard.

SIMPSON, JOHN, son of James and Mary Simpson, was born in Newtown or Buckingham township, Bucks county, Penn'a, about 1744. His parents went South, and were residing in North Carolina in 1783, and in Georgia in 1791. He learned blacksmithing, and, in 1763, settled on the Susquehanna in what was then Upper Paxtang township, Lancaster, now Dauphin county. On the 15th of August, 1775, he was commissioned second lieutenant of Capt. James Murray's company, in the Fourth Battalion of Associators of Lancaster county. On the 28th of January, 1777, Lieut. Colonel Cornelius Cox, of the battalion, ordered him to remain in the "Continental Smith shop" at Bristol. He served during the greater part of the Revolution, towards its close in command of a company of militia, when he returned to his farm. In the Spring of 1793 he removed to Huntingdon, Penn'a, where he died on the 3d of February, 1807, in his sixty-third year. Capt. Simpson married May 7, 1776, Margaret Murray, daughter of Capt. James Murray. They had two sons, James and John, and six daughters, four of the daughters respectively married to John Patton, George Anshutz, Daniel Africa (father of Hon. J. Simpson Africa), and William Curry.

SNODGRASS, JAMES, the son of Benjamin Snodgrass, was born near Doylestown, Bucks county, Penn'a, July 23, 1763. He graduated at the University of Penn'a in 1783, and was for a brief time a tutor therein. He studied theology under direction of the Rev. Nathaniel Irwin, then pastor of the church at Neshaminy, and licensed to preach the Gospel by the Presbytery of Philadelphia, in December, 1785. After preaching about a year and a half in destitute places in the central and northern parts of New York, on the 16th of October, 1787, he accepted the call of the Hanover congregation of May previous, and until his ordination on the 13th of May, 1788, he gave his attention to that church. At his installation there were present of the Presbytery of Carlisle, the revered and honored ministers, Revs. John Elder, John Hoge, John Linn, John Craighead, Robert Cooper and Samuel Waugh. His pastorate extended over a period of fifty-eight years, and he was the last who ministered at Hanover. His death occurred July 2, 1846, and he lies interred in the old Hanover church graveyard. The Rev. Snodgrass was twice married. His first wife Martha Davis, born November 12, 1760, died December 20, 1828; his second wife Nancy, born in 1770, died January 24, 1839, and both are interred in the same graveyard. In appearance Mr. Snodgrass was tall, erect and athletic; hair dark, which changed to an iron grey in his last years; of pleasing countenance, amiable and sociable, and in his mode of living temperate, simple and regular. "His sermons were methodical, clear, scriptural, spiritual and evangelical; his voice and enunciation were good." As a minister he was dearly beloved and highly revered.

STEWART, LAZARUS, the second son of James Stewart and Margaret Stewart, was born in Hanover township, now Dauphin county, Penn'a, in 1734. His maternal grandfather, Lazarus Stewart, was one of the earliest settlers on the Swatara, and the owner of large tracts of land. The grandson was well grounded in the essentials of a good English education, and was raised a farmer. In 1755 he raised a company for the Provincial service in Braddock's campaign, and during the subsequent French and Indian war performed valiant service. The part Captain Stewart took in the transactions at Conestoga and Lancaster in December, 1763, has made him a prominent personage in the history of Pennsylvania during that period. He subsequently, in company with a number of Hanover families, removed to Wyoming, where he took sides with the Connecticut settlers. In the Revolution he was an active partisan, but fell at the head of his troops in that terrible onslaught the Massacre of Wyoming, July 3, 1778. Capt. Stewart was one of the bravest of the heroes of "Seventy-six," although impetuous and rash at times. Despite all the calumny Quaker historians can heap on his prominent position in the history of the Province, there are thousands who honor and revere his memory for the part he took in the defense of their ancestors from the Indian's tomahawk and scalping knife.

TRIMBLE, JAMES, was born in the city of Philadelphia, July 19, 1755. His father died when he was quite young, leaving a store, which his widow carried on, assisted by her son. When, at the age of fifteen, the secretary of the Provincial land office, James Tilghman, becoming cognizant of the business qualifications of young Trimble, secured him a clerkship in his office, or rather an apprenticeship therein. In 1775 he was a clerk in the office of the Provincial council, and upon the appointment of Colonel Matlack as the first Secretary of the Commonwealth, March 6, 1777, James Trimble became Deputy Secretary, and so continued, by successive re-appointments, down to January 14, 1836, when he was displaced under the administration of Gov. Ritner. During his residence in Harrisburg Mr. Trimble became quite prominent in local and church affairs. For many years he served as trustee and treasurer of the Presbyterian church. He served in public capacity sixty-six years, and his removal no doubt hastened his death, which took place January 25, 1836, in his eighty-first year. His remains are interred in the Harrisburg cemetery. He married April 22, 1782, Clarissa, widow of John Hastings. Her maiden name was Claypoole, and a descendant of Oliver Cromwell. She died at Lancaster, Feb. 6, 1810. Mr. Trimble's records are models of neatness, his papers elaborately endorsed, and filed with great care. The judgment of his contemporaries "that he was a faithful public servant, a man of unimpeachable integrity, of obliging manners, respected by the community at large, and beloved by his family, to whom he had greatly endeared himself by his kindness and affection."

WALKER, THOMAS, son of James Walker, was born in Paxtang township, Dauphin county, Penn'a, 1789. He was brought up a farmer, but about 1810 removed to Harrisburg and began merchandizing. He was captain of the "Harrisburg Volunteers" who in 1814 marched to the defense of Baltimore. He was appointed by Gov. Hiester prothonotary of the county, March 10, 1821, which he held until Jan. 17, 1824. He was elected sheriff the latter year, commissioned Oct. 18, 1824. He died on the 19th of March, 1843, in the fifty-fourth year of his age, and is buried in Paxtang Church graveyard. Captain Walker was an ardent patriot, a popular officer, and an active, enterprising citizen. His wife Mary, born in 1788, died April 1, 1839, and is interred by his side.

NOTES AND QUERIES.—LIV.

OLD STYLE CLOCKS.—I have an upright old-fashioned clock which runs for twenty-eight days. Has upon its face the sun, moon and stars. Months, days, hours and minutes are all told. It was made by "J. Jameson, Columbia." There is no date. It was bought by my father in Harrisburg about 1815. It would no doubt be interesting to many to find out the history of Jameson and his works.

H. A. G.

THE RICHMOND (*Va.*) STANDARD.—There is not a periodical in the Union that is doing such valiant service in the harvest field of history as this most excellent journal. Its columns come freighted with the treasures which our learned friend R. A. Brock, Esq., librarian of the Virginia Historical Society, so industriously collates. The *Standard* is being thus made a rich repository of Virginia History, Biography and Genealogy, and the student of the Future will refer more frequently to its columns than to any work now in existence relating to the Old Dominion. Mr. Brock is sweeping the entire State confining himself to no one locality, and we are astonished at the vast amount of material which comes to his hands. We have one suggestion, however, that Mr. James, the talented editor of the *Standard* transfer the articles as fast as they appear in its columns to page form and print a *limited* number of copies in that shape at intervals of say every two months. They will be eagerly sought for.

SNODGRASS, REV. JAMES (N. & Q., xlvii).—In Sprague's Annals we find this brief memoranda relative to the last official duty of this revered minister of Old Hanover: "He continued in the active discharge of his office until the 25th of May, 1845, when disabled by disease. The only service he attempted afterwards was in May, 1846, at the funeral of his son-in-law, as well as friend and physician, Dr. William Simonton. After the coffin had been lowered to its final resting place, he addressed the people for a few minutes, 'leaning on the top of his staff.' He then sat down upon a tombstone, and having remained a short time to recruit his strength, attempted to walk the distance of a few hundred yards to his own dwelling, but on arriving at the gate, he found it impossible to proceed further—he was carried to his bed, and from this time he gradually declined until the 2d of July, when, in the full possession of his mental faculties and in the joyful hope of a better life, he gently fell asleep, in the eighty-fourth year of his age."

SEVENTY YEARS AGO.—A native of Harrisburg whose recollection goes back over "five and sixty years," gives us a reminiscence which has the merit of being pleasant reading, and a valuable contribution to our local history. He writes:

"Mr. John Wright, the fourth Postmaster at Harrisburg, lived on Front street in the house now owned by J. Brisbin Boyd, next above the house once owned by Stofel Sees, a coachmaker. Mr. Wright, before he became Postmaster, taught school in Mulberry street, in a house adjoining the tavern and hatter shop owned and kept by George Henning, opposite the residence of Adam Boyd, Esq. It was an old white house, with high steps and small porch, and afterwards occupied as a coach manufactory by a Mr. Sommers, who left Harrisburg for Lancaster. It was in the school-room of Mr. W. that I first saw a cannon stove, such as afterwards was used to burn coal in, but in it wood was used. In those days wood alone was used for fuel, and was burned in thick ten plate stoves that were a long time getting hot and a long time in getting cold. The stage always drove from Berryhill's tavern to the postoffice on Front street to receive the mail, and among the horses in the team, as I recollect, was a large black one, very vicious and to keep him from biting the others he was driven with a strong muzzle. About this time, or shortly afterwards, Richard Hilman, called "Big Dick," who bore a very striking resemblance to General Washington, drove six horses in the Philadelphia stage, and that feat was considered a most attractive performance. The house occupied by Mr. Wright had been owned and occupied by Mr. Stacy Potts, a Quaker gentleman, a member, from Dauphin county, of the House of Representatives, and who subsequently removed to Trenton, New Jersey, where he died." It may be added to this allusion to Mr. Potts, that he was a thorough believer in and writer upon balloons as a means of travel. The *Oracle*, in 1792–93, contains many articles upon this subject from his pen. We never heard, however, of his practising aerial feats.

BIOGRAPHICAL HISTORY OF DAUPHIN COUNTY—VI.

WALLACE, WILLIAM, the eldest son of Benjamin Wallace and Elizabeth Culbertson, was born in Hanover township, Lancaster, now Dauphin county, Penn'a, in October, 1768. He received a classical education, studied law at Harrisburg under Galbraith Patterson, and was admitted to the bar at the June term, 1792. He became interested in the Harrisburg and Presqu' Isle Land Company and about 1800 removed to Erie, in the affairs of which place and in the organization of the county he took an active and leading part. About 1810 he returned to Harrisburg, and partly resumed his profession. He was nominated by the Federalists for Congress in 1813, but was defeated. He was elected the first president of the old Harrisburg Bank, and was burgess of the borough at his death, which occurred on Tuesday, May 28, 1816. His remains are interred in Paxtang church graveyard. Mr. Wallace married first, in 1803, Rachel, daughter of Dr. Andrew Forrest. She died at Erie in 1804. He married secondly, in 1806, Eleanor Maclay, daughter of the Hon. William Maclay, who died at Harrisburg in 1823. Mr. Hamilton describes him as "a polite, urbane man of slight frame and precise address." He was the father of the venerable and revered Mrs. Mary DeWitt, widow of Rev. Dr. DeWitt.

The following were the children of Benjamin Wallace and Elizabeth Culbertson:

   i. William, b. Oct., 1768; d. May 28, 1816.
   ii. Benjamin, b. Apr. 14, 1773; d. Aug. 22, 1833.
   iii. Jane, b. Apr. 9, 1775; d. Jan., 1790.
   iv. James, b. ―――― 1777; d. ―――― 1782.
   v. John C., b. Feb. 14, 1779; d. Dec., 1827.
   vi. Alexander Cox, b. Jan. 28, 1782; d. July 3, 1806.

WEIRICK, JACOB, the son of Christian and Margaret Weirick, was born in Bethel township, Lancaster, now Lebanon county, in 1754. He received a fair English education and was brought up as a farmer. During the Revolution he served as a non-commissioned officer in Colonel Greenawalt's battalion, was taken prisoner at Long Island, but shortly after paroled. Upon the organization of the county of Dauphin, he became influential in political affairs and was elected sheriff in 1790. He was a member of the Legislature from 1795 to 1797 and from 1802 to 1806, serving a longer period than any of his successors. About 1807 he removed to Canton township, Washington county, Penn'a, where he purchased a fine tract of land. In his new home he became quite prominent and was twice elected to the House of Representatives. He died at his residence in Washington county, on the 17th of September, 1822, aged sixty-eight years.

WEISE, ADAM, was born in New Goshenhoppen, now Montgomery county, Penn'a, December 23, 1751. On the 2d of February, 1772, he married Margaret Elizabeth Wingerd, of Heidelberg township, Berks county, and the following year removed to Hagerstown, Md. At the breaking out of the Revolution he entered the service as sergeant in the Maryland cavalry. In 1782, Mr. Weise removed to Upper Paxtang township, and settled on the Wiconisco creek, on the road now leading from Cross-Roads to Berrysburg. In 1788, he left the valley and located in Bethel township, Berks county, but about 1796, returned to his old place on the Wiconisco. In 1802 he took up his residence in Millersburg, having previously been appointed by Gov. Mifflin a justice of the peace, an office he held over thirty-four years. His first wife dying March 29, 1828, Mr. Weise married in August following Mrs. Mary Kuehly, of Union county, who died on the 10th of September, 1830. In December that year he married his third wife, Mrs. Catharine Patton, who survived her husband thirty years. 'Squire Weise died October 5, 1833, in his eighty-second year, and was interred in David's Reformed church graveyard. Mr. Weise was a faithful officer and a good citizen.

WIESTLING, SAMUEL CHRISTOPHER, was born in Colba, on the river Saale, in the Duchy of Magdeburg, Lower Saxony, on the 4th of June, 1760. After the usual preparatory studies he entered the University of Leipsic, where he remained seven years. Going to Amsterdam, after examination he received the appointment of assistant surgeon in the Dutch navy. Sailing on a man-of-war for the West Indies, an accident befel the vessel, but with others was rescued by a passing ship, and taken to Philadelphia. Here, in company with a medical friend and comrade named Hoerner, it was proposed to visit the frontier German settlements, in Pennsylvania. They subsequently retraced their way to Philadelphia, but found the vessel on which they were to sail had departed. At this juncture, a gentleman from near the Trappe, Montgomery county, learning of the presence of Dr. Wiestling, sought him requesting him to visit his home. Here he began the practice of medicine, and two years after, in 1790, married Anna Maria Bucher of that locality. About 1792 he removed to Dauphin county and located on a farm at the foot of the first ridge of the Blue mountains, five miles from Harrisburg. There he continued his profession until 1811, when finding a large country practice too laborious, he came to Harrisburg. In 1817 he was stricken with paralysis, which terminated his medical career. He died on the 2d of April, 1823, in his sixty-third year. Dr. Wiestling was an experienced physician, and his practice was extensive and successful. His life was active and useful, and his loss at the time was considered an irreparable one, such was the confidence and esteem in which he was held. He left three sons in the profession, *Samuel C.*, *Joshua M.* and *Benjamin J.*, the latter of whom survives, as also his son *George P.*

WINEBRENNER, JOHN, was born in Frederick county, Md., March 25, 1797. He was partly educated in the Glades school in Frederick, and partly at Dickinson College, Carlisle. He studied for the ministry under Rev. Mr. Helfenstein, in Philadelphia, and was ordained by the Potomac Synod of the Reformed Church in September, 1820, at Hagerstown. That year he was called to Salem church at Harrisburg, at the same time ministering to Shoop's, Wenrick's and the Frieden's churches in the neighborhood. It was during his pastorate that the present church edifice, Third and Chestnut streets, was erected. Mr. Winebrenner ministered there from October 22, 1820, to March 23, 1823, when owing to his religious views on revivals, Sunday schools, anti-slavery and the temperance movement, with the allowing of non-ordained persons to preach in his pulpit, becoming obnoxious to his congregation, a seperation took place. In a number of pamphlets he issued, Mr. Winebrenner vigorously defended his principles from the attacks made right and left by his opponents; and he did not cease therefore "to preach the word." Subsequently his energies were devoted to the establishment of a new denomination, called by him the Church of God, but known in early years as Winebrennarians. He met with a remarkable success, and, although but fifty years have passed since the Rev. John Winebrenner promulgated the doctrines of baptism by immersion and the washing of feet, the ministers of that Church number probably five hundred and the membership well on to sixty thousand. Mr. Winebrenner was the author of a number of religious and controversial works, those on "Regeneration," "Brief Views of the Church of God," and a volume of "Practical and Doctrinal Sermons," being the more important. He edited for several years the *Gospel Publisher*, now the *Church Advocate*. In the early years of his ministry he was an uncompromising opponent of human slavery. The Rev. Mr. Winebrenner died at Harrisburg on the 12th of September, 1860, at the age of sixty-three. Over his remains in the Harrisburg cemetery the denomination have erected a handsome monument.

WHITEHILL, GEORGE, the son of John Whitehill, was born in Salisburg township, Lancaster county, in the year 1760. His father owned land in Paxtang on which the son subsequently settled. He received a good education, and entered mercantile pursuits. He began the hardware business at Harrisburg about 1800, and was quite successful. He was appointed by Governor Snyder, one of the associate judges of the county of Dauphin, October 20, 1817, but on the 30th of July, 1818, with his colleague, Obed Fahnestock, resigned, owing to the commissioning of Judge Franks as president of the court by Governor Findlay that year. Judge Whitehall died at Harrisburg on the 7th of January, 1821. His wife, Abigail, born in 1762, died April 12, 1825. They are both buried in Paxtang church graveyard.

WOOD, NICHOLAS BAYLES, son of James Wood, was a native of Vermont, born April 2, 1792. He was well educated, and came to Harrisburg about 1809, teaching school in the neighborhood. He subsequently took charge of the school of Abiathar Hopkins, who had entered into law partnership with Francis R. Shunk. In the meantime he studied under Mr. Hopkins and was admitted to the Dauphin county bar in October, 1818, and soon acquired an extensive practice. He was appointed by Gov. Shulze Deputy Attorney General for Dauphin county January, 1824, serving until January, 1827. Mr. Wood died at Harrisburg, Saturday, September 1, 1832. aged thirty-nine years. He was a gentleman of fine abilities, and enjoyed the esteem and confidence of his fellow citizens. He married, Dec. 5, 1822, Catharine, daughter of Henry Beader, Esq., who survived.

WRIGHT, JOHN, was a native of Ireland, born about 1745. He came to America in early life and located in New Jersey, where he probably taught school until the opening of the war of the Revolution. He held the position of a quarter master of the New Jersey troops during the struggle for Independence, and at the close of the conflict, settled at Patterson in that State, from which place he removed to Harrisburg about the year 1797, and opened on the 10th of August of that year "an English school in the German school house" there. On the removal of John Wyeth as postmaster by President Adams in 1798, Major Wright was appointed to that office. This he took charge of in connection with his school, holding the office until his death, which occurred on the 4th of January, 1814. He married, at Trenton, N. J., August 14, 1778, Rose Chambers, daughter of Alexander Chambers, one of the leading merchants of that town during the last half of last century. Her mother, Elizabeth Chambers, was one of the matrons who received Washington at the bridge at Trenton, on the 21st of April, 1789. Mrs. Wright was one of Harrisburg's most estimable women, and, on the death of her husband, succeeded to the postoffice, which she retained until her death in March, 1822 (see N. & Q. viii). The venerable widow of the late John M. Forster, Esq., is the only child of Mr. Wright's who survives. Major Wright was an ardent patriot, an excellent teacher, a faithful officer, an active, energetic citizen and one of the leaders of public opinion seventy and eighty years ago.

WYETH, JOHN, a native of Cambridge, Mass., was born March 31, 1770. He was apprenticed to the printing business in the office of the *American Recorder* at Charlestown. In 1788 he went to St. Domingo as foreman on a newspaper, but left during the Insurrection of 1791. The following year he came to Harrisburg, where he was engaged with Major Eli Lewis on the *Harrisburg Visitor*. Purchasing this paper in connection with John W. Allen, a printer, *The Dauphin Oracle and Harrisburg Visitor* appeared in October, 1792, files of which are in existence. In 1793 Mr. Wyeth was appointed postmaster but removed in 1798 by President Adams' Postmaster-General, who was of the opinion that "the position of editor of a newsyaper was incompatible with the office." In addition to the keeping of a book store, and the publishing of pamphlets and books, Mr. Wyeth continued the *Oracle* until 1827, when it was continued by his son, Francis, who conducted it with ability for several years.

Mr. Wyeth subsequently removed to the city of Philadelphia, where he died on the 23d of January, 1858, at the age of eighty-eight years. For one-third of a century Mr. Wyeth was widely known. He was an active, enterprising citizen and a gentleman of superior attainness. He was universally respected for his integrity and uprightments.

NOTES AND QUERIES.—LV.

OLD STYLE CLOCKS (N. & Q. liii.)—H. A. G. wants to know about an "old style clock." In the year 1818 Jacob Jameson, then a single man opened a clock and watch repairing shop along Front street, between Locust and Walnut streets, in the borough of Columbia. He first had his shop on the west side of the street, near where the Continental hotel stands. From thence he removed nearly opposite on the east side of the street. At this time Mr. J. must have been quite a young man, and if he learned his trade in Columbia, it was probably with John Maus, a bachelor, who carried on where Zeller's saloon now is, on Front street above Walnut. Maus was in the habit of getting on periodical sprees, in one of which he hung himself to a fence stake below the town. His family were very respectable, and he left an aged mother to mourn his untimely end. She was the last of the family and died about thirty years ago.

I have no doubt Mr. Jameson came from that good old Scotch-Irish Presbyterian stock of Revolutionary times, who settled in Donegal near Conewago creek and Elizabethtown. They were in Col. Lowrey's Battalion at Brandywine. Jacob Jameson was First Lieutenant in Capt. McGlaughlin's volunteer military company in Columbia. He was full of life and fond of military display.

About 1820 he married Maria Brubaker, a beautiful and attractive young lady of Columbia. He removed from this place to Dayton, Ohio, about the year 1823, at which place he died fifty years ago. His widow was residing there a year ago, and perhaps is still living. The case of this clock was probably made by John S. Atlee, of this place. He was the uncle of Dr. John L. Atlee, of Lancaster. I infer from this date that the Jameson clock did not come into Col. G.'s family until after 1818.

SAMUEL EVANS.

Columbia, Pa., July 12, 1880.

OAK DALE FORGE.

After Andrew Lycans, the first house built at Oak Dale Forge was erected by Henry Shoffstal for Joel Ferree, of Lancaster county, then of the Lycans' tract, about the year 1771. Its location was about seventy-five yards N. W. of where the present bridge crosses the Wiconisco creek. The property was purchased by Mr. Ferree from Jane Lycans, the widow of the old pioneer. On the death of the former, it became the property of Isaac Ferree, of Lancaster county, whose son Isaac, jr., moved into it in 1800. At the period when Andrew Lycans lived on the forge property there was an Indian village on the land now owned by Henry Bohner, and the spring at his house is the head of the run which empties into the head of the Forge dam and called the "Indian town run." This Indian town property when it was abandoned by the Indians was taken up by Joel Ferree, first named.

When the house was built by Mr. Shoffstall, there were few settlers in the neighborhood. There were, however, Shott (now Kottka) George Buffington, near Buffington's church, John Nicholas Hoffman, and Philip Umholtz, near Gratz. In Williams' Valley, the nearest person was Conrad Updegraff at (now) Williamstown, and next Daniel Williams, who had a grist mill there, at or near on the property now owned by Martin Blum, east of Williamstown. Another person about this time, by the name of Daniel Hain, built a saw-mill where the Summit Branch R. R. crosses the creek at Lykens taking the water from Rattling creek, by a race to Wiconisco creek.

Oak Dale Forge was built about the year 1828, by James Buchanan who, at the same time, or the year following, built six or seven houses for his workmen. The houses were located on the south side of the creek, and were occupied by John Ginter, Thomas Nutt, George Conner, Samuel Boon, Joseph Dunlap and others. Mr. Buchannan came from Harrisburg. He subsequently moved to Baltimore, where he died. He kept a store at the Forge and also the postoffice, which latter was established about 1830, the mail being carried by pack-horse. Previous to that time the postoffice was at Millersburg, each neighbor taking his turn to bring the mail from there weekly.

From 1795 to 1800 there were only three houses built between the Forge and Lykens. One was located on the property now of Henry Bohner, and then occupied by Joel Ferree, the younger, who died at Baltimore, in the war of 1812. The second house built by George Setzler on the property now of Isaac Seebolt. The third on property now owned by John Wallace, erected by Peter Shoffstall and occupied by him for a time, subsequently by Peter Minnich. This cabin stood near the old house on Wallace's farm, and was in later years occupied by Solomon Shoffstall, who erected the present old log house on the premises.

The first election held in the valley or in Lykens township, was probably in Gratz about the year 1815. Hoffman's church was the first place of religious worship.
H. B. H.

CAPTAIN BENJAMIN WALLACE.

The families of Wallace who settled in the Swatara region of Pennsylvania, emigrated from county Antrim, Province of Ulster, Ireland, and made location on Swatara, Manada, Bow creeks, between the years 1738 and 1743. We find the names of Andrew, James, Michael, William, John, Robert and Benjamin Wallace of the first generation on the assessments of Paxtang, Derry and Hanover, as early as 1749, and some of the same names continuously to this day. The descendants of these early inhabitants in the female line are quite a marvel, whilst those of the male have shrunk in undue proportion.

The ancestor of Benjamin Wallace was James, who married before he emigrated, 1737-38, and located on the Swatara. He was driven from his home by the Indians in 1756. In 1759 he was again upon his farm as appears by receipts for taxes.

Benjamin was born in 1738—at the time of the raid about eighteen years of age—and as his father's refuge was "the Irish settlements near the Delaware," his son formed such acquaintance there as led him to choose two of his three wives from the daughters of his father's friends. He married, firstly, Letice, who was daughter of John, who was son of James Ralston and Mary Cummock, of Northampton county. She dying, left one child, Mary Wallace, who married James B. Wilson, of Hanover. They removed to Erie about 1800. She died there in 1844 at the age of eighty-five. Captain Wallace married, secondly, in 1767, Elizabeth, daughter of John Culbertson and Ann McNair. When the Revolution occurred, Mr. Wallace entered with the spirit of his race. He held a command in the battle of Long Island, taken prisoner at Fort Washington in November, 1776; captive for nearly a year, when he was exchanged and returned to his family. In December, 1777, he makes application for the discharge of his brother Michael Wallace, who had been "put under guard" for the reason that he had obtained "a warrant for a substitute in Boyd's battalion, for abuse." The Supreme Executive Council granted the application and discharged his brother. In what this "abuse" consisted we are not informed. We do not further hear of him in public or private life until 1780, when he was appointed a magistrate. In the affairs of the Hanover church, on Bow creek, he appears to have taken a deep interest, as his name is found upon nearly all the papers relating to it from 1783 to 1792. In 1785, upon the formation of Dauphin county, he was appointed one of the judges. He retained this station until the adoption of the Constitution of 1790, when the mode of constituting courts was changed. He, however, continued in the commission of the peace until his death.

Mr. Wallace seems to have been a gentleman of fair culture, experienced in public affairs and had a considerable estate. Through his own merits, aided by the importance of his family connection, he was a person influential in the events of his period. He married a third wife in 1784, Rebecca Rush Stamper, widow, daughter of Jacob Rush and one of the sisters of the distinguished Dr. Benjamin Rush. By this marriage there was no family. His family by the Culbertson connection was William, the first president of the Harrisburg bank, Dr. John Culbertson, a physician of great repute in Erie, Major Benjamin, U. S. A., and Alexander, a lawyer, who died young. William and John left descendants. Judge Wallace died December 8, 1803, and is buried in Hanover graveyard on Bow creek. He was taught the trade of wheelwright. The fathers of one hundred years ago never omitted training their sons in some useful avocation.

H.

MARRIAGES IN PAXTANG.

1807–1839.

[We are indebted to Mr. W. Frank Rutherford for the accompanying "Record of Marriages in Paxtang," as kept by Rev. James R. Sharon, from 1807 to 1839, a period of thirty-three years." Concerning the Rev. Sharon, we hope ere long to present a biographical sketch, contenting ourself with this remark—his faithful records of marriages, baptisms, communicants and deaths in Paxtang congregation during his pastorate, show him to have been a painstaking, laborious and God-fearing minister of Christ. That these records have been so carefully preserved is indeed a cause for congratulation. We are confident that the portion herewith presented will be highly prized.]

1807.

June 2. William Espy and Susannah Gray.
June 4. William Boyd and Martha Cowden.
Oct. 31. John Rogers and Dinah Carson.

1808.
April 4. William Moorhead and Jane Wilson.
June 29. John Lyons and Mary Maclay.

1809.
March 30. John Latta and Letitia Stephen.

1810.
Nov. 22. Daniel Elliot and Esther Dickey.

1811.
Feb. 22. William Larned and Dorcas Dickey.
Oct. 29. Benjamin Jordan and Mary Crouch.

1812.
March 24. Robert Simmons and Sarah Ward.
March 24. William Gillmor and Elizabeth Cowden.

1813.
March 4. Thomas Reid and Agnes Ross.
December —. Joseph Sherer and Mary Snodgrass.

1816.
Feb. 29. Matthew Snoddy and Jane Wilson.
April 25. Alexander Piper and Ann Elder.
May 28. Joseph Wallace and Sarah E. Cummins.
June 26. William McNitt and Maria Musgrave.
October 15. ——— Henderson and ——— Shaw.
Dec. 14. David Espy and Rebecca Allen.

1817.
May 20. Williamson Harrison and Jane McKinney.

1818.
Dec. 20. William Boon and Margaret Mahargue.

1819.
Nov. 16. John Cochran and Hannah Cowden.

1820.
March 2. Robert Elder and Elizabeth Sherer.
March 2. John Elder and Jane Ritchey.
May 10. John Hart and Mary Gordon.

1820.
May 30. Joseph Jordan and Mary Cowden.
June 13. John Graham and Martha Sherer.

June 13. Elias Drisbaugh and Rebecca Grove.
Nov. 8. Alexander Hannah and Ann Wilson.

1823.

March 6. John Duncan and Mary McKinsey.

1824.

June 8. Robert Elder and Sarah Sherer.
Oct —. John P. Rutherford and Eliza Rutherford.

1825.

June 14. George Kunkel and —— Campbell.
Dec. 8. David Elder and Julia Sherer.

1826.

Oct. 10. John Elder and Mary Thompson.

1827.

March 6. John McFarland and Elizabeth Fisher.
August 2. John Nevins and Eleanor Ewing.

1828.

May —, Joseph Burd and Harriet Bailey.

1829.

March 3. Dr. —— Stough and Catharine Ann McCammon
March 12. Joshua Elder and Eleanor Sherer.
March 17. Joshua Elder and Eliza Murray.
Jan 2. John Collier and Margaret Rutherford.

1830.

June 1. Joseph Gray and Jane Gray.

1835.

Jan. 5. Martin Kendig and Sarah Seebaugh.

1833.

Feb. 21. George Failen and Eliza Hatton.
June 30. John Lingle and Ruth Mahargue.
—— William Paxson and —— Campbell.

1834.

April 15. Hugh Wilson and Martha Rutherford.
May 27. Matthew Brown and Rebecca McClure.

1835.

Oct. 1. David McKibbin and Rachel McCammon.

1836.
March 10. Michael Whitley and Jane Simonton.
March 10. Daniel Kendig and Sarah Rutherford.
March 17. Samuel S. Rutherford and Mary Rutherford.
1837.
June 19. Robert Wilson and Elizabeth Gray.
Sept. 16. George W. Simmons and Elizabeth Bates
1838.
April 19. John Hamaker and Mary Ann Sherer.
May 29. Jacob Light and Catharine Brooks.
Sept. 11. James McGaughy and Esther Gray.
1839.
Jan. 1. Joshua Elder and Mary Gillmor.
Feb. 28. Abner Rutherford and Ann Espy.

NOTES AND QUERIES.—LVI.

ORTH FAMILY.—On the left bank of the Danube, about fifteen miles east of Vienna, is the village of Orth, containing about three thousand inhabitants. About the year A. D. 1200, one Henry Orth owned the village and estate surrounding it. It remained in the family for several successive generations, when the proprietor, about the close of the Seventeenth century, sold out and removed to Moravia, one of the Northern Provinces of Austria. The family cannot be traced from Moravia to the Rhine. The first of the family emigrated from the Palatinate to Lancaster, now Lebanon county, about the year 1725. Balzer Orth, born in 1703, who took up a large tract of land in 1742, and had administered to him the oath of allegiance April 11, 1755, died on the 20th of October, 1788. Among his children were Balzer and Adam. The former had among others:

    i. Gottlieb, who was the grandfather of Hon. Godlove S. Orth, of Indiana.
   ii. Joseph.
  iii. Maria Barbara, b. Nov. 9, 1768, m. 1st Mathias Morrett, a Huguenot, and had a daughter—Elizabeth, m. John Egle; 2d, Martin Light, of Lebanon, and had issue. She died May 14, 1851, at the residence of John Egle, near Decatur, Ill.

The younger, Adam Orth, married and left issue as follows:
  i. *Henry*, the ancestor of the name in this locality, and concerning whom we shall refer at another time.
  ii. *Rosina*, m. ——— Smith.
  iii. *Maria Elizabeth*, m. 1st, John Keller; 2d, ——— Shaffner.
  iv. *Catherine*, m. John Gloninger.
  v. *Regina*, m. David Krause.

No doubt the Hebron church records at Lebanon, if properly preserved, will give further genealogical information of the Orths.

CAPTAIN J. SHERER'S COMPANY, 1776.

[We herewith present another of those valuable rolls of the soldiers of the Revolution. The company and its officers belonged to the Paxtang Battalion of Associators, commanded by Colonel James Burd, of Tinian, concerning whom we hope ere long to present a sketch of his eventful life and services. The captain of the company was Joseph Sherer, whose farm adjoined Colonel Burd's, near Highspire, reference to whom was made in N. & Q. No. liii. Captain Sherer's company was in active service during the whole of the Spring and Summer of 1776, and a number of the men were wounded in a skirmish with a party of British cavalry near Amboy, N. J.

A true return of Capt. Joseph Sherer's Company of the Fourth Battalion of Lancaster County, Commanded by Col. James Burd, Esq., March 25th, 1776.

Captain.
Sherer, Joseph.
1st Lieutenant.
Collier, James.
2d Lieutenant.
Rutherford, Samuel.
Ensign.
Hutchinson, Samuel.
Sergeants.
Larue, Henry,
Sherer, Samuel,
McClure, Richard,
McKinney, Henry.
Privates.
Alleman, John,
Boal, Michael,
Bowman, John,
Brown, Benjamin,
Boyd, Samuel,
Brunson, Barefoot,
Brunson, William,

Dimsey, John,
Finney, John,
Fulton, William,
Gilmor, John,
Gray, George,
Gray, John,
Gray, Joseph,
Gray, Robert,
Harbison, Adam,
Hutchinson, Joseph,
Kerr, William,
Larue, George,
Mayes, Thomas,
Mahon, James,
Mahon, John,
McClure, Andrew,
McClure, Alexander,
McClure, Rowan.
McClure, William,
McCord, James,
McCoy, Charles,

McKillip, Hugh,
Means, Adam,
Means, James,
Means, John,
Morrison, Roger,
Murray, William,
Reed, Hugh,
Rennick, Thomas,
Roan, Stewart,
Rutherford, James,
Rutherford, John,
Sheets, Leonard,
Sherer, John,
Smith, Joseph,
Smith, William,
Sterrett, Robert,
Steel, John,
Stewart, John,
Stuart, William,
Thome, James,
Wilson, sr., John,

Brunson, Daniel,
Carson, George,
Chambers, Maxwell,
Chambers, Robert,
Coulter, John,

McFadding, Samuel,
McKinney, James,
McKinney, John,
McKinney, Matthew,

Wilson, jr., John,
Wilson, John,
Wolf, Michael,
Wylie, Samuel.

CAMPBELL FAMILY OF AMERICA.

Duncan Campbell (of the lineage of the noble branch of Breadalbane) was born in Scotland, married there in 1612, Mary McCoy, and removed with his wife in the same year to Ireland. They had issue among other children a son John (2), born 1621; married 1655, Grace, daughter of Peter Hay, and had issue:

   i. Dugald (3). His descendants settled in Rockbridge county, Va.

   ii. Robert (3), born 1656; married 1695, ———. His descendants settled in Orange (now Augusta) county, Va., in 1740.

   iii. John (3), born 1656; died 1734; married ———; emigrated from Ireland to Lancaster county, Pa., in 1726. Had issue:

     i. Patrick (4), born 1690; "a strong churchman." Removed from Pennsylvania to Virginia in 1738.

     ii. John (4), born 1692; minister at York, Pa.; died 1764; married ———.

     iii. Robert (4), died in Virginia; married ———, and had issue—five children—four daughters and one son, the last dying young. The name of only one daughter—Rebecca—has been transmitted.

     iv. James (4), died in England.

     v. David (4), removed from Pennsylvania to Augusta county, Va., in 1741; married there Margaret Hamilton.

Issue of Rev. John (4) and ——— Campbell:

   i. James (5), born 1731; removed to Virginia in 1760.

   ii. Ellen (5), born 1733; died 1735.

   iii. Frances (5), born 1737.

   iv. John (5), lawyer, born 1740; died 1797; married Ellen Parker, and had issue:

     i. Rev. *John* (6) minister, educated in England; had charge first of the parish of York, and afterwards of that of Carlisle, Pa.; married ———, and left issue—sons and daughters.

     ii. Francis (6).

   iii. James (6), removed to Chillicothe, O.; married the sister of the mother of Hon. Fredk. Watts, of Carlisle, Pa. (her maiden name desired), and read law with the father of Mr. Watts; died about 1807, at York, Pa; a man of brilliant talents. Left issue—sons and daughters.

   iv. Parker (6), born 1768, at Carlisle; married Elizabeth Calhoun (died 1846, in N. O., La.), of Chambersburg, Pa.; died 1824, in Washington, Pa. The venerable the Hon. Fredk. Watts, of Carlisle, Pa., in a recent letter testifies to his ability as a lawyer—" there was not a more distinguished member of the bar of Western Pennsylvania, of his day, than Parker Campbell. He ranked with the distinguished trio—James Ross, Henry Baldwin and Steele Semple. He left issue—sons and daughters—among the former, Parker (bred a civil engineer), banker, Richmond, Va. (Incidents in the legal career of Parker Campbell are requested from any gentleman who may possess such traditions.)

   The above is extracted from a more extended genealogy, which appeared in the *Standard*, of Richmond, Va., July 10, 1880, prepared by the writer, who is also in possession of further material. Additions to the above, and correspondence with all interested, solicited, with the purpose of ultimate publication, in book form of the genealogy as perfected.

   The arms of Duncan Campbell, preserved by his descendants are: *Quarterly first and fourth gyronny of eight or. and sa. for Campbell; second, or. fesse chegny, ar. and az. for Stewart; third, ar. a lymphad, her sails and oars in action all sa. for Lorn.*

   Gen. Wm. Campbell, the hero of the battle of King's Mountain, and many other distinguished men of the South and West, are believed to have descended from Duncan Campbell, as above.

   Richmond, Va.   R. A. BROCK.

[We commend the foregoing to the attention of our correspondents, and shall be grateful if those having any information whatever concerning the family of Campbell will forward it to us, that we may render whatever assistance we can to the labors of the learned historian, who makes the earnest request. Quite a number of the name settled at an early period in this county, and the village of Campbellstown, now in Lebanon county, was founded and named for a prominent member of that family. With what data we already have, and may by this publication secure, the opportunity will be afforded us to contribute our quota to Mr. Brock's genealogical budget.]

THE FAMILY OF AYRES.

This name, however it may spelled—Eyre, Ayre, Ayer, Ayres, &c.,—is derived from county Wiltshire, England. Of its position, Sir Bernard Burke says: "The old Wilts family of Eyre enjoyed for several centuries the highest distinction within its native county, and was of consideration in the State; most of its chiefs having had seats in Parliament, and two of them learned in the law, upon the Bench—one a Lord Chief Justice of the Common Pleas. A branch, too, which emigrated to Ireland, attained the Peerage of the Kingdom." The foregoing references include Sir William Ayre, who was one of fifty persons constituting the body guard of Henry VIII., and Sir Gervase Eyre, who was slain in defending Newark Castle, for Charles I.; the peerage is now extinct by failure of issue.

The name was carried to Ireland by Col. John Eyre, an officer of the English army, sent by Cromwell, in 1649; and who, after the rebellion ended, was authorized to locate there on eight hundred acres, and his descendants still maintain "Eyrecourt Castle," in county Galway. From this the name reached the Ulster district.

Samuel Ayres (Eyre or Eyres) brought his family to America about 1744, landing in Philadelphia. Following the Scotch-Irish path, he went to "Deep Run church," now in Bucks county, where he died. His family retraced its steps to within a dozen miles of Philadelphia, and settled permanently at what is now Beth-ayres station, on the new route to New York (so named by Franklin Ayres Comly, president N. P. R. R., a descendant.)

Here William Ayres, the eldest child and only son, married a Scotch lassie, Mary Kein, and his sisters also became the maternal ancestors of families prominent in Montgomery county fifty years ago. William had three sons and two daughters. Two of the sons married sisters names Yerkes, and some of their descendants still occupy the old locality.

In 1773 William Ayres relinquished his farm to his children, Samuel and Charles, and started westward with the remainder of his family. The move is wholly inexplicable to us. He was then about fifty-three years old, he left a property which he had cultivated for twenty-five years, and he was going—where? Imagination cannot, in 1880, call up in all its roughness, the condition of things between Philadelphia and their future home in 1773! Roads that were not roads, pack-horses, stopping places far distant from each other, tenting over night, &c., and to be contrasted with parlor cars, lightning speed and good living.

Suffice it, that (*wherever* it was they intended going) my great-grandmother vowed she *would not* climb the rugged Indian path over Peter's mountain, twelve miles above "Harris' Ferry." It was October, too, the nights were doubtless frosty, and the prospect gave intimations of going further and faring worse. In this dilemma, however, they found one John Black, who had located a cabin there, on land which old Bertram Galbraith had surveyed for him in the previous June—two hundred and twenty-seven acres. Black sold this property to William Ayres, October 30, 1773, for the sum of £100.

If the reader will recollect that this transaction antedates the organization of Dauphin county a dozen year, and that the Capital was then only a river crossing and an Indian trading post; that the nearest town worthy of the name was Lancaster, nearly fifty miles distant; and that their new home must have been in the midst of "the forest primeval," it will be seen that the father of the family upheld his indomitable Scotch-Irish blood in sharing with his brethren of the same faith those labors, trials and untold privations which resulted in making the wilderness to blossom as the rose.

Only two years pass by, when the rising war-cloud at Lexington and Bunker Hill attracts the patriotic hearts of the Susquehanna region, and William Ayres gives up his only help, his son John, who marched with Capt. Matthew Smith's company to join Washington's army at Cambridge, in June, 1775. [For these and other facts of a similar nature, I am, in common with the people of Dauphin county, indebted to the indefatigable and accomplished Editor of *Notes and Queries*, whose ability to resurrect facts which all his predecessors overlooked, have given him a well-earned reputation among the historians of our time.] Having returned from Cambridge on account of sickness, in November or December of the same year, we find John Ayres again enlisted, now in Captain James Murray's company, which marched to Amboy, and was present at the battle of Long Island, and the subsequent campaign through the Jerseys.

But strangely, too, the father also joined the son, in Captain Richard Manning's company, together with William Forster and his son James, both of whom afterwards became intermarried with the Ayres'. Who it was that remained to attend to the farming operations must be left to conjecture—unless the women did it.

In 1780 the elder daughter, Margaret (1754–1824) was married to William Forster, Rev. John Elder, officiating. The Forsters—with the Carsons, Reeds, McKees, Armstrongs and others—were among the very earliest settlers along the Susquehanna, in this section, their location being noted on Scull's map of the Province of Pennsylvania, January 1, 1759.

In 1781, the son, John Ayres, found an attractive flower at the mouth of the Mahoning (Danville), Northumberland county; and Mary, daughter of General William Montgomery, a settler from Chester county, became his wife. The matrimonial contagion having started in the family, even Peter's mountain was no barrier to the advances of James Reed, who carried off the youngest child, Esther (Hetty) Ayres (1756-1830), and Parson Elder was called upon, March 31, 1782.

But the marriage bell soon struck a funeral knell, and death claimed the venerable mother, Margaret Richmond Ayres (1726-178-) and her daughter-in-law, John's wife; both were buried in the old graveyard near Dauphin, and thus consecrated the ground where most of the family are buried. William Ayres, the father, did not long survive the loss of his partner, and met his death by accidental drowning at McAllister's mill, during one of his accustomed errands there, during the winter of 1784-5, aged about sixty-five.

John Ayres meanwhile succeeded to the property, and on April 2d, 1786, married Jane Lytle, of Lytle's Ferry, whose family history will be detailed in another chapter. Of this union there was issue: Sarah Eleanor (1787-1864), William (1788-1856), who married Mary Elizabeth Bucher; Mary (1790-1868); Margaret (1793-186/) married James Forster; John Lytle (1795-1857); Matilda Willis (1797-1872) married William Armstrong; Eliza Jane (1806-1830). Of these children, the best known to the people of the county, was William, who became an attorney at the Dauphin bar, and a well-known citizen of Harrisburg.

In a former contribution to *Notes and Queries*, I exhibited the facts in detail that William Ayres, the father, changed the old Indian path over Peter's Mountain—the same which terrified his wife and so altered his plans—to something like a road; that his son John made the grade still less; and that finally the grandson, William, made it entirely practicable and easy.

The after life of the Ayres' was simply that of their day, except that their house at the eastern base of the mountain, became a sort of "free-lunch" station for everybody going over the mountain. Not being at an avaricious bent, this location was their ruin; because they could refuse no one, and their hospitality was largely imposed upon. John Ayres lived to reach his seventy-fourth year, and died in 1825; he was the last survivor, but one, of the Revolutionary patriots in his neighborhood. His wife died suddenly at Harrisburg, in 1831, aged sixty-four.

The family was intimate with the best society at Harrisburg. The main road to the Upper End passing their door, gave them an incidental acquaintance which their neighbors did not enjoy, and on this account their hospitality at home was reciprocated largely at Harrisburg.

The blood of the family was pure Scotch-Irish, and it was not lacking in the energy and courage nor in the large-heartedness and religious instinct of that nationality. But the name has disappeared in the county, the people of to-day reap the fruit of their labor and vicissitude in the past; and in common with their worthy cotemporaries, they simply *deserve the remembrance* that history bestows.

GEORGE B. AYRES.

NOTES AND QUERIES.—LVII.

EARLY EXPLORATIONS OF THE SUSQUEHANNA.—I am partial to the very early period of our colonial history, and have made what to me are exceedingly interesting discoveries if they can be so called, one of which is the descent of the northeast branch of the Susquehanna in 1614, by the three Dutchmen, one of whom, named Kleynties, furnished Captain Hendricksen the information contained in his map of the Susquehanna in 1616 (see pp. 10, 11, Col. Hist, N. Y., vol. i). I conclude that they descended as far as present Pittston, and thence over the portage and down the Lehigh, where they met Capt. Hendricksen and were ransomed, "*giving for them kittles, beads and merchandize*," (Col. Hist. N. Y., vol. i, p. 14). An error which nearly all investigators have fallen into, is in considering the river indicated on Capt. Hendricksen's map as a tributary of Delaware bay; this was an error of the captain's, which remained uncorrected for many years afterward; when by examination of the later maps you will find the river and towns transferred bodily over to the Chesapeake. The earliest map in which this transfer appears is Vischers, 1656. In the Fall of 1615, Stephen Brule, a Frenchman, and interpreter of Champlain's reached the Chemung river, at present Waverly, where he found a great Indian town on the so-called Spanish Hill, and the next Summer passed down the Susquehanna to the sea. His account unfortunately was very brief, found in Champlain's works, 1619. These were undoubtedly the first white men who ever saw the Susquehanna river after Capt. Smith in 1608. J. S. CLARK.

EARLY CORRESPONDENCE.—The following letter of John Harris "to Col. James Burd at Tinian," calls up the query—what Capt. Patterson is this? He seems to have raised the first company in the

Province for the army, but did not go into service. Can any one answer our question?

"PAXTANG, *20th Nov., 1775.*

"SIR: When I informed you yesterday that the poor men that had some venison Taken from them at Mr. Carver's Lately, they were Bringing to me ag't their inclination. I did not mean to Deprive you or Mr. Shippen of s'd venison, but told you that if Capt. Patterson or any Gentleman in your Company made Soe free they were welcome. As you informed me how the affair was, & that Captn. Patterson had pd or was to pay the s'd men for their venison, & made a present of it to you for Mr. Shippen. Upon the whole I pd nothing for it nor will I ever have it, and the men should not Desire me to ask any of the Gentlemen who had their venison for pay After they were pd by Captn. Patterson for it. I send my boy with s'd venison to yr house on purpose, & shall never be Displeased unless you'l not receive it for the use Intended by y'self and Captn. Patterson, as I would cheerfully send it to Mr. Shippen myself knowing he is in a bad state of health, (If I had Rec'd it.)

"Martin Housar goes Past William's this day with his waggon, I expect, to Newport, thro' Lancaster, & can carry it for you. I send you the Late paper, with my own & my wife's Compliments to y'rself and Madam Burd. I am, Sir, y'r most Humble Servant,

"JOHN HARRIS."

"DUTCHLAND IN AMERICA."

The foregoing is the title of a two-column article which appeared some time since in the columns of a prominent newspaper in the city of New York. The article betokens either such ignorance and stupidity or downright maliciousness, that it demands a serious reply. We consider it a duty we owe the State of our nativity—and an ancestry of whom several millions of the citizens of Pennsylvania and other States of the Union, have reason to be proud—to correct such egregious blunders or willful prevarications. In doing so we shall review as briefly as possible the history of the German settlers of our State.

The origin of the German population in Pennsylvania dates back to the latter part of the Seventeenth century. As early as 1684, Francis Daniel Pastorius, of whom the poet Whittier has sung so sweetly, with a colony of Germans settled and laid out Germantown, near to the metropolis. These came from Cresheim, Germany, and were in religious opinions and proclivities, allied to the Quakers.

Other colonies followed, settling in different parts of the Province. It was not, however, until the years 1709 and 1710 that the emigration of the Germans was of any magnitude. For two or three years previous, Queen Anne of England gave refuge to thousands of the Palatinates, who, oppressed by the exactions of the French, were forced to flee from their homes. It is stated that in the month of July, 1709, there arrived at London six thousand five hundred and twenty German Protestants. Transportation was gratuitously given many to America, through the aid of the Queen and the government of England. The vast majority were sent at first to New York, from whence many reached the confines of Pennsylvania, a Province, the laws of which were more tolerant than those of any of the new Colonies. Among these German emigrants were Mennonites, Dunkards German Reformed and Lutherans. Their number was so great during the subsequent years, that James Logan, secretary to the Proprietary, wrote: "We have of late great number of Palatines poured in upon us without any recommendation or notice, which gives the country some uneasiness, for foreigners do not so well among us as our own English people." Two years afterwards, Jonathan Dickinson remarks "We are daily expecting ships from London, which bring over Palatines in number about six or seven thousand. We had a parcel who came out about five years ago, who purchased land about sixty miles from Philadelphia, and prove quiet and industrious. Some few came from Ireland lately, and more are expected thence. This is besides our common supply from Wales and England. Our friends do increase mightily, and a great people there is in the wilderness which is fast becoming a fruitful field."

These emigrants settled principally in Montgomery Berks and Lancaster counties. They were well educated, and brought with them their ministers and school-masters; the latter very frequently, when there was a want of supply of the former, read sermons and prayers.

Between the years 1720 and 1725 a large number of Germans, who had previously settled in Schoharie county, New York, descended the Susquehanna river on rafts to the mouth of the Swatara, ascending which stream, already settled by the Scotch-Irish, they took up their abode near the waters of the Tulpehocken, Berks county. The celebrated Conrad Weiser, to whom we shall refer on a future occasion, was of this party of colonists.

From 1725, for a period of ten years there was another great influx of Germans of various religious opinions, Reformed, Lutherans, Moravians, Swenkfelders and Roman Catholics. By a letter of Secretary James Logan in 1725, it appears that many of these settlers were not over scrupulous in their compliance with the regulations of the Land Office. He says, and perchance with much truth: "They come in in crowds, and as bold, indigent strangers from Germany, where many of them have been soldiers. All these go on the best vacant tracts, and seize upon them as places of common spoil." He again says: "They rarely approach me on their arrival to propose to purchase," and adds, "when they are sought out and challenged for their right of occupancy, they allege it was published in Europe that we wanted and solicited for colonists, and had a superabundance of land, and, therefore, they had come without the means to pay." In fact, those who thus "squatted" without titles acquired enough by their thrift in a few years to pay the land which they had thus occupied, and so, generally, they were left unmolested. Secretary Logan further states: "Many of them are Papists—the men well armed, and as a body a warlike, morose race." In 1727, he writes: "About six thousand Germans more are expected (and also many from Ireland), and these emigrations," he "hopes may be prevented in the future by act of parliament, else *these Colonies will in time be lost to the Crown.*" The italics in the last sentence are our own. To us it seems like a prophecy.

From 1735 to 1752 emigrants came into the Province by thousands. In the autumn of 1749 not less than twenty vessels with German passengers to the number of twelve thousand arrived at Philadelphia. In 1750, 1751 and 1752 the number was not much less. Among those who emigrated during these years were many who bitterly lamented having forsaken their native land for the Province of Pennsylvania. At that time there was a class of Germans who had resided some time in Pennsylvania, well known by the name of Neulander, who made it their business to go to Germany and prevail on their countrymen to sacrifice their property and embark for America. In numerous instances, persons in easy circumstances at home, with a view to better their condition, came to America, but to their sorrow found that their situation was rendered none the better, but in many cases so much worse as to be absolutely wretched. Others again who had not the means of paying their passage across the Atlantic, were, on their arrival at Philadelphia, exposed at public meeting to serve for a number of years to pay their passage. Those thus disposed of were termed *Redemptioners*. The Palatine Redemptioners were usually sold at ten pounds for from three to five years servitude. In almost every instance the time for which they sold was honestly served out, while many subsequently, by dint of industry and frugality, rose to positions of wealth and importance in the State. That stalwart statesman of Western Pennsylvania, John Covode, used to pride himself on being the descendant of a Redemptioner.

In later times, say from 1753 to 1756, the Germans having become numerous, and therefore powerful as "make-weights" in the political balance, were much noticed in the publications of the day, and were at that period in general and very hearty co-operation with the Quakers then in rule in the Assembly. From that time onward, although not so numerous, almost all the German emigrants landed in Pennsylvania.

The assumption by the writer of the article referred to that any appreciable portion of the present German population of the Commonwealth are the descendants of the Hessians who were brought here by the British government to put down the rebellion of 1776, is as impudent as it is false. All of the German Mercenaries, as they are called, who were prisoners of war and stationed in Pennsylvania according to Baron Reidesel, who was one of the commanders, were properly accounted for, and were returned to their own country upon the evacuation of New York by the British. *They did not remain*, as it was a condition entered into by the English Government with the Landgrave of Brunswick, the Duke of Hesse Cassel, and the petty princes of Hanau and Waldeck, that a certain price was to be paid for every man killed, wounded or missing. Before the official proclamation of peace, the Hessian prisoners were on their way to New York, by direction of the Supreme Executive Council of Pennsylvania. Some few deserted and some eventually returned to America, after their transportation to Germany, but the bald assertion that the origin of the large German population of Pennsylvania is due to the settlement of those hired mercenaries of England, cannot be supported, and shows the profoundest historical ignorance and audacious stupidity.

That the Germans of Pennsylvania have been so uniformly successful in acquiring wealth is due to their industry, to their thrift and to their knowledge of agricultural pursuits. If some portions of Pennsylvania are the garden-spots of America, they have been made so by the Germans who have tilled them—who have indeed "made the wilderness to blossom as the rose." Not anywhere in the New England States, in New York, nor in the South are farms so well tilled, so highly cultivated, as in the sections of Pennsylvania where the Germans predominate; and we assert, without fear of contradiction, that more works on agriculture, more papers devoted to farming are taken and read by the so-called "Pennsylvania Dutch" farmers than by the farmers of any other section of the Union. That our German citizens are not "content to live in huts," is palpably certain, and whoever will go into the homes of the farmers will find evidence of both refinement and culture, and although their barns are capacious because their dwellings are not castles, they should not be accused of indifference to their own domiciles. At the present time it is rare to find a farm-house in the old German settlements that does not contain a double parlor, sitting-room, dining-room, kitchen and out-kitchen, with six or eight bed rooms. This is more general in the counties of Berks, Lancaster, Lebanon, Dauphin and Cumberland, than among the New England settled counties of the North and West—the Quaker counties of Chester and Bucks, in Pennsylvania—and to go to New England, the latter are not to be mentioned in comparison.

Of the Pennsylvania German language or idiom we will not speak except to state, that at the present time there are few persons speaking this *patois* who are unable to speak and read English. Those who are not conversant with English are of recent importation from the Fatherland. Because the Dunkards and other religious bodies retain the peculiar views of their ancestors, they are accused of being unprogressive—of preserving the customs and general characteristics of the race—which is far from the truth. Next to the Scotch-Irish, no race has left such a high and lofty impress upon this nation as the German. There is less ignorance and superstition in the German counties of Pennsylvania than will be found in any agricultural region East, West, North or South. Because some old plodding farmer who prefers remaining on his farm, attending to his cattle and grain, caring little of going beyond the county town in his visits, his disinclination ought not to be imputed to either his ignorance or to his being close-fisted. In the German counties one rarely meets with an individual who has never been "to town" and we venture an opinion that both in the New England States and in New York are there many persons who have never visited the county-seat; and as for visiting Boston and New York city, where one farmer has visited those metropolises, we assert that two Pennsylvania German farmers have seen their own city of Philadelphia.

German opposition to common schools has been a terrible bugaboo to very many outside of Pennsylvania who never understood the occasion of it. Foremost among the opponents of the free school system were the Quakers, the opposition arising from the fact that having had schools established for many years, supported by their own contributions, they were opposed to being taxed for the educational maintenance of others. Precisely similar were the objections in the German districts. As stated in the outset of this article, the German emigrants brought their school-masters with them and schools were kept and supported by them. More frequently the church pastor served as teacher, and hence when the proposition came to establish the system of public education the people were not prepared for it. But that was nearly fifty years ago, and to the credit and honor of the German element in Pennsylvania, Governor George Wolf, the father of the free school system, and Governor Joseph Ritner and William Audenreid, the earnest advocates of the same, were of German descent. The opposition died away in a few years, and a glance at the school statistics of Pennsylvania would open the eyes of our Yankee friends, and astonish the descendants of Diedrick Knickerbocker. The present system and management of public education in our State—yes, this "Dutchland in America"—is in the lead in the Union, and figures and facts will bear us out in our assertion.

Of the domestic manners and customs of the Pennsylvania Germans we shall have little to say, but the charge that "bundling" surv ves to the present day among them, is simply absurd. Despite all that may be said in regard to this custom, it was a rare circumstance (and we have it from good authority) seventy-five years ago, and all knowledge of it was obtained from the staid New England people and the *low* Dutch of New York. According to the Rev. Samuel Peters, who published a "History of Connecticut" nearly a hundred years ago, that custom "prevailed in New England for one hundred and sixty years, while most of the New England genealogies and histories refer to it as occurring there. Stiles, in his history of it, states that the custom was not only brought over from Holland by the Dutch emigrants to New York, but blames New England for propagating it, and refers incidentally to the fact, that "the conatgion" reached in time the German settlements in Pennsylvania. To fasten its origin or prevalence to a great extent upon the Pennsylvania "Dutch" is a violation of fact. If it was a rare occurrence seventy-five years ago, propriety and good manners have obliterated the evil borrowed from the East, where we are inclined it is still indigenous.

Sectarian strife is not as frequent among the Germans as among the Irish and Welsh, and to accuse them of "Hiberni-phobia," would be tantamount to charging the English and other foreigners, who settled in Pennsylvania with "Germani-phobia." The Pennsylvania Dutch are not exclusive by any means, and the frequent marriages of their daughters to the town lads repel this insinuation.

Look on the German element in Pennsylvania—so frequently and inappropriately called Dutch—and there will be found industry, honesty, energy, progress, ei terprise, wealth, intelligence—in short all those characteristics which go to make up educated and useful citizens—a population of which any State in the Union might well be proud.

NOTES AND QUERIES—LVIII.

REV. JOHN EWING, D. D.—An incident has come to us relative to this gentleman which is well worthy a place in *N. & Q.* The Rev. Dr. Ewing was the pastor of the First Presbyterian church of Philadelphia, and afterwards the Provost of the University of Pennsylvania. It was his daughter Elizabeth who married Robert Harris, of Harrisburg. Dr. Ewing was in London previous to the Revolutionary war on business connected with the University. He was invited to dine where the celebrated Dr. Johnson was one of the company. Dr. Johnson was late in coming, and when dinner was announced, ate, as his custom was, voraciously. Whilst he was thus indulging, a conversation was being carried on between Dr. Ewing and a person next to him on the subject of American literature. At length Dr. Johnson turned about and said rather rudely to Dr. Ewing: "What do you know about literature in America; you have no books." "Oh, yes," Dr. Ewing blandly replied, "we have read *The Rambler.*" This reply pacified Dr. Johnson, and he afterwards presented to Dr. Ewing a bamboo cane, which is now in possession of Dr. Ewing's grandson, G. W. Harris, Esq.

"THE SOLDIER'S TALE."—From Tennessee, and from a descendant of the Dixons, of Dixon's Ford, we have this: "H. R." is just a little wrong in regard to any of the characters being fictitious. Ellery Trueman was an officer in the same regiment that Robert Dixon was in, and was wounded at the battle of Quebec where Robert Dixon was killed. So you see he was a *real* character. I have heard my grandmother Dixon say this often; and that Emily Raymond was not a myth. She told in my hearing time and again that she distinctly remembered the day of her Uncle Roan's funeral, when Emily Raymond fainted and was carried to her aunt's residence insensible; and also that she was present at old John Dixon's when Emily snatched the bones and rushed out of the house homewards. As for William Bertram, our dear grandmother has often said she knew him as well as any one she was ever acquainted with. I have heard her say that their names were as familiar to her as those of her own Aunt and Uncle Roan. They were as real characters as Robert Dixon, Lindley Murray or John Roan or any of the other characters in "The Soldier's Tale."

[In regard to these characters, we can only venture this opinion. The names of Ellery Trueman and Emily Raymond are fictitious, although they may represent real individuals. The Christian names are unusual, and we have never come across them among the early Scoth-Irish settlers. We have the entire roll of Captain Matthew Smith's company, which went to Quebec and in which was Robert Dixon, who fell in front of that stronghold. Third Lieutenant William Cross, of Hanover, was the only officer wounded. No doubt our fair correspondent's informant had heard the stories in her childhood, and the weaving of them by Mr. Darby into a tale impressed her with the idea that, as Roan and Dixon and Murray were real living characters, concerning whom we all have knowledge, the others were also real, hero and heroine. 'H. R.' did not doubt the correctness of the incidents—only that the characters were mythical.]

PRE-HISTORIC REMAINS.—The following was copied verbatim from a note made in his pocket almanac, by the late Judge Atlee: "On the 24th of May, 1798, being at Hanover (York county, Pennsylvania), in company with Chief Justice McKean, Judge Bryan, Mr. Burd, and others, on our way to Franklin, and taking a view of the town, in company with Mr. McAllister, and several other respectable inhabitants, we went to Mr. Neese's tan-yard, where we were shown a place near the currying-house, from whence (in digging to sink a tanvat), some years ago, were taken two skeletons of human bodies. They lay close beside each other, and measured about eleven feet three inches in length; the bones were entire, but on being taken up and exposed to the air, they presently crumbled and fell to pieces. Mr. McAllister and some others mentioned that they and many others had seen them; and Mr. McAllister, who is a tall man, about six feet four inches high, mentioned that the principal bone of the leg of one of them, being placed by the side of his leg, reached from his ankle a considerable way up his thigh, pointing a small distance below the hip bone."

HUMMELSTOWN.—When Frederick Hummel laid out his town on the Swatara, he called it Fredericktown, but after his death, which occurred at the opening of the war for Independence, the inhabitants changed it to its present name—Hummelstown. We have before us the assessment list of Fredericktown in 1771, and that of Hummelstown in 1779, from which it will be seen that in the eight years supervening there was no increase in the number of inhabitants. Whether this was due to the war which was then going on, and which will account for the absence of either "freemen" or "single men," we cannot say. The absence of the name Hummel in the last list is in striking contrast to the late census return which we are told number ninety-four of the name. The Hummels then resided on the adjoining farm to the town and are included in the other portions of Derry tax lists. In 1779 it is well known that there were a large number of gunsmiths at Hummelstown making arms for the continental army. They are perchance also included in the Derry assessment proper

Frederick Town, Derry Township, 1771.

Peter Shot,	Jacob Hammer,	Christopher Bogner,
Jacob Reigart,	Adam Baum,	Melchor Reigart,
Widow Wetherhold,	Barnard Fridley,	John Philips,
Sebastian Creas,	Jacob Myer,	Henry Wieser,
Fred. Hummel,	Henikle Shwoontz,	Andrew Hearauf.
Widow Eurick,	Peter Hiney,	

Freemen.

Hanickle Evart,	Thos. Flack,	Jacob Fridley.
William Grab,		

Hummelstown, Derry township, 1779.

Elizabeth Clooney,	Peter Fridley,	Nicholas Smith,
Jacob Deery,	Joseph Ferree,	Adam Baum,
James Dainy,	Widdow Haupt,	Widdow Fetherhold,
Ludwick Emerick,	George Lauer,	Adam Gambel,
David Eatly,	Jacob Ricard,	Michael Spade,
John Fergison,	Martin Rise,	—— Hall.
Martin Fridley,	Peter Spade,	

ROLL OF CAPTAIN RUTHERFORD'S COMPANY, 1776–7.

[For the roll of the following company of Associators, we are indebted to Mr. Silas Rutherford. Of the commanding officer of this body of patriots of the Revolution, we propose to refer at length on another occasion. The company was in active service throughout the campaign in the Jerseys during 1776, and the roll as here given was as the company stood when they assembled at Middletown on the 12th of August, 1777, preparatory to their participation in the campaign around Philadelphia. The four additional names are on the roll for September of that year, probably joining the company prior to the Battle of Brandywine.]

Captain.	Sergeant.	Corporals.
Rutherford, John.	Graham, John,	Swineford, John,
Lieutenant.	Jones, Benjamin.	Weiser, Jacob,
McClure, Jonathan.	Chambers, Elisha,	Ritter, Adam,
Ensign.	Newhouse, Philip.	Miller, Jacob.
Sherer, Samuel.		

Drummer.
Swineford, George.
Privates.
Allison, Richard,
Barnett, Samuel,
Bell, John,
Boyd, William,
Castle, Frederick,
Cochran, James,
Cochran, Samuel, sr.,
Cochran, Samuel, jr.,
Conway, Francis,

Dougherty, Dennis,
Galey, James,
Grogan, Charles,
Herron, Robert,
Hogan, William,
Kennedy, Dr. Robert,
Light, Ludwig,
Little, John,
McAllister, Tobias,
McCord, James,
McWhorter, Robert,

Miller, John,
Morrison, James,
Neighbor, Abraham,
Packer, Jesse,
Pancake, George,
Pancake, Peter,
Raredon, Simon,
Sheattel, Michael,
Steever, Michael,
Smith, John,
Woodside, John.

[Joined the company Sept., 1777.]

Cisler, Samuel,
Yeager, Andrew.

Snyder, Leonard,

Swineford, Albright,

YE ANCIENT INHABITANTS—VIII.

West End of Derry.—1755.

Adam Bown,
Mathew Laird,
William Spencer,
Hugh Black,
Thos. Black,
Jas. Irland,
John Laird,
Adam Talker,
Robert Talker,
Wm. Breading,
David Camble,
Jas. Russell,
Moses Patterson,
John Cook,
John Crockens,
John Penelton,
Wm. Thompson,
Lawrence Magill,
Isaac Pennington,
Moses Camble,
Jas. Wiley,
Wm. Starrett,
Sam'l Morrow,
Robert Ramsey,

Jas. Walker,
Sam'l Wilson,
Wm. McCobb,
Wm. Drening,
Jas. Sample,
Thos. Park,
Robt. Breadshaw,
Mathew Wilson,
Joseph Cander,
Stophel Shoop,
Adam Wagner,
Jas. Carithers,
Peter Pearsh,
John Singer,
Jacob Catts,
Daywalt Baker,
Geo. Bomach,
Henry Carber,
Anthony Wiry,
Peter Spangler,
Peter Glassbloss,
David Etter,
Edward Martin,
John Tyce,

John Fleming,
Geo. Bare,
Francis Newcommer,
Henry Hart,
Jacob Albright,
Deter Kinder,
Mocks Pidle,
Jas. Chambers,
Jas. Clark,
Thomas Hall,
Robert Wilson,
John Karr,
John Vanlear,
Jas. McCaye,
Jas. Shaw,
Robt. Corithers,
John Were,
Hugh Corithers,
Geo. Weetaberger,
Robt. Armstrong,
Andrew Hershaw,
Martin Brand,
Jas. Rusell,
Jacob Bronck.

Freemen.

Jas. Snody,
Jas. Harris,
Robert Bready,
Thos. Carr,

John Bowman,
John Clark,
Robert McKee,
Jas. Findleer,

Jas. McCormag,
Wm. Findley,
Wm. McClary.

ADAM BAUM, *Col'r.*

West End of Derry.—1757.

Robert Taylor,
David Campble,
Thomas Hall,
Robert Wilson,
Moses Paterson,
Jno. Vanlear,
Joseph Cander,
James Nelson,
Jno. Fleming,
Saml. Reed,
Robt. Bradshaw,
Wilson Thompson,
Lewis Morrow,
Wm. Starratt,
Robt. Ramsey,
Robt. Walker,
Mathew Wilson,
Jas. Clark,
Jno. Karr,
Thomas Karr,
Robert Caruthers,
James Shaw,
Geo. Frey,
Widow Sample,
Thos. Parks,
Moses Campbel,

Jas. Finton,
Jno. Clark,
Jno. James,
Jas. Vanlear,

Larence Magill,
Jno. Pennelton,
Jno. Cooke,
Jas. Russel, jur.,
Isaac Pennelton,
Jas. Russel,
Wm. Bredy,
Jno. Lard,
James Chambers,
Stofel Soop,
Hugh Caruthers,
James Caruthers,
Wolry Hipsher,
Peter Spangler,
Edward Martin,
Simon Singer,
Jno. Singer,
Peter Grosles,
Adam Wagner,
Moses Wilson,
Jas. Ireland,
Alex. McCormag,
Robt. Armstrong,
Mathew Lard,
Conrad Wiseler,

Freemen.

Geo. Philip Sherger,
Jas. Snoddy,
Allx. Rannex,
Saml. McCormack,

Saml. Walker,
Francis Newcomm,
Peter Kinter,
Geo. Wesberry,
Jno. Greap,
Melchar Flenshabauch,
Robt. McKee,
Anthony Wiry,
Anthony Blackny,
Adam Dalker,
Fredrick Gencel,
Hugh Black,
Thos. Black,
Wm. Spencer,
Mich'l Huber,
Jno. Tyce,
Jas. Walker,
Geo. Bever,
Handel Vence,
Adam Baum,
Henry Heart,
Widow McKee,
Wm. Drennan,
Jno. Croket,
Martin Brand.

Wm. McCleery,
Edward Queen,
Cornelous Queen,
John Bowman.

ROBERT CARUTHERS, *Collr.*

MOSES GILLMOR.

Moses Gillmor was born in the townland of Burt, parish of Templemore, county of Donegal, six miles from the city of Londonderry, province of Ulster, Ireland, about the year 1749. Until his seventeenth year he remained in Ireland, when he came with an uncle to America, settling in Hanover township, Lancaster, now Dauphin county, Penna. Prior to the Revolution he returned to Ireland on business connected with his father's estate, but the breaking out of the war delayed his return until about 1783. The next year, November, 1784, according to Parson Elder's marriage record, he married Isabel Wallace, third daughter of Robert and Mary Wallace, of Hanover. Upon the laying out of the town of Harrisburg in 1785, Mr. Gillmor purchased a lot on Market square, built a house and established himself in the mercantile business, which he successfully carried on a number of years. Mr. Gillmor was prominent in political affairs, and in the church of which he was one of the founders, the First Presbyterian, he was an elder for thirty-four years. Mr. Gillmor died at Harrisburg, June 10, 1825, aged seventy-six years, and with his wife Isabel (born in 1755, died Sept. 16, 1828) is buried in Paxtang church graveyard. Their children were:

i. *Thomas*, b. 1785; d. 1793.
ii. *Mary*, b. 1787; d. 1793.
iii. *William*, b. 1789; d. Aug. 28, 1856.
iv. *Robert*, b. 1791; d. Nov. 13, 1867.
v. *Margaret*, b. 1793; d. 1839.

Of these William Gillmor was the only one who married. His wife was Isabella, daughter of Capt. James Cowden. Robert Gillmor was well known to most of our citizens. He was a gentleman of the old school, of strict integrity and honored by all who knew him.

Concerning Moses Gillmor the following description of him and estimate of his character, as given by the Rev. Dr. Robinson in his " Historical Discourse on the Ruling Elders of the First Presbyterian Church," are a fitting close to this sketch. " He was a gentleman of remarkably fine personal appearance, tall and well proportioned, grave and dignified, and wore, as was customary with gentlemen of his standing in society, the cocked hat, short breeches and silver-buckled shoes of that and the earlier revolutionary age. He was a man of stately bearing and courtly manners, and his tall manly form, clothed in the dress peculiar to gentlemen of the olden times, would command involuntary respect. He was a most worthy citizen and a man of sterling integrity, sincere, incorrupt and straightforward in all his dealings. In Christian character he was decidedly old side; and in this day of so much that is easy, fictitious and sensational in religious life and manners, he would, no doubt, be regarded severely cold and puritanic; but in him and his associates there was in their reverent and high-toned piety, a solid realness that could well do without the more attractive, but less substantial piety of many in modern times.

"Many incidents are still rehearsed that illustrate the character of this good and strong-minded man. When selling merchandise he was often heard to tell his customers, ' Tak it, if ye like, if not, ye'll perhaps find something better at some other place.' The precenter was one day greatly troubled to find a tune of the right metre for the psalm that was to be sung. After failing once or twice, the voice of Mr. Gillmor was heard from another part of the church, ' Tut, man, tak anither tune.' "

NOTES AND QUERIES.—LIX.

RECUSANT INDIAN TRADERS IN 1749.—For some reason a great many Indian traders did not take out a license in the year 1748. At the August term (Lancaster county) the following named persons were indicted for their neglect:

Robert Dunlap,	Samuel Chambers,	James Lowrey,
James Crowly,	Peter Corbet,	Thomas Mitchell,
John Traner,	George Croghan,	John Owens,
Joseph Campbell,	Samuel Cuzzins,	Alexander Morehead,
William Blythe,	Thomas McKee,	John Galbreath,
Paul Pierce,	*Simon Girty*,	John Potts,
Andrew Akins,	John Findley,	Peter Shaver,
Hugh Crawford,	John Lee,	Dennis Sullivan,
James Dunning,	Daniel Lowrey,	Charles Williams.

This was a large number, and many of them were respectable and influential citizens. Their neglect to take out a license was doubtless a technical informality. The names are quite familiar ones, and they can be readily traced from Chickies' creek through the Donegals, Dauphin and Cumberland counties. Thomas Harris, an Indian trader, who resided at Conewago creek, a few miles above Elizabethtown, was foreman of the grand jury that indicted these traders.

SAMUEL EVANS.

THE GARFIELD FAMILY.—The purpose of these papers is to keep up a connection between the past and present. Information of the character herewith adds to the knowledge of the history of the whole country. Readers will therefore find an excuse for us in departing from our usual local status in its publication. As soon as it can be obtained it is our purpose to follow this pedigree with authenticated data relating to a Welsh Quaker, who came over in 1670, settled on Delaware, and was in Pennsylvania in 1680, bearing the name of Hancock, from whom the General, so prominent at present, descends in the seventh generation. A correspondent of the Worcester *Spy*, Mass., writes to that paper of the Garfields:

Edward Gearfield (spelled as it is recorded on the Watertown records), came to this country from England, and died June 14, 1672, aged ninety-seven. His son, Edward, jr., had two wives—first Rebecca ——, the mother of all his children, and, second, Joanna, the widow of Thomas Buckminster, of Muddy river.

Edward Garfield, jr., died in 1672, and his inventory amounted to

£457 3s. 6d. He was one of the earliest proprietors of Watertown, and was selectman in 1638, 1655 and 1662.

His son, Benjamin Garfield, born in 1653, admitted freeman in 1690, was representative in Watertown to the great and general court nine times between 1689 and 1717, and he held numerous municipal appointments. He had two wives—Mehitable Hawkins and Elizabeth Bridge—by the second wife he had a son Thomas, born December 12, 1680, who was a prominent citizen of Weston. He married Mercy Bigelow, daughter of Joshua and Elizabeth (Flagg) Bigelow, and had twelve children. The third, Thomas, married Rebecca Johnson, of Lunenberg, and had:

(1) Solomon, born July 18, 1743, and married May 20, 1766, to Sarah Stimson, of Sunbury; these were the great grandfather and grandmother of General James A. Garfield.

(2) Rebecca, born September 23, 1745; married October 1, 1765, to David Fiske.

(3) Abraham, born April 3, 1748, died August 15, 1775, in the Revolutionary army.

(4) Hannah, born August 15, 1750.

(5) Lucy, born March 3, 1754.

General Garfield's ancestry, summed up, is as follows: 1, Edward; 2, Edward, jr.; 3, Samuel; 4, Benjamin; 5, Thomas; 6, Thomas; 7, Solomon; 8, Thomas; 9, Abraham; 10, James Abraham Garfield."

A. B. H.

YE ANCIENT INHABITANTS—IX.

West Hanover Assessment.—1772.

Saml. Allen,
Joseph Allen,
John Andrews,
William Allen,
Philip Brand,
William Brown,
Philip Brown,
James Beard,
William Brisban,
Saml. Brown,
Joseph Barnet,
William Branden,
Matthew Barnet,
John Cooper,
Wm. Cathcart,
John Crawford,
Wm. Crane,
Joseph Crane,

Jas. Huchison, jr.,
John Huchison,
Robert Humes,
James Johnson (Taylor)
James Johnson,
Robt. Kennédy,
Thos. Kennedy,
Alex. Kid,
James McMullen,
James McClure,
Thos. McCord,
Bernard McNutt,
John McCord,
Wm. McCullough,
John Mitchel,
John McCown,
Richard McCown,
Thos. McElhenny,

Wm. Rippeth,
John Rodgers,
James Rodgers,
Thos. Rippeth,
James Robinson,
John Stuart,
Hugh Stuart (Paxtang),
Daniel Shaw,
Andrew Stast,
John Snider,
Robt. Sturgeon,
Thos. Strain,
Isaac Skiles,
Samuel Stuart,
William Snodgrass,
Samuel Starrat,
Mathew Snoday,
George Taylor, jr.

Richard Crawford,
George Crane,
Richard Dermond,
Peter Ebersole,
James Finney,
James Finney, jr.,
Thos. Finney,
David Ferguson,
Saml. Ferguson,
Susanah Finney,
John French,
Hugh Glen,
John Graham,
Timothy Green, Esq.,
John Hutchison,
Robt. Hutchison,
Mike Houk,
William Hill,
John Hay,
Isaac Hannah,
John Snoday.

James Reney,
James McCormick,
James Finney,
Saml. Agnew,
James McNight,

John Bringhold,
Thos. Tompson,
John Moody,
Wm. Brown,

David Moody,
Robert Martin,
John McCormick,
James McClenahan,
Thos. McNair,
Francis McClure,
Henry McCormick,
Widow McGuire,
Thos. McClure,
George Peters,
Robert Porterfield,
James Park,
Jacob Pruner,
Jacob Richard,
Melchor Rhime,
Wm. Rogers,
Jeremiah Rodgers,
Andrew Rodgers,
Thos. Robinson,
Saml. Robinson,

Freemen.

James Humes,
Joseph Pitt,
John Rippith,
Aaron Cotter,
James Wilson,

Inmates.

Wm. Ramage,
Wm. Moorhead,
Robt. Dalton,
Gilbert Keneday,

John Templeton,
Wm. Thompson,
Mathew Thorton,
Wm. Thorn,
John Thompson,
John Trousdale,
Michael Vanleer,
Moory Woods,
Danl. Monderly,
Robert Wallace,
James Willson (creek)
Hugh Wilson,
Idcole Wolf,
Andrew Wallace,
William Wright.
James Wilson,
James Wilson, jr.,
Thos. Walker,
Joseph Wilson,
Benjamin Wallace,

John Pruner,
James Williams,
Richard Robinson,
Joseph McClure.

Robert Halley,
James McFarland,
Wm. McClure.

WM. TROUSDALE,
Collector of West Hanover.

NOTES AND QUERIES.—LX.

HANOVER PATRIOTISM IN 1774.

We herewith publish for permanent record, by request, the text of the Hanover Resolves of June 4, 1774:

"At an assembly of the inhabitants of Hanover, Lancaster county, held on Saturday, June 4, 1774, Colonel Timothy Green, chairman, to express their sentiments on the present critical state of affairs, it was unanimously resolved,

1st. That the recent action of the Parliament of Great Britain is iniquitious and oppressive.

2d. That it is the bounden duty of the people to oppose every measure which tends to deprive them of their just prerogatives.

3d. That in a closer union of the colonies lies the safeguard of the liberties of the people.

4th. That in the event of Great Britain attempting to force unjust laws upon us by the strength of arms, our cause we leave to heaven and our rifles.

5th. That a committee of nine be appointed who shall act for us and in our behalf as emergencies may require.

The committee consisted of Colonel Timothy Green, James Carothers, Josiah Espy, Robert Dixon, Thomas Coppenheffer, William Clark, James Stewart, Joseph Barnett and John Rodgers."

The foregoing declarations are worthy of perpetual record. They furnished the text of the resolves at Middletown, Col. Burd chairman, and other portions of the Scotch-Irish settlements of Lancaster and the Kittatinny Valley, and struck the key-note of the proceedings which eventuated in the separation of the colonies from England. It is worthy of remark in this connection that while Philadelphia and the lower counties were hesitating and doubting, the Scotch-Irish districts were firm yet dignified in their demands for justice and in the denunciation of British tyranny and wrong. These Hanover resolves preceded those of the Mecklenburg convention, showing that the liberty-loving Scotch-Irish of Pennsylvania were the head and front of the American Rebellion of 1776.

FAMILY GENEALOGIES.

The Springfield (Mass.) *Republican*, alluding to some comments of the London *Spectator* on a novel of English life and manners, thus discourses of an observation of the *Spectator*. That paper said: "Of the utility of family pride to writers of fiction there can be no question, for we have only to observe how dull and helpless American story-tellers are for want of such a resource." Possibly; although Cooper is not dull nor Hawthorne helpless; but one was enough of an "aristocrat" to be roundly hated in his neighborhood and much abused in the papers of his day, and Hawthorne was at pains to use such family pride as came in his way, with exquisite effect in the House of the Seven Gables. Miss Pyncheon does up a package in her little store with all the pangs a duchess might feel, and all of her awkwardness. The mistake of the British reviewer probably lies quite as much in concluding that family pride is absent in this country as in assuming that poor American novels are dull because of its lack.

It is now nearly a round century since John Adams noted that the colonists showed "greater care over their originals" than people of the same quality in England, and Lord Houghton ninety years later, with a surprise which shows the bare patches broad culture may leave, noted in an admirable review article, written after his second visit to America, that the literature relating to pedigrees was altogether larger in this country than in England, cutting a wider swath through the community, and that people in general were at more trouble here than there to know their ancestry accurately. To an Englishman, who knew that there were no titles to secure by this care, and no settled estates whose reversionary interest might make a marriage certificate and a baptismal registry, the bridge over which distant cousins pass to great wealth, this attention to ancestry, to one's "originals," as Adams put it, was as unexpected as it was astonishing. The simple fact appears to be that, with no ruling and property-laden class whose pedigrees keep themselves, there is here a diffused desire to keep family records; and by preserving a family line indulge in a gentle family pride which has led already to a number of family books and hundreds of smaller monographs. As Lord Houghton observes, there are few English pedigree writers who deem it worth their while to trace out collateral lines; the central and ruling stock absorbs attention, while American toilers in the same field deal with all branches of a family alike, and go to what this excellent English authority calls "extraordinary" pains to establish collateral relationships.

It is tolerably plain that this pain and trouble implies at least interest in one's family. Family pride, pure and simple, is a thing which a great many Americans would feel some shame at acknowledging. Of the two, an American is quite as willing to be an "ancestor," as Marshal Lannes styled himself in talking to the undistinguished princeling of an ancient house—as to have ancestors. To a Presidential candidate now, too many grandfathers would be a decided handicap. One or possibly two is about all that can be considered safe. But one has to watch American public life but a short time to see that family connections play an important part in affairs, and to perceive that a large share of the public men of to-day are descended from or related to the public men of yesterday. The new men are numerous. The way is open and the path is clear; but the old men have left their descendants well to the front. John Fiske says that the first thing a cataloguer learns is that if one man in a family has written a book some other man has, too, and it takes short reading in Congressional directories to show that the familiar names lie by twos and fours and sixes to its pages. Their presence is out of all proportion less than under an aristocracy. This is a matter of course, but it is altogether larger than is to be expected under a pure democracy, were it not that profound thinkers have pointed out that the influence of families swaying affairs by sheer transmitted influence is likely to be as strong in a republic as in an aristocracy, where this force is recognized by titles. At the Chicago convention the chairman, Hoar, came of a family in public life for more than a generation; Conkling, the prominent figure on the floor, had a father and grandfather known before him, and he is by marriage connected with a family who for three generations has shared in the government of New York State. Don Cameron, another leader, succeeded his father. Blaine's name recalls his connection with a leading Pennsylvania family in earlier days, and his relationship with the Ewings, of Ohio, is matter of public report. Sherman traces his name to the family which gave Roger Sherman to the Continental Congress. These things lie on the surface. The list could be extended almost indefinitely. To family pride in its technical English sense probably none of these men would plead guilty, and probably, too, none of them are wholly free from it.

GEN. JOHN KEAN.

Gen. John Kean was one of the earliest settlers of Harrisburg; one of the first Judges of Dauphin county; a County Commissioner for eight years; two terms State Senator from Dauphin and Berks counties; Registrar General of Pennsylvania; Elector in 1800, voting for Mr. Jefferson for President, and for many years a Justice of the Peace at Harrisburg.

His family have preserved brief notes, prepared by himself, of his public transactions, including some personal incidents. The information here given is drawn from that source. He was the son of John Kean, born in Ireland, 1728, who came to America 1742, served as a Captain in the Revolution, died at Harrisburg, 1801, aged 73. His wife, Mary Dunlap, was born 1721, died at Harrisburg, 1819, aged 98. The only son of this union was John, who was born in Philadelphia, October 3, 1762. His father was located in Dauphin (then Lancaster) in 1775; in 1780, John, junior, was called into service, and was with the army until after the taking of Yorktown. Upon his discharge he was placed with Mr. Clunie, a merchant, at Hummelstown, second sheriff of Dauphin county, at a salary of $100 a year and boarding. In this period he taught himself conveyancing and surveying. In

1785, he came to Harrisburg, as partner of Clunie. Of that period he states: "Where from the vast number of people crowding to this new place, and no houses being yet erected, I was compelled to take lodging with a Dr. Sterling, a mile above town. We came in April—we erected a house, and in August opened shop. Our sales quite excelled our expectations." In 1786, he was appointed a Justice of the Peace. He states: "From this period I may date any troubles I have had—as I could no longer attend store, the partnership was dissolved."

In 1786 he married his first wife, Mary, daughter of Hon. Robert Whitehill, of Cumberland county. In 1787, he was elected a county commissioner. Having lost his first wife he married in 1789, secondly, Jane, daughter of Capt. John Hamilton. In 1788, he was one of the members of "the Harrisburg Conference," held at "the Compass," the old ferry-house, at Paxton and Vine streets. He notes, 1790, "I was deeply interested in the progress of schools, churches, fire companies, the formation of a library, improvement of streets, and for sanitary precautions." He was of the first managers of the Library company, established in 1787; of the trustees of the Harrisburg Academy 1788; treasurer of the Presbyterian congregation; chosen Captain of our first volunteer company upon the resignation of Gen. Hanna, and President of the first fire company. In 1792, being appointed a judge, "I purchased a black suit and $60 worth of law books. Nature had furnished me with a frowning look, which with a black coat on was construed into a wise one; but I did my duty to the public satisfaction." In 1793, Harrisburg was visited with an "epidemic resembling yellow fever, which carried off great numbers, including my good friend, Mr. Hamilton." In 1796, he purchased, "with John Elder, jr., New Market Forge, about three miles from Palmyra, for $22,000, and removed thence." A few years before he had been elected to the State Senate, and was re-elected in 1798—serving until 1802. In 1805, he was appointed by Governor McKean Registrar General at a salary of $1,333.33, serving for three years. He removed to Philadelphia in 1810, was a merchant there —returned to Harrisburg in 1813, was again appointed Justice of the Peace by Gov. Snyder, and died December 9, 1818, aged fifty-six years, one of the most active and influential of the early citizens of Harrisburg. He was a brother-in-law by his marriages of Col. Richard M. Crain, Hugh Hamilton, Esq., James Alricks, Gen. Jacob Spangler and Moses Maclean, Esq. He left no male descendants. Two of his daughters are living, residents of this city.

A. B. HAMILTON.

AN EARLY SETTLER IN CLARK'S VALLEY.

[A gentleman who has recently been through the length and breadth of Clark's Valley sends us the following:]

Ludwig Minsker, an emigrant from the Palatinate, located in Clark's Valley in 1750. He built his cabin on a run near the place where the house of John Hocker, jr., now stands. He was a man of great courage, and the Indians of the neighborhood fearing him never molested him or his family.

It was subsequent to Braddock's defeat, that hostile Indians crossed over the mountains and spread death and desolation on the frontiers. While out hunting during the spring of 1756, Ludwig observed the trail of the marauding savages. Knowing that if they discovered his cabin, his wife and child, in his absence, would be killed, he hastened home and quickly devised means for their protection. It was too late to go below the mountains, for he would be overtaken. Having in his house a chest six feet long he bored a sufficient number of holes in it to admit air; then, taking it upon his shoulder, waded up the run some distance, placing it in a sequestered nook. Returning to his cabin he took his wife and child (the latter but six months old) in the same way to the chest to conceal his trail, where the dense foliage covered their hiding place. It was ten days before the hostiles had left the valley, and during all that time Mrs. Minsker and her child were safely secured in the huge chest, her husband, in the meantime, keeping guard in the neighborhood of their cabin, hunting and carrying provisions to the refugees.

One autumn, while Ludwig was carrying toward his cabin half of a good sized hog he had butchered, an Indian stealthily came up behind him, quickly severed the lower part, exclaimed, "hog meat very good meat, Indian like him," and scampered off to the woods.

The child who was concealed with his mother in the chest became Ludwig the second. He married a daughter of Thomas Cairn, and built his cabin at a spring on the Third mountain, on property now belonging to Harry Zeiders, who is a descendant of the first Ludwig. It is only a few years since that the cabin was torn down.

Prior to the Revolution, a friendly Indian had his cabin on the north side of Peter's mountain, near the spring which supplies the water-trough on the pike. Here he lived for years unmolested. One evening, in the fall of the year, Mrs. Minsker, while standing in the doorway, heard a loud moan, resembling that of some one in extreme agony. She told her husband, who replied that it was the cry of a panther. Still listening, she found by direction of the sound that the person was going up the mountain—but Ludwig to quiet her said she must be mistaken, it was only the cry of the panther. The ensuing summer, the cows remained out beyond the usual time and the children were sent in search of them. Going up the mountain they came to what was then called and still known as the "King's Stool," when they found a skeleton lying under it. Informing their father of the fact, Ludwig examined the remains—found by the hunting shirt which was intact that it was the Indian referred to. It appeared that some ill-disposed whites had gone to the cabin of the Indian and wantonly shot him—but did not kill him. With his little strength remaining the poor Indian crawled up and then down the side of the Fourth mountain across Clark's Valley; then up the Third mountain to the "King's Stool"—where he died from exhaustion. The rock alluded to is a huge boulder heaved on the top of another, and as high as the tallest trees.

The foregoing facts were gathered from the lips of Mrs. Mary Minsker, widow of the third Ludwig Minsker, now in her seventy-seventh year, and whose mental faculties are yet vigorous.

W. W. GEETY.

NOTES AND QUERIES.—LXI.

THE POSTMASTERS OF HARRISBURG.—It has so frequently been asserted within the past half year that John Wyeth was the first postmaster here, that "*Notes and Queries*" fears the error of such a statement will interfere with well established facts that are locally interesting. They are that

1. John Montgomery was first postmaster, appointed in 1792.
2. John W. Allen, appointed August, 1793.
3. John Wyeth, appointed October, 1793.
4. John Wright, appointed 1802.
5. Mrs. Wright took the office at his death, in 1814, who held it until 1822, when James Peacock was appointed.
6. James Peacock, who was succeeded in office by the following gentlemen:
7. Isaac G. McKinley.
8. Andrew J. Jones.
9. John H. Brant.
10. Dr. George W. Porter.
11. George Bergner.
12. Gen. Joseph F. Knipe.

13. George Bergner.
14. Henry Gilbert, *ad interim.*
15. M. W. McAlarney, the present incumbent.

DATES OF ARRIVALS OF THE ANCESTORS OF SOME OLD FAMILIES.—
The following partial list of arrivals of the ancestors of some of the old Dauphin county families—German, Swiss and French emigrants—is worthy of preservation:

Beader, Philip Jacob, Oct. 20, 1744; Buehler, Christian, Sept. 22, 1752; Buehler, Ulrich, Sept. 23, 1734; Bomberger, Henry, Sr. and Jr., Sept. 3, 1739; Buehler, Geo. Ernst, Sept. 3, 1739.

Dock, Balthaser, Sept. 13, 1749; Dock, Jacob, Sept. 17, 1750; Doll, Casper, Aug. 27, 1739.

Egle, John, Sept. 21, 1742.

Greenawalt, Hans Philip, Sept. 15, 1749; Gross, Christian, Aug. 28, 1750; Gross, Christian, Oct. 5, 1736.

Hummel, Adam, Sept. 19, 1732; Hummel, Thomas, Sept. 1, 1736.

Kapp, Michael, Sept. 16, 1751.

Kunkel, John, Sr. and Jr., Sept. 16, 1748; Kunkel, Adam, Sr. and Jr., Sept. 16, 1748. [These were brothers.]

Mumma, John Conrad, Oct. 13, 1747; Miller, John Peter, Sept. 9, 1751; Mumma, Jacob, Sr. and Jr., Sept. 11, 1731.

Ott, Hans Nicholas, Sept. 15, 1749; Ott, Hans Ulrich, Sept. 15, 1749; Ott, Philip, Sept. 21, 1732; Ott, Jacob, Sept. 18, 1733; Orth, Adam, August 19, 1729.

Rahm, Melchoir, Oct. 17, 1749.

Seyforth, John, Sept. 16, 1751; Sees, Christopher, Oct. 16, 1722; Sees, Balthaser, Oct. 5, 1737; Seiler Family, Aug. 30, 1749.

Thomas, Durst, Sept. 16, 1736; Thomas, Jacob, Sept. 16, 1736; Thomas, Martin, Sept. 16, 1736; Thomas, John and Peter, Jan. 10, 1739.

Ziegler, Hans George, Sept. 19, 1750; Ziegler, George, Sept. 25, 1751.

THE FORMATION OF DAUPHIN COUNTY.

[A proposition to divide the county of Lancaster was discussed about the commencement of the Revolution, but that ordeal of arms for several years quieted the agitation for the formation of a new county. When, towards the close of the war, the courts were crowded with business, when military fines were being sued out against non-associators, compelling many of the citizens from remote sections of the county to appear at the county town, the question of the formation of a new county embracing that portion of Lancaster county north of the Conewago with a portion of the county of Berks, seriously disturbed not only the citizens of both counties, but the Assembly, and petitions, pro and con, were frequently presented. The county of Berks was early in the field, they were not in favor of a dismemberment, and at the session of 1782, several remonstrances bearing upon this point had the effect of confining the new county enterprise to Lancaster county alone. At the ensuing session of the Assembly the subject of a division was again agitated—when the following petition, prepared by Judge Jasper Yeates, of Lancaster, was presented. The memorial was of no avail, however, and the matter being constantly brought to the attention of the legislative body, two years subsequently the county of Dauphin was erected. The remonstrance, however, is worth preserving as a part of the history of those times:]

To the Honorable the Representatives of the Freemen of the Commonwealth of Pennsylvania, in General Assembly met:
The Remonstrance and Petition of Divers Freeholders and Others, Inhabitants of the County of Lancaster, Most Humbly Sheweth:

That your petitioners conceive themselves bound to remonstrate against the prayers of two petitions proposed to the Legislature at the last session respecting a division of the said county of Lancaster, and beg leave to suggest to your *Honorable Body* the following remarks:

That a frequent division of counties must naturally occasion a distrust in the faith of government—persons who, confiding in the acts of the Legislature, having purchased landed property near a county town long established by law, suffering considerable losses from such division.

That the creating new counties necessarily tends to increase the public expenses, and to derange in some sort the policy of a government.

That nothing but the most manifest public expedience arising from the welfare of the community at large, independent of individual interests, can justify such measures in an old established county; and that tho' the bringing the courts of justice near to the doors of every man may in some wise conduce to his private interests, yet in other instances a remoteness of the station may be in some degree advantageous, as it tends to repress a litigious spirit in many who might be desirous of vexing their neighbors at law at a much less expense.

Your petitioners beg leave further to observe, that as to the petition which points out the precise limits of a new county attaching thereto a part of Berks county, your petitioners concur fully in the state of facts submitted to your honorable House by the inhabitants in general of the said county of Berks in their late petition and remonstrance, to which we humbly refer you.

As to the erecting of a county town at Harris' Ferry, we submit to the wisdom of the Legislature the propriety, expedience or justice of the measure. If a central situation has been ever deemed most eligible and convenient to the public at large for the cite of a county town, the spot proposed is deficient in this particular, the western boundary not exceeding one mile. If the trade of the back country on the Susquehanna is the real object of the petitioners, the *streams of traffic* will equally find their way to the capital of the State, whether there be a new county town erected pursuant to their wishes or not; and if the inhabitants who live beyond Peter's mountain find themselves aggrieved by their remote situation, it is submiteed to the Legislature whether it would not be more natural and easy to attach that settlement to Northumberland county. It is apprehended with due deference to the sense of your *Honorable House*, that measuring the petition for a county town at Harris' Ferry by the large scale of national good, and detracting therefrom a few individual interests, the prayer of that petition will be thought utterly inadmissible.

Your petitioners take the liberty of adding that the present bounds of the county of Lancaster are not found to be inconvenient or unreasonable.

That it will be utterly impracticable by the House to gratify the wishes of individuals in every instance when they complain of being aggrieved.

And that when the division of counties is forced as a measure, of course your Honorable House will have much of their time engrossed by petitions for such divisions from the interested views of private people, which the claims of the public demand for objects of much greater magnitude.

That in the present exhausted state of the country at large, when the public demands occasion the levying of heavy taxes, it would be highly grievous to many that new assessments should be laid for the purpose of building court house and jail, and other expenses incident to a new county; for tho' many have signed the petition, it may fairly be presumed there are many others within the several districts averse to such additional impositions.

Whereupon your petitioners most humbly pray that your Honorable Body, upon full deliberation had of the two petitions herein first before noted, will not grant the prayers thereof or either of them.

And your petitioners as in duty bound will ever pray, etc.

"KIHTOTENING MILLS" OR FORT HUNTER.

It frequently occurs in the story of the early settlements of this part of Pennsylvania, that family records become important in ascertaining dates or establishiug a controverted point. There has been a good deal of confusion respecting the Chambers brothers, who made the first settlement at what is now known as "Fort Hunter," Dauphin county, alluded to in the valuable contribution of Samuel Evans, Esq., of Columbia, which we take pleasure in presenting before proceeding with the story we have in hand:

"BENJAMIN CHAMBERS.—In 1724, a road was laid out from Chambers' mill on Susquehannah, at Kihtotening hill, to the Pine ford on the Swatara, thence to Lancaster. William Reinnock, James Armstrong, Hugh Black, Samuel Smith, Samuel Scott and Joshua Towl were the viewers. Armstrong probably lived in Lykens valley, Smith lived at Conoy creek, Scott, where the Lancaster pike crosses Big Chickies creek, and Towl, who was coroner of Lancaster county, lived in Hempfield township.

"The present turnpike from Harrisburg to Lancaster probably occupies a portion of this old road. Although this mill is designated as Benjamin Chambers', it is not conclusive evidence that he resided there. It establishes, however, the fact of the location of his mill and that it was erected prior to 1734.

In B. Chambers' letter to James Tighlman in 1774 (see Penna. Archives O. S. vol. iv., page 535) he says he was living at "Fawling Spring on Canogogige" before Cresap's raid, which was in 1736. While at Samuel Blunston's at Wright's Ferry, Thomas Penn sent for Mr. Chambers, who arrived there, when Penn gave him permission to build a corn mill on "Cedar Spring in the Manor of Loudun," in 1736. He probably removed west of the river in 1735. At this time he was aged twenty-three years. (See Penna. Archives O. S., vol. i., page 519.) He was, therefore, twenty-one years of age when application was made to the court to lay out the road from his mill to Lancaster. At this time it would seem that he had no design of removing to the west side of the river. Mr. Hamilton gives the year 1724 as the time he settled at Fort Hunter. This is evidently an error. He was probably misled by confounding the Benjamin Chambers who ran the temporary boundary line between Penn'a and Maryland and the miller. From Mr. C.'s letter to which I have referred, he was evidently well acquainted with the Scotch-Irish settlers in Donegal, and made frequent visits to Wright's Ferry and the vicinity. His familiarity with the topography of that locality would seem to warrant this inference.

"His visits to the neighborhood of Wright's Ferry, were not on

business strictly. His visits became very frequent to the old Indian trader, James Patterson, who lived three miles below Wright's Ferry. He married Mr. Patterson's daughter Sarah, between the years 1734 and 1736. Colonel James Chambers, of Revolutionary fame, was the only child by this marriage. His wife died probably in a year or two after their marriage.
SAM'L EVANS.

We have examined the article prepared by Mr. Hamilton, to which allusion is made. It is there stated that the brothers Chambers " are heard of about 1720, at the mouth of Fishing Creek, whether at what is now known as Little Conewago dividing Dauphin from Lancaster county, or Fishing Creek at Hunter's, we have no means of determining, more probably the latter.

"Subsequently, in 1725-26, a title under the fashion of the period was acquired at the mouth of Fishing Creek." This was undoubtedly at Fort Hunter. Having examined the subject thus far, we thought it best to ascertain upon what Mr. Hamilton founded his statement, and for that purpose "interviewed" him. He promptly answered all that we desired, remarking that the error was made in 1872, when he prepared and published his ephemeral papers on Fort Hunter. It consisted in the statement that Benjamin Chambers, with others, came to this, then Province, as 'adventurers in ye old Pennsylvania Comp'y'—why called 'old' eighteen years after Penn landed at Upland, is calculated to puzzle the present generation of inquirers. Benjamin, however, appears to have been one of its managers, as he is called upon by the council to lay 'his acc's before ye council on the 4th mo., 1704.' Whether he ever got them settled to his own, and to the satisfaction of his superiors does not appear, but we soon hear of his complaining to the same council of two Swede ministers who were about to set up a ferry' (over the Schuylkill as one may suppose), 'after he had made such conveniences as ye like had never been known in these parts.'"

Very soon after this appeared, a letter was received from Hon. Eli K. Price, of Philadelphia, to Mr. Hamilton, correcting the statement, too late, however, to repair the error, with any probability that sufficient interest was awakened in the subject to suppose that any one would make the correction for permanent reference.

Mr. Price writes: "The Benjamin Chambers spoken of as here in 1704, was not of your Dauphin or Cumberland heroes. *That* B. C. came here with, or soon after Wm. Penn; and the Swede's ferry referred to was afterwards "Gray's ferry," over the Schuylkill near Bartram's garden. He was a justice of the peace, sheriff of Philadelphia in 1682, *a Friend*, and did not fight. Your hero was always a fighter down to the Revolution, and was living in 1776. *Our* B. C. *died 1716.* In that year his estate was divided among his heirs—he had no children—the daughters and grandchildren of his brother John Chambers. One granddaughter of John married John Bartram and the other, Humphrey Marshall, and their sons were the botanists. *Our* B. C. came from England, *yours* came from County Antrim, Ireland, about 1720, then seventeen years old.

"Mr. Garrard's historical memoirs of Charlotte Chambers makes the same mistake you do."

Mr. Lewis H. Garrard published his memoir in 1856. He was a great grandson of Benjamin Chambers and of Sarah Patterson, as stated by Mr. Evans. The tradition in the family was, as told by Messrs. Garrard and Hamilton, and as both of them had access to family records and traditional narrative, it is not surprising that they were not aware of this error, that, owing to the exact coincidence of names, had fastened itself in the history of the connexion. General James Chambers, of Loudoun iron works, Franklin county, married Catharine Hamilton, only daughter of John Hamilton, who was the great grandfather of Mr. A. Boyd Hamilton.

Benjamin Chambers, one of these four brothers, was about seventeen years of age when the family came to Fort Hunter, 1725-26, fixing the year of his birth in 1708; another authority fixes it in 1703. He may have "prospected" in 1730, west of the Susquehanna, and been struck with the beauty and advantages of "Fawling Spring," (Chambersburg), but could not have made a permanent settlement until some years after this date; as the following record, furnished by Mr. Evans, would appear to prove:

"1735, May term court of Lancaster county, at Quarter Sessions, Samuel Maynes made complaint of assault and battery against John Chambers, John Chambers, Benjamin Chambers, Robert Chambers and Robert Miller.

"John Chambers plead guilty and was fined two shillings. The other defendants discharged. It would seem, therefore, that the four brothers Chambers were living at the mill on Fishing Creek, Paxtang, in 1735. Joseph Chambers died there in 1748. Samuel Hunter married his widow Catharine."

This is a scrap of historical information that future historians of Franklin county would do well to preserve. It may conflict with several cherished traditions, yet it is a true record of the common way of settling border controversies. It was over forty miles from "Kihtotening mills" to Lancaster, and must have cost in addition to the "two shillings" fine, a good deal of time and money. "Notes and Queries" is pretty well satisfied that there need not be further controversy upon this particular point, of the time or of the persons who were the original owners of the romantic neighborhood, well known as "Fort Hunter."

NOTES AND QUERIES.—LXII.

LOUISBURGH.—This name bestowed upon our town at the formation of the county of Dauphin by the then Chief Justice, Thomas McKean, was used in all official advertsements for at least three years, 1785 to 1788. The citizens, however, in deference to the founder, insisted on Harrisburg, and after the borough was incorporated Louisburgh was never mentioned.

SCRAPS OF LOCAL HISTORY.—We are indebted to our industrious friend and antiquary, Samuel Evans, Esq., of Columbia, for the following notes. Although seemingly of little importance, such facts as here embodied frequently give a clue to more valuable details and occurrences which otherwise would be left merely to tradition:

"At the August term 1735, of the court of Lancaster, Henry Jones was indicted for assaulting Peter Allen, the old Indian trader who resided along the eastern slope of the mountain, not far from Chambers.'

In 1732 a road was laid out from Donegal meeting house to Lancaster. The viewers were Patrick Campbell, John Mitchell, Randle Chambers, William Allison, Geo. Stuart and James Smith.

In 1737 a road was laid out from James Galbreath's mill on the Swatara creek to intersect the road at Harris Ferry to Lancaster at Thomas Harris on Conewago creek.

Thomas Gardner took up five hundred acres in Paxtang, March 4, 1733.

Henry Martin, two hundred acres on branch of Swatara, three miles above Castle's mill, May 26, 1737.

Thomas Sharp, two hundred acres on south side of Swatara, next Wm. Harbison, August 22, 1734.

Anthony Pretter, six hundred acres in Swatara Valley, south side of the creek, March 15, 1736.

In 1731 Peter Allen was licensed to keep a public house. In 1720 he settled in Donegal about a mile northeast from the furnaces below Marietta, and commenced trading with the Indians. It was likely he was still living there in 1731.

In October, 1734, he received a patent for four hundred acres in Paxtang, next Ketachtenny hills. He probably had the surveys for this tract of land made a few months before he received his patent. John Harris, I think, was the first and only person who was licensed to sell rum west of Donegal township previous to 1734, except perhaps William Dunlap, who kept a trading post on the Swatara, in 1730. Robert Dunning was also licensed the same year to sell rum, but at this time he lived along the Big Chickies creek.

McCombs, Davenport and Bizallion probably sold rum under a license also at an earlier date.

[We are not certain as to Robert Dunning, unless, there were two of the same name. There was a Robert Dunning residing west of the Susquehanna as early as 1728, and we infer that to him the license spoken of was issued.]

THE CAMPBELL FAMILY OF AMERICA.

To Mr. Brock's inquiries (N. & Q. lvi.), we have been able to send forward the following:

In the graveyard of Old Derry church, there is a tombstone with this inscription:

"Here lies | ye body of JOHN | CAMPBELL, who died | Febry 20, 1734, aged 79."

This is undoubtedly John (3) Campbell of the genealogy, the ancestor of the family in Pennsylvania.

Close by this tomb is a stone with the following, with inscriptions as rendered:

"Underneath this stone lies entombed | JAMES CAMPBELL's Dust you see | Who was as healthy and as strong | As many that may be | But now by death whom ,all devours | Is laid up in this cell | With crawling worms and reptiles base | He is obliged to dwell | You that these lines do look upon | May also call to mind | That death will be your certain fate | Therefore improve your time | He died May 31, 1777 | About the age of 80. | Also | *Agnes* his second wife | Who died April 3, 1757 | About the age of 50." | "In memory of | James Campbell Junr. | who departed this life | August 25, 1757 in the 33d | Year of his Age." | "In | Memory | of JAMES | CAMPBELL, | who depar | ted this | Life June 10, | A. D. 1783. | Aged 26 years."

These are the only epitaphs to the name Campbell appearing in Derry, but the name Patrick Campbell is among the assessments of Donegal township for 1725 and 1726, which at that period included Derry township.

Samuel (1) Campbell, of Derry (doubtless related to the above), died in October, 1747. (His will proved November 3, 1747.) He left a widow and the following children:

i. Hugh, (2) married and had issue: I. Elizabeth, (3) II. Samuel, (3)
ii. Mary, (2) married Thomas *Bowman* and had issue: I. Jean, (3) II. Elizabeth, (3) III. William, (3) IV. Jean, (3) married

James Clark and had issue: I. John (4) II. Samuel, (4) III. Isabella, (4) IV. Jean. (4)

Francis (5) Campbell ("The Campbell Family of Europe and America"), born 1727, married first, —— and had issue:
  i. Robert (6).
  ii. John (6), Episcopal minister of ability and learning, educated in England; had charge of the parish of York, and afterwards that of Carlisle, Pa., for thirty years, and died at Carlisle, May 16, 1819, aged 67 years; married and had issue: *i.* Frances, (7) married James Armstrong, of Williamsport, Pa., father of Hon. William H. Armstrong; *ii.* Elizabeth, (7) married June 26, 1813, Colonel Washington, son of Captain Andrew Lee, of the Revolution (N. & Q., No. xxv.); *iii.* Jane, (7) died unmarried.

The James Campbell who removed to Chillicothe, Ohio, was of a different family from that under notice. He was from Shippensburg or Chambersburg, Pa.

James (6) Campbell ("The Campbell Family of Europe and America") married Cassandana, eldest daughter of General Henry Miller (N. & Q., No. xxii.). He was an officer of the Revolution, studied law with William Lewis (Mr. David Watts, father of Hon. Frederick Watts, was a fellow-student in the same office and also married a daughter of General Miller). He was a practicing lawyer at York, Pa., as early as 1798. He died at Natchez, Miss., leaving issue:
  i. Sarah Miller, (7) died unmarried in 1849.
  ii. Henry McConnell, (7) an officer of artillery in the war of 1812; distinguished at Lundy's Lane and Chippewa; died unmarried on the eastern shore of Maryland.
  iii. Julianna Watts, (7) died unmarried in 1878.

Nancy, (7) daughter of Parker (6) and Elizabeth (Calhoun) Campbell ("The Campbell Family of Europe and America"), married Samuel, son of John Lyon, of Carlisle, Pa. Their daughter, Ellen (8) married Dr. —— Nichols. She conducted a seminary for young ladies near Baltimore.

[We print the foregoing in the hope of obtaining further additional data.]

OUR FIRST INHABITANTS.

A much respected friend and antiquary who has been devoting many years to the elucidation of our Indian history, gives us in reply to some inquiries the following interesting facts touching upon the Susquehannas, with promises that at some future time we shall hear from him in detail:

* * * I appreciate fully your difficulty in securing dates for a history of the Susquehannas. In connection with other tribes I have had them in my eye for several years and have only within the last few days reached satisfactory conclusions as to the salient points of their history. My friend Dr. Shea, who has done so much to elucidate Indian history, has as regards the Susquehannas, added to the confusion which previously existed. The terms Andastes, Andastogue, Gandastogue, etc., as used in the Jesuit Relations and other French works at different dates, covered a wide field, and a great number of tribes ; certainly as far east as the Susquehannas of your neighborhood ; as far north as the Carantowaunais near Tioga Point, and as far west as the western extremity of Lake Erie.

Finally the pressure from the Iroquois on the North and civilization on the East compelled the greater number to remove West of the Alleghenies.

The remnant that remained became subject to the Iroquois, who placed an Onedia vice-gerent to rule over them, as was their custom with all subjugated tribes. The Virginians made nearly as bad work with the name Susquehanna as our French friends did with that of Andaste and also of the Dutch who called nearly everything Minquas. The fact is that these tribes were all divided into confederacies, embracing from three to six distinct tribes. One of these confederacies almost entirely unknown, consisting of four distinct tribes was in 1632, governed by four kings, in thirty villages, and estimated at thirty thousand persons. (This probable was double the number at that date.) The four great towns named Tonhoga, Mosticum, Shaunetowa, and Usserahak were located on the upper waters of the Potomac in your State.

One of these tribes, Mowhacks, or *maneaters*, Mr. Neill, in his founders of Maryland, very kindly advises us were the *Mohawks of New York*, and yet they are placed on the Potomac and afterward on the James in several early maps. Another of these tribes Massomacks, the learned Gallatin, and all modern writers confound with the Iroquois of New York. They are the same mentioned by Smith in 1608 as Massowomacks, West of the Susquehannos, which term, as used by Smith, probably included the Eries or a portion of them. These last are also mentioned in Fleet's Journal, 1632 (Founding of Maryland), as Hirechenes and who lived a three day's journey from the Mosticums, "*one of our confederate nations.*" The Hirechenes were the Erich-ronons of the "Relations." All of those tribes yielding to the pressure from the east and north, retired to the Ohio and south of Lake Erie, including the best part of the Susquehannas (or what there was left of them), and under a great variety of names fought desperately for their existence against the terrible Iroquois. They were called Shawanese, Satanas, Torgenhas (by La Salle), Ontouagannha, Erich-ronons, Andastogue-ronons (see La Hontan's map), and a great variety of other names arising from the great numbers of fragments of tribes. Your friends, the Susquehannas, re-appear at the western extremity of Lake Erie as the Andastogue-ronons above, on several maps in company with the Eries. In 1673 the Iroquois begged piteously of Gov. Frontenac to assist them against the Andastoques, the sole enemies remaining on their lands (Col. His. N. Y., ix. 110), and these were their former enemies whom they had driven from New York and from the whole length of the Susquehanna. The war against them existed in 1668, '70, '71, '72 and '73 certain, and just at this point I propose to open up one of the most interesting chapters in our provincial history, and account for the whereabouts of La Salle during that interesting period. I have lately obtained evidence that I am quite certain will effectually clear up this very dark period, and settle a controversy that has puzzled our scholars for a generation.

DEATHS IN PAXTANG CONGREGATION.

[From the record of Rev. Mr. Sharon, alluded to in N. & Q. lv., we have the following list of deaths in Paxtang congregation. Those marked with a * are on the original list designated as Elders of the church. The date given is that of the burial: where the date of death is known, we insert it in brackets. We also append age.]

1809.

March 8 [6]. James Rutherford, 62.
June. Mrs. Awl.

1810.

January [9]. Isabella Larned (wf. Wm).
January [18]. Margaret Rutherford, 73.
October [10]. James Cowden, 74.

1813.

May 8. Susanna Rutherford, 63.
July [26]. Josiah Espy, 71.
August [17.] Mary J. Elder, 63.

1814.

August 12 [10.] Ann Elder Stephen, 47.

1815.

November 25 [23]. Mary Fulton, 45.

1816.
March [17]. John Allison, 46.
April [18]. Elizabeth Gray, 72.
September [23]. Elizabeth Sherer, 55.

1818.
August 19 [18]. Margaret Cowden.
September [29]. Robert Elder,* 77.
September. Mrs. McClure.

1819.
May [30]. John Gray, 66.

1821.
Margaret Allison.
William Calhoun.

1822.
July [16]. James Cochran, 80.
July 16. Jane Gray.
July [17]. Peggy Sherer, 34.

1823.
January 4. Mary Foster.
March [12]. Sarah Wilson, 70.
April 9. Jane Harrison.

1824.
March 11 [4]. Joseph Sherer, 38.
April 17. Williamson Harrison.
August 10. John C. Thompson.

1825.
March. Margaret Rutherford, 73.

1826.
February. Isabella Buffington.
February [25]. Sarah Kearsley, 72.
May 24. James Cowden.
May 28. Elizabeth Wiggins.

1827.
January 2. Edward Crouch.*
March 2. William Calhoun.
October [19]. Robert Elder, 86.

1829.
May 28. David Ritchey.

1831.
December [3] John Ritchey,* 56.

1833.
September 7. Hannah Calhoun.
November [26]. Samuel Rutherford,* 65.

1834.
February 20. Anne Gordon.
Frederick Hatton.

1835.
October 15. John Gilchrist, sen.
Elizabeth Wilson.

1836.
November [23]. Sarah Elder (wf. Robt.), 40.

1837.
April 2. Eleanor Elder (wf. Joshua), 35.

1838.
July. John McCammon,*

1839.
July 21. Robert McClure,*

1840.
April. David Espy.
July 7. Mary Hatton.

1841.
November. Eliz. Wilson (wf. Henry).
Sarah Kendig.
Ann Espy.

NOTES AND QUERIES—LXIII.

HEROES OF THE REVOLUTION.

[We present herewith the rolls of the companies of Captains Jacob Fridley and Richard Manning—the former raised in the neighborhood of Hummelstown, the latter in Upper Paxtang. These companies served faithfully during the compaign of 1776, and were present at Trenton and Princeton.]

Roll of Capt. Jacob Fridley's Company.

A true return of Capt. Jacob Fridley's company of the 4th Battalion of Lancaster county, commanded by Col. Jas. Burd, Esq., May 27, 1776.

Captain.
Fridley, Jacob.
1st Lieutenant.
McFarland, Jno.
2d Lieutenant.
Hover, Matth's.
Ensign.
Blessing, Philip.
Privates.
Boehler, Jacob,
Bell, Saml,
Brouster, Chas.
Byer, Jno.
Chambers, Rowland,
Zimmer, Nich's.

Currey, Jas.
Derry, Jacob,
Dunbar, John,
Ernest, Stopel,
Fishborn, Peter,
Fishborn, Philip,
Fridley, Bern'd,
Fridley, Peter,
Harris, Jacob,
Hummel, Fredk.
Hummel, Valentine,
Kecker, Philip,
Kisner, Jacob,
Krosklos, Better,

Laird, John,
Laird, Wm.
Lower, Geo.
Miller, Henry,
Montgomery, Alex.
Rouse, Martin,
Rowland, Thos.
Shad, Lodwk,
Spidel, Jacob,
Spode, Mich'l.
Spidel, Maxwell,
Suitle, Joney,
Wethhold, Jno.
Wilson, Wm.

Roll of Capt. Richard Manning's Company.

A true return of Capt. Richard Manning's of the 4th Battalion of Lancaster county, commanded by Jas. Burd, Esq., March 13, 1776.

Captain.
Manning, Richard.
1st Lieutenant.
Forster, Thomas.
2d Lieutenant.
Martin Samuel.
Ensign.
Burke, Elijah.
Privates.
Armstrong, Robt.
Ayers, John,
Ayers, William,

Bonnel, Jno.
Cain, Charles,
Cain, Neal,
Clemens, Samuel,
Crague, Aaron,
Forster, James,
Forster, William,
Foulks, William,
Goudy, Jno.
Hulins, Thomas,
Higgins, John,
Jones, Hugh,

Leech, Wm.
Martin, Alex.
McCord, Robt.
McCreight, Jas.
McMullen, Jno.
McMullen, Wm.
Reynolds, Alex.
Parkers, Moses,
Shields, Bernard,
Smith, Jno.
Stiver, Mich'l.
Troster, Stephen.

JAMES BURD, Col. 4th Battalion, Lancaster county.

CAPTAIN JAMES MURRAY.

James Murray was born in Scotland about 1729. His father William Murray, emigrated to America and settled on Swatara creek between the years 1731 and 1735. About the same time came Robert Murray, the father of Lindley Murray, the grammarian, and we are of the opinion that they were brothers—especially so since two of the sons of William Murray, Samuel and William, accompanied Robert Murray to the Carolinas about the year 1755.

In 1768 James Murray took out a patent for the tract of land on which he resided, located in Upper Paxtang Township, and then surveyed to him.

In 1775 he was chosen a member of the committee of safety for his township, and on the 8th of November of that year took his place in the general committee for Lancaster county. On the 4th of July, 1776, at a military convention, representing the Fifty-three battalions of the Associators, he was present as one of the captains for that county. A roll of his company was printed in the first number of *Notes and Queries*. With John Rodgers and John Harris, on the 8th of July, 1776, by appointment of the Provincial Conference, he superintended the election held at Garber's mill for the Sixth district of Lancaster county, to make a choice of delegates to the convention that assembled on the 15th of the month, and which framed the first constitution of the State. During that and the following year he was almost in constant active military service with his company. He commanded one of the companies of the Tenth Battalion, Lancaster county militia, and was with the expedition up the West Branch in 1779. The exposures to which Capt. Murray was subjected during the Revolutionary struggle brought on an attack of rheumatism, from which for many years prior to his death he was a constant sufferer. He died at his residence in Upper Paxtang on the 15th of March, 1804, aged 75 years. The *Oracle* pays this tribute to his memory. It will be seen, however, that Ireland is given as the place of his nativity. His family, however, claim that he was born in the Land of the Thistle:

"This worthy man was born in Ireland, and at three years of age he came to this country. He was an active and useful character (especially during the Revolutionary war). In the year 1786 he was violently attacked by rheumatism and other complaints; ever since he has been confined to his bed in extreme bodily pain. He was, however, cheerful and agreeable with his friends, patient and resigned to the Divine will, and endured the chastisements of his Heavenly Father without murmuring. He was a tender and indulgent father, and a good brother, neighbor and friend and a useful member of society. Trusting in the mercies of God, through Christ Jesus, he cheerfully resigned his breath and his body to be committed to the silent dust, attended by a respectable number of neighbors and friends—there to rest till the last trumpet sounds—'Blessed be the dead who die in the Lord.'"

Captain Murray married Rebecca McLean, a native of Scotland. Their children were:

i. *Margaret*, m. John Simpson, of Paxtang.

ii. William, removed to Virginia.
iii. Annie, m. Samuel Davidson.
iv. Rebecca, m. Samel Brown, of Hanover.
v. Isabella, m. Robert Chambers.
vi. John, who settled on Chillisquaque creek, Northumberland county. He was a member of the House of Representatives from 1807 to 1810, and served as a member of Congress, 1817 to 1821. He married Margaret, a daughter of Col. John Murray (*N. & Q. lii*). Of Capt. John Murray's brothers, Samuel and William removed, as stated, to South Carolina, Thomas settled at Muncy, and John, afterwards known as Col. John Murray, resided for many years prior to his death on an adjoining farm immediately above Dauphin.

THE BRITISH PRISONERS AT LANCASTER IN 1776.

[Lancaster, York and Reading were the principal places for the confinement of British prisoners during the war for Independence. Various causes are assigned why these localities were thus honored (?). Carlisle was another point which was thus distinguished, especially during the British occupancy of Philadelphia. As a general thing the officials were not placed in close confinement, but comfortably quartered, as the following letter will show, in private houses. As a matter of course there was more or less surveillance—but as a general thing the British officers fared better than those of the Patriot army in the hands of the British. The letter herewith printed for the first time was from the committee of Lancaster county to the committee of York county:]

"IN COMMITTEE FOR LANCASTER COUNTY.
March 19, 1776.

GENTLEMEN: We received last night a Letter from the Committee of Safety of the Province of Pennsylvania, accompanied with their Resolutions & those of the Congress respecting the Officers who are Prisoners here. In Consequence of the Authority delegated to us, to make the best arrangement we could, as to this Distribution, we beg leave to mention to you that we have pitched upon the Town of York for the Place of Residence of Captains Strong & Livingston—Lieutenants Wittington, Thompson & Thomas, & Ensign Gordon of the 26th Regt.—of Capt'n Robertson of the Royal Emigrants, of Capt'n Chase of the Navy. Lieutenant McDonnel of the 26th Regt. is absent in Philad'a by the Permission of the Hon'ble Congress. Cap'n Campbell has also leave to go to Philad'a to visit Mrs. Campbell who is indisposed. Should they return here they will also be fixed amongst you. The Officer's Servants accompany them. The other Officers are stationed at Carlisle. All the Military Gentlemen start from this Place on Friday next under the escort of two of us.

We think it is our Duty to give you the earliest Intelligence we possibly can of this measure, that you may take the proper Steps with Respect to their Plans of Lodging & such necessary precautions as must inevitably result from our Appointment. Permit us to quote a Passage from the Congress' Letter to us. "Upon the whole, Gentlemen, you have judged rightly in supposing every measure you have taken to render the Situation of our Prisoners as comfortable as possible, would be agreeable to us. As men they have a right to all the Claims of Humanity;—As Countrymen, tho' Enemies, they claim something more. You have Therefore the Thanks of The Congress." Need we suggest to you, Gentlemen, that your Interesting yourselves in Behalf of those officers who are to reside amongst you in procuring them such private Lodging, necessary accommodations as they may want, will particularly oblege those Gentlemen & this Board? Your own feelings, we are persuaded, will render this Intimation perfectly unneccessary.

We have to apologise to you for the liberty we have taken to open Your Letter from the Committee of Safety. Some Doubts arose with Respect to our Taking of the Parole of the Prisoners before they left this Borough. We recurred to your Letter for a Solution of our Difficulties. The common cause we are engaged in must serve as our excuse.

You will please to forward the Letter herewith sent to the Committee of Cumberland County by Express. We are directed to transmit our Letters as early as possible.
We are Gentlemen very truly,
Y'r most Ob'd't Humble Serv'ts.

IN THE REVOLUTION.

The following is a copy of a letter written by Col. William Gibbons, who owned one of the ferries at Paxtang, and purchased supplies for the army during the darkest hours of the war. He came from Nantmeal township, Chester county, where he owned large tracts of land. His residence at Paxtang may have been only a temporary one:

"PAXTANG, *March 9, 1779.*

"Friend, and Good Neighbor Gardner:

"There is that Greedy, extorting Disposition amongst us here; even of those who call themselves Whigs, And some Tories and Jew

Whigs, that grain is very hard to be purchased—Some denying that they have any to spare—Others say that it is promised—Some will not sell unless for the rising price, until their call for their money, so that near home I cannot purchase grain for my family, and have not two weeks' bread for my house. Therefore request you to get my grain threshed for me and keep it; only what you may need for your own use. And pray do me the favor to request my good neighbors, John and Jarred Irwin to keep what appertains to me.

"I have offered Col. Greenawalt and other men of Distinction what Commissions they would please to charge to buy grain for me—they say they can do nothing in that way unless I can furnish hard money, of which I have none.

"I intend soon going to Lebanon and getting Col. Greenawalt along with me, to go through that neighborhood, and if possible to purchase what grain may suffice my family until harvest, and if I am so happy as to succeed, Shall then be willing to sell what grain I have with you.

"I do not expect my wheat yield well; But hope I have a considerable quantity of Rye, which is good enough for me, and I suppose for any man that sets a Right value on his Liberty, if the fortune of War gives that turn to our affairs. Sooner would I eat Rye Bread to my dying day than meanly surrender my Liberty and Sell Posterity.

"With sincerity do I wish this may find you and all my former Good Neighbors in Good health and unanimous for the support of the American States.

"I remain, with sincere regard, Your Friend.

"WILLIAM GIBBONS."

Col. Greenawalt lived in Lebanon and commanded one of the Lancaster county Battalions of militia at Brandywine.

SAM'L EVANS.

Ang. 27. 1880.

NOTES AND QUERIES—LXIV.

MCKINNEY.—We have been furnished the following memoranda from the Readington (N. J.) Church Records, which will, perchance, supplement considerable genealogical information connected with this locality:

Mordechai McKinney, son of Mordechai McKinney, married Agnes Bodein [Bodine]. Their children were:

i. John, baptized Oct. 9, 1753.
ii. Marytje, bap. Dec. 27, 1755.
iii. Catrina, bap. Feb. 12, 1758; m. Joseph Hall.
iv. John, bap. March 2, 1760; m. Elizabeth Wyckoff, and had children as follows: *Rebecca*, m. John Stephens; *Peter Sudaford* [Studdeford]; *Mary; Nicles Wickoff;* and *Aletta Sudaford.*
v. Mordechai, bap. April 15, 1764.
vi. Angenietje, bap. May 18, 1766.
vii. Willem, bap. July 11, 1768.
viii. Antje, bap. August 12, 1770.

A portion of this family removed at an early period to Northumberland county, from whence several of its members came to this county, locating at Middletown. The late judge McKinney belonged to this family. If any one can supply the subsequent records we shall be under many obligations.

BAPTISMS IN PAXTANG CONGREGATION.

1807–1830.

[With the exception of the record of Rev. Mr. Sharon's "communicants admitted to Paxtang congregation" during his ministry, and the baptisms from 1831 to 1842, which we shall omit for the the present, the following closes the official record of that faithful and devoted pastor. The data herewith presented possesses more than a transient interest and value—it will be highly appreciated by many families genealogically connected—and although many of the individuals named are yet traversing the busy walks of life, we are confident this record will be just as interesting to them as to the readers of *Notes and Queries.*]

1807.

June 28. Samuel Gray.
Sept. —. James Anderson.
Sept. —. David T. Caldwell.

1808.

April 6. Catharine Ann McCammon.
April 6. Polly Bowman.
April 24. James Rutherford.
April 24. Thomas Bell Allison.
July 24. Elizabeth Gray Espy.
August 21. Jane Chamberlain.

Sept. 15. John Wiggins Smith.
Sept. 15. Thomas Michael Whitley.
Oct. 21. Wallace Calhoun.
Dec. 4. Margaret Rutherford.
Dec. 4, John Wyeth Barned.

1809.

April 9. Ann McClure.
April 9. George Ross.
April 9. Catharine Carson.

1810.

June 24. Josiah Espy.
June 24. Joseph Ross.
August 5. Mary Rutherford.
August 11. Mary Gray.

1811.

April 7. Margaret Mary Hayes.
May 5. John Carson.
August 22. Samuel Rutherford.
August 25. Joseph D. Jones.
October 31. Priscilla McClure.

1812.

August 15. ——— Ross.
August 15. Lydia C. Allison.
August 15. Sarah Rutherford.
August 15. Ann Espy.

1813.

April 19. George Carson.
May 9. Robert Walker Taylor.
July 11. Isabella Campbell.

1814.

June 13. Eleanor Gray.
June 13. Abner Rutherford.
June 13. Andrew Wilson.

1815.

January —. George Washington Simmons.
August 20. James Cowden.
August 20. Sophia Carson.
October 30. William Stewart Culbertson.

1816.

June 20. Hiram Rutherford.
June 20. Robert Culbertson.
June 20. Isamiah Hayes.
July 11. Cyrus Findley.

1817.

April 14. Joseph Campbell.
May 21. Margaret Clifton Jones.
September 19. Esther Gray.
September 19. John Simmons.
September 19. Mary Rutherford.
December 8. John Wallace Cowden.
December 8. Josiah Espy.

1818.

May 10. Ira Harris Jones.
May 10. Mary Ann Sherer.
June 28. William Carson.
June 28. Jacob Carson.
June 28. Mary Ann Hayes.
June 19. Amelia Brady.
December 7. ––––– Harrison.
December 29, Sarah Wilson Foster.

1819.

June 20. Maria Harris Jones.
April —. Edward Crouch Jordan.
October 16. Cyrus Green Rutherford.
December 31. William Espy.
December 31. Levi Boon.
December 31. Margaret Cowden.
December 31. James Cowden Gillmor.
December 31. Mary Ann Harrison.

1820.

January 9. Jane Whitley Simmons.
February 2. James Sharon Mahargue.
September 3. Martha McClure Forster.
December 3. Harriet Harrison.

1821.

May 6. John Ritchie Elder.
September 6. Harriet Carson.

1822.

January 3. Sarah Montgomery Peffer.
January 3. Ira Jones.
January 3. Eliza Jones.
May 11. Elizabeth Sherer,
May 11. Nancy Ainsworth Mahargue.
May 11. ——— Harrison.
May 14. Thomas Jefferson Jordan.
May 14. Thomas Grier Hood.
June —. Ann Maria Espy.
August 14. John Gordon Hart.
September 20. William Kerr Cowden.
September 20. Alexander Boon.
October 19. Sarah Stanley Thomson.

1823.

February 1. Samuel Elder.
February 22. Robert Gilchrist & Simmons.

1824.

April 11. Harriet Newell Cupples.

1825.

February 2. William Allen.
March 27. ——— Hart.

1826.

May 1. Mary Ann Barnett.
May 19. David Espy Moore.
May 22. Thomas Wilson Buffington, Elizabeth Slaymaker Buffington.
May 22. Isabella Fulton Buffington.
June 9. James Cowden Jordan.
July 3. Sarah Elder Cowden.
October 28. William Gillmor.
December 22. Samuel Sherer Elder.
December 22. James Elder.

1827.

January 10. David Espy.
November 10. Keziah Hart.

1828.

Aug. 22. Edward Crouch Cowden.
March 1. Samuel Silas Brisbin Rutherford.
March 1. William Swan Rutherford.

1830.

July 18. Josiah Reed Elder.

PARSON ELDER AND THE PAXTANG BOYS.

[The following extracts relating to the Rev. John Elder and the Paxtang Boys, we glean from the correspondence of Thomas Elder, youngest son of the brave old minister of frontier times, in possession of his daughter, Mrs. Boude. During his life-time the younger Mr. Elder was frequently queried as to the main facts in the life of his father—and when important replies were made, copies thereof properly taken and preserved. Parkman in his "Conspiracy of Pontiac," Redmond Conyngham in his "Historical Papers," and Charles Miner in his "History of Wyoming," expressed themselves under many obligations to Thos. Elder for the valuable information contributed by him. The extracts given are not only valuable, but interesting, as giving some facts which have not heretofore been made public. As we have in preparation a "Record of the Elder Family," we reserve a notice of Col. Thomas Elder for another time.]

[*From Charles Miner the Historian of Wyoming, to Thomas Elder.*]
September 21, 1843.

* * I am greatly struck with the evidences of learning, talent and spirit displayed by your father. He was beyond doubt *the most* extraordinary man of Western Pennsylvania. I hope some one may draw up a full memoir of his life and a narrative, well digested, of his times. * *

May 12, 1843.

* * He was a very extraordinary man, of most extensive influence—full of activity and enterprise, learned, pious and a ready writer. I take him to have been of the old Cameronian blood. Had his lot been cast in New England he would have been a leader of the Puritans. * *

[*Thomas Elder to Redmond Conyngham.*]
May 30, 1843.

* * My father had a good and very handsome face. The features were regular, yet no one feature prominent—good complexion, with blue eyes. In speaking with an old and estimable gentleman last Saturday about my father, I asked his recollection of his face. He replied: I remember him perfectly, indeed, as well as if he was now before my eyes, and say that he had as good a face as could be found in ten thousand. He was a portly, long straight man, over six feet in height, large frame in body, with rather heavy legs. * * * * * As to the letter of the 17th March, 1764,

which was written by my father, you have my consent to use it in connection with the materials and facts you are in possession of; your judgment and discretion will best advise what use to make of it. It is probable it was written to Doctor F. Allison, though possibly to Doctor Ewing—Allison, Ewing, Tennent and my father were then and up to the time of their several deaths, very intimate and close friends. * *

[The letter in question is entitled "Letter from a gentleman in one of the back counties to a friend in Philadelphia," and was written by Rev. Mr. Elder.]

[*Thomas Elder to Charles Miner.*]

May 12, 1843.

* * At the time the British army overrun New Jersey, driving before them the fragments of our discouraged, naked and half-starved troops, and without any previous arrangement, the Rev. Mr. Elder went on Sunday as usual to Paxtang Church. The hour arrived for church service, when, instead of a sermon, he began a short and hasty prayer to the Throne of Grace; then called upon the patriotism of all effective men present, and exhorted them to aid in the support of Liberty's cause and the defense of the country. In less than thirty minutes a company of volunteers was formed. Colonel Robert Elder, the parson's eldest son, was chosen captain. They marched next day, though in winter—my brother John at sixteen years was among the first. My brother Joshua, sub-lieutenant of Lancaster county, could not quit the service he was employed in, but sent a substitute.

The disaffected and tories around (who were very saucy) raised a story on the old man's prayer of this Sunday, and though not a word of it true never gave offense. That he begged for and implored Heavenly aid to give success to the American cause. "We beseech Thee, through our Lord and Saviour Christ, mercifully to give us triumph, yet not ours but Thy blessed will be done. And, oh, Lord God of the Universe; if Thou art unwilling by Divine grace to assist us, *do stand aside and let us fight it out!*"

I met with an old Dutchman lately, a friend that I had not seen for years—a Whig. We had some wine, when he gave me many anecdotes, and this among the rest and he told it well.

[*Thomas Elder to Mr. Miner.*]

May 12, 1843.

My father did not talk broad Scotch—a dialect, however, always pleasing to me. He talked and spoke much as we do now, but grammatically. By the way, there was no little Puritan feeling about him. He, from the first outbreak of the Revolution, was a warm and active Whig—was Chairman of the Committee of Public Safety for this part of then Lancaster county, which extended to the Northumberland county line.

NOTES AND QUERIES.—LXV.

MINSKER, LUDWICK (N. & Q. lix).—On the roll of Capt. John Murray's company, Miles' regiment, 1776–1778, occurs the name of Ludwig Minsker, private, with the remark, died in service November 24, 1776. Capt. Murray's company was enlisted in what is now the northern portion of Dauphin county. L.

WILSON, HENRY.—Henry Wilson, a native of Harrisburg, who represented the Northampton and Lehigh district in Congress from 1823 to 1826, died at Allentown, August 19, 1825. Can any one give us proper information as to Henry Wilson and his family. All that we have been able to glean concerning him is that his father was a cabinet maker, who died early in life, leaving Henry and one or two other children.

A GOOD WORK.—The present year being the fiftieth anniversary of the Church of God, the organ of that religious denomination, the *Church Advocate*, is publishing a valuable series of historical and biographical sketches. The histories of the various elderships are especially interesting, while the recent extended sketch of the Rev. John Winebrenner, prepared by Dr. Geo. Ross, is a valuable contribution to Pennsylvania biography. If not already organized, it is in contemplation the forming of an historical society—and with such progressive spirits as Messrs. Ross, Redsecker, Forney and others of that young, though influential denomination, it must prove successful. As one of the Reformers of the first half of the present century, the history of the eventful life of Rev. John Winebrenner should be brought to their early attention. It deserves to be well and carefully written. Either of those mentioned are able for the task. Their present work—the preservation of the historic records of their Church—is commendable.

THE LYTLE FAMILY.

The name of Lytle—spelled also Litle and Little—is found among the Earliest Scotch-Irish settlers in Lancaster county, Penna., who located more particularly in the townships of Rapho and Donegal.

My ancestor's name was Joseph Lytle—not the Joseph Lytle who, in Nov., 1775, was elected a member of the Revolutionary "Committee of Observation and Correspondence," but from data in my possession, must have been a cousin to him.

Marietta was then known as "Anderson's Ferry," and was a point of great importance until the bridge constructed at Columbia diverted the trade across the river and reduced the ferry. My impression is that Joseph Lytle had been interested in the river transit business, and desiring a new field of labor he decided upon a location northward, as we shall see presently.

Meanwhile he had married Sarah Morrison, a lassie of his own nationality. Their first child was a daughter, whom they named Jane, and with her began a list of names having no originals that I can trace within the family; quite an exception to the custom of primitive times. A second daughter was named Elizabeth, and then a son, John.

An important event now occurs, in the removal of the family from Marietta to the locality on the Susquehanna river, afterwards known as "Lytle's Ferry." Here Joseph Lytle arrived with his family in the fall of 1779, just a month after his future relatives, the Ayres', had arrived at Peter's mountain.

It may be opportune to remark, that in early times, when the country bordering the river was in its unbroken state of nature the route of travel—mostly of emigrants from Lancaster, Chester and the lower counties, seeking new homes and wider opportunities on the north and west branches of the Susquehanna—was found to be practicable for along the eastern shore only, for about twenty-five miles above Harris' Ferry. Beyond that, the extremely rugged condition, the difficulty of crossing numerous streams which emptied into the river, the inaccessible mountain spurs, and other reasons were sufficient to necessitate crossing to the western shore where the obstacles to passage were comparatively few or more easily surmounted. Indeed, there was no opening from Lytle's Ferry to Sunbury, save the "Indian Paths"—nothing like a road.

Repeating, for the sake of its proper connection, what I have already contributed to N. & Q. (xxxi.) I record that this property was obtained through warrants originally issued to John Kroker (1766) Samuel Hunter (1767) and Joseph Lytle (7th Nov., 1773), and comprised a fraction over two hundred acres. Geographically, it was situated about four miles north of Halifax, and about two miles south of Millersburg, in what is now Halifax township, and a half mile below Berry's mountain. The tract was surveyed December 3d, 1773, by Bertram Galbraith, and named in his draft "Fairview."

Noting the addition of a daughter, Mary, in 1774, the family history is silent for twelve years. But as the intervening time was momentous in our country's history—the Revolutionary period—we can easily imagine that, situated as they were on the main line of communication in Central Pennsylvania, and hearing continually from the "seat of war," they shared in excitements of which their neighbors were perhaps ignorant; fed passing detachments of troops who rested at the Ferry, and enjoyed little privacy and less quietude.

In 1794, John Lytle, then twenty-two years old, went out as cornet with his neighbors John Ayres and James Reed, in a cavalry company, when military force was summoned to suppress the Whiskey Insurrection in Western Pennsylvania.

The death of Joseph Lytle occurred prior to April 17, 1795 (according to family data), but the actual date is unknown. He was taken ill suddenly and a messenger was sent to Lancaster for his family physician.

After the father's death, the ferry was purchased by John Lytle and Michael Bower. In April, 1806, they sold to William Moorehead (father of the well-know Moorehead brothers, of Philadelphia and Pittsburgh), the ferry taking his name, it having borne the name of *Lytle* for nearly thirty-three years. He relinquished it about 1814 and it became "Montgomery's Ferry," and is only remembered as such at this day.

The first marriage in this Lytle family was that of the eldest child, Jane, (1767–1831) to John Ayres, farmer, (N. & Q. lvi.) on the 2d of April, 1786. The second, that of Elizabeth (1770–1852) to David Watson, merchant, of Watsontown, Northumberland county, January 24, 1797.

The third, was that of the youngest child, Mary (1774–1848) who married John McCleery, a merchant, of Halifax, September 23d, 1802.

The fourth marriage was one in high life when the dashing son, Major John Lytle (1772–1808) led to the altar "the agreeable and lovely Miss Elizabeth Green"—according to the *Oracle of Dauphin* —third daughter of Col. Timothy Green, of Green's Mills (now Dauphin) who was a conspicuous character in the history of Lancaster and Dauphin counties. This distinguished affair of January 10, 1805, was conducted by Rev. Nathaniel R. Snowden, who married Elizabeth and Mary also.

The aged mother, surviving her husband thirty-two years, died July 3d, 1822, at John McCleery's, at the advanced age of ninety-one and was buried at Watsontown. Her husband was buried at Dauphin.

The Lytles were widely known in their day, and were inter-married with some of the best families of Dauphin and Northumberland counties, many of their descendants still living in the latter. In common with the grand old names of the early times, they did their full share in developing the resources of Dauphin county, and laying the foundations of society and business as we find it matured in the glory of to-day. GEORGE B. AYRES.

AN EARLY ROLLING MILL.

The first mill in the United States to roll bars and puddle iron was located on Redstone creek, at a place called Plumstock, in Fayette county, Pennsylvania. The enterprise was undertaken by Colonel Isaac Beeson, who employed two Welshmen, brothers, being skilled workmen, who where prohibited by an English statute from leaving their country, and thus compelled to smuggle their passage across the Atlantic. This rolling mill was erected in 1816. The first bar iron rolled in New England was at the Boston iron works, on the mill dam in Boston, 1825, and that the first puddling in New England was done at the same place by Lyman Ralston & Co. in 1835.

The first mill for rolling bar iron in the section of country surrounding Harrisburg, Pa., was erected on the Conedoguinet creek, about one mile from its mouth, near the village of Neidigstown, now Fairview, Cumberland county, on the present site of the rolling and nail mills of the Messrs. McCormick, by Messrs. Gabriel Hiester and Norman Callender, of Harrisburg, in 1833, who carried on the mill until the death of Mr. Hiester the following year (1834.) His son, A. O. Hiester, then purchased Mr. Callender's interest in the works and conducted the business for a number of years successfully. He then disposed of the mill to Jared Pratt, from Massachusetts, who erected the first nail mills in connection with the rolling mill in this part of the country. Mr. Pratt was a thorough business man with much enterprise. He also established a rolling mill on the Le Barron lot occupying the buildings formerly erected by William Le Barron. Mr. Pratt continued the rolling of boiler and bar iron and the manufacture of nails on a large scale for some years, and then sold both of the mills to James McCormick, Sen., Esq.

The rolling of bar iron attracted many visitors to the mill of Messrs.

Hiester & Callender, who had never witnessed the manufacture of bar iron by rolling it. It was a novel sight to see the red hot bars passing through the rollers, bending in graceful curves like great fiery serpents,—the people being accustomed to hear of or see all the iron that was made into bars slowly forged into different sizes by the great hammers at the forges, which were located mostly on large creeks, and were propelled by water, as steam engines were not introduced into the interior of the country until a later period. The only forges near Harrisburg were that owned and carried on by the late Jacob M. Haldeman on Yellow Breeches creek near its mouth, and the other one on the same stream at Lisburn, Cumberland county. The forge of Mr. Haldeman has not been in operation for many years, but the one at Lisburn has been until quite recently. It was said that when Harrisburg was a smaller and quieter town the hammers of the forge at Lisburn, some six or seven miles away, could be distinctly heard at the lower end of Front street, on a still morning, the sound following the course of the creek. A. BURNETT.

NOTES AND QUERIES.—LXVI.

AN EARLY ROAD.—In April, 1784, a road was directed to be laid out from Rev. John Elder's house " at ye foot of ye Blue mountain " beginning at Rev. J. Elder's house, thence to John Thompson's field, thence to Robert Cochran's lane, thence to Paxtang creek, thence to South Branch of Paxtang creek, thence to Samuel Sturgeon's field, thence to Joseph Martin's field, thence opposite meeting house, thence to provincial road on Spring creek, 5 miles and 58 perches long. Can anyone inform us where the residence of Rev. John Elder then was?

RODDY, JAMES, (N. & Q. xli.)—James Hutchinson took up some land along the little Chickies, about a mile above its junction with big Chickies, in 1749. This tract was known as " Denmark." It was bounded by Chickies creek, and the farms of James Mitchell, Jane Stewart, James Roddy and Thomas Brown. Roddy must have joined on the west side, and his land ran to the creek. In 1745 the farm of James Patterson between the creeks, was bounded by James Roddy's land which must have run to the creek to do so. Roddy was in Donegal in 1723. The year the name disappears I am not able to determine. S. E.

HARRISBURG IN 1784.—We copy from a Philadelphia newspaper the following advertisement:

HARRISBURG
A NEW TOWN.

The subscriber having laid out a *Town* on the banks of the Susquehanna, adjoining the Ferry (commonly called Harris' Ferry) he now offers for sale or on ground rent, for such term of years as may be agreed upon a number of LOTS in said town. This spot of ground seems designed by nature for the seat of a town; it's healthy, pleasant, high situation—it's easy communication by water with a large part of the country—it's lying on the *main road through the Continent*, and from Philadelphia to Ft. Pitt, and all the back country—points it out as one of most convenient and best spots for a town in the interior parts of the State of Pennsylvania. The town may be accommodated with a very fine dock, at a small expense, there being a natural canal, defended on both sides by limestone banks at its entrance into the Susquehanna, where boats and craft will lay safe at all times. There being a great deal of fine clay for making bricks and earthen ware, also a great plenty of wood which will be furnished on very low terms, encouragement will be given to brick makers, potters and other tradesmen. For terms apply to

JOHN HARRIS.

A FAVORITE SHADE TREE SEVENTY YEARS AGO.—About one hundred years ago the Lombardy poplar was introduced into the United States, and for sixty or seventy years was almost the only shade tree planted. The trees stood like great tall sentinels around nearly all the better farm houses, and in double rows were placed along the avenues leading to rural mansions occupied by the wealthy. The first Lombardy poplar trees introduced into Harrisburg were by Robert Harris, Sen., and Gen. John A. Hanna, about 1790, and were brought from New Jersey by these gentlemen. Mr. Harris planted his in front of the Harris residence on Paxtang street, lately known as the "Black Horse Tavern," demolished during the past summer. Gen. Hanna planted his in front of his residence on Front street, corner of Strawberry alley, now the residence of his grand-daughter, Mrs. John H. Briggs. As the Lombardy poplar grows from cuttings as the willow does, many were thus propagated. Mr. Harris planted a row on the river bank below Indian alley, also a row on each side of Second street below Vine. Several were placed in front of the old Presbyterian church, then located on the corner of Second street and Cherry alley. Mr. Duncan had one on Chestnut near Second, and

Robert Sloan planted two on Chestnut near Third. There were several on Second street above Locust street, and in other parts of the borough. These trees all grew to be quite tall, but being unsuitable for the streets of a populous town, were gradually removed until none remained. For some years they were a thing of the past, until the late Governor Shunk planted one in the Capitol park near to the Mexican monument. It has, however, been of slow growth, owing to the naturally thin soil.

The Lombardy poplar, which graced the surrounding yards of the best residences throughout the country at one time, has almost disappeared for some reason, probably because it was deficient in giving shade, and was thought unsafe on account of its great height and the brittle nature of the tree in violent storms of wind. A. BURNETT.

YE ANCIENT INHABITANTS—X.

"*Return of ye West Side of Derry—1758.*"

Albright, Jacob, renter from John McNeel at 1 d ℔ year.
Armstrong, Robert.
Chambers, Arthur, exe'r to Estate of James Chambers, dec.
Carson, William & John, inmate with Jane McConaghey.
Chambers, Widdow, poor widow.
Carithers, Hugh.
Clark, James.
Carithers, James, shoemaker.
Coutes, Jacob, a waste plantation.
Candour, Joseph.
Carithers, Robert.
Chambers, Arthur.
Chambers, Robert.
Campble, Moses, shoemaker.
Crockat, John, renter from James Todd at £1 10s ℔ year, deeded land.
Blackburn, Widdow.
Blasley, Antoney, mason.
Bughman, Michail, waste land.
Bell, Thomas, blacksmith.
Breden, William.
Black, Hugh.
Black, Thomas.
Barndt, William, fled, poor man.
Brand, Martin.

Baum, Adam, gunsmith.
Barsh, Peter, weaver.
Bombugh, George, tailor.
Bevor, George, waste.
Baker, Deval, two tracts of waste land, Joyning.
Boman, John, weavar, renter from James Clark at £1 10s ℔ year.
Dalkar, Adam.
Drenon, William.
Edly, David, tailor.
Fray, George.
Fleck, Alexander.
Fleming, John.
Gengel, Michail, living on Adam Dalkar's land.
Hover, Michail, Jun., renter at £7 ℔ year.
Hipsheer, Ulry.
Hummel, Frederick.
Hamaker, Adam, weavar.
Hall, Thomas.
Hershaw, Andrew, Jun., waste land Deeded.
Hovar, Michail, renter from Hugh Hays for the 3d Bushal.
Hays, Hugh, waste land.
Hart, Widdow.
Harris, John, Esq., deeded land.
Ireland, James.
Kerr, John, deeded land.
Kindar, Deeter, weavar.
Leard, John.
Leard, Matthew.
Landies, Felix, deeded land, 200 acres, 100 in possession, one grist mill.
Morrow, Samuel, weavar.
Morrow, Lewis.
Newcomar, John, wagon maker.
Nickelson, Culbart.
Nilson, James, weavar, renter from David Ramsey at £8 ℔ year.
Neelson, Robert, renter from Jacob Righar at £4 ℔ year.
Newcomer, Francis.
Parks, Thomas, wagon maker & renter from Widow Sample at £14:17s ℔ year.
Patterson, Moses, renter from Mr. Stevenson at £5 ℔ year.
Porterfield, John, fled.
Ridals, James, cropper with Widow Blackburn, poor.
Robens, William, poor.

Reed, Samuel, renter with Mr. Stevenson at £8 ℔ year.
Russall, James.
Russall, James, Junear.
Ramsey, Robert.
Robertson, Andrew, renter from Widdow Hall at £3 ℔ year.
Stoall, Mathias, poorman.
Straker, William, renter from Hendry Little at £4-10 ℔ year.
Shoop, Stophal.
Stirrat, William.
Shaw, Danial, shoemaker, fled; on Mr. Stevenson's land.
Spensar, William.
Stall, Mathias, nailer.
Stevenson, Mr., waste.
Spinglar, Deeter, shoemaker.
Singar, Simon.
Singar, John, fled.
Stevenson, Mr., a waste plantation.
Stevenson, Mr., a waste plantation.
Sample, Widdow, tavernkeeper, deeded 100 acres to 2 Neagors, 1 aged 60 the other 12 years.
Spidal, Mack, weavar.
Shaw, James,
Stirratt, Alexander, blacksmith.
Tagart, James, poor man.
Taylor, Robert, tavernkeeper, deeded.
Tice, John.
Taylor, Robert, a tract of waste land.
Vanlear, John.
Vance, John.
Wyle, widdow, poor woman.
Wilson, John, a tract of waste land.
Wastberey, George, fled.
Wolfle, Conrod.
Waganor, Adam, weaver.
Wilson, Mathew.
Walker, Robert, renter from Thomas Rutherford at £10 ℔ year.
Wilson, deeded 130 acres & 30 acres by warrant.
Walker, Samuel & James, renters from Widow Sample at £4 ℔ year.
Young, Samuel, fled, poor.
McGill, Lorrance, renter from Mr. Stevenson at £4 ℔ year.
McConnell, Edward, living on Mr. Stevenson's land.
McLean, Hector.

McCormick, Samuel.
McClure, John, fled, poor.
McComb, William, renter from Widdow Sample at £3 ⅌ year.
McKee, Widow.
Weirick, Anthony.

Freemen.

Harris, James, taylor.
Shanklin, George.
Strikar, Lorrance.
Cosler, Frederick, blacksmith.
Campble, John.
McCullough, John, weaver.
Riddle, Tristram.
Vanlear, James.
Queen, Thomas.
Hendry, James, blacksmith.
Snoddy, James, gunsmith.
Waugh, John, blacksmith.
Laney, Andrew, wheelwright.
Finton, James, schoolmaster.
Philopsager, George.
Clark, Samuel.
Walker, James.
Bowman, John.

a True Return,
ADONIUS WEIRICK,
Constable.
ROBERT TAYLOR,
Coll'r.

NOTES AND QUERIES—LXVII.

CONTRIBUTIONS TO THE HISTORY OF THE CUMBERLAND VALLEY.— We present with this number of *Notes and Queries* the first portion of the promised historical and genealogical data relating to the beautiful valley " West of ye Sasquehannah." In about two weeks we propose giving another installment—and shall from time to time present the additional information which may come to our hands. There is much to be done in researches among the musty records of the past, ere justice be done to the early history of the Cumberland Valley—

and the same applies to every section of our State. Since 1720 much of the important history of Pennsylvania belongs to and centers in that portion beyond the three original counties. To gather up this genealogical and biographical history is an arduous task, but there be some who feel it a duty so to do. We are confident that this labor will be duly appreciated by the descendants of the early pioneers, and induce those interested to assist in the preservation of everything relating to those ancestors and early frontier times.

THE ROBBER LEWIS.—In the diary of the late Samuel James McCormick, who lived two miles south of Doubling Gap, I find the following:

"On Tuesday, the 20th of June, 1820, the sheriff of Franklin county arrived with a party in search of David Lewis (the robber) and early the next morning proceeded to the mountain southeast of the Sulphur Springs, where they discovered a cave or den, where they found blankets and other articles known to belong to Lewis. But according to the best information the inhabitants had decamped on the Thursday before."

This you will observe was only about three weeks before Lewis' death. The cave, badly fallen to ruin, is still shown to the visitors at the Springs. It was known that Lewis had a cave somewhere in the mountain to which he fled from time to time during the years 1816–20, but its locality was not discovered before June, 1820.

J. B. SCOULLER.

EARLY COURT CASES.—At the February court, held at Lancaster, 1756, John Bayley, a runaway servant of the Rev. John Elder, was ordered to serve Mr. Elder eighteen months over and above his time. This was generally called "runaway time."

Andrew Lycans, of Hanover township, was indicted at the November term, 1742, for an assault and battery upon Joseph Ripeth. James Armstrong, Esq., was one of the witnesses. Lycans was like a good many of the frontier settlers, he took the law into his own hands and was brought up on a short turn.

In 1754 Constable James Clark returned John Harris for selling rum by the small.

Constable Andrew Johnson, of Paxtang, returned Samuel Hunter also, for selling rum by the small.

Thomas Clark, of Derry, returned James Galbraith for selling rum by the small.

James Sempel, John Harris and Moses Potts had no license.

July 15, 1753, Samuel Hunter was indicted for keeping a disorderly house.

S. E.

CAPTAIN JAMES CALDERWOOD.—"This is to certify that Captain James Calderwood and Rachel Sprigue were joined together by me in holy matrimony on the 12th day of May, 1777; also that David Watson and Rachel Calderwood (the widow of the aforesaid Capt. James Calderwood) were joined together by me in holy matrimony on the 24th of October, in the year of our Lord 1779. Given under my hand at big Spring the 9th day of February, 1784.
WILLIAM LINN, V. D. M."

Captain Calderwood was commissioned an ensign in Capt. Robert Adams' company, Col. Wm. Irvine's (Sixth Penn'a) Battalion, May 1, 1776, and accompanied the Battalion to Canada. He had been appointed quartermaster of the Battalion, and acted as such from the 9th of January until his appointment by Gen'l Gates as Lieutenant on board the fleet on Lake Champlain, August 1, 1776. He served with such ability as to be specially noticed by General Gates. On his return from the Canada campaign he raised an independent company in Cumberland county, and joined Col. Christian Febiger's Eleventh Virginia regiment, and was mortally wounded and died upon the field of Brandywine, at the head of his company, Sept. 11, 1777.
JOHN B. LINN.

THE FIRST ROAD THROUGH THE VALLEY.—A road was laid out in part, commencing at Harris' Ferry in 1736, which was intended to run to the Potomac. In 1743 the direction of this road was somewhat changed, which was finally confirmed in 1744. It began "at river at Harris Ferry, thence to James Silvers' spring, thence three miles west, thence to Randall Chambers' spring, west five miles, and thence to Archibald McCallester's run, thence to Robert Dunning's spring, thence to Shippensburg, thence to Raynold's spring, thence to Conogocheaque creek, thence to the Falling Spring, thence to John Mushel's spring, thence to Thomas Armstrong's spring, being sixty miles ten perches to temporary line." Randall Chambers, Robert Dunning, Robert Chambers, Benjamin Chambers and John McCormick were the viewers. The old Indian traders seemed to have always located at or near a spring which was a source of attraction and relief to the hunters, both white and savage.

Benjamin Chambers was probably then settled at "Falling spring." It was in one of Penn's manors, and he was only allowed by them to locate there temporarily, as was James Patterson, the Indian trader, and his father-in-law, who settled in "Manor," in Lancaster county, seventeen years before the land was open to settlers.
SAMUEL EVANS.

THE FIRST SCOTCH-IRISH SETTLERS IN THE VALLEY.—The recent celebrations of the settlement of the Cumberland Valley were based, perchance, on the presumption that the first settlers came in 1730. We have but little doubt that ten years prior there were isolated settlements between the Susquehanna and the Conecocheague, for in 1729, when the county of Lancaster was organized, which then included Cumberland county, there were "over Sasquehannah," Hendricks, Macfarlane, Silvers, Parker and others, pioneers who claimed a residence of from five to ten years. If Richard Parker and his family, concerning whom and his descendants mention is made elsewhere, located on the Conedoguinet near Carlisle in 1725, there certainly must have been a good many settlers between him and the Susquehanna. He would not venture that distance from civilization, unless the land had not already been taken up by actual settlement. The argument that the lands not being surveyed until after 1730, there were no occupants, will not hold good, for it is well known that the pioneer preceded the surveyor by from ten to fifteen years. There were numerous settlers in York county as early as 1721, and it is reasonable to suppose that the South Mountain was no barrier to the occupancy of the fine fertile lands of the Valley. Emigrants did not wait for the purchase of the lands by the Proprietaries from the Indians, especially the Scotch-Irish, who were "not wanted" where the lands had already been acquired, but were directed to push to the utmost frontier. This early settlement of the Cumberland Valley is a subject fraught with much interest, and those devoted to its history should make the research which will undoubtedly verify what we have stated. In writing up the history of our own locality, we have not been unmindful of the information received concerning others, and trust by the time we shall have made further research into the Scotch-Irish immigration, that we may arrive at more accurate data relative to the settlement of the Cumberland Valley.

FRANKLIN COUNTY IN THE WAR OF 1812-14.—The following letter which has never been published is well worth preservation, breathing forth as it does that spirit of unselfish patriotism which characterized the yeomanry of the Cumberland Valley from the earliest to the latest period of its existence. Captain Dunn's company, it is stated by McCauley (History of Franklin County, p. 150, 2d edition), was not called into service until March, 1814. It became part of Col. James Fenton's regiment, the Fifth Pennsylvania, and did faithful service in the battles of Chippewa and Lundy's Lane. The complete roll of the company can be found in McCauley's history, pages 151-152.

BENJ. M. NEAD.

FANNET'S BURGH, }
FRANKLIN COUNTY, }   *15 June, 1813.*

Sir: Being authorized by a volunteer company of riflemen in the Sixty-fourth Regiment, 2d Brigade, 7th Division Penn'a Militia to inform your Excellency that they have made a tender of service to you for six months or what time such corps are wanted. We offered our services in the regular way to our respective brigade inspector, William McClelland, Esq., who has no doubt reported us before this time.

The present communication is to inform you of the great anxiety the company are in to receive marching orders, which we hope will be in your power to give us very soon, when if we meete the Enemy of our Country I have no doubt but the result will be Highly Honorable to ourselves and the State to which we belong. The Company Consists of 50 men all Armed & Equiped ready at any time you may think proper to order us to take the Field. We have made no stipulations where we will march to, and will therefore not hesitate a moment to meete the Enemy within the United States, but will, without those Limits with ardor seek and with the determination belonging to Freemen punish the unprovoked Invaders of our Country, with the assurance that you will (by giving us Marching Orders) give us an opportunity of displaying our Patriotism to our Country.

Very Respectfully,
Your Obedient Servant,
SAMUEL DUNN,
Capt. Rifle Company.

GOV'R SNYDER.

THE JOHNSTONS OF ANTRIM TOWNSHIP.

South of Greencastle, near Shady Grove, Franklin county, on the Beatty farm, now Witmer's, in a secluded spot some distance from the road, is the graveyard of one of the oldest families west of Conecocheague—that of the Johnstons. Several of the graves are well marked with large marble slabs, inscriptions from the principal of which we give herewith:

James Johnston | born | in the north of Ireland | Died A. D. 1765. | From documents still extant he settled on | the land on which he | died, as early as 1735 | and was probably the | first white settler in | what is now Antrim | township, Franklin county.

The "documents still extant" are the application and warrant for survey, and we are inclined to the belief that James Johnston settled there about 1730, but whether then, or at the period given on his tombstone, there is no doubt of his preceding the Chambers brothers by two or three years. Close by this grave is the following:

Sacred | to the memory of | Doctor Robert Johnston | who departed this life | on the 25th Nov., 1808 | aged 58 years, 4 months | and 4 days.

Born on the 21st of July, 1750, Dr. Johnston became one of the most prominent surgeons of the Revolvtionary era. He was appointed surgeon of the Sixth Penn'a Battalion, Col. William Irvine, January 16, 1774, and continued in service until 1781, when he was ordered by the commander-in-chief to leave the regimental service and assist the wounded officers and soldiers of the American army, prisoners in the British hospital at Charleston, S. C. He was a member of the Society of the Cincinnati, and retained the friendship of his fellow officers during life, many of whom sought his medical advice and skill long after his professional retirement. During the so-called Whiskey Insurrection in 1794, Gen. Washington and the members of his staff were the guests of Dr. Johnston, the President going out of his way to meet his old friend. Near to the grave of Dr. Johnston is that of his brother:

Col. Thomas Johnston | died Dec., 1819 | in the 75th year of his | age. | Martha Beatty | wife of Col. T. Johnston | died August, 1811. | Both possessed qualities of the | heart that insured the respect | and esteem of all their acquaintances.

Thomas Johnston was another hero of the Revolution. He was an early associator; was an ensign in the Flying Camp; appointed January 21, 1777, first lieutenant in the State Regiment, Col. Bull, afterwards Col. Walter Stewart's, and subsequently in the re-arrangement, transferred to the Thirteenth Penn'a. At the close of the war he was commissioned colonel in the militia. He was a gentleman of dignified manners, very hospitable, and respected by all who came in contact with him.

The Johnstons were true representative men of the Valley, and deserve to be held in grateful memory by every Pennsylvanian.

CAPT. WILLIAM HENDRICKS AND HIS COMPANIONS.

The First Company Raised in the Cumberland Valley, 1775.

The echoes of the thundering at Lexington, on the 19th of April, 1775, had scarcely ceased reverberating along the Kittatinny hills ere the brave sons of the Valley, under the gallant Hendricks, were on the march to the relief of the beleagured city of Boston. Capt. William Hendricks was the grandson of Tobias Hendricks, an Indian trader, and probably the first actual white settler in the Valley, who located at what is now known as Oyster's Point, two miles west of Harrisburg. Here Tobias Hendricks died in November, 1739, leaving a wife Catharine, and children, Henry, Rebecca, Tobias, David, Peter, Abraham and Isaac. William Hendricks was probably the son of Henry who retained the " old place," and where our hero was born. The company of Capt. Hendricks was raised in about ten days, and as soon as the officers received orders was on the march Eastward, reaching camp the first week in August, 1775. When the Quebec expedition was decided upon by the commander-in-chief, the companies of Matthew Smith, of Paxtang, and William Hendricks, of Pennsboro, were detached from Col. Thompson's battalion of riflemen and ordered " to go upon the command with Colonel Arnold." For the particulars of this expedition we must refer our readers to Judge Henry's narrative, who was a volunteer in Capt. Smith's company. The gallant Hendricks fell in front of Quebec, and his remains were interred in the same enclosure with those of the lamented General Montgomery. The following is a list of Hendricks' company, those escaping being designated by a *. Some of those captured were probably killed or wounded or died in captivity, as many never returned. Of those who did, some re-enlisted ; while others were disabled for life owing to the severe exposure incident to the winter's march through the wilderness of Maine, or the hardships and sufferings endured in captivity :

Captain.
Hendricks, William, killed at Quebec.
Lieutenants.
McClellan, John, died on the March,
Nichols, Francis,
Francis, George,
Sergeants.
Gibson, Dr. Thomas,
Crone, Henry,
Greer, Joseph,
McCoy, William.
Privates.
Agnew, Edward,
Albright, George,*
Anderson, Thomas,
Baker, Philip, w.,
Blair, John,
Burns, Alexander,
Burns, Peter,
Campbell, John, k.,
Carlisle, Daniel,
Carswell, John,
Casey, Roger,
Cashey, Joseph,
Chambers, John,
Cooke, Thomas,

Cone, John,
Craig, John,*
Cummings, Matthew,*
Eckles, Arthur,*
Frainer, Peter,
Furlow, Francis,
Gammel, William,
Gardner, John,
Graham, Daniel,
Greer, James,
Greer, Thomas,
Hardy, John,
Hardy, Elijah,*
Henderson, John, w.,
Hogg, James,
Ireland, James,
Kenny, Dennis, k.,
Kirkpatrick, William,*
Lynch, Richard,
Lamb, David,*
Lesley, Thomas,
Loraine, John,*
McChesney, John, w.,
McClellan, Daniel,
McClure, Richard,
McCormick, Henry,*
McEwen, Henry,
McFarlane, Archibald,

McGuire, Barnabas,
McLin, John,
McMurdy, John,
Mason, Jacob,
Maxwell, Philip,
Morrison, George,
Morrow, George,
Martin, Edward,
Murdock, Thomas,
North, Daniel,
O'Hara, Daniel,
O'Hara, William,
Ray, John,
Reed, James,
Rinehardt, George,
Rodden, Edward,*
Shannon, William,*
Smith, William,*
Snell, William,
Steel, Robert,
Sweeny, Hugh,*
Sweeny, Edward,*
Swaggerty, Abraham, w.,
Taylor, Matthew,*
Turpentine, Henry,*
Young, Michael,*
Witherop, Thomas,*
Wright, Joseph.*

NOTES AND QUERIES—LXVIII.

THE FIRST AMERICAN FLAG RAISED IN THE BRITISH CHANNEL.—
In December, 1820, the executors of Capt. Gustavus Conyngham, presented to the State of Pennsylvania the first flag of the United States of America that was raised in the British Channel. It was said to have been made under the direction of Benjamin Franklin for the sloop Surprise, commanded by Capt. Conyngham, in 1776. This flag was in the possession of the State at the reception of La-Fayette in 1825, and was placed back of the Speaker's chair upon that memorable occasion. Inquiry has been made of us concerning its existence and if possible to obtain a description thereof. What is especially desired, is to obtain information as to whether the flag contained the rattlesnake emblem or the stars. There are a number of our readers who were present at the LaFayette Reception who may perchance call this to mind, and if any such can do so, we will be under many obligations.

AN HISTORIC BIBLE.

In Kercheval's History of the Valley of Virginia, among the accounts given of Indian massacres "about the year 1760," we find the following:

"At the attack on George Miller's family, the persons killed were a short distance from the house spreading flax in a meadow. One of Miller's little daughters was sick in bed. Hearing the firing she jumped up, and looking through a window and seeing what was done, immediately passed out at a back window, and ran about two or three miles down to the present residence of David Stickley, Esq., and from thence to George Bowman's, on Cedar creek, giving notice at each place. Col. Abraham Bowman, of Kentucky, then a lad of 16 or 17, had but a few minutes before passed close by Miller's door, and at first doubted the little girl's statement. He however armed himself, mounted his horse, and in riding to the scene of action, was joined by several others who had turned out for the same purpose, and soon found the information of the little girl too fatally true.

"The late Mr. Thomas Newell, of Shenandoah county, informed the author that he was then a young man; his father's residence was about one mile from Miller's house; and hearing the firing, he instantly took his rifle, and ran to see what it meant. When he arrived at the spot, he found Miller, his wife and two children weltering in their blood and still bleeding. He was the first person who arrived, and in a very few minutes Bowman and several others joined them. From the scene of murder they went to the house and on the sill of the door lay a large folio *German Bible,* on which a fresh killed cat was thrown. On taking up the Bible it was discovered *that fire had been placed in it; but after burning through a few leaves,* the weight of that part of the book which lay uppermost, together with the weight of the cat, had so compressed the leaves *as to smother and extinguish the fire.*"

In a note to the above the author says: " This Bible is now (1833) in the possession of Mr. George Miller, of Shedandoah county, about one and a half miles south of Zane's old iron works. The author saw and examined it. The fire had been placed about the center of the 2d book of Samuel, burnt through fourteen leaves, and entirely out at one end. It is preserved in the Miller family as a sacred relic or memento of the sacrifice of their ancestors."

The above Bible is at this writing (October 16th, 1880) in the possession of Rev. Joel Swartz, D. D., of Harrisburg, who is a near relative of the Miller family, and a native of the valley where the events referred to occurred. He was also, when a boy, familiarly acquainted with the author of the history of the valley.

The Bible has the following imprint: *Tubingen, Verlegts Johann Georg Cotta, 1739.*   CHARLES L. EHRENFELD.

STACY POTTS.

From 1790, for a period of almost sixteen years, the subject of this sketch was notably prominent in political and public affairs in Pennsylvania. A truly representative man, he deserves grateful recognition at our hands. His life was an eventful one, but the data at present within our reach prevents us from giving little more than a summary of the main incidents in his remarkable career.

Thomas Potts, the ancestor of Stacy Potts, was a Quaker who emigrated from England with his wife and children, in company with Mahlon Stacy and his family, in the ship Shield, and landed at Burlington, New Jersey, in the Winter of 1678, she being in the first ship that went so far up the Delaware. Stacy was a leading man in the Society of Friends and in the government of West Jersey. The families of Stacy and Potts intermarried, and thus the two names were interchanged in both. Mahlon Stacy owned a plantation of eight hundred acres on both sides of Assunpink creek, which he sold in 1714 to William Trent, of Philadelphia, from whom the city of Trenton took its name.

At Trenton, in 1731, Stacy Potts was born. He received a good education and learned the trade of a tanner, a business which he successfully carried on at least up to the time of the Revolution. At this period, Mr. Potts resided on the west side of King (now Warren) street, Trenton. This building has some historic interest. It is stated that Daniel Lanning, who on the morning of the 26th December, 1776, was guide to the American army to Trenton, had a few days previously been taken prisoner by a scouting party of Hessians, carried to Trenton and confined there. Watching an opportunity, when there was a commotion among the guard, he slipped out, sprang over a fence, and escaped to the house of Stacy Potts, who took him in and concealed him that night. The next morning he passed out of the town in safety, and a few days thereafter challenged the Hessian sentries as the battle of Trenton opened.—*Raum's History of Trenton, p. 157.*

On the day of that disaster to the British arms, Col. Rall, the Hessian commander, who was wounded in the early part of the engagement was carried into his headquarters, the house of Mr. Potts, and died there. Lossing, in his Field-Book of the Revolution, states that it was a tavern. Mr. Potts never kept an inn, but it may have been occupied as such at a more recent period.

In 1784 the building was occupied by the President of Congress. It was taken down in the year 1857.

Mr. Potts seems to have been a very enterprising and public spirited citizen. In 1776, besides owning a tannery, he built the steel works on Front street, Trenton, and after the close of the Revolution was largely interested in the erection of a paper mill in the same locality. This was prior to the publication of Collins' Bible. In December, 1788, it was advertised by its proprietors, Stacy Potts and John Reynolds, as " now nearly completed." The manufacturers issued earnest appeals for rags in one of their publications, presenting " to the consideration of those mothers who have children going to school, the present great scarcity of that useful article, without which their going to school would avail them but little."

Mr. Potts took a warm interest in the invention of John Fitch, and was one of the company formed to assist that famous inventor in his experiments, and he, with others were instrumental in obtaining for Fitch fourteen years exclusive privilege on the Jersey side of the Delaware.

About this period, Stacy Potts came to Harrisburg. It is difficult to divine what were his motives in leaving his native town where he was very popular, and with his ample competency, remove to this then new town on the Susquehanna. His second marriage may perchance have had somewhat to do with his removal from Trenton. Coming to Harrisburg he made large purchase of land and whether it was due to this fact or his agreeable manner, Stacy Potts became quite prominent, was chosen to the Legislature in 1791 and in 1792. During the mill-dam troubles of 1793-5, Mr. Potts was quite active, and was one of the committee of citizens who were willing to take upon themselves all responsibility by the destruction of the obnoxious dam. He served as burgess of the borough and was a member of the town council. From 1799 to 1801 he again represented Dauphin county in the Legislature.

Mr. Potts' sudden departure from Harrisburg is really as inexplicable as his coming to it. He seems to have gone to Trenton about 1805. It is stated that he walked, accompanied by his youngest son, the entire distance, and that when they arrived at the bank of the river opposite Trenton, and before crossing the bridge, then newly erected, the boy remarked: "I like the looks of that place; I think I shall live there all my life."

Stacy Potts subsequently became Mayor of Trenton, an office he held for several years. He died in that city, April 28, 1816, in his 85th year.

Mr. Potts was thrice married. We have no knowledge as to his first wife. He married, about 1790, Miss Gardner, of Philadelphia, a Presbyterian lady of superior intelligence. She died at Harrisburg in 1799. His third wife was Mrs. Mary Boyd, widow of John Boyd, of Harrisburg. She survived her husband many years, died at Harrisburg, September 25, 1844, aged 84 years. Mrs. Boyd was the daughter of George Williams, and had by her first husband James Rutherford and George Williams Boyd, the ancestors of the Boyd family of Harrisburg. Mr. Potts had issue by his first and second wife. *Stacy, jun.*, who married Polly, daughter of Leonard Sommers, of Harrisburg, was a lawyer of ability and died at Philadelphia in 1831, aged 53 years. *Rebecca* married George Sherman, editor of the Trenton "Federalist." *Anna* married William Potts, of Trenton. *Stacy Gardiner*, born at Harrisburg, in November, 1799, became one of the Justices of the Supreme Court of New Jersey, a position he held some years. He was a gentleman of prominence in public and private life, and died at Trenton in 1865.

During his entire residence at Harrisburg Stacy Potts was deeply interested in its growth and prosperity. He owned most of the ground which is now included in the Fifth, Sixth and Seventh wards of our city, and some of it yet remains in the possession of his descendants at Trenton. That portion of the river front between Herr and Calder streets was originally named Potts' town, from his ownership of the ground contiguous. While in the Legislature, Mr. Potts was a strong advocate for the permanent establishment of the seat of government of the State at Harrisburg, when it was fully decided to remove it from Philadelphia. The divided counsels of the Dauphin county representatives alone prevented it at that time, and Lancaster was agreed upon. He, however, lived to see the Capital fixed on the banks of the Susquehanna. Mr. Potts must have been an individual of decided character—a strong advocate for the right. He was a gentleman of unquestioned ability, and an enterprising and energetic citizen.

CAPTAIN JAMES BEATTY.

Prior to the laying out of the town of Harrisburg, came James Beatty and family, locating there. From the family record in the possession of his descendants we have this entry: "That my children may know the place of their nativity, I, James Beatty, was born in the Kingdom of Ireland, and County of Down, Parish of Hillsborough and Townland of Ballykeel Ednagonnel, in the year of our Lord, 1746; and came to America in the year 1784. My wife, Ally Ann Irwin, was born in said kingdom, county and parish, and Townland of Tillynore, within two miles of Hillsborough, three of Lisburn, three miles of Dromore, and six miles of Bally-nahinch,* and ten of Belfast, which last place we sailed from the 27th of June, 1784." In the Fall of this year he was settled at Harrisburg, and thus became one of its *first* inhabitants.

It may not be out of place in this connection to refer to the ancestors of James Beatty. After the battle of the Boyne, there was a large influx of Scotch families into the north of Ireland. Among them was that of James Beatty who located in the county of Down. The building he erected known as "Sycamore Lodge" is yet standing and has never been out of the occupancy of a James Beatty. It was here that the subject of our sketch was born. The first James Beatty was the head of a very large family, some of whose descendants remain in the land of their nativity, but the greater portion are scattered over many States of the Federal Union. He was a covenanter of the old school, and a prominent member of the Anahilt Congregation—near which Church repose the remains of himself, and a portion of the five or six generations following.

---

*Means "Town of the Island."

His son, William Beatty, was the father of Captain James Beatty. He died at Ballykeel-Ednagonnel in February, 1784, and was buried in Anahilt Glebe. "The grave," writes one of his descendants, "is covered with a flat tombstone, and with the exception of the name, nothing can be traced, owing to the wear and tear of the weather and the continual friction of passing feet. The central portion of the stone has been worn perfectly smooth." William Beatty married, in 1741, Mary McKee, and had issue:

   i. George, b. 1743; d. 1815; m. Mary Blackburn.
   ii. James, b. 1746; d. 1794; m. Alice Ann Irwin.
   iii. Agnes, b. 1751; d. 1844; m. Robert Finlay.
   iv. Jane, b. 1753; d. 1777, unm.
   v. Mary, b. 1758; d. 1847; m. James Nelson.

A few months after the death of his father, James Beatty, his wife and children came to America. He became the purchaser of a number of lots in the town of Harrisburg, some of which remain in possession of his descendants. He became quite prominent in his adopted home, and held several official positions under the borough charter. He died on the 1st of December, 1795, at the age of forty-eight, comparatively a young man. He was buried in the Presbyterian graveyard, of which Church he held membership.

Captain Beatty married, in 1768, Alice Ann Irwin, daughter of Gawin Irwin and Mary Brereton, of Tullynore. She died in Harrisburg, June, 1805. They had children as follows, all born at Ballykeel-Ednagonnel:

   i. Mary Brereton, b. July 14, 1769; d. in Ashland county, O., March 2, 1853; m. Patrick Murray.
   ii. Nancy, b. May 2, 1771; d. at Steubenville, O., May 7, 1839; m. Samuel Hill.
   iii. Gawin Irwin, b. Sept. 13, 1773; d. Dec. 14, 1843.
   iv. Rebecca, b. Dec. 4, 1775; d. 1819; m. Daniel Houseman.
   v. Alice Ann, b. Feb. 12, 1777; d. May 14, 1841, in Ashland county, O.; m. John Downey.
   vi. William, b. June 30, 1778; d. Sept. 3, 1790.
   vii. Sarah, b. Oct. 6, 1779; d. Aug. 4, 1861, at Ashland, O., unm.
   viii. George, b. Jan. 4, 1781; d. March 10, 1862, from whom the family of this name, now residing at Harrisburg, descends.

In personal appearance Capt. Beatty was about five feet eight inches, thick set, florid complexion, dark hair and blue eyes. He was an active and energetic business man, and his death was a great loss to the young town.

NOTES AND QUERIES.—LXIX.

THE FIRST TELEGRAPH DISPATCH.—The first telegraphic dispatch shown to the citizens of Harrisburg was brought from Washington City by the late Isaac G. McKinly, then one of the proprietors and editors of the *Democratic Union*, now the *Patriot*, in 1841. It was a long narrow strip of white paper, bearing the characters indented by the machine. The telegraph was then first introduced, the wires, however, only extending from Baltimore to Washington. The dispatch was a great curiosity, and attracted a small crowd on the street where it was shown.   A. B.

WALLACE, BENJAMIN (N. & Q. lv.)—An Erie correspondent gives us the following data: Benjamin Wallace was born in Ireland in 1727. He married his first wife, Lettice Ralston, 1761. Their child, Mary Wallace, married James B. Wilson, of Hanover, in 1803, removing, the same year to Erie, Pa., where she died in May, 1874, at the age of eighty-five. The children of Benjamin Wallace and Elizabeth Culbertson (his second wife) were as follows:

   i. William, b. Oct., 1758; d. May 28, 1816.
   ii. John Culbertson, b. February 14, 1779; d. Dec., 1827.
   iii. Benjamin, b. April 14, 1773; d. Aug. 22, 1833.
   iv. Jane, b. April 9, 1775; d. Jan., 1790.
   v. James, b. 1777; d. 1782.
   vi. Alexander Cox, b. Jan. 28, 1782; d. July 3, 1806.

Benjamin Wallace (iii) was a major in the U. S. Army.

REV. MR. ROAN'S SUBSCRIPTION OR ACCOUNT BOOK.—Recently there has been placed in our hands the account book of the Rev. John Roan, which contains the subscription of the members of his congregations at Derry, Paxtang, and Mount Joy, from 1745, the beginning of his ministry, until the close of his eventful life in 1775; also his marriage record from 1754 to 1774. The list of members is important, from the fact that the first tax list in existence is 1749, while this goes to show who resided within the bounds of his different congregations as early as 1744. The marriage record is exceedingly valuable, and we have no doubt that it will be as highly prized as that recently published of the Rev. John Elder. Besides these important additions to our historical and genealogical knowledge, the accounts go to disprove many of the statements made by Webster and other historians concerning the Rev. John Roan. As soon as it is possible to prepare these contributions, we shall lay them before our readers.

AT TRENTON AND PRINCETON.

[We have recently found the following list of those Lancaster county companies which were in actual service at the battles of Trenton and Princeton. This list, however, does not include all the troops from this section which were in the field during 1776. Col. Cunningham's battalion, as also a portion of Col. Green's and Col. Burd's were at Long Island and Fort Washington, where they suffered severely in killed and wounded. Those companies marked with a * were from what is now Dauphin county, those † from Lebanon—the remainder, so far as we have information, probably from what is now Lancaster county proper. Of those from Dauphin county we have in our possession the rolls of Capts. Brown, Cowden, Koppenheffer, Manning, McQuown, Murray, Reed, Sherer and Fridley. Among their descendants ought be found those of the Capts. Boyd, Campbell, McCallen and McKee. These with the rolls of other companies which were in the service during 1776 and subsequent years, it is earnestly to be hoped may be secured, and the names of all the patriots of the Revolution be preserved unto us.

"*List of Captains whose companies of Militia went to Jersey in August, 1776, Were Absent till Jan. and Feb., 1777. Muster Rolls of Lancaster County Militia, 1776.*

Adams, Isaac,
*Boyd, John,
Boyd, Samuel,
*Brown, William,
*Campbell, Robert,
*Cowden, James,
Crawford, Christopher,
†Doebler, Albright,
Evans, Joshua,
Graeff, Andrew,
Hollinger, Christian,
Hoofnagle, Peter,
Johnston, ——,
Jones, John,
King, Jacob,
*Koppenheffer, Thos.,
*Manning, Richard,

*McCallen, Robert,
*McQuown, Richard,
*McKee, Robert,
Morgan, David,
*Murray, James,
Morrison, James,
Martin, Alex.,
Musser, George,
Peden, Hugh,
*Reed, John,
Ross, ——,
*Sherer, Joseph,
Steele, William,
Page, Nathaniel,
Parry, William,
Paxton, ——,
*Fridley, Jacob,

Tweed, John, Lieut.-Comdt.
Watson, James, company Comd. by Lieut. John Patton,
†Weaver, Henry,
Whiteside, Thomas,
Wilson, Dorrington, Commanded by Lieut. John Echman,
Withers, John,
Wright, Joseph,
Yeates, Jasper.
Zantzinger, Paul,
Ziegler, Frederick,
Zimmerman, Bernard.

THE FIRST RAILROAD AND CARS AT HARRISBURG.

The location, construction and completion of the first railroad that is to terminate or pass a town or village is an important event, and of course creates great curiosity and anxiety among the inhabitants of the place and surrounding country. When the Harrisburg and Lancaster road was being located in 1835, much opposition was manifested by the farmers on surveying the road, at having their farms "cut up" or divided. The road, however, was partly completed at different points during the following year. In August, 1836, it was finished as far as Middletown, terminating here at Paxtang street.

As cars were soon needed, Messrs. Wm. Calder, Sen., & Co., had a car built by Eben Miltimore at his coach shop, then located on the corner of Chestnut street and River alley. The building, formerly a large brick stable, was erected and used by Joshua Elder many years previous, who owned the property and had kept the principal store in the town. The car was a plain open four wheel car, similar, though smaller, to the present excursion cars of the street railroad now used. When finished it was taken down to the railroad and a trial trip was made two or three miles down the road, with two horses attached to it by a short tow-line, as the track between the rails could not be used for horses. Of course the car was well filled with men and boys, eager to enjoy their first ride on the rails, the writer being one of the number. A short time after, in September, a locomotive engine was brought from the State road (which had been previously constructed) from Columbia on a flat in the canal, and landed at Middletown, from whence it was run here; and during the time, Saturday and Sunday, excursions were run to Middletown and back about every two hours, with the car built by Mr. Miltimore. The small car was crowded all the time—Governor Ritner, the heads of the State Department and prominent citizens were first treated to a ride.

As very few had seen a locomotive, it was an object of great curiosity, and many funny remarks were made by different individuals among the crowd which assembled on Paxtang street during the trial trips of the engine. One colored man said to his wife, "Jane, now you sees what fire and water des." This locomotive was made in England, and was one of the first placed on the State road. It was called the "John Bull," and would be a diminutive novelty now. It was a small, black affair, with two driving wheels, the piston connected inside of the wheel. The first locomotives put on the Harrisburg and Lancaster road were built by Mathias Baldwin, of Philadelphia, and were named after the three or four principal towns along the road. They had but two driving wheels, with the crank and piston inside; were used for both freight and passengers.

The next engines purchased were two built by Messrs. Norris & Sons, of Philadelphia, and were used for hauling freight trains. They were named Henry Clay and David R. Porter, were heavier and lower than the first ones, having but two driving wheels with the piston connected to the driving wheels on the outside, as they are now constructed.

The road was not fully completed until some time in 1838, owing to the slow work on the tunnel near Elizabethtown. During its construction the passengers were conveyed around in stage coaches, the writer having made the trip in the summer of 1837. The Cumberland Valley railroad was completed about the same period (1837) except the erection of the bridge over the river. Their first locomotives were brought from Columbia on the canal, and landed on the McCormick lot at Second and Vine streets, and were hauled over the Market street bridge by six Cumberland county farm-horses.

Bells were first used on the locomotives; the first brought here for the Cumberland Valley railroad had whistles, and when they were being conveyed over the bridge, the writer heard some of our prominent citizens who had gathered at the toll-house discussing the matter, aver that the whistle could be heard a distance of five miles.

A. BURNETT.

MARRIAGE RECORD OF HEBRON CHURCH.

[We are indebted to Dr. George Ross, of Lebanon, for the following marriage records of the Quittapahilla or Hebron Moravian Church, near Lebanon, who obtained them through the Rev. L. P. Clewell, present minister there. The records, as will be seen, although somewhat meager, cover sixty years—1751 to 1811. They include the names of the ancestors of the Orths, Buehlers, Kelkers, and others familiar to this locality, and we consider them a valuable contribution to the Genealogical history of our country.]

1751.

March 17. Henry Xander and Mary Pristarju, by Rev. Christian Rauch.

1753.

Jan'y 12. Daniel Heckadorn and Susanna Kunzlien.

1754.

May 1. John Ebermann and Maria Xander, by Rev. Geo. Neiser.

1756.
Feb'y 24. Philip Meurer and Anna Maria Schasters.
1757.
May 24. Adam Orth, oldest son of Balther Orth, and Catharine, oldest daughter of Peter Kucher, by Rev. Geo. Neiser.
1758.
Aug. 8. George Wambler and Elizabeth Strahaus, by Rev. Philip Meurer.
1759.
May 9. Adam Faber (widower) and Elizabeth Spitler (widow), born Meulin, by Rev. Boehler.
1761.
June 30. Casper Kieth (widower) of Heidelberg, and Anna Maria Stephan, born Schirmer, by Rev. Boehler.
1762.
May 4. George Hederick (widower) and Elizabeth Ohrich, by Rev. Franz Boehler.
1763.
April 26. Balzar Orth, and Rosina Kucher, by Rev. Langoard.
April 26. Jacob Scherzer, and Barbara Stoehr, by Rev. Zahm.
1765.
April 30. Philip Uhrig and Margaret Hederig, by Rev. Langoard.
1767.
Nov. 24. Abraham Friedrick and Maria Barbara Buehler, by Rev. Zahm.
1769.
Feb'y 28. Philip Faber, Adam Faber's son, and Magdalena Stoehr, Philip Stoehr's daughter, by Rev. Zahm.
1770.
September 18. Ehrhart Heckedorn, Daniel Heckedorn's son, and Catharine Meilin, by Rev. Zahm.
1773.
Aug. 3. John Abraham Borroway, from Mount Joy, and Elizabeth Uhrich, by Rev. Bader.
Nov. 2. John Friedrick, son of Abraham Friedrick, from Mount Joy, and Julia Anna Buehler, by Rev. Bader.
1779.
April 13. John Kunzlein, from Mount Joy Congregation, and Joanna Buehler, by Rev. Bader.

Nov. 23. Isaac Borroway, of Mount Joy, and Anna Johana Uhrich, by Rev. Bader.

1785.

March 31. Frederick Stohler, of Donegal, and Catharine Uhrich, of Hebron, by Rev. Michler.

1786.

April 22. Jacob Lanius, from Yorktown, and Barbara Friedrick, born Buehler, by Rev. Augustus Klings Ohr, of Lititz.

1789.

November 15. Daniel Brozman, from Graceham on the Monocacy, Md., and Anna Maria Spieker, maiden name Buehler, by Rev. Gottlieb Senseman.

1793.

July 21. Andrew Kapp, from Shaefferstown, and Susanna Shoebel by Rev. Christopher Gottlieb Peter.

1795.

Nov. 3. Gottlieb Orth and the unmarried sister Sarah Steiner, by Rev. John Molther.

1797.

Oct. 8. Jacob Widmer, a Menomite from Chamberstown, and the unmarried Hannah Orth, by Rev. John Christian Fritz.

1799.

March 17. John Frederick Williams and the maiden Rebecca Flor, by Rev. John Christian Fritz.

Nov. 13. Conrad Bremer (widower) and the maiden Rebecca Kuehner, by Rev. J. C. Fritz.

Nov. 17. Mr. Peter Gloninger and the maiden Elizabeth Zerman, by Rev. J. C. Fritz.

1800.

April 15. Michael Uhrich and Susanna Kapp, maiden name Krause, by Rev. John C. Fritz.

Oct. 29. Nathaniel Kohler (single) and Maria Bruecher (single) by Rev. J. C. Fritz.

Dec. 28. Jacob Kiefer and Dorothea Gilbert, maiden, by Rev. J. C. Fritz.

1801.

Dec. 27. William Weitzel (single) youngest son of the long departed Martin Weitzel, farmer, and Anna Maria, born Fellberger, his wife, and Elizabeth Rudy, youngest daughter of the departed Abraham

Rudy, and Catharine, his wife, born Huber, at present wife of Geo. Glossbrenner, by Rev. Nathaniel Braun. The stepfather, Geo. Glossbrenner, and Sister Braun were witnesses.

1802.

Jan. 4. Philip Xander, shoemaker and farmer, youngest son of Jacob Xander and Susanna, his wife, born Williams, born Oct. 13, 1782. and Catharine Jaeger, born 1782, oldest daughter of Christian Jaeger, by Rev. Nathaniel Braun. In the presence of the parents, Sister Braun, and other relatives.

Jan. 24. Peter Gardi and Anna Rosina Williams by Rev. N. Braun.

June 13. Jacob Steiner aged 23, and Sabina Hats, aged 32, from Hanover, seventeen miles from here, by Rev. N. Braun.

July 4. John Kelker youngest son of Rudy Kelker and Maria, his wife, born Weitman, and Barbara Zimmerman, oldest daughter of the departed Adam Zimmerman and Barbara, his wife, born Fisher, by Rev. N. Braun.

Aug. 11. Henrich Seiler, aged 23, and Catharine Feyerabend, aged 19, by Rev. N. Braun.

Sept. 4. Geo. Pfeffer and Margaret Steiner.

1804.

May 22. Simon Schut and Magdalena Schark, both of Lutheran Church, by Rev. Blech.

1805.

Aug. 4. Philip Uhrich and Elizabeth Goldman, by Rev. Blech.

1805.

Dec. 22. Nathaniel Koehler and Mariah Kaufman, by Rev. Ludwig Huebener.

Aug. 30. John Tshudy and Mariah Schaffner, by Rev. Ludwig Huebener.

1809.

Jan. 24. John Stiles, a gunsmith, near Millerstown, and Catharine Benigna Kloz, by Rev. Ludwig Huebener.

1810.

May 27. Jacob Uhrich and Hannah Goldman, by Rev. Ludwig Huebener.

1811.

Jan. 20. John Bucher, Dr. Bucher's oldest son, near Cornwall, and the maiden Regina Schmidt, by Rev. Ludwig Huebener.

NOTES AND QUERIES.—LXX.

[CONTRIBUTIONS TO THE HISTORY OF THE CUMBERLAND VALLEY.— The articles comprising the present issue of *Notes and Queries* are chiefly of a biographical character, but assuredly of great value and interest. They are principally of and concerning men of whom little has been said, but the prominence of their eventful lives require full details. They were indeed "Men of Mark" in their day and generation, and we hope to give biographical memoranda of many others, representative men of the Cumberland Valley, whom it is the duty of the present to properly enbalm in print. As to the early settlement of the valley, we seek no controversy when we simply present the facts within reach. We claim it both as a right and a duty, as a faithful historian, to give such authentic data as we may find, whether it conflicts with either our own or the long cherished views of others. We do not claim to be an historical iconoclast, yet no one should find fault if tradition and legend, or current history should be wiped out through patient labor and industrious research among the musty archives of the past. Let us accept what is in store without grumbling.]

CULBERTSON.—Robert Culbertson, of Kennett, Chester county, Penna., in his will dated March 21, 1762, proven May 3, 1762, gives to his wife Jean one-third of the estate; to his son Samuel "all that he owes me and £20," also "my negro lad James, on these conditions, that he shall take my dear wife, Jean Culbertson, and all of his sisters that shall be at my decease living, unto Cumberland county, in this Province, and their take proper cair of his said mother, Jean Culbertson, unto her decease and his sisters unto their day of marriage, otherwise the lad to be a part of my wife's thirds of my estate." To his son-in-law, Alexander Porter, he left five shillings, and to each of the children of his daughter, Elizabeth Porter, five shillings. To his daughters, Jean, Mary, Martha, Isabella and Sarah Culbertson, he bequeathed the remainder of his estate. G. C.

SILVERS OF SILVERS' SPRING.—Not taking into consideration the location of Indian traders such as Letort, Chartier and others, to the west of the Susquehanna, among the earliest permanent settlers in the Cumberland Valley was James Silvers, a native of the north of Ireland, who from a letter written by James Steel to the Proprietary's Secretary, James Logan, appears to have gone "over Sasquahannah" in 1724. Under date of 11th 12 mo., 1724–5," his "loving friend" Logan is informed that "James Silver, of whom I wrote thee has gone over Sasquahannah." This was no doubt the James Silvers who was located at the spring bearing his name and whose land was among the earliest surveys in the Cumberland Valley. As " others " are mentioned, we may in time be able to gather information as to them. It is to be regretted that we have no further data relative to James Silvers. He seems to have been a person of prominence in the valley, a man of indomitable enterprise if not of courage. What has become of his descendants we know not—they have all disappeared from the locality. Several of the name are buried in the graveyard at Silvers' Spring Church, and perchance the bones of the old pioneer are resting in the same enclosure. If any of our readers can furnish us any information concerning the family, we shall be pleased to receive it.

REV. WILLIAM LINN, D. D.

WILLIAM LINN was born in Lurgan township, (now in Franklin county) Penn'a, February 27, 1752. His father and grandfather bearing the same name came from the north of Ireland in 1732, and are included in the taxables of Lurgan for the year 1751, as William Linn, Sr., and William Linn, Jr. Dr. Linn's mother, Susanna Trimble, died in the fort at Shippensburg where the people had gathered after Braddock's deafeat, in July, 1755. The latter removed, in 1775, to Buffalo Valley, now Union county. The present families in Cumberland and Franklin are descendants of Jane McCormick, second wife of William Linn, Jr.

Dr. Linn was early placed at a grammar school under George Duffield, D. D., and his preparation for college was superintended by Rev. Mr. Smith. He graduated at Princeton in 1772, in a class of formidable ability, embracing such names as William Bradford, Attorney General of the United States, Aaron Burr, Vice-President, Dr. Samuel E. McCorkle, of Dickinson college, etc. At the Junior contest in 1771, Burr and Linn took the prizes in reading, Bradford and Linn those for public speaking, and on graduation day the palm for eloquence as between Burr and Linn was in doubt. (*See Davis' Life of Burr.*)

After leaving college, Mr. Linn studied under Revd. Robert Cooper, pastor of Middle Spring. He was married Jan'y 10, 1774, to Rebecca Blair, daughter of Rev. John Blair, pastor of the Three Springs (1742–1748), whose descendants have left the impress of their ability upon the political history of the country. His son James

Blair was attorney General of the State of Kentucky for twenty years, and father of Francis P. Blair, Sr., the noted journalist of the days of Andrew Jackson.

After a tour of supply among the frontier settlements, Mr. Linn became pastor of Big Spring congregation, (now Newville, Cumberland county,) and upon the breaking out of the Revolutionary war was appointed chaplain to Col. Robert Magaw's (5th) and Col. William Irvine's (6th) Battalions, Feb. 15, 1776. "A military discourse delivered at Carlisle, March 17, 1776, to Col. Irvine's Battalion of Regulars, and a very respectable number of the inhabitants, by William Linn, A. M., chaplain, published by the request of the officers from Psalm xx. 7; 'Some trust in chariots, and some in horses,' &c.," is still extant, labelled thus in his own handwriting, and was republished at Carlisle on the centennial of its delivery, March 17, 1876. He accompanied the battalions to New York, and his classmate, Philip V. Fithian, who was chaplain to a New Jersey battalion, in his journal speaks of meeting him frequently with officers of Magaw's battalion. After the capture of Magaw's battalion at Fort Washington, Nov. 16, 1776, he seems to have returned home and resumed his charge.

He served the congregation at Big Spring about six years, and was then elected President of Washington College on the Eastern shore of Maryland. After remaining there a year, on account of the sickly state of his family, he resigned, and accepted a call from the Presbyterian church of Elizabethtown, N. J., where he remained until 1786, when he removed to New York, and settled in the Collegiate Dutch church of that city. On the 1st of May, 1789, he was elected the first Chaplain of the House of Representatives of the United States under the Constitution of 1787.

During the last decade of the last century he was considered the foremost pulpit orator of New York city—his oration before the Society of the Cincinnati upon the death of General Washington placing him notably beyond his pulpit compeers of that day. Failing health compelled him to resign his charge in New York and he retired with his family to Albany, where he died in January, 1808. His published works are "Sermons, historical and characteristical," 12 mo., 1791; "Signs of the Times," 1794, etc.

A manuscript containing outlines of the sermons he preached at Newville in 1779 and 1780, now before me, contains ample evidence of his ability as a sermonizer, before he was transferred to the more extensive theater of his life at New York. A cotemporary critic says, "his eloquence was for the most part natural, impressive and commanding, though at times he had too much vehemence in his manner." The latter remark reminds me of what I heard his youngest step-brother say, many years ago: That he could hear him preach a mile away from Big Spring.

His children were all noted women and men of their day.

Mrs. Charles Brockden Brown, wife of the first American novelist.

John Blair Linn, D. D., of First Presbyterian church of Philadelphia.

Mrs. Simeon Dewitt, authoress of " Justinea."

Mrs. William Keese.

Mary Linn.

William Linn, Esq., the " Roorback " of Gen. Jackson's time.

Mrs. John W. Peters.

James Henry Linn, Esq., of Albany.

Judge Archibald L. Linn, of Schenectady, member of Congress, 1841–3.   JOHN B. LINN.

COLONEL ROBERT MAGAW.

Col. Magaw, who resided in Carlisle, was quite noted as a lawyer as early as 1772, when he traveled the circuit as lawyers then did, and was then largely concerned in suits in Northumberland county. On the 14th of July, 1774, he was appointed upon the county committee and a deputy to meet the deputies from other counties of the Province at Philadelphia to concert measures preparatory to the General Congress. Following the reception of the news of Bunker Hill, he was commissioned June 25, 1775, Major of Col. William Thompson's Battalion, and marched with it to Cambridge, where he took part in the operations connected with the siege of Boston, until he was commissioned, January 3, 1776, Colonel of the 5th Pennsylvania Battalion. He immediately returned home from Boston, organized and recruited his battalion, and on the 11th of June, 1776, was ordered with his battalion to New York. He encamped on the ground on which Fort Washington was erected, and began, under the direction of Col. Rufus Putnam, the erection of that fortress, and with its misfortunes his military career was indissolubly linked, saving his assistance in covering the retreat of the army from Long Island on the night of the 29th of August.

As remarked by Mr. De Lancey in his able and thorough article upon " Mount Washington and its capture, November 16, 1776," in the Magazine of American History, N. Y., for February, 1877, " perhaps no question growing out of any single event of the Revolution were discussed with more vigor at the time, or have given rise to more controversy since than these. Each of the officers, Washington,

Greene and Magaw have had their enemies and opposers, friends and defenders." From the calm and dispassionate discussion of these questions, by such able historians as Mr. De Lancey and Prof. Henry P. Johnston in his "Campaign of 1776," (Memoirs of Long Island Historical Society, vol. iii.;) Col. Magaw's fame for cool personal bravery and good conduct, comes forth unsullied, and we gratefully leave it in their keeping.

Fort Washington stood on the east side of the Hudson river, on a commanding site on the line of what is now 183d street (New York city) two hundred and thirty feet above the Hudson. It was a large five-sided structure with bastions commanding the passage of the Hudson, in connection with Fort Lee opposite, on the west side, on the summit of the Palisades on the Jersey side. The obstructions in the river between the two forts, consisted mainly of a line of vessels chained together, loaded with stone, and then sunk and anchored just below the surface of the river.

When it was determined on the 16th of October to abandon New York Island, Col. Magaw was left in command of the garrison at Fort Washington, while the army marched to King's Bridge and afterwards to White Plains. Howe not being able to force Washington into an engagement turned his attention to Fort Washington, and on the 15th of November had it invested, when he sent a messenger to Magaw, demanding its surrender in peril of massacre if his demand was not complied with within two hours. Magaw's reply is historical, but as the original was found some years since by Dr. Murray among Magaw's papers, and will no doubt be deposited as an inestimable relic among the archives of the Cumberland Valley Historical Society for the benefit of the present generation, it is well to reprint the noble answer of the Carlisle lawyer of one hundred years ago.

When Magaw received Howe's summons he at once dispatched a note to General Greene at Fort Lee with the intelligence, saying to him, "we are determined to defend the post or die." He then replied to the summons as follows:

"*To the Adjutant General of the British Army:* SIR: If I rightly understand the purport of your message from General Howe, communicated to Col. Swoope, this post is to be immediately surrendered, or the garrison put to the sword. I rather think it is a mistake than a settled resolution in General Howe, to act a part so unworthy of himself and the British Nation. But give me leave to assure his Excellency, that actuated by the most glorious cause that mankind ever fought in, I am determined to defend this post to the very last extremity.   ROBERT MAGAW,
                            Colonel Commanding."

The sequel is well known. "Magaw disposed of his men to the best advantage, considering the great extent of his outside lines and his numbers, and did his duty faithfully," says De Lancey. Col. Baxter fell sword in hand at the head of the Pennsylvania Associators. Cadwalader fought bravely, but overwhelming numbers swept all before them into the Fort, and Magaw, after much parley, surrendered. —Thus 2,637 enlisted men and 221 officers, the greater part from Pennsylvania, and nearly half of them well drilled troops, were lost to the cause. The officers were placed on Long Island. The Dutch Reformed and Presbyterian churches in New York were turned into prisons, where and in the sugar house prison on Liberty street, the privates were compelled to perish by hundreds, by slow starvation and loathsome disease, which brutal keepers took little trouble to alleviate.—[Prof. Johnston]. Col. Magaw remained a prisoner on Long Island until his exchange, October 25, 1890. (Gen. William Thompson, also of Carlisle, captured at Three Rivers in Canada, was exchanged with Col. Magaw for the Hessian Major General De Riedesel, taken at Burgoyne's surrender.) For an interesting account of some years of this captivity, the reader is referred to the Memoirs of Alexander Graydon, the first Prothonotary of Dauphin County. Graydon (who was a captain in Shee's battalion, taken at the same time) says Magaw comforted his captivity on Long Island by taking of its fair daughters a wife, Miss Marietta Van Brunt, a daughter of Rutgers Van Brunt. Dr. Murray has a letter from his father-in-law to Col. Magaw, congratulating him on his safe arrival at Carlisle. This letter is dated May 17, 1780; he was therefore paroled before he was exchanged. In a letter addressed to President Reed, dated at Carlisle, April 19, 1781, he explains the cause of his retiring from service: "On my return from near four years' captivity, I found the infantry of the Pennsylvania Line about to be reduced to six regiments, and that the number of officers was more than competent; and considering that it would show but false patriotism to insist for my rank as a general officer, in prejudice to one of more experience, I sent down my intimation to be returned as a retiring officer, which was done accordingly."

After Col. Magaw retired the service he took great interest in military matters in Cumberland county. He organized and commanded a volunteer company in Carlisle. He was also elected a member of the Assembly. He died at Carlisle, January 7, 1790, and is buried in Meeting House Spring graveyard, two miles west of Carlisle. In the *Carlisle Gazette and Western Repository of Knowledge*, of January 13, 1790, a full account of the imposing cortege that followed the dead Colonel to his tomb, amid the booming "of minute guns fired by the artillery during the procession. At the grave a thepatic discourse was delivered by Rev. Dr. Davidson. Three volleys from the infantry closed the scene."

Col. Magaw owned two stone houses on the southeast corner of the public square in Carlisle. The smallest of the two lately owned by Wm. Biddle, Esq., has been coated with plaster since. In this house General Washington lodged when he came to Carlisle, on the occasion of the Whiskey Insurrection, in October, 1794, and boarded at the stone tavern nearly opposite.

Col. Magaw left two children, Van Brunt and Elizabeth Magaw. He had two brothers, Rev. Samuel Magaw, Vice-President of the University of Pennsylvania, and Dr. William Magaw, Surgeon of the 1st Penn'a Continental Line, who built and resided in the large stone mansion lately owned by Dr. McDowell in Mercersburg. Dr. William Magaw died at his son's house in Meadville, May 1, 1829, aged eighty-five, and his descendants are among the prominent people of that place.   JOHN B. LINN.

THE HOGES OF HOGESTOWN.

When William Penn and his eleven associates bought the land now comprising the State of New Jersey, the first Governor under the Proprietors was Robert Barclay, one of the original purchasers, who was a Scotchman and a Quaker. Under him many Scotch settled in that Province.

WILLIAM HOGE, a native of Musselburgh, Scotland, came to America shortly after 1682. On the same ship came a family consisting of a Mr. Hume, his wife and daughter, from Paisley. On the passage the father and mother both died, and young Hoge took charge of the daughter and landed at New York, where he left the girl with a relative, and settled himself at Perth Amboy, N. J. He subsequently married the daughter, Barbara Hume, removed to Penn's Three Lower Counties, now the State of Delaware; from thence to Lancaster county, Pennsylvania, and thence to the Valley of Virginia, about three miles south of Winchester, where he and his wife lived and died.

Many of the descendants of William Hoge and Barbara Hume became distinguished both in Church and State, but their oldest son John, never went to Virginia to reside. He was born at Perth Amboy, went with his father to the Three Lower counties, and there married Gwenthleen Bowen, a native of Wales.

JOHN HOGE and his wife removed to East Pennsboro' township, then Lancaster, now Cumberland county, about the year 1730 (probably three or four years previous), where he afterwards purchased a considerable body of land from the Penns. He died there, probably toward the latter end of October, 1754, his will being probated on the 19th of the month following. He mentions therein his wife "Gweenthleen" and children—*John, Jonathan, David, Benjamin, Mary, Elizabeth,* and her daughter Rachel, *Sarah, Rebecca* and *Abigail.*

JOHN HOGE, the eldest of the sons, graduated at Nassau Hall (Princeton) in 1748, became a Presbyterian minister, was ordained in 1755, and became quite distinguished in the Church. He was one of the first members of the Huntingdon Presbytery. Webster in his *History of the Presbyterian Church,* makes the astonishing statement that he was a son of William Hoge instead of a grandson, and confounds him with the Virginia Hoges. He died the 11th day of February, 1807, aged about eighty.

JONATHAN HOGE, born July 23, 1725, received a liberal education and was brought up a farmer. He was a justice of the peace from 1764 to the Revolution; was a member of the Constitutional Convention of July 15, 1776; member of the Assembly in 1776, and again from 1778 to 1783; member of the Supreme Executive Council from March 4, 1777, to November 9, 1778, and from November 3, 1784, to October 20, 1787; member of the Council of Safety from October to December, 1777; one of the commissioners to remove the public loan office in September, 1777; one of the committee to superintend the drawing of the Donation Land Lottery, October 2, 1786; member of the Board of Property in 1785-6; and by Gov. Mifflin appointed one of the Associate Judges of Cumberland county, August 17, 1791. Judge Hoge died of paralysis on the 19th of April, 1800. He was a prominent and influential man—his entire life was an active and busy one.

DAVID HOGE was sheriff of Cumberland county, and took a very active part in the Revolutionary contest. He owned the land where the borough of Washington, Penn'a, now stands, and laid out that town in 1780. He never resided there, but his two sons, William and John, went there in 1781, and owned the lots and sold them. This John was second lieutenant in Col. William Irvine's (Sixth) Battalion, and captured in the Canada campaign, at Three Rivers, June 8, 1776. He was not exchanged until 1779. In 1783 he was chosen a member of the Council of Censors under the constitution of 1776, and was one of the members of the Convention of 1790. He was chosen to the State Senate in 1791 and again in 1794. He was a Federalist, while his brother, William Hoge, was a Republican or Democrat, and represented his district in Congress during the whole of Jefferson's administration.

BENJAMIN HOGE, the youngest of the first John Hoge's children, died early in life and unmarried. As to the daughters we have no accurate data. All of the old stock of the Hoges, and their connections, the Walkers, are buried in the graveyard at Silvers' Spring church, near where they lived, They bore a prominent part in the affairs of their day and generation—and left their impress on the History of the Valley.

CAPTAIN JAMES POE.

Within four miles of Greencastle, Franklin county, less than a quarter of a mile from the station of the Cumberland Valley railroad, known as "Kauffman's Cross Roads" and in plain sight of the passer-by—to the left journeying southward—is a cluster of tall trees, the shadows of which fall upon the lichen-covered tombstones of an ancient burial ground known as "Brown's mill graveyard." Near the northern end of the enclosure is a tombstone of rather more imposing proportions than its fellows, surmounted, by a broad stone slab which bears the following inscription:

Sacred
To the memory of
James Poe, Esq.,
A patriot of the Revolution of 1776,
A Sincere Friend an Honest Man,
and
A Professor of the Christian Religion,
Who departed this life June 22d, 1822,
Aged 74 years.

James Poe, if not a native, became a resident of old *Hopewell* or new *Antrim* township, Cumberland county, at a very early period of his life. As early as the 26th of July, 1764, although but a lad of sixteen years, he is said to have been one of the party of settlers which under the command of Lieut. (afterwards General) James Potter, pursued the savages who had massacred the schoolmaster and scholars at Guitner's school-house a few miles southwest of what is now Marion station. In common with a majority of his fellow settlers, Poe was a martial spirit, and when the war for Independence became an established fact, he was among the first to offer his service to his country, and attached himself to the militia of Cumberland county in 1776. At the beginning of the year 1777 he became captain of an infantry company, raised in Antrim township, which subsequently was attached and became the Third company of the Eighth battalion of militia commanded by Col. Abram Smith—John Johnston, Lt. Col.; Thomas Johnston, adjutant; Thomas Campbell, quartermaster. In regard to the details of the services of this battalion there is no record at present known, but that it was in continual service—suffering severe losses—from the latter part of 1777, until the middle, at least, of 1780, there can be no doubt. In speaking of the Eighth and other battalions of Cumberland county militia, McCauley, in his history (2d edition, p. 141), says that no rolls of these battalions " could be found," and he gives none. For the purpose of preservation, therefore, since it has not been published, the roll of Captain Poe's company as it stood prior to the 23d of October, 1777, is subjoined:

Roll of the Third Company in the Eighth Battalion of Cumberland County Militia.

Commissioned Officers.
James Poe, Captain.
James Patton, 1st Lieut.
Jacob Statler, 2nd Lieut.
James Dickson, Ensign.
    Sergeants.
James Crawford,
John Hopkins,
Samuel Statler.
    Corporals.
William Newell,
Alex. Drybaugh,
John Lord.
    Privates.
John McAdo,
William McDonald,
John Anderson,
James Roddy,
William Cook,
Jacob Seller,
Henry Snively,
Archibald Bachman,
William McKee.
Daniel McKissek,
John Pachore,
William Meanor,
John Gibson, Jr.,
Robert McClellan,
Henry Grindle,
Thomas Dunlop,

David Witherspoon,
Arch. Kosky,
Robt. Cooper,
James Watson,
Humphrey Fullerton,
Thomas Gibson,
Robert Johnston,
James Kennedy,
Henry Sites,
Thomas Dowler,
Emanuel Statler,
John Leaney,
Thomas Lucas,
Conrad Fisher,
Jacob Grindle,
William Nisbet,
James McKee,
Andrew Reed,
Andrew Gibson,
George Dickso,
John Holliday,
James Carlow,
Philip Swarts,
Peter Whitmore,
Richard Hopkins,
James Reed,
Patrick Cavit,
John Thompson,
Hugh McCay,

John Grindle,
Jacob Baucord,
Joseph Lowrey,
Andrew Smith,
Michael McDonall,
William Kelly,
John Brown,
Robert Patton,
Jeremiah Callahan,
James Ross,
James Smith,
Peter Dougherty,
Thomas Reed,
Stoffle Sites,
Gabriel Carpenter,
Robert Thompson,
William Beatty,
William McClellan,
William Ray,
Joseph Alender,
John Woods,
Henry Kooly,
Dennis McDonall,
Peter Koon,
William Rankin,
James Evans,
John Statler.
Samuel Hill,
James Reynolds.

At the close of the war Captain Poe returned to his home in Antrim township, and was residing there when Franklin* county was created in 1784. He was married to a daughter of General James Potter of Revolutionary fame, and it was at the homestead of the

Poes that General Potter died in the fall of 1789, whilst upon a visit to his daughter.

Captain Poe's military services were supplemented in after life by no inconsiderable services of a civil character. On the 22d of October, 1783, he was appointed by the State authorities as "Commissioner of Taxes" for Cumberland county. In 1785 he was chosen first County Commissioner of the new county of Franklin, and served in that capacity during the years 1785–86–87, with John Work and John Beard as colleagues. He was a second time chosen County Commissioner in 1797, and served three years longer. In 1796 he was chosen a representative for Franklin county in the Assembly for the session of 1796–97. He subsequently served in the Assembly for three successive terms longer, from 1800 to 1803. Under the act of 21st of March, 1808, Franklin county was made an independent Senatorial district, and Captain Poe, was chosen first Senator under this apportionment. He served in the Senate from Dec., 1811, to Dec., 1819. With the close of his last Senatorial term closed his public service. He retired to his home in the country, and on the 22d of June, 1822, passed quietly away at the ripe old age of 74.

In this connection it may not be inappropriate to say a word in memory of a gallant son of Captain Poe whose untimely death the aged father was called upon to mourn ere the inexorable monarch claimed him too for his own. I speak of Adjutant Thomas Poe who, when the second war Great Britain begun, resigned the position of deputy surveyor for Franklin county, to which he had been appointed in 1809, to enter the army. His qualifications secured for him the position of adjutant of the 5th Pennsylvania regiment (from Franklin county), Col. James Fenton commanding. His career was short but brilliant, his daring conduct soon won for him a name. Upon one occasion, it is said, that single handed he quelled a dangerous mutiny among the troops by the mere force of his will, and in his last battle his gallant and intrepid bearing won the admiration of all. He fell mortally wounded at the battle of Chippewa, July 6, 1814, and died a few days after. Peace to the ashes of father and son.
BENJ. M. NEAD.

OLIVER POLLOCK.

Of this distinguished citizen of Pennsylvania very little indeed can be learned from the published histories of the United States, and that little is confined to the histories of the Mississippi Valley in which section the most active part of his life was passed. The loss of family papers in 1863 at Bayou Sara, La., has left his early history in the dark. He was born in Ireland about 1740. Emigrated to Cumberland county, Penna., about 1760. He was then associated with James Pollock, who was, in 1776, one of the commissioners of Cumberland county, and by his signature is supposed to have been at that time an aged man. James had also a son named John Pollock, who must have been born before 1756, as he was sent to Philadelphia in 1776 to draw £600 from the Committee of Safety, for the use of the commissioners of Cumberland county. In 1807, Oliver Pollock advertised for sale several thousand acres of land, "being part of the estate of James Pollock, deceased, late of the borough of Carlisle, and part of the estate of the subscriber." (But he had a son James killed in his youth at Silvers' Spring by his horse, as he rode him to water. This property may have been owned partly by his son James.)

In 1762–4, Oliver Pollock removed to Havana, Cuba, and engaged in mercantile pursuits, in connection with an eminent house in that city. Here he at once applied himself to the study of the Spanish language, in which he soon became proficient. Being a Roman Catholic, he became acquainted, on his arrival at Havana, with Father Butler, President of the Jesuit College. Through his influence he was brought into close relations with Don Alexander O'Reily the Governor General of Cuba, whose friendship he retained through life. In 1762, France had ceded her Louisiana territory to the King of Spain. Thither the thoughts of Pollock were early turned, and before 1768 he had removed to the town of New Orleans, then a place of about 3,000 souls, but offering a fine opening for mercantile transactions. Here, about 1765, he was married to Miss Margaret O'Brien, an extended account of whom will be found in the *Carlisle Gazette* of January, 1799. She was born in Ireland in 1746, and was descended from a noble family by both her parents, O'Brien of the house of Clare, and Kennedy of Ormond, whose sons were distinguished in the service of the Kingdom of Great Britain. She died at Carlisle, Penn'a, January 10, 1799, aged 52 years.

Having settled at New Orleans, and purchased some property there, Pollock soon established a high reputation in mercantile circles, making frequent voyages to the cities on the Atlantic coast of America. In 1769 he went to Baltimore, Md., purchased and fitted out a brig, which he named the Royal Charlotte, loaded her with flour and set sail for New Orleans. Meanwhile O'Reily had been appointed by the King of Spain to be Captain General and Governor of the Province of Louisiana, with directions to take immediate possession of that country then in a state of insurrection. On the 17th of August, 1779, O'Reily arrived at New Orleans with 3,000 troops. The population of the town being thus doubled, the food became scarce, the provisions O'Reily had ordered to be forwarded failed to arrive, and a famine was imminent.

At this important juncture Pollock arrived with his load of breadstuff at New Orleans. The last barrel of flour sold had that day brought thirty dollars. With that generosity which afterwards marked his relations with the Colonies, Pollock at once placed his entire cargo of flour at the disposal of the Governor, requesting O'Reily to fix the price. This the Governor refused to do. Pollock tells the rest of the incident thus: "I then said, that as the king had 3,000 troops there and the inhabitants were in distress for flour, I did not mean to take advantage of that distress and I offered my flour at fifteen dollars or thereabouts, per barrel, which he readily agreed to; and observed that he would make a note of it to the king, his master, and that I should have a fine trade there so long as I lived; and I did enjoy that as long I stayed in the country." Thus he laid the foundation of his large fortune which subsequently he placed at the disposal of the United Colonies.

In 1775, when the conflict between the United Colonies and the mother country began, among the many merchants from the Colonies residing in New Orleans, Pollock was the most prominent and energetic. His sympathies were at once enlisted in favor of the Colonies, and his services rendered secretly and effectively. On the 10th of July, 1776, Don Bernardo de Galvez, then Colonel of the Regiment of Louisiana was appointed Provisional Governor of Louisiana, succeeding Governor Unzaga, February 1, 17,7. He was a young man of talent, energy and character, the son of then Viceroy of Mexico, and the nephew of the Spanish Secretary of State.

Pollock was introduced to Don Galvez by Gen. Unzaga, with the assurance that "if the Court of Spain was going to take part with Great Britain, Oliver Pollock should not remain in the country twenty-four hours, but if the reverse, that they were going to take part with France, Oliver Pollock was the only man that he could confide in the colony"—meaning as an English merchant.

Pollock and Galvez became very intimate and warm friends. In the expeditions which Galvez commanded against the British possessions during the war between Spain and England, Pollock accompanied, doing personal service and largely aiding the armies of Spain.

His reputation as a financier and a zealous patriot had already become so well known in Philadelphia that on the 12th of June, 1777, the Secret Committee of the United States, among whom were Franklin, Morris and Lee, appointed him Commercial Agent of the United States at New Orleans, at the same time directing him to ship at once to Philadelphia $50,000 worth of goods, blankets, &c., for the use of the army.

Pollock had become very much interested in the efforts of Virginia to take possession of the Illinois Country. When, in 1778, General George Rogers Clarke was despatched by Governor Jefferson, with a small force to reduce the English posts at Vincennes and Kaskaskia, Pollock had already forwarded to Fort Pitt, by Col. Gibson, a large quantity of gunpowder obtained from the King's store, part of which furnished Clarke with his ammunition.

In January, 1778, after Don Galvez had publicly recognized Pollock's official character as United States agent, the Governor of Virginia ordered Pollock to draw bills on France for $65,000 to aid Clarke. In order to meet these drafts, Virginia had proposed disposing of large quantities of tobacco stored in several localities in the Eastern counties. But this tobacco the traitor Arnold destroyed during his raid into Virginia. The State thus being made powerless at the time to meet her engagements to Pollock, the bills were returned to him protested, and his creditors seized his property. During this year he had also borrowed from the royal treasury, through Don Galvez, $70,000 in specie, which was expended for the furtherance of Clarke's campaign and the defense of the Virginia and Pennsylvania frontiers. For this amount he gave his own individual bond.

During the time of his appointment as U. S. Agent, from 1777 to 1783, he made advances to the government of Virginia, and also to the United States, on the basis of his own credit, of over three hundred thousand dollars in specie. His private fortune was great. He was supported by the first mercantile houses of Europe, as well as the South, and the wealth of many Spanish officers, his friends, was at his disposal. "But at that era the hand of America was comparatively of *straw*, her exchequer was of *paper*, but her promise was of *gold*." How it resulted with Pollock as its agent is readily seen.

The Secret Committee of the United States in Philadelphia, embarrassed him very seriously by failing to respond to his drafts. By their directions he made extensive purchases—borrowed and forwarded to Willing & Morris large sums of money, and pledged his own property for the amount. The committee expressly stipulated that he should draw on them in favor of whom he pleased, with assurances that his drafts should be paid. They also pledged him that cargoes of flour should be shipped to him in the several vessels he employed, and that other remittances should be made for future purchases. These promises they failed to make good. In reply to his appeal for remittances, they wrote him July 19, 1779, recognizing his claims, his sacrifices, and his faithfulness to duty, but *lamenting their inability to fulfil their pledges.* That which would have crushed most men, only stimulated him to greater exertions to sustain his own credit. Leaving a respectable American citizen named Patterson in his place as a hostage, he parted from his family in 1781 and went to Richmond and Philadelphia. Appealing to Congress, then in session, and to the Assembly of Virginia, he was met with irritating delays and failures. Meanwhile, May 20, 1783, Congress appointed him United States Agent at the Havanas, whither also Galvez had been transferred—having been succeeded by Miro as Governor of Louisiana. Leaving his claims before Congress, in the hands of an attorney, he at once embarked for the Havanas. Here new dangers assailed him. Galvez, although transferred to Havana, had not yet arrived. Unzaga was still in command. The bills of credit drawn for Virginia were sent to Havana for collection. Meanwhile, Virginia had ceded Illinois to the United States, who had also assumed all the cost of Clarke's campaign. In May, 1784, one year from the date of his appointment as United States Agent at Havana, Spanish soldiers entered his house, his property, house carriage, mules, negroes and even the money due him and in the hands of creditors, some $10,000, were seized by the command of Unzaga, himself placed under arrest, and all correspondence between him and the United States prohibited. He immediately had his family shipped to Philadelphia, borrowing for that purpose money from a Mr. Thomas Plunket, an American resident at Havana, and remained in close custody for eighteen months until Don Galvez arrived at Havana. Through his influence he was released, after first executing a bond to Don Gardoquia, the Spanish Minister to the United States, to pay him the amount of the French drafts on his arrival in Philadelphia. Galvez, however, did not allow him to depart without other evidences of his friendship, and he furnished him with a certificate testifying that during Pollock's residence in New Orleans as Agent of the United States, " he acted in favor of the soldiers and citizens of his own nation with all the zeal and love which becomes a true patriot, supplying them with provisions, and assisting them whenever they wanted it with his own credit or with ready money, the Congress bills not being current there, in all which he spared neither pains nor trouble to obtain the end proposed to himself and to give every assistance in his power, soliciting loans in the name of the United States and obtaining $79,087, which are yet owing and unpaid. That, in the expedition I made against the forts of his Britannic majesty, he attended me in person until the surrender."

Upon his arrival in Philadelphia, he at once appeared before Congress then in session. Here he was met with the slanderous charge that he was endeavoriug to make enormous profits by his claim, that the demand he made to cover the bills which he had drawn on Spain was for specie, whereas the money had been disbursed in paper money. To a sensitive nature this return for the unflagging zeal and vast sacrifices he had made, was galling beyond measure. But consciousness of rectitude in all his transactions as Agent, sustained him, and gave fresh vigor to his purpose. He fortunately learned that General George Rogers Clarke was in New York. He readily found him and obtained the following certificate, which silenced his slanderers and procured his immediate relief:

"*These are to certify* to whom it may concern, that the bills I drew when I commanded the Virginia troops in the Illinois country upon Mr. Oliver Pollock, Agent for the United States at New Orleans, where considered by me to be for specie, as the respective bills expressed in dollars and cents, and that the services of Mr. Pollock rendered upon all occasions in paying those bills, I considered at the same time and now to be one of the happy circumstances that enabled me to keep possession of that country.

"Given under my hand and seal this day at New York, the 2d of July, 1785. GEORGE R. CLARKE."

December 18, 1785, Congress awarded to Mr. Pollock over $90,000 with interest, to cover the claims for which he had been arrested, and for which his hostage remained in New Orleans.

But the money was not in the treasury and the award of Congress was not paid until 1791. Meanwhile Pollock's energies were not dormant. He resolved to return to New Orleans and relieve his hostage. Fitting out a vessel in Philadelphia, and loading it with flour, he sailed to Martinique, where he disposed of the cargo and laid in another. Then he sailed to New Orleans, where he remained eighteen months. Engaging once more in mercantile pursuits, his energies and good fortune soon enabled him to pay—in 1790—all the claims by Galvez and others, and once more a free man he turned his face toward Philadelphia.

In 1791–2 Pollock returned to Cumberland county and purchased the property now known as Silvers' Spring. Here his wife died and was buried in 1799, and here his son James was killed. In 1797 he became a candidate for Congress, but was defeated by General John Andre Hanna, of Dauphin county.

In 1804 he was again an aspirant for congressional honors in the Congressional district composed of Cumberland, Dauphin, Mifflin and Huntingdon counties. He and David Bard, of Huntingdon, against Gen. Hanna, of Dauphin, and Robert Whitehill, of Cumber-

land. As Pollock and Whitehill were both from the same county neither were elected, the vote being as follows:
Oliver Pollock, 1700; Robert Whitehill, 1514; David Bard, 3245; Jno. A. Hanna, 2931.

The vote of Cumberland county shows Pollock's popularity. It was as follows: Pollock 1367, Whitehill 614, Bard 1168, Hanna 462.

In 1806 he was again nominated, but withdrew in favor of Whitehill, on the score of friendship, and the probability that a similar vote and non-election of either candidate would result.

November 8th, 1805, Pollock was married in Baltimore, Maryland, to Mrs. Dady, and in 1806 removed to that city where he resided until 1820, when his second wife having died he removed to the home of his son-in-law, Dr. Samuel Robinson, at Pinckneyville, Wilkinson county, Mississippi, where he died full of years, December, 17, 1823.

By his first wife he had five children. He left no known descendants excepting those of his daughter Mary, who married Dr. Robinson. From the few letters of Mr. Pollock in the hands of the writer, it is evident that his fortune had been so reduced by the Revolutionary war, that May 30, 1800, he became for a while, like Robert Morris, an inmate of the debtor's prison. HORACE EDWIN HAYDEN.

NOTES AND QUERIES.—LXXI.

THE LATE JOHN G. RIPPER.—In the *Deutsche Pionier*, edited by that erudite scholar and antiquary, H. A. Rattermann, is a biographical sketch of the late John George Ripper, from the pen of the editor. Through the kindness of the Rev. J. G. Pfuhl, we are enabled to present a translation of certain portions thereof, which we are confident will be as interesting to the readers of *Notes and Queries* as it is to us:

"On the 23d of July there died at Harrisburg, Penn'a, John George Ripper, the founder and editor of the 'Pennsylvania *Staats Zeitung*.' With him, perhaps, the last of the editors of the old school passed away, where the editor and his subscribers were not only personally acquainted with each other, but were to a great extent confidential friends.

"In olden times it was an indispensable necessity for the editor of a newspaper to visit his subscribers once a year. He had therefore to make more or less extensive journeys, and as there were no railroads, he usually went horseback. In these travels the "newspaper man" gathered new subscribers, collected his subscriptions, inquired about the well being of the people, the condition of the harvest, and the state of business generally. Inquiry was likewise made concerning the political views of the people, their social and religious circumstances, etc. In this way an intimate relationship grew up between the editor and his readers, which is wholly unknown in our day.

"The announcement was made in the paper when and where the man with the stove-pipe' (Ripper always called himself thus in his paper), would make his appearance. It can easily be surmised that he was very successful collecting the 'luppele' (bank-notes), and most heartily welcomed to the homes of the people. Whenever he entered, if at meal time, he was invited to partake; and if late in the evening, he found a welcome lodging place. He was seldom permitted to leave a house without a refreshing drink, whether it was wine, apple cider, whisky or a cup of coffee, tea or bowl of milk, and then he left with a hearty pressure of hands, and (auf Wiedersehn) with a promise of return the next year.

"A faithful report of such a trip was always afterward found in the paper, in connection with the different receipts of subscription money. These would be read, how 'Peter' was still well; how 'Betsey had presented her Michael with a stout, fat boy;' how the apple trees of 'Hans' gave promise of an excellent crop; how the corn of 'Sam' looked splendidly; how the family prospered; how the stock of cattle was, etc. But, if one of the subscribers had disappeared without settling his bill, which not unfrequently happened, his name usually appeared under a 'gallows.' In the same manner delinquent subscribers were treated, who promised from year to year to pay, but did not.

"In short, editor and reader were befriended, became better acquainted, and stood in closer relationship than they do nowadays. To this species of 'newspaper men' of the old type, Ripper, or 'the man with the stove-pipe,' belonged. Every year he traveled over a territory which was larger than that of Germany. The characteristics of his subscribers were reflected in his paper. True and sturdy, but honest and frank, were its tone and speech. It was written in half Pennsylvania-German style, and thus it was easier understood by its readers than if it had been in the purest and most elegant German. The character of an editor can be thus judged with reliable certainty from his paper. If this shows firmness, then the editor is likewise no wavering reed, and *vice versa*. In a word, in the case of Ripper, all three, editor, paper and reader, were in perfect harmony."

DAUPHIN COUNTY IN THE REVOLUTION.

"A muster roll of Captain William Brown's Company of Militia of Colonel Timothy Green's Battalion of Lancaster County—destined for the camp in the Jerseys, August 31, 1776:

Captain.
Brown, William.
1st Lieutenant.
Wilson, James.
2d Lieutenant.
McCormick, Henry.
3d Lieutenant.
Rogers, Andrew.
Sergeants.
Barnet, William,
Hutchison, John,
Wilson, James,
Stuart, James.
Corporals.
Barr, Charles,
Gaston, Alex.
Porter, David.
Privates.
Calhoun, David,
Carter, John,
Cathcart, John,

Cooper, John,
Crain, William,
Freckelton, Robert,
Hill, Robert,
Hutchison, Joseph,
Jamison, John,
Johnston, James, (1)
Johnston, James, (2)
Kennin, Hugh,
McNair, Thomas,
McCoy, Neil,
McClure Francis,
McClure, James,
McMullen, James,
McClure, John,
McClure, Martin,
McNitt, Barnard,
Martin, Thomas,
Patterson, John,
Porter, Charles,

Rogers, Jeremiah,
Rogers, William,
Sinclair, Duncan,
Shoddy, Matthew,
Snodgrass, John,
Starritt, John,
Starritt, Samuel,
Stewart, James,
Sturgeon, Robert,
Templeton, John,
Thompson, James,
Thompson, William,
Umberger, Leonard,
Vance, David,
Wallace, James,
Wallace William,
Watson, David,
Wilson, James,
Wilson, Joseph,
Wright, William,

THE DAUPHIN COUNTY BAR IN 1789.

From the current number of *The Penn'a Magazine of History and Biography,* we cull the following which some one has resurrected from the *Freeman's Journal* of March 4, 1789:

"*From a lawyer who could not attend Dauphin Court to his friend a lawyer at Harrisburg.*

"At Dauphin Court, tho' fond of sport,
 The prospect is so barren,
I can't attend, my dearest friend,
 Where there's more crow than carrion.

"There's *Wilkes,* and *Andre, John* and *Joe*
 And *Peter,* too, so pliant,
If you but flinch and stir an inch
 They're sure to nab your client.

"There's Father *Smith* and Brother *Yeates,*
 And little *Tom* and *Stephen,*
When one sits down the other prates
 And so they both are even.

"With hooks and crooks and musty books
 Whilst candles waste in sockets,
The court perplex and juries vex,
 And pick their client's pockets.

"When court is out, away they scout,
  Sworn enemies to quiet,
Drink wine at *Crab's*, kiss dirty drabs,
  And spend the night in riot."

The editor of the *Penn'a Magazine* prefixes the following queries:
" Who can tell who the lawyers are who are referred to in the doggerel—names in italics? And what does the writer mean by saying " Where there's more crow than carrion ?" Does he mean more lawyers than there are suits to try ? Is the Stephen mentioned Stephen Chambers, who was killed in a duel with Dr. Rieger? When did that duel take place?"

As to the meaning of the line " Where there's more crow than carrion," there is no difficulty—the *crow* are lawyers and the *carrion* are clients.

Now as to the gentlemen alluded to. From the organization of the court in 1785, until the May term, 1789, the following persons were admitted to the Dauphin county bar: May term, 1785—Stephen Chambers, John W. Kittera, John Clark, Joseph Hubley, John A. Hanna, James Riddle, John J. Henry, Peter Huffnagle, Jacob Hubley, James Biddle, Collinson Reed, George Ross and John Reily. August term, 1785—Jasper Yeates, Robert Magaw, Thomas Hartley, Thomas Smith, David Grier, Thomas Duncan, John Caldwell, Andrew Dunlap and William Montgomery. May term, 1786—William Graydon and Charles Smith. August term, 1786—James Smith and James Hamilton. November term, 1786—William R. Atlee. May term, 1787—James Hopkins. August term, 1787—Richard Wharton. November term, 1787—George Fisher. February term, 1788—George Eckert. May term, 1788—William Bradford, Edward Burd and John Spayd. August term, 1788—Matthias Barton.

" *Wilkes* " was John Wilkes Kittera. He was a son of Thomas Kittera, of East Earl township, Lancaster county. He graduated at Princeton College in 1776, afterwards studied law, and was admitted to the Lancaster bar in 17—. He was a member of Congress from 1791 until 1801, a period of ten years. At the close of his Congressional life, he was appointed U. S. District Attorney for the eastern district of Pennsylvania, and removed to Philadelphia, where he died. He was a man of fine personal appearance.

"*Andre*" was John Andre Hanna. Mr. Hanna was a native of New Jersey, and a graduate of Princeton. He married Mary Reed Harris, a daughter of John Harris, the founder. He served in Congress from 1797 to 1805 in which year he died, at the age of about forty-four. He was a brigadier general of the militia in the Whiskey Insurrection, and took a prominent part in the political affairs of the day. He was an anti-Federalist, and the compeer and colleague of Gallatin,

Smilie and others of that school. His descendants reside in this city.
"*John*" was Captain John Reily, concerning whom see *N. & Q.* No. liii.

"*Joe*" was undoubtedly John Joseph Henry, of Lancaster, afterwards presiding judge of this judicial district. He was the author of the "Expedition to Quebec," having been a volunteer in Capt. Matthew Smith's company from Paxtang in 1775, and which accompanied Arnold's expedition to Quebec. As we have a biographical sketch of Judge Henry in preparation, we shall make no further allusion.

"*Peter*" was Peter Huffnagle, of Lancaster. He commanded a company of Associators in the War of the Revolution, and was a man of prominence in Lancaster county, but he seems to have been overlooked by Mr. Harris in his Biographical History of Lancaster county.

"Father *Smith* was James Smith, of York, a signer of the Declaration of Independence.

"Brother *Yeates*" was Jasper Yeates, of Lancaster. Mr. Yeates was one of the most eminent lawyers of his day. He was admitted to the bar in 1765. He took an active part in the affairs of the Revolution, was one of the delegates to the Pennsylvania Convention of 1787 which ratified the Federal constitution. He was appointed a judge of the Supreme Court in 1791, and was the author of one of the State reports. He died March 13, 1817, aged 72 years.

"Little *Tom*," was Thomas Duncan, of Carlisle. Upon the death of Judge Yeates, Gov. Snyder appointed him to the Supreme bench. Judge Duncan later in life removed to Philadelphia where he died in November, 1827. Mr. Harris in his reminiscences of the Bar of Dauphin county, gives us this sketch : " Mr. Duncan was a man of polished manners, neat and careful in dress, and never rude or wantonly disrespectful to others. He and Mr. David Watts were the rival practitioners at Carlisle. I have heard of an anecdote which somewhat illustrates their respective characters. On one occasion in court, when Mr. Watts was annoyed by a remark of Mr. Duncan, he said, " You little (using some offensive expression) I could put you in my pocket." "Then," said Mr. Duncan, " you would have more law in your pocket than ever you had in your head." Judge Duncan, as may be inferred, was of small stature ; "his voice was weak, and some times quite shrill in pleading." His knowledge of law, however, was superior.

"*Stephen*" was Stephen Chambers, of Lancaster, and a brother-in-law of John Joseph Henry. He was admitted to the bar in 1780, and became one of the leading lawyers of the county courts of Lancaster, Dauphin and Northumberland. He was a member of the

Pennsylvania convention of 1787, which ratified the Federal constitution. He was fatally wounded in a duel with Dr. Reiger, of Lancaster, on Monday, May 12, 1789, on a challenge of Dr. R. for an affront received by him at a tavern. On the day of the duel " when each had fired one pistol without effect, the seconds interfered and proposals of accommodation were made, which Reiger could not be persuaded to agree to. Each then presented a second pistol. Chambers' snapped, but Reiger's discharged a ball through both his antagonist's legs." Mr. Chambers died on the Saturday following (May 17). The affair caused great excitement at the time, for the latter was much beloved not only by the entire profession, but by the community generally.

"*Crab's*" was William Crabb, who subsequently removed to Middletown. He probably kept the tavern at the corner of Vine and Paxtang streets, afterwards kept by Nicholas Ott and others.

NOTES AND QUERIES—LXXII.

THE SETTLEMENT OF THE CUMBERLAND VALLEY.—We trust our friends "over ye Sasquahannah" will take the facts relative to the *actual* settlement of the beautiful historic Cumberland Valley as philosophically as possible. On this side of the river, recent researches have exploded all our views concerning the settlement here, notwithstanding writers before us, historians of celebrity, had led us to form the opinions which we had held a number of years. Our friend Rupp was an indefatigable historian, and with the documents then accessible (the Provincial Records and Archives had not at that time been published) he made perchance as good use of his material as possible. For his labors, he is certainly deserving of proper recognition, and frequently is an authority—but with the newer light we are in possession of, we must confess that many of Mr. Rupp's assertions are unsubstantiated. Again, because Mr. Rupp has not said thus and so, it should not be taken for granted that statements founded upon recently published or discovered documents should not be correct.

We have little doubt that prior to the year 1700 such traders as Letort and others had traversed the Cumberland Valley from the Susquehanna to the Potomac, but that they did so would be no argument that the Valley was settled prior to 1700. Yet when, as in the case of Silvers and others who, when the Provincial land office was opened for the sale of lands across the river, in 1732, were the first to request warrants for their "improved" lands, we must naturally infer that they had been prior settlers. Coupled with this, if there are extant certain statements which go to show that these men went "over Sasquahannah" about 1725, or before that, we should accept these dates as the periods when their *actual* settlements were begun.

Silvers, and Parker, and Macfarlane, and Kelso were no traders, as Chartier and Letort, but finding the west side of the river far preferable to the east side thereof, they pushed thitherward and located, permanently of course, or we would not find them where we do when it was necessary to take out their warrants for land.

John Harris had no land surveyed him until 1732, and yet he located at this point in 1707; then as an Indian trader, with authority "to cultivate fifty acres of land." In 1718 we find his name with quite a number in Conestoga township, Chester county, assessment list, who in the changes of townships and counties, subsequently appear in West Conestoga, Chester county, Donegal, Lancaster county, and Paxtang, Lancaster county. And yet these persons had no land surveyed or warranted to them during a period of fourteen to fifteen years, simply from the fact that west of the Conewago hills, the Proprietaries gave no authority to sell, the lands not having been purchased from the Indians. No one will deny that *they* were actual settlers. This will apply to those who went into the Cumberland Valley. We have no theories of our own to advance—we have given the historic data as we have found it. Our own views would be at wider variance with current history, yet we always refrain from giving our opinion unsubstantiated by good authority.

FITHIAN'S JOURNAL.

PREFATORY NOTE.—Philip Vicars Fithian, who kept the Journal from which the following extracts are taken, was a graduate of the class of 1772 in the College of New Jersey—a class noted for its ability and for the subsequent prominence of many of its members, Aaron Burr, William Bradford, William Linn, D. D., &c. Mr. Fithian was licensed to preach by the First Presbytery of Philadelphia, Nov. 6, 1774. On April 4, 1775, he received an honorable dismission from the Presbytery, as there were no vacancies within its boundaries, and recommended as a candidate in good standing. He left his home at Greenwich, N. J., May 9, 1775, on horseback, for a tour through Delaware, Maryland, Pennsylvania and Virginia, in company with Andrew Hunter, also his classmate, taking notes of people and places in journal form, addressed to Miss Elizabeth Beatty (sister of Major John, Dr. Reading and Erkuries Beatty, subsequently prominent officers of the Pennsylvania Line). After his return, Oct. 25, he was married to Miss Beatty and in the following June accepted the appointment of chaplain to Col. Newcomb's Battalion of New Jersey Militia, and died in camp at Fort Washington, of dysentery, October 8, 1776. (*Beatty Family Record, page 55*). He kept a journal up to within a few weeks of his death, embracing the battle of Long Island and the subsequent skirmishing at York Island. His last entry, Sunday, Sept. 22 is: "Many of our Battalion sick; our lads grow tired and begin to count the days of service which remain." I am indebted to his grand-niece, Miss Josephine C. Fithian, of Woodbury, N. J., for the use of the Journal.   JOHN BLAIR LINN.

YORKTOWN.

May 17, 1775.—A considerable village; the principal street near half a mile in length. The houses a great part of the way very near and joining each other, many of them are large and fine, three stories high. There are three considerable public buildings; the Court house, English church and Dutch Meeting house. The inhabitants are enthusiastic in the American Cause and united almost without exception. Many were on the common and in different parts of the town exercising themselves (*i. e.* going through the manual at arms).

Fifteen miles from York is a small village called Berwick or Abbottstown. One Dutch Lutheran church with a cupola; all the houses built with square logs. An old kind Dutch landlady gave our horses for breakfast a dish of "Spelts;" they are a coarse species of wheat. Our horses, however, were not over fond of new and harsh grain. On the Conewago is another settlement of the Scotch-Irish. Mr. Hunter has some relatives here; we dined with one of them, who were highly civil to us. Twenty-two miles from York is a small village called Huntersville. There is a Presbyterian meeting house now belonging to Mr. Thompson. Marsh creek is a fine brook, low banks are lined with tall sycamores.

THE BLUE MOUNTAINS.

May 18.—Here we arrived late last night at a small log house. A smart, neat young landlady, a spry, gowden-haired, buxom maid; several sturdy waggoners; huge hills on every side. We are at what is called Nicholson's Gap. We jog on over the rugged hills. A middle aged, dropsical Dutch woman, with her face muffled up in the mumps, boiled up for our breakfast a little coffee in the sugar and milk; indeed it made good broth. From the mountain to Elizabeth or Hagerstown is a level country and good land.

HAGERSTOWN.

A considerable village; it may contain two hundred houses; some of them are large and neat, built with stone or brick, but the greater part of the houses are built with logs neatly squared, which indeed make a good house. There are many stores here and many mechanics, and it is a place of business. The inhabitants are chiefly Dutch. East and southeast of this town the Blue mountains appear like thick hazy thunder clouds just above the horizon in Summer. There is here a Dutch Lutheran church and they are now building an English church. Frederick is the county town, so that they have no court house. We made from this village to the Potowmack in company of Betsy Vanleer and Dr. Magaw. The river here is eighteen rods over. We were in Virginia by six. We were in the Province of Pennsylvania this morning; we have passed through the colony of Maryland and are now in Virginia. Distance twenty-seven miles.

May 19.—We lodged with Mr. Vanleer. He told us when we were leaving his house and about paying our bill, that a clergyman's money would not pass with him. We are now in Berkeley county, 80 miles above Alexandria, 87 from Baltimore. We arrived among Mr. Hunter's relations. He introduced me to his mother, sister, brothers.

MARTINSBURG.

The county town of Berkeley, has lately been taken from Frederick. This village derives its name from Col. Martin, a nephew of Lord Fairfax. It is yet in infancy. Two years ago the spot was high woods. There are now perhaps thirty houses. They have already built a prison of stone, and strong, and are making a court house of no inconsiderable size and elegance. Probably, if American liberty be established, for which we are now contending even in blood, this with many other infant villages, in a series of years, will be populous and wealthy towns, especially if the navigation of this long river can be effected.

May 20—We visited Mr. Vance, minister of Tuscarora congregation. He gave us liberty to visit and preach in the neighboring vacancies. He lives at the foot of the North mountain, partakes, I believe, of the Virginian spirit, and hands round the "sociable bowl." We dined at Captain Mitchell's.

Sunday, May 21.—Mr. Hunter and I preached at Falling Water meeting house. It stands on Potowmack, is well situated; and I am told is a numerous society. The people gave good attention, sang the Scotch or as they call them David's Psalms. The congregation is chiefly made up of country Irish and half Scotch, most of them Presbyterians. We dined at one Bowland's. Two wagons fully loaded went past, going with families to the back settlements.

WINCHESTER.

May 22.—The county town of Frederick, twenty-nine miles from Martinsburg. It is a smart village nearly half a mile in length, and several streets broad and pretty full. The situation is low and disagreeable. There is a pleasant hill northeast from the town, at a small distance a large stone Dutch Lutheran church with a tall steeple. In the town is an English church. North of the town are the ruins of an old fort wasted and crumbled down by time. The land is good, the country pleasant, the houses in general large. Rode to-day to Stevensburg distance 37 miles.

STEVENSBURG.

May 23—A small village well situated. Four taverns kept in this town. One large store kept by Mr. Holmes, where I am to lodge. With Mr. Hunter I rode out with the intention of visiting Mr. Hoge, the late minister here. He is now from home at Redstone over the Allegany mountains.

May 24.—Before dinner Col. Isaac Zane, Burgess of this county, came to the store with Miss Betsy McFarland, his kept and confessed mistress, and their young son and heir. Mr. Zane is a man of first rank here, both in property and office. He possesses the noted Malbron Iron Works, six miles from this town. He is with regard to politicks, in his own language, a "Quaker for the Times." Of an open, willing conversation; talks much and talks sensibly on the present connections. He is a patriot of a fiery temper. In Dunmore county he is Colonel of the Militia, one of the Burgesses in this; but he scorns to have a wife.

After dinner with Mrs. Holmes and Andrew, I walked out of town a mile to a lovely farm of Mr. Whitehead's, an old gray-haired batchelor. He is a singular character, an Englishman of Yorkshire by birth. Left home early and has been through America with a set of pictures and magic lantern by which he has made a fortune. His house is small, but the walls on every side are crowded with maps, paintings and well chosen pictures.

May 26.—Dined with us an old starched Dutch Lutheran clergyman. He professed to be a scholar and has attempted to institute a small Academy in this county. Towards evening, came in from Staunton, Mr. Porterfield and his wife. They invited me strongly to make them a visit; they tell me the doctrine of universal restitution is making great headway in their congregations.

Sunday, May 28.—Opickon church; a large and genteel society, mostly Irish. I preached two sermons, the people very attentive.

From this town may be seen six counties (and there are but few such prospects in America) Hampshire, Dunmore, Culpepper, Farquar, Loudoun, Frederick. The mountains on a smoky or dusky sky day appear vastly beautiful, like a fine well designed and finished piece of painting.

May 31.—Mr. Glass was blessed while he was filling up his family, so far as to have eight daughters in continual succession and but three sons. I visited a brother of his a mile off at the head of Opickon creek, a solid lusty farmer; lives next to a clean well-filled garden; a small, brown, brisk, tidy, very sociable wife. A little spruce well turned daughter. Several visits we made to-day, among others to one Colville. He is clerk for the Society, raises the tune, and in the primitive genuine Presbyterian whine and roll. Begins the first note of the music with a deep strained gutteral from the last word of the reading without any intermissions. This, however, in these Societies, is universal. I am here under the necessity of close study, as the people here do not allow of reading sermons.

Sunday, June 4.—Cedar Creek church, six miles from Stevensburg, northwest. All here are full Quakers. I preached twice; the assembly very attentive, I made very little use of my notes, which is a vast almost essential recommendation here. Preach without papers produce casuistic divinity; seem earnest and serious, and you will be listened to with patience and wonder. Both your hands will be seized and almost shook off, so soon as you are out of the church, and you will be claimed by half of the society to honor them with your company after sermon. Read your sermons, and if they be sound and sententious as Witherspoon's, copious and fluent as Hervey's; and read off with the ease and dignity of Davies; their backs will be up at once, their attention all gone, their noses will grow as red as their wigs. And (let me whisper this) you may get your dinner where you breakfasted. Please keep your seats, said an old greyheaded gentleman, when worship was concluded; he took off his hat and made a collection. Well I must go home with this venerable prop of the church. His wife is old and flaxen haired as he. Both are hearty, lusty and nimble. In this happy condition of life and friendship by Hymen's blessing they have lived together fifty-five years. They have three daughters at home, virgins, and well risen in years. Have some books, much poultry. Mr. Colville lives within four miles of the North Mountain on the bank of Cedar creek, a small deep brook. The bank of this creek on the other side of the house is forty feet high, and in some places wholly perpendicular. They told me a melancholy story. A neighbor of theirs, some years ago, was riding in the night and lost his way on the other side of this creek, he alighted from his horse, and, doleful mishap, blundered over this bank, fell to the bottom and died.

Monday, June 5.—We breakfasted heartily and soundly on the richest products of a fat farm. Boiled milk, highly buttered, and fine cheese of two kinds, one made last summer, the other last week. We passed one freeman talking politicks and religion. These good people are full warm for election and reprobation in its strictest sense. Mr. Colville gave me yesterday's collection. I seem gratified to find that when the number at church was so small so many remembered me. There was thirty-four pieces of silver in cut money, quarters of dollars, pistareens and half-bits. The whole donation, however, for the two sermons was three dollars, 1£, 2s. 6d. After dinner I visited old Mrs. Sarah Vance. She was in her early life acquainted with Mr. Hunter, of Cohansie, and once they were on the borders of being married, before Mr. Hunter went to the grammar school. But said the honest woman, he was born to a better fortune. On my way home I called in to visit one Mr. Wilson, an intelligent, agreeable person lately from Ireland. He wears the short, trite, yellow wig.

Four o'clock at Stevensburg.—This is Whitsun-Holiday. The village is full of people. Men busy mustering, women in the streets and at the doors looking on; all things festive.

Tuesday, June 6.—The drum beats, and the inhabitants of this village muster each morning at five o'clock. After dinner with Captain Holmes and Captain Hunter, I rode to Winchester. The court was sitting. Mars, the great God of Battle, is now honored in every part of this spacious colony, but here every presence is warlike—every sound is martial—Drums beating, pipes and bag pipes playing, and only sonorous and venic tunes. Every man has a hunting shirt, which is the uniform of each company. Almost all have a cockade and buck-tail in their hats to represent that they are hardy, resolute and invincible natives of the woods of America. The county committee sat. Among other resolves they passed this resolute and trying determination, "That every member of this county between sixteen and sixty years of age shall appear every month at least in the field under arms, and it is recommended to all to muster weekly for their improvement."

Wednesday, June 7.—Election! Election! Election! Oh! this election and reprobation. It is damnation, *nolens volens*, said an old crafty buckskin to me this day. I am much troubled with these doctrines. Poor, unmeaning persons, perplexed with a fictitious, airy fury, and never in expectation of full satisfaction, till the die is cast.

Thursday, June 8.—We see many every day traveling out and in to and from Carolina, some on foot with packs, some on horseback, and some in large covered waggons. The road is here much frequented and the country for one hundred and fifty miles further west thickly inhabited. To-day, for the first time; I went through the "new exercise," gave the word and performed the action, *Libris Doctoribusque amotis.* One Shipe of this town was backward this morning in his attendance with the company of Independents. A file was sent to bring him. He made resistance, but was compelled at length, and is now in great fear and very humble since he heard many of his townsmen talk of tar and feathers.

Saturday, June 10.—Last night by some daring villain, Lord Fairfax's office was broken open and robbed. The money was not found but many suits of my lord's and Colonel Martin's best clothes were taken, many pairs of shoes, shiffs, linen, &c. The same evening near this town ten horses were stolen.

OPICKON CHURCH.

Sunday June 11.—A numerous assembly. Mr. Hoge present. He is a lusty, well made man. Captain Holmes introduced me to him and he received me kindly. Invited me to the session house and home with him after worship. I proposed and strongly urged him to preach at least once, but he wholly declined it. Several store keepers and people of note were from Winchester, many members of the English church, and all gave good attention. Sometimes, at particular sentences, I could observe every eye to be fixed and the whole house in silence. Then, when the sentiments cooled, one would cough, another would ogle some woman, a third would cough, another would take snuff, &c. After sermon I rode home with Mr. Hoge. He is remarkably chatty, and in some cases facetious; has the reputation, I believe justly, of a sound, well-meaning man. I grieve for his present state; he has a large family, no way of supporting it, has been dismissed from this Society near three years. He is anxious of being reinstated, and is jealous of my having an intention to supplant him.

Monday, June 12.—The opinion of his Reverence on politicks is blank. He rode with me to Mr. Glass'. Mr. Glass gave me for my five sermons five dollars and many thanks. He proposed I should stay with them a year on trial, but I objected on Mr. Hoge's case.

A report came to town pretty well confirmed that in the upper part of Augusta some few days ago was committed a base murder. A gentleman traveling towards Carolina was assaulted and stabbed many places in the breast and afterwards robbed of cash about £110. Soon after the murder, while the unhappy victim was yet bleeding but quite dead, two gentlemen from the northward came up, saw the dead body, and looking about at some distance, they discovered a person washing his hands and clothes in a brook; they seized him; at first he denied the fact; but when he was bound and threatened he owned that he had destroyed the man and robbed him for his money which was upwards of an hundred pounds. They then carried the dead body and the murderer back to a tavern, kept by a widow woman, at a small distance, and desired her to take the charge of all and carry on the prosecution as he there acknowledged before witnesses that he was the murderer. The woman, however, obstinately refused in every respect. They then asked for a rope, called several as witnesses of his acknowledgement of the murder; took him out from the house and without the formality of a legal trial hung him dead themselves. After having thus secured him, they left the murdered body, the money, and an account of their procedure with the widow and proceeded on their journey.

This causes much speculation. It is an action so circumstanced and so unprecedented, that I know not how to give my opinion, and yet I cannot make a strong objection nor bring one single reason than from thinking such conduct necessary.

Tuesday, June 13.—Many servants and negroes are running off. One was brought into town this day with a huge iron collar on his neck, a long, heavy chain on his feet; and the poor victim was on his way to a scene of usage less inferior to Papal Purgatory.

Wednesday, June 14.—Early this morning Mr. Emmitt, of this town, teased me to agree and stay in this society. I told him I respect and love the people, but am not clear with respect to Mr. Hoge's case. The independent company met and mustered diligently. Many men of note are warm in the cause, as especially Col. Hite, a man of influence and property in the neighborhood.

Evening.—I visited Major Stevens, the proprietor of this town. He and his wife both urged me by many arguments to agree and stay in this society. I would stay gladly if I should not injure Mr. Hoge.

June 15. Before noon I made a visit to Mr. Wilson, an elder in this society. Mr. Wilson is a plain able farmer, very old and stout; a full and strong example that this place is healthy. Afternoon, with Mr. Holmes, visited Col. Hite. His general characteristics are wealth and honesty. He entertained us merrily with humor, toddy and music.

In town a most furious hurly burly; Mr. McGinnis formerly a Baptist preacher but now a constable had apprehended a. fellow on suspicion of stealing his horse. When we rode up a large mob were together. A posse was dispatched for a woman said to be his companion; in about an hour with much reluctance she came *Magna Caterva Comitante.* Both are remarkably impudent, and it is said by all are well known characters.

You a preacher, damn you, said the culprit yesterday. You a preacher, a teacher of good. Yes, you are the picture, the imp of folly and mischief, an hypocrite ingrate—you apostate. McGinnis ran up to him in rage and beat him with his whip, and on application to the magistrate he put in his mouth an iron gag.

Friday, June 16.—Larkins was sent to prison well secured, the woman was degraded and dismissed. Dined with us a Mr. Root, a lawyer from Winchester. He is a warm patriot.

WINCHESTER.

Saturday, June 17.—This town in arms, all in hunting shirt uniform, and bucktails in their caps. Indeed they make a grand figure. I arrived in Martinsburg a little before evening. Mr. Hunter just arrived from Jersey. He tells me that the negroes in Pittsgrove have murdered Mrs. Sherry and many are in this conspiracy. Here slaves are running off daily, servants skulking about and pilfering houses, and many other things weekly. Riots on many occasions most parts of the continent, and in every place much anxiety and doubt, and almost total inattention to business. These, however, are only some of the most beautiful outlines of "*civil discord.*"

Sunday, June 18.—Over the North mountain I rode to Mr. Vance's meeting house at Back creek. The sacrament was administered. Ninety-three communicants. Vast assembly. This North mountain is very high, at the top almost bare. The view below on each side is rich and beautiful. On each side we see ridges of hills, and ridges on ridges still succeed till you cross the Allegany.

Monday, June 19.—Rode to the Rev. Johns, near Potowmack; rode nine miles.

Tuesday, June 20, 1775.—Rose by 3, rode over Potowmack, the bottom solid rock, high banks of 40 feet hard rock. Then through a small blind road to Mr. King's meeting house of Upper West Connecocheague [the church is now gone, but the graveyard still marks the place, 2 miles northwesterly from Mercersburg]. The Presbytery [Donegal] met. Mr. Black gave the sermon. Present Messrs. Cooper, Thompson, Hoge, McFarquar. Correspondents, McPherin, Craighead, Ray, Vance. Candidates, Black, Keith, McConnel, Hunter and myself. Students, Wilson, Linn, Waugh, Boyd. So much company in these woods seems agreeable.

The land here is good and a fine creek through it. Tall timber and near the North Mountain. Distance rode to-day 22 miles—Mr. Black's. He lives West under the North Mountain. Has a smart pleasant wife and sweet child. I had her pleasant society. Mr. Black and I played for our diversion and amusement many airs on the German flute. We recollected and chatted over our peregrinations, since we parted. All was simple, sociable and friendly.

Wednesday, June 21.—By 9 at Presbytery; many *pros* and *cons.*, repartees and break-jaw compliments passed. Nothing was done for us and we passed the day in dullness, only now and then a ramble among the trees.

Evening—we returned with friendly Mr. Black* and passed it in music and friendship.

Thursday, June 22.—At the Presbytery by nine. They gave us our appointments. Mr. Keith over the Allegheny. I have the following: Next Sabbath, the 4th in June, at Cedar Springs [now Mifflin, Juniata co.] First Sabbath in July at Northumberland. Second at Buffalo Valley, Third at Warrior Run. Fourth at Bald Eagle. Fifth at Chillisquaque. First in August in Penns Valley. Second, West Kishacoquillas. Third, East Kishacoquillas. Fourth, Shirley. A vast stony woods round. At eleven I left the Presbytery and rode to Mr. King's within a mile of Fort Loudoun ; dined ; Mr. Keith along. We rode on North into Path Valley. Mr. Keith left me at twelve miles, on his way to Bedford.

[Here ends all that relates to Cumberland Valley. The balance of the Journal contains curious notices of customs and prominent persons. Dr. Plunket, Mrs. Scull, Esq. Brown, Fleming, &c., and old Northumberland county, more proper for publication in papers of that locality ; but if a desire for more is expressed it will be furnished for *Notes and Queries*.   JOHN BLAIR LINN.]
Bellefonte, Pa.

---

* Probably John Black of class of 1771, who died in 1802.

www.ingramcontent.com/pod-product-compliance
Lightning Source LLC
Chambersburg PA
CBHW060909300426
44112CB00011B/1403